Marketing Essentials

SECOND EDITION

SALLY DIBB Open University Business School

LYNDON SIMKIN Oxford Brookes University

Australia • Brazil • Japan • Korea • Mexico • Singapore • Spain • United Kingdom • United States

CENGAGE
Learning·

Marketing Essentials, Second Edition
Sally Dibb and Lyndon Simkin

Publishing Director: Linden Harris

Publisher: Andrew Ashwin

Development Editor: Annabel Ainscow

Editorial Assistant: Lauren Darby

Production Editor: Alison Cooke

Production Controller: Eyvett Davis

Typesetter: S4Carlisle Publishing Services

Cover design: Adam Renvoize

Text design: Design Deluxe, Bath

For product information and technology assistance, contact **emea.info@cengage.com.**

For permission to use material from this text or product, and for permission queries, e-mail **emea.permissions@cengage.com.**

British Library Cataloguing-in-Publication Data
A catalogue record for this book is available from the British Library.

ISBN: 978-1-4080-7368-1

Cengage Learning EMEA
Cheriton House, North Way Andover, Hampshire, SP10 5BE United Kingdom

Cengage Learning products are represented in Canada by Nelson Education Ltd.

For your lifelong learning solutions, visit **www.cengage.co.uk**

Purchase your next print book, e-book or e-chapter at **www.cengagebrain.com**

Printed in United Kingdom by CPI Antony Rowe
Print Number: 06 Print Year: 2015

Marketing

Marketing's focus is on delivering customer satisfaction and also value to both customers and the marketer's own organization.

In addition, it falls on the Marketing function to identify threats and opportunities and to be the provider of market insights to the organization and its leadership.

Marketers must select the most appropriate opportunities to pursue, the markets to serve and the products or services to support.

For these priority pursuits, marketers must identify a target market strategy, a compelling and differentiated proposition to take to market and a customer engagement plan.

Marketing programmes should be created which maximize competitive advantage, appeal to target customers and provide adequate returns to the organization.

The marketing programmes need to attract new customers and also retain existing customers, while leveraging the latest advances in the marketer's toolkit.

This remit requires considerable investment, so marketing activities must be well planned and assessed for their effectiveness and contribution to the organization's fortunes.

All of these activities should be undertaken ethically and in a responsible manner.

These are the sentiments which guide the structure and content of *Marketing Essentials* and which should underpin the work of all marketers.

Sally Dibb and Lyndon Simkin
The Open University/Oxford Brookes, 2012

Contents

NOTE Each chapter contains a Summary, Key Links, a list of Important Terms, Discussion and Review Questions, Recommended Readings, an Internet Exercise and an Applied Mini-Case.

Preface

Marketing affects everyone: we are all consumers. Most businesses depend on marketing to provide an understanding of the marketplace, to identify opportunities, and to ensure that their products and services satisfy the needs of customers and that they are competing effectively. There is little doubt that marketing is an important part of today's society and commerce. Marketing matters! It is important, therefore, that marketers are well trained and are equipped with the skills required.

In the majority of business schools and colleges in the UK, Eire, Benelux and Scandinavia, *Marketing: Concepts and Strategies*, the big sister of *Marketing Essentials*, has been used to introduce undergraduate and MBA students to the nature and scope of marketing. Many CIM students also depend on this text to guide their studies.

The first edition of *Marketing: Concepts and Strategies* appeared in 1991, just after Sally and Lyndon joined the fast-growing Warwick Business School and were introduced to American co-authors Bill Pride and 'OC' Ferrell. Since then, this text has become the leader in its market. Whether for undergraduates seeking a comprehensive introduction to marketing, MBAs requiring a grounding in marketing analysis or marketing management, or students in colleges wishing to pass degrees and diplomas, *Marketing: Concepts and Strategies* is used by lecturers and teaching staff to provide an accessible, topical and enlightening insight into the world of marketing. *Marketing: Concepts and Strategies* is also recommended by the Chartered Institute of Marketing.

Marketing Essentials was developed for shorter courses and where the 800+ pages from its big sister text would be too much. However, it still manages to provide a good insight into the use and tools of marketing, including the core marketing analyses, marketing strategy and marketing management. This edition of *Marketing Essentials* has been totally revised to reflect the current core themes of marketing in terms of academic content but also – given the authors' wide-ranging consultancy and research experience outside the lecture theatre – from a practitioner's perspective. In particular, since the last edition appeared, the world for marketers has gone digital, consumers communicate readily with each other via social media, marketing has become more aligned to ethical, responsible and sustainability issues and marketing as an academic discipline has become more critical and reflective; all of which are developments under-pinning this new edition.

Changes for the second edition

Marketing is a quickly evolving discipline in a rapidly changing world. The second edition of *Marketing Essentials* strives to explain the nature of marketing and the importance of understanding the complexities of the marketplace. In so doing, the intention as ever is for the text to be easy to read, informative, interesting and topical. To this end, there has been a major restructuring of the 15 chapters and accompanying web materials.

Each Part has improved scene-setting openers to explain the interrelationships of the many concepts and strategies introduced. Leading practitioners have contributed to these openers in order to emphasize the importance of strategic marketing. Each Part concludes with a full-length strategic case study. The Parts follow a logical structure, which adheres to the premise that for effective marketing there must first be analysis of the marketplace, then the recommendation of a marketing strategy, and finally the production of marketing programmes with control processes to manage implementation of the desired strategy.

Every chapter has been updated in terms of the current research and thinking in the area, the latest statistics and industry figures where relevant, and to reflect the views of the leading academics and practitioners who have kindly reviewed the chapters, provided thought-provoking quotes and suggested the recommended readings in their area of expertise as additional references. Chapter openers have been redesigned and the concluding pages of each chapter provide an Applied Mini-Case, a Case Study, an Internet Exercise and Key Links to related chapters.

The principal aim of *Marketing Essentials* has always been to provide a book that students find easy to use and that reflects accurately the current thinking in the world of marketing. There have been extensive changes to the second edition – these have been made in order to reflect students' needs, suggestions by peers and the current developments in marketing as identified by practitioners, the journals and at conferences. There is improved material addressing marketing strategy, targeting and positioning; customer relationship management practices; e-marketing and the growth of digital; social marketing applications; there are more e-exercises; better cross-referencing between related concepts and chapters; and numerous practitioner insights and boxes describing marketing managers' real-world use of key concepts.

The biggest changes reflect how for marketers the world has gone digital; social media networking has provided consumers with easy communication about brands and product experiences and removed some control from marketers about what is communicated about their propositions; sustainability and responsibility are high on the agenda; and recession has forced a re-think of how marketers ply their trade. These developments have steered this re-write of *Marketing Essentials*. Along with a growing critical reflection of marketing's deployment and impact by many academics.

Ancillaries for tutors include PowerPoint visual aids, test bank software, case answers and a student/tutor CourseMate. CourseMate support for all users of *Marketing Essentials* and *Marketing: Concepts and Strategies* includes PowerPoint visual aids; student quiz tests web links with case companies, brands and topics; extra cases; suggested examination formats and questions; selected course outlines and syllabus proposals; Q&A topics and solutions; financial analyses in marketing; full glossary of important terms; topical insights and evolving concepts. For these features, please visit the supporting CourseMate.

As ever, *Marketing Essentials* is supported by comprehensive indexing, a full glossary of important terms appearing in the margins of the relevant chapters and cross-referenced in the subject index, questions for discussion and full listing of the key terms and jargon detailed chapter by chapter.

The running order of Marketing Essentials, second edition

PART ONE   **Marketing Defined and Marketing in Context** – An introduction to the nature and scope of marketing and the marketing process, marketing strategy and the understanding of competition.

PART TWO   **Understanding Markets** – The forces of the marketing environment, consumers and business-to-business buying behaviour, target marketing and brand positioning, customer relationship management and marketing research.

PART THREE   **Developing Marketing Programmes** – The ingredients of the marketing mix: products, developing products and portfolios, services; channels and channel management; pricing; promotion (marketing communications); and, branding.

PART FOUR   **Managing Marketing** – Marketing planning, controls, implementation and metrics.

Acknowledgements

This text would not have happened without the support and encouragement of original American co-authors Bill Pride and O.C. Ferrell; the team at Cengage Learning; the comments and enthusiasm from fellow marketing lecturers at Warwick, The Open University and Oxford Brookes; colleagues in the Academy of Marketing; and, above all, the feedback from our students past and present.

Specific thanks for insights, material, great experiences, lots of stimulation and very interesting challenges must go to Alan, Richard, Ross and colleagues at Lockheed Martin; Lesley, Rohit, Umesh, Vijay, Shilen and colleagues at Tilda; Siobhan, Willie, Steve and colleagues at Nynas; Ian and Peter at Fujitsu; Anne at Willis; Jim, Andrew and colleagues at Raytheon; Andy at QinetiQ; Anette at GfK; Victoria at the ABS; Shelley at Republic; Silvia and colleagues at Inter-IKEA, as well as to Dave Chaffey, Peter Jackson, John Wringe, Adam Morgan and Robert Bean. Special mention must be made of Annabel and Brendan at Cengage, without whom we would not have this edition.

Special mention must go to our children, Rosalie, Samantha, Mae, Abby, James and Bex. They are our motivation.

Sally Dibb and Lyndon Simkin
Kenilworth, 2012

About the authors

Sally Dibb and Lyndon Simkin each spent around twenty years at the leading UK university management centre, Warwick Business School, teaching undergraduates, MBAs and executives the basics of marketing, advanced strategic marketing, marketing management, buyer behaviour, marketing communications and marketing research. Sally then moved to head up Marketing and research at the innovative Open University Business School as Professor of Marketing, where she also established and co-directs the Institute for Social Marketing. Lyndon left Warwick to join fast-moving Oxford Brookes Business School as Professor of Strategic Marketing and Research Lead.

Sally and Lyndon's research focuses on market segmentation, marketing planning, Social marketing applications, marketing strategy operationalization and teaching methods, in which areas they have published extensively in the academic journals in the UK and USA. They co-chair the Academy of Marketing's SIGs in Market Segmentation and CRM, and are both Associate Editors of the *Journal of Marketing Management*. Lyndon is a member of the Research Committee of the Academy, while Sally is a trustee of the research charity Alcohol Research UK.

In addition to being joint authors of *Marketing Essentials* and its big sister *Marketing: Concepts and Strategies* and *Marketing Essentials,* they produced the innovative *The Marketing Casebook: Cases and Concepts* (Thomson) in 1994 and 2001, mixing real-world cases with overviews of theory, and in 1996 and 1998 *The Market Segmentation Workbook* and *The Marketing Planning Workbook* (both published by Thomson), aimed at assisting marketing practitioners to reassess their target markets and understand the complexities of marketing planning. These workbooks were based on their consultancy experiences with organizations as diverse as ABB, Accenture, AstraZeneca, GalaCoral, Calor, EDF Energy, E.on, Ernst & Young, Fujitsu, Geocell, GfK, IKEA, JCB, McDonald's, Nynas, QinetiQ, Raytheon, Royal SunAlliance, Tilda and Willis. Both *Workbooks* have been translated and published in China and Russia. In 2001, Sally and Lyndon published the revision aid, *Marketing Briefs* (Elsevier Butterworth – Heinemann), revised in 2004. While primarily targeted at students preparing for examinations in marketing, *Marketing Briefs* is also ideal for providing time-pressured managers with concise and topical insights into the core concepts and tools of strategic marketing. The acclaimed *Market Segmentation Success: Making It Happen!* was published by Routledge in America 2008, in which year Cengage published the very popular *Marketing Planning* title, aimed at practicing marketers. In 2009, the first edition of *Marketing Essentials* was published, targeting college courses introducing the subject of marketing. The latest version of their main text, *Marketing: Concepts and Strategies*, came out in 2012.

Walk-through tour

Part Opener text, a figure, and short case study in a box, and the main text describes what is in each chapter, to help the reader

Strategic Cases
to facilitate debate and understanding

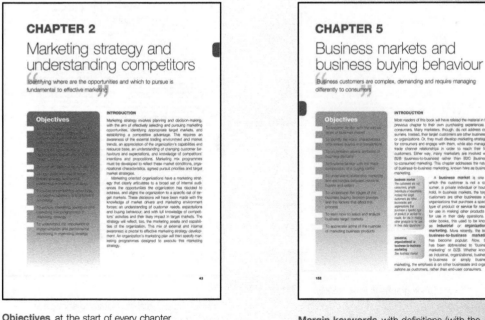

Objectives at the start of every chapter
Introduction text at the start of every chapter

Margin keywords with definitions (with the glossary keywords emboldened in the main text and available online)

Chapter Opener box feature to help introduce the theme of the chapter

Figures and Tables are helpfully scattered throughout the text, to aid understanding

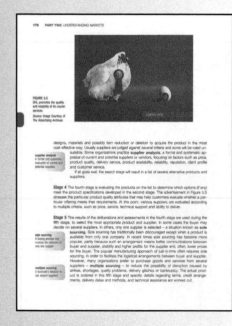

Concepts Figures photographs to illustrate key marketing concepts

Topical Insight real-life feature to showcase current development

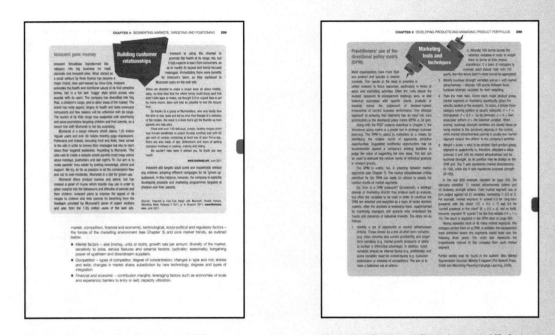

Building Customer Relationships real-life
feature to enhance understanding

Marketing Tools and Techniques real-life feature
to demonstrate the approaches of practitioners

Summary feature at the end of every chapter to
emphasise key learnings

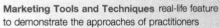

Key Links to other chapters

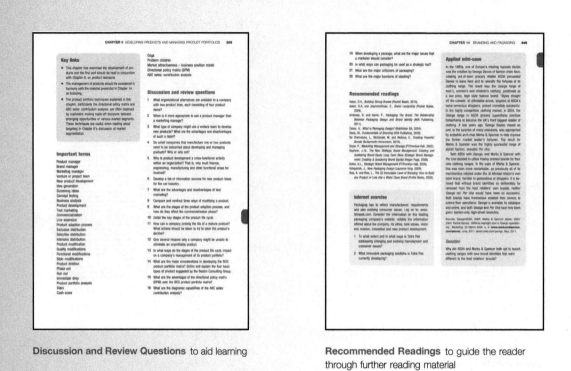

Discussion and Review Questions to aid learning

Recommended Readings to guide the reader through further reading material

Useful Internet Exercises to cement understanding

Applied Mini-Cases to close each chapter

Case Study at the end of each chapter designed to force consideration of key themes and learnings

Notes at the end of the book (relating to superscript numbers within the main chapters)

Glossary of key terms and jargon

DIGITAL SUPPORT RESOURCES

Dedicated Instructor Resources

To discover the dedicated instructor online support resources accompanying this textbook, instructors should register here for access:
http://login.cengage.com

Resources include:

- Instructor's Manual
- ExamView Testbank
- PowerPoint Slides

Instructor access

Instructors can access CourseMate by registering at **http://login.cengage.com** or by speaking to their local Cengage Learning EMEA representative.

Instructor resources

Instructors can use the integrated Engagement Tracker in CourseMate to track students' preparation and engagement. The tracking tool can be used to monitor progress of the class as a whole, or for individual students.

Student access

Students can access CourseMate using the unique personal access card included in the front of the book.

Student resources

CourseMate offers a range of interactive learning tools tailored to the second edition of *Marketing Essentials* including:

- Online cases and self-test questions
- Interactive eBook
- Games
- Videos
- Glossary
- Flashcards
- Links to useful websites

PART ONE
Marketing defined and marketing in context

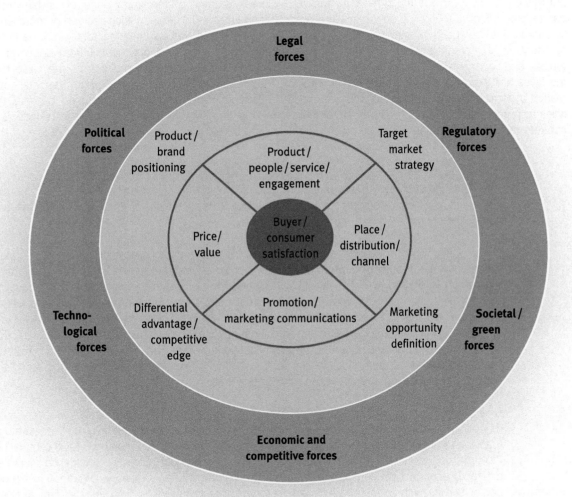

Marketing centres on a set of processes for creating, communicating and delivering value to customers; for managing customer relationships; and, for providing direction to an organization based on market insights. Marketing consists of individual and organizational activities that facilitate and expedite satisfying exchange relationships in a dynamic environment through the creation, distribution, promotion and pricing of goods, services and ideas.

The simple premise of marketing is that to be successful, any organization must understand its customers' requirements and satisfy them in a manner that gives the organization an edge over its competitors, and by staying abreast of changing market dynamics it will continue to offer compelling propositions to these targeted customers. This involves offering the 'right' marketing mix of product, people, service, pricing, promotion and distribution channel. Marketing depends, therefore, on constant updating of ideas and market knowledge. Customers are often surprisingly fickle and modify their needs and wants; rivals alter their strategies; and, forces in the marketplace regularly change. There is, though, much more to marketing than serving customers through marketing programmes.

Marketing's core focus is indeed the understanding and ongoing satisfaction of targeted customers, but marketers must provide much more for their organizations. Effective marketing should analyze markets in order to be able to maintain customer interest and satisfaction, combat competitors, identify opportunities and recognize threats. Marketers should be the 'eyes and ears' for their organizations regarding market dynamics. Having determined which opportunities to pursue and having agreed the mix of target markets to prioritize, marketing should create target

customer engagement strategies, establish the 'wow factor' and ensure there is a robust basis for competing. Marketing programmes should be developed appropriate for the successful execution of this strategy. Therefore, marketing as a process and in terms of its activities involves marketing analysis, marketing strategy and marketing management, as explored in *Marketing Essentials*.

The term 'customer' should be treated loosely. While in commercial settings, it means consumers in consumer markets, or business customers in business marketing, the importance of understanding and satisfying those audiences served or represented in the public and voluntary sectors is just as important. Such organizations benefit from adopting the marketing concept and process ... they also must strive to stay ahead of changing environmental conditions, maximize use of their resources to deliver their aims, compete for attention, and seek to understand and satisfy their audiences and stakeholders.

Part One of *Marketing Essentials* introduces the nature and scope of marketing and the marketing process, marketing strategy and competitive forces. The aim of Part One is to define marketing and enable readers to appreciate its context.

Chapter 1, 'The Marketing Concept', defines marketing; establishes its importance to organizations and to consumers; and outlines the major components of marketing strategy – notably marketing opportunity analysis, target market selection, competitive advantage and the development of marketing programmes designed to implement the marketing strategy. The discussion also examines the concept of marketing orientation within an organization. The chapter establishes the ethos of *Marketing Essentials*, describes the structure of the text and presents an overview of the marketing process. Important concepts presented in Chapters 1 and 2 are deliberately repeated throughout the book. It is important for the reader to understand and accept them before progressing to the following chapters.

Chapter 2, 'Marketing Strategy and Understanding Competitors', presents an overview of marketing strategy and the strategizing process. This chapter aims to highlight which strategic marketing considerations help to ensure that a product or service is marketed for the benefit of the organization as well as its targeted customers. The product or service should be marketed differently enough from competitors' marketing programmes to provide the organization's product or service with a perceived advantage over these competitors. The chapter first explores what is marketing strategy and the importance of organizational mission, goals and corporate strategy. The discussion next turns to assessing organizational opportunities, capabilities and SWOT issues, as well as identifying strategic objectives. The chapter addresses the all-important role of identifying market segments, targeting and brand positioning in marketing strategy: the development of clear target market priorities. The chapter then focuses on competitive strategies for marketing: the role of competition, its ramifications for strategy, competitive positions and warfare strategies. The link between marketing objectives and marketing mix programmes is examined, along with implementation and performance monitoring.

By the conclusion of Part One of *Marketing Essentials,* readers should understand what is meant by the terms *marketing, marketing orientation, marketing strategy* and the *marketing process.* The essential themes in Part One are developed further as the text continues.

Tilda

1. What excites me most about marketing?

Things that excite me most about marketing are what made me choose marketing as a career in the first place. Understanding consumer needs and wants, and unearthing insights that motivate consumers of diverse backgrounds to behave quite similarly, have been two of the most exciting aspects of my career as a marketer.

I have been fortunate to work on brands and with consumers, across Asia, the UK, Continental Europe and North America. My work has given me the opportunity to interact with consumers – in focus groups, in stores and in social gatherings, from very diverse ethnic and socio-economic backgrounds. What fascinates me is the work I have done in finding out how consumers of diverse backgrounds approach brands and categories in a similar way, albeit for different reasons. I will give an example that illustrates this point.

Working on a project for the laundry product category for Unilever in India, my team and I discovered that women engaged in doing the family laundry, from either end of the diverse socio-economic spectrum, had some things in common. Most women from the educated upper income families as well as those at the very bottom end of the spectrum wanted to 'delegate' the task of laundry. The upper end consumers had busy lives as they were in professional jobs and wanted someone/something that would magically get laundry done. Those at the bottom end were struggling to survive and laundry was a chore they could not afford to spend time on. We called these consumers 'task delegators'. Interestingly many consumers in the middle got immense satisfaction out of doing chores like laundry, as they derived self-fulfilment out of providing for their families. We called these consumers 'task participators'. These insights helped us craft offerings under different brands at different price points. Consumer propositions built on such sound insights can withstand the vagaries of the fast moving consumer goods (FMCG) market.

2. What are the biggest challenges for marketing?

Marketing as a function faces some interesting challenges in today's climate:

i. Increasing focus on very short term financial results

This is a result of pressure from the stock markets and the need to show good quarterly results. FMCG and food companies with Venture Capital funding sometimes have added pressure to show quick profits. The current economic climate is also putting pressure on some medium and small companies to show good results to keep the banks off their backs if they have borrowings.

While good financial results are indeed very important, if these are achieved by curtailing investments in the area of marketing, which is considered 'discretionary' spend by some companies, it results in the company/brand entering a vicious cycle of decline that is difficult to come out of. It is far more difficult and expensive to regain a lost consumer than to acquire a new one.

ii. Consumer and corporate apathy towards marketing.

For this, the marketing fraternity has no one, but itself, to blame. Shallow understanding of consumer needs, over stratification of categories in a bid to get more shelf space, perennial promotional 'offers' that reduce consumers' faith in pricing, are but some examples of activities that have resulted in consumer and corporate apathy. Lack of 'big ideas' is challenging marketing as a function on many company boards, resulting in lack of continuous investment in this area.

iii. Seismic changes in consumers' lives due to the Internet

a. The way we consume media is changing dramatically. From an era of one-way communication, we are moving to one of greater two-way interaction. This has implications for the way marketers communicate their brand messages. Increasing numbers of consumers do not want to be 'sold' to. They want brands to understand them and help make their lives easier in an interactive way.

b. More and more consumers are buying products and services online. The UK is one of the fastest growing Internet economies. This has profound implications for marketers in terms of 'route to market' or channel decisions.

3. What does marketing contribute?

Despite all the challenges and the changes in the way we consume media and shop for goods and services, marketing as a function should continue to represent the end consumer in any company. Marketing should have its finger on the consumers' pulse and should enable companies to take the correct medium and long term decisions on products/services – quality, price, range, availability, innovation, etc.

The day the marketers of any company start to think that their role is ONLY to plan the next promotion or increase of shelf space, they run the risk of sowing the seeds of slow long term decline.

VIJAY VAIDYANATHAN
HEAD OF MARKETING, TILDA LTD.

Mattel takes on the world

Strategic case

Mattel, with US$5.8 billion in annual revenues, is the world leader in the design, manufacture and marketing of children's toys. The company's major toy brands include Barbie, with more than 120 different Barbie dolls, Fisher-Price, Disney entertainment lines, Hot Wheels and Matchbox cars, Tyco Toys and Polly Pocket, plus many well-known games, including Scrabble (International), Outburst and Rebound. The company markets toys and games bearing the names of children's favourites Barney, Bear in The Big Blue House, Blue's Clues, Dora The Explorer, Sesame Street, Winnie The Pooh, Angelina Ballerina, Thomas and Friends, Toy Story, Harry Potter, Rugrats and the Wild ThornBerrys.

In addition, Mattel promotes global sales by tailoring toys for specific international markets, instead of simply modifying established favourites from the company's base in the United States. The company's headquarters are in El Segundo, California, but Mattel also has offices in 36 countries. In fact, the company markets its products in more than 155 countries throughout the world. 46 per cent of gross sales stem from its worldwide division, outside its native USA.

Mattel's marketing prowess and reach have paid off. For example, in a poll conducted by the annual Power Brands study, Mattel had strong popularity among consumers: as many as four out of ten people said that if they were shopping for toys, Mattel would be the preferred brand. Retailers also singled out Mattel as the number-one performer, mentioned six out of ten times. This survey proved that both children and adults are enthusiastic about Mattel and its line of products. The Mattel and Fisher-Price names also topped a survey of consumers who were asked about their brand preferences when buying toys in discount stores or superstores, also mentioning Barbie and Hot Wheels repeatedly.

Customer orientation at Mattel

Mattel's management philosophy focuses on satisfying the customer's needs and wants. For example, Mattel redesigned Barbie to more naturally reflect a 'normal' athletic woman in an attempt to meet demands for a more realistic doll. Barbie has also taken on many different professions in order to reach a wider audience. These product modifications and extensions are designed to meet consumer and social demands while still accomplishing company objectives. Likewise, some Hot Wheels cars now display the logos of famous racing teams and major championships around the world, in an attempt to meet consumer demand for more merchandise related to this popular televised sport.

Mattel's pursuit of interactive multimedia is an attempt to adapt to the shorter span of time that young girls want to spend playing with Barbie and other dolls and more traditional toys. Increasingly, children are turning to more interactive toys sooner than was the case in previous years, and Mattel's acquisition of The Learning Company was designed to meet this demand. This acquisition, however, did not prove profitable for Mattel, and the company eventually sold the division. This acquisition and disposal demonstrates the company's awareness of evolving customer trends and also a ruthless management of its portfolio against clearly laid-down performance measures.

As another indicator of its commitment to customers, Mattel employs marketing research to ensure that its strategy and tactics match customer desires. This is combined with product research and development in an effort to release new products yearly, based on these consumer needs and wants. An addition to the Mattel product lines included the innovative construction and activity set called Ello, now receiving significant marketing communications support. The product is meant to compete with Lego AG and draws girls to building toys, which have traditionally been marketed almost exclusively to boys. Mattel research teams watched girls play with pipe cleaners, scissors, glue, paper and cardboard. The results indicated that girls wanted to make panels and tell stories about the space created. The idea behind Ello is to build a house or figures using interconnecting plastic shapes, allowing girls to build and create while engaging in social play. Product development ensures Mattel's portfolio never stagnates: for example the very engaging *Sing-a-me-jigs* were voted toy of the year in 2011.

Mattel's core products

Mattel believes its products are among the most widely recognized toy products in the world. Mattel's portfolio of brands and products are grouped in the following categories:

> *Mattel Girl and Boy Brands* – including Barbie® fashion dolls and accessories ('Barbie®'), Polly Pocket®, Little Mommy®, Disney Classics®, and Monster High® (collectively 'Other Girls Brands'), Hot Wheels®, Matchbox®, Battle Force 5®, and Tyco R/C® vehicles and play sets (collectively 'Wheels'), and CARS™, Radica®, Toy Story®, Max Steel®, WWE® Wrestling, and Batman® products, and games and puzzles (collectively 'Entertainment').
>
> *Fisher-Price Brands* – including Fisher-Price®, Little People®, BabyGear™, and View-Master® (collectively 'Core Fisher-Price®'), Dora the Explorer®, Go Diego Go!®, Thomas and Friends®, Sing-a-ma-jigs™, and See 'N Say® (collectively 'Fisher-Price® Friends'), and Power Wheels®.
>
> *American Girl Brands* – including My American Girl®, the historical collection, and Bitty Baby®. American Girl Brands products are sold directly to consumers via its catalogue, website, and proprietary retail stores.

Mattel's children's publications are also sold to certain retailers.

Source: **http://files.shareholder.com/downloads/MAT/ 1327761574x0x455252/1587E36E-D23A-4783-8AC3-A3ADE3FE9A6F/ 2010_Mattel_Annual_Report_Bookmarked_.pdf**, July 2011.

Barbie

The first Barbie doll sported open-toed shoes, a pony-tail, sunglasses, earrings and a zebra-striped bathing suit, with fashions and accessories also available for the doll. While buyers at the annual Toy Fair in New York City took no interest in the Barbie doll, the little girls of the time certainly did. The intense demand seen at the retail stores was insufficiently met for several years: Mattel simply could not produce Barbie dolls fast enough. Barbie is one of Mattel's major product lines, accounting for more than 50 per cent of its total sales. Around the world, Barbie-related merchandise from Mattel is worth a staggering US$3.6 billion at retail prices, making it by far the number one girl's brand globally.

March 1999 marked the 40th anniversary of Barbie. It also heralded a new Barbie campaign, called 'Be Anything', which focused on encouraging girls to become anything, from athletes to computer experts to dreamers. A Barbie doll is barely present in the Be Anything advert, and not one of Barbie's accessories appears. The whole campaign is an attempt to retain the interest of girls for another two years after the usual post-Barbie age of seven and to make Barbie more 'real' to these older girls.

However, by August 2002, Barbie's popularity had waned and she failed to make the list of the top five best-selling dolls. Mattel reacted by introducing a line of My Scene dolls, which includes a multicultural Barbie, aimed at older girls referred to as 'tweens'. The 'tween' market is comprised of girls between ages 8 and 12 who would rather watch MTV than play with dolls. A website at **www. myscene.com** engages girls in the lives of four friends living in the 'big city' through short 'shows' and music videos. Other efforts targeted at 'tweens' include a crime-solving crew called the Mystery Squad and the Barbie Doll as Elle Woods, which is a tribute to the blonde character in the MGM Pictures movie *Legally Blond 2: Red, White and Blonde*. These lines gave Barbie a new lease of life: recently she stood for election in the US Presidential elections, supported by a full PR campaign! The Barbie collection has been enlarged to include the professions typically entered by female graduates, as Mattel strives to portray a very modern angle for the brand. By the time of her 2009 50th birthday, Barbie's sales were soaring and are now providing 7 per cent year-on-year growth.

Hot Wheels

With millions of boys aged 5–15 collecting Hot Wheels cars, this line of small die-cast vehicles is now involved with almost every racing circuit in the world, including NASCAR (the

National Association for Stock Car Auto Racing), Formula One (F1), NHRA (the National Hot Rod Association), CART (Championship Auto Racing Teams), AMA (American Motorcycle Association) and many other circuits. This immense popularity has created a group of young collectors: the average boy collector owns more than 40 Hot Wheels cars.

Hot Wheels celebrated its 35th anniversary in 2003 with a massive marketing campaign called the Hot Wheels Highway 35 World Race. Mattel then created a story-based and character-based package that included collectible cars, racetracks, comic books, home videos, a video game, a television network special and an on-line race. The idea was to appeal to the many different age groups of collectors Mattel has acquired in more recent years. The 45th anniversary is expected to be a major focus of energy, for Mattel's marketers and consumers alike.

Fisher-Price

Acquired in 1993 as a wholly owned subsidiary, Fisher-Price is the umbrella brand for all of Mattel's infant and pre-school lines. The brand is trusted by parents all over the world and appears on everything from children's software to eyewear, and from books to bicycles. Some of the more classic products include the Rock-a-Stack and Little People play sets. New favourites include Power Wheels vehicles and Rescue Heroes, a line of fire-fighter action figures. Through licensing agreements, the brand also develops character-based toys such as Sesame Street's Elmo and Big Bird, Disney's Winnie The Pooh and Mickey Mouse, and TV favourites Dora The Explorer and Thomas and Friends.

Fisher-Price has built trust with parents by creating products that are educational, safe and useful. In recent years, the brand has earned high regard for innovative car seats and nursery monitors. While not toys, these baby and toddler products are sold to parents already familiar with the company's reputation and these are often retailed in the same stores as Mattel's toys. The company continues to innovate in its core business, too: one project includes collaboration with Microsoft to develop an activity table that teaches children from infants to pre-schoolers using 'smart technology'.

International sales

Under CEO Robert A. Eckert's leadership, Mattel has maintained its strategy of strong expansion overseas, with non-US sales fast approaching half of the company's total. These international sales are in Europe (52 per cent), Latin America (30 per cent) and Asia-Pacific (11 per cent). The international segment has benefited from Mattel's strategic focus on globalization of brands, including improved product availability, better alignment of worldwide marketing and sales plans, plus strong product launches.

Products marketed internationally are generally the same as those developed and marketed in the domestic US market, with the exception of American Girl Brands, although some are developed or adapted for particular international markets. Mattel's products are sold directly to retailers and wholesalers in most European, Latin American, and Asian countries, and in Australia, Canada, and New Zealand, and through agents and distributors in those countries where Mattel has no direct presence.

Worldwide, Mattel's most recognized product continues to be Barbie. In a study conducted by Interbrand and published in *Business Week,* Barbie was the only Mattel brand that made the overall list of the '100 Best Global Brands'. However, the traditional Barbie doll is not receiving a warm welcome in some international markets. The Malaysian Consumers' Association of Penanghas tried to ban Barbie because of her non-Asian appearance and the lack of creativity needed to play with her. Government agencies in other countries, such as Iran, are carrying out similar campaigns against Barbie.

Ethics and responsibility at Mattel

Like most organizations, Mattel has recognized the different responsibilities it has to various stakeholders, including customers, employees, investors, suppliers and the community. These stakeholders have some claim, or stake, in Mattel's products, markets and business outcomes. Mattel demonstrates a commitment to economic, legal, ethical and philanthropic responsibilities.

Mattel's core products and business environment can present ethical issues. For example, since the company's products are designed primarily for children, the company must be sensitive to children's rights. In addition, the international environment often complicates business transactions, especially in the areas of employee rights and safety in manufacturing facilities. Different legal systems and cultural expectations about business can create ethical conflict. The use of technology may also present ethical dilemmas, especially with regard to consumer privacy. Mattel has recognized these potential issues and has taken steps to strengthen its commitment to business ethics and social responsibility. Advances in technology have created special issues for Mattel's marketing efforts. Mattel has recognized that because it markets to children, it has the responsibility to communicate with parents about its corporate marketing strategy. The company has taken special steps to inform both children and adults about its philosophy regarding Internet-based marketing tools, such as the Hot Wheels website.

At the **Barbie.com** website, parents are encouraged to read and follow the suggestions provided by Mattel on Internet safety. This parents' page provides tips for creating rules and regulations for their children's use of the Internet. There is also an example of an Internet Safety Promise for children and parents to complete, forming a type of 'contract' to engage in smart, safe and responsible behaviour when surfing the Internet.

Today, Mattel faces many marketing opportunities and threats, including the rate at which children are maturing and abandoning toys, the role of technology in consumer products, purchasing power and consumer needs in global markets. Mattel has much sales growth potential, especially in the international markets. For a company that began with two friends making picture frames, Mattel has demonstrated marketing dexterity and the ability to keep abreast of market developments.

Questions for discussion

1 Describe the importance of branding and brand portfolios to Mattel's business strategy.

2 Outline the role of product development in Mattel's fortunes.

3 What environmental forces have created challenges for Mattel as its continued expansion moves it into global markets?

References: **http://files.shareholder.com/downloads/MAT/1327761 574x0x455252/1587E36E-D23A-4783-8AC3-A3ADE3FE9A6F/2010_Mat tel_Annual_Report_Bookmarked_.pdf**, July 2011; and Toys R Us stores, 2011.

CHAPTER 1

The marketing concept

Satisfying and retaining customers better than rivals

Objectives

To define marketing

To appreciate the context of marketing and marketing orientation

To explain the marketing process

To understand the importance of marketing

To gain insight into the basic elements of the marketing concept and its implementation

To understand how the marketing concept has evolved and some of the current 'hot' themes

To appreciate the major components of a marketing strategy and the marketing mix

To gain a sense of general strategic marketing issues, such as market opportunity analysis, target market selection and marketing mix development

To grasp the ethos and structure of this book

INTRODUCTION

Marketing's primary aim is the identification of target markets and the satisfaction of these customers, now and in the future. In most organizations, marketing fulfils an analytical function, provides strategic direction and executes a set of tactical activities designed to attract and retain the targeted customers to the organization's products or services. Marketers should strive to be the 'radar' or 'eyes and ears' for their organizations in terms of assessing opportunities, identifying threats and preparing their colleagues for the evolving challenges in the marketplace. There is much more to marketing than creating an advertisement, producing an eye-catching price promotion, jazzing up a website or developing a brand.

Organizations with a marketing orientation have more than a few staff engaged in marketing activities. Such organizations have a sound awareness of customers' needs and buying behaviour, of competitors' offerings and strategies, and of market trends. They take steps to ensure they know how these market conditions will evolve. In addition, they orientate their operational practices and coordinate their interfunctional thinking around these market conditions.

Effective marketing involves an analytical process combining marketing analysis, strategizing and the creation of marketing programmes designed to implement a designated marketing strategy. Marketing opportunity analysis is a pivotal part of marketing, involving the determination of emerging and existing market opportunities and the choice of which to address. At the heart of a marketing strategy is the formation of a target market strategy and a basis for competing in order to focus on the opportunities prioritized by the organization.

Most members of the general public think of 'advertising', 'marketing research' or 'sales persuasion' when the term 'marketing' is mentioned. These brief introductory comments explain that there is in fact much more to marketing. This first chapter of *Marketing Essentials* is designed to define marketing and explain its role.

Attention-getting marketing for condoms

A major aim for marketers is to create awareness of their products amongst their targeted audiences, often through advertising and other forms of marketing communications. Not too long ago, advertisements were rarely seen for condoms. A mix of changing social attitudes, concerns about sexually transmitted diseases and campaigns to combat teenage pregnancies have led to a range of brands turning to mainstream TV and press advertising. Even so, this surge in marketing activity has not been without its critics.

Mates, launched by Richard Branson in 1987, is now part of Ansell Healthcare, the original manufacturers of Mates for the Virgin brand. Ansell trades in France with the Manix brand, and the USA and Australia with its Lifestyles range. In two decades, Mates has become the No 2 condom brand in the UK, challenging Durex. A recent ploy by Mates was to target women with a separate range of condoms, branded Pleasure. This new brand launch was placed next to cosmetics and haircare products in supermarkets and pharmacies, rather than among other condom lines. Arguably this was smart marketing, placing condoms in unexpected parts of stores. In targeting women, Mates moved away from the traditional target audience, male purchasers. By persuading retailers to display the range among beauty products, the company strived to achieve an edge over its competitors in a way which demonstrated an affinity with the purchasing behaviour of its target customers. Mates' marketers were seeking to grow market share and to take advantage of changing attitudes to condoms. Recently, Mates has innovated in terms of designs, messages and added value, including a range incorporating a vibrating ring. Maintaining an emphasis on safety, reliability and health, Mates nevertheless has a policy of constant product development supported by provocative advertising. Any new launch or campaign inevitably attracts critics for such a socially and culturally sensitive product category.

A few years ago, a storm of protest accompanied US brand Trojan broadcasting UK TV advertisements for its Shared Pleasure brand, showing a couple having sex. The first adverts ran in the commercial breaks of TV reality show *Big Brother*, which attracted a viewing profile similar to the target market profile for the brand. Trojan gained approval from the UK's Broadcast Advertising Clearance Centre for a post-9.00 p.m. watershed showing of the 20-second adverts. Trojan claimed that this marked the first time an orgasm had been shown in a UK television advert. The advert, made by agency Media Therapy, apparently showed people captured at the height of pleasure, linking to the Shared Pleasure brand name. Building on the back of a poster campaign, this advertising was bound to court controversy, receiving complaints to the Advertising Standards Authority that the campaign was offensive, demeaning to women, pornographic and not suitable for television audiences. While the brand-building creativity may have been clever, Trojan's marketers nevertheless caused uproar in certain circles.

Courtesy of Mates Healthcare

Sources: 'Trojan under fire for "her pleasure" ad', *Marketing Week*, 4 April 2004, p. 8; 'Trojan to screen first orgasm ad', *Marketing*, 26 April 2004, p. 6; 'Mates', *Marketing Week*, 3 June 2004, p. 10; 'Why is safe sex unpalatable?', *Marketing*, 8 April 2004, p. 15; **www.mates.co.uk**, 1 February, 2011; **www.ansell.com**, 1 February, 2011. Photo: Courtesy of Mates Healthcare

This chapter first overviews the concept of marketing orientation before developing a definition of marketing. The focus then moves on to consider why people should study marketing and why marketing is important. The chapter proceeds to explore the marketing concept and examines several issues associated with successful implementation. The chapter explains the importance of an analytical process to effective marketing, from analysis to strategy formulation to the creation of marketing programmes. Mates – see 'Opener' box – analyzed the purchasing behaviour of its targeted consumers before developing the marketing strategy for its Pleasure range of condoms. How the marketing concept has evolved and topical themes are highlighted. The chapter concludes by discussing the organization and running order of this text.

The concepts and strategies discussed throughout this book are applicable to consumer goods and services, business-to-business products and services, public sector organizations, as well as to not-for-profit and many social sector organizations. As explained in the Part Opener, the term 'customer' in the definitions of marketing should be treated somewhat loosely. While in commercial settings, it means consumers in consumer markets, or business customers in business marketing, the themes explored in *Marketing Essentials* extend beyond such parameters. The understanding and satisfying of audiences served or represented is just as important in the public and voluntary sectors. Such organizations benefit from adopting the marketing concept and process, as they also must strive to stay ahead of changing environmental conditions, maximize use of their resources to deliver their aims, compete for attention and seek to understand and satisfy their audiences and stakeholders.

Like all the chapters in *Marketing Essentials*, this one contains detailed topical illustrative examples in highlighted boxes, presents cases for discussion, suggests Internet exercises at its conclusion, lists at the end all the key terms presented in the chapter, provides discussion and review questions to emphasize the key themes and offers suggested further reading choices. In addition, as the principal definitions are introduced in the text, they are repeated in the margins for ease of understanding, glossary-style. If you have not yet done so, before tackling the chapters you should read the Preface to this book in order to understand the perspective, structure and chapter components of *Marketing Essentials*.

Marketing explained and defined

Marketing orientation

marketing orientation
A marketing-oriented organization devotes resources to understanding the needs and buying behaviour of customers, competitors' activities and strategies, and of market trends and external forces – now and as they may shape up in the future; inter-functional coordination ensures that the organization's activities and capabilities are aligned to this marketing intelligence

An organization exhibiting a **marketing orientation** is said to have a sound understanding of customer needs, buying behaviour and the issues influencing the purchasing choices of customers. A marketing-oriented organization also has a shrewd appreciation of competitors and external marketing environment forces and trends.[1] In addition to comprehending these customer, competitor and marketing environment issues, a marketing-oriented organization ensures its operations, personnel and capabilities are aligned to reflect these external drivers. A truly marketing-oriented organization understands these current issues, but is also focused on identifying how they will evolve, so ensuring that the organization's strategy and capabilities are modified to reflect not just current market requirements but also future market conditions.

A marketing-oriented organization, therefore, devotes resources to understanding the needs and buying behaviour of customers, competitors' activities and strategies and market trends and external forces (now and as they may shape up in the future). Inter-functional coordination ensures that the organization's activities and capabilities are aligned to this marketing intelligence.

Not all organizations can claim to have a marketing orientation. For example, some are purely sales led, concentrating on short-term sales targets, whereas other organizations are production oriented, choosing to emphasize product development and production efficiency in their business strategy. Few experts would argue against maximizing sales or seeking leading-edge production practices, or indeed the adoption of best-practice financial and human resource approaches.

Similarly, the adoption of a marketing orientation is highly desirable. A marketing orientation is of significant benefit to an organization, as it facilitates a better understanding of customers and helps a business to prepare for external market developments, threats and opportunities. It is difficult to contemplate a scenario where a marketing orientation would not be beneficial to an organization.

An organization practising the concepts explained in *Marketing Essentials* is well on the way to having a marketing orientation; but it is important that inter-functional coordination aligns the activities within the organization and also the leadership team to the marketplace, and specifically to customer buying behaviour, competitive pressures and marketing environment forces, and to the evolving nature of these market conditions. The use of some of marketing's concepts and an understanding of the role of marketing in attracting and satisfying customers, are not enough on their own to establish a marketing orientation. However, failure to comprehend the core concepts of marketing will make a marketing orientation impossible to achieve. The focus of this text, therefore, is on explaining the core concepts of marketing which are the entry point requirements for going on to establish a marketing orientation.

It is possible for an organization lacking a full marketing orientation to nevertheless deploy and benefit from aspects of the marketing toolkit as described in the following chapters. For instance, many businesses have an adequate understanding of their customers, but not all have fully grasped their competitors' strategies or the forces present in the external marketing environment. Obviously, it is better not to operate in ignorance of these external pressures, which may create threats or opportunities. The definition of marketing *per se* is not, therefore, the same as the definition of marketing orientation.

Marketing defined

Asking members of the public to define marketing is an illuminating experience. They will respond with a variety of descriptions, including 'advertising', 'selling', 'hype', 'conning people', 'targeting' and 'packaging'. In reality, marketing encompasses many more activities than most people realize and depends on a wealth of formal concepts, processes and models beyond the soundbites just listed. Since it is practised and studied for many different reasons, marketing has been, and continues to be, defined in many different ways, whether for academic, research or applied business purposes. This chapter examines what is meant by the term **marketing**.

marketing
Individual and organizational activities that facilitate and expedite satisfying exchange relationships in a dynamic environment through the creation, distribution, promotion and pricing of goods, services and ideas

> Marketing consists of individual and organizational activities that facilitate and expedite satisfying exchange relationships in a dynamic environment through the creation, distribution, promotion and pricing of goods, services and ideas.
>
> *Dibb, Simkin, Pride and Ferrell in Marketing: Concepts and Strategies*

The basic rationale of marketing is that a successful organization requires satisfied and happy customers who return to the organization to provide additional custom. In exchange for something of value, typically payment or a donation, the customers receive a product or service that satisfies their needs. Such a product has an acceptable level of quality, reliability, customer service and support, is available at places convenient for the customer at the 'right' price and is promoted effectively by means of a clear message that is readily comprehended by the customers in question. For example, in return for quenching thirst at affordable prices with a reliable product that is widely available in easy-to-use containers, Coca-Cola receives a great deal of money from customers. Unfortunately for companies and their marketers, customers' requirements change as their needs alter, marketing messages infiltrate their thinking, friends and colleagues discuss purchases, and competing products are pushed by rival organizations. In the dynamic world of marketing, an effective solution to satisfying customer needs rarely has longevity. High-specification cassette decks no longer satisfy the majority of music lovers' needs, nor for many consumers do compact disc players, so MP3 players and music downloads now dominate the product ranges of firms like Sony. Marketers must constantly assess their customers' requirements and competitors' propositions, being prepared to modify their marketing activity accordingly. An assessment of marketing opportunities is an ever evolving process requiring regular revision and updating.

> Marketing is the management process responsible for identifying, anticipating and satisfying customer requirements profitably.
>
> *Chartered Institute of Marketing*

Understanding customers and anticipating their requirements is a core theme of effective marketing.[2] So, too, is understanding general market trends and developments that may affect both customers' views and the activities of organizations operating in a particular market. These factors may include social trends, technological enhancements, economic patterns and changes in the legal and regulatory arena, as well as political influences. These are often termed the forces of the **marketing environment**. Compared with five years ago, for example, look at how many companies now produce products in 'environmentally friendly' packaging in line with the social trend of the 'green consumer'. Or, owing to recession, consider how many brands now have value versions. An organization does not have a marketplace to itself. There are direct competitors, new entrant rivals, substitute products offering alternative solutions to a customer's specific need. Construction-equipment giant JCB markets trench-digging equipment to utilities and local authorities. The growth of subterranean tunnelling robotic 'moles' for pipe laying, requiring no trench digging, is a substitute for the traditional JCB backhoe loader and a major competitive threat. The competitive context is of fundamental importance to marketers of any good or service. The internal resource base of the business which drives its strengths and weaknesses will determine which market opportunities are viable for the organization to pursue. Marketing, therefore, depends on the successful analysis of customers, the marketing environment, competition and internal capabilities.

marketing environment
External changing forces within the trading environment: laws, regulations, political activities, societal pressures, economic conditions and technological advances

> The aim of marketing is to make selling superfluous. The aim is to know and to understand the customer so well that the product or service fits him/her and sells itself!
>
> *US management guru Peter Drucker*

With an understanding of these aspects of the marketplace, an organization must then develop a marketing strategy. Even the mighty global organizations such as GM/Vauxhall, DuPont or Unilever choose not to offer a product for every type of consumer or customer need. Instead, they attempt to identify groups of customers where each separate group, or 'market segment', has 'similar' needs. Each group of customers may then be offered a specifically tailored product or service proposition and a 'marketing mix' programme. The Ford Kuga off-roader appeals to a separate group of customers than does the Ford Focus town car, and it is marketed totally differently. In developing unique marketing programmes for individual market segments – groups of customers – an organization must prioritize which particular groups of customers it has the ability to serve and which will provide satisfactory returns. Organizations have limited resources, which restricts the number of segments in a market which can be targeted. In deciding which segments to target, an organization must be clear about the image – or brand *positioning* – it intends to offer to each group of customers. The organization should endeavour to serve those customers it targets in a manner that gives it an edge over its competitors. Knowing how to group customers sensibly into homogeneous market segments; determining which to target; selecting a suitable positioning; and seeking superiority over rivals, are some of the core elements of marketing strategy.

> The marketing concept holds that the key to achieving organizational goals lies in determining the needs and wants of target markets and delivering the desired satisfaction more efficiently and effectively than the competition.
>
> *US marketer Philip Kotler*

Once a company has devised a marketing strategy, its attention must switch to marketing mix programmes.[3] As consumers of food brands, audio products or banking services, all readers of this text will have experienced the marketing mix programmes of major companies such as Cadbury's, Apple or Barclays. These are the tactical actions of marketing departments, which are designed to implement the desired marketing strategy by attracting, engaging and continuing to serve targeted customers. The product or offer must be clearly defined in line with target customer needs; service levels and guarantees must be determined; pricing and payment issues decided; channels of distribution established to make the product or service available; and promotional strategies devised and executed to communicate with the targeted customers. These tactical aspects of marketing programmes – often referred to as *the marketing mix* – must be supported with carefully managed controls in an organization to ensure their successful execution and the monitoring of their effectiveness.

Marketers must understand their markets – customers, competitors, market trends – and their own capabilities before developing marketing programmes. A marketing strategy must be determined that reflects the analyses, before the marketing programmes that will be used to action the recommended strategy are specified. **A**nalysis first, then **S**trategy decisions with, finally, the formulation of marketing **P**rogrammes: the *ASP* of the marketing process. The focus must be on providing customer satisfaction, but in a manner that leads to the organization's successful performance. For example, by addressing customers' needs and adopting a marketing culture incorporating clear controls, construction equipment manufacturer JCB has enjoyed the most successful financial returns in the company's history.

The intention of this introductory marketing text is to comprehensively explore these facets of marketing and thus provide a sound conceptual basis for understanding the nature and activities of marketing. There are many definitions of marketing, since it is not a pure science. However, certain core ingredients of the various definitions collectively indicate the basic priorities of marketing:

- satisfying customers
- identifying/maximizing marketing opportunities
- targeting the 'right' customers
- facilitating exchange relationships
- staying ahead in dynamic environments
- endeavouring to beat and pre-empt competitors
- utilizing resources/assets effectively
- increasing market share
- enhancing profitability or income
- satisfying the organization's stakeholders.

These aims form the objectives for many marketing directors and marketing departments. They are featured throughout this book, which formally adopts two definitions of marketing by the American Marketing Association. As already stated, *Marketing consists of individual and organizational activities that facilitate and expedite satisfying exchange relationships in a dynamic environment through the creation, distribution, promotion and pricing of goods, services and ideas.* Along with the Association's more process-driven explanation;

> *Marketing. Noun. An organizational function and a set of processes for creating, communicating and delivering value to customers and for managing customer relationships in ways that benefit the organization and its stakeholders.*

Marketing indeed must be viewed as a process… of analysis to gain market insights, strategy decisions to make choices, and the management of marketing programmes in order to implement the desired marketing strategy. A definition of marketing must acknowledge that it relates to more than just tangible goods, that marketing activities occur in a dynamic environment and that such activities are performed by individuals as well as organizations.[4] The ultimate goal is to satisfy targeted customers and stakeholders, seeking their loyalty and consumption, in a way that adds value for the organization and its stakeholders. This should be achieved in a manner that is differentiated in the view of customers and stakeholders vis-à-vis competitors' marketing, that provides an organization with a competitive edge over rivals and that is updated regularly to reflect market forces and developments. To be in a position to satisfy targeted customers or stakeholders, much work is required by those tasked within the organization and their external partners to conduct the required marketing analyses, develop sensible marketing strategies and create appropriate marketing programmes to take to market... repeatedly and regularly.

The definitions of marketing explored

Marketing consists of individual and organizational activities that facilitate and expedite satisfying exchange relationships in a dynamic environment through the creation, distribution, promotion and pricing of goods, services and ideas.

Marketing consists of activities

The marketing of products or services effectively requires many activities. Some are performed by producers; some are accomplished by intermediaries, who purchase products from producers or from other intermediaries and resell them; and some are even performed by purchasers. Marketing does not include all human and organizational activities, only those aimed at facilitating and expediting exchanges. Table 1.1 lists several major categories and examples of marketing activities, as ultimately encountered by the consumer or business customer, who remains at the 'sharp end' of such decisions and marketing programmes. Note that this list is not all-inclusive. Each activity could be sub-divided into more specific activities.

TABLE 1.1 Possible decisions and activities associated with marketing mix variables

Marketing mix variables	Possible decisions and activities
Product	Develop and test market new products; modify existing products; eliminate products that do not satisfy customers' desires; formulate brand names and branding policies; create product guarantees and establish procedures for fulfilling guarantees; provide customer service; plan packaging, including materials, sizes, shapes, colours and designs
Place/distribution	Analyze various types of distribution channels; design appropriate distribution channels; select appropriate channel members and partners; design an effective programme for dealer relations; establish distribution centres; formulate and implement procedures for efficient product handling; set up inventory controls; analyze transportation methods; minimize total distribution costs; analyze possible locations for plants and wholesale or retail outlets; manage multiple channels to market
Promotion (marketing communications)	Set promotional objectives; determine major types of promotion to be used; select and schedule advertising media; develop advertising messages; measure the effectiveness of advertisements; recruit and train salespeople; formulate payment programmes for sales personnel; establish sales territories; plan and implement sales promotion efforts such as free samples, coupons, displays, competitions, sales contests and cooperative advertising programmes; prepare and disseminate publicity releases; evaluate sponsorships; provide direct mail; and establish websites and a digital presence
Price	Analyze competitors' prices; formulate pricing policies; determine method(s) used to set prices; set prices; determine discounts for various types of buyer; establish conditions and terms of sales; determine credit and payment terms; understand the consumers' notion of value
People	Manipulate the marketing mix and establish service levels, guarantees, warranties, expertise, sales support, after sales back-up, customer handling requirements, personnel skills training and motivation (people as marketers); make products and services available (people as intermediaries); provide a market for products (people as consumers); manage customer retention

Marketing is performed by individuals and organizations

All organizations perform marketing activities to facilitate exchanges. Businesses as well as not-for-profit and public-sector organizations, such as colleges and universities, charitable organizations, community theatres and hospitals, perform marketing activities. For example, colleges and universities and their students engage in exchanges. To receive instruction, knowledge, entertainment, a degree, the use of facilities and sometimes room and board, students give up time, money and perhaps services in the form of labour; they may also give up opportunities to do other things! Many organizations engage in marketing activities. Various police forces have surveyed their communities in order to prioritize services and reassure the general public that people's concerns will be addressed. Politicians now conduct analyses before determining strategies; they think of target markets rather than just the electorate. Even the sole owner of, and worker in, a small corner shop decides which products will sell, arranges deliveries to the shop, prices and displays products, advertises and serves customers.

Marketing facilitates satisfying exchange relationships

exchange
The provision or transfer of goods, services and ideas in return for something of value

For an **exchange** to take place, four conditions must exist.

1 Two or more individuals, groups or organizations must participate.

2 Each party must possess something of value that the other party desires (for example, cash for a product or a donation for a charitable cause).

3 Each party must be willing to give up its 'something of value' to receive the 'something of value' held by the other party. The objective of a marketing exchange is to receive something that is desired more than that which is given up to get it – that is, a reward in excess of costs.

4 The parties to the exchange must be able to communicate with each other to make their 'something of value' available.[5]

Figure 1.1 illustrates the process of exchange. The arrows indicate that the parties communicate and that each has something of value available to exchange. Note, though, that an exchange will not necessarily take place just because these four conditions exist. Nevertheless, even if there is no exchange, marketing activities have still occurred. The 'somethings of value' held by the two parties are most often products and/or financial resources, such as money or credit. When an exchange occurs, products are traded for other products or for financial resources.

customer satisfaction
A state that results when an exchange meets the needs and expectations of the buyer

An exchange should be *satisfying* to both the buyer and the seller. In fact, in a study of marketing managers, 32 per cent indicated that creating **customer satisfaction** was the most important concept in a definition of marketing.[6] Marketing activities should be oriented towards creating and maintaining satisfying exchange relationships. To maintain an exchange relationship, the buyer must be satisfied with the goods, service or idea obtained in the exchange; the seller must be satisfied with the financial reward or something else of value received in the exchange.

Maintaining a positive relationship with buyers is an important goal for a seller, regardless of whether the seller is marketing cereal, financial services or construction plant. Through buyer–seller interaction, the buyer develops expectations about the seller's future behaviour. To fulfil these expectations, the seller must deliver on promises made. Over time, a healthy buyer–seller relationship results in interdependencies between the two parties. The buyer depends on the seller to furnish information, parts and service; to be available; and to provide satisfying products in the future.

Marketing occurs in a dynamic environment

The marketing environment consists of many external changing forces within the trading environment: laws, regulations, political activities, societal pressures, changing economic conditions and technological advances. Each of these dynamic forces has an impact on how effectively marketing activities can facilitate and expedite exchanges. For example, the development and acceptance

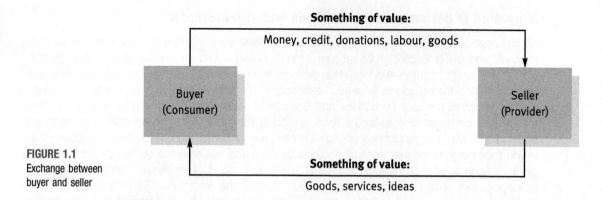

FIGURE 1.1
Exchange between buyer and seller

of the Internet in home or mobile PCs has given organizations another vehicle through which to promote and distribute their products. Another example is the impact EU regulations have had on reducing distribution headaches within much of Europe.

Marketing involves products, distribution, promotion, pricing and people

Marketing means more than simply advertising or selling a product; it involves developing and managing a product that will satisfy certain needs. It focuses on making the product available at the right place, at the right time, at a price that is acceptable to customers and with appropriate people and service support. It also requires transmitting through marketing communications the kind of promotional information that will help customers determine whether the product will in fact be able to satisfy their needs.

Marketing focuses on goods, services and ideas

product
A good, service or idea

good
A physical entity that can be touched

service
The application of human and mechanical efforts to people or objects in order to provide intangible benefits to customers

idea
A concept, philosophy, image or issue

The word 'product' has been used a number of times in this chapter. For purposes of discussion in this text, a **product** is viewed as being a good, a service or an idea. A **good** is a physical entity that can be touched. A Ford Focus, a Sony MP3 player, Kellogg's Cornflakes, a bar of Lux soap and a kitten in a pet shop are examples of goods. A **service** is the application of human and mechanical efforts to people or objects in order to provide intangible benefits to customers. Services such as air travel, dry cleaning, hairdressing, banking, medical care and childcare are just as real as goods, but an individual cannot actually touch or stockpile them. Marketing is utilized for services but requires certain enhancements in order to be effective (see Part Three). **Ideas** include concepts, philosophies, images and issues. For instance, a marriage counsellor gives couples ideas and advice to help improve their relationships. Other marketers of ideas include political parties, charities, religious groups, schools and marketing lecturers.

An organizational function and a set of processes for creating, communicating and delivering value to customers and for managing customer relationships in ways that benefit the organization and its stakeholders

The more recent definition suggested by the American Marketing Association came as a welcome addition, as for over two decades we have presented marketing to our students as an analytical process of analysis, strategizing and then programmes for implementation in our *marketing process*. This process is relevant to not only those organizations with consumers or business customers. Given that all organizations have stakeholders which must be influenced and satisfied, this process is suitable for any organization, including those in the third sector.

The marketing process

Marketers spend much of their time managing existing products, target markets and marketing programmes. Even with such so-called 'steady-state' operations, the dynamic nature of marketing leads to continual changes in the marketing environment, competitors and their activities, as well as in customers' needs, expectations, perceptions and buying behaviour. Without a sound understanding of these issues, marketing strategies and their associated marketing programmes cannot be truly effective. Marketers must, therefore, undertake analyses of these market conditions. As changes in the marketplace occur, marketers should revise their marketing strategies accordingly. Any strategy modifications will necessitate changes to the organization's marketing programmes.

marketing process
Analysis of market conditions, the creation of an appropriate marketing strategy, the development of marketing programmes designed to action the agreed strategy and, finally, the implementation and control of the marketing strategy and its associated marketing programmes

This analytical process of marketing analyses, strategy formulation and the creation or modification of marketing programmes is necessary for existing activities and target markets. This marketing process is also required when an organization contemplates entering new markets, launching new or replacement products, modifying the brand strategy, changing customer service practices, rethinking advertising and promotional plans, altering pricing or evaluating distribution policies. Unexpected sales patterns also require such a process of understanding, thinking and action. This is the **marketing process:** the analysis of market conditions, the creation of an appropriate marketing strategy and the development of marketing programmes designed to execute the agreed strategy, as depicted in Figure 1.2. Finally, as part of this process, the implementation of the marketing strategy and its associated marketing programmes must be managed and controlled.

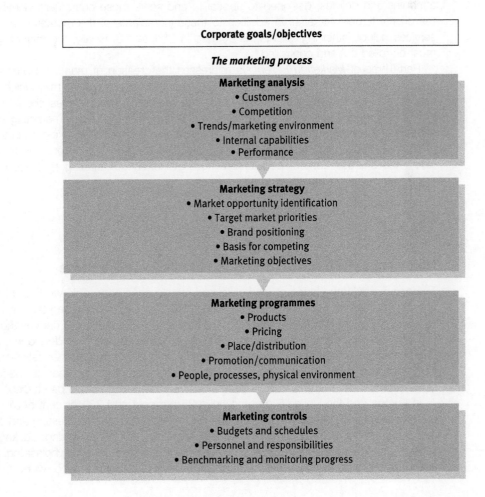

FIGURE 1.2
The marketing process

Source: © Sally Dibb and Lyndon Simkin

With an understanding of customers' needs, buying behaviour, expectations and product or brand perceptions, marketers are able to create marketing programmes likely to attract, satisfy and retain customers. With an appreciation of competitors' activities and plans, the marketing programmes are more likely to combat rivals' marketing programmes and to differentiate an organization's product. Without an awareness of changes in the marketing environment, it is unlikely that the specified marketing programme will be sustainable in the longer term. As trading environment changes occur, it is important that an organization's capabilities are modified in order to reflect market conditions and likely demands. The marketing analysis stage of the marketing process is, therefore, of fundamental importance.

Equipped with an awareness of the marketplace made possible through marketing analyses, a marketing strategy may be derived. This involves selecting the opportunities to be pursued and devising an associated target market strategy. Few organizations have adequate financial, managerial and employee resources to address all of the possible marketing opportunities that exist: there must be some trade-offs. This generally involves selecting only some of the opportunities to pursue and focusing on specific target markets. Having made these decisions, marketers must ensure that they develop a compelling brand positioning and that they create a strong basis for competing versus their rivals, aimed specifically at attracting customers in the prioritized target markets. These strategic recommendations should then translate into specific marketing objectives, designed to hone the creation of marketing programmes.

In most organizations the majority of the budget, time and effort within the marketing function is devoted to creating and managing marketing programmes. These programmes revolve around specifying product, people, promotion (communication), pricing and place (distribution channel) attributes and policies, designed to appeal to and serve those customers identified as being in the priority target market(s). In addition to these ingredients of the marketing mix, marketers of services include other ingredients, as detailed in Chapter 13. Finally, the marketing programmes must be rolled out and controlled.

Part Three of *Marketing Essentials* addresses the creation of marketing programmes. These chapters examine extensively each of the ingredients of the marketing mix, which are the essentials for a marketing programme. However, the marketing programmes should not be created before marketers have fully analyzed the market and then devised a marketing strategy. These aspects of marketing analysis and marketing strategy are, therefore, explored in the early stages of *Marketing Essentials,* in Parts One and Two. The chapter running order is also structured to reflect the syllabus content popular on most mainstream marketing modules and courses at diploma and degree level.

The importance of marketing

Marketing activities are carried out in many organizations

The commercial importance of marketing and its relevance as a topic worth studying are apparent from the definitions of marketing just presented. The use of marketing techniques and the development of a marketing orientation should enable an organization to understand its customers and stakeholders better, address competitors' activities and market developments, and effectively harness its capabilities. The results should be enhanced customer satisfaction and retention, improved market share in key target markets and stronger financial performance. This section discusses several less obvious reasons why marketing should be studied.

In Europe and the United States between 25 per cent and 33 per cent of all civilian workers perform marketing activities. The marketing field offers a variety of interesting and challenging career opportunities, such as strategic planning, personal selling, advertising, packaging, transport, storage, marketing research, product development, creative design, wholesaling, retailing, marketing planning and consultancy. In addition, many individuals who work for not-for-profit

FIGURE 1.3
Promotion of a non-profit organization.

copyright © Jeans for Genes, www. jeansforgenesday. org

organizations – such as charities or health agencies – engage in marketing activities. Marketing skills are used to promote political, cultural, religious, civic and charitable activities. The advertisement in Figure 1.3 encourages support of the Jeans for Genes campaign, a non-profit organization. Whether a person earns a living through marketing activities or performs them without reward in non-business settings, marketing knowledge and skills are valuable assets. For both commercial and non-profit organizations there are needs to satisfy, exchanges to expedite, changing circumstances to monitor and decisions to make. Even a country benefits from marketing, as described in the Marketing insight box below.

Marketing activities are important to organizations and the economy

An organization must sell products in order to survive and grow. Directly or indirectly, marketing activities help to sell an organization's products. By doing so, they generate financial resources that can be used to develop innovative products. New products allow a company to satisfy customers' changing needs more efficiently, which in turn enables the company to generate more profits. Charities and other not-for-profit organizations use marketing to generate revenues and funds.

Europe's highly complex economy depends heavily on marketing activities. These help produce the profits that are essential not only to the survival of individual organizations but also to

Ireland: marketing a country

Topical insight

How do you develop a marketing strategy for a country? This was a question faced by the Irish government during difficult times in the 1960s and 1970s. The challenge was to build the Irish economy to match the affluence enjoyed by some of its European neighbours. At the time, Ireland was viewed as being backward and unattractive for investment by international corporations. The Industrial Development Authority (IDA) played an important role in developing the country's economy, moving it away from its traditional over-reliance on agriculture. Today, with well over a third of the country's GDP coming from industry, and services also accounting for approaching a third, agriculture's contribution has fallen to just 10 per cent.

Marketing and good promotion alone were not responsible for this turnaround. The Irish government realized that to attract investment from overseas it had to provide a stable economy, desirable residential suburbs, modern road and air infrastructure, state-of-the-art telecommunications and, crucially, a well-qualified, dynamic and motivated workforce. These improvements took some time to achieve, but today the companies located in Dublin and around Ireland's airports testify readily to the excellent infrastructure, communications, workforce and tax breaks. The Irish workforce is one of the best educated and most highly prized in Europe.

Having improved the amenities, infrastructure and the workforce, the perceptions of investors overseas had to be addressed. In order to instigate this change, the IDA established a clear strategy by pinpointing attractive sectors for growth and actively encouraging growth businesses in those areas. Consumer products, electronics, healthcare and financial services were some of the key targets. Once

decisions about growth priorities had been made, the aim was to develop a marketing programme based around the particular assets that Ireland was able to offer. For example, promotional material focused on – among other things – the young, highly educated workforce, the low rates of corporate taxation, excellent digital and satellite telecommunications systems and a stable currency with low inflation. The attractive countryside and vibrant cultural scene also featured prominently in the IDA's branding of Ireland.

Considerable care was taken to ensure that the propositions developed matched the requirements of the businesses targeted. This provided many overseas businesses with substantial, tangible reasons for establishing a base in Ireland, bringing with them the investment the country so badly craved. Leading computer manufacturers, pharmaceutical businesses, financial corporations and telecommunications businesses are just some of those who have located facilities in the country: over 1000 well-known organizations have chosen Ireland ahead of other locations for their European operations.

After the recent meltdown of the Irish economy following the global financial crisis, there is once more the need to develop a marketing strategy for Ireland. Most of the work of the past 20 years must be repeated and reinforced, in order to ensure continued inward investment. The marketing toolkit will play a significant part in the overhaul of Ireland's target market strategy, positioning and new-look measures to attract global businesses to locate in the country.

Sources: Irish Embassy, London; Industrial Development Authority (IDA); 'Facts about Ireland', IDA, 1995, 1996, 1999, 2003, 2008, 2011; **http://www.idaireland.com**, 2 February 2011.

the health and ultimate survival of the economy as a whole. Profits are essential to economic growth because without them organizations find it difficult, if not impossible, to buy more raw materials, recruit more employees, attract more capital and create the additional products that in turn lead to more profits.

Marketing knowledge enhances consumer awareness

Besides contributing to a country's economic well-being, marketing activities permeate everyone's lives. In fact, they help to improve quality of life. Studying marketing activities enables the costs, benefits and flaws of marketing to be evaluated. The need for improvement and ways to accomplish changes can be determined. For example, an unsatisfactory experience with a guarantee may lead consumers to demand that laws be enforced more strictly to make sellers fulfil their promises. Similarly, there may be the desire for more information about a product – or more accurate

TABLE 1.2 Popular marketing myths

Myths	Strongly agree	Somewhat agree	Neither agree nor disagree	Somewhat disagree	Strongly disagree
Marketing is selling	34%	14%	26%	18%	8%
Marketers persuade	21%	25%	20%	11%	23%
Dealers' profits significantly increase prices consumers pay	21%	32%	12%	8%	27%
Marketing depends on advertising	44%	17%	12%	9%	18%
Strategic planning has nothing to do with marketing	19%	19%	21%	17%	24%

information – before purchase. Understanding marketing leads to the evaluation of the corrective measures – such as laws, regulations and industry guidelines – that may be required to stop unfair, misleading or unethical marketing practices. The results of the survey presented in Table 1.2 indicate that there is a considerable lack of knowledge about marketing activities, as reflected by the sizeable proportion of respondents who agree with the myths in the table.

Marketing costs consume a sizeable proportion of buyers' incomes

The study of the marketing discipline emphasizes that many marketing activities are necessary to provide people with satisfying goods and services. Obviously, these marketing activities cost money. A family with a monthly income of £2000, of which £600 goes towards taxes and savings, spends about £1400 on goods and services. Of this amount, typically £700 goes towards marketing activities. Clearly, if marketing expenses consume that much income, it is necessary to know how this money is used.

Business performance

Marketing puts an emphasis on satisfying customers. Marketing analyses should lead an organization to develop a marketing strategy that takes account of market trends, aims to satisfy customers, is aware of competitive activity and targets the right customers with a clear positioning message. In so doing, an organization should benefit from customer loyalty and advantages over its rivals, while making the most efficient use of resources to effectively address the specific requirements of those markets it chooses to target. Hence, marketing should provide both a financial benefit and a greater sense of well-being for the organization.

The marketing concept and its evolution

Some organizations have tried to be successful by buying land, building a factory, equipping it with people and machines, and then making a product that they believe consumers need. However, these organizations frequently fail to attract buyers with what they have to offer because they defined their business as 'making a product' rather than as 'helping potential customers satisfy their needs and wants'. Such organizations have failed to implement the marketing concept. It is not enough to be product-led, no matter how good the product. An organization must be in tune with consumer or business customer requirements.

marketing concept
The philosophy that an organization should try to provide products that satisfy customers' needs through a coordinated set of activities that also allows the organization to achieve its goals

According to the **marketing concept**, an organization should try to provide products that satisfy customers' needs through a coordinated set of activities that also allows the organization to achieve its goals. Customer satisfaction is the major aim of the marketing concept. First, an organization must find out what will satisfy customers.

With this information, it then attempts to create satisfying products. But the process does not end there. The organization must continue to alter, adapt and develop products to keep pace with customers' changing desires and preferences. The marketing concept stresses the importance of customers, and emphasizes that marketing activities begin and end with them.[7]

In attempting to satisfy customers, organizations must consider not only short-term, immediate needs but also broad, long-term desires. Trying to satisfy customers' current needs by sacrificing their long-term desires will only create future dissatisfaction. For instance, people want efficient, low-cost energy to power their homes and cars, yet they react adversely to energy producers that pollute the air and water, kill wildlife or cause disease or birth defects. To meet these short- and long-term needs and desires, a company must coordinate all its activities. Production, finance, accounting, personnel and marketing departments must work together.

The marketing concept is not another definition of marketing. It is a way of thinking: a management philosophy guiding an organization's overall activities. This philosophy affects all the efforts of the organization, not just marketing activities, and is strongly linked to the notion of marketing orientation. However, the marketing concept is by no means a philanthropic philosophy aimed at helping customers at the expense of the organization. A company that adopts the marketing concept must not only satisfy its customers' objectives but also achieve its own goals, or it will not stay in business long. The overall goals of an organization may be directed towards increasing profits, market share, sales or a combination of all three. The marketing concept stresses that an organization can best achieve its goals by providing customer satisfaction. Thus, implementing the marketing concept should benefit the organization as well as its customers.

production era
The period of mass production following industrialization

The evolution of the marketing concept

The marketing concept may seem an obvious and sensible approach to running a business. However, business people have not always believed that the best way to make sales and profits is to satisfy customers. A famous example is the marketing philosophy for cars widely attributed to Henry Ford in the early 1900s: 'The customers can have any colour car they want as long as it's black.' The philosophy of the marketing concept emerged in the third major era in the history of business, preceded by the **production era** and the **sales era.** Surprisingly, it took nearly 40 years after the **marketing era** began before many organizations started to adopt the marketing concept. The more advanced marketing-led companies have now entered a spin-off from the marketing era: the **relationship marketing era**. More recently, there have been several significant developments for marketers, most notable of which are value-based marketing, digital marketing and the associated surge in consumer-to-consumer communication, the growth of social marketing applications, and the emergence of so-called critical marketing.

sales era
The period from the mid-1920s to the early 1950s when competitive forces and the desire for high sales volume led a company to emphasize selling and the sales person in its business strategy

marketing era
The period in which product and aggressive selling were no longer seen to suffice if customers either did not desire a product or preferred a rival brand, and in which customer needs were identified and satisfied

The production era   During the second half of the nineteenth century, the Industrial Revolution was in full swing in Europe and the United States. Electricity, railways, the division of labour, the assembly line and mass production made it possible to manufacture products more efficiently. With new technology and new ways of using labour, products poured into the marketplace, where consumer demand for manufactured goods was strong. This production orientation continued into the early part of the last century, encouraged by the scientific management movement that championed rigidly structured jobs and pay based on output.

relationship marketing era
In which the focus is not only on expediting the single transaction but on developing ongoing relationships with customers to maintain lifetime share of wallet

The sales era   In the 1920s, the strong consumer demand for products subsided. Companies realized that products, which by this time could be made quite efficiently, would have to be 'sold' to consumers. From the mid-1920s to the early 1950s, companies viewed sales as the major means of increasing profits. As a result, this period came to have a sales orientation. Business people believed that the most important marketing activities were personal selling and advertising.

The marketing era By the early 1950s, some business people began to recognize that efficient production and extensive promotion of products did not guarantee that customers would buy them. Companies found that they first had to determine what customers wanted and then produce it, rather than simply making products first and then trying to change customers' needs to correspond to what was being produced. As organizations realized the importance of knowing customers' needs, companies entered into the marketing era – the era of customer orientation.[8]

The relationship marketing era By the 1990s, many organizations had grasped the basics of the marketing concept and had created marketing functions. However, their view of marketing was often largely transaction based. The priority for marketing was to identify customer needs, determine priority target markets and achieve sales through marketing programmes. The focus was on the individual transaction or exchange. It should be recognized that long-term success and market share gains depend on such transactions, but also on maintaining a customer's loyalty and on repeatedly gaining sales from existing customers. This requires ongoing, committed, reassuring and tailored relationship-building marketing programmes.

Relationship marketing refers to 'long-term, mutually beneficial arrangements in which both the buyer and seller focus on value enhancement through the creation of more satisfying exchanges'.[9] Relationship marketing continually deepens the buyer's trust in the company and, as the customer's confidence grows, this in turn increases the company's understanding of the customer's needs. Successful marketers respond to customers' needs and strive to increase value to buyers over time. Eventually this interaction becomes a solid relationship that allows for cooperation and mutual dependency

As the era of relationship orientation developed, it became clear that it is not only relationships with customers that are important. Suppliers, agents, distributors, recruiters, referral bodies (such as independent financial advisers recommending financial services companies' products), influencers (such as government departments, national banks or the EU), all should be 'marketed to' in order to ensure their support, understanding and resources. The internal workforce must be motivated and provided with a clear understanding of a company's target market strategy, marketing mix activities and, indeed, of the corporate strategy and planned direction. Hence, the current era is moving away from transaction-based marketing and towards nurturing ongoing relationships.[10]

From the 1990s, lifetime value (of the customer) became a buzz term for marketers. This concept is linked to relationship marketing, said by many observers to be the new paradigm for marketing. This evolution of marketing, from focusing on individual transactions with customers to building ongoing relationships and repeat business, has been very important for the success of many organizations. Until relatively recently, relationship marketing was the main significant change in how the discipline has been perceived. In the last few years, however, there have been several new trends for marketing, each of which has stretched the bounds for the discipline, adding complex new dimensions and further shaping the marketing paradigm:

value-based marketing
Value-based marketing recognizes that marketing must prove its long term financial worth and be accountable to organizations, which involves showing that marketing enables both the creation of short-term customer value and longer-term value for shareholders.

Focus on value-based marketing Since the late 1990s, marketing has been through a period of reflection, amidst demands that the discipline demonstrates its credibility and proves its contribution to organizational goals. **Value-based marketing** recognizes that marketing must prove its long-term financial worth and be accountable to organizations. This involves showing that marketing enables both the creation of short-term customer value and longer-term value for shareholders.

The growth of consumer-to-consumer (C2C) communications in the digital era This has significant consequences for brands and marketers, for consumers and for society in general. Previously, brand managers largely controlled what information was available to consumers and business customers. These customers based their decisions about brands and products on the marketing and sales information communicated to them by brand managers. Today, **consumer-to-consumer (C2C) communication** is routine, enabled by the digital era generally and social media in particular. Consumers readily and rapidly share views, experiences and information with one another. A positive or negative customer experience is tweeted instantly, blogged or shared on Facebook with many potential fellow consumers. Such messaging, whether positive or negative, has moved beyond the control of marketers. Many consumers trust and value the views of their peers far more than the views of brand managers, advertising messages or media reviews. The surge of C2C communication has redefined the boundaries and created huge new challenges for marketers. The role of C2C interaction and communication is picked up throughout this edition of *Marketing Essentials*.

Digital media, the surge in Internet usage and the uptake of personal mobile communications and information provision, have fostered changing consumer behaviours, greater consumer-to-consumer influence on brands and purchasing decisions, and business-to-business interaction. These developments have created an entirely new domain for marketers, known as **digital marketing.**

This domain encompasses the use of the Web and mobile phones, as well as radio, TV and other forms of digital media, to attract, engage and build relationships with customers and other target audiences. The immediacy, intimacy and customization of many Internet and mobile digital communications and customer interactions have transformed the ability of marketers to target customer groups and individuals with bespoke propositions and nurture an ongoing relationship. While the digital era poses significant challenges to marketers, most marketers recognize its exciting potential. The implications of digital are explored throughout this text.

Social marketing's adoption of marketing's toolkit in non-commercial settings Social marketing: uses tools and techniques from commercial marketing to encourage positive behavioural changes, such as quitting smoking, reducing alcohol consumption, minimizing anti-social behaviours or reducing carbon footprint. The health and well-being of individuals, society and the planet are at the core of social marketing. The social marketing field now provides interesting career opportunities for marketing professionals interested in applying marketing analyses, notably in terms of understanding behaviours of a particular audience or social group (Chapter 4), developing targeting strategies (Chapter 6) and in creating programmes to communicate with such audiences (Chapter 13). Rising interest in these applications reflects the increasing importance of the strategic marketing process to a growing set of audiences and stakeholders beyond those from traditional commercial markets. The growth of social marketing is also reflected throughout this edition of *Marketing Essentials*.

Most readers of this book will be students undertaking a business studies degree or marketing qualification. Some readers will be students on more general management degrees who do not inhabit the world of commercial marketing managers. For either audience, this text demonstrates how the marketing philosophy permeates many aspects of our lives and society, including in the overtly non-commercial realms of social marketing. As the second marketing insight reveals, marketing principles extend much further than promoting Kellogg's Cornflakes, the iPhone, McDonald's burgers and JCB diggers.

---

consumer-to-consumer (C2C) communication
Consumer-to-consumer (C2C) communication is now routine, enabled by the digital era and social media in particular. Consumers readily and rapidly share views, experiences and information with each other. A positive or negative customer experience is tweeted instantly, blogged or shared on Facebook with potentially very many fellow consumers.

digital marketing
The use of particularly the Web and mobile phones, as well as radio, TV and any other form of digital media to attract, engage and build relationships with customers and other target audiences.

social marketing
Social marketing uses tools and techniques from commercial marketing to encourage positive behavioural changes, such as quitting smoking, reducing alcohol consumption, minimizing anti-social behaviours or reducing carbon footprint. The health and well-being of individuals, society and the planet are at the core of social marketing.

An alternative view of the scope for marketing: social marketing

Topical insight

The Institute for Social Marketing (ISM) was established 30 years ago with the aim of improving the health and well-being of individuals and society through social marketing research. Now based at the University of Stirling and the Open University, ISM is interested in social marketing's use of tools and techniques from commercial marketing to encourage positive behaviour changes, such as quitting smoking or reducing carbon footprint.

Key priority research areas for ISM include alcohol and alcohol marketing, tobacco control, sustainability and sustainable consumption, faith and community partnerships, problem gambling, health, well-being and life of quality, ageing, food and nutrition.

This agenda differs from the common perception of marketing that is widely held by the general public. This implies there is more scope for applying marketing principles than only for the marketing of FMCG supermarket products, financial services, holiday packages or condoms!

ISM explains the purpose of social marketing and about its use of commercial marketing ideas:

> Social marketers are interested in human behaviour. They seek to understand why we live our lives as we do, sometimes healthily as when we eat a good diet or take regular exercise and at other times unhealthily as when we smoke or binge drink. Given that more than 50 per cent of premature deaths are attributable to such individual lifestyle decisions, there is enormous potential for any discipline that can progress thinking in this area. Social marketing brings a unique perspective to the issue.
>
> Marketing is typically concerned with behaviour in the limited area of consumption and the marketplace. However, from the discipline's beginnings, marketers have argued that their behaviour change thinking can also be applied to other contexts; as Wiebe famously argued, you can sell brotherhood like soap. So, just as Big Tobacco can use marketing to encourage smoking, so 'social marketing' can do the reverse. The same

principles – of understanding the consumer, strategic thinking and building satisfying relationships based on emotional as well as rational benefits – can be brought to bear.

Social marketing also recognizes that, although commerce brings many benefits, it can also cause harm to both the individual and society. Tobacco, which kills half of its long term users, provides an extreme example of this, but other industries like alcohol and food are also coming under scrutiny. Social marketing's understanding of both the commercial and social sectors puts it in a unique position to provide realistic critiques, and identify intelligent solutions. This forms an important part of the growing field of critical marketing.

These realities informed Lazer and Kelly's original definition of social marketing: Social marketing is concerned with the application of marketing knowledge, concepts and techniques to enhance social as well as economic ends. It is also concerned with the analysis of the social consequences of marketing policies, decisions and activities.

http://www.open.ac.uk/oubs/ism, January 2012.

Readers may be surprised to learn that those fighting obesity, smoking, alcohol abuse, problem gambling are using ideas from commercial marketing in their efforts. Just as in commercial settings, social marketers must understand the attitudes, perceptions and behaviour of those they are targeting, before creating strategies to tackle these problems areas. Once decisions about who to target have been made, well articulated and carefully communicated propositions are needed to engage with these audiences. In these respects, the development and execution of a social marketing strategy has many similarities with commercial marketing practice.

Sources: **http://www.open.ac.uk/oubs/ism**; **http://www.management.stir. ac.uk/about-us/institute-of-social-marketing**; Philip Kotler and Nancy Lee (eds), *Social Marketing: Influencing Behaviors for Good*, 3rd Edition, Thousands Oaks: Sage Publications Inc, 2007; Douglas Evans and Gerard Hastings (eds), *Public Health Branding: Applying Marketing for Social Change*, Oxford: Oxford University Press, 2008.

The emergence of critical marketing Although this cannot really be described as a paradigm shift in the sense of relationship marketing, critical marketing nevertheless warrants consideration. Those interested in this field agree that critical marketing is difficult to define. **Critical marketing:** is espoused by individuals who challenge orthodox views that are central to the core principles of the discipline. Sometimes this involves promoting radical philosophies and theories in relation to the understanding of economies, society, markets and consumers, which may have implications for the practice of marketing. In some instances, the assumptions at the heart of many of the core principles of the discipline are challenged. Critical marketing is connected with the growing area of critical management.

critical marketing
Critical marketing involves challenging orthodox views that are central to the core principles of the discipline. Sometimes this involves promoting radical philosophies and theories in relation to the understanding of economies, society, markets and consumers, which may have implications for the practice of marketing. Critical marketing is connected with the growing area of critical management.

While a detailed exploration of critical marketing is beyond the scope of this text, it is right to highlight the alternative views that exist about the domain and the activities associated with it. Once readers are familiar with the core concepts associated with effective marketing, they might also wish to explore the views of critical marketers.[11] This group is interested in issues such as postmodernism; the biological base for consumer behaviour; the connections between marketing activities and society (including social marketing), such as sustainable marketing; anti-globalization challenges to marketing; ecofeminism; and the inter-connection of cultural studies and consumer research. Although many of these themes are not explored in detail here, a more detailed examination of aspects of social marketing is included. In addition, reflections on marketing in practice are incorporated throughout this book, contributing to the critical marketing debate around the distinction between theory and practice.

A further aspect of critical marketing that warrants consideration relates to concerns that marketing sometimes has damaging consequences and that marketers are not always aware of these outcomes.[12] For example, some critics argue that marketing is responsible for heightening consumerism and generating 'must have' attitudes amongst consumers. This has resulted in negative consequences for society in relation to carbon footprint, the use of scarce resources, landfill, state spending priorities and even on changing societal values. Although there are divergent opinions on these matters, there can be little doubt that marketing influences consumption and that these patterns have significant impacts for the environment, for society and for consumers. These and other impacts of marketing, including a discussion of some of the ethical issues facing marketers, are considered later in this edition.

Implementing the marketing concept

A philosophy may sound reasonable and look good on paper, but that does not mean it can be put into practice easily. The marketing concept is a case in point. To implement it, an organization must focus on some general conditions and recognize several problems. Because of these conditions and problems, the marketing concept has yet to be fully accepted by some organizations.

Because the marketing concept affects all types of business activities, not just marketing activities, the top management of an organization must adopt it wholeheartedly. High-level executives must incorporate the marketing concept into their philosophies of business management so completely that it becomes the basis for all the goals and decisions that they set for their companies. They should also convince other members of the organization to accept the changes in policies and operations that flow from their acceptance of the marketing concept. Costs and budgetary controls are important, products and manufacturing essential, and personnel management necessary; but all are to no avail if the organization's products or services are not desired by the targeted customers.

As a first step, management must set up a system for capturing information that enables it to discover customers' real needs and to use the information to create satisfying products. Because such a system is usually expensive, management must be willing to commit money and time for development and maintenance. Without an adequate information system, an organization cannot be customer oriented.

Management's second major task is to structure the organization appropriately. If a company is to satisfy its customers' objectives as well as its own, it must coordinate all its activities. To achieve this, the internal operations and the overall objectives of one or more departments may need restructuring. If the head of the marketing unit is not a member of the organization's top-level management, he or she should be. Some departments may have to be abolished and new ones created. Implementing the marketing concept demands the support not only of top management but also of managers and staff at all levels within the organization.

Even when the basic conditions of establishing an information system and reorganizing the organization are met, the organization's new marketing approach may not work perfectly, for the following reasons:

- There is a limit to a company's ability to satisfy customers' needs for a particular product. In a mass-production economy, most business organizations cannot tailor products to fit the exact needs of each customer.

- Although a company may attempt to learn what customers want, it may be unable to do so, and when the organization does identify customers' needs correctly, it often has a difficult time developing a product that satisfies those needs. Many companies spend considerable time and money researching customers' needs and yet still create some products that do not sell well.

- By striving to satisfy one particular segment of society, a company sometimes dissatisfies other segments. Certainly, government and non-business organizations also experience this problem.

- An organization may have difficulty maintaining employee morale, particularly if restructuring is needed to coordinate the activities of various departments. Management must clearly explain the reasons for the various changes and communicate its own enthusiasm for the marketing concept.

Adoption of the marketing philosophy takes time, resources, endurance and commitment.

The essentials of marketing

Marketing analyses

From these brief introductory comments, it should be evident that marketing can enhance an organization's understanding of its customers, competitors, market trends, threats and opportunities. Marketing should direct an organization's target market strategy, product development and communication with its distribution channels and customers. In order to carry out these activities, marketing personnel need access to good quality marketing intelligence about the following issues:

- customers
- competitors
- marketing environment forces
- the organization's capabilities, marketing assets and performance.

As will be seen later in this book, there are other marketing analyses which can be carried out, but these just mentioned are the essential building blocks for the development of marketing strategies and the creation of marketing programmes. The majority of the chapters in Parts One and Two of *Marketing Essentials* address these marketing analyses, which are the foundation of the marketing process.

marketing strategy
The selection of which marketing opportunities to pursue, identification of associated target market(s), creation of a basis for competing and 'wow' positioning, and the development and maintenance of an appropriate marketing mix to satisfy those in the target market(s)

marketing mix
The tactical 'toolkit' of the marketing programme; product, place/distribution, promotion, price and people variables that an organization can control in order to appeal to the target market and facilitate satisfying exchange

Marketing strategy

To achieve the broad goal of expediting desirable exchanges, an organization's marketing managers are responsible for developing and managing marketing strategies. A **marketing strategy** involves selecting the best opportunities to pursue, identify an appropriate target market (the group of people the organization wants to reach), develop a competitive edge, and create and maintain a suitable **marketing mix** (the product, place [distribution], promotion, price and people) that will satisfy those customers in the target market. A marketing strategy articulates a plan for the best use of the organization's resources and directs the required tactics to meet its objectives.

When marketing managers attempt to develop and manage marketing activities, they must deal with three broad sets of variables:

1 those relating to the marketing mix
2 those inherent in the accompanying target market strategy
3 those that make up the marketing environment.

The marketing mix decision variables – product, place/distribution, promotion, price and people – and the target market strategy variables are factors over which an organization has control. As Figure 1.4 shows, these variables are constructed around the buyer or consumer. The marketing environment variables are political, legal, regulatory, societal, technological and economic and competitive forces. These

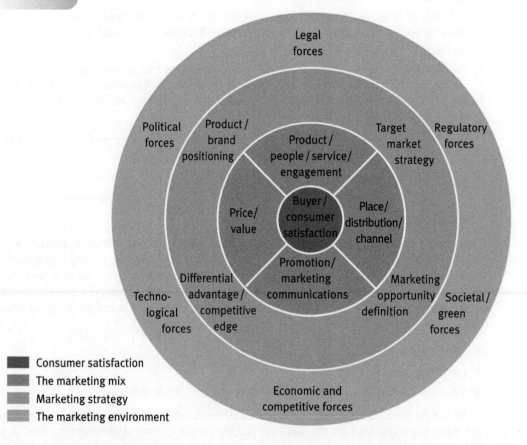

FIGURE 1.4
The marketing environment, marketing strategy, the marketing mix and customer satisfaction; consumers and organizations are affected by the forces of the marketing environment; organizations must determine a marketing strategy, implemented through the ingredients of the marketing mix, which aims to satisfy targeted customers

factors are subject to less control by an organization, but they affect buyers' needs as well as marketing managers' decisions regarding marketing mix variables.

To develop and manage marketing strategies, marketers must focus on several marketing tasks: marketing opportunity analysis and marketing analyses, the determination of a marketing strategy and target market selection, marketing mix development and management of the programmes that facilitate implementation of the marketing strategy. Figure 1.5 lists these tasks, along with the chapters of this book in which they are discussed.

Marketing opportunity analysis	Chapters
• Marketing strategy and competitors	2
• The marketing environment	3
• Consumer buying behaviour	4
• Business markets	5
• Marketing research	7

Target market strategy	Chapters
• Marketing strategy	2
• Market segmentation and prioritization	6
• Product and brand positioning	6/14
• Competitive advantage	2

Marketing mix development	Chapters
• Product, branding, packaging and service decisions	8/9/10
• Place (distribution and marketing channel) decisions	11
• Promotion (marketing communications) decisions	13/14
• Pricing decisions	12

Marketing management	Chapters
• Marketing planning, controls, implementation and metrics	15

FIGURE 1.5
Marketing tasks, analysis, strategy and programmes for implementation and control

marketing opportunity
One that exists when circumstances allow an organization to take action towards reaching a particular group of consumer or business customers

Marketing opportunity analysis A **marketing opportunity** exists when circumstances allow an organization to take action towards reaching a particular group of customers. An opportunity provides a favourable chance or opening for a company to generate sales from identifiable markets for specific products or services. For example, during a heatwave, marketers of electric fans have a marketing opportunity – an opportunity to reach customers who need electric fans. Various 'no frills' airlines have entered the rapidly growing market for low-priced scheduled air travel, as consumers have demonstrated their liking for this alternative to high-priced full-service airlines or charters. Bluetooth and wireless connectivity are creating numerous opportunities for computer manufacturers and online service providers, as wireless access to the Internet offers users greater flexibility. Most new products or services reflect the identification by marketers of a marketing opportunity.

Marketers should be capable of recognizing and analyzing marketing opportunities. An organization's long-term survival depends on developing products that satisfy its customers. Few organizations can assume that products popular today will interest buyers ten years from now. A marketing-led organization can choose among several alternatives for continued product development through which it can achieve its objectives and satisfy buyers. It can modify existing products (for example, by reducing salt content and additives in foods to address increasing health consciousness among customers), introduce new products (such as e-readers like Kindle, pay-as-you-talk mobile phone packages or digital flat-screen TVs) and delete some that customers no longer want (such as disc cameras or cassette decks). A company may also try to market its products to a greater number of customers, persuade current customers to use more of a product or perhaps expand marketing activities into additional countries. Diversification into new product offerings through internal efforts or through acquisitions of other organizations may be viable options for a company. For example, Sony has established itself as a major supplier of business laptop and desktop computers, diversifying from its base of consumer home entertainment products; while Virgin has entered financial services. An organization's ability to pursue any of these alternatives successfully depends on its internal characteristics and the forces within the marketing environment. These strategic options are discussed further in Chapter 2 of *Marketing Essentials*.

Internal organizational factors The primary factors inside an organization to be considered when analyzing marketing opportunities and devising target market strategies are organizational objectives, financial resources, managerial skills, organizational strengths and weaknesses, and cost structures. Most organizations have overall organizational objectives. Some marketing opportunities may be consistent with these objectives; others may not, and to pursue them is hazardous. Frequently, the pursuit of such opportunities ends in failure, or forces the company to alter its long-term objectives. The links with corporate strategy and an organization's mission are discussed in Chapter 2.

An organization's financial resources constrain the type of marketing opportunities it can pursue. Typically, an organization avoids projects that might bring economic catastrophe. In some situations, however, a company must invest in a high-risk opportunity, because the costs of not pursuing the project are so great. Thus, despite an economic recession and reduced house and road building, construction equipment manufacturer JCB has continued to launch new ranges and enter new markets.

The skills and experience of management also limit the types of opportunity that an organization can pursue. A company must be particularly cautious when exploring the possibility of entering unfamiliar markets with new products. If it lacks appropriate managerial skills and experience, the business can sometimes acquire them by recruiting additional managerial personnel. Most organizations at some time are limited in their growth plans by a lack of sufficient managers with suitable skills and market insights.

Like people, most organizations have strengths and weaknesses. Because of the types of operation in which a company is engaged, it will normally have employees with specialist skills and technological information. Such characteristics are a strength when launching marketing strategies that require them. However, lack of them may be a weakness if the company tries to compete in new, unrelated product areas. A major IT services company altered its strategy to focus on winning more business for IT infrastructure management from existing clients rather than from attracting new clients. This required a different set of selling skills, and managers with the ability to nurture relationships and exploit emerging sales opportunities within a client company. The revised target market strategy resulted in redundancies among the existing salesforce, and the recruitment of account managers with the necessary skills and interpersonal abilities.

An organization's cost structure may be an advantage if the company pursues certain marketing opportunities, and a disadvantage if it pursues others. Such factors as geographic location, employee skills, access to raw materials and type of equipment and facilities can all affect cost structure. Previous investment levels and priorities will have ramifications for the current cost structure. As discussed in Chapter 2, the cost structure of an organization may provide a competitive advantage over rivals, or may place a business at a competitive disadvantage.

Marketing environment forces   The marketing environment, which consists of political, legal, regulatory, societal, technological and economic/competitive forces, surrounds the buyer (consumer) and the organization's marketing mix (see Figure 1.4), impacting on both. Each major environmental force is explored in considerable depth in Chapter 3. Marketers know that they cannot predict changes in the marketing environment with certainty. Even so, over the years marketers have become more systematic in taking these forces into account when planning their competitive actions.[13] An organization that fails to monitor the forces of the marketing environment is likely to miss out on emerging opportunities at the expense of rivals with the foresight to examine these market drivers.

Marketing environment forces affect a marketer's ability to facilitate and expedite exchanges, in four general ways:

1 They influence customers by affecting or regulating their lifestyles, standards of living, preferences and needs for products. Because a marketing manager tries to develop and adjust the marketing mix to satisfy consumers or business customers, the effects of environmental forces on customers also have an indirect impact on the marketing mix components.

2 Marketing environment forces help determine whether and how a marketing manager can perform certain marketing activities. They may force marketers to cease certain practices or to adopt new strategies.

3 Environmental forces may affect a marketing manager's decisions and actions by influencing buyers' reactions to the company's marketing mix.

4 Marketing environment forces may provide an organization with a window of opportunity over rivals that fail to notice the market development or that take no action themselves.

Equally, market drivers may provide competitors with such an opportunity ahead of a marketer's own organization.

Although forces in the marketing environment are sometimes viewed as 'uncontrollables', a marketing manager may be able to influence one or more of them. However, marketing environment forces fluctuate quickly and dramatically, which is one reason why marketing is so interesting and challenging. Because these forces are highly interrelated, a change in one may cause others to change. For example, from Freons in fridges to additives in foods, most consumers have become increasingly aware of health and environmental issues. Manufacturers have altered product specifications and production methods to reflect this awareness. Legislators and regulatory bodies have also responded to expert and consumer opinions with new regulations and informal agreements, forcing companies to rethink their manufacturing and marketing policies.

Even though changes in the marketing environment produce uncertainty for marketers and at times impede marketing efforts, they can also create opportunities. After the 1989 oil spills, for example, more companies began developing and marketing products designed to contain or dissipate spilled oil. The BSE beef crisis gave producers of other meats significant opportunities. Environmental concerns have encouraged car manufacturers to develop emission-free engines. Rising mobile phone usage and improvements to network technologies have enabled various information providers to tailor their services for sports fans or stock-market investors. Recession has led to a growth in demand for domestic vacations, at the expense of more expensive flight-based holidays. Thus, a marketer must be aware of changes in environmental forces so that they can capitalize on the opportunities they provide. The marketing environment is discussed more fully in Chapters 3 of *Marketing Essentials*.

target market
A group of people for whom a company creates and maintains a marketing mix that specifically fits the needs and preferences of that group

Target market selection A **target market** is a group of people for whom a company creates and maintains a marketing mix that specifically fits the needs and preferences of that group.[14] When choosing a target market, marketing managers try to evaluate possible markets to see how entering them would affect the company's sales, costs and profits. Marketers also attempt to determine whether the organization has the resources to produce a marketing mix that meets the needs of a particular target market, and whether satisfying those needs is consistent with the company's overall objectives and mission. The size and number of competitors already marketing products in possible target markets are also of concern.

Marketing managers may define a target market as a vast number of people or as a relatively small group. For example, Ford produces cars suitable for much of the population – although specific models are quite narrowly targeted, such as the family runaround Focus or the executive Mondeo. Porsche focuses its marketing effort on a small proportion of the population, believing that it can compete more effectively by concentrating on an affluent target market desiring sports coupés. Although a business may concentrate its efforts on one target market through a single marketing mix, organizations often focus on several target markets by developing and deploying multiple marketing mixes. Reebok, for example, markets different types of shoes to meet the specific needs of joggers, walkers, aerobics enthusiasts and other groups.

Target market selection is crucial to generating productive marketing efforts. At times, products and organizations fail because marketers do not identify the appropriate customer groups at which to aim their efforts. Organizations that try to be all things to all people typically end up not satisfying the needs of any customer group very well. It is important for an organization's management to designate which customer groups the company is trying to serve and to have adequate information about these customers. The identification and analysis of a target market provide a foundation on which a marketing mix can be developed. As will be explored in the next chapter, it is important to strive to develop an advantage over competitors in the markets targeted.

Marketing programmes

In order to make the devised marketing strategy become a reality, marketers must specify the set of marketing mix ingredients forming the marketing programme for implementing the agreed marketing strategy. These marketing mix decisions occupy the majority of marketers' time and account for the bulk of a marketing department's budget. However, as previously explained, before the marketing mix is specified, marketers should undertake sufficient marketing analyses and reflect the findings of these analyses in their marketing strategy.

Marketing mix development Traditionally, the marketing mix was deemed to consist of four major components: product, place (distribution), promotion and price. Increasingly, a fifth component is viewed as 'people', who provide customer service and interact with customers and organizations within the supply chain. These components are called 'marketing mix decision variables' because a marketing manager decides which type of each component to use and in what amounts. A primary goal of a marketing manager is to create and maintain a marketing mix that satisfies consumers' needs for a general product type. Note that in Figure 1.4, the marketing mix is built around the buyer – as is stressed by the marketing concept and definition of marketing. Bear in mind, too, that the forces of the marketing environment affect the marketing mix variables in many ways.

Marketing mix variables are often viewed as controllable variables because they can be changed. However, there are limits to how much these variables can be altered. For example, because of economic conditions or government regulations, a manager may not be free to adjust prices daily. Changes in sizes, colours, shapes and designs of most tangible goods are expensive; therefore such product features cannot be altered very often. In addition, promotional campaigns and the methods used to distribute products ordinarily cannot be changed overnight. People, too, require training and motivating, and cannot be recruited or sacked overnight, so customer service is not always flexible.

Marketing managers must develop a marketing mix that precisely matches the needs of the people – or organizations in business-to-business marketing – in the target market. Before they can do so, they have to collect in-depth, up-to-date information about those needs. The information might include data about the age, income, ethnic origin, sex and educational level of people in the target market; their preferences for product features; their attitudes towards competitors' products; and the frequency and intensity with which they use the product. Armed with these kinds of data, marketing managers are better able to develop a product, service package, distribution system, promotion programme and price that will satisfy the people in the target market.

This section looks more closely at the decisions and activities related to each marketing mix variable (product, place/distribution, promotion, price and people – the '5Ps' of the marketing mix). Table 1.1 contains a list of the decisions and activities associated with each marketing mix variable.

product variable
The aspect of the marketing mix that deals with researching consumers' product wants and designing a product with the desired characteristics

The product variable A product can be a good, a service or an idea. The **product variable** is the aspect of the marketing mix that deals with researching consumers' product wants and designing a product with the desired characteristics. It also involves the creation or alteration of packaging and brand names, and may include decisions about guarantees, repair services and customer support. The actual manufacturing of products is not a marketing activity, but marketing-oriented businesses look to marketers to specify product development requirements that reflect customer needs and evolving expectations.

Product-variable decisions and related activities are important because they directly involve creating products and services that satisfy consumers' needs and wants. To maintain a satisfying set of products that will help an organization achieve its goals, a marketer must be able to develop new products, modify existing ones and eliminate those that no longer satisfy buyers or yield acceptable profits. For example, after realizing that competitors were capturing large shares of the low-calorie market, Heinz introduced new product items under its Weight Watchers name. To reflect greater use of microwave ovens, rice company Tilda introduced its steam-in-a-pouch range of quick-cook microwavable sachets.

place/distribution variable
The aspect of the marketing mix that deals with making products available in the quantities desired to as many customers as possible and keeping the total inventory, transport and storage costs as low as possible

The place/distribution variable To satisfy consumers, products must be available at the right time and in a convenient location. In dealing with the **place/distribution variable**, a marketing manager seeks to make products available in the quantities desired to as many intended customers as possible, and to keep the total inventory, transport and storage costs as low as possible. A marketing manager may become involved in selecting and motivating intermediaries (wholesalers, retailers and dealers), establishing and maintaining inventory control procedures, and developing and managing transport and storage systems. Many organizations distribute their products through multiple channels, now typically including the Web, adding to the complexity of marketing management but providing exciting opportunities.

promotion variable
The aspect of the marketing mix that relates to marketing communications used to inform one or more groups of people about an organization and its products

The promotion variable   The **promotion variable** relates to communication activities that are used to inform one or more groups of people about an organization and its products. Promotion can be aimed at increasing public awareness of an organization and of new or existing products. In addition, promotion can serve to educate consumers about product features or to urge people to take a particular stance on a political or social issue. It may also be used to keep interest strong in an established product that has been available for decades. The advertisement in Figure 1.6 is an example. Marketers increasingly refer to the promotion variable in the marketing mix as 'marketing communications'. Recently, this has become even more important for marketers, as they struggle to understand the power of growing consumer-to-consumer communications about their brands, made possible by social media and the Web.

price variable
The aspect of the marketing mix that relates to activities associated with establishing pricing policies and determining product prices

The price variable   The **price variable** relates to activities associated with establishing pricing policies and determining product prices. Price is a critical component of the marketing mix because consumers and business customers are concerned about the value obtained in an exchange. Price is often used as a competitive tool; in

FIGURE 1.6
Promoting an established brand. Champagne house Moët & Chandon uses its heritage in its advertising to reinforce its brand appeal
Source: Courtesy of Moët Hennessy UK Ltd

fact, extremely intense price competition sometimes leads to price wars. For example, airlines like Aer Lingus, British Airways and Virgin Atlantic are engaged in ruthless price cutting in the battle for transatlantic routes. Price can also help to establish a product's image. For instance, if Chanel tried to sell Chanel No. 5 in a two-litre bottle for £3 or €4, consumers would probably not buy it because the low price would destroy the prestigious image of this deluxe brand. Linked to the notion of perceived value, recent recession has placed even greater emphasis on the pricing ingredient of many organizations' marketing programmes.

The people variable Product, place/distribution, promotion and price are traditionally the principal elements of the marketing mix: the '4Ps'. Marketers of services include people as a core element, along with other ingredients (see Chapter 10), arguing the case for there being '5Ps'. Whether part of the product element or a separate element of the marketing mix, there is no doubt that people are important, and are integral to providing customer service. As marketers, they manipulate the rest of the marketing mix. As intermediaries in the marketing channel, they help make products and services available to the marketplace. As consumers or organizational purchasers, they create the need for the field of marketing. In the marketing mix, the **people variable** reflects the level of customer service, advice, sales support and after-sales back-up required, involving recruitment policies, training, retention and motivation of key personnel. For many products and most services, personnel interface directly with the intended purchaser and are often perceived by such consumers as being part and parcel of the product offering.

people variable
The aspect of the marketing mix that reflects the level of customer service, advice, sales support and after-sales back-up required, involving recruitment policies, training, retention and motivation of key personnel

Developing and maintaining an effective marketing mix is a major requirement for a strong marketing strategy. Thus, as indicated in Figure 1.5, a large proportion of this book (Chapters 8 to 13) focuses on the concepts, decisions and activities associated with the components of the marketing mix. It is the marketing mix that readers, as consumers, will most frequently have experienced for products and services purchased. It is important to remember, however, that analysis must precede the development of a marketing strategy, which in turn must be formulated before the marketing mix is determined for a product or a service.

Marketing management

marketing management
A process of planning, organizing, implementing and controlling marketing activities to facilitate and expedite exchanges effectively and efficiently

Marketing management is the process of planning, organizing, implementing and controlling marketing activities to facilitate and expedite exchanges effectively and efficiently. Effectiveness and efficiency are important dimensions of this definition. *Effectiveness* is the degree to which an exchange helps achieve an organization's objectives. *Efficiency* is the minimization of resources an organization must spend to achieve a specific level of desired exchanges. Thus, the overall goal of marketing management is to facilitate highly desirable exchanges and to minimize as much as possible the costs of doing so.

Marketing planning is a systematic process of assessing opportunities and resources, determining marketing objectives, developing a marketing strategy and constructing plans for implementation and control. Planning determines when and how marketing activities will be performed and who is to perform them. It forces marketing managers to think ahead, to establish objectives and to consider future marketing activities. Effective marketing planning also reduces or eliminates daily crises. Marketing planning and the management of the execution of the resulting marketing plan are intrinsic aspects of marketing management.

Organizing marketing activities refers to developing the internal structure of the marketing unit. The structure is the key to directing marketing activities. The marketing unit can be organized by function, product, region, type of customer or a combination of all four.

Proper implementation of marketing plans hinges on the coordination of marketing activities, motivation of marketing personnel and effective communication within the unit. Marketing managers must motivate marketing personnel, coordinate their activities and integrate their activities, both with those in other areas of the company and with the marketing efforts of personnel in external organizations, such as advertising agencies and marketing research businesses. An organization's communication system must allow the marketing manager to stay in contact with high-level management, with managers of other functional areas within the company and with personnel involved in marketing activities both inside and outside the organization.

The marketing control process consists of establishing performance standards, evaluating actual performance by comparing it with established standards and reducing the difference between desired and actual performance. An effective control process has the following four requirements:

1 The control process should ensure a rate of information flow that allows the marketing manager to quickly detect differences between actual and planned levels of performance.

2 The control process must accurately monitor different kinds of activities and be flexible enough to accommodate changes.

3 The control process must be economical so that its costs are low, relative to the costs that would arise if there were no controls.

4 Finally, the control process should be designed so that both managers and subordinates can understand it. To maintain effective marketing control, an organization needs to develop a comprehensive control process that evaluates marketing operations at regular intervals. The authors' other titles, including *Marketing Planning* (Cengage), *Market Segmentation Success: Making It Happen!* (The Howarth Press/Routledge) and *Marketing: Concepts and Strategies* (Cengage) explore the operationalization of marketing strategies and marketing control processes in more detail.

The organization of this book

The structure of this book adheres to the principle that it is important to analyze markets and marketing opportunities, then develop marketing strategies and construct marketing programmes that implement the desired marketing strategy, before ensuring suitable controls are in place to manage the roll-out of the strategy and programmes: the marketing process. Marketing analyzes develop a thorough understanding of the marketplace, focusing particularly on customers, competitors and market trends. This knowledge of the marketplace provides a sound basis from which to devise marketing strategies. These strategies should determine marketing opportunities to pursue, identify attractive target markets, and develop a clear brand positioning and basis for competing. In order to implement the recommended target market strategy, marketing programmes must be designed with marketing mix combinations and control processes to ensure effective implementation. This marketing process, as presented in Figure 1.2, is fundamental to sound marketing practice.

What does each part of this book cover?

The first Part of *Marketing Essentials* provides an explanation of the marketing concept, presents the marketing process and overviews the principles of marketing strategy:

- Part One: Marketing Defined and Marketing in Context

The second Part explores the essential marketing analyses for assessing the forces of the external trading environment, developing an understanding of consumers and business customers, while producing a target market strategy:

- Part Two: Understanding and Targeting Customers

Having explored the core marketing analyses and requisites for developing a marketing strategy, Part III provides the examination of the ingredients of the marketing mix, starting with product and service issues, then covering channels, pricing, marketing communications and branding:

- Part Three: Marketing Programmes

Part Four explores aspects of marketing management, including marketing planning, controls, managing implementation and performance metrics:

- Part Four: Managing Marketing

Marketing Essentials also offers:

- an indexed margin/glossary of key terms
- full subject and name indexing
- extended cases to enhance readers' understanding of key topics
- Internet-based exercises
- questions for discussion
- recommended further reading on each topic
- detailed illustrative examples in every chapter
- up-to-date statistics for the marketing industry
- support material on its own website
- Various auxilliaries are also available to tutors on the companion website.

Summary

Organizations that practise marketing do not necessarily have a *marketing orientation*. Organizations with a marketing orientation have a sound awareness of customers' needs and buying behaviour, of competitors' offerings and strategies, and of market trends. They also take steps to ensure they know how these market conditions will evolve. Crucially, they orientate their operational practices and coordinate their inter-functional thinking around these market conditions. In order to have a marketing orientation, it is necessary to adopt a range of marketing concepts and techniques. To practise marketing and to benefit from the activities of marketing, however, it is not necessary for an organization to have a fully developed marketing orientation. A few managers, whether or not in an organization's marketing function, utilizing the concepts described in this book, will make a significant contribution to the organization's fortunes and its understanding of its marketplace.

Marketing consists of individual and organizational activities that facilitate and expedite satisfying exchange relationships in a dynamic environment through the creation, distribution, promotion and pricing of goods, services and ideas. Marketing is an organizational function and a set of processes for creating, communicating and delivering value to customers and for managing customer relationships in ways that benefit the organization and its stakeholders.

Marketing opportunity analysis involves reviewing both internal factors (organizational objectives and mission, financial resources, managerial skills, organizational strengths, organizational weaknesses and cost structures) and external ones in the *marketing environment* (the political, legal, regulatory, societal, technological and economic/competitive forces).

An *exchange* is the provision or transfer of goods, services and ideas in return for something of value. Four conditions must exist for an exchange to occur: (1) two or more individuals, groups or organizations must participate; (2) each party must have something of value desired by the other; (3) each party must be willing to give up what it has in order to receive the value held by the other; and (4) the parties to the exchange must be able to communicate with each other to make their 'somethings of value' available. In an exchange, products are traded either for other products or for financial resources, such as cash or credit. Through the exchange, the recipient (the customer) and the provider (the organization) must be satisfied (leading to *customer satisfaction*). *Products* can be *goods, services or ideas*.

The *marketing process* is the analysis of market conditions, the creation of an appropriate marketing strategy, the development of marketing programmes designed to action the agreed strategy and, finally, the implementation and control of the marketing strategy and its associated marketing programme(s). Organizations contemplating entering new markets or territories, launching new products or brands, modifying their strategies or manipulating their marketing programmes, should use this sequential analytical process. Even steady-state markets and products encounter changing market conditions, and marketers should continually analyze and then modify their marketing strategies and marketing programmes accordingly.

It is important to study marketing because it permeates society. Marketing activities are performed in both business and non-business organizations. Moreover, marketing activities help business organizations generate profits and income, the life-blood of an economy. Even organizations without 'customers' have to maximize the deployment of their resources, address trends, identify stakeholders and develop compelling propositions to satisfy these stakeholders. The study of marketing enhances consumer awareness. Marketing costs absorb about half of what the consumer spends. Marketing, practised well, improves business performance.

The *marketing concept* is a management philosophy that prompts an organization to try to satisfy customers' needs through a coordinated set of activities that also allows the organization to achieve its goals. Customer satisfaction is the major objective of the marketing concept. The philosophy of the marketing concept emerged during the 1950s, as the *marketing era* succeeded the *production era* and the *sales era*. As the 1990s progressed into the *relationship marketing era*, a focus on transaction-based marketing was replaced by relationship marketing. Recent significant advances in the field of marketing relate to demands for *value-based marketing*, growing *consumer-to-consumer communication* and *digital marketing*, the growth of *social marketing* applications and the challenges posed to the discipline by critical management scholars theorists in the form of *critical marketing*. To make the marketing concept work, top management must accept it as an overall management philosophy. Implementing the marketing concept requires an efficient information system and sometimes the restructuring of the organization.

The essentials of marketing are that there are marketing analyzes, a marketing strategy, marketing programmes centred around well-specified marketing mixes, plus marketing management controls and implementation practices. *Marketing strategy* involves selecting which marketing opportunities to pursue, analyzing a target market (the group of people the organization wants to reach), and creating and maintaining an appropriate *marketing mix* (product, place/distribution, promotion, price and people) to satisfy this target market. Effective marketing requires that managers focus on four tasks to achieve set objectives: (1) marketing opportunity analysis, (2) target market selection, (3) marketing mix development and (4) marketing management.

Marketers should be able to recognize and analyze *marketing opportunities*, which are circumstances that allow an organization to take action towards reaching a particular group of customers.

A *target market* is a group of people or organizations for whom a company creates and maintains a marketing mix that specifically fits the needs and preferences of that group. It is important for an organization's management to designate which customer groups the company is trying to serve and to have some information about these customers. The identification and analysis of a target market provide a foundation on which a marketing mix can be developed.

The five principal variables that make up the marketing mix are product, place/distribution, promotion, price and people: the '5Ps'. The *product variable* is the aspect of the marketing mix that deals with researching consumers' or business customers' wants and designing a product with the desired characteristics. A marketing manager tries to make products available in the quantities desired to as many customers as possible, and to keep the total inventory, transport and storage costs as low as possible – the *place/distribution variable*. The *promotion variable* relates to marketing communications used to inform one or more groups of people about an organization and its products. The *price variable* refers to establishing pricing policies and determining product prices. The *people variable* controls the marketing mix; provides customer service and often the interface with customers, facilitates the product's distribution, sale and service; and – as consumers or buyers – gives marketing its rationale. Marketing exists to encourage consumer satisfaction.

Marketing management is a process of planning, organizing, implementing and controlling marketing activities to facilitate and expedite exchanges effectively and efficiently. Marketing planning is a systematic process of assessing opportunities and resources, developing a marketing strategy, determining marketing objectives and developing plans for implementation and control. The operationalization of the marketing plan is a core element of marketing management. Organizing marketing activities refers to developing the internal structure of the marketing unit. Properly implementing marketing plans depends on coordinating marketing activities, motivating marketing personnel and communicating effectively within the unit. The marketing control process consists of establishing performance standards, evaluating actual performance by comparing it with established standards, and reducing the difference between desired and actual performance.

Key links

At the end of each chapter summary, a 'Key links' box will steer readers to any chapters that are directly related.

Given that this is an introductory chapter, the other chapters of *Marketing Essentials* are all relevant links.

Specifically, Chapter 2 is required reading associated to this chapter.

Important terms

Marketing orientation
Marketing
Marketing environment
Exchange
Customer satisfaction
Product
Good
Service
Idea

Marketing process
Marketing concept
Production era
Sales era
Marketing era
Relationship marketing era
Value-based marketing
Consumer-to-consumer (C2C) communication
Digital marketing
Social marketing
Critical marketing
Marketing strategy
Marketing mix
Marketing opportunity
Target market
Product variable
Place/distribution variable
Promotion variable
Price variable
People variable
Marketing management

Discussion and review questions

1   What is meant by marketing orientation?

2   What is marketing? How did you define marketing before you read this chapter?

3   Why should someone study marketing?

4   What is the marketing process? Why should the process be so sequenced?

5   Discuss the basic elements of the marketing concept. Which organizations use this concept? Have these organizations adopted the marketing concept? Explain your views.

6   Identify several organizations that obviously have not adopted the marketing concept. What characteristics of these organizations indicate non-acceptance of the marketing concept?

7   What is consumer-to-consumer communication and why is it now so important to marketers?

8   Give an overview of what is meant by social marketing.

9   Briefly outline some issues of importance to critical marketers.

10 Describe the major components of a marketing strategy. How are these major components related?

11 Identify the tasks involved in developing a marketing strategy.

12 What are the primary issues that marketing managers consider when conducting a market opportunity analysis?

13 What are the variables in the marketing environment? How much control does a marketing manager have over environmental variables?

14 Why is the selection of a target market such an important issue?

15 Why are the elements of the marketing mix known as variables? What are these variables?

16 What type of management activities are involved in marketing management?

17 Why is it important to adhere to the principle of analyses first, then marketing strategy development, followed ultimately by programmes for implementing the recommended marketing strategy?

Further readings

In addition to the general marketing introductory texts recommended at the end of this chapter, readers studying for marketing examinations or wishing to put into practice these concepts of marketing may find the following books useful:

● *Marketing Briefs: a Study and Revision Guide,* Sally Dibb and Lyndon Simkin (Oxford: Elsevier Butterworth-Heinemann), 2004.
As implied in the title, this is a revision aid, complete with brief overviews of concepts, illustrative examples and cases, trial questions and revision guidance.

● *The Marketing Casebook,* Sally Dibb and Lyndon Simkin (London: Thomson), 2001.
For readers requiring concise summaries of essential concepts and explanatory applied cases.

● *Marketing Planning,* Sally Dibb and Lyndon Simkin (London: Cengage), 2008.
Aimed at marketing practitioners and offering a step-by-step guide to undertaking planning.

● *Market Segmentation Success: Making It Happen!,* Sally Dibb and Lyndon Simkin (New York: The Haworth Press/Routledge), 2008.
Aimed at marketing practitioners undertaking market segmentation and devising a target market strategy.

● *Marketing: Concepts and Strategies*, Sally Dibb and Lyndon Simkin (London: Cengage), 2012.
An abbreviated version of this text, useful for revision purposes.

Recommended readings

Baker, M., *Marketing: An Introductory Text* (Westburn, 2007).
Baker, M. and Saren, M., *Marketing Theory: a Student Text* (Sage, 2010).
Boone, L. and Kurtz, D., *Contemporary Marketing* (Cengage, 2011).
Day, G.S., *The Market Driven Organization: Attracting and Keeping Valuable Customers* (Free Press, 1999).
Hart, S., *Marketing Changes* (Thomson Learning/Cengage, 2003).
Jobber, D., *Principles and Practice of Marketing* (McGraw-Hill, 2009).
Kotler, P. and Armstrong, G., *Principles of Marketing* (Pearson, 2010).

Internet exercise

Seat cars used to be cheap and cheerful. Under VW's ownership the marque has been repositioned as sporty but good value. The range of cars is well specified, produced to VW's high standards, reasonably quick, but keenly priced. Take a look at Seat's website at: www.seat.co.uk or www.seat.com

1 How user-friendly is the site?

2 To what extent does the site provide the information required by someone seeking additional product information in order to construct a shortlist of possible car models to purchase?

3 Consider the decision-making process of a car buyer: to what extent is this website reflecting the issues considered by car buyers?

Applied mini-case

The market for crisps (potato chips) is dominated by global giants such as P&G and PepsiCo. Brands including Pringles, Walkers and KP are household names. So what of Salty Dog? Never heard of these hand-cooked crisps? Salty Dog was voted one of the 'cool brands' of 2010/11 (www.saltydog-grrr.com). They are produced by a very small-scale operation, run from a barn deep in the Chiltern hills in the UK. Since their launch in 2002, sales have been way ahead of forecasts and exports are heading to France, Germany, Norway, Belgium and even China. So far so good, but in order to grow, the company has to attract major retailers and pub/bar chains, and broaden the brand's appeal among consumers – not easy tasks. Worse, the company is now attracting the attention of the major players in this market, which are unlikely to stand back and permit Salty Dog to steal their market shares.

Question

As a newly recruited marketing manager for Salty Dog, what would be your priorities? How would you explain these to the owners of Salty Dog?

Case study

Sweden's IKEA marches on

When Swedish home furnishings retailer IKEA opened its first store in the UK, a retail shed near the M6 at Warrington, curious shoppers found queues jamming nearby roads, parking spaces at a premium and retailing analysts by the score. With just one store, IKEA had the UK furniture industry on its toes: large retail groups and manufacturers alike feared large market share losses. With the opening of a national network of 19 IKEA-branded stores, IKEA has conquered yet another territory. Such an impact is not confined to the UK market. The leading five countries for IKEA are Germany, the UK, the USA, France and Sweden, but global expansion is extensive... just check out details of store openings on **www.ikea.com**.

IKEA has grown from one store in 1958 to 282 stores in 26 countries belonging to the IKEA Group, and 34 stores franchised in another 16 countries; with sales of 23.8 billion Euros and 699 000 000 customer visitors each year. 198 000 000 copies of the famous IKEA catalogue are distributed annually. Close to 70 per cent of sales are from within Europe, but expansion in North America, South-East Asia and Australasia is now increasing sales in the rest of the world – despite some initial franchising difficulties in certain territories. IKEA's distinctive catalogue is produced in-house and now printed in nearly 50 languages. IKEA is perhaps one of the world's most successful retailers, with a brand name that is known, recognized and discussed; a retail concept that stands for value, style and quality; everything for the home under one roof, with easy parking, children's play areas and cafés – in fact, 'a day out!'

As the company succinctly stated in its advertising:

IKEA: the furnishings store from Sweden

More for your money

IKEA is more than just furnishing ideas. It's a day out for all the family.

Most of the time, beautifully designed home furnishings are created for a small part of the population – the few who can afford them. From the beginning, IKEA has taken a different path. We have decided to side with the many.

That means responding to the home furnishing needs of people throughout the world. People with many different needs, tastes, dreams, aspirations ... and wallets. People who want to improve their home and create a better everyday life.

For IKEA, helping create a better everyday life means offering a wide range of home furnishings in IKEA stores. Home furnishings that combine good design, good function and good quality with prices so low that as many people as possible can afford them.

Source: IKEA

IKEA's huge volumes – 10 000 items in a typical store – cheap out-of-town sites and dedication to keeping costs low through self-assembly packs mean that, unlike many competitors, the company can cope with any troughs in consumer spending. Low prices have been the key to IKEA's success, but price alone cannot create an international long-term marketing success story. Products are updated consistently to match consumers' expectations and lifestyles. In-store service and staff training are integral to the IKEA shopping experience. Store sites are chosen to maximize catchment areas, to make access easy for shoppers and to bring the brand name to the attention of the whole community. Logistics give IKEA an edge, with carefully managed ordering and delivery reducing both stock holdings and stock-outs. Promotion emphasizes the 'style without expense' philosophy and the IKEA name. The result has been a country-by-country revolution as staid furniture markets have been rejuvenated with the entry of IKEA. Shoppers intending to buy just a sofa return home with a sofa, a chair, some lamps and a general excitement about a new store where they can buy home furnishings at unbelievable prices. The IKEA vision is simple: 'Good design and function at low prices'.

The latest strategic developments for IKEA include entering eastern European markets, developing new IKEA formats and expanding its mail-order/electronic ordering. Eastern Europe has been a recent target for expansion, with IKEA stores opening in Poland, the Czech Republic and Hungary. Russia, Greece and Turkey have witnessed recent expansion. The company is also sourcing furniture from eastern European

manufacturers, which now supply 15 per cent of its range. As an experiment, the standard 'big box' IKEA concept was brought to a smaller stage with the New York opening in Manhattan of the first IKEA Marketing Outpost, a 720-square-metre (7500-square-foot) 'boutique', significantly smaller than the normal 19 000-square-metre (200 000-square-foot) IKEA superstore. Even more unusual was the decision – in this test concept – to offer only a selected, themed, reduced range at any point in time. For example, IKEA Cook showcases the company's kitchen-related merchandise. In early 2008, Coventry in the UK saw the opening of IKEA's first ever 'vertical store': built on the city centre site of a former grocery superstore, the constrained site has led IKEA to develop a new-look format that retails on three levels with parking on three others. Its city-centre location enabled more scope for IKEA's well known catering outlets, including an on-street pavement café. IKEA is now also recognizing the growing use of the Internet and is developing sales tools to utilize this new technology.

IKEA has its ideals and operating philosophies: standards matter. IKEA has a forceful, well-directed marketing strategy actioned through primarily one tightly developed marketing mix for the core superstore operation. The result is a successful, expanding company, satisfied target customers, highly motivated personnel and unhappy competitors. Despite global economic problems, the company is going from strength-to-strength.

Questions for discussion

1 Explain why IKEA is successful.

2 Why has IKEA developed new formats?

3 In what ways does IKEA deploy the marketing concept?

Sources: **www.ikea.com**, 1 February, 2011; **www.ikea.co.uk**, 2004; Helen Jones, 'IKEA's global strategy is a winning formula', *Marketing Week*, 15 March 1996, p. 22; Jennifer Pellet, 'IKEA takes Manhattan!', *Discount Merchandiser*, October 1995, pp. 22–3; 'IKEA', *Retail Business*, March 1995, pp. 78–81; Jonathan Pell, 'IKEA successfully penetrates east European consumer markets', *Central European*, June 1994, pp. 13–14; IKEA Facts, 1990 and 1992; B. Solomon, 'A Swedish company corners the business: worldwide', *Management Review*, 80 (4), 1991, pp. 10–13; IKEA HQ, 1998; **www.ikea.com**, 2007; IKEA Coventry store, 2008 and 2011; IKEA Delft (strategy HQ), 2009/10.
Reproduced with kind permission from Ikea

CHAPTER 2

Marketing strategy and understanding competitors

"Identifying where are the opportunities and which to pursue is fundamental to effective marketing"

Objectives

- To define marketing strategy and explore the relationship with a company's organizational mission, goals and corporate strategy

- To assess organizational opportunities, capabilities and the SWOT analysis

- To consider strategic objectives

- To appreciate the role of target market strategy and brand positioning in marketing strategy

- To examine competitive advantage, competitive positions and differential advantage

- To explore marketing objectives and marketing mix programmes in marketing strategy

- To understand the importance of implementation and performance monitoring in marketing strategy

INTRODUCTION

Marketing strategy involves planning and decision-making, with the aim of effectively selecting and pursuing marketing opportunities, identifying appropriate target markets and establishing a competitive advantage. This requires an awareness of the external trading environment and market trends, an appreciation of the organization's capabilities and resource base, an understanding of changing customer behaviours and expectations, and knowledge of competitors' intentions and propositions. Marketing mix programmes must be developed to reflect these market conditions, organizational characteristics, agreed pursuit priorities and target market strategies.

Marketing oriented organizations have a marketing strategy that clearly articulates to a broad set of internal audiences the opportunities the organization has decided to address, and aligns the organization to a specific set of target markets. These decisions will have been made with the knowledge of market drivers and marketing environment forces; an understanding of customer needs, expectations and buying behaviour; and with full knowledge of competitors' activities and their likely impact in target markets. The strategy will reflect, too, the marketing assets and capabilities of the organization. This mix of external and internal awareness is pivotal to effective marketing strategy development. An organization's marketing plan will then specify marketing programmes designed to execute this marketing strategy.

Diversification of a brand: Coca-Cola's move into clothing

SassiSam Girlie Gossip Files focuses on fashion, beauty, lifestyle and pop culture. According to its creator, 'Sassi is a self-proclaimed shopaholic who loves all things fun and girlie and I have created a website and blog that embodies this ideal. Everything is from Sassi's perspective, she's your online virtual friend'. This is what Sassi had to say about a well-known brand in a blog:

> I know this is a completely random ad campaign to post and you may not even know that Coca-Cola have a fashion collection, but they do in Brazil and this is their 2011 ad campaign.
>
> The reason why I'm posting this campaign is from a branding perspective, as you know I'm obsessed with branding, and you seriously couldn't get a more perfect on-brand campaign than this one for Coca-Cola. It is exactly what you would imagine a Coca-Cola Fashion campaign to look like, it's so on-brand it just doesn't seem real!
>
> Featuring Brazilian models Ana Paula Scopel, Iuri Jasper, Leonardo Alberici, Reinaldo Berthoti and Renata Sozzi at the beach, where else, having fun in the sun which is the Coca-Cola brand message from the beginning of time!

http://www.sassisamblog.com/2010/08/08/coca-cola-clothing-springsummer-campaign/

Source: Image courtesy of Rex Features Ltd.

So why has Coca-Cola extended the well-known brand for soft drinks into new territory? In general, Coca-Cola has enjoyed the effects of massive growth in global soft drinks sales. However, towards the end of 1998, for the first time in many years, the company failed to hit its expected 7–8 per cent annual volume growth. Following this disappointing performance, senior managers were quick to deny that the core soft drinks business had reached maturity, blaming economic problems in key markets for the difficulties. The launch of Coca-Cola Ware was not, they stated, because of difficulties with the core business. Instead, the company sees the clothing as a promotional activity, an extension of Coca-Cola's licensing programme, which raises the profile of the brand around the world and is a core ingredient of the brand's strategy. Sassi's recent blog indicates that Coca-Cola's strategy is working; it also illustrates the power of digital communications in today's marketplace. The new clothing range certainly added an extra dimension to the company's existing licensing activities. With 250 licensees offering some 10 000 different items in 40 different countries, the precedent for such an arrangement was well established.

The clothing range, which comprises casual clothing and accessories, was test marketed prior to being launched globally. The target market for the jeans, woven clothing and knitwear is teenagers and young adults. According to US spokeswoman Susan McDermott, 'This is an integrated approach to create a fashion line with a cohesive feel and a sense of lifestyle'. Coca-Cola Ware is sold through department stores, fashion boutiques and specialist 'active' wear shops. The company has been quick to stress that the range is used to support and communicate Coca-Cola brand values, rather than to detract from the company's core products of soft drinks. This is a similar brand-building approach to that adopted by construction equipment giants CAT and JCB, whose footwear and clothing ranges have done much to raise the profile of their brands. Jaguar also entered the fray, with a range of men's clothing competing with the likes of Boss and Armani. However, some industry experts warn about the dangers of devaluing the core brand, suggesting that the fashion market is notoriously difficult to enter.

The extension of familiar brands into clothing is not a new trend. However, in a highly competitive market already saturated with well-known fashion house labels, success is difficult to achieve. One brand extension expert believes that brands seeking such a move must exhibit three crucial strengths: expertise, image and reputation. Few would deny that the classic and timeless brand of Coca-Cola possesses these qualities. Certainly Sassi's Brazilian endorsement implies that Coca-Cola Ware is creating the right impression. All marketers strive to promote their brands. Coca-Cola's marketers hope Coca-Cola Ware will lead to thousands of walking 'adverts', raising the profile of this already ubiquitous and successful brand. Nevertheless, the move into clothing was a significant diversification from the company's soft drinks business.

Sources: **www.Coca-Cola.com**, 2004, 2007, 2011/12; Amanda Wilkinson, 'Is Coke hip?', *Marketing Week*, 28 January 1999, pp. 26–9; Julia Day, 'Coke plans global clothing brands', *Marketing Week*, 21 January 1999, pp. 37–42; 'Jaguar drives in UK men's clothing market', *Marketing Week*, 18 March 1999, p. 7.; **http://www.colacorner.com/vintageitems.html**, 12 February 2011; **http://www.coca-colastore.com**, 12 February 2011; **http://www.sassisamblog.com/2010/08/08/coca-cola-clothing-springsummer-campaign**, 12 February 2011.

This chapter aims to highlight which strategic marketing considerations help to ensure that a product or service is marketed for the benefit of the organization as well as its targeted customers. The product or service should be marketed differently enough from competitors' marketing programmes to provide the organization's product or service with a perceived advantage over these competitors in shrewdly selected target markets. These core components of marketing strategy are illustrated in Figure 2.1 and are clearly of great concern to the business described in this chapter's opener, Coca-Cola, as it chose to diversify into clothing.

The chapter first explores how to develop marketing strategies and then discusses strategic market planning, stressing the importance of organizational mission, goals and corporate strategy. The discussion next turns to assessing organizational opportunities and resources, as well as identifying strategic objectives and strategic focus. The chapter addresses the all-important role of identifying market segments, targeting and brand positioning in marketing strategy: the development of clear target market priorities. The chapter then focuses on competitive strategies for marketing: the role of competition, its ramifications for strategy, competitive positions and warfare strategies. The link between marketing objectives and marketing mix programmes is examined, along with implementation and performance monitoring.

Marketing strategy defined

Companies typically have a top-level *corporate strategy* setting the agenda for the business's over-arching strategy, which is in many cases related to a *strategic market plan* or *business plan*. In order to achieve the objectives in the corporate strategy and to meet the needs of the strategic market plan, they also have a *marketing strategy*. This is operationalized through the *marketing plan*. Although the focus of this chapter is marketing strategy, this chapter first explores the relationships and nature of corporate strategy, a strategic market plan, marketing strategy and marketing plans. A later chapter explores marketing planning in more detail.

Marketing strategy articulates the best uses of an organization's resources and tactics to achieve its objectives. It states which opportunities are to be pursued by an organization, indicates the specific markets towards which activities are to be targeted, identifies the types of competitive advantage that are to be developed and exploited, and provides direction for marketing programmes.[1] Implicitly, as described in Figure 2.1, the strategy requires clear objectives and a focus in line with an organization's corporate goals; the 'right' customers must be targeted more effectively than they are by competitors, and associated marketing programmes should be developed to implement the marketing strategy successfully.[2]

strategic market plan
An outline of the methods and resources required to achieve an organization's goals within a specific target market

A **strategic market plan** is an outline of the methods and resources required to achieve an organization's goals within a specific target market. It takes into account not only marketing but also all the functional aspects that must be coordinated, such as production, IT, logistics, finance and personnel. Environmental issues are an important consideration too. The concept of the strategic business unit is often used to

Organizational mission, goals and corporate strategy

Organizational opportunities and capabilities
- Environmental scanning
- Customer and competitor analysis
- Marketing opportunities
- Capabilities and resources

Strategic objectives
- Intense growth
- Diversified growth
- Integrated growth
- Maintenance

Target market strategy and brand positioning
- Market segmentation
- Priority target markets
- Brand positioning
- Differential advantage

Marketing objectives

Marketing programmes for implementation
- Marketing mix tactics
- Operational controls

Performance assessment and benchmarking

FIGURE 2.1
The components of marketing strategy

strategic business unit (SBU)
A division, product line or other profit centre within a parent company

define areas for consideration in a specific strategic market plan. Each **strategic business unit (SBU)** is a division, product line or other profit centre within a parent company. Each sells a distinct set of products to an identifiable group of customers, and each competes with a well-defined set of competitors. Each SBU's revenues, costs, investments and strategic plans can be separated from those of the parent company and evaluated. SBUs operate in a variety of markets, which have differing growth rates, opportunities, degrees of competition and profit-making potential. Construction giant JCB, for example, includes the Compact Division for smaller machines, which is a strategic

FIGURE 2.2
British Gas strives to market the appeal of its range and services

Source: Image courtesy of The Advertising Archives

business unit. Strategic planners, therefore, must recognize the different performance capabilities of each SBU and allocate resources carefully. They must also ensure that the SBUs complement each other for the greater good of the overall business.

The strategic planning process should be guided by a marketing-oriented culture and processes in the organization.[3] A **marketing plan** includes the framework and entire set of marketing activities to be performed; it is the written document or blueprint for specifying, implementing and controlling an organization's marketing activities and marketing mixes. Thus, a strategic market plan is not the same as a marketing plan – it is a plan of all aspects of an organization's strategy in the marketplace.[4] A marketing plan, in contrast, deals primarily with implementing the marketing strategy as it relates to target markets and marketing programmes.[5] The marketing plan states which are priority target markets and details the marketing programmes, specifying also time-frames, budgets and responsibilities.

> **marketing plan**
> The written document or blueprint for specifying, implementing and controlling an organization's marketing activities and marketing mixes

Figure 2.3 shows the components of strategic market planning. The process is based on the establishment of an organization's overall goals, and it must stay within the bounds of the organization's opportunities and resources. When the organization has determined its overall goals and identified its resources, it can then assess its opportunities and develop a corporate strategy. Marketing objectives must be designed so that their achievement will contribute to the overall corporate strategy and so that they can be accomplished through efficient use of the company's resources. For example, IT services company Fujitsu wants to be the dominant provider of IT solutions and outsourcing to government and the public sector, along with certain commercial sectors such as financial services. The marketing function in Fujitsu must identify opportunities

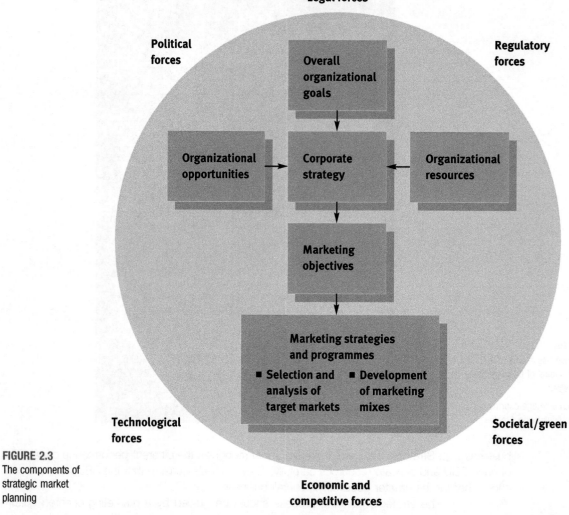

FIGURE 2.3
The components of strategic market planning

to pursue in these sectors, specifying target market prospects, developing appropriate services and marketing messages, engaging with potential clients, building relationships and helping to win individual pieces of business within the organization's priority sectors. In some organizations, marketers steer the development of the strategic market plan because they are the holders of market knowledge. In other organizations, the board of directors develops the strategic market plan and marketers focus on devising marketing strategies capable of achieving the aims of the top-line strategic market plan.

To achieve its marketing objectives, an organization must develop a marketing strategy, or a set of marketing strategies, as shown in Figure 2.3. To operationalize a marketing strategy, a marketing mix must be developed. Most marketers refer to their marketing mix activities as their **marketing programme**. Marketing programmes centre around a detailed marketing mix specification and include internal controls and procedures to ensure that they are implemented effectively. Through the process of strategic market planning, an organization can develop marketing strategies that, when properly implemented and controlled, will contribute to the achievement of its marketing objectives and its overall goals. To formulate a marketing strategy, the marketer identifies and

marketing programme
A marketer's marketing mix activities and implementation processes designed to operationalize the marketing strategy

analyzes opportunities and the associated target market, and develops a marketing mix to satisfy individuals in that market. Marketing strategy is best formulated when it reflects the overall direction of the organization and is coordinated with all the company's functional areas.

As indicated in Figure 2.3, the strategic market planning process is based on an analysis of the broader marketing environment. As detailed in Chapter 3, marketing environment forces can place constraints on an organization and possibly influence its overall goals; they also affect the amount and type of resources that a business can acquire. However, these forces can create favourable opportunities as well – opportunities that can be translated into overall organizational goals and marketing objectives. For example, when oil prices declined during the second half of the 1980s, consumers viewed cars with high petrol consumption more favourably. This situation created an opportunity for manufacturers of large vehicles, such as BMW and Volvo. More recently, hefty fuel price rises have created opportunities for fuel-efficient brands and alternative energies: vehicle manufacturers with capabilities in these areas have benefited.

Marketers differ in their viewpoints concerning the effect of marketing environment variables on planning and strategy development. Some take a deterministic perspective, believing that companies must react to external conditions and tailor their strategies and organizational structures to deal with these conditions. According to others, however, companies can influence their environments by choosing in which markets to compete, lobbying regulators and politicians, striving to modify social views, joining forces with trade bodies for campaigning purposes and so forth. They can also change the structures of their industries, engaging in activities such as mergers and acquisitions, demand creation or technological innovation.[6]

Regardless of which viewpoint is adopted, marketing environment variables play a part in the creation of a marketing strategy. When environment variables affect an organization's overall goals, resources, opportunities or target markets, they also affect its marketing strategies, which are based on these factors. Marketing environment forces more directly influence the development of a marketing strategy through their impact on consumers' needs and desires, as well as their effect on competitors' plans, and how they impact on other organizations in their supply chain. In addition, these forces have a bearing on marketing mix decisions. For instance, competition strongly influences marketing mix decisions. The organization must diagnose the marketing mix activities it performs, taking into account competitors' marketing mix decisions, and develop a differential advantage to support a strategy. Thus, as Honda and Toyota entered the luxury car market with the Acura and Lexus models, European car makers BMW, Mercedes and Jaguar had to change their marketing strategies to maintain their market shares. They did so by lowering prices, introducing new models and creating brand-building marketing communications campaigns to compete with the new Japanese models.

Organizational mission, goals and corporate strategy

Central to the strategic market plan is a clear view of the organizational mission, goals and corporate strategy. A company's organizational goals should be derived from its mission – the broad, long-term tasks that the organization wants to accomplish. Computer producer Dell has three parts to its mission, co-created by its employees:

- CUSTOMER SATISFACTION: We are an established company striving to satisfy customers by meeting their demands of quality, responsiveness, and competitive pricing. Each customer is #1.
- TEAM SATISFACTION: Management and employees are committed to cooperating as a team for the purpose of profitability and gratification of a job well done.

● COMMUNITY SATISFACTION: We will provide jobs in a clean, safe, environmentally sound atmosphere and be an active participant in community affairs.

When a company decides on its mission, it really answers three questions:

1 What is the company's core business/areas of activity?
2 How should these evolve?
3 What behaviours are required and expected?[7]

Although these questions seem very simple, they are in fact three of the hardest, yet most important, for any organization to answer.

Creating or revising a mission statement is very difficult because of the many complex variables that must be examined. However, having a mission statement can greatly benefit the organization in at least five ways.[8] A mission statement:

1 gives the organization a clear purpose and direction, keeping it on track and preventing it from drifting

2 describes the unique aim of the organization that helps to differentiate it from similar competing organizations

3 keeps the organization focused on customer needs rather than its own abilities. This ensures that the organization remains externally rather than internally focused

4 provides specific direction and guidelines to top managers for selecting alternative courses of action. It helps them decide which business opportunities to pursue, as well as which opportunities not to pursue

5 offers guidance to all employees and managers of an organization, even if they work in different parts of the world. As a result, the mission statement acts like 'glue' to hold the organization together.

A company's mission and overall organizational goals should guide all its planning efforts. Its goals should specify the ends, or results, that are sought. Examples of organizational goals include profit, return on investment, an increase in market share, an increase/decrease in the number of active markets, the desire to enter specific market sectors, to develop a particular reputation and track record, to contribute to society in specific ways and to touch employees in a manner desired by them. Organizations can also have short-term and long-term goals. Companies experiencing financial difficulty may be forced to focus solely on the short-term results necessary to stay in business, such as increasing cash flow by lowering prices or selling off parts of the business. Other organizations may have more optimistic long-term goals. In many cases, companies that pursue long-term goals have to sacrifice short-term results to achieve them. Businesses that are successful over time tend to have a longer-term, market-share-driven strategy, rather than a short-term, 'profits only' sales-led emphasis.

An organization in serious financial trouble may be concerned solely with short-run results needed for remaining viable and fending off creditors. There is usually, for example, an airline or major retailer being forced by cash shortages to take drastic action to stay in business. Lowndes Queensway, once the UK's largest retailer of carpets and furniture, had to renegotiate its financing several times with city institutions, alter payment and credit lines and terms with its suppliers, and ultimately identify which of its 500 superstores should be closed to save costs. The company went into receivership despite all its efforts and ceased trading. Woolworths followed a similar path, while more recently HMV and Waterstones turned to a major store closure programme in order to remain trading. On the other hand, some companies have more optimistic goals. Often manufacturers, such as General Motors, have goals that relate to return on investment. A successful company, however, may want to sacrifice the current year's profits for the long run and at the same time pursue other goals, such as increasing market share.

corporate strategy
A strategy that determines the organization's vision and goals, and how they are to be addressed, in which markets, with what advantages over competitors, and so aligning resources in key functions accordingly across the business

Corporate strategy determines the organization's vision and goals, and how best to utilize resources and capabilities in the areas of production, logistics, finance, research and development, human resources, IT, sales, business development and marketing to reach the organization's goals. A corporate strategy determines not only the scope of the business but also its resource deployment, differential advantages and overall coordination of its functional areas, people and their activities. The term 'corporate' in this context does not apply only to corporations: corporate strategy is used by all organizations, from the smallest sole proprietorship to the largest multinational corporation. Corporate strategy is that created centrally and at the top of the organization's decision-making, in order to satisfy the aims of owners, investors and directors.

Corporate strategy planners are concerned with issues such as diversification, internationalization, acquisitions and mergers, competition, differentiation, interrelationships among business units and environmental issues. Strategic planners attempt to match the resources of the organization with the various opportunities and risks in the external environment. Corporate strategy planners are also concerned with defining the scope and role of the strategic business units of the organization so that they are coordinated to reach the ultimate goals desired.

While not the focus of *Marketing Essentials*, it is important to recognize that the marketing strategy, marketing plan and marketing mix programmes actioned by an organization's marketers must reflect the aims and ethos of the overall corporate plan. Unfortunately, in some instances those empowered to deliver marketing programmes are unaware of or are unconcerned about the nuances of the organization's overall corporate plan, and may even be pursuing a course of action that is at odds with the leadership team's sense of purpose. In some businesses, this reflects the paucity of analysis behind corporate planning, and the failure to involve senior marketers in such strategy development. In most organizations, the forces of the external marketing environment, competitors' strategies and evolving customer expectations are poorly assessed. In other cases, only an organization's marketers are aware of these issues and have the relevant marketing intelligence to be able to suggest likely scenarios. It is therefore essential that those responsible for establishing corporate plans tap into this expertise and knowledge within the marketing function, just as it is essential for marketers to devise target market strategies and marketing programmes that properly reflect the direction desired by the corporate strategy.

Organizational opportunities and resources

There are three major considerations in assessing opportunities and resources:

1 evaluating marketing opportunities
2 environmental scanning (discussed in Chapter 3)
3 understanding the organization's capabilities and assets.

An appreciation of these elements is essential if an organization is to build up a sustainable differential advantage or competitive edge.

Marketing opportunities

marketing opportunities
circumstances and timing that allow an organization to take action towards reaching a target market

A **marketing opportunity** arises when the right combination of circumstances occurs at the right time to allow an organization to take action towards reaching a target market. Government concerns about energy supplies have provided the turbine makers for wind farms with an opportunity that a few years ago did not exist. An opportunity provides a favourable chance or opening for an organization to generate sales from identifiable markets. For example, in reaction to the overwhelming growth in cereals and other foods containing oat bran – which some researchers believe helps lower cholesterol levels – the Quaker Oats Company developed an advertising campaign to remind consumers that Quaker porridge oats have always contained oat bran. Increasing concerns about cancer and heart disease gave Quaker a marketing opportunity to reach consumers who are especially health-conscious by touting the health benefits of its oats.

strategic window
A temporary period of optimum fit between the key requirements of a market and the particular capabilities of a company competing in that market

The term **strategic window** has been used to describe what are often temporary periods of optimum fit between the key requirements of a market and the particular capabilities of a company competing in that market.[9] A few years ago, there was much interest in organically grown/produced foods, with retailers increasing shelf-space in response to growing consumer demand. Often more expensive than non-organic versions, economic meltdown and tightening consumer spending reduced consumer interest and retailers' displays accordingly … the window of opportunity had closed for certain organic lines.

The attractiveness of marketing opportunities is determined by market factors such as size and growth rate; by political, legal, regulatory, societal, economic and competitive, and technological marketing environment forces; by internal capital, plant, and human and financial resources; and, by expected financial performance.[10] Because each industry and each product is somewhat different, the factors that determine attractiveness tend to vary for different leadership teams, as illustrated in Table 2.1.

market requirements
Requirements that relate to customers' needs or desired benefits

Market requirements relate to customers' needs or desired benefits. Market requirements are satisfied by components of the marketing mix that provide buyers with these benefits. Of course, buyers' perceptions of what requirements fulfil their needs and provide the desired benefits determine the success of any marketing effort.

Marketers must devise strategies to out-perform competitors by finding out what product attributes buyers use to select products. An attribute must be important and differentiating if it is to be useful in strategy development. When marketers fail to understand buyers' perceptions and market requirements, the result may be failure. Toyota had failed to attract prestige-led car purchasers, even though it produced well-specified executive cars. The brand image was not at-

TABLE 2.1 Examples of dimensions for attractiveness

Mobile phone operator	Leisure industry company	Insurance business
• Disposable income	• Profitability	• Profit potential
• Willingness to spend on mobiles	• Market growth potential	• Sales level
• Interest in value-added services	• Market share	• Income potential
• ARPU/revenue/profitability – the financial worth of the opportunity	• Differentiator possible	• Longevity of opportunity
• Customer share likely in three years	• Competitive intensity	• Size of market
• Loyalty level	• Certainty of customer demand	• Market growth prospects
• Size of the market	• Barriers to entry as blockers to rivals	• Differential advantage possible
• Competitive intensity – degree of competition	• Expanding the company's footprint within the market	• Exclusivity possible
• Potential growth		• Competitive situation favourable
• Market share now		• Insurer support
		• Supplier partnership/resource
		• Endorsements
		• Similar markets – adaptable capabilities
		• Ease of entry
		• Quality of customers
		• Resources/expertise required

tractive enough to these target customers. As a result, Toyota created its highly successful Lexus marque, focusing on the brand values desired by these customers.

Environmental scanning

environmental scanning
The process of collecting information about the marketing environment to help marketers identify opportunities and threats, and assist in planning

Environmental scanning is the process of collecting information about the marketing environment to help marketers identify opportunities, prepare for impending threats and assist in planning. Some companies have derived substantial benefits from establishing an environmental scanning (or monitoring) unit within the strategic planning group, as part of their marketing planning activity, or by including line management in teams or committees to conduct environmental analysis. This approach engages management in the process of environmental forecasting and enhances the likelihood of successfully integrating forecasting efforts into strategic market planning.[11] Results of forecasting research show that even simple quantitative forecasting techniques out-perform the unstructured intuitive assessments of experts.[12]

Environmental scanning to detect changes in the environment is extremely important if an organization is to avoid crisis management. A change in the external marketing environment can suddenly alter an organization's opportunities or resources. Reformulated strategies may then be needed to guide marketing efforts. For example, after the global banking crisis led to tighter consumer spending and less disposable income, many brands had to re-think their propositions and seek ways for demonstrating value-for-money. Environmental scanning should identify new developments and determine the nature and rate of change.

Capabilities and assets

capabilities
A company's distinctive competencies to do something well and efficiently

A company's **capabilities** relate to *distinctive competencies* that it has developed to do something well and efficiently. A company is likely to enjoy a differential advantage over its rivals in an area where its competencies out-do those of its potential competitors.[13] Often a company may possess manufacturing or technical skills that are valuable in areas outside its traditional industry. For example, defence giant Lockheed Martin provided military customers with sensors and data analytics relevant also to the owners of fleets of commercial vehicles, interested in optimizing fuel performance and carbon footprints. Capabilities can be classified in terms of **marketing assets**, highlighting capabilities that managers and the marketplace view as beneficially strong. These capabilities can then be stressed to the company's advantage. Marketing assets are commonly classified as either customer-based, distribution-based or internal. *Customer-based* assets include capabilities that are customer-facing, such as brand image and reputation, product quality and customer service expertise; *distribution-based assets* relate to marketing channel issues and may involve density of dealers and geographic coverage, the responsiveness of distributors, after-sales support and logistical capabilities; *internal marketing assets* are operational, process and resource capabilities, including skills, experience, economies of scale, technology, working practices and people resources.[14] It is essential for a business to take time to assess its capabilities and assets, and to map these alongside identified opportunities. Research findings suggest that the mix of these capabilities and assets affects the types of strategy that should be pursued.[15] Table 2.2 depicts the capabilities that certain companies believe are the most important in their respective sectors. The capabilities and marketing assets that are viewed as being essential for success vary dramatically between industries and sectors, reflecting the nuances of their operations and characteristics.

marketing assets
Customer, distribution and internal capabilities that managers and the marketplace view as beneficially strong

TABLE 2.2 Examples of capabilities

Mobile phone operator	Leisure industry company	Insurance business
• Network coverage • Network quality • Voice/data roaming • Attractive tariffs • Fair billing • Products/services/value added services • Distribution (sales) network • Brand awareness (strong image) • Innovativeness • Quality of marketing staff and their outputs • Customer orientation	• IT capability • Expertise and skills of the company's people • Marketing skills and effectiveness • Market insights/business information • Management bandwidth/focus • Ability to fund • Ability to serve/provide customer service • Long-term commitment • Suitable track record	• Expertise/skills • Brand awareness/presence • Reputation • Relationship with key supplier • Creation of differentiators • Access to distribution channel • Quality of service • Link to trade associations • Sales process and skills • Marketing/communication • Service ability (spread of base) • Resources: IT • Resources: financial • Resources: people • Customer empathy/partnership • Long-term commitment • Resources: adaptability • Delivery/process – cost effective solution • Experience/credibility • Existing customers

SWOT analysis
The examination of an organization's strengths and weaknesses, opportunities and threats, usually depicted on a four-cell chart

SWOT analysis SWOT analysis (strengths, weaknesses, opportunities, threats) is one of the most simplistic used by marketers; fundamentally it is little more than a set of checklists. However, it cannot be ignored in a book such as this owing to its popularity and widespread use. The strengths it refers to relate to those internal operational, managerial, resource and marketing factors that managers believe provide a strong foundation for their organization's activities and for their ability to compete effectively in the marketplace. Many marketers treat the notion of marketing assets as a means for classifying strengths. Weaknesses are those aspects of the organization, its products and activities in the marketplace that place the organization at a disadvantage vis-à-vis competitors and in the view of targeted customers. Best practice indicates that an organization should strive to remedy such faults, particularly those that may be exploited by rivals. An analysis of strengths and weaknesses is a fundamental aspect for developing a marketing strategy, as an organization must have an awareness of its capabilities and how these map out against competitors' strengths and weaknesses.

The other elements of the SWOT analysis are opportunities and threats, which are external-facing issues of the trading environment. As explained in Chapter 1, at the forefront of the marketing concept is marketing opportunity analysis. A sound appreciation of marketing environment forces and evolving market trends is essential for a marketing-oriented organization. It is difficult to contemplate a scenario in which an organization lacking such an external awareness is able to develop a truly meaningful marketing strategy. As described above, marketing environmental scanning identifies numerous issues that marketers must consider when developing marketing strategies. These market developments may offer opportunities for marketers to exploit or they may be the cause of threats to the fortunes of an organization. As explained in more detail in the next chapter, an awareness of the marketing environment may lead to strategic windows of opportunity. The SWOT analysis, in its simplistic way, has the benefit of placing an organization's strengths and weaknesses in the context of the identified opportunities and threats, so implying the extent to which an organization is capable of leveraging an opportunity or fending off an apparent threat. The SWOT analysis can be an effective scene-setting tool, but *only* if the guidelines detailed in the Marketing Tools and Techniques box below are followed.

Strategic objectives and strategic focus

Ansoff matrix
Ansoff's product–market matrix for determining competitive strategies: market penetration, market development, product development or diversification

Having evaluated the overall corporate vision, those responsible for devising the marketing strategy must build on their analysis of opportunities and internal capabilities by analytically assessing the most promising directions for their organization and marketing activity. Ansoff developed a well-known tool, the market–product matrix, popularly known as the **Ansoff matrix**, to assist in this decision-making, as depicted in Figure 2.4. A business may choose one or more competitive strategies as the basis for its **strategic objectives**, including intense growth, diversified growth and integrated growth. This matrix can help in determining growth that can be implemented through marketing strategies. Its underlying principles often assist marketers in identifying sources for growth by addressing whether there are the following types of opportunities:

strategic objectives
Includes intense growth, diversified growth or integrated growth

– Existing customers – existing products/programmes.

– Existing customers – new products/programmes.

– New customers – existing or new products/programmes.

– Adjacent/new markets – existing or new products/programmes.

These are the categories of growth most often discussed by leadership teams, who traditionally shy away from the diversification option included in Ansoff's work. This is a pity, as there are examples of very successful corporations targeting unrelated markets with great success, such as Samsung's belated move into cellphones, Apple's diversification from computers to audio and then media players, or Fujitsu's manufacturing (under many other brands) of flatscreen televisions.

FIGURE 2.4
Ansoff's competitive strategies

Source: H.I. Ansoff, The New Corporate Strategy (New York, NY: John Wiley & Sons, 1988), p. 83. Reproduced by permission of the Ansoff Family Trust

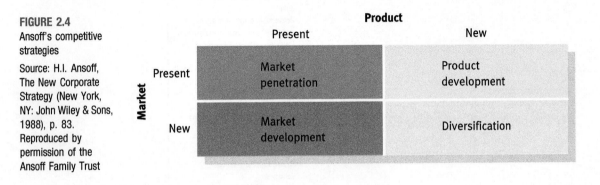

Practitioners' use of SWOT analysis

Marketing tools and techniques

The SWOT analysis is a very simplistic tool, yet it appears in most marketing plans and is popular with boards of directors because it conveys so much information: strengths (S) on which to build, weaknesses (W) to rectify, opportunities (O) to consider and threats (T) to address.

The first SWOT depicted is typical. This was produced by a brainstorming workshop involving 25 sales and marketing personnel. Workshops are often used to generate SWOTs; alternatively, individual managers may spend a few minutes producing them – for example, while killing time at an airport. The problems in the example are that:

- the lists were not ranked in order of importance, only listed in the order they were suggested

- many of the bulleted points are vague or ambiguous

- there is no validation or evidence to support these points being included, only the personal judgement of the managers present at the meeting

- the implications are not detailed

- there are far too many non-prioritized points listed to act upon.

By contrast, the following SWOT grid for a major insurance company has a more manageable set of issues, although the points are still horrendously ambiguous. Such ambiguity in practice would need rectifying. For example, what 'network' is a strength – IT, branch, broker, distribution geographically – and in what way?

STRENGTHS	WEAKNESSES
Experience and quality of people	Multiple image
Safety/environmental standards	Inconsistent site presentation
Brand heritage – low price perception	Brand equity value
Co-op mode of operation	Inflexible logistics
Teamwork/alignment	Lack of maintaining business
New concept	investment
Merchandizing	High break-even cost
Category management structure	Lack of flexible resources
Store locations	Inflexible technology
Streamlined organization	Inconsistent focus on retailing/lack of
Fully integrated company	selling structure
Ability to change quickly	Staff turnover
Dealer Loyalty	Quality of data and analysis
	Inadequate benchmarking
	Consumer research
	Reactive rather than proactive
	Communication – quality/mode
	Poor succession planning
	Cost control
	Total overheads too high
	Too many non-performing sites

OPPORTUNITIES	THREATS
Dealer buying group	Industry restructuring
Customer loyalty promotion	– by store categories
Optimizing distribution e.g. push/pull	– by supplier/retailer alliances/JVs
Market growth of forecourt	Lack of loyalty programme
convenience	Government transport policy
Synergies for services with other	Lack of shop image and investment
brands	Majors targeting smaller dealers
Green products	Cost of environmental legislation
European purchasing agreements	Control of costs
Joint venture on payment card	Continued low margins
Detailed economical analysis for sites	Failure to capture convenience
Concessions/rebranding	market growth
Alcohol/fast food/bakeries	
Technology	
Small profitable dealers (brand standards)	
Cost effective store and design	
More and better use of consumer/customer research industry data	
Active selling by sales attendants	
Optimization of site opening hours	
Promoting underperforming sites/ micro marketing	
Margin enhancement through loyalty scheme	
Alliance with shop retailers	
Market attrition	
Linking site to local community	
Co-op portfolio management	
Differentiation through customer service excellence	
Closer supplier relations	
Telesales	

SWOT Grid for an Insurance Business

	STRENGTHS	WEAKNESSES
Internal issues	Brand recognition Expertise in underwriting Network British, leading UK market Wide product range	Share price Press reports → Media targeting Uncertainty re. direction/market segments Poor product differentiation Cost base Wide network
External issues	Profitable markets still far from mature Broker loyalty Business unit focus strategy Technology Joint ventures with 3rd parties, such as major retailers entering fin/servs	Regulation Solvency Share price and ownership Negative press Losing customers Competitors – many mergers taking place Our markets are desirable to Euro-rivals Changing weather patterns
	OPPORTUNITIES	THREATS

Effective SWOTs should adhere to the following essential guidelines:

- Be as focused as possible – no huge lists.
- Use teamwork to generate a range of opinions, then verify with external stakeholders (e.g. channel members, suppliers, customers) and benchmark against any available marketing research or customer satisfaction audit data.
- Concentrate on a customer orientation in allocating priorities: deal first with issues of importance to customers, particularly weaknesses that rivals could exploit.
- Strengths and weaknesses are more revealing when benchmarked against key rivals.

- Use an analysis of the macro marketing environment (see Chapter 3) as input to the opportunities and threats.
- Rank the points listed in order of importance: senior managers assume lists presented to them to be prioritized.
- Have supporting evidence, otherwise exclude the issue from the list.
- Be honest! Include bad news, too, such as major weaknesses to rectify and nasty threats to now combat. All too often, managers only wish to communicate opportunities and supporting strengths to their superiors, yet it is unfixed weaknesses which will ruin a strategy and ignored threats which will damage the organization's performance.

Having produced the top-line SWOT depicted lower left, the insurance company team then debated in detail each point in order to clarify the issues, verify their importance and discuss the implication of each issue to the business. This discussion led to a prioritization of tasks to action. This phase is crucial if the SWOT is to help direct a business's thinking.

By following these guidelines, this insurance business eventually produced a meaningful, objective SWOT that led to specific action programmes, notably to address the stated weaknesses and steer the board's thinking about possible opportunities to consider.

Source: © Dibb/Simkin.

Note: a more extensive explanation of this technique is offered in either *The Market Segmentation Workbook* (Dibb and Simkin) *or The Marketing Planning Workbook* (Dibb, Simkin and Bradley), both originally published in 1996 by Thomson, and in *Marketing Planning* (Dibb and Simkin), published by Cengage in 2008.

---

intense growth
Growth that occurs when current products and current markets have the potential for increasing sales

Ansoff's original work identified categories for growth:

Intense growth

Intense growth can take place when current products and current markets have the potential for increasing sales. There are three main strategies for intense growth – market penetration, market development and product development.

market penetration
A strategy of increasing sales of current products in current markets

Market penetration **Market penetration** is a strategy of increasing sales in current markets with current products. For example, Coca-Cola and PepsiCo try to achieve increased market share through aggressive advertising and brand building.

market development
A strategy of increasing sales of current products in new markets

Market development **Market development** is a strategy of increasing sales of current products in new markets. For example, a European aircraft manufacturer was able to enter the US market by offering Eastern Airlines financing that Boeing could not match. Evian devised a new use for its mineral water by developing its Brumisateur, an atomiser spray for the skin.

product development
A strategy of increasing sales by improving present products or developing new products for current markets

Product development **Product development** is a strategy of increasing sales by improving present products or developing new products for current markets. PepsiCo and Coca-Cola both have new container sizes, low-calorie/low-sugar/low-carb versions and vending machine services.

Diversified growth

diversified growth
Growth that occurs when new products are developed to be sold in new markets

Diversified growth occurs when new products are developed to be sold in new markets. Companies have become increasingly diversified since the 1960s, although many European businesses are reluctant to 'gamble' in what are for them unchartered markets. Diversification offers some advantages over single-business companies, because it allows businesses to spread their risk across a number of markets. More important, it allows them to make better and wider use of their management, technical and financial resources. For example, marketing expertise can be used across businesses, which may also share advertising themes, distribution channels, warehouse facilities or even salesforces.[16] The three forms of diversification are horizontal, concentric and conglomerate.

horizontal diversification
A process that occurs when new products not technologically related to current products are introduced into current markets

Horizontal diversification **Horizontal diversification** results when new products that are not technologically related to current products are introduced to current markets. Sony, for example, diversified from electronics to movie production through its purchase of Columbia Pictures. The purchase gave Sony a library of 2700 films, including *Ghostbusters 2* and *When Harry Met Sally*, as well as 23 000 television episodes, which it has used to establish its line of video tapes and DVDs.[17]

concentric diversification
A process that occurs when new products related to current products are introduced into new markets

Concentric diversification In **concentric diversification**, the marketing and technology of new products are related to current products, but the new ones are introduced into new markets. For instance, Sony developed business PCs and laptops based on its consumer flatscreen and electronics products, and then successfully used its established position in business computers to tackle the home computing market. Apple's now famous and hugely successful move into consumer media players and smart phones leveraged capabilities from its business computing heritage.

conglomerate diversification
A process that occurs when new products unrelated to current technology, products or markets are introduced into new markets

Conglomerate diversification **Conglomerate diversification** occurs when new products are unrelated to current technology, products or markets, and are introduced into markets new to the company. For example, Bass, the British brewer and pubs business, acquired the American Holiday Inn hotel chain. Laura Ashley, the UK clothing and furnishings company, moved into the fragrance market with Laura Ashley No. 1. Samsung diversified into everything from air conditioning and construction equipment to shipbuilding, home entertainment centres and mobile phones.

integrated growth
Growth that occurs in three possible directions: forwards, backwards or horizontally

Integrated growth

Integrated growth can occur in the same industry that the company is in and in three possible directions: forwards, backwards or horizontally.

1   A company growing through forward integration takes ownership or increased control of its distribution system. For example, a shoe manufacturer might start selling its products through wholly owned retail outlets.

2 In backward integration, a company takes ownership or increased control of its supply systems. A newspaper company that buys a paper mill is integrating backwards.

3 Horizontal integration occurs when a company takes ownership or control of some of its competitors, such as BMW's acquisition of Mini, or Ford's purchases of Land Rover, Jaguar, Volvo and Aston Martin (most of which were subsequently sold-off).

An absolutely crucial part of developing both a corporate strategy and a marketing strategy is the need to seek competitive advantage over rivals and the associated importance of gaining competitor intelligence. In developing strategies, an organization must consider the competitive positions in the marketplace and formulate marketing strategies and tactics accordingly. Some authors have adopted warfare analogies to describe the strategic options for competing in a market.[18] This chapter later examines the concept of competitive positions.

Target market strategy and brand positioning

Central to achieving a company's corporate vision is the need to build up a loyal customer base of satisfied customers. Tesco did not overtake Sainsbury's by chance – it developed a clear marketing strategy based on a desire to fully satisfy a carefully targeted set of market segments. Tesco is continuously upgrading its stores, adding new services and product lines, even new markets such as financial services and banking, and innovating with channels of distribution through Tesco Metro and Tesco.com, with the aim of addressing its targeted segments' customer needs. Market segmentation is at the core of robust marketing strategy development. As explained in Chapter 6, this involves identifying customer needs, expectations, perceptions, decision-making and buying behaviours, so as to group those customers who will be satisfied and marketed to in a similar manner into homogeneous groups or segments. One segment will differ from another in terms of customer profile and buying behaviour, and also with regard to the sales and marketing activity likely to satisfy these customers; but within a particular segment customers will share similar needs, buying behaviour and expectations. Without a thorough understanding of customers, therefore, it is difficult to produce a marketing strategy. Developing an understanding of customers is explored in Chapters 4 and 5.

Taking the time to objectively and sensibly group a market's customers into meaningful market segments is a discipline many organizations are only now discovering, particularly in business-to-business markets. Most of the fast movers, market leaders and successful brands in a marketplace base their marketing strategies on carefully honed market segmentation analyses. It is important to remember that the process of market segmentation involves more than simply grouping customers into segments or groups. Shrewd targeting of certain segments and the development of a clear brand positioning are part of the market segmentation process. **Brand positioning** is the creation of a desirable, distinctive and plausible image for a brand that will have strong appeal for the customers in a target market segment. The basis of Chapter 6's coverage – identifying segments, deciding which to target and developing desirable positionings – is one of the foundations of a marketing strategy.

brand positioning
The creation of a desirable, distinctive and plausible image for a brand in the minds of targeted customers

target market strategy
The choice for which market segment(s) an organization decides to develop marketing programmes

A **target market strategy** is the choice of which market segment(s) an organization decides to prioritize and for which to develop marketing programmes. An organization must first have agreed an over-riding corporate strategy and decided on which opportunities to focus, as described above. The selected target markets should be appropriate for this selection of opportunities, within the stated corporate strategy. Organizations must identify priority target markets that are worthwhile targeting with bespoke marketing mix programmes: product, price, place (distribution), promotion and people. Even the mighty Ford or General Motors has to decide which segments in the car and van markets to pursue, opting not to have models aimed at all buyers in the market. It is important to balance current core target markets with those offering future viability.

Once determined, in each target market an organization must strive to emphasize to those targeted customers the relevance and applicability of its product and marketing mix proposition. This is achieved through all ingredients of the marketing mix, but specifically through developing a distinctive, plausible and memorable brand positioning, such as BMW's 'The Ultimate Driving Machine'. This positioning imagery is communicated to targeted customers primarily through the promotional mix, packaging and design, but product attributes, pricing, choice of distribution and customer service provision must also support the positioning strategy. An upmarket restaurant, for example, requires a suitably lavish ambience, slick service, quality food, appropriate location and a suitable price to match its branding and promotional campaigns. It is important to agree on the target market strategy and required brand positioning before developing the marketing programmes destined to implement this strategy. These marketing mix activities must reflect the marketing analyses and target market strategy requirements rather than being merely a continuation of previous marketing mix activities.

Competitive advantage

competitors
Organizations viewed as marketing products similar to, or substitutable for, a company's products, when targeted at the same customers

Competitors are generally viewed by an organization as those businesses marketing products similar to, or substitutable for, its products when targeted at the same customers. In order to persuade customers to purchase an organization's products in preference to those products marketed by its **competitors**, leading strategists argue that it is necessary to develop a **competitive advantage**. Competitive advantage is the achievement of superior performance vis-à-vis rivals, through differentiation, to create distinctive product appeal or brand identity; through offering customer value and achieving the lowest delivered cost; or by focusing on narrowly scoped product categories or market niches so as to be viewed as a leading specialist. The creation of a competitive advantage is a core component of the development of a marketing strategy. It is not easy to achieve, as rivals often have sensible strategies, good products and customer service and smart marketing programmes.

competitive advantage
The achievement of superior performance vis-à-vis rivals, through differentiation to create distinctive product appeal or brand identity; through providing customer value and achieving the lowest delivered cost; or by focusing on narrowly scoped product categories or market niches so as to be viewed as a leading specialist

Marketing strategist Michael Porter identified the so-called **generic routes to competitive advantage**, claiming them to result in success for companies competing for position in any particular market. Although created over 30 years ago, this framework is still appropriate and highly directional for companies seeking to examine thoroughly their likely basis for competing. As depicted in Figure 2.5, these three generic strategies are as follows.

generic routes to competitive advantage
Cost leadership, differentiation and focus; not mutually exclusive

1 *Cost leadership.* This involves developing a low cost base, often through economies of scale associated with high market share and economies of experience, to give high contribution. This high financial contribution can then be used to further develop the low cost base. Very tight cost controls are essential to the success of this strategy. Generally, within a single market, only one competitor is secure in adopting this strategy for creating a competitive advantage: the organization with the lowest cost base and best experience curve.

2 *Differentiation.* Companies adopting a differentiation strategy strive to offer product and marketing programmes that have a distinct advantage or are different to those offered by competitors. Differentiation can be achieved on a number of fronts, including creative and innovative product or brand designs, or novel distribution channel, pricing and customer service policies. This theme is taken further when marketers seek a *differential advantage*, as discussed later in this chapter.

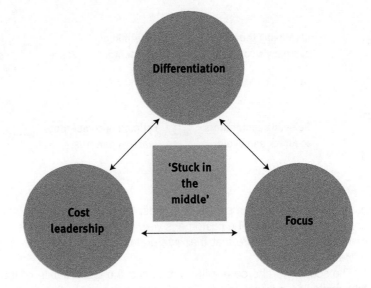

FIGURE 2.5
Porter's generic routes to
competitive advantage

3 *Focus.* Companies must maintain close links with the market so that product and marketing effort are designed with a particular target group in mind. Typically of small size, unable to achieve cost leadership or maintain significant differentiation, such companies succeed by effectively meeting customer needs that may be being missed by larger players in the market and by gaining a reputation for being experts or specialists in their narrowly defined area of activity.

Failure to achieve any of these strategies can result in companies becoming 'stuck in the middle', with no real competitive advantage. It is not usually possible to simultaneously follow all three generic strategies for competitive advantage, but it is common for businesses to gain cost leadership while also differentiating their proposition, and also for organizations to seek both a focused and a differentiated approach. Discounter Aldi adopts a cost leadership and a differentiated approach for developing a competitive advantage, as does no-frills airline easyJet. Sports coupé manufacturer Porsche adopts a focused and differentiated approach to defining a competitive advantage. It is sometimes more difficult to create a focused and cost leadership approach, as niche players rarely have the necessary scale economies, but it is not impossible. Companies or brands failing to master at least one of Porter's dimensions invariably struggle to compete or indeed to survive in the medium-term.

Competitive positions and differential advantage

competitive set
All competing
organizations and brands,
irrespective of size and
history, including
substitutable solutions to
customers' needs, as
defined by the target
market customers

In order to compete effectively, marketers should seek to develop a differential advantage. In order to ensure this will be effective, marketers must understand the nature of the **competitive set** and also identify those rivals with which to do battle. The competitive set includes all competing organizations and brands, irrespective of size and history, including substitutable solutions to customers' needs, as defined by target market customers. Leading marketing strategists David Aaker and Michael Porter both argue that the scoping of the competitive set in many organizations is too limited. Ask most management teams who are their competitors and they will simply name the leading few organizations and brands in the market, ignoring smaller fast-moving rivals, probable new entrants to the market or substitutable solutions to their customers' needs offered by dissimilar organizations. It is often the case that when a company's customers are asked to

FIGURE 2.6
Steps in analyzing competitors

Source: Veronica Wong, 'FT MBA course notes', Warwick Business School, 1996, copyright © Professor Veronica Wong

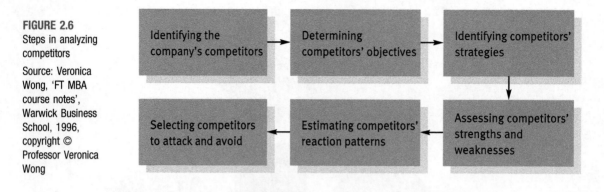

name the competing companies or brands, they list a few names not routinely considered by the company's marketers. The customer's view of his or her options is of paramount importance and marketers should ensure that their interpretation of the competitive set is shared by their target market customers.

The scoping of the competitive arena and the identification of the competitive set are important marketing analysis tasks. Competitors are outside the control of an organization, so the forces of competition are generally included within the forces of the *marketing environment*, as part of what is termed the 'micro marketing environment'. This concept is described in Chapter 3, which discusses further the forces of the competitive environment.

For the identified competitive set, marketers should assess the objectives and strategies of these rivals, their strengths and weaknesses, and determine how competitors are likely to react to their own marketing strategy and programmes. In effect, this leads to a decision about which competitors to 'fight', which to avoid antagonizing and which to treat as unimportant. Veronica Wong (after Kotler) suggests that competitor-aware marketers should be able to answer six key questions, as described in Figure 2.6. Marketers require these insights into competitors.

Before examining the concept of differential advantage, this chapter looks at the increasingly popular use of warfare analogies in identifying the relative threat posed by the competitors in a market. While *Marketing Essentials* is not intended to be a marketing strategy text, analysis of the competition is a core principle for effective marketing and, as explained in Chapter 1, without a thorough appreciation of the competitive arena an organization cannot have a marketing orientation.

Competitive positions

Evidently it is important to understand the nature of competition. This involves more than a cursory examination of like-for-like major rivals. Most organizations consider only similar companies or brands to be their competitors. As shown in Figure 2.7, there are other facets of competition that must be evaluated. What of the smaller players that may one day emerge as dominant in a market or specific segment? Why not pre-empt such an outcome by developing a strategy to destroy them while still only a small rival? What about the new entrant into the marketplace? Could its appearance have been foreseen? What actions are required to minimize its threat? How did Nokia or Moto fend off the entry of Samsung in the mobile market? Did they even anticipate Samsung's entry? Citroën did, while now defunct Rover did not! What of innovative solutions to customers' problems?

JCB produces construction equipment that digs trenches for pipes and cables. Micro-bore tunnelling moles lay pipes without the need for a trench. Such moles – substitute competition – could be missed by JCB's marketers as a competitive threat without a rigorous analysis of the forces of the competitive environment. Web-comms posed a threat to BT, who then went online in order to remain competitive. The iPhone threatened Samsung, which then developed a successful range of rival smart phones.

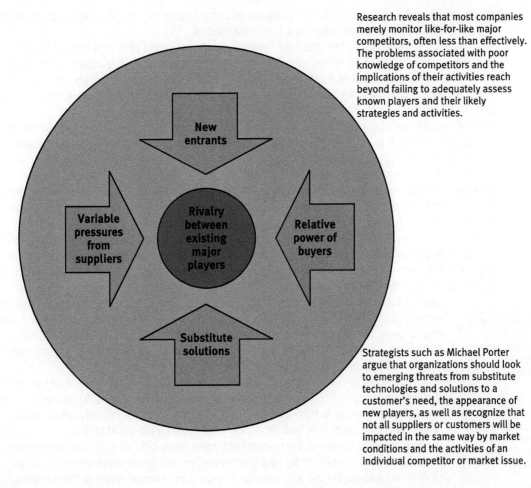

Research reveals that most companies merely monitor like-for-like major competitors, often less than effectively. The problems associated with poor knowledge of competitors and the implications of their activities reach beyond failing to adequately assess known players and their likely strategies and activities.

Strategists such as Michael Porter argue that organizations should look to emerging threats from substitute technologies and solutions to a customer's need, the appearance of new players, as well as recognize that not all suppliers or customers will be impacted in the same way by market conditions and the activities of an individual competitor or market issue.

FIGURE 2.7
Forecasting market potential and sales

The power of suppliers and of consumers can also vary per company and act as a competitive force, particularly if one organization encounters greater supply problems or more severe customer bargaining than its rivals face from their suppliers and customers. These competitor categories are in addition to the like-for-like rivals considered by most organizations to be their competitors.

Figure 2.7 is particularly useful for scoping the nature of a market place. This framework still offers management teams a very smart approach for assessing their competitive arenas. Porter defined **five competitive forces** that together determine competition in an industry or market:

five competitive forces
Together these determine competition in an industry or market: rivalry amongst existing like-for-like players; the threat of new entrants; the threat of substitute solutions; the bargaining power of buyers; and the bargaining power of suppliers

1 rivalry among existing like-for-like players
2 the threat of new entrants
3 the threat of substitute products or services as a solution to customers' problems or needs
4 the bargaining power of buyers
5 the bargaining power of suppliers.

Many marketing directors find this framework ideal for persuading their colleagues to consider competitive threats from more than just like-for-like rivals. Similarly, most marketing dissertations use Porter's framework in order to provide the perspective for describing the competitive pressures prevalent in a particular market.

In addition to realizing the importance of examining all categories of competitors, it is necessary to understand what must be known about rivals. Most companies can describe their competitors: who, where, with what and at what price. However, few organizations genuinely understand their rivals' strategies or endeavour to predict their rivals' reaction to moves they themselves may make. Very few companies attempt to identify those individual competitors it is sensible to avoid in a head-to-head marketing campaign or those most likely to be vulnerable to attack at low risk to the company's resource base. It is prudent to avoid head-to-head conflict with a similarly sized and resourced adversary, or one bigger and better resourced. It is more desirable to identify the weaknesses of more vulnerable competitors and address these through the proposed marketing mix programmes. No marketing strategy should be formulated without a shrewd analysis of competitors. For some companies, carrying out this kind of analysis has recently been made more complex by the fact that they operate in both the physical and digital marketplace.[19]

Many marketers view their marketplace as a battlefield, opting to compete on only certain fronts, engaging with carefully selected opponents, where there is a perceived differential advantage over the enemy. This warfare analogy has become increasingly popular and hinges on identifying the competitive positions of the various businesses competing in a market segment.[20] The categories of **competitive positions** – competitors' roles in the marketplace that influence their marketing strategies and programmes – include the market leader, market challengers, fast movers, market followers and market nichers. These should be identified within each target market segment: a market challenger in one market segment may be a follower or even absent in a second market segment.

competitive positions
Competitors' roles in the marketplace, which influence their marketing strategies and programmes

In the world of market shares, there has to be one, and only one, **market leader**: the player enjoying individually the largest slice of the market. In some business-to-business markets, a market leader can have a majority of industry sales, particularly when patent protection or technical innovation gives it an advantage over competitors. In most markets, however, the market leader may have only 10 to 20 per cent of the market's sales. The market leader has the highest market share and retains its competitive position by expanding the total market or expanding market share at the expense of its rivals, while protecting or defending current market share by retaining its customer base. In this context, the market leader, although successful, perhaps has the most difficult task: it must find strategies to increase market size and market share, as well as maintaining strategies to defend its current share. The marketing programmes necessary for maintaining ongoing relationships with existing customers are quite different to the marketing programmes used to attract and entice potential customers.

market leader
The single player enjoying the largest individual share in the market

Behind the market leader are competing companies, which are market challengers, fast movers, market followers or market nichers. **Market challengers** are non-market leaders that aggressively attack rivals, including the market leader, to take more market share. In most instances, these players are number two, three and perhaps four in a market, aspiring to market leadership. When Virgin entered the transatlantic market, its intention was to steal BA's market leadership. It is important to remember that to qualify as challengers these companies must be proactive and aggressive in their sales and marketing rather than passively reinforcing the existing hierarchy. **Fast movers** are smaller rival companies not yet destined to be major challengers, but growing rapidly on a smaller scale. A new entrant may have only 2 per cent of the market – but what is to stop it from increasing its share to 8 per cent within two years? A business may only have 4 per cent of the market, but three years ago it only had 1 per cent. What is to prevent it from having 8 per cent or 19 per cent in three years' time? The market leader and key challengers should take steps to prevent such continued growth.

market challengers
Non-market leaders that aggressively try to capture market share from their rivals

fast movers
Smaller rival companies not yet destined to be major challengers, but growing rapidly on a smaller scale

Market followers are low-share competitors without the resources, market position, research and development, or commitment to challenge for extra sales and market

market followers
Low-share competitors without the resources, market position, research and development, or the commitment to challenge for extra sales and market share

share. These companies tend to be the 'me-too, also-rans' in a market, whose raison d'être is to do as before and simply survive. In boom times these players can latch on to the success of their larger rivals, but in recession – or when faced with larger rivals' product innovations – they often struggle to achieve sales. Most markets also contain **market nichers**: companies that specialize by focusing on only a very narrow range of products such as Sock Shop or Saab, or on a select band of consumers, such as Body Shop or Porsche. Nichers survive by finding a safe, small, profitable market segment – often apparently too small to attract the market leaders and challengers. Nichers specialize and can genuinely prepare a marketing mix that exactly matches their target customers' needs. They are vulnerable to market downturns, the entry of rival nichers and the sudden attention of the major players in the marketplace, as happened to Porsche when the North American target market hit a recession and Japanese rivals appeared with cheaper, fast, two-seater sports coupés.

market nichers
Companies that specialize by focusing on only a very narrow range of products or on a select band of consumers

A market leader must defend its position, while simultaneously seeking more market share. Only a market leader should consider **defensive warfare** as a strategic foundation. Strong defence involves striking a balance between waiting for market developments or competitor activity and proactively parrying competitors' actions. As market leader, the company must remember that a false sense of security and passive inactivity lead to disaster: the best defensive strategy is the courage to attack; and strong moves by competitors should always be blocked, never ignored. To defend its market share, a market leader must treat existing customers well and attentively, and never take them for granted. The marketing mix must be updated continually and target customers' needs must regularly be considered. New markets, products and opportunities should always be sought and evaluated. Occasionally, if faced by a strong challenger in a small or declining market, a market leader should consider divesting and concentrating resources in its other markets. Others may have to turn to defensive warfare when attacked by the market leader or challengers, but only the market leader should build a strategy around the desire to defend its current position.

defensive warfare
A policy of striking a balance between waiting for market developments or competitor activity and proactively parrying competitors' actions

A challenger has to attack for market share, but on what basis? The leader, and perhaps other challengers, will be strong and rich in resources. A challenger's attack must be well thought out and not suicidal in terms of the company's medium-term future. A few years ago, few observers could accept the logic in Sainsbury's attacking market leader Tesco on the basis of price. Price anyway was not the core facet of Sainsbury's service-led culture, nor was Tesco the weakest of rivals to choose to fight. In **offensive warfare**, the main consideration is the market leader's strength: where are there any chinks in the leader's armour? A challenger seeking market share must identify a weakness in the leader's marketing mix and in other challengers' marketing programmes, and develop a genuine corresponding strength. With such a differential advantage or competitive edge, the challenger's resources may well be sufficient to steal ground successfully from the leader and the other challengers. Any attack, however, should be on a narrow front, where the challenger is perceived by the target customers to have an advantage and where resources can be focused. If no real weakness in the market leader exists, a challenger may attack head-on. Such an attack can be successful only if there are numerous, very weak market followers, if the leader is slow to react and if a price-cutting war does not result. In the last situation, the leader's resource base may fend off the challenger's attack.

offensive warfare
A policy whereby challengers aggressively seek market share by identifying any weaknesses in the leader's and other challengers' marketing mixes and developing a genuine corresponding strength

Followers are vulnerable, but careful monitoring of market segments, marketing environment forces and competitive trends can help ensure their survival. They must serve exactly only a few market segments, specializing rather than diversifying in terms of products and markets, and making prudent use of what research and development resources are available. Nichers must watch for signs of competitor threats and possible changes in target segment customers' needs, and they may need to consider product development and, ultimately, diversification. Their marketing mixes must be tailored exactly to meet the expectations of their target segment.

All organizations should know, for all their markets and target segments, which companies occupy these competitive positions. They must alter their strategies and marketing programmes

competitor scanning
The monitoring of competitive positions and competitors' strategies

competitive positions proforma
A tool for scoping the competitive set, helping a company to understand the competitive positions in its target markets and diagnosing the effectiveness of a marketing strategy

accordingly. Organizations should also review their rivals' marketing strategies and marketing programmes: many companies are surprisingly predictable. Response to rivals' pricing policies, frequency of new product launches, entry into new markets and timing of promotional campaigns, for example, can often be accurately anticipated. In this way, **competitor scanning** – the monitoring of competitive positions and competitors' strategies – helps to establish more realistic marketing goals, develop successful strategies and programmes, and pre-empt nasty shocks caused by competitors' actions.[21] The leading marketing strategists agree that it is essential to understand competitors' strategies, their strengths and weaknesses in satisfying customers, and any differential advantages they hold that must be combated.[22] The **competitive positions proforma** has been developed by the authors of *Marketing Essentials*, in conjunction with many organizations such as JCB, HSBC, Fujitsu, EDF and IBM, as a way of scoping the competitive set, helping a company in understanding the competitive positions in its target markets and diagnosing the effectiveness of a marketing strategy. This particular tool for practitioners is described in the Marketing Tools and Techniques box on page 67.

Differential advantage

differential advantage
An attribute of a brand, product, service or marketing mix that is desired by the targeted customer and provided by only one supplier

If a marketing mix is developed that matches target market needs and expectations and is superior to those offered by competitors, there is a real – or perceived – differential advantage. A **differential advantage** is an attribute of a brand, product, service or marketing mix that is desired by the targeted customer and provided by only one supplier: it is a unique edge over rivals in satisfying this customer. If successful in developing a differential advantage, an organization is likely to have its differential advantage copied by rivals. Direct Line innovated in selling car insurance over the telephone, cutting out the broker. This more convenient and cheaper service was very popular with customers, gaining market leadership for Direct Line. Very high profits followed. Rivals caught up, offering their own telephone-based direct selling of car insurance. Nevertheless, Direct Line developed a sizeable and successful customer base, which is still proving difficult for competitors to win back.

Achieving a differential advantage – or competitive edge – requires an organization to make the most of its opportunities and resources while offering customers a satisfactory mix of tangible and intangible benefits.[23] When striking a balance between customer requirements on the one hand and company resources on the other, competitor activity must also be monitored. For example, there is little sense in promoting speedy distribution to customers if several large competing organizations offer a faster service. An understanding of competitors and customers' perceptions of companies' propositions is an essential part of identifying a differential advantage. Once determined, it is sensible to maximize the use of any differential advantage in the marketing mix, particularly in the promotional mix and all marketing communications.

There are many different sources of differential advantage that companies can pursue. It is important to ensure that the promoted differential advantage is:

● unique to the one organization, otherwise it is not a differential advantage, only a strength or capability
● desirable to the targeted customer
● not simply the expected marketing mix taken for granted by the target market
● not simply an internal perception by a team of marketers.

For example, a new range may be superior to the company's former product range, but compared to competitors' products may offer few benefits to the customer. The marketers could be guilty of identifying the new range's advantages over the former range, wrongly, as offering a differential advantage.

Practitioners' use of competitor intelligence: the Dibb/Simkin competitive positions proforma

Marketing tools and techniques

The understanding of competition is not generally strong in most organizations. Managers may be able to name their rivals, and these businesses' products, price points and outline promotional activity, but rarely are managers able to suggest rivals' next moves or to identify an individual competitor's strengths or weaknesses. Therefore, managers cannot be taking into account the capabilities and market standing of such rivals when they construct their own target market strategies. The result could be a significant waste, as a company's marketing programme may fail to enable the company to set itself apart from its principal rivals. Worse, the company may be incapable of combating its rivals' marketing strategies.

The ultimate goal in marketing is to produce a differential advantage: something desired by targeted customers and only offered by a single supplier. Failure to analyze rivals means that the creation of a differential advantage is going to occur only by chance, rather than due to knowledge of competitors' strengths and weaknesses.

The strategists also point to the need to address an organization's own weaknesses. In particular, a management team should be aware of which rivals are best placed to exploit any weaknesses in the organization or in its marketing mix. Over time, the competitive set will change, as new entrants and substitution solutions to customers' requirements emerge. The relative strengths and weaknesses of competitors will alter, too, often rapidly. The competitive set must be monitored closely and not just occasionally.

Chapter 7 identifies methods for collecting competitor intelligence. Once the competitive set has been defined – through the customer's eyes – and some knowledge has been built up about these brands, a useful tool to deploy is the competitive positions proforma.

This technique is based on warfare analogies and assumes that the analysis is replicated for each individual target market segment. Within each segment, it is necessary to allocate the competitive set – which may include substitutes and possible new entrants – into the following categories.

- *Market leader*. Only ever one in a segment: the player or brand with the biggest market share. The market leader should (1) expand the total market, (2) expand its own market share and (3) protect existing market share. The market leader has to defend and attack.

- *Market challenger*(s). Non-market leaders that want to be the leader! Aggressively attacking for market share gains by investing in new product development, establishing distribution, promotional activity, field force increases or price incentives.

- *Market follower*(s). Low-share rivals without resources, market position, R&D or commitment to challenge. The 'me-too' smaller players in a market segment.

- *Market nicher*(s). Companies that specialize in terms of market/product/customers, by finding a safe, profitable niche or narrowly defined segment.

- *Market fast mover*(s). Smaller players with intentions to be much bigger. A rival not yet large enough to be classed as a challenger, but one worth watching or 'knocking out' before it is too late.

One column of the proforma is completed for each market segment. A company should include itself within the columns. In this way, a management team may assess the business's relative performance across market segments and identify rivals making gains in more than one segment. In this context, the technique is of great value to the board of a company and not only to marketing managers.

Marketing-oriented businesses repeat this analysis every few months, in order to reveal movements within the columns and to identify fast movers, new entrants or emerging substitute competition. The changing strengths and weaknesses of rivals also become apparent. If a company is not moving up the column – or 'league table' – it is likely that its marketing strategy and/or marketing programme are inappropriately specified. Remedial action should be taken.

The competitive positions

For reasons of commercial confidentiality, the identities of the cited retailers have been disguised.

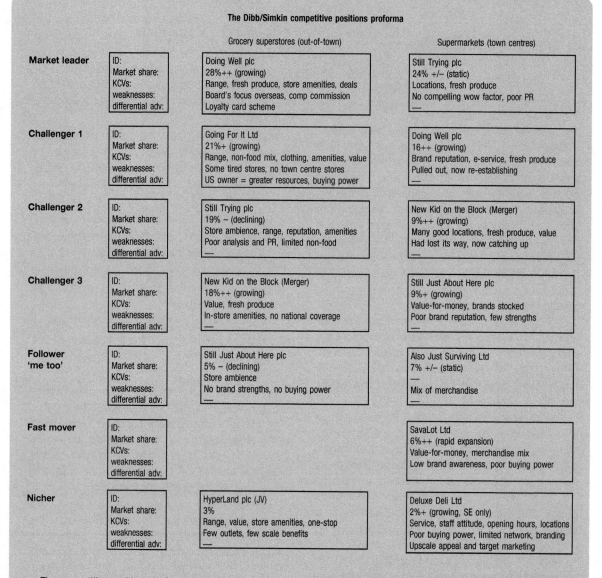

The Dibb/Simkin competitive positions proforma

		Grocery superstores (out-of-town)	Supermarkets (town centres)
Market leader	ID: Market share: KCVs: weaknesses: differential adv:	Doing Well plc 28%++ (growing) Range, fresh produce, store amenities, deals Board's focus overseas, comp commission Loyalty card scheme	Still Trying plc 24% +/– (static) Locations, fresh produce No compelling wow factor, poor PR —
Challenger 1	ID: Market share: KCVs: weaknesses: differential adv:	Going For It Ltd 21%+ (growing) Range, non-food mix, clothing, amenities, value Some tired stores, no town centre stores US owner = greater resources, buying power	Doing Well plc 16++ (growing) Brand reputation, e-service, fresh produce Pulled out, now re-establishing —
Challenger 2	ID: Market share: KCVs: weaknesses: differential adv:	Still Trying plc 19% – (declining) Store ambience, range, reputation, amenities Poor analysis and PR, limited non-food —	New Kid on the Block (Merger) 9%++ (growing) Many good locations, fresh produce, value Had lost its way, now catching up —
Challenger 3	ID: Market share: KCVs: weaknesses: differential adv:	New Kid on the Block (Merger) 18%++ (growing) Value, fresh produce In-store amenities, no national coverage —	Still Just About Here plc 9%+ (growing) Value-for-money, brands stocked Poor brand reputation, few strengths —
Follower 'me too'	ID: Market share: KCVs: weaknesses: differential adv:	Still Just About Here plc 5% – (declining) Store ambience No brand strengths, no buying power	Also Just Surviving Ltd 7% +/– (static) — Mix of merchandise
Fast mover	ID: Market share: KCVs: weaknesses: differential adv:		SavaLot Ltd 6%++ (rapid expansion) Value-for-money, merchandise mix Low brand awareness, poor buying power
Nicher	ID: Market share: KCVs: weaknesses: differential adv:	HyperLand plc (JV) 3% Range, value, store amenities, one-stop Few outlets, few scale benefits —	Deluxe Deli Ltd 2%+ (growing, SE only) Service, staff attitude, opening hours, locations Poor buying power, limited network, branding Upscale appeal and target marketing

The competitive positions proforma identifies:

- the key players and their relative positions
- current successes and probable reasons
- the KCVs (key customer values or needs) each rival is good at serving – rivals' customer-facing strengths that must be addressed
- any differential advantages (DAs) to fear – these must be combated
- the company's own standing, which should improve over time
- emerging and fast-moving rivals, including substitute solutions to customers' needs
- the evolving competitive set with which to do battle, and how!

The proforma, therefore, is a 'call to action' to a company's marketers and leadership teams. In addition, the technique acts as a diagnostic over time of a business's successes or failures in terms of its marketing strategy and programmes.

Note: The Dibb/Simkin competitive positions proforma is copyright Sally Dibb and Lyndon Simkin. A more extensive explanation of this technique is offered in *The Market Segmentation Workbook* (Dibb and Simkin) and *The Marketing Planning Workbook* (Dibb, Simkin and Bradley), both originally published in 1996 by Thomson (London), or in *Marketing Planning* (Cengage, 2008).

Low price should also be avoided as a differential advantage at the centre of a marketing programme unless a company genuinely has the scale economies to maintain a low cost base and offer cost leadership. Only one company in any market can occupy this platform, as explained by Porter's generic routes to achieving a competitive advantage. Others are vulnerable to being undercut and losing their apparent differential advantage. Jet's lowest price proposition was undermined by Esso's highly effective Tigerwatch lowest price guarantee. Low price can be utilized as a short-term tactic – to off-load excessive stocks, for example – but should not form a basis for competing unless it can be defended against all challenges.

If there is no observable differential advantage, an organization must look to its strengths over its rivals. While not unique, these will still form the foundation for its ability to compete effectively. The SWOT analysis assists marketers in identifying their strengths and capabilities. The composite

basis for competing
A company's combined strengths as identified in a SWOT analysis and any differential advantage, which should form the leading edge of the company's marketing strategy

of any differential advantage with any strengths is a company's **basis for competing**, which should form the leading edge of the organization's marketing strategy. For some companies, such as 3M, innovativeness is the basis for competing, while for others, like Vidal Sassoon hair salons, image plays an important part. The Body Shop concentrates on environmentally friendly cosmetics, whereas for multiplex cinemas the basis for competing is the choice of multiple screens at one location. Some of these ways of gaining an edge are easier to sustain than others. For example, many UK companies that have traditionally focused on low price have found this advantage difficult to maintain in the long term.[24] The airline industry is just one to be plagued by periodic price wars, with many companies turning instead to flexibility and customer service as the basis for competing, while others have adopted a value-based strategy.

Identifying differential advantage There is a straightforward sequence that marketers follow when attempting to identify a differential advantage:

1　Identify the market's segments.

2　Establish what product and service attributes are desired and demanded by customers in each segment.

3　Decide which of these attributes the company in question offers.

4　Determine which attributes the company's competitors offer.

5　Consider what the marketplace perceives the competitors' genuine strengths to be.

6　Identify whether any gaps exist between customer expectations of the product/service on offer and perceptions of the competitors' marketing programmes.

7　Consider whether any gaps identified in step 6 are matched by the company and its own offerings. If the company is able to match one or more of these gaps, the potential exists for a differential advantage to be developed.

8　Question whether any of these potential advantages for the company can be emphasized through sales and marketing programmes.

9　Consider the sustainability of these advantages for the company. How easily and quickly can competitors catch up? Is it possible for the company to defend these advantages?

10　If there are no current advantages for the company, given the gaps identified between competitors' propositions and customer expectations, consider which areas offer potential for developing a future differential advantage.

11　In order to maximize any existing or potential differential advantages, detail the changes the company must make to its research and development, engineering, sales and marketing activities.

It is important to remember that companies frequently examine their relative strengths and weaknesses in relation to their rivals. A strength is not the same as a differential advantage. For example, many rivals may also have strong brand awareness, products that perform well, loyal distributors or high profitability. A differential advantage is something that targeted customers want and value, and that only one supplier is able to provide.

Marketing objectives

Once an organization has agreed which marketing opportunities are worth pursuing and on which target markets to focus marketing and sales activities, the organization must ensure that its marketing strategy specifies its core marketing objectives. These marketing objectives are typically defined in terms of which are the most desirable market segments to target and, for each of these priority market segments, what market share is being sought and thereby what sales volumes or levels are expected to be achieved.

Marketers must specify a raft of performance metrics, including customer satisfaction or brand awareness measures, profitability and financial contribution – or in retailing, sales per square metre of selling space. Marketing objectives may include various product and market developments that marketers expect to achieve. These developments may include new product launches, new territory or market segment entry, the creation of innovative distribution channels or partnerships with marketing channel members. Without specification of these expectations it is difficult to ensure a fit with the organization's overall corporate strategy. It is impossible, too, to monitor ongoing performance or benchmark the effectiveness of the recommended marketing strategy against competitors' strategies.

Marketing mix decisions

As mentioned in Chapter 1, marketers must decide which products or services to offer to selected target markets, the attributes, specifications, performance characteristics and designs of these products, and the levels of customer service required to support them and to encourage customer satisfaction. In addition, prices must be set, payment terms and mechanisms agreed; distribution channels have to be chosen and distribution channel members orchestrated, in order to ensure product availability at places appropriate for the targeted customers. These customers must be made aware of the product through promotional activity – marketing communications – and their interest in the product maintained through promotional campaigns. These product, people, price, place and promotion decisions are what are termed the marketing mix decisions. They occupy the majority of marketers' time and account for most of a marketing department's budget.

Part Three of *Marketing Essentials* explores in detail the ingredients of the marketing mix, and the tactical toolkit utilized by marketers in developing marketing programmes designed to implement their recommended marketing strategy and target market strategy.

These product, people, price, place/distribution and promotion issues should be determined only after the marketing strategy has been agreed. The marketing strategy itself should be developed only after the core marketing analyses have been undertaken addressing market trends, marketing environment forces, customer buying behaviour, competition, opportunities and capabilities. The marketing process outlined in Chapter 1 requires analysis, strategy formulation and then the specification of a marketing mix to facilitate the implementation of the desired target market strategy. Marketing programmes created from the ingredients of the marketing mix are part of the creation of an effective marketing strategy. Without the specification of marketing mixes, marketing strategies will not be effectively operationalized.

Implementation and performance monitoring

Marketing programmes depend on a detailed marketing mix specification: product, place/distribution, promotion, price and people issues. In addition, marketing programmes require the specification of budgets for actioning the desired marketing mix recommendations. These budgets must reflect the anticipated sales from the sales forecast and the trends inherent in the targeted market segments. Sales and marketing personnel must know of their responsibilities in implementing the recommended marketing programmes. There may be a requirement on colleagues outside the sales and marketing functions or on senior executives. Schedules must be determined so that it is clear when specific marketing mix activities are expected to occur.

It is essential that the implementation of a marketing strategy is managed and facilitated. This involves specifying by whom, when, how and at what cost the desired marketing mix programmes will be actioned. There may be internal marketing issues to address, such as those connected with the sharing of marketing intelligence and strategies; communication channels within the business; hierarchical support and resources. Finally, marketing must demonstrate its worth. Marketing programmes should be evaluated against predetermined performance measures to ensure their effective implementation and success in terms of the desired marketing objectives detailed within the marketing strategy.

Summary

Companies typically have a top-level over-arching corporate strategy and an associated strategic market or business plan. A marketing strategy is created with which to achieve the corporate strategy, which generally is operationalized via the annual marketing plan. *Marketing strategy* identifies which opportunities are to be pursued, indicates the specific markets towards which activities are to be targeted, defines the types of competitive advantage that are to be developed and exploited, and provides direction for marketing programmes. A marketing strategy aims to target customer segments of most benefit to an organization in a manner that best utilizes the organization's capabilities, provides a differential advantage over competitors and matches the organization's corporate goals.

A company's *strategic market plan* is an outline of the methods and resources required to achieve an organization's overall goals within specific target markets; it takes into account all the functional areas of a business unit that must be coordinated. A *strategic business unit (SBU)* is a division, product line or other profit centre within a parent company, and is used to define areas for consideration in a specific strategic market plan. The process of *strategic market planning* yields a marketing strategy that is the framework for a marketing plan. A *marketing plan* includes the framework and entire set of activities to be performed; it is the written document or blueprint for specifying, implementing and controlling an organization's marketing activities and marketing mixes. The marketing plan executes the marketing strategy, which in turn should help to deliver the over-arching corporate strategy.

Through the process of strategic market planning, an organization can develop marketing strategies that, when properly implemented and controlled, will contribute to achieving the organization's overall goals. The marketing mix and associated implementation processes designed to operationalize the marketing strategy are the organization's *marketing programme*. Most marketing programmes centre around a detailed marketing mix specification and include internal controls and procedures to ensure that they are implemented effectively. Marketing environment forces are important in – and profoundly affect – the strategic market planning process. These forces imply opportunities and threats that influence an organization's overall goals.

Central to the marketing strategy is a clear view of the corporate mission and goals. These may well be developed separately to the marketing strategy but the marketing strategy must aim to reflect the overall corporate vision. A company's organizational goals should be derived from its *mission* – that is, the broad, long-term tasks that the organization wants to achieve. These goals should guide planning efforts and specify the ends, or results, that are sought. *Corporate strategy* determines the means for utilizing resources in the areas of production, logistics, finance, research and development, human resources, IT and marketing to reach the organization's goals.

There are three major considerations in assessing opportunities and resources: (1) evaluating marketing opportunities, (2) environmental scanning and (3) understanding the company's capabilities and assets. A *marketing opportunity* arises when the right combination of circumstances occurs at the correct time, allowing an organization to take action towards reaching a target market. An opportunity offers a favourable chance for the company to generate sales from identifiable markets. A *strategic window* is a temporary period of optimum fit between the key requirements of a market and the particular capabilities of a company competing in that market. Market requirements relate to customers' needs or desired benefits. *Market requirements* are satisfied by components of the marketing mix that provide buyers with these benefits. *Environmental scanning* is the process of collecting information about the marketing environment to help marketers identify opportunities and threats, and assist in planning. A company's *capabilities* relate to distinctive competencies that it has developed to do something well and efficiently. A company is likely to enjoy a differential advantage in an area in which its competencies and *marketing assets* out-do those of its potential competition. Marketing assets are a categorization of an organization's strengths or capabilities in terms of customer-facing assets; distribution-based assets; and internal, operational or resource assets.

The *SWOT analysis* is little more than a set of checklists, but it is a popular tool for analyzing the capabilities of an organization in terms of strengths and weaknesses, and for linking identified opportunities and threats to these capabilities. As long as the analysis identifies the most important issues – supported with validation – and managers consider appropriate actions to address the emerging priorities, the SWOT analysis is useful for identifying necessary actions. It is important that any weaknesses that could be leveraged by competitors are rectified, and that managers strive to pre-empt any threats identified.

Having evaluated the overall corporate vision, those responsible for devising the marketing strategy must build on their analysis of opportunities and internal capabilities by analytically assessing the most promising directions for their business and its marketing activity. *Ansoff's matrix* for determining competitive strategies is a suitable tool, offering four options: market penetration, market development, product development or diversification. Strategic objectives that can be implemented through marketing include intense growth, diversified growth and integrated growth. *Intense growth* includes *market penetration, market development or product development. Diversified growth* includes *horizontal, concentric and conglomerate diversification. Integrated growth* includes forwards, backwards and horizontal integration.

Integral to achieving a company's corporate vision is the need to develop a loyal customer base of satisfied customers. It is essential to continuously improve the company's marketing programmes so as to address evolving target market customer needs and expectations. The market segmentation process of segmentation, targeting and positioning is a core element of a recommended marketing strategy. *Brand positioning* is the creation of a desirable, distinctive and plausible image for a brand that will have strong appeal for the customers in a target market segment. A *target market strategy* is the choice of which market segment(s) an organization decides to prioritize and for which to develop marketing programmes.

The *competition* faced by a company are those organizations viewed as marketing products similar to, or substitutable for, a company's products, when targeted at the same customers. Strategists argue that organizations should work to attain a *competitive advantage*. While not always possible to achieve, success without a competitive advantage is unlikely in most markets. Competitive advantage is the achievement of superior performance vis-à-vis rivals: through differentiation to create distinctive product appeal or brand identity; through providing customer value and achieving the lowest delivered cost; or by focusing on narrowly scoped product categories or market niches so as to be viewed as a leading specialist. The so-called *generic routes to competitive advantage* are cost leadership, differentiation and focus, and are not mutually exclusive: while it is not possible to pursue all three routes to creating a competitive advantage, many businesses successfully pursue two of these routes.

It is important to understand the nature of competition and to utilize this knowledge in determining a marketing strategy. Aspects of the marketing strategy should be purposively designed to maximize any weaknesses in competitors' activities and pre-empt any impending moves from rivals. As defined by Porter's *five competitive forces*, competitors should not be viewed only as like-for-like rivals: new entrants, substitute products or services, and the bargaining power of suppliers and of buyers can all form competitive threats or opportunities. The competitive set must be defined by marketers, ensuring it reflects customers' views of direct alternatives and substitute options.

In developing strategies, an organization should consider the *competitive positions* in the marketplace. The *market leader* must both defend its position and seek new sales opportunities. Attack may prove the best form of defence. *Market challengers* must aggressively seek market share gains but carefully select the basis on which to attack: a chink in the leader's armour, for example, or a quick response to changing consumer needs. *Fast movers* may be small but they have the potential to win market share from rivals and should be combated. *Market followers* are the 'me-too, also-rans', prone to be squeezed in times of recession or in response to challengers' aggression. *Market nichers* specialize in terms of product and customer segment: they can very successfully tailor their marketing to their customers' needs but are vulnerable to competitors' entry into their target segments. To compete successfully, any organization needs to consider the principles of *defensive* and *offensive warfare* and to understand its competitors' strategies through *competitor scanning*. The competitive positions proforma is an increasingly popular tool for evaluating competition across a company's segments or markets.

An organization should strive for a *differential advantage* or competitive edge in its markets. A differential advantage is an attribute of a brand, product, service or marketing mix that is desirable to targeted customers and provided by only one supplier. Marketers should emphasize the desirable attributes of a company's marketing mix that their target customers consider unmatched by competitors. The combined strengths, as identified in a SWOT analysis, and any differential advantages make up the *basis for competing*, which should form the leading edge of a company's marketing strategy.

A marketing strategy must specify its core marketing objectives, typically defined in terms of market segments, to address desired market shares, customer satisfaction or brand awareness measures, profitability and financial contribution, plus any planned product and market developments. Without specification of objectives it is difficult to assess the performance of the marketing strategy or to ensure its fit with the overall corporate strategy.

The ingredients of the marketing mix – product, place/distribution, promotion, price and people issues – should be determined only after a marketing strategy has been specified. The marketing strategy must be decided only after the essential analyses of marketing – market trends, the marketing environment forces, customer buying behaviour, competition, opportunities and capabilities – have been undertaken. Analysis should come first, then strategic thinking and, finally, determination of implementation programmes, as explained in Chapter 1's examination of the marketing process.

Marketing programmes depend on detailed marketing mix specifications, but also on the determination of budgets for implementing these marketing mix requirements. These budgets must reflect the sales forecast and trends in the targeted market segments. Sales and marketing personnel should take responsibility for implementing the marketing plan's recommendations, and schedules for marketing mix activity must be established. Implementation of a marketing strategy has to be facilitated, which involves specifying by whom, when, how and at what cost the desired marketing programmes will be implemented. These programmes must be evaluated against predetermined performance measures.

Key links

The content of this chapter examining marketing strategy must be read after having understood the scope of marketing and the marketing process as outlined in Chapter 1. Other links include:

- Chapter 3's explanation of the forces of the macro and micro marketing environment and the importance of environmental scanning.

- Chapter 6's discussion of the market segmentation process, central to developing a target market strategy.

Important terms

Marketing strategy
Strategic market plan
Strategic business unit (SBU)
Marketing plan
Marketing programme
Corporate strategy
Marketing opportunity
Strategic window
Market requirements
Environmental scanning
Capabilities

Marketing assets
SWOT analysis
Ansoff matrix
Strategic objectives
Intense growth
Market penetration
Market development
Product development
Diversified growth
Horizontal diversification
Concentric diversification
Conglomerate diversification
Integrated growth
Brand positioning
Target market strategy
Competitors
Competitive advantage
Generic routes to competitive advantage
Competitive set
Five competitive forces
Competitive positions
Market leader
Market challengers
Fast movers
Market followers
Market nichers
Defensive warfare
Offensive warfare
Competitor scanning
Competitive positions proforma
Differential advantage
Basis for competing

Discussion and review questions

1 Why should an organization develop a marketing strategy? What is the difference between strategic market planning and the marketing plan?

2 Identify the major components of strategic market planning and explain how they are interrelated.

3 In what ways do marketing environment forces affect strategic market planning? Give some specific examples.

4 What is a mission statement? Why must marketing strategists understand their organization's corporate strategy?

5 What are some of the issues that must be considered in analyzing an organization's opportunities and resources?

How do these issues affect marketing objectives and marketing strategy?

6 Why is marketing opportunity analysis necessary? What are the determinants of marketing opportunity?

7 What are the components of a SWOT analysis?

8 In relation to resource constraints, how can environmental scanning affect a company's long-term strategic market planning? Consider product costs and benefits affected by the environment.

9 What is the difference between market penetration, market development and product development?

10 Why do you think more companies are diversifying? Give some examples of diversified businesses.

11 Target marketing – the market segmentation process – is at the heart of a marketing strategy. Why must this be so?

12 What is competitive advantage?

13 Why should companies attempt to understand the strategies of their competitors? Explain your views.

14 How can a market leader best defend its competitive position?

15 What are the strengths of a market nicher? In what way is a nicher vulnerable?

16 What is meant by the term differential advantage? How does this relate to the concept of competitive advantage?

17 Why must a marketing strategy include detailed marketing objectives?

18 In what ways should implementation of a marketing strategy be managed and facilitated?

Recommended readings

Aaker, D. and McLoughlin, D., *Strategic Marketing Management* (Wiley, 2010).
Baker, M., *Marketing Strategy and Management* (Palgrave Macmillan, 2007).
Cravens, D. and Piercy, N., *Strategic Marketing* (McGraw-Hill, 2008).
Dibb, S. and Simkin, L., *Market Segmentation Success* (The Haworth Press/Routledge, 2008).
Littler, D. and Wilson, D., *Marketing Strategy* (Butterworth-Heinemann, 1995).
Moutinho, L. and Southern, G., *Strategic Marketing Management: a Process-Based Approach* (Cengage, 2009),
Porter, M.E., *Competitive Strategy: Techniques for Analyzing Industries and Competitors* (The Free Press, 1980 and 2004).
West, D., Ford, J. and Ibrahim, E., *Strategic Marketing: Creating Competitive Advantage* (OUP, 2010).

Internet exercise

Consider a large, well-known company with which you have regular dealings, such as a major retailer, financial institution or hotel group. Or select a supplier whose products you purchase frequently, such as Apple, Nestlé, Sony or Vodafone. Log on to the selected organization's website.

Ignore the investors' pages, corporate information pages, PR releases and so forth. Look at the site from the perspective of a customer and access only the customer-relevant pages (those to do with products, services, offers, customer services, stockist location and so on).

1 What customer-relevant information is offered by the website you have chosen?

2 In what ways is the website striving to make the organization appear 'special' or particularly good?

3 Given the website material, how would you interpret the selected strategy for this organization? What is its apparent sense of purpose and what seem to be its leading priorities?

Applied mini-case

Over a decade ago, Korean car manufacturer Daewoo entered the European market with wacky advertising, innovative dealer arrangements and value-for-money cars. While based on dated car designs, the company nevertheless made reasonable inroads into the small and medium-sized car sectors. As part of Korea's well-publicized economic woes, conglomerate Daewoo headed for bankruptcy. The car business was acquired by strategic partner General Motors of the USA in 2002.

General Motors ayway had to consider how to roll out its Chevrolet marque in Europe. Should it try to sell existing Chevrolet models in Europe, or develop more European-looking models for European consumers? Should Chevrolet establish a new dealer network in Europe, be sold alongside the Vauxhall and Opel ranges in existing GM dealers, or be retailed by third parties or through the Internet? Or should the Daewoo range of cars and dealers in Europe be rebadged as Chevrolet? Perhaps a mix of these options would be preferable? These questions were not easy to answer and General Motor's senior managers agonized for some time to determine their strategy.

Question

As the senior marketer tasked to assess the market's probable response to these options, what steps would you take?

St Andrew's healthcare: a charity's marketing strategy

Case study

St Andrew's Healthcare in Northampton
is the market leader in many types of mental health care in the UK. In addition to its large site in Northampton, St Andrew's has created satellite facilities in the south-east of England. As a leading specialist provider, the organization's patients are referred to its hospitals from throughout the UK and beyond. In its own words:

A charity leading innovation in mental health...
St Andrew's is the UK's largest not-for-profit mental healthcare charity.

We offer specialist services for men, women, adolescents and older people across:

● Mental healthcare

● Learning disability

● Acquired brain injury

● Progressive and neurodegenerative conditions

By putting our service users' needs at the heart of everything that we do, we have built a culture encouraging innovative practices, leading clinical expertise and forward-thinking attitudes. Through this, St Andrew's is fast-becoming a national centre of excellence.

http://www.stah.org/,
12 February, 2011

As a charity, its focus is not on helping mental health sufferers in the community, or charity shop-style fundraising, or increasing the general public's awareness of mental health issues – other charities and bodies address these important tasks. St Andrew's Healthcare is a fully specified hospital with leading experts, state-of-the-art care pathways and an eminent reputation within the mental health care profession. St Andrew's divisions address everything from adolescent learning difficulties through to major behavioural problems, with patients requiring secure accommodation and lengthy treatment programmes. It has a specialist unit dealing with brain injuries and, through an on-site partner, also offers clinic facilities for patients needing to 'dry out'. Its staff are recognized as being leading-edge thinkers.

The St Andrew's brand reputation is based on the quality of its care, its multiple care pathways and its ability to relate to patients, their families, and to the medical staff or personnel in social services who refer patients to the hospital. St Andrew's has charitable status, but strives to set its fees sufficiently high to permit it to provide the high-quality care that is at the core of its ethos, and to continually reinvest in its facilities and treatment programmes.

Despite its success, its diversity of operations places significant demands on its capital spending: wards and facilities require modernizing, newly devised care programmes may require remodelled facilities, the expansion of demand led by reduced state provision of mental health facilities pressurizes the organization's caring professionals to provide expanded facilities. Private-sector commercial businesses have entered the more financially lucrative parts of the market. St Andrew's must defend its position in these segments, as fee income from these activities is required to support the hospital as a whole and to cross-subsidize other segments of the market deemed less financially attractive by new-entrant competitors. In order to defend its market share in these segments, the hospital has to develop marketing strategies and devote resources to marketing programmes designed to maintain the loyalty of referring GPs, medical consultants and social workers. The requirement is growing to tailor marketing messages to a growing mix of audiences. Commercially minded competitors are developing 'glitzy' marketing programmes and St Andrew's has to maintain its visibility to key stakeholders in this quickly evolving marketplace.

While some patients deal directly with the charity, the vast majority are referred from the National Health Service (NHS). St Andrew's has a reputation for being able to deal with difficult patients suffering from complex problems. However, the NHS is moving towards fragmented buying, with numerous regionalized buying consortia of medics able to purchase services – such as those offered by St Andrew's – from a variety of providers. In addition to the medical staff diagnosing the patients' problems and recommending appropriate courses of treatment, the NHS has risk assessors, financial managers and professional purchasing executives, who all are involved in the decisions concerning which treatment programme to purchase and from which provider. For St Andrew's and other suppliers to the NHS, such formalized purchasing and group buying centre dynamics complicate the marketing activity and the engagement programmes the charity runs with its 'customers'. For the patient, to his/her family, to the referring medical staff and the numerous administrators involved, St Andrew's must develop bespoke messages, marketing communications and client-handling programmes. This complex buying centre must be addressed for St Andrew's to operate with full bed occupancy, in order to fulfil its mission to truly help those suffering with mental health problems.

The organization has responded to these market forces by developing a corporate strategy and a marketing strategy, by allocating resources to producing and implementing marketing programmes, and by recruiting a set of marketing managers to support the various divisions' marketing activities.

Questions for discussion

1 For a non-profit organization such as St Andrew's Healthcare, what aspects of a marketing strategy will be the most important?

2 Why are organizations such as St Andrew's Healthcare turning to marketing and the development of marketing strategies?

3 In what ways would a marketing strategy benefit St Andrew's Healthcare?

Sources: St Andrew's Healthcare, 2004–9; James Watkins, director of marketing and strategy, St Andrew's Healthcare, 2003–9; *Marketing Briefs*, Sally Dibb and Lyndon Simkin (Oxford: Elsevier Butterworth-Heinemann), 2004; **http://www.stah.org**, February, 2011.

PART TWO
Understanding Markets

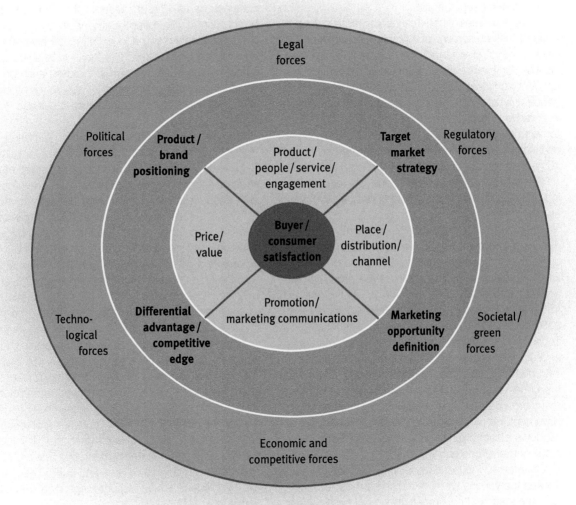

As explained in Chapter 1 of *Marketing Essentials*, a major role for marketers is to help in identifying opportunities to pursue and threats to combat. An assessment of external market drivers and dynamics – known as the forces of the marketing environment – is of fundamental importance not only to marketers but to anyone inside an organization involved with strategic planning.

Customers should be at the centre of the marketing process. Organizations – whether for-profit or not-for-profit – must target specific groups of customers, stakeholders or audiences, understand their needs and endeavour through their marketing activities to satisfy these customer needs.

Part II of *Marketing Essentials* examines the concept of the marketing environment before exploring thoroughly the nature of consumer buying behaviour and buying processes, and purchasing behaviour in business markets.

Having developed an understanding of a marketplace and particularly the customers within, marketers must then develop a target market strategy. This should identify which customers they wish to target, what positioning they intend to use and which approach will provide an advantage over competitors. Part II includes, therefore, an explanation of target market strategy selection and the all-important concept of market segmentation.

There are times when managers' existing knowledge of their customers is sufficient for marketing decision-making, or when they are content to trust their intuition. On many occasions, however, marketers may not feel confident with the level of marketing intelligence available and will instigate marketing research in order to fill any gaps in their understanding of customers, competitors or market trends. The nature, uses and types of marketing research are introduced in the final chapter of Part II of *Marketing Essentials*.

Part II explores the essential concepts for developing an understanding of markets and a target market strategy.

Chapter 3, 'The Marketing Environment', examines the many forces at work in a market over which consumers and organizations have little or no control but which tangibly affect the nature of the products and services marketed. These forces of what is termed 'the macro marketing environment' include economic, political, legal, regulatory, societal and technological impacts. Competitive forces – 'the micro marketing environment' – often have a more specific impact on individual organizations. The chapter also examines the concept of environmental scanning, the process many organizations use to address the marketing environment, before discussing the concept of strategic windows of opportunity created by the forces of the marketing environment.

Chapter 4, 'Consumer Buying Behaviour', describes the various types of consumer buying behaviour, the stages of consumer buying decision-making and the different categories of buying decisions. The chapter examines how personal, psychological and social factors influence the consumer buying decision process. Chapter 4 explains why marketers must understand consumer buying behaviour and use their understanding to determine a target market strategy.

Having an understanding of customers' buying is fundamental to the marketing concept and to developing a marketing orientation. The chapter concludes by examining the growth in consumer-to-consumer interaction, often via social media, and the implications for buying behaviour.

Chapter 5, 'Business Markets and Business Buying Behaviour', familiarizes readers with the various types of business markets, identifies the major characteristics of business-to-business buyers and transactions, outlines the attributes of business-to-business demand and presents the concept of the buying centre. The chapter emphasizes the notion of relationship marketing and exchanges between business buyers and sellers. The focus then shifts to the stages of the business buying process and the factors that influence it. The chapter concludes by examining how to select and analyze business target markets.

Chapter 6, 'Segmenting Markets, Targeting and Positioning', explains the core aspect of developing a marketing strategy: the process of target market strategy selection. The chapter commences by defining the concept of a market and outlining the various types of markets. The focus then shifts to how organizations segment markets, how they make targeting decisions and prioritize target markets, and how they determine a brand or product positioning strategy for each segment selected as a target market. The chapter also highlights the role of customer relationship management (CRM) in handling effectively the most important customers within targeted segments.

Chapter 7, 'Marketing Research', explains the importance of research in marketing decision-making, distinguishes between research and intuition in solving marketing problems, and outlines the basic steps for conducting formal marketing research. The fundamental methods of gathering data for marketing research are examined. The chapter then introduces the wide variety of available marketing research tools and explains their relative pros and cons. The chapter also considers ethical issues regarding marketing research.

By the conclusion of Part II of *Marketing Essentials*, readers should understand the concepts of the marketing environment, buying behaviour in consumer and business-to-business markets, the fundamentals of target market strategy selection, and the nature and use of marketing research.

Adsearch

1. What excites me most about marketing

For a market researcher, who is now seen as the more fashionable customer insight specialist, excitement has to be about insight … getting to the bottom of what makes the customer tick, spending time with them, understanding the way they think and the way they talk and what it all means for the brand. It has also, for me, been about making mistakes, as we all do … misreading the messages and misinterpreting them and maybe learning from your mistakes: wrong product, wrong time, wrong place, wrong price. It is also about being excited by the markets to research that you think will be dull and boring and which turn out otherwise. I may wish that all my clients brewed cask conditioned ale and that I could research it (and drink it) till the cows come very slowly home, but the real excitement can come from insight into markets which you think might be rational and aren't necessarily so: like dry cleaning where it turned out that a lot of customers were terrified of the person behind the counter making personal judgements or possibly sniffing their dirty clothes, or the possibility of their clothes going in a vat with your clothes or even my clothes! Sometimes excitement comes from dealing with consumers who aren't like you and can't be like you, and the insights they bring: older or younger than you, more up market or down market, or from a different ethnic group.

2. What are the biggest challenges for marketing?

For me, the biggest challenge to my part of marketing is that the consumer is wising up to market research: they know or think they know as much as we do, and for all I know they may be right. In focus groups it is now common for respondents, as we call them, to second guess what we are trying to do and answer for the brand or for the greater British public, rather than for themselves. A typical comment will start with the words 'people won't like that idea' and my world weary response is 'try to forget people and tell us what you feel' or 'forget people – it's your money they are after'. And connected to that point we are in danger of running out of market research virgins – proper customers, those who have never been to a market research group and can still speak as real people and think as real people with all their emotional and functional faculties intact. Not many of those about, unfortunately.

3. What does marketing contribute?

Marketing helps sell stuff to people: no more and no less … let's not forget this!

PETER JACKSON
MANAGING DIRECTOR
ADSEARCH MARKET RESEARCH

Strategic case

Birmingham women's hospital: giving birth – the consumer's choice!

The provision of maternity services is an area of health care which most people encounter at some point in their adult life. Despite being a significant life event, until relatively recently most women in the UK having a baby had very little control over the health care side of the maternity experience. The type of care on offer was largely outside a patient's control and usually determined more by locality than by patient choice. The characteristics of antenatal care, the maternity unit where delivery took place and even the position adopted during labour, were all likely to be predetermined by others.

In recent years, much has changed. The Government's *Changing Childbirth report* compiled in 1992 indicated that women should be offered choice in their maternity provision. Regulatory changes, allowing General Practitioners (doctors) more flexibility in where they are allowed to refer their patients, have helped foster a greater sense of choice. More recent Government initiatives to increase patient control over these decisions have underlined this change. Social changes have led to people becoming more proactive in making decisions about issues affecting their lives. As consumers, for example, they are more likely than ever to change their bank account, shop around for insurance or buy products over the Internet. Social media and the Web enable consumers – patients in this case – to share good and bad experiences with each other very quickly and widely, impacting on the choices of others. In such an environment, it is no surprise that women are increasingly likely to exert control over maternity decisions. This tendency has been supported by advances in technology which have made information about maternity services much more readily available.

Today's expectant mother and her partner now have far more control over the antenatal and birthing process than previously. There is greater flexibility in the style of antenatal care on offer. Perhaps the most significant issue is that women can now choose the hospital unit at which they deliver their baby. This is important because it is the characteristics of the unit, more than any other factor, which impact upon the maternity care received.

It is now common practice for medical staff to encourage women to write their own birth plans. This document describes the patient's preferences for all aspects of delivery, from pain relief to monitoring and intervention. The patient's desire to exercise some form of control over this important life event is consistent with changes in how people live. Women have grown accustomed to exercising control over other aspects of their lives and careers: this expectation has been extended to the antenatal and birth experience. From the patient's viewpoint, the provision of maternity care is just like any other service.

How busy a maternity unit becomes is now partly affected by the preferences of expectant mothers. A greater level of hospital responsiveness is required to ensure that the needs and wants of these patients are met. Hospitals and their staff must be more aware of 'consumer' expectations, demands and information requirements. One implication is that many hospital units have been forced to devote far greater attention to the ways in which they are branded and perceived in the maternity 'marketplace', requiring improved marketing communications and more tailoring of information.

Ensuring that the services provided are acceptable to patients is a complex task. While the provision of good quality patient care is paramount, the service on offer extends beyond the purely medical. In addition to the medical provision, units have to provide appropriate facilities with a mix of amenities to cater for patients and their visitors. The hospital environment should be amenable to the well-being of its users. Appropriate processes must be in place to control the smooth flow of patients through the unit. The mix of medical and support staff has to be carefully managed to ensure that units can cater for the peaks and troughs associated with demand for maternity services.

The role of information

The decision process involved in making choices about antenatal and delivery care is driven by the availability of information. Women making these decisions acquire this information from a variety of informal and formal sources. Some will rely on previous experiences of childbirth, either their own or those of their friends and acquaintances. Others will discuss the options with their family doctor or midwife. Some will consult the increasing array of pregnancy and birth related publications or tune-in to a relevant television programme or radio broadcast. Overall, an increasingly diverse array of sources is available. Pregnancy books, parenting magazines, specialist websites, midwife groups and organizations dealing with birth issues, all provide advice on how this can be achieved. Google *Birmingham Women's Hospital* and review the mix of information sources offered in seconds, from the hospital's own web pages, to NHS and Government sources, plus the views of many specialist information providers focusing on medical issues. Comparable statistics and patient comments are freely available.

The BirthChoiceUK website (**http://www.birthchoiceuk. com**) was set up to help parents make informed choices about their maternity care. The website objectives are:

BirthChoiceUK is a voluntary organization which helps women choose their maternity care through information provided by way of its website **www.BirthChoiceUK.com**. It provides information and maternity statistics for each maternity unit in an accessible form for parents to help them know what questions to ask locally and to decide where to plan to have their baby. There are also summaries and analyzes of maternity statistics for the four countries of the UK which are of use to policy makers, health professionals and maternity activists.

http://www.birthchoiceuk.com, 2011

The BirthChoiceUK website encourages prospective parents to visit their chosen unit and there are tips on the kinds of questions to ask about facilities and services. Guidance is given on the booking-in process. The website also provides additional features designed to support those seeking further information. Further reading is offered on a variety of issues and a range of maternity-related research findings is explored. An extensive reference list of publications supporting the information provided is also available. Finally, the website provides web links, among others, to:

- NCT Pregnancy and Babycare: The National Childbirth Trust offers advice on pregnancy, birth and parenthood.

- AIMS (Association for Improvements in Maternity Services): details on maternity choices.

- Independent Midwives' Association: register enabling patients to contact a local independent midwife.

- Association of Radical Midwives: information about birth choices.

- Home Birth Reference Site: guidance for those considering a home birth.
- MIDIRS (Midwives' Information and Resource Service): provides a series of Informed Choice Leaflet for patients and healthcare professions and the Informed Choice database.
- The VBAC (Vaginal Birth After Caesarean): information on the birth options for mothers who have previously delivered by caesarean section.
- Sheila Kitzinger: author who campaigns for women's rights in childbirth.

Birmingham women's hospital

Birmingham Women's NHS Foundation Trust (BWNFT) is a Centre of Excellence for specialist healthcare to women and their families in Birmingham and the West Midlands.

Established in 1994, we are proud of being one of only two Trusts in the UK specializing primarily in women's health care. We provide a focussed range of health care services, primarily, though not exclusively, to women and their families. These are maternity and fetal medicine services; neonatal care; gynaecology and fertility services; regional clinical and laboratory genetics; and imaging and pathology services. The Trust enjoys strong and effective partnerships with our Universities, playing a leading role in education and training and research and development.

Our mission is clear, Birmingham Women's NHS Foundation Trust will:

'Continue to be a leading provider of local, regional and national importance providing a specialist range of distinct, but interrelated services, delivering excellent healthcare, education, training and research, and contributing to the health and wellbeing of the people we serve'.

Source: Birmingham Women's Hospital, July 2011

Birmingham Women's Health Care NHS Trust, which manages Birmingham Women's Hospital, was established in 1994. The unit provides care exclusively for women and is a teaching hospital linked to Birmingham University's Medical School and the University of Central England's nursing programme. As a regional referral unit, the hospital provides maternity services for the local community in Birmingham and for more complex cases from the West Midlands as a whole. The Trust operates antenatal clinics, offers pre-pregnancy counselling and specializes in care for patients following miscarriage or bereavement. There is also an assisted conception unit, which provides fertility treatment. In addition, the Trust runs a foetal medicine unit which offers specialist care in relation to various foetal

and maternal conditions, has a 43 cot Neonatal Intensive Care Unit to treat sick and premature babies, and provides care in the areas of genetics and gynaecology.

The hospital is also home to the regional Human Milk Bank, offering a service for collecting and pasteurizing donor breast milk. The donated milk is circulated to neonatal units in the Midlands and further afield for premature and sick babies whose mothers are unable to breast feed. The managing Trust also hosts the Cancer Intelligence Unit, the West Midlands Public Health Observatory and the NHS National Genetics Education and Development Centre.

With an income annually around £80 million, the hospital looks after 50 000 patients each year and carries out over 3 000 operations. The abilities of its 1 500 staff, the hospital's practices, its reputation and success rates, in 2008 enabled the hospital to achieve Foundation status, placing the unit among the elite of UK hospitals. While this has resulted in a re-naming of the Trust to Birmingham Women's NHS Foundation Trust, the hospital remains branded as Birmingham Women's Hospital. The mission is simple, 'to be a place that women and families choose first, and where people want to work'.

Birmingham Women's Hospital Basic Features

Number of beds	149
Births per midwife per year	33
Births per bed per day	1.20
Home births	1%
Obstetrician available 24 hours	Yes
Paediatrician available 24 hours	Yes
Epidural pain relief 24 hours	Yes

Source: Birmingham Women's Hospital, July 2011

Birmingham Women's Hospital is a large unit, responsible for the delivery of around 7000 babies each year. Not all women who deliver their babies at the hospital attend the unit for their antenatal care. Some patients are completely or predominantly looked after by their local midwife and family doctor, while others may have some or all of their antenatal care at the unit. The delivery statistics for Birmingham Women's Hospital are, to a degree, influenced by the number of complex cases referred to the unit from elsewhere. The delivery suite itself is able to cater for all kinds of births, ranging from different forms of normal delivery including water births, through to caesarean section and instrumental delivery – the use of forceps and venthouse. A full range of pain relief options is generally available and women have the opportunity to visit and look around the unit prior to their expected due date. The patient's wishes are genuinely regarded as a key priority when determining the characteristics of care.

There is a strong focus on the provision of information for patients and visitors. Information leaflets on a wide range of topics are freely available on stands in the public areas of the hospital. There are many noticeboards and e-displays providing information on areas such as blood donation and NHS Direct (the telephone helpline which members of the public can call with queries about their health). There is also a feature on the hospital's Assisted Conception Unit, together with leaflets seeking sperm donors. The provision of information in different languages helps cater for the diverse ethnic catchments. For example, the 'Your Guide to the NHS' leaflet is available in many different Asian languages. Some leaflets are specific to maternity patients, who receive a *welcome* pack at their booking-in visit. This pack contains information about the antenatal period, a free pregnancy magazine and various product samples and coupons deemed appropriate for expectant mothers. A second pack containing further leaflets, product information and samples targeted at new mothers and their babies is offered to patients who deliver at the hospital. A typical pack might include leaflets on breastfeeding and the dangers of cot death, together with samples of nappy cream, detergent or fabric conditioner. There is also an option to receive a further two packs during baby's first year.

The information theme is a particular focus in the hospital's innovative health shop. This area, which is located close to the main entrance, provides a wealth of information leaflets and posters about health-related issues and voluntary groups. The 'shop' is open to patients, the public and staff seeking information on a wide range of topics.

Providing the care desired by patients

As the emphasis on choice in maternity services increases, there is more pressure on hospitals to be responsive. Women are increasingly likely to review and compare a number of alternative care providers. Although quality of care will almost certainly remain the paramount consideration, many other aspects of the antenatal and delivery experience are likely to influence the decisions which are made. The implications for units such as Birmingham Women's Hospital are clear. In particular, the need to understand and respond to the expectations of patients and other stakeholders is greater than ever. The hospital has also to devote more resources to creating a brand reputation and managing its multi-channel communications to prospective parents, through an increasing array of marketing communications channels and information sources.

Questions for discussion

1 Given the nature of the 'buying process' for maternity care, what are the main influencing factors on users' decision-making when selecting a hospital?

2 In what ways does the hospital respond to its customers' requirements?

3 What is the role of the Internet in patients' search for information? How must Birmingham Women's Hospital respond to the role of the Web?

CHAPTER 3

The marketing environment

Marketers must have insights into their emerging market challenges, many of which will not be of their making but which will impact hugely on their practices

Objectives

- To understand the concept of the marketing environment and the importance of environmental scanning and analysis

- To explore the broad forces of the macro marketing environment: political forces relevant to marketers, the influence of laws on marketing practices, the impact of government regulations and self-regulatory agencies, societal issues important to marketers, the effects of new technology on society and marketing activities, economic and competitive factors and their impact on organizations and customers' willingness and ability to buy

- To examine the company-specific micro marketing environment forces: the competitive pressures facing an organization, in terms of the supply chain, marketing intermediaries, competitors and from other publics

- To understand the role of the marketing environment in marketing opportunity analysis and the importance of strategic windows in marketing strategy

INTRODUCTION

This chapter explores the external forces that impact on an organization's trading and ability to satisfy its customers. These forces, over which organizations rarely have any direct control, are termed the *marketing environment* and fall into two categories: the macro and the micro forces of the marketing environment. Most senior marketers believe that the marketing function should provide market insights to an organization, framing opportunities and threats, and acting as the 'radar' for colleagues in other functions. A fundamental part of such a remit is to develop an understanding of the forces of the marketing environment.

The very broad forces are the *macro marketing environment:* the political, legal, regulatory, societal, technological and economic/competitive forces that impact on all organizations operating in a market and on their ability to carry out their affairs. Authors have increasingly distinguished these broad forces from an additional set of more company-specific external forces termed the *micro marketing environment* forces. These micro marketing environment forces are largely aspects of the competitive arena.

After defining the marketing environment and considering why it is necessary for marketers to *scan* and analyze these forces, each of these macro and micro forces is discussed. Awareness of these issues and trends may create *strategic windows* of opportunity. Ignorance of such forces jeopardizes an organization's ability to perform well and may leave the organization more vulnerable to the actions of more aware competitors.

Regulatory influence: the EU single market

In 1947 the launching of the Marshall Plan presented a blueprint for the economic reconstruction of a Europe devastated by the Second World War. This led in 1948 to the creation of the Organization for European Economic Co-operation (OEEC), the precursor of today's economic union. In March 1957 the Treaty of Rome was signed to establish the European Economic Community (EEC). By 1973, with the arrival of Denmark, Ireland and the UK, the EEC had grown to nine member states. Greece joined in 1981 and Portugal and Spain in 1986 to create the 'Euro 12'. The momentous signing of the Maastricht Treaty in 1992 established the European Union (EU) and by 1 January 1993 the European single market was at last a reality. The single market is defined by the EU as 'an economic area within which persons, goods, services and capital have unrestricted freedom of movement, which entails not only the elimination of customs barriers, but also of technical, tax and legislative obstacles'. By 2007, membership had swelled to 27 countries, including many eastern European countries, such as the Czech Republic, Estonia, Hungary, Latvia, Lithuania, Poland, Slovakia and Slovenia, plus Mediterranean countries Cyprus and Malta. Bulgaria and Romania joined in 2007. Applicant countries include Turkey, Croatia, Serbia, Bosnia, Montenegro, Albania and Macedonia, leaving only Norway and Russia as major countries not seeking membership.

The single market has had a significant impact on the populations of member and non-member trading states, as well as on marketers representing their companies. With the removal of so many bureaucratic barriers on 1 January 1993, professionally qualified personnel could seek employment without retraining in other member states; companies could tender for government contracts throughout the EU; imports and exports became subject to far fewer restrictions, less 'red tape', reduced customs controls and allowed much freer movement within and between EU states. Immigration and travel have become much quicker and simpler than before. Health and safety working regulations have been harmonized, as have air travel regulations and even standards for mobile phone networks and VAT collection. The creation of the euro – the currency to which many member states are now signed up – further simplified cross-border business transactions and travel arrangements.

The EU has many critics, not least due to its Common Agricultural Policy (CAP), which takes more than half of the entire EU budget, is a significant drain on the resources of the richer member states and is currently being renegotiated. There are moans about the often top-heavy bureaucracy of European government in Brussels; and the inevitable formalization of a great number of working practices when so many countries' rules and regulations are combined to form a single, cohesive approach. The financial conditions that must be met in order to participate in the euro, and the apparent flouting of these conditions by certain 'major league' member states, have added to the criticisms. The inclusion of seemingly 'weaker' eastern European economies has concerned people in the western European economies, which may well cross-subsidize these new member economies. However, there are few marketers who would claim that in the years since the harmonization of Europe in 1993, doing business across Europe has not been simplified, opening up significant marketing opportunities for many businesses and presenting new competitive threats. The recent expansion of EU membership – doubling the number of consumers inside the single market – is of great interest to marketers. The EU continues to present new challenges and a reason to rethink marketing strategies. There is little doubt that the EU is an external factor in the marketing environment of most businesses and consumers that cannot be ignored, providing trading opportunities, increasing competitive threats, creating significant bureaucracy and regulation with which to deal, and presenting European products to a global market.

Source: iStock, 06-27-06 © Ufuk ZIVANA

Sources: EU policy documents, 1990–2007; *Europe in Figures*, Eurostat, Luxembourg, 1995; *Europe on the Move, From Single Market to European Union, Internal Market* – all EU, Brussels, publications; the BBC, 2007; *The EU at a Glance*, February, 2011.

The EU has a tremendous impact on the decisions and activities of marketers. The regulations and legal directives produced by the EU, plus the financial implications of many of its policies – such as the CAP and the criteria for participating in the euro – are aspects of the macro marketing environment. This chapter discusses both macro and micro forces, commencing with the broader macro issues. It includes a discussion of why and how marketers scan the forces of the marketing environment. The chapter concludes with an examination of how an understanding of these marketing environment forces assists a company in identifying strategic windows, maximizing marketing opportunities and recognizing impending threats.

Examining and responding to the marketing environment

marketing environment
The external forces that directly or indirectly influence an organization's acquisition of inputs and generation of outputs, comprising six categories of forces: political, legal, regulatory, societal, technological and economic/competitive

The **marketing environment** consists of external forces that directly or indirectly influence an organization's acquisition of inputs and generation of outputs. Inputs might include personnel, financial resources, raw materials and information. Outputs could be information such as advertisements or packages, goods, services and ideas. As indicated in Chapter 1 and as shown in Figure 1.4, the broad marketing environment consists of six categories of forces: political, legal, regulatory, societal, technological and economic/competitive. Although there are numerous environmental factors, most fall into one of these six categories. These are termed the 'macro forces' of the marketing environment as they affect all organizations operating in a particular market. In addition, many authors have identified a set of issues termed the 'micro forces' of the marketing environment. These micro forces are more situation- and organization-specific, including the organization's internal environment, suppliers, marketing intermediaries, buyers, competitors and the organization's publics ... they tend to be centred on competitor issues directly impacting on a specific organization.

Whether they fluctuate rapidly or slowly, environmental forces are always dynamic. Changes in the marketing environment can create uncertainty, threats and opportunities for marketers. Although the future is not very predictable, marketers can estimate what will happen, although some fail to do so, thus negatively affecting the performance of their businesses. Astute marketers continually modify their marketing strategies in response to the dynamic environment. Marketing managers who fail to recognize changes in environmental forces leave their companies unprepared to capitalize on marketing opportunities or to cope with threats created by changes in the environment.

Organizations that cannot deal with an unfavourable environment are at risk of going under.[1] The 1990 Persian Gulf Crisis caused huge increases in the price of petrol, repeated in 2004 following the start of the last Gulf War. Civil war in the former Yugoslavia had tragic implications for the peoples of that region and an economic impact on the tour operators who specialized in holidays to the Yugoslav coast. The BSE beef crisis affected farmers, meat producers and supermarkets. Genetically modified (GM) foods caused a more recent storm with implications for food manufacturers and supermarkets. The activities of terrorists have had a significant impact on companies and the general public in many countries, with tourism and airline operators being particularly badly affected. Sub-prime mortgages have led to huge economic troubles, impacting on consumers' spending potential and their priorities. Recent political upheaval in Egypt has disrupted the tourism industry there, tour operators marketing holidays to the country, and consumers planning to holiday there. Monitoring the marketing environment is crucial to an organization's survival and to the long-term achievement of its goals.

Environmental scanning and analysis

To monitor changes in the marketing environment effectively, marketers must engage in environmental scanning and analysis. **Environmental scanning** is the process of collecting information about the forces in the marketing environment. Scanning involves: observation; keeping 'an ear to the ground'; perusal of secondary sources, such as the Web, business, trade, government and general interest publications; and marketing research. However, managers must be careful not to gather so much information that sheer volume makes analysis impossible. **Environmental analysis** is the process of assessing and interpreting the information gathered through environmental scanning. A manager evaluates the information for accuracy, tries to resolve inconsistencies in the data and, if warranted, assigns significance to the findings. Through analysis, a marketing manager seeks to describe current environmental changes and to predict future changes. By evaluating these changes, the manager should be able to determine possible threats and opportunities linked to environmental fluctuations. Understanding the current state of the marketing environment and recognizing the threats and opportunities arising from changes within it, help marketing managers assess the performance of current marketing efforts and develop marketing strategies for the future. The Marketing Tools and Techniques box below describes how organizations often conduct an analysis of the marketing environment.

environmental scanning
The process of collecting information about the forces in the marketing environment

environmental analysis
The process of assessing and interpreting the information gathered through environmental scanning

---

Practitioners' assessment of the macro marketing environment

Marketing tools and techniques

The marketing environment forces are not obviously part of an individual manager's routine job specification, particularly within the marketing function. However, businesses must monitor these forces through environmental scanning in order to pre-empt possible problems caused by unfavourable market developments, but also in order to leverage any emerging opportunities ahead of competitors. The identification of strategic windows and the chance to take first mover advantage are desires among senior managers and marketers.

The forces of the micro marketing environment and competitive pressures are usually evaluated within a marketing team's analysis of competition (see Chapter 2). Companies must examine the macro forces, too, however. Many managers refer to this macro marketing environmental analysis as a PESTLE analysis: political, economic, societal, technological, legal and environmental. While research indicates that many fail to examine the opportunities and threats from the marketing environment, 'best practice' companies typically adopt one of three approaches to assessing their marketing environments.

1 Individual managers or small work groups are allocated to each of the macro forces: social, economic, legal, regulatory, political, technological. As 'champions' for their allocated topic, such managers collate intelligence from stakeholders, employees and external sources in order to build up a picture of the key trends and developments. These managers either suggest the emerging implications for their business and make recommendations, or they present their findings at a sales and marketing meeting or to senior managers for their debate and consideration. The development of company intranets has significantly assisted the networking so important for the collation of topical and relevant information.

2 The task of assessing the marketing environment may be handed to external consultants. This is not common, as few consultancies know enough about all of the forces of the macro marketing environment, or about the organization in question, to judge likely implications. However, in certain industries, such as automotive, IT and pharmaceuticals, such is commonplace.

3 An organization may intermittently stage workshops to which cross-functional and multi-hierarchical personnel are invited. For example, R&D personnel may be aware of technological trends, the company secretary of legal or

regulatory issues, the salesforce of economic or social forces and so on. Typically, each of the macro marketing environment forces is discussed in turn, in a 'brainstorming' exercise. Certain themes or 'hot topics' then emerge to be debated further within the workshop. The company then allocates an individual manager or creates a small taskforce to examine a particular issue in more detail, in order to subsequently develop an action plan based on more information.

Some companies invite external experts, suppliers, partners or even customers to such a workshop. If these external opinions are not sought as part of the workshop, any planned activity by the business resulting from this workshop-based analysis must await some external validation after the workshop.

Such sessions are an excellent way in which a business can harness the expertise across its functions and within its marketing channel in order to prioritize actions that should minimize the impact of a negative external development or maximize an emerging opportunity.

In this type of forum, the senior management team – supported by functional experts and channel partner personnel – brainstormed the key issues from the macro marketing environment for a leading insurance business. The priorities emerged as shown in the list (right).

While some of these forces, such as the weather, were outside the influence of the business, many of them could be addressed. Indeed, while the weather could not be altered, the company did decide to re-examine its exposure to flood plain customers and modified its policy cover accordingly.

Within each of these rather broad-brush summary bullets lay much detail to explore and to discuss. An example of a resulting action was to more closely manage the activities of the field salesforce, harnessing the latest mobile office technology solutions and customer relationship management field systems. As a result, the already low level of client complaints for inappropriate selling approaches virtually disappeared, and the highly ethical stance in controlling the salesforce bolstered the company's brand reputation and thereby its ability to recruit high-calibre personnel. This strategy also reflected the growing litigious culture among consumers and thereby addressed another of the trends identified during the workshop.

It is important to have a good mix of inputs – market information and personnel – to any assessment of the macro forces of the marketing environment, and to solicit the views of stakeholders other than those participating in the session. For example, partners, channel members,

market analysts, industry experts or consultants and even customers, are all useful sources both for marketing intelligence and for checking out suggested action plans. It is better not to only involve marketers.

Having identified the key issues – the macro marketing environment forces – currently of relevance, the business must consider the implications. The 'So what does this mean to us and to our business?' question has to be answered. Is the issue a threat or an opportunity? What resulting actions must be taken? Certain trends and developments may pose a threat, while other forces may be creating an opportunity. Sometimes, the same issue is both an opportunity and a threat. In the above example, had this company failed to implement changes to its field force's working practices, it would not have bolstered its reputation or improved the completion rate of its sales representatives. Worse, rivals may have been able to steal a march and measures designed to minimize the likelihood of client litigation would not now be in place.

The macro marketing environment for a leading insurance company

- Stock market (worthless investments, own share price/company value)

- New/more regulations (FSA, Gov, EU, within client sectors, accountancy)

- Over/under capacity in the industry/key sectors

- Many mergers and changes to the competitive set

- Structural changes in the sector and for clients

- Emerging compensation culture amongst clients and brokers

- Customers' expectation of better advice

- Greater role for technology (CRM, online quotes/claims, e-business)

- Distribution channel developments (role of brokers, e-commerce, tele-business, retailer new entrants)

- Recruitment problems/inability to make the sector attractive

- Global warming/changes to weather: greater claims

© Dibb/Simkin

Note: a more extensive explanation of this technique is offered in either *The Market Segmentation Workbook* (Dibb and Simkin) or *The Marketing Planning Workbook* (Dibb, Simkin and Bradley), both originally published in 1996 by Thomson, London, or in the authors' newer titles *Market Segmentation Success: Making It Happen!* (The Haworth Press/Routledge, 2008) and *Marketing Planning* (Cengage Learning, 2008).

JCB, the construction equipment producer, allocated to individual managers the task of monitoring aspects of the macro marketing environment: political, legal, regulatory, societal (particularly the Green movement), technological, economic and competitive. A small committee met to prepare short papers and presentations to interested colleagues. When the laws relating to roadworks were amended, making contractors responsible for the safety of their sites and the long-term quality of the re-laid road surface, JCB recognized that many of its customers would have to alter their working practices as a result. So the company produced guides to assist these contractors in responding to the new legislation. In so doing, JCB was able to enhance its image and reputation as a leading player in the industry, and at the same time promote its products.

Responding to environmental forces

In responding to environmental forces, marketing managers can take two general approaches: accept environmental forces as uncontrollable or confront and mould them. If environmental forces are viewed as uncontrollable, the organization remains passive and reactive towards the environment. Instead of trying to influence forces in the environment, its marketing managers tend to adjust current marketing strategies to environmental changes. They approach marketing opportunities discovered through environmental scanning and analysis with caution. On the other hand, marketing managers who believe that environmental forces can be shaped adopt a pro-active approach. For example, if a market is blocked by traditional environmental constraints, marketing managers may apply economic, psychological, political and promotional skills to gain access to it or operate within it. Once they identify what blocks a marketing opportunity, marketers can assess the power of the various parties involved and develop strategies to try to overcome environmental forces.[2]

FIGURE 3.1

The growing social awareness of healthy eating and the problems of obesity have created opportunities for many products, including Innocent smoothies and other products promising to help you get your 'five a day' of fresh fruit and veg

Source: Image Courtesy of The Advertising Archives

In trying to influence environmental forces, marketers may seek to either create new marketing opportunities or extract greater benefits relative to costs from existing marketing opportunities. For instance, a company losing sales to competitors with lower-priced products may strive to develop technology that would make its production processes more efficient; greater efficiency would allow it to lower the prices of its own products. Political action is another way of affecting environmental forces. UK retailers, for example, successfully lobbied government to permit longer Sunday trading and legal opening of retail outlets all day. Airlines such as bmi lobbied government ministers to persuade the EU to enact its 'open skies' policy, providing more routes and landing slots for its planes. A proactive approach can be constructive and bring desired results. However, managers must recognize that there are limits on how much an environmental force can be shaped and that these limits vary across environmental forces. Although an organization may be able to influence the enactment of laws through lobbying, it is unlikely that a single organization can significantly increase the national birth rate or move the economy from recession to prosperity!

Generalizations are not possible. It cannot be stated that one of these approaches to environmental response is better than the other. For some organizations, the passive, reactive approach is more appropriate, but for other companies, the aggressive approach leads to better performance. What is certain is that ignorance of the forces of the marketing environment leads to problems and creates opportunities for rivals. The selection of a particular approach depends on an organization's managerial philosophies, objectives, financial resources, customers and human skills and on the specific composition of the set of environmental forces within which the organization operates.

The rest of this chapter explores in detail the macro and micro marketing environment forces, and then examines the link between an understanding of these issues and marketing opportunity analysis.

Political forces

The political, legal and regulatory forces of the marketing environment are closely interrelated. Legislation is enacted, legal decisions are interpreted by the courts, and regulatory agencies are created and operated, for the most part, by people elected or appointed to political offices or by civil servants. Legislation and regulations (or the lack of them) reflect the current political outlook. Consequently, the political force of the marketing environment has the potential to influence marketing decisions and strategies.

Marketers need to maintain good relations with elected political officials for several reasons. When political officials are well disposed towards particular companies or industries, they are less likely to create or enforce laws and regulations unfavourable to these companies. For example, political officials who believe that oil companies are making honest efforts to control pollution are unlikely to create and enforce highly restrictive pollution control laws. In addition, governments are big buyers, and political officials can influence how much a government agency purchases and from whom. The UK government's liking of public–private partnerships for financing capital projects such as schools and hospitals has created significant opportunities for construction companies Carillion and Laing O'Rourke or outsourcing specialists such as Capita and Fujitsu. Finally, political officials can play key roles in helping organizations secure foreign markets.

Many marketers view political forces as beyond their control; they simply try to adjust to conditions that arise from those forces. Some organizations, however, seek to influence political events by helping to elect to political office individuals who regard them positively. Much of this help is in the form of contributions to political parties. A sizeable contribution to a campaign fund may carry with it an implicit understanding that the party, if elected, will perform political favours for the contributing company. There are, though, strict laws governing donations and lobbying in most countries and, increasingly, ethical considerations for donor marketers.

Legal forces

A number of laws influence marketing decisions and activities. This discussion focuses on pro-competitive and consumer protection laws and their interpretation.

Procompetitive legislation

procompetitive legislation
Laws enacted to preserve competition and to end various practices deemed unacceptable by society

Office of Fair Trading
UK government office set up to oversee the trading practices of organizations and individuals in the UK

Competition Commission
An independent body in the UK that investigates monopolies to determine whether they operate against the public interest

Procompetitive legislation is enacted to preserve competition and to end various practices deemed unacceptable by society – for example, monopolies and mergers. In the UK, the Department for Business, Innovation and Skills (BIS) and the director general of the **Office of Fair Trading** (OFT) can refer monopolies for investigation by the **Competition Commission**, an independent body whose members are drawn from a variety of backgrounds, including lawyers, economists, industrialists and trades unionists. The legislation defines a monopoly as a situation in which at least a quarter of a particular kind of good or service is supplied by a single person or a group of connected companies, or by two or more people acting in a way that prevents, restricts or distorts competition. Local monopolies can also be referred to the Commission. If the Commission finds that a monopoly operates against the public interest, BIS has power to take action to remedy or prevent the harm that the Commission considers may exist. Alternatively, the director general of the Office of Fair Trading may be asked to negotiate undertakings to remedy the adverse effects identified by the Commission. The government believes that the market is a better judge than itself of the advantages and disadvantages of mergers, so most take-overs and proposed mergers are allowed to be decided by the companies' shareholders. However, when too much power would be placed in the hands of one organization, company or person, the government will insist on a Competition Commission appraisal. If the Commission believes it is against the public interest for a take-over or merger to proceed, then it will prohibit or limit any agreement between the companies or organizations involved. For example, when Morrisons acquired rival supermarket chain Safeway, the deal was permitted only on the basis that a number of Safeway stores were sold to a third party, ultimately Waitrose. The EU has a commissioner responsible for competition. In recent years, the commissioner has ruled on anti-competitive practices in many industries, from airlines to financial services, forcing companies to alter their trading practices and encouraging competition from a broader base of organizations.

Under the Financial Services Act of 1986, the director general of the Office of Fair Trading is required to consider the implications for competition of rules, regulations, guidance and other arrangements and practices of the regulatory bodies, investment exchanges and clearing houses. The director general must report to BIS whenever a significant or potentially significant effect on competition has been identified. This legislation is for the protection of investors, and the secretary of state may refuse or revoke recognition of the organization or require it to make alterations to its activities.

Under anti-competitive practices legislation, the director general of the Office of Fair Trading can investigate any business practice, whether in the public or private sector, that may restrict, distort or prevent competition in the production, supply or acquisition of goods or services. The Secretary of State has power to take remedial action. With the introduction of the Restrictive Trade Practices Act 1976, if two or more people who are party to the supply of goods or services accept some limitation on their freedom to make their own decisions about matters such as prices or conditions of sale, the Office of Fair Trading must be notified and such an agreement must be registered. Once an agreement has been registered, the director general is under a general duty to refer it to the Restrictive Practices Court, and the court must declare the restrictions in it contrary to the public interest unless the parties can satisfy the court that the public interest is not an issue. The vast majority of agreements never reach the court because parties elect to give up the restrictions rather than go through such a procedure.

Within the European Union, the objective of the competition policy is to ensure that there is free and fair competition in trade among member states and that the government trade barriers, which the Treaty of Rome seeks to dismantle, are not replaced by private barriers that fragment the Common Market. The EU has powers to investigate and terminate alleged infringements and to impose fines. The Treaty of Rome prohibits agreements or concertive practices that may affect trade among member states, and aims to prevent restriction or distortion of competition within the Common Market.[3] Most countries have similar procompetitive legislation. For example, in the United States the Sherman AntiTrust Act prevents monopolistic situations, the Clayton Antitrust Act specifically prohibits price discrimination, and the Federal Trade Commission Act broadly prohibits unfair methods and empowers the Federal Trade Commission to work with the Department of Justice to enforce the provisions of the Clayton Antitrust Act. The Wheeler–Lea Act essentially makes unfair and deceptive acts or practices unlawful, regardless of whether they incur competition. The Robinson–Patman Act deals with discriminatory price differentials.[4]

Consumer protection legislation

The second category of regulatory laws – consumer protection legislation – is not a recent development. However, consumer protection laws mushroomed in the mid-1960s and early 1970s. A number of them deal with consumer safety, while others relate to the sale of various hazardous products such as flammable fabrics and toys that might injure children. In the UK, the Fair Trading Act 1973 provides a mechanism – headed by the director general of the Office of Fair Trading – for the continuous review of consumer affairs, for actions dealing with trading practices that unfairly affect consumers' interests, for action against persistent offenders under existing law and for the negotiation of self-regulatory codes of practice to raise trading standards. Consumers' interests with regard to the purity of food, the description and performance of goods and services, and pricing information are safeguarded by the Food Act 1984, the Medicines Act 1968, the Misrepresentations Act 1967, the Trade Descriptions Act 1968, the Prices Act 1974, the Unfair Contract Terms Act 1977, the Sale of Goods Act 1979 and the Supply of Goods and Services Act 1982. The marking and accuracy of quantities are regulated by the Weights and Measures Act 1985. The Consumer Credit Act 1974 provides comprehensive protection for consumers who enter into credit or hire transactions. The Consumer Protection Act 1987 implements a harmonized European Union code of civil law covering product liability, creates a general criminal offence of supplying unsafe consumer goods, makes it an offence to give any misleading price indication and consolidates the powers provided under safety-related acts. The Financial Services Act 1986 offers greater protection to investors by establishing a new regulatory framework for the industry. Currently, legislation is pending concerning the production, packaging, supply and use of food.

In addition, consumer advice and information are provided to the general public at the local level by the Citizens Advice Bureau, and the Trading Standards or Consumer Protection departments of local authorities, and in some areas by specialist consumer advice centres. The independent, non-statutory National Consumer Council, which receives government finance, ensures that consumers' views are made known to those in government and industry. Nationalized industries and utilities have consumer councils whose members investigate questions of concern to the consumer, and many trade associations in industry and commerce have established codes of practice. In addition, several private organizations work to further consumer interests, the largest of which is the **Consumers' Association** funded by the subscriptions of its membership of over one million people. The association conducts an extensive programme of comparative

Consumers' Association
A private organization, funded by members' subscriptions, that works to further consumer interests

testing of goods and investigation of services; its views and test reports are published in its monthly magazine *Which?* and other publications.

Interpreting laws

Laws certainly have the potential to influence marketing activities, but the actual effects of the laws are determined by how marketers and the courts interpret them. Laws seem to be quite specific because they contain many complex clauses and sub-clauses. In reality, however, many laws and regulations are stated in vague terms that force marketers to rely on legal advice rather than their own understanding and common sense. Because of this vagueness, some organizations attempt to gauge the limits of certain laws by operating in a legally questionable way to see how far they can go with certain practices before being prosecuted. Other marketers, however, interpret regulations and statutes very conservatively and strictly to avoid violating a vague law. Although court rulings directly affect businesses accused of specific violations, they also have a broader, less direct impact on other businesses. When marketers try to interpret laws in relation to specific marketing practices, they often analyze recent court decisions, both to understand better what the law is intended to do and to gain a clearer sense of how the courts are likely to interpret it in the future.

Regulatory forces

Interpretation alone does not determine the effectiveness of laws and regulations; the level of enforcement by regulatory agencies is also significant. Some regulatory agencies are created and administered by government units; others are sponsored by non-governmental sources.

Government

In the UK, the Department for Environment, Food and Rural Affairs (DEFRA) develops and controls policies for agriculture, horticulture, fisheries and food; it also has responsibilities for environmental and rural issues and food policies. The Department for Employment and Learning controls the Employment Service, employment policy and legislation, training policy and legislation, health and safety at work, industrial relations, wages councils, equal opportunities, small businesses and tourism, statistics on labour and industrial matters for the UK, the Careers Service, and international representation on employment matters and educational policy. DEFRA controls policies for planning and regional development, local government, new towns, housing, construction, inner-city matters, environmental protection, water, the countryside, sports and recreation, conservation, historic buildings and ancient monuments. The Export Credit Guarantee Department is responsible for the provision of insurance for exporters against the risk of not being paid for goods and services, access to bank finance for exports and insurance cover for new investment overseas.

The Office for National Statistics prepares and interprets statistics needed for central economic and social policies and management; it coordinates the statistical work of other departments. The Department for Business, Innovation and Skills (BIS) controls industrial and commercial policy, promotion of enterprise and competition in the UK and abroad, and investor and consumer protection. The Department of Transport is responsible for: land, sea and air transport; rail network regulation; domestic and international civil aviation; international transport agreements; shipping and ports industries; navigation issues, HM Coastguard and marine pollution; motorways and trunk roads; road safety; and overseeing local authority transport.

These examples of British government departments are not unusual. Similar administrative bodies exist in most countries. Increasingly in the EU, political, legal and regulatory forces are being harmonized to reflect common standards and enforcement.

Local authorities

The functions of UK local authorities are far-reaching; some are primary duties, whereas others are purely discretionary. Broadly speaking, functions are divided between county and district councils on the basis that the county council is responsible for matters requiring planning and administration over wide areas or requiring the support of substantial resources, whereas district councils on the whole administer functions of a more local significance. English county councils are generally responsible for strategic planning, transport planning, highways, traffic regulations, local education, consumer protection, refuse disposal, police, the fire service, libraries and personal social services. District councils are responsible for environmental health, housing decisions, most planning applications and refuse collection. They may also provide some museums, art galleries and parks. At both county and district council level, arrangements depend on local agreements.

Most countries in Europe have a similar structure: resource-hungry issues with wide-ranging social and political consequences are controlled centrally. Planning and service provision within the community are viewed as being better controlled at the local level by the actual communities that will experience the advantages or problems resulting from such decision-making. The European Union aims to establish commonly accepted parameters for planning, service provision and regulation and a framework to assist in inter- and intra-country disputes.

Non-governmental regulatory forces

In the absence of governmental regulatory forces and in an attempt to prevent government intervention, some organizations try to regulate themselves. For example, many newspapers have voluntarily banned advertisements for telephone chat services used for undesirable activities, even though such services are technically not illegal. Trade associations in a number of industries have developed self-regulatory programmes. Even though these programmes are not a direct outcome of laws, many were established to stop or stall the development of laws and governmental regulatory groups that would regulate the associations' marketing practices. Sometimes trade associations establish codes of ethics by which their members must abide, or risk censure by other members or even exclusion from the programme. For example, many cigarette manufacturers agreed, through a code of ethics, not to promote their products to children and teenagers. The Ofcom Code of Advertising Standards and Practice aims to keep broadcast advertising 'legal, decent, honest and truthful'.[5]

Self-regulatory programmes have several advantages over governmental laws and regulatory agencies. They are usually less expensive to establish and implement, and their guidelines are generally more realistic and operational. In addition, effective industry self-regulatory programmes reduce the need to expand government bureaucracy. However, these programmes also have several limitations. When a trade association creates a set of industry guidelines for its members, non-member organizations do not have to abide by them. In addition, many self-regulatory programmes lack the tools or the authority to enforce guidelines. Finally, guidelines in self-regulatory programmes are often less strict than those established by government agencies.

Deregulation

Governments can drastically alter the environment for businesses. In the UK, the privatization of the public utilities created new terms and conditions for their suppliers and sub-contractors. The state's sales of Jaguar and Rover in the car industry and of British Airways created commercially lean companies that suddenly had new impetus to become major competitors in their industries. In the European Union, deregulation has created opportunities across borders and also new threats. Car manufacturers were previously able to restrict certain models to specific countries. They placed rigorous controls on their dealers, forbidding them to retail cars produced by rival manufacturers in the same showroom or on the same site. Many of these controls have since been swept aside.

Societal forces

Societal forces comprise the structure and dynamics of individuals and groups and the issues that engage them. Society becomes concerned about marketers' activities when those activities have questionable or negative consequences. For example, in recent times, well-publicized incidents of unethical behaviour by marketers and others have perturbed and even angered consumers, notably in connection with banks' policies and resulting economic meltdown. When marketers do a good job of satisfying society, praise or positive evaluation rarely follows. Society expects marketers to provide a high standard of living and to protect the general quality of life. This section examines some of society's expectations, the means used to express those expectations, and the problems and opportunities that marketers experience as they try to deal with society's often contradictory wishes.

Living standards and quality of life

Most people want more than just the bare necessities; they want to achieve the highest standard of living possible. For example, there is a desire for homes that offer not only protection from the elements but also comfort and a satisfactory lifestyle. People want many varieties of safe and readily available food that is also easily prepared. Clothing protects bodies, but many consumers want a variety of clothing for adornment and to project a certain image to others. Consumers want vehicles that provide rapid, safe and efficient travel. They want communications systems that give information from around the globe – a desire apparent in the popularity of products such as smart phones, social media, mobile devices and the 24-hour news coverage provided by cable and satellite television networks and by the Internet. In addition, there is a demand for sophisticated medical services that prolong life expectancy and improve physical appearance. Education is expected to help consumers acquire and enjoy a higher standard of living.

Society's high material standard of living is often not enough. Many desire a high degree of quality in their lives. People do not want to spend all their waking hours working: they seek leisure time for hobbies, voluntary work, recreation and relaxation. Quality of life is enhanced by leisure time, clean air and water, unlittered beaches, conservation of wildlife and natural resources and security from radiation and poisonous substances. A number of companies are expressing concerns about quality of life. Consumers, too, are expressing concern over 'Green' issues such as pollution, waste disposal and the so-called greenhouse effect … sustainability and issues around carbon footprint are now centre stage. Society's concerns have created both threats and opportunities for marketers. For example, one of society's biggest environmental problems is lack of space for refuse disposal, especially of plastic materials such as disposable nappies and Styrofoam packaging, which are not biodegradable. In the United States, several cities have passed laws banning the use of all plastic packaging in stores and restaurants, and governments around the world are considering similar legislation. This trend has created problems for McDonald's and other fast-food restaurants, which have now developed packaging alternatives. Other companies, however, see such environmental problems as opportunities. Procter & Gamble, for example, markets cleaners in bottles visibly made of recycled plastic.[6] Environmentally responsible, or green, marketing is increasingly extensive. For example, the German companies Audi, Volkswagen and BMW are manufacturing 'cleaner' cars that do not pollute the atmosphere as much as traditional ones. BP launched a 'green' diesel fuel with hardly any noxious emissions. Italian chemical companies are investing billions to reduce toxic wastes from their plants, and British industry is investing equally large sums to scrub acid emissions from power stations and to treat sewage more effectively.[7]

Green movement
The trend arising from society's concern about pollution, waste disposal, manufacturing processes and the greenhouse effect

The **Green movement** is concerned about these environmental issues. Several years ago few consumers were concerned about the well-being of their natural environment – their planet. Resources were not seen as scarce, pollution was barely acknowledged and people had a short-term, perhaps selfish, perspective. Now there is a growing awareness that is affecting everyone: consumers, manufacturers and legislators. Supermarket shelves are rapidly filling with packaging that can be recycled or reused, and products for which manufacturing processes have altered. Children are now taught in the classroom to 're-educate' their parents to take a more responsible view of the earth's environment. The changes are not just in the supermarkets and schools, with ever more households sorting their rubbish into various containers for collection by local authorities striving to recycle growing amounts of trash.

The rising importance and role of the green aspect – sustainability – of the societal forces must not be underestimated. Changes in the forces of the marketing environment require careful monitoring, and often demand a clear and effective response. Since marketing activities are a vital part of the total business structure, marketers have a responsibility to help provide what members of society want and to minimize what they do not want.

Consumer movement forces

consumer movement
A diverse collection of independent individuals, groups and organizations seeking to protect the rights of consumers

The **consumer movement** is a diverse collection of independent individuals, groups and organizations seeking to protect the rights of consumers. The main issues pursued by the consumer movement fall into three categories: environmental protection, product performance and safety and information disclosure. The movement's major forces are individual consumer advocates, consumer organizations and other interest groups, consumer education and consumer laws.

Consumer advocates take it upon themselves to protect the rights of consumers. They band together into consumer organizations, either voluntarily or under government sponsorship. Some organizations, such as the Consumers' Association, operate nationally, whereas others are active at local levels. They inform and organize other consumers, raise issues, help businesses develop consumer-oriented programmes and pressure legislators to enact consumer protection laws. Some consumer advocates and organizations encourage consumers to boycott products and businesses to which they have objections. For marketers, it is better to work with such activists than to incur their displeasure.

Educating consumers to make wiser purchasing decisions is perhaps one of the most far-reaching aspects of the consumer movement, which is now impacting on a growing number of organizations (see Figure 3.2). This is a motive of the Fairtrade Organization, as detailed in the marketing insight box (see page 97). Increasingly, consumer education is becoming a part of school curricula and adult education courses. These courses cover many topics – for instance, what major factors should be considered when buying specific products, such as insurance, housing, cars, appliances and furniture, clothes and food. The courses also cover the provisions of certain consumer protection laws and provide the sources of information that can help individuals become knowledgeable consumers.

Technological forces

The word technology brings to mind creations of progress such as mobile phones, computers, the Web, superconductors, lasers, GM foods, wind farms, cloning and organ transplants.

FIGURE 3.2
Npower's 'energy smart' campaign capitalizes on a growth in concern for natural resources and technological advancements in monitoring energy consumption

Source: Image Courtesy of The Advertising Archives

technology
The application of knowledge and tools to solve problems and perform tasks more efficiently

Even though such items are outgrowths of technology, none of them is technology. **Technology** has been defined as the application of knowledge and tools to solve problems and perform tasks more efficiently.[8] Often this knowledge comes from scientific research. The effects of technology are broad in scope and today exert a tremendous influence on everyone's lives. Technology grows out of research performed by businesses, universities and not-for-profit organizations. Much of this research is paid for by governments, which support investigations in a variety of areas, including health, defence, agriculture, energy and pollution. Because much centrally funded research requires the use of specialized machinery, personnel and facilities, a sizeable proportion of this research is conducted by large commercial organizations or research institutions that already possess the necessary specialized equipment and people.

The rapid technological growth of recent decades is expected to continue. Areas that hold great technological promise include digital electronics, artificial intelligence, superconductors, materials research and biotechnology. Current research is investigating new forms of memory chips and computers that will think for themselves or be more responsive to their specific users' characteristics. Because these and other technological developments will clearly have an impact on buyers' and marketers' decisions, it is important to discuss here the effects of technology on society and marketers, and to consider several factors that influence the adoption and use of technology.

The impact of technology

Marketers must be aware of new developments in technology and their possible effects because technology does affect marketing activities in many different ways. Consumers' technological knowledge influences their desire for goods and services. To provide marketing mixes that satisfy consumers, marketers must be aware of these influences. For example, the Web has led to easy access for consumers to comparative information about products and brands, while providing marketers with an important channel for communications and selling. The massive growth of digital media and social networking is impacting on all markets and marketers' practices, as they battle to keep pace with the associated changing consumer behaviours and societal implications. Within marketing departments, technology has enabled far more sophisticated customer profiling and engagement through increasingly sophisticated CRM (customer relationship management)

Brands and consumers embrace Fairtrade

Topical insight

Fairtrade labelling was created in the Netherlands in the 1980s, with coffee from Mexico being the first recipient of the eco-label.

Fairtrade exists to guarantee that the suppliers of products consumed in the developed world, based in the developing regions, benefit from a fair price. By negotiating better deals, improving the negotiating power and marketing expertise of farmers and producers, and seeking a greater proportion of the retail price, the movement helps sustain development and is largely welcomed by the leading development agencies. A core aim is to minimize dramatically fluctuating prices that, when low, force farmers into crippling debt or out of production. More information is available at **www.fairtrade.org.uk**.

Now there are around twenty organizations around the world, including the Fairtrade Foundation, overseeing the labelling of Fairtrade products. Over 500 Fairtrade-certified producer groups in 40 countries have helped many impoverished and vulnerable regions. In order to achieve this, the movement must lobby retailers, the media and consumers to purchase or support Fairtrade products. In the UK there are now over 3000 Fairtrade retail and catering products (up from 1500 in 2006), from tea to fruit, roses to footballs, snacks to wines. One key product receiving such high-profile attention is coffee.

Leading coffee houses Costa Coffee, Prêt à Manger and Starbucks have retailed Fairtrade coffees for a while, but now it is the turn of the major manufacturers. Until relatively recently, most Fairtrade products were niche brands produced by marginal manufacturers. Now, even the giants of the global food industry have embraced the movement, reflecting the growing interest in ethical trading by consumers and major retail chains.

First, Nestlé announced a Fairtrade addition to its Nescafé brand. Today there is a full range of Nescafé Partners Blend Coffee lines, supported with some innovative branding (**www.growmorethancoffee.co.uk**). Before its launch, however, rival Kraft stole a march by introducing a Fairtrade coffee range under its well-known Kenco brand. Kenco Sustainable Development comprised two lines: a filter pack and an espresso bean pack. First available to consumers in restaurants, hotels, coffee shops and vending machines, then through supermarkets. Both Kenco lines carry an eco-label from sustainable agriculture organization the Rainforest Alliance, which guarantees that the beans are from certified farms. Kraft also reformulated its flagship brands Maxwell House and Kenco Really Smooth so that they contain at least 5 per cent certified beans, but they do not carry the eco-label. Now all of the major supermarket groups, many buying groups and even the discounters stock Fairtrade or ethically sourced coffee lines.

Did growing consumer interest in Fairtrade encourage these manufacturers to launch the new lines? Were moves by the more socially aware retailers responsible? Had lobbying by organizations such as the Rainforest Alliance or Fairtrade Foundation created the necessary swell of positive public opinion? Were Kraft and Nestlé simply reaping the rewards of their environmental scanning of market trends? In reality, a mix of these drivers combined to create the impetus for these products and the growth of other companies' Fairtrade products.

Sources: **www.growmorethancoffee.co.uk**, 28 February 2011; Kraft, 2004; **www.fairtrade.org.uk**, 28 February 2011; Mark Sweeney, 'Kraft beats Nestlé to launch of fair trade coffee', *Marketing*, 7 July 2004, p. 1; 'Starbucks and Fairtrade' at **www.starbucks.co.uk**, 28 February 2011.

---

systems. These are three of the most dramatic illustrations in recent years of how markets and marketing have changed as a result of new technology and associated consumer behaviours. The various ways in which technology affects marketing activities fall into two broad categories:

1 effects on consumers and society in general
2 influences on what, how, when and where products are marketed.

Effects of technology on society Technology determines how consumers as members of society satisfy their physiological needs. In various ways and to varying degrees, eating and drinking habits, sleeping patterns, sexual activities and healthcare are all influenced both by existing technology and by changes in technology. Right now, many consumers seek technology solutions for the planet's sustainability needs and carbon problems. Technological developments have improved standards of living, thus creating more leisure time; they have also enhanced information, entertainment and education. Nevertheless, technology can detract from the quality of life through undesirable side-effects, such as unemployment, 'coach potato' lazing around, cyber-bullying, polluted air and water and other health hazards. Some people believe that further applications of technology can soften or eliminate these undesirable side-effects. Others argue, however, that the best way to improve the quality of our lives is to decrease the use of technology.

Effects of technology on marketing   Technology also affects the types of product that marketers can offer. The introduction and general acceptance of cassette tapes and compact discs drove most manufacturers of vinyl long-playing (LP) albums out of business or forced them to invest in new technology. Yet this technology provided new marketing opportunities for recording artists and producers, record companies, retailers and those in related industries. More recently, music downloads from the Web have created a new set of opportunities and challenges for marketers in the music industry, while giving greater flexibility and immediacy to consumers. The following items are just a few of the many thousands of existing products that were not available to consumers 20 years ago: webcams, digital cameras, mobile phones, ultra-light laptop computers, high-resolution televisions, hand-held video cameras, the Internet, mobile media applications, kindles, skype and social networks. All of these are products that have transformed lifestyles and people's access to information.

Computer technology helps make warehouse storage and keeping track of stored products more efficient and, therefore, less expensive. Often, these savings can be passed on to consumers in the form of lower prices. Because of technological changes in communications, marketers can now use a variety of media to reach large masses of people more efficiently. The development and widespread use of fax, e-mail and text messaging, for example, allowed marketers to send their advertisements or sales specifications directly to selected groups of customers who want their products. In recent years the Internet has permeated the lives of many, bringing a world of information into the home and allowing consumers to shop for products online. Facebook, LinkedIn and other digital social media networks have revolutionized how consumers find out about events, products, services, brands and how they share their views. Technological advances in transport enable consumers to travel further and more often, to shop at a larger number of stores, or to broaden their options. Changes in transport have also affected producers' ability to get products to retailers and wholesalers. The ability of present-day manufacturers of relatively lightweight products to reach any of their dealers within hours via express-delivery services would astound their counterparts of 50 years ago. Geographical boundaries for markets have been revolutionized thanks to transport, communication and customer engagement technological changes.

The adoption and use of technology

technology assessment
A procedure by which managers try to foresee the effects of new products and processes on their company's operation, on other commercial organizations and on society in general

Through a procedure known as **technology assessment**, some managers try to foresee the effects of new products and processes on their company's operation, on other organizations and on society in general. With the information gained through a technology assessment, management tries to estimate whether the benefits of using a specific kind of technology outweigh the costs to the business and to society at large. Increasing numbers of companies are encouraged to proceed in this direction as carbon footprint pressures and corporate social responsibility (CSR) policies drive change. Although available technology could radically improve their products or other parts of the marketing mix, some companies may put off applying this technology as long as their competitors do not try to use it. The extent to which an organization can protect inventions stemming from research also influences its use of technology. The extent to which a product is secure from imitation depends on how easily others can copy it without violating its patent. If new products and processes cannot be protected through patents, a company is less likely to market them and make the benefits of its research available to competitors. How a company uses – or does not use – technology is important for its long-term survival. An organization that makes the wrong decisions may well lose out to the competition. Poor decisions may also affect its profits by requiring expensive corrective action. Poor decisions about technological forces may even drive a company out of business.

When a company's marketers undertake an assessment of the marketing environment they will identify many aspects of technology pertinent to their own industry, markets and products, presenting both opportunities and threats. To illustrate just some implications from technological change, here some of the most significant developments for marketers of all types are highlighted. Five aspects of technology ahead of all others warrant further discussion in terms of their implications for how marketing has itself altered: customer relationship management (CRM), Internet marketing, mobile marketing, social media and digital marketing. In practice, these are now all viewed as facets of what has come to be termed digital marketing, except for CRM.

CRM

There is nothing more important for marketers than identifying prospective customers, engaging effectively with them, building ongoing relationships and managing the varied personnel across the many functions in a typical company who interact with customers. In today's multi-media and multi-channel environment, managing a relationship with a customer across the many ways in which s/he can interact with the brand or the company is very challenging, but also presents numerous opportunities for achieving more business. CRM illustrates well how technology has impacted on marketers. Not too long ago it was an arduous and manual paper-driven task to keep track of contacts with customers and to build up profiles of a company's customers or customer segments. Now CRM packages and suppliers provide off-the-shelf or bespoke approaches to managing customer contacts and relationships.

Business Link, the official UK government service providing business advice, explains[9] that, 'customer relationship management helps businesses to gain an insight into the behaviour of their customers and modify their business operations to ensure that customers are served in the best possible way'. In essence, CRM helps a business to recognize the value of its customers and to capitalize on improved customer relations. The better you understand your customers, the more responsive you can be to their needs. CRM can be achieved by:

● Finding out about customers' purchasing habits, opinions and preferences.

● Profiling individuals and groups so as to market more effectively and increase sales.

● Changing the way a company operates, to improve customer service and marketing.

Therefore using technology to improve CRM makes good business sense. There are many IT solutions to CRM available.

Many software companies offer CRM applications that integrate with existing customer data and sales management packages. Cut-down versions of such software may be suitable for smaller businesses. While not tailored to a company's unique customer base, product portfolio and marketing environment, such solutions are readily available and popular. Some users want to have a more customized and bespoke software solution, and are prepared to pay more for such benefits. If a company does not wish to fully outsource its operation, it may opt to select a managed solution, in effect renting a customized suite of CRM applications as a bespoke package. Some companies opt to fully outsource their CRM requirements to IT services businesses. Application service providers, such as Accenture Interactive, can provide web-based CRM solutions, increasingly harnessing the benefits of cloud computing which frees up an organization from having to provide its own IT infrastructure. Such providers host their clients' CRM operations for them. Outsourcing is a significant commitment and tends to be an option for larger corporate clients.

CRM involves data capture about customers and their buying habits, analysis and profiling of such behaviours, so that tailored propositions and communications may be created in order to maintain an ongoing relationship and continue to interest customers in the company's brand, products and activities. IT and software have routinized this aspect of customer handling in many organizations. There are even CRM apps for Blackberry users and most businesses now utilize such ready-made packages. CRM will be explored in more detail in Chapter 6.

> **CRM**
> Data capture about customers and their buying habits, analysis and profiling of such behaviours, so that tailored propositions and communications may be created in order to maintain an ongoing relationship and continue to interest customers in the company's brand, products and activities.

The Internet

A decade ago, the Internet was big news for marketers and eMarketing was a buzz word. This was the process of creating, distributing, promoting and pricing products for targeted customers in the digital environment of the Internet. The Internet impacted largely in three ways: (a) for distributing products, as an alternative marketing channel to retail stores or trade depots; (b) for marketing communications, as an additional option to sales promotion, traditional advertising, public relations or personal selling; and (c) as a means for finding out information about markets, competitors, market trends and customers. Internet marketing was deemed to be a part of what was termed direct marketing. In recent years, the speed of technological innovation, social acceptance of such advances and their deployment by marketers, have rapidly taken this aspect of marketing to new heights. Now more generally termed digital marketing, this also encompasses mobile marketing and social media. There is no doubt about the extent to which the Internet has altered the bounds for consumers, business customers, marketers and brands.

Digital marketing

Digital marketing tools and techniques are used by marketers to improve their proposition to customers and overall competitiveness, with a value adding website and interrelated digital marketing techniques to drive traffic, conversion, positive experience and referrals. These techniques include website, online public relations, e-mail, blogs/microblogs, social networks, podcasts, wikis and search engine management to ensure preferential web search.

> **digital marketing**
> Digital marketing tools and techniques are used by marketers to improve their proposition to customers and overall competitiveness, with a value adding website and interrelated digital marketing techniques to drive traffic, conversion, positive experience and referrals.

According to a recent Gartner analyst report on IT spending trends, five out of the top ten Chief Information Officer (CIO) priorities involve investment in digital marketing properties.[10] Yet there is a bewildering and fast-evolving landscape of digital marketing touch points for marketers to understand … consumers have a growing selection of Web and mobile options for learning about products, services and brands, and sharing opinions and views directly with fellow consumers. Two very important aspects of digital marketing are mobile marketing and social media.

Mobile marketing

A more traditional definition of mobile marketing is marketing activity in a moving manner or encountered by consumers on the move, such as moving advertising boards at sports events or stations, but increasingly the term stands for marketing via a mobile device such as a smartphone, to provide customers with time and location sensitive, personalized information

mobile marketing
A set of practices that enables organizations to communicate and engage with their audience in an interactive and relevant manner through any mobile device or network.

that promotes goods, services and ideas. The Mobile Marketing Association defines **mobile marketing** as, '*a set of practices that enables organizations to communicate and engage with their audience in an interactive and relevant manner through any mobile device or network*' (**www.mmaglobal.com**).[11] Many brand managers currently are launching apps and developing interactive websites suitable for smartphones, laptops on the move and interactive points at a host of locations. Technology now permits ready and immediate access to customers wherever they are, whenever and irrespective of whatever they are doing. Whether searching for flight information whilst in a meeting or taxi, paying a utility bill when watching TV, betting on a sports result over dinner or Googling for the answer to a pub quiz question, instant hooking up whenever and wherever to the digital community is now routine, providing marketers with a selection of mobile possibilities.

Social media and networks

Twitter, Facebook, Digg, MySpace, LinkedIn, Bebo and YouTube are familiar to most readers of this text and to most marketers. Insight consultants Gartner examined 400 social media cases, concluding that, '... social-media technologies, such as social networking, wikis and blogs, enable collaboration on a much grander scale and support tapping the power of the collective in ways previously unachievable'.[12] As explained in Chapter 1, the emergence of social media and networking has radically shifted the boundaries for marketers and consumers, not least because they have taken a great deal of communication about brands and products out of the hands of marketers and into the hands of consumers, who easily may share their experiences and views with each other.

social media
Social media incorporate the online technology and methods through which people can share content, personal opinions, different perspectives and insights, using text, images, audio and video, via social networks, video and photo sharing, micro-blogs, wikis and news aggregators.

Social media offer a way to more effectively reach audiences and engage them in commercial transactions, but also the social/third sector is able develop low cost conversational communication strategies. **Social media** incorporates the online technology and methods through which people can share content, personal opinions, swap different perspectives and insights, using text, images, audio and video. Social networking sites such as Facebook are one form of social media; others include wikis, video sharing such as YouTube, photo sharing on sites like Flickr, news aggregators typified by Digg, social bookmarking, online gaming and micro-blogging on presence apps such as Twitter.

Economic and competitive forces

economic and competitive forces
Factors in the marketing environment – such as the effects of general economic conditions; buying power; willingness to spend; spending patterns; types of competitive structure, competitive tools and competitive behaviour – that influence both marketers' and consumers' decisions and activities

The **economic and competitive forces** in the marketing environment influence both marketers' and customers' decisions and activities. This section first examines the effects of general economic conditions, also focusing on buying power, willingness to spend and spending patterns. Then the discussion moves to the broad competitive forces, including types of competitive structure, competitive tools and some methods for monitoring competitive behaviour. The strategic importance of understanding and evaluating the competitive arena has been discussed in Chapter 2.

General economic conditions

The overall state of the economy fluctuates in all countries. Table 3.1 presents some economic measures of performance for Europe. These changes in general economic conditions affect – and are affected by – the forces of supply and demand, buying power, willingness to spend, consumer expenditure levels and the intensity of competitive behaviour. Therefore, current economic conditions and changes in the economy have a broad impact on the success of organizations' marketing strategies.

TABLE 3.1 Some economic measures of performance for europe

DATA ON WESTERN EUROPEAN COUNTRIES[†]

		Units	Austria	Belgium	Denmark	France	Germany	Ireland	Italy	Netherlands	Norway	Spain	Sweden	Switzerland	United Kingdom
A	Total population, 2006[1]	millions	8.27	10.51	5.43	63.39	82.44	4.24	58.46	16.33	4.64	44.40	9.05	7.46	60.59
A	Population growth at annual rates														
	Population growth 06/05[1]	%	1.1	1.1	0.4	3.8	-0.1	2.5	1.5	0.4	0.7	2.3	0.6	1.0	0.6
	Population growth 06/96[1]	%	3.9	3.5	3.2	9.2	1.0	16.6	2.2	5.2	5.9	12.9	2.5	6.0	3.8
A	Population by sex and age, 2006[1]														
	Male	%	48.6	48.9	49.5	48.6	48.9	49.8	48.5	49.5	49.6	49.4	49.6	49.0	49.0
	Female	%	51.4	51.1	50.5	51.4	51.1	50.2	51.5	50.5	50.4	50.6	50.4	51.0	51.0
	Under 15	%	15.9	17.0	18.8	18.5	14.1	20.4	14.2	18.2	19.6	14.2	17.3	16.0	17.7
	15–64	%	67.6	65.8	66.0	65.3	66.6	68.5	66.3	67.5	65.7	69.0	65.4	68.0	66.3
	65+	%	16.5	17.2	15.2	16.2	19.3	11.1	19.5	14.3	14.7	16.8	17.3	16.0	16.0
A	Births, 2005[2]	per 000	9.5	11.3	11.9	13.1	8.3	14.8	9.4	11.5	12.3	10.7	11.2	9.8	12.0
A	Marriages, 2005[2]	per 000	4.8	4.1	6.7	4.3	4.7	5.0	4.3	4.5	4.8	4.8	4.9	5.4	4.7
A	Inhabitants per sq. km, 2006[1]	no.	100	347	128	99	236	61	199	482	15	89	22	188	251
A	Number of households, 2006[3]	000s	3 475	4 482	2 517	27 490	39 178	1 288	23 600	7 146	2 010	15 976	4 400	3 115	24 800
	Persons per household[3]	no.	2.4	2.3	2.2	2.3	2.1	3.1	2.5	2.3	2.3	2.7	2.1	2.3	2.4
B	Commonly used unemployment rate, 2006 Proportion of labour force	%	6.8	12.4	4.4	9.0	10.8	4.4	6.8	5.5	3.5	8.5	5.3	3.3	2.9
C	Civilian employment by main sectors[4]														
	Agriculture	%	3.0	1.3	3.0	4.1	2.8	8.0	5.0	2.0	4.0	5.3	2.0	4.6	1.4
	Industry	%	27.0	24.5	21.0	24.4	33.4	29.0	32.0	19.0	22.0	30.1	24.0	26.3	18.2
	Services	%	70.0	74.2	76.0	71.5	63.8	64.0	63.0	79.0	74.0	64.6	74.0	69.1	80.4
D	Strikes, 2006[5] Working days lost per 1,000 employees	no.	—	—	476	699	—	10	549	31	12	783	9	3	158
B	Gross Domestic Product (local currency, constant 2000 prices[6])														
	Total, 2006	billions	233.6	301.9	1 431.9	1 593.3	2 183	170.8	1 255.8	457.3	1 840.1	768.7	2 594.9	464.0	1 209.3
	Per capita	000s	28.3	28.7	263.7	25.1	26.5	40.3	21.5	28.0	396.6	17.3	286.7	62.2	20.0
B	Gross fixed capital formation, 2006 (local currency, constant 2000 prices[6]) Proportion of GDP	%	20.9	20.5	23.5	20.3	19.6	25.4	20.9	20.5	20.4	29.1	18.1	22.1	17.9

TABLE 3.1 Continued

Notes: † Where data for the reference period were not available, the most recent were used. All countries use the Euro except for Denmark (DKK), Norway (NOK), Sweden (SEK), Switzerland (CHF) and UK (GBP) [1] Data for Austria, Germany, Italy, Sweden and Switzerland are for 2005; the population growth for these countries is based on 2004 and 1995 respectively. [2] Data for France are 2000 estimates. [3] Data for Switzerland are for 2000. Data for Ireland are for 2002. Data for Austria, Germany, Italy, Norway, Spain and Sweden are for 2005. [4] Data for Belgium are for 2003, data for Denmark, Netherlands and Spain are for 2004. Data for the UK are for 2006. Data for all other nations are prior to 2003. All data are estimates. [5] Data for Belgium and Germany are unavailable. Data for France are for 2004. [6] Data for UK are in 2003 prices. Data for Belgium and Norway are in 2004 prices. Data for Ireland are in 2005 prices.

Sources: A *European Marketing Pocket Book*, WARC; Local sources.
B OECD Main Economic Indicators © OECD, September 2007.
C CIA World Fact Book', (*www.cia.gov/cia/publications/factbook*), 2007.
D 'Strikes and Lockouts — Days not worked', International Labour Office (ILO) 2007.

MEMBER STATES OF THE EUROPEAN UNION

Full Members
Austria, Belgium, Bulgaria, Cyprus, Czech Republic, Denmark, Estonia, Finland, France, Germany, Greece, Hungary, Ireland, Italy, Latvia, Lithuania, Luxembourg, Malta, Netherlands, Poland, Portugal, Romania, Slovenia, Slovak Republic, Spain, Sweden, United Kingdom.

Candidate Countries
Croatia and Turkey are the next candidate countries, along with Macedonia. Albania, Bosnia and Herzegovina, Montenegro and Serbia are now viewed as probable members to join the EU.

		Austria	Belgium	Denmark	France	Germany	Ireland	Italy	Netherlands	Norway	Spain	Sweden	Switzerland	United Kingdom
A	**Consumption per capita per year**													
	Beer, 2003	litres	110.6	96.2	96.2	35.5	117.5	141.2	30.1	78.7	50.5	78.3	54.2	58.1	101.5
	Wine, 2003	litres	29.8	23.0	32.6	48.5	23.6	15.2	47.5	19.6	12.4	30.6	16.6	40.9	20.1
	Spirits, 2003	100% alc., litres	1.4	1.4	1.1	2.4	2.0	2.0	0.4	1.5	0.8	2.4	0.9	1.6	1.8
B	Chocolate confectionery, 2005	kg	9.4	11.0	7.7	6.8	11.1	3.9	4.3	4.5	8.5	3.1	6.8	10.7	10.2
	Sugar confectionery, 2005	kg	3.8	4.2	8.9	3.4	5.9	1.7	2.2	7.5	4.6	2.7	11.7	3.2	5.6
	Biscuits and other baked goods, 2005[1]	kg	8.2	5.9	9.1	8.6	7.7	3.4	3.6	14.5	—	6.6	3.5	8.1	15.7
C	**Media and telecommunications, 2006[2]**														
	Daily newspapers – weekly reach[3]	%	73.7	56.7	79.7	18.4	73.7	56.9	64.1	72.5	90.9	41.8	93.0	90.7	62.9
	Radio – weekly reach[3]	%	83.6	82.2	95.9	83.3	79.3	86.0	84.8	91.3	97.8	56.3	94.0	90.7	90.4
	TV – weekly reach[3]	%	69.2	91.3	93.1	95.9	75.4	91.0	95.4	96.5	90.4	87.9	88.2	92.8	93.8
	Household penetration:														
	Telephone mainlines	%	75.9	76.6	—	86.0	—	87.8	85.3	—	—	76.1	93.0	88.4	93.1
	Mobile phones	%	87.5	80.4	94.0	79.3	77.9	86.4	88.0	86.3	94.2	80.3	93.0	81.0	84.7
	Personal computers	%	64.3	66.4	—	52.9	47.0	63.3	36.3	78.2	69.0	40.8	70.0	77.5	56.9
	Internet	%	49.9	55.2	78.8	42.6	43.9	44.7	31.6	71.5	69.0	28.8	70.0	70.9	56.9
C/D	**Indicators of living standards**														
	Physicians, 2003[4]	per '000 popn.	3.4	3.9	2.9	3.4	3.4	2.8	4.2	3.1	3.1	3.2	3.3	3.6	2.2
	Life expectancy at birth, 2005[5]	years	79.5	79.5	77.9	80.7	79.0	77.7	80.4	79.0	80.1	80.3	80.5	81.3	79.2
	Infant mortality, 2005	per '000 live births	4.2	4.4	4.4	3.7	3.9	4.0	4.2	4.9	3.2	4.1	2.4	4.2	4.9
	Health expenditure, 2003	% of GDP	7.5	9.4	9.0	10.1	11.1	7.3	8.4	9.8	10.3	7.7	9.4	11.5	8.0
	Public spending on education, 2002[7]	% of GDP	5.7	6.3	8.5	5.6	4.8	4.3	4.7	5.1	7.6	4.5	7.7	5.8	5.5
C	**Vehicles**														
	Total motor vehicles, 2005[1]	000s	5 647	5 862	4 134	36 039	54 519	2 139	38 224	8 494	2 523	27 657	4 615	5 369	32 897

E	**The retail grocery trade, 2000**													
	Grocery store numbers		6 417	9 891	3 026	37 559	64 230	9 118	107 669	4 663	4 564	59 689	4 834	6 223	33 348
	Market share by store type:														
	Hypermarkets	%	12	14	19	52	25	19	18	5	4	33	18	19	53
	Large supermarkets	%	17	46	25	25	17	35	18	39	18	17	38	32	24
	Small supermarkets	%	44	29	37	11	39	11	21	19	47	18	29	25	12
	Superettes	%	27	8	17	4	14	34	19	9	28	18	13	19	11
	Traditionals	%	—	3	1	—	4	—	18	—	2	13	2	5	—
D	**International tourism, 2004[8]**														
	Arrivals	% of popn.	223.4	124.2	61.8	118.5	22.3	164.7	63.4	59.1	77.6	120.7	85.2	89.0	45.8
	Departures	% of popn.	78.4	134.9	85.3	33.3	90.4	127.6	39.9	101.5	56.5	11.5	154.4	156.9	106.0

Notes: **In each category, where data for the reference period were not available, the most recent have been used.**

1   Data in italics are for 2004.
2   Data in italics are for 2005.
3   Data for Austria, Germany, Ireland, Italy and Spain are daily reach.
4   Data for Belgium, Denmark, Sweden and Switzerland are for 2002; data for France, Ireland and Italy are for 2004.
5   Data for Belgium and Spain are for 2004; data for France and UK are 2006 estimates.
6   Data for Denmark and Italy are for 2004; data for France are 2006 estimates.
7   Data for the UK are for 2006.
8   All data for Belgium and Germany; arrivals data for Sweden and Switzerland; and departures data for Netherlands and Norway are all for 2003. Departures data for Switzerland are for 2002.

Sources: A *World Drink Trends 2005*, WARC; Commissie Gedistilleerd/WARC.
B CAOBISCO.
C *European Marketing Pocket Book 2007*, WARC; Local sources.
D *World Development Indicators 2006*, World Bank.
E Nielsen.

business cycle
Fluctuations in the economy that follow the general pattern of prosperity, recession, depression and recovery

Fluctuations in the economy follow a general pattern often referred to as the **business cycle**. In the traditional view, the business cycle consists of four stages: prosperity, recession, depression and recovery.

prosperity
A period during which unemployment is low and total income is relatively high

Prosperity   During **prosperity**, unemployment is low and total income is relatively high. Assuming a low inflation rate, this combination causes buying power to be high. To the extent that the economic outlook remains prosperous, consumers are generally willing to buy. In the prosperity stage, marketers often expand their marketing mixes (product, place/distribution, promotion, price and people) to take advantage of the increased buying power. They sometimes capture a larger market share by intensifying distribution and promotion efforts.

recession
A period during which unemployment rises and total buying power declines

Recession   Unemployment rises during a **recession**, so total buying power declines. The pessimism that accompanies a recession often stifles both consumer and business spending, as is the case as this edition of *Marketing Essentials* is produced. As buying power decreases, many consumers become more price- and value-conscious; they look for products that are basic and functional. For instance, people ordinarily reduce their consumption of more expensive convenience foods and strive to save money by growing and preparing more of their own food. Individuals buy fewer durable goods and more repair and do-it-yourself products. During a recession, some companies make the mistake of drastically reducing their marketing efforts and thus damage their ability to survive. Obviously, marketers should consider some revision of their marketing activities during a recessionary period. Because consumers are more concerned about the functional value of products, a company must focus its marketing research on determining what product functions buyers want and then make sure that these functions become part of its products. Promotional efforts should emphasize value and utility.

depression
A period during which unemployment is extremely high, wages are very low, total disposable income is at a minimum and consumers lack confidence in the economy

Depression   A **depression** is a period in which unemployment is extremely high, wages are very low, total disposable income is at a minimum and consumers lack confidence in the economy. Governments have used both monetary and fiscal policies to offset the effects of recession and depression. Monetary policies are employed to control the money supply, which in turn affects spending, saving and investment by both individuals and businesses. Through the establishment of fiscal policies, the government is able to influence the amount of saving and expenditure by adjusting the tax structure and by changing the levels of government spending. Some economic experts believe that the effective use of monetary and fiscal policies can completely eliminate depressions from the business cycle, although the credit crunch at the end of the decade posed some challenge to this view.

recovery
The stage of the business cycle in which the economy moves from depression or recession to prosperity

Recovery   **Recovery** is the stage of the business cycle in which the economy moves from depression or recession to prosperity. During this period, the high unemployment rate begins to decline, total disposable income increases and the economic gloom that lessened consumers' willingness to buy subsides. Both the ability and the willingness to buy rise. Marketers face some problems during recovery – for example, the difficulty of ascertaining how quickly prosperity will return and of forecasting the level of prosperity that will be attained. During this stage, marketers should maintain as much flexibility in their marketing strategies as possible to be able to make the required adjustments as the economy moves from recession to prosperity. Fluctuations in economic conditions have a significant impact on marketers' activities and fortunes.

Consumer demand and spending behaviour

Marketers must understand the factors that determine whether, what, where and when people buy. Chapters 4 and 5 look at the behavioural factors underlying these choices, but here the focus is on the economic components: buying power, willingness to purchase and spending patterns.

buying power
Resources such as goods, services and financial holdings that can be traded in an exchange situation

Buying power   The strength of a person's **buying power** depends on the size of the resources that enable the individual to purchase, as well as on the state of the economy. The resources that make up buying power are goods, services and financial holdings. Fluctuations of the business cycle affect buying power because they influence price levels and interest rates. For example, during inflationary periods, when prices are rising, buying power decreases because more pounds or euros are required to buy products. The major financial sources of buying power are income, credit and wealth. From an individual's viewpoint, **income** is the amount of money received through wages, rents, investments, pensions and subsidy payments for a given period, such as a month or a year. Normally, this money is allocated among taxes, spending for goods and services, and savings. However, because of the differences in people's educational levels, abilities, occupations and wealth, income is not distributed equally in any country.

income
The amount of money received through wages, rents, investments, pensions and subsidy payments for a given period

Marketers are most interested in the amount of money that is left after payment of taxes. After-tax income is called **disposable income** and is used for spending or saving. Because disposable income is a ready source of buying power, the total amount available in a country is important to marketers. Several factors affect the size of total disposable income. One, of course, is the total amount of income. Total national income is affected by wage levels, rate of unemployment, interest rates and dividend rates. These factors in turn affect the size of disposable income. Because disposable income is the income left after taxes are paid, the number of taxes and their amount directly affect the size of total disposable income. When taxes rise, disposable income declines; when taxes fall, disposable income increases. Disposable income that is available for spending and saving after an individual has purchased the basic necessities of food, clothing and shelter is called **discretionary income**. People use discretionary income to purchase entertainment, holidays, cars, education, pets and pet supplies, furniture, appliances and so on. Changes in total discretionary income affect the sales of these products – especially cars, furniture, large appliances and other costly durable goods. The marketers of such products must monitor factors likely to alter their target customers' discretionary income.

disposable income
After-tax income, which is used for spending or saving

discretionary income
Disposable income that is available for spending and saving after an individual has purchased the basic necessities of food, clothing and shelter

Credit enables people to spend future income now or in the near future. However, credit increases current buying power at the expense of future buying power. Several factors determine whether consumers use or forgo credit. First, credit must be available to them. Interest rates, too, affect consumers' decisions to use credit, especially for expensive purchases such as homes, appliances and cars. When credit charges are high, consumers are more likely to delay buying expensive items. Use of credit is also affected by credit terms, such as the size of the down payment and the amount and number of monthly payments. Many marketers offer 'interest-free credit' or low interest rates as part of the marketing proposition for their products.

wealth
The accumulation of past income, natural resources and financial resources

A person can have a high income and very little wealth. It is also possible, but not likely, for a person to have great wealth but not much income. **Wealth** is the accumulation of past income, natural resources and financial resources. It may exist in many forms, including cash, securities, savings accounts, jewellery, antiques and property. Like income, wealth is distributed unevenly. The significance of wealth to marketers is that as people become wealthier they gain buying power in three ways: they can use their wealth to make current purchases, to generate income and to acquire large amounts of credit. Buying power information is available from government sources, trade associations and research agencies. One of the most current and comprehensive sources of buying power data is the Office for National Statistics (http://www.statistics.gov.uk) and the *National Income, Expenditure and Output Surveys*. The EU's Eurostat (http://epp.eurostat.ec.europa.eu) provides similar data across member states of the EU. Income, wealth and credit equip consumers to purchase goods and services. Marketing managers should be aware of current levels and expected changes in buying power in their own markets because buying power directly affects the types and quantities of goods and services that consumers purchase, as explained later in the discussion of spending patterns. Just because consumers have buying power, however, does not necessarily mean that they will buy. Consumers must also be willing to use their buying power. Marketers must encourage them to do so.

willingness to spend
A disposition towards using buying power, influenced by the ability to buy, expected satisfaction from a product and numerous psychological and social forces

Consumers' willingness to spend People's **willingness to spend** is, to some degree, related to their ability to buy – that is, people are sometimes more willing to buy if they have the buying power. However, a number of other elements also influence willingness to spend. Some elements affect specific products; others influence spending in general. A product's absolute price and its price relative to the price of substitute products influences almost everyone. The amount of satisfaction currently received or expected in the future from a product already owned may also influence consumers' desire to buy other products. Satisfaction depends not only on the quality of the functional performance of the currently owned product, but also on numerous psychological and social forces.

Factors that affect consumers' general willingness to spend are expectations about future employment, income levels, prices, family size and general economic conditions. If people are unsure whether or how long they will be employed, willingness to buy ordinarily declines. Current realignment following the global banking crisis and the credit crunch have caused high

consumer spending patterns
Information indicating the relative proportions of annual family expenditures or the actual amount of money spent on certain kinds of goods and services

levels of uncertainty for many consumers and businesses, altering spending patterns and willingness to buy. Willingness to spend may increase if people are reasonably certain of higher incomes in the future. Expectations of rising prices in the near future may also increase willingness to spend in the present. For a given level of buying power, the larger the family, the greater the willingness to buy. One of the reasons for this relationship is that as the size of a family increases, a larger amount of money must be spent to provide the basic necessities of life to sustain the family members. Finally, perceptions of future economic conditions influence willingness to buy. For example, rising short-term interest rates cool consumers' willingness to spend.

comprehensive spending patterns
The percentages of family income allotted to annual expenditures for general classes of goods and services

Consumer spending patterns Marketers must be aware of the factors that influence consumers' ability and willingness to spend, but they should also analyze how consumers actually spend their disposable incomes. Marketers obtain this information by studying consumer spending patterns. **Consumer spending patterns** indicate the relative proportions of annual family expenditures or the actual amount of money spent on certain kinds of goods and services. Families are usually categorized by one of several characteristics, including family income, age of the head of household, geographic area and family life cycle. There are two types of spending pattern: comprehensive and product-specific.

product-specific spending patterns
The annual monetary amounts families spend for specific products within a general product class

The percentages of family income allotted to annual expenditures for general classes of goods and services constitute **comprehensive spending patterns**. Comprehensive spending patterns or the data to develop them are available in government publications and in reports produced by the major marketing research companies and by trade associations. **Product-specific spending patterns** indicate the annual monetary amounts families spend for specific products within a general product class. Information sources used to construct product-specific spending patterns include government publications, trade publications and consumer surveys. A marketer uses spending patterns to analyze general trends in the ways that families spend their incomes for various kinds of product. Analyzes of spending patterns yield information that a marketer can use to gain perspective and background for decision-making. However, spending patterns reflect only general trends and thus should not be used as the sole basis for making specific decisions.

Assessment of competitive forces

Few organizations, if any, operate free of competition. Broadly speaking, all companies compete with each other for consumers' money. In other walks of life, such as the public sector or third sector, organizations may compete for attention, people's time or involvement, goodwill, donations or payment. In commercial settings, a business generally defines **competition** as those organizations marketing products that are similar to, or can be substituted for, its own products in the same geographic area or marketing channel. For example, a local Tesco or Aldi supermarket manager views all grocery stores in a town as competitors, but almost never thinks of other types of local or out-of-town stores (DIY or electrical, for example) as competitors. This section considers the types of competitive structure and the importance of monitoring competitors.

competition
Those companies marketing products that are similar to, or can be substituted for, a given business's products in the same geographic area or marketing channel

Types of competitive structure   The number of organizations that control the supply of a product may affect the strength of competition. When only one or a few companies control supply, competitive factors will exert a different sort of influence on marketing activities than when there are many competitors. Table 3.2 presents four general types of competitive structure: monopoly, oligopoly, monopolistic competition and perfect competition.

monopoly
A market structure that exists when a company turns out a product that has no close substitutes or rivals

A **monopoly** exists when a company turns out a product that has no close substitutes or rivals. Because the organization has no competitors, it completely controls the supply of the product and, as a single seller, can erect barriers to potential competitors. In reality, the monopolies that survive today are some utilities, such as telephone, electricity and some railways (in many countries), and cable companies, which are heavily regulated. These monopolies are tolerated because of the tremendous financial resources needed to develop and operate them; few organizations can obtain the resources to mount any competition against a local electricity producer, for example. An **oligopoly** exists when a few sellers control the supply of a large proportion of a product. In this case, each seller must consider the reactions of other sellers to changes in marketing activities. Products facing oligopolistic competition may be homogeneous, such as aluminium, or differentiated, such as cigarettes and cars. Usually, barriers of some sort make it difficult to enter the market and compete with oligopolies. For example, because of the enormous financial outlay required, few companies or individuals could afford to enter the oil-refining or steel-producing industries. Moreover, some industries demand special technical or marketing skills that block the entry of many potential competitors.

oligopoly
A market structure that exists when a few sellers control the supply of a large proportion of a product

monopolistic competition
A market structure that exists when a business with many potential competitors attempts to develop a differential marketing strategy to establish its own market share

Monopolistic competition exists when an organization with many potential competitors attempts to develop a differential marketing strategy to establish its own market share. For example, Levi has established a differential advantage for its blue jeans through a well-known trademark, design, advertising and a quality image. Although many competing brands of blue jeans are available, this company has carved out its market share through use of a differential marketing strategy. **Perfect competition**, if it existed at all, would entail a large number of sellers, not one of which could significantly influence price or supply. Products would be homogeneous, and there would

perfect competition
A market structure that entails a large number of sellers, not one of which could significantly influence price or supply

TABLE 3.2 Selected characteristics of competitive structures

Type of structure	Number of competitors	Ease of entry into market	Product	Knowledge of market	Examples
Monopoly	One	Many barriers	Almost no substitutes	Perfect	Non-privatized railways, many government departments
Oligopoly	Few	Some barriers	Homogeneous or differentiated (real or perceived differences)	Imperfect	Airlines, petroleum retailers, some utility providers
Monopolistic competition	Many	Few barriers	Product differentiation with many substitutes	More knowledge than oligopoly; less than monopoly	Jeans, fast food, audio-visual
Perfect competition	Unlimited	No barriers	Homogeneous products	Perfect	The London commodity markets, vegetable farms

be full knowledge of the market and easy entry. The closest thing to an example of perfect competition would be an unregulated agricultural market. Few, if any, marketers operate in a structure of perfect competition. Perfect competition is an ideal at one end of the continuum, with monopoly at the other end. Most marketers function in a competitive environment that falls somewhere between these two extremes.

Competitive tools Another set of factors that influences the level of competition is the number and types of competitive tools used by competitors. To survive, an organization uses one or several available competitive tools to deal with competitive economic forces. Once a company has analyzed its particular competitive environment and decided which factors in that environment it can or must adapt to or influence, it can choose among the variables that it can control to strengthen its competitive position in the overall marketplace. Probably the competitive tool that most organizations grasp is price. Bic, for example, markets disposable pens and lighters that are similar to competing products but less expensive. However, there is one major problem with using price as a competitive tool: competitors will often match or beat the price. This threat is one of the primary reasons for employing non-price competitive tools that are based on the differentiation of market segments, product offering, service, promotion, distribution or enterprise.[13]

By focusing on a specific market segment, a marketer sometimes gains a competitive advantage. For instance, Saab cars and Porsche sports coupés are narrowly targeted at specific groups of consumers. Most manufacturers try to gain a competitive edge by incorporating product features that make their brands distinctive to some extent. Companies use distinguishing promotional methods to compete, such as advertising and personal selling. Competing producers sometimes use different distribution channels to prevail over one another. Retailers may compete by placing their outlets in locations that are convenient for a large number of shoppers. Dealers and distributors offer wide ranges, advice and service.

competitor monitoring
The process by which a company studies the actions of its major competitors in order to determine what specific strategies they are following and how those strategies affect its own; also used by marketers as they try to develop competitive advantages, adjust current marketing strategies and plan new ones

Monitoring competition Marketers in an organization need to be aware of the actions of major competitors. They should monitor what competitors are currently doing and assess the changes occurring in the competitive environment, as explained in Chapter 2. **Competitor monitoring** allows organizations to determine what specific strategies competitors are following and how those strategies affect their own. It can also guide marketers as they try to develop competitive advantages and can aid them in adjusting current marketing strategies, as well as in planning new ones. Information may come from direct observation and product testing of competing products, or from sources such as the Web, sales people, customers' feedback and marketing research, trade publications, media comments, online postings, syndicated marketing research services, distributors, supply chain feedback and marketing studies. Unfortunately, less ethical information sources for competitor insights sometimes are utilized. An organization needs information about competitors that will allow its marketing managers to assess the performance of its own marketing efforts. Comparing their company's performance with that of competitors helps marketing managers recognize strengths and weaknesses in their own marketing strategies. Data about market shares, product movement, sales volume and expenditure levels can be useful. However, accurate information on these matters is often difficult to obtain.

Competition exists in most markets and situations. Even charities compete with one another and with manufacturers for consumers' attention and financial commitment. Marketing places an emphasis on meeting consumers' needs and offering satisfaction. To be successful, however, competing organizations need to identify unique marketing programmes; otherwise all rival products and services will merely replicate each other. The search for a competitive edge over competitors is central to effective marketing strategy. As well as monitoring direct competitors, marketers should be aware of new entrants coming into a market with competing propositions, and of the danger of substitute products or services being developed. Marketers' strategic understanding of competition was addressed in Chapter 2.

The micro marketing environment

macro marketing environment
The broader forces affecting all organizations in a market: political, legal, regulatory, societal/green, technological and economic/competitive

Many authors, notably Michael Porter,[14] have made a distinction between the very broad forces of the **macro marketing environment** discussed up to now in this chapter – political, legal, regulatory, societal, technological, economic/competitive – and a set of more company-specific forces often termed the **micro marketing environment** forces. The distinction, put simply, is that the broad macro forces have an impact on every organization operating in a particular market, from manufacturers to distributors to customers, and such an impact is largely universally felt by such organizations. The micro forces, on the other hand, are still forces external to the organization and not directly controllable, but often have an organization-specific impact subject to the characteristics and status of the individual business. For example, a new entrant competitor might only target customer segments currently served by certain existing rivals and not impinge on the activities of other competitors.

micro marketing environment
The more company-specific forces reflecting the nature of the business, its suppliers, marketing intermediaries, buyers, all types of competitors – direct, substitute and new entrant – and its publics

The core aspects of the micro marketing environment

Although categorizations vary among authors, the core aspects of the micro marketing environment worthy of note include the organization itself, suppliers, marketing intermediaries, buyers, competitors and publics (see Figure 3.3).

The organization It is necessary when creating and implementing marketing strategies and marketing mix programmes to consider the reaction, attitudes and abilities of the internal environment: top management, finance, research and development, purchasing, manufacturing, sales and marketing, and logistics. The marketing function's recommendations must be consistent with senior management's corporate goals; be conveyed to other functions within the organization; and reflect colleagues' views, input, concerns and abilities to implement the desired

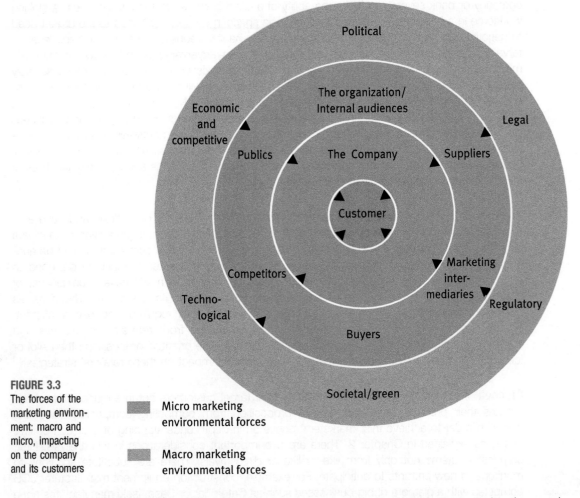

FIGURE 3.3
The forces of the marketing environment: macro and micro, impacting on the company and its customers

Micro marketing environmental forces

Macro marketing environmental forces

marketing plan. Marketers must be aware of these organizational factors, monitor them and modify their actions accordingly to ensure internal take-up of their ideas and plans.

Suppliers Most organizations source raw materials, components or supplies from third parties. Without the understanding and cooperation of these other organizations, a business would fail to deliver a quality product or service that satisfies its customers' needs. Marketers must be aware of aspects of supply that might affect the way in which their organization functions in satisfying its customers. These forces could include supplier innovations; deals with rivals; supply shortages, delays or quality concerns; strikes or recruitment difficulties; legal actions or warranty disputes; supply costs and price trends; new entrants into the supply chain; or anything prone to altering the business's receipt of its required supplies.

Marketing intermediaries Some businesses sell directly to their targeted customers. Most, though, utilize the skills, network and resources of intermediaries to make their products available to the end-user customer. Intermediaries are discussed later (see Part Three) and include resellers such as retailers, wholesalers, agents, brokers, dealers; as well as physical distribution companies responsible for logistical needs; providers of marketing services such as advertising agencies or packaging design consultancies; and financial facilitators of credit lines and export guarantees. Without the smooth cooperation of such intermediaries, an organization is unlikely to be able to deliver its products as required by its customers. For example, the collapse of a credit company or bank severely reduces the ability of a client business to fund its activities. A striking workforce in a business's preferred road haulage space in company will lead to the urgent need to negotiate alternative logistical support with a new haulier, requiring time and perhaps legal intervention given existing contractual arrangements. An advertising agent's new account win might be that of a direct rival to an existing client. The existing client business might sensibly choose to find a different advertising agency, but this move will have a penalty in terms of management time and perhaps the timely execution of a planned advertising campaign.

In each of these examples, shrewd awareness of developments by an organization's marketers would have reduced the likelihood of any impediment to its own activities and ability to serve its own customers. Failure to pick up on any of these events would have resulted in a loss of business as the marketers and colleagues in other business functions sought alternative lines of credit, haulage agreements or advertising expertise.

Buyers Customers are central to the marketing concept. They are often fickle and have ever changing requirements, needs and perceptions, which marketers must understand, anticipate and satisfy. As Chapters 4 and 5 describe, consumers and business customers should be analyzed, and the marketing programme developed by a set of marketers must be designed to satisfy these customers' requirements. Each individual organization will have a unique set of resources, skills, marketing programmes and products to offer its customers. Therefore, as customers' needs evolve, separate businesses will find that their required response is different. As the consumer came to demand more customer service from retailers, John Lewis and Sainsbury's have been better placed to upgrade their service-oriented propositions than Aldi or Iceland. This micro environmental force has had a variable impact on these retailers' strategies.

Competitors Marketers must strive to satisfy their target customers but in a manner that differentiates their product, brand and overall proposition from competing companies' marketing mixes. In order to achieve this, marketers require an in-depth understanding of their competitive arena, as explained in Chapter 2. There are two important considerations in this analysis. First, competition stems not only from like-for-like or direct rivals. There are substitute solutions to monitor and new entrants to anticipate. For example, construction equipment manufacturer JCB competes with a plethora of big businesses such as Caterpillar or Case. Iseki manufactures none of the same equipment, but it produces a micro-bore tunnelling 'mole' that lays pipes without the need to dig trenches, thus rendering the need for a JCB backhoe loader digger redundant. Such substitute competition can seriously erode an organization's market position if not observed and combated. Kindle e-readers have been a non-store competitor for book shop chains such as Waterstones. Facebook has become a rival to long landline-based phone conversations or sometimes meeting face-to-face in a club or bar.

The second consideration is the organization's own position: resources, market standing, capabilities, strengths and any competitive edge held over rivals. These characteristics are different for each organization, so the impact of any competitive activity will vary between businesses. Marketers must be aware of direct, substitute and new entrant competitor activity but should also gauge the likely impact of competition on their own business in the context of a sound understanding of their capabilities and standing as explained in Chapter 2.

In terms of the micro marketing environment, competitors are external forces beyond the direct control of marketers. The impact of a particular competitor will vary for one organization to the next or for one brand to the next in the same market. These are the reasons why competition is included in Porter's view of the micro marketing environment.

Publics The micro marketing environment also includes any group – public – that does or could impact on an organization's ability to satisfy its target customers and achieve its corporate objectives.[15] These include: financial bodies such as banks, investment houses, financial analysts or shareholders; newspaper, magazine, radio, television or Web media that carry features about a business, its products and activities; government bodies that may intervene over operating or consumer issues; consumer and pressure groups; neighbourhood publics such as residents adjacent to a large manufacturing plant; the general public, whose view of an organization must be assessed and taken into account when developing marketing programmes; and internal publics such as the workforce. Most businesses are increasingly recognizing the importance of communicating effectively with these sets of people. The growth of social media and networks such as Facebook or LinkedIn has made communication with publics more straightforward, but has also significantly increased the risk of groups of consumers or other parties instigating discussions about a company's products, services or practices, and not necessarily constructively or positively.

The notion of relationship marketing outlined in Chapter 1 is designed to emphasize the need to address more publics than solely customers through marketing programmes and communications. In order to achieve this effectively, however, it is necessary for an organization to understand these micro marketing environment forces.

The marketing environment and strategic opportunities

strategic windows
Major developments or opportunities triggered by changes in the marketing environment

When changes occur in the marketing environment they can trigger major developments. If large enough, such changes are called **strategic windows** or paradigm shifts.[16] If market leaders have failed to spot the underlying development or evolutionary change, rivals may have an opportunity to gain an advantage over established companies and brands by 'stepping through the open window'. The established company must strive to 'close the window' with its own proposition speedily enough to pre-empt competitors' inroads. For example, global recession created opportunities for value brands at the expense of premium brands, many of which had to work hard to re-engineer their propositions in order to maintain relevance for their customers and to 'close the window' on their upstart rivals. Failure to monitor the marketing environment and take appropriate action invariably results in an organization being unable to react to the change quickly enough to keep out competitors.

Opening strategic windows

Marketing strategists believe there are six broad causes of strategic windows opening, as described below.[17]

New technology Duracell overtook market leader EverReady because it took advantage of new lithium technology before EverReady modified its product range. Direct Line gained leadership in the car insurance market because it turned to direct selling via telephone call centres before any of the major insurance companies recognized this evolving use of technology. Motorola and Nokia, once dominant in mobile phones, were overtaken by smart phone technologies such as Android and the iPhone.

New markets Security services and logistics company G4S (then Securicor) was quick to spot the likely take-off of the mobile phone market, taking the majority share in the then leading network provider Cellnet (now O$_2$). Racal did the same with Vodafone. This awareness of new markets enabled Securicor/Cellnet (O$_2$) and Vodafone to firmly establish themselves as multi-faceted communications businesses.

New distribution channels Ocado, the online grocery retailer, has no supermarkets. Unlike established players such as Tesco or Sainsbury's, it entered the grocery market directly on an eCommerce platform, negating the need to create a store network in order to serve consumers across much of England.

Market redefinition NCR – National Cash Registers – used to dominate the market for providing electronic cash tills in retailers' stores. As retailers discovered the convenience of stock management through barcodes and EPoS systems, they turned to more sophisticated systems. Retail management's desire to monitor and record detailed sales data altered the buyer's requirement for in-store technology. ICL (Fujitsu) and Nixdorf were quick to spot this change and build on their computer industry resources to develop all-in retail systems that incorporated the cash till with much more. This redefinition of the market eroded NCR's once dominant position while giving rivals a marketing opportunity.

New legislation and regulation Laws, regulations and international agreements create strategic windows. The 'open skies' policy of the EU has created route opportunities for smaller airlines once precluded from hubs by state-protected national airlines. Privatization of the UK rail network enabled Stagecoach and Virgin to diversify their businesses into rail services. Growth of the EU presented new trading opportunities in eastern Europe for EU member states, but not all companies were quick to recognize the opportunities for business growth in this region.

Financial and political 'shocks' Sudden changes in currency prices, interest rates, trade agreements, inflation, unemployment levels, protectionist policies or political leadership can have a major impact on business. A new government might decide to privatize state-owned assets or regulate an industry's activities more tightly. A trade war between states will impact on organizations operating in such markets. The UK's approach to addressing the global financial crisis has been very different under the Conservative/LibDem Coalition than had there been a Labour Government, with implications for many companies serving the public sector which faced large budget cuts and job losses.

The importance of keeping a lookout for the strategic window

Often managers only notice sales dips months after a marketing environment force has created a problem. In the meantime, this has created a window for competitors to enter. While there are many psychological factors that can hinder managerial activity, such as a preference for retrenchment and an aversion to change,[18] a common problem is simply the failure to formally and routinely monitor the forces of the marketing environment through environmental scanning – the process of collecting and analyzing information about the forces of the marketing environment. An organization must determine which aspects of the marketing environment – macro and micro – to monitor and how. Strategists believe a regular and routinized system enables identification of strongly signalled issues, which senior management or a marketing function can then prioritize for more detailed investigation. Clearly, given the vast array of issues examined in this chapter, it is not feasible or desirable for a set of managers to address every conceivably pertinent facet of the trading environment. However, failure to examine the marketing environment is a major problem for many poorly run organizations lacking a marketing orientation.

As described in the Marketing Tools and Techniques box (see page 86), companies opt for different solutions.[19] Some require line managers to undertake environmental scanning in addition to their other responsibilities. Occasionally, a strategic planner undertakes such monitoring, although this head office position is often too divorced from the organization's operations to identify which crucial core forces to investigate. Consultancies may be handed the task. A few large companies have created a bespoke marketing environment unit of cross-functional managers responsible for researching, analyzing, disseminating and recommending. This ensures scanning occurs but is costly and, again, can be too removed from a company's operations. More frequently, marketing planning identifies core trends and evolving forces to monitor.[20]

Marketing planning is practised in most medium-sized and large companies, and part of the cross-functional, multi-hierarchical team's remit is to report annually on marketing environment forces likely to have implications for the organization.

Some companies have no more than a box in the centre of an open-plan office in which any manager can deposit marketing environment information stemming from press comments, customer feedback, dealer observations, trade show intelligence, analysts' reports or any other inputs. This material is sifted regularly, summarized and circulated, with individual issues followed up as determined necessary by managerial judgement. Other organizations have formalized this approach using e-mail newsletters, intranet boards or a wiki for personnel and sites within the organization, often globally, with interactive dialogue aiding the understanding of the environmental forces noted.

PEST analysis/PESTLE analysis
PEST is a popular name for an evaluation of the marketing environment, looking at political – including legal and regulatory issues – economic, social and technological developments, and assessing the implications of such issues. Another term used by marketers is PESTLE – political, economic, societal, technological, legal and environmental forces.

No matter how it is orchestrated, it is essential that the marketing environment is monitored thoroughly and regularly.[21] This must translate into managerial recommendations when necessary, with target market strategies and marketing programmes reflecting the issues identified. Such an analysis is often termed by marketing managers as a **PEST analysis**, looking at political (P) – including legal and regulatory issues – economic (E), social (S) and technological (T) developments, and assessing the implications of such issues, or it is referred to as a **PESTLE analysis** (political, economic, societal, technological, legal and environmental issues). An understanding of the marketing environment – macro and micro forces – is essential for a rigorous and meaningful assessment of marketing opportunities.

Without such an analysis, any recommended marketing strategy is unlikely to take account of newly opening strategic windows. Competitors may be offered the chance to make inroads and the organization may fail to benefit from potential marketing opportunities. Threats will go unnoticed until they are damaging a company's revenues.

Summary

The *marketing environment* consists of external forces that directly or indirectly influence an organization's acquisition of inputs (personnel, financial resources, raw materials, information) and generation of outputs (information, packages, goods, services, ideas). Generally, the forces of the marketing environment are divided into two categories: macro and micro. The macro marketing environment comprises political, legal and regulatory forces, societal forces, including concerns for the earth's natural environment, and technological forces. Along with economic forces and trends, these macro, broader, aspects of the marketing environment have an impact on manufacturers and their customers. The forces of the micro marketing environment are more company-specific and include the organization's internal environment, suppliers, marketing intermediaries, buyers, specific competitors and publics.

To monitor changes in these forces, marketers should practise environmental scanning and analysis. *Environmental scanning* is the process of collecting information about the forces in the marketing environment; *environmental analysis* is the process of assessing and interpreting the information obtained in scanning. This information helps marketing managers predict opportunities and threats associated with environmental fluctuation. Marketing management may assume either a passive, reactive approach or an active, aggressive approach in responding to these environmental fluctuations. The choice depends on an organization's structure and needs, and on the composition of the environmental forces.

The political, legal and regulatory forces of the marketing environment are closely interrelated. The current political outlook is reflected in legislation and regulations, or the lack of them. The political environment may determine what laws and regulations affecting specific marketers are enacted, and how much the government purchases and from which suppliers; it can also be important in helping organizations secure foreign markets.

Legislation affecting marketing activities can be divided into *procompetitive legislation* – laws designed to preserve competition and to end various practices deemed unacceptable by society – and consumer protection laws. In the UK, the Restrictive Trade Practices Act and the Competition Act sought to prevent monopolies and activities that limit competition; while legislation such as the Financial Services Act, the Sale of Goods Act and the Consumer Credit Act was directed towards more specific practices. Consumer protection laws generally relate to product safety and information disclosure. The actual effects of legislation are determined by how marketers and the courts interpret the laws.

Regulatory agencies influence most marketing activities. For example, in the UK the *Competition Commission* and the *Office of Fair Trading* (being merged) usually have the power to enforce specific laws and some discretion in establishing operating rules and drawing up regulations to guide certain types of industry practice. Self-regulation by industry represents another regulatory force; marketers are more in favour of this type of regulation than government action, because they have more opportunity to take part in creating the guidelines. Self-regulation may be less expensive than government regulation, and its guidelines are often more realistic. However, such regulation generally cannot assure compliance as effectively as government agencies.

Societal forces refer to the structure and dynamics of individuals and groups, and the issues that concern them. Many members of society want a high standard of living and a high quality of life, and they expect business to help them achieve these goals. Of growing concern is the well-being of the earth, its resources, climate and peoples. The *Green movement* is increasing general awareness of the natural environment and sustainability, and is altering product design, manufacture, packaging and use. The *consumer movement* is a diverse collection of independent individuals, groups and organizations that attempt to protect the rights of consumers. The major issues taken up by the consumer movement fall into three categories: environmental protection, product performance and safety, and information disclosure. Consumer rights organizations inform and organize other consumers, raise issues, help organizations develop consumer-oriented programmes and pressure legislators to enact consumer protection laws. Some are quite formally organized, such as the *Consumers' Association*.

Technology is the knowledge of how to accomplish tasks and goals. Product development, packaging, promotion, prices and distribution systems are all influenced directly by technology. Several factors determine how much and in what way a particular organization will make use of technology. These factors include the company's ability to use technology;

consumers' ability and willingness to buy technologically improved products; the business's perception of the long-term effects of applying technology; the extent to which the company is technologically based; the degree to which technology is used as a competitive tool; and the extent to which the business can protect technological applications through patents. Many organizations conduct a *technology assessment*. For marketers, technological forces of the marketing environment have provided significant consequences in recent years, particularly in terms of more sophisticated *customer relationship management* systems, eMarketing with web-based communications and selling, *mobile marketing* and *social media* fostering greater consumer-to-consumer communication about products, brands and companies' activities. The *digital marketing* era has radically impacted on marketing.

The *economic forces* that can strongly influence marketing decisions and activities are general economic conditions, buying power, willingness to spend, spending patterns and *competitive forces*. The overall state of the economy fluctuates in a general pattern known as the *business cycle*. The stages of the business cycle are *prosperity, recession, depression and recovery*.

Consumers' goods, services and financial holdings make up their *buying power*—their ability to purchase. The financial sources of *buying power* are *income*, credit and wealth. After-tax income used for spending or saving is called *disposable income*. Disposable income left after an individual has purchased the basic necessities of food, clothing and shelter is called discretionary income. It is important to identify levels of *wealth*. Two measures of buying power are: effective buying income (which includes salaries, wages, dividends, interest, profits and rents, less taxes); and the buying power index (a weighted index consisting of population, effective buying income and retail sales data). The factors that affect consumers' *willingness to spend* are product price, the level of satisfaction obtained from currently used products, and expectations about future employment, family size, income, prices and general economic conditions. *Consumer spending patterns* indicate the relative proportions of annual family expenditures, or the actual amount of money spent, on certain kinds of goods and services. *Comprehensive spending patterns* specify the percentages of family income allotted to annual expenditures for general classes of goods and services. *Product-specific spending patterns* indicate the annual amounts families spend for specific products within a general product class.

Competition is a fundamental concern for all marketers. Although all businesses compete for consumers' spending, a company's direct competitors are usually the organizations in its geographic area marketing products that resemble its own or which can be substituted for them. The number of businesses that control the supply of a product may affect the strength of competition. There are four general types of competitive structure: *monopoly, oligopoly, monopolistic competition* and *perfect competition*. Marketers use *competitor monitoring* to determine what competitors are currently doing and to assess the changes occurring in the competitive environment.

Increasingly, marketers make a distinction between the broader trading *macro marketing environment* forces – political, legal, regulatory, societal, technological, economic/competitive – and the more company-specific forces of the *micro marketing environment*. Micro forces include the organization in question, its suppliers, marketing intermediaries, buyers, business-specific competition – direct, substitute and new entrant rivals – and the various publics of an organization: financial bodies, media, government, consumer and pressure groups, neighbours, the general public and the internal workforce.

Changes in the marketing environment often create *strategic windows* that, if they are not quickly identified, can enable rivals to gain an edge. There are six key causes of the creation of strategic windows, all aspects of the macro or micro marketing environment: new technology, new markets, new distribution channels, market redefinition, new legislation and regulation, plus financial and political 'shocks'. Often, managers fail to notice sales dips until months after the impact of an aspect of the marketing environment. This may be because they are averse to change and prefer retrenchment, but often it stems from a lack of environmental scanning. Strategists believe a regular and routinized assessment of the marketing environment is essential prior to the formulation of any target market strategies or marketing mix programmes. Practitioners often term such an assessment a *PEST analysis* or *PESTLE analysis*. Companies adopt different solutions to monitoring the marketing environment, it can be carried out by: line managers, strategic planners, consultants, specialist units or be incorporated as an integral part of the annual marketing planning process. It is essential that the marketing environment – macro and micro forces – is monitored continually in order to maximize marketing opportunities and fend off competitors' actions.

Key links

Marketers must analyze the marketing environment in order to identify opportunities and minimize threats. This chapter should be read in conjunction with:

- Chapter 1, examining marketing opportunity analysis.
- Chapter 2, the overview of marketing strategy development.

Important terms

Marketing environment
Environmental scanning
Environmental analysis
Procompetitive legislation
Office of Fair Trading
Competition Commission
Consumers' Association
Societal forces
Green movement
Consumer movement
Technology
Technology assessment
Customer relationship management
Mobile marketing
Social media
Digital marketing
Economic and competitive forces
Business cycle
Prosperity
Recession
Depression
Recovery
Buying power
Income
Disposable income
Discretionary income
Wealth
Willingness to spend
Consumer spending patterns
Comprehensive spending patterns
Product-specific spending patterns
Competition
Monopoly
Oligopoly
Monopolistic competition
Perfect competition
Competitor monitoring

Macro marketing environment
Micro marketing environment
Strategic windows
PEST analysis/PESTLE analysis

Discussion and review questions

1 Why are environmental scanning and analysis so important?

2 How are political forces related to legal and regulatory forces?

3 Describe marketers' attempts to influence political forces.

4 What types of procompetitive legislation directly affect marketing practices?

5 What is the major objective of most procompetitive laws? Do the laws generally accomplish this objective? Why or why not?

6 What types of problem do marketers experience as they interpret legislation?

7 What are the goals of the Competition Commission? How does the Commission affect marketing activities?

8 Name several non-governmental regulatory forces. Do you believe that self-regulation is more or less effective than governmental regulatory agencies? Why?

9 How is the so-called 'Green movement' altering the shape of business?

10 Describe the consumer movement. Analyze some active consumer forces in your area.

11 What does the term 'technology' mean to you?

12 How does technology affect you as a member of society? Do the benefits of technology outweigh its costs and dangers?

13 Discuss the impact of technology on marketing activities.

14 What factors determine whether an organization adopts and uses technology?

15 In what ways can each of the business cycle stages affect consumers' reactions to marketing strategies?

16 What is the current business cycle stage? How is this stage affecting businesses in your area?

17 Define income, disposable income and discretionary income. How does each type of income affect consumer buying power?

18 How is consumer buying power affected by wealth and consumer credit?

19 How is buying power measured? Why should it be evaluated?

20 What factors influence a consumer's willingness to spend?

21 What are the principal types of competition?

22 What differentiates the forces of the micro marketing environment from those of the macro marketing environment?

23 Why must marketers monitor changes in supplier and marketing intermediary practices?

24 Why should marketers not only track direct, like-for-like competitors? What other types of competitor are there?

25 Why should marketers be aware of their organization's publics?

26 How does an assessment of marketing environment forces assist in marketing opportunity analysis?

27 What are the main causes of the opening of strategic windows?

28 How can a business instigate environmental scanning?

Recommended readings

Blythe, J. and Megicks, P., *Marketing Planning: Strategy, Environment and Context* (FT Prentice-Hall, 2010).

Dibb, S. and Simkin, L., *Marketing Planning* (Cengage, 2008).

Drucker, P., *Management in Turbulent Times* (Butterworth-Heinemann/Pan, 1994).

Palmer, A., Worthington, I., Hartley, B. and Mulholland, M., *The Business and Marketing Environment* (McGraw-Hill, 1999).

Porter, M.E., 'How competitive forces shape strategy', *Harvard Business Review*, March–April 1979, pp. 137–45.

Worthington, I. and Britton, C., *The Business Environment* (FT Prentice-Hall, 2009).

Applied mini-case

Until recently, excepting the low-sugar variants, few observers would have included the producers of the leading colas as aiding healthy diets or encouraging greater awareness of obesity issues. First, the leading suppliers launched low-carb versions, and now they are proactively striving to educate consumers. Coca-Cola, for example, launched a major initiative to encourage people to exercise more. Coke launched an anti-obesity campaign under the title 'Active Lifestyle', engaging with young people through a variety of media. The initiative aimed to promote the route to a healthy lifestyle through a combination of effective hydration, a balanced diet and physical activity. Today, its website has a wide array of health-related messages and educational campaigns (**http://www.coca-cola.co.uk**).

Sources: Coca-Cola, 2004; Ben Bold, 'Coca-Cola debuts healthy living initiative in UK', *Marketing*, 1 July 2004, p. 1; **http://www.coca-cola.co.uk/?kid=sr3_43523989_go&WT.srch=1**, 18 February 2011.

Question

As Coca-Cola's marketing manager, how would an understanding of the marketing environment have led to the *Health* initiatives now promoted on its web pages? How might the company have monitored the forces of its marketing environment?

Internet exercise

Choose the websites of key government departments, EU departments or of leading regulatory bodies and learn more about the ways in which their activities and powers impact on marketers and consumers. For example, log on to the websites for the Competition Commission and the Office of Fair Trading at: **www.competition-commission.org.uk** and **www.oft.gov.uk**

1 What are the implications of these organizations' powers and recommendations for marketers?

2 In what ways do the activities of these bodies impact on consumers?

The world of rice: external challenges for Tilda's marketers

Known as the 'Prince of Rice', basmati can only be grown in one place on earth – at the foothills of the Himalayas. It is here where the combination of unique climate and soil conditions allow basmati to truly flourish. We select the highest quality pure basmati from over 10 000 independent farmers, all of whom we know by name.

www.tilda.com, February, 2011

Tilda is rightly proud of basmati rice, which it is largely responsible for introducing to the UK and many other markets. Today, basmati accounts for 46 per cent of all UK rice sales, or around £72m, much of which comes from Tilda. Something of a 'supergrain', being gluten-free and low in fat, basmati is a delicate, light, fluffy grain with a wonderful aroma, literally translated it is 'the fragrant one'. However, with the need to help protect the single annual harvest, a fairplay buying policy with farmers, storing grains until they are suitably mature, and Tilda's long-held belief in providing consistency to the consumer's experience with extensive and fastidious milling techniques, comes a high price. Compared with many other rices, basmati is far from cheap and Tilda's is premium-priced to reflect the quality of its famously blue-bagged basmati.

A difficulty of premium-pricing is that if external factors force changes to supply costs or to the availability of quality rice, there are difficulties in raising further retail prices or in maintaining such prices, especially if the harvest leads to inferior grains in a particular season. In recent years, Tilda's marketers have faced a number of challenges, none of which has been in their control or a result of Tilda's decisions.

A couple of years ago, the world's rice harvest was poor, with basmati badly affected. Tilda has no control over the rains and climatic conditions necessary for a good harvest. The quality of the grain was poorer, but there was also much lower volume available to purchase from the farmers. Inevitably, raw material prices soared. Tilda had to almost double its retail prices in order to cover the costs of acquiring adequate tonnages and for the extra milling activities required to provide discerning consumers with an appropriate cooking and taste experience. Sales dropped, as many consumers were priced out of buying this 'Prince of Rice'. No-one could have predicted the poor harvest and huge rise in world rice prices.

Owing to rice shortages, largely caused by poor harvests, the Indian Government had to protect supplies of this staple food for its own population. As basmati in its purest form comes only from the foothills of the Himalayas, any ban on exports from India would catastrophically impact on the basmati part of Tilda's rice business. Tilda's stock pile of reserves was just adequate to cover the period of the ban, but the company's marketers and executives felt significant pressure from this regulatory pressure thousands of miles from its Essex milling base.

Tilda's sourcing of basmati, from farmers the company knows and who nurture their rice using traditional methods, precludes the use of GM rices. However, a leading competitor allowed GM grains to enter its supply chain, causing negative publicity for rice in the press and in Government circles, not only for its own brand but for rice in general. Although Tilda had no link with this adulterated rice, the company had to invest significant time and resources to explaining this and to reassuring its retail stockists.

The global economic meltdown has caused many consumers to revaluate their consumption patterns and spending priorities. Tilda has many ranges and brands, catering for most rice-eating communities and consumer segments, but its flagship brand, Tilda basmati, is premium priced and branded to reflect its status amongst rices. Few observers predicted the credit crunch or its longer-term implications on global finances and consumer priorities. Most premium brands, such as BMW or John Lewis, have worked very hard to re-engineer the propositions to provide relevance and value for target consumers. Upmarket grocer Waitrose is now well-known for its *Essentials* range and competitive pricing comparison for 1000 brands versus Tesco. Tilda's marketers also had to come up with a value-based proposition, launching its *Everyday Rice* range.

The above examples are aspects of Tilda's macro marketing environment, but micro marketing environmental forces are also important for Tilda's marketers. The economic crisis has forced retailers to re-think their strategies and merchandising, putting pressure on suppliers such as Tilda to reduce prices and margins offered to trade customers, the major supermarkets. Many retailers are seeking ways for reducing their carbon footprints to reflect social and regulatory pressures, in turn demanding lower delivery miles, environmentally responsible packaging and altered manufacturing processes from their suppliers, such as Tilda. Such buyer pressures are commonplace for marketers examining the micro environment. The rise of own label has been an issue for Tilda and its leading branded competitors such as Uncle Ben's, Veetee or

Kohinoor, and is an example of the competitive forces within the micro marketing environment.

Readers should not think that the marketing environment brings little good news to a company's marketers. The increased attention by Government, nutritionists, medics, educationalists, the media and many food producers to healthier eating presents an opportunity for Tilda, as many health experts and nutritionists believe rice to be preferable to other carbs such as potatoes and pasta. Within the rice arena, basmati has specific health-attributes, being gluten-free, low in fat, very low in sodium, with no cholesterol and containing all eight essential amino acids. Perfect for diabetic sufferers and very useful in many diets as an alternative to chips or butter-filled jacket potatoes, there is a window of opportunity for rice producers such as Tilda caused by obesity scares and healthier eating social marketing initiatives from various state bodies, medics and the media.

These are just a few examples of how external forces impact on one large food company, but Tilda is far from being alone in facing such a diverse and never-ending set of externally-derived challenges, many of which flair up unexpectedly. The demands on marketers in such companies are to identify such issues and raise awareness of their concerns, where possible in advance of any negative impact on customer demand, performance or brands; and, to provide suggestions for how best to navigate such market conditions. Inevitably, even the most tuned-in marketers on occasion are caught out by surprising events. In such circumstances, the expectation is that marketers will quickly evaluate and propose a plan for addressing the issue in question. All organizations face a myriad of challenges from their marketing environments. It should be the onus of marketers to be the 'eyes and ears' for their organizations, so as to foster an understanding of the issues and their implications.

Questions for discussion

1 Which of the issues faced by Tilda's marketers would cause them the most concern and why?

2 What approaches could a company such as Tilda adopt in order to develop a sound appreciation of changes to its marketing environment?

3 Why might marketers struggle to gain appropriate insights into aspects of their marketing environments?

Sources: **http://www.tilda.com**, February 2011; **http://www.waitrose.com/footer/corporateinformation**, February, 2011; **http://www.riceassociation.org.uk**, 20 February 2011; **http://www.rice-trade.com/rice-nutritional-facts**, 20 February 2011, Tilda, 2012.

CHAPTER 4

Consumer buying behaviour

"Getting into the heads and hearts of consumers is the fundamental requirement of marketing"

Objectives

- To understand the different types of consumer buying behaviour

- To recognize the stages of the consumer buying decision process and understand how this process relates to different types of buying decisions

- To explore how personal factors may affect the consumer buying decision process

- To learn about the psychological factors that may affect the consumer buying decision process

- To examine the social factors that influence the consumer buying decision process

- To understand why it is important for marketers to attempt to understand consumer buying behaviour and the role of this behaviour in marketing strategy

- To appreciate the growing role of consumer-to-consumer communication and the digital environment regarding buying behaviour.

INTRODUCTION

The decision processes and actions of people involved in buying and using products are termed their **buying behaviour**.[1] **Consumer buying behaviour** is the buying behaviour of ultimate consumers – those who purchase products for personal or household family use. Consumer buying behaviour is not concerned with the purchase of items for business use. The next chapter of *Marketing Essentials* examines business or organizational buying behaviour.

> **buying behaviour**
> The decision processes and actions of people involved in buying and using products

> **consumer buying behaviour**
> The buying behaviour of ultimate consumers – those who purchase products for personal or household use

There are important reasons for marketers to analyze consumer buying behaviour. The success of a company's marketing strategy will depend on how buyers react to it. As Chapter 1 indicated, the marketing concept requires companies to develop a marketing mix that meets customers' needs. To find out what satisfies customers, marketers must examine the main influences on what, where, when and how consumers buy. Having a good understanding of these consumer buying behaviour factors enables marketers to satisfy customers better because they are able to develop more suitable marketing strategies. Ultimately, this information helps companies compete more effectively in the marketplace.

Although marketers try to understand and influence consumer buying behaviour, they cannot control it. Some critics credit them with the ability to manipulate buyers, but marketers have neither the power nor the knowledge to do so. Their knowledge of behaviour comes from what psychologists, social psychologists and sociologists know about human behaviour in general.

Raleigh cycles to stay in touch with consumers

From its 19th century roots as a British bicycle company, Raleigh has developed a worldwide reputation for marketing sturdy, comfortable, steel-frame bicycles. The firm, named for the street in Nottingham, England, where it was originally located, was a trend-setter in designing and manufacturing bicycles. Despite being an iconic brand, the company has to keep a close eye on changing consumer tastes and behaviour. As a result of these insights and inspired by the European tradition of getting around by bike, Raleigh is developing new models for contemporary consumers that are lighter, faster and better. New owners Accell plan to accelerate these developments.

Raleigh's marketers know how important it is for consumers to find out about and try out their products. In recent years they have stepped up the practice of bringing demonstration fleets to public places where potential buyers can hop on one of the company's bicycles and pedal for a few minutes. The idea is to allow consumers who enjoy bicycling to actually experience the fun feeling of riding a Raleigh. As Raleigh seeks to increase its share of the US bike market, it is sending representatives out to visit bicycle races and meet cyclists in cities and towns across America. The company wants to encourage discussion about Raleigh and about cycling in general, so that it can gain feedback on Raleigh products and on the factors which influence purchase.

To stay in touch with current and potential customers, Raleigh is increasingly active in social media. It has several thousand fans who visit its Facebook page to see the latest product concepts and post their own photos and comments about Raleigh bicycles. It also uses Twitter to keep customers informed and answer questions about its bicycles and upcoming demonstration events. The company's main blog communicates the latest news about everything from frame design and new bike colours under consideration to product awards and racing activities.

By listening to customers and showing that it understands the daily life of its target market, Raleigh is developing a better understanding of consumer buying in this marketplace, and wheeling toward higher sales.

© Matt Bristow / Alamy

When someone decides to buy a new bicycle, there are many factors directing their choices and numerous underlying motivations. Raleigh must understand these behaviours and influences. Any set of marketers has a responsibility to explore the buying behaviour of intended purchasers and those consumers expected to return for more. Chapter 4 begins by examining the types of decision-making in which consumers engage. The chapter then analyzes the major stages of the consumer buying decision process and the personal, psychological and social factors that influence it. How the growth of social media and consumer-to-consumer communication is changing how individuals buy is considered next. Finally, the chapter examines why marketers must develop a good understanding of consumer buying behaviour.

Types of consumer buying behaviour

Different consumers have a varied and wide range of needs and wants. The acquisition of products and services helps these consumers to satisfy their current and future needs. To achieve this objective, consumers make many purchasing decisions. For example, people make many decisions daily regarding food, clothing, shelter, medical care, education, recreation or transport. When making these decisions, they engage in decision-making behaviour. The amount of time and effort, both mental and physical, that buyers expend in decision-making varies considerably from situation to situation – and from consumer to consumer. Consumer decisions can thus be classified into one of three broad categories: routine response behaviour, limited decision-making and extensive decision-making.[2]

Routine response behaviour

routine response behaviour
Behaviour that occurs when buying frequently purchased, low-cost, low-risk items that need little search and decision effort

A consumer practises **routine response behaviour** when buying frequently purchased, low-cost, low-risk items that need very little search and decision effort. When buying such items, a consumer may prefer a particular brand, but will probably be familiar with several brands in the product class and view more than one as acceptable. The products a consumer buys through routine response behaviour are purchased almost automatically. For most buyers, the time and effort involved in selecting a bag of sugar or a bar of soap is minimal. If the supermarket has run out of the preferred brand, the buyers will probably choose an alternative brand instead.

Limited decision-making

limited decision-making
Behaviour that occurs when buying products purchased only occasionally, for which a moderate amount of information gathering and deliberation is needed

Buyers engage in **limited decision-making** when they buy products occasionally and when they need to obtain information about an unfamiliar brand in a familiar product category. This type of decision-making requires a moderate amount of time for information gathering and deliberation. For example, when a new Wii game is launched aimed at teenagers, buyers may seek additional information about the new product, perhaps by asking a friend who has tried the game or seen it reviewed. Similarly, if a well-known brand appears in a new form, the consumer will take extra time to consider whether to buy it.

Extensive decision-making

extensive decision making
Behaviour that occurs when a purchase involves unfamiliar, expensive, high-risk or infrequently bought products for which the buyer spends much time seeking information and comparing brands before deciding on the purchase

The most complex decision-making behaviour, **extensive decision-making**, comes into play when a purchase involves unfamiliar, expensive, high-risk or infrequently bought products – for instance, cars, homes, holidays or personal pensions. The buyer uses many criteria to evaluate alternative brands or choices, and takes time seeking information and comparing alternative brands before making the purchase decision.

impulse buying
Behaviour that involves no conscious planning but results from a powerful, persistent urge to buy something immediately

Impulse buying By contrast, **impulse buying** involves no conscious planning but a powerful, persistent urge to buy something immediately. Self-control failure is one factor that appears to affect whether or not consumers indulge in this kind of buying.[3] As the Marketing Insight box explains, research suggests that consumers are increasingly engaging in impulse buying. Sophisticated point of sales (POS) displays are part of the reason. For some individuals, impulse buying may be the dominant buying behaviour. Impulse buying, however, often provokes emotional conflict. For example, a young woman buying a new outfit for clubbing, may later regret the expense because a friend has purchased the same item or she only uses the outfit once. Marketers often capitalize on the tendency towards impulse buying – for example, by placing magazines and confectionery next to supermarket checkout counters.

How point of sale is changing how we shop

Topical insight

When did you last buy something that you spotted on promotion? Consumers who make such purchases are often responding to a point of sale promotion (POS). There is evidence that we are all becoming more impulsive in our shopping behaviour. We are more likely to buy items on impulse and there has been a trend away from carefully planned shopping trips. Research findings suggest that for the purchase of clothing, food, toiletries, computer games, PDAs, MP3 players, mobile phones and home electronics there are increasing levels of impulse buying.

POS tools are an important element in this picture. In the past POS tools were mostly used to offer one-off promotions, such as buy one, get one free. Now a new generation of POS is working much harder to educate consumers about product features, explain how they work, or to deliver messages about product fit with people's lifestyle. Asda recently promoted Johnson & Johnson baby bath products using a branded bath and rubber duct tray. As the Asda baby products buyer explained 'It brings some theatre to the area without taking up precious selling shelf space, highlights that it's a new product and demonstrates what the product actually is'. Meanwhile Burberry has been streaming live images of its fashion shows direct to video walls in its stores. Such a move is designed to inspire consumers about the brand, the image it creates, and how this might fit into their lives.

Technological advances, such as the development of digital signage, are increasing the possibilities for POS.

Fashion retailer New Look has added in-store screens that can promote new lines while entertaining store visitors at the same time. The real beauty is that messages can be tailored to suit the location and store catchment, and can be readily changed to reflect new offers. Customers in the Birmingham store benefit from fitting room cameras allowing them to see the clothes they are trying from all sides; while those in Dublin can upload a photo to create their own fashion magazine cover, which is shown on the store's screens.

Other developments include 3D signage and augmented reality displays. Toy manufacturer Lego has created a system where customers can put a product box next to a screen to show an image of the constructed product. Lego customers who use the screens are so excited by these new displays that they have increased what they spend by up to 40 per cent. Mobile barcode technology is also allowing consumers to interact more closely with the brands they buy at the point of purchase. Customers can use their camera phones to snap the on-shelf codes, then use it to connect with information on the brand's website. In some cases, manufacturers like H & M are combining this approach with barcode coupons sent via SMS.

Sources: Kate Hilpern, 'POS persuasion', *The Marketer*, May 2011, pp. 28–32; Caroline Parry, 'Enthusiastic for listless shopping',*Marketing Week*, 4 March 2004, pp. 30–1; shopping habit surveys, 2007, Touchwood in Solihull, 2012.

Variations in decision-making behaviour

The purchase of a particular product does not always elicit the same type of decision-making behaviour.[4] In some instances, buyers engage in extensive decision-making the first time they purchase a certain kind of product but find that limited decision-making suffices when they buy the product again. If a routinely purchased brand no longer pleases the consumer, either limited or extensive decision processes may be used to switch to a new brand. For example, if the batteries that a family buys to power electronic gadgets such as digital cameras become used up too quickly, a different brand may be chosen in future.

consumer buying decision process
A five-stage process that includes problem recognition, information search, evaluation of alternatives, purchase and post-purchase evaluation

The consumer buying decision process

A major part of buying behaviour is the decision process used in making purchases. The **consumer buying decision process**, shown in Figure 4.1, includes five stages:

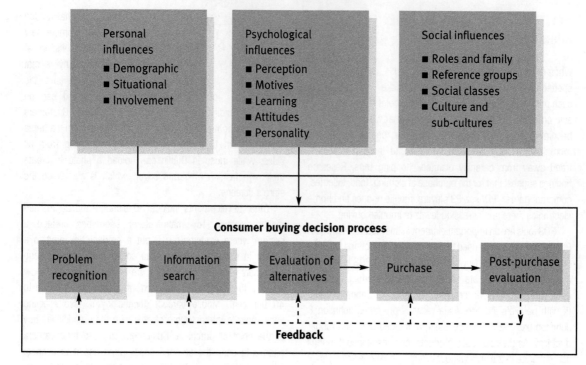

FIGURE 4.1
The consumer buying decision process and possible influences on the process

1 problem recognition

2 information search

3 evaluation of alternatives

4 purchase

5 post-purchase evaluation.

Although a detailed understanding of these stages is needed, a number of general observations are also pertinent. First, the actual act of purchasing is only one stage in the process; the process begins several stages before the purchase itself. Second, not all decision processes lead to a purchase, even though the diagrammatical process implies that they do. A consumer may stop the process at any time. It is also possible that a different sequence of stages will be followed, with buyers revisiting certain stages. Finally, consumer decisions do not always include all five stages. People engaged in extensive decision making usually go through all stages of this decision process, whereas those engaged in limited decision making and routine response behaviour may omit certain parts, leaping from problem recognition (need) to purchase.

Stage 1: Problem recognition

Problem recognition occurs when a buyer becomes aware that there is a difference between a desired state and an actual condition. For example, consider a sales manager who needs to keep a record of appointments. When, at the end of the year, her old diary is finished, she recognizes that a difference exists between the desired state (a current diary) and the actual condition (an out-of-date one). She therefore makes the decision to buy a new diary.

Sometimes a person has a problem or need but is unaware of it. Some consumers may be concerned about their weight but may not be aware that low-calorie options exist for favourite

FIGURE 4.2
Along with the Web, travel agents provide a valuable source of information for consumers selecting a holiday
Photo © Royalty-Free / CORBIS

products. Marketers use sales staff, advertising, sales promotion and packaging to help trigger such need recognition. This is why travel agents often advertise package holidays immediately after the Christmas and New Year holidays. People who see the advertisements may realize that now is a good time to plan their summer holidays. The speed of consumer problem recognition can be either slow or rapid, depending on the individual concerned and the way in which need recognition was triggered.

Stage 2: Information search

After recognizing the problem or need, the buyer (if continuing the decision process) searches for information about products that will resolve the problem or satisfy the need. For example, after people have recognized the need to plan their holiday, they may search for information about different tour operators, travel options and possible locations. Information is acquired over time from the consumer's surroundings and, ever more frequently, on the Internet. The impact the information has will depend on how the consumer interprets it.

internal search
One in which the buyer searches his or her memory for information about products

external search
One that focuses on information not available from the consumer's memory

There are two aspects to information search. In the **internal search**, buyers search their memory for information about products that might solve the problem. If they cannot retrieve enough information from their memory to make a decision, they seek additional information in an **external search**. The external search may involve communicating with friends and colleagues, comparing available brands and prices, looking at offers on the Internet, reading reviews on social networking sites or reviewing press advertisements. An individual's personal contacts – friends, relatives, associates – are often viewed as credible sources of information because the consumer trusts and respects them. A consumer study has shown that word-of-mouth communication often impacts more strongly on consumer judgements of products than printed communications. Using marketer-dominated information sources, such as sales staff, advertising, packaging, corporate websites, in-store demonstrations and displays, typically does not require much effort on the consumer's part. Buyers can also obtain information from public sources – for instance, government reports, news stories, the Internet, consumer publications and reports from product testing organizations. Many companies use public relations to try to capitalize on these sources because consumers often perceive them as factual and unbiased. The external search is also characterized by the extensiveness, manner and order in which brands, stores, attributes and sources are considered. For example, a man buying a new suit for work may look at or try on several styles at a number of clothing outlets before reaching a final decision.

Consumer groups are increasingly demanding access to greater quantities of relevant product information. However, research shows that buyers make poorer choices if overloaded with too much information.[5] Improving the quality of information and stressing features important to buyers in the decision process may help buyers make better purchase decisions.

How consumers use and process the information obtained in their search depends on features of the information itself, namely availability, quantity, quality, repetition and format. If all the necessary information for a decision is readily to hand, either in-store or online, consumers may have no need to conduct an internal information search and the decision process may be easier.[6] However, adequate information may not always be available, and consumers may have to make do with whatever data are to hand. For example, a motorist replacing a broken windscreen following a road accident may not have enough time to review all relevant sources of information because the car is needed again urgently.

Repetition Repetition, a technique well known to advertisers, increases consumer learning of information. When seeing or hearing an advertisement for the first time, the recipient may not grasp all its important details but learns more as the message is repeated. Nevertheless, even when commercials are initially effective, repetition eventually causes 'wear-out': consumers pay less attention and respond less favourably to the advertisement than they did at first.[7] Consumers are more likely to be receptive to repetition when making a low-involvement purchase. **Involvement** refers to the level of interest, emotion and activity the consumer is prepared to expend on a particular purchase. For example, a consumer who buys a potting compost for their garden, may have very low interest in the product itself but may elect to buy the particular brand because it has been discounted at their local garden centre.

involvement
The level of interest, emotion and activity the consumer is prepared to expend on a particular purchase

Format The format in which information is transmitted to the buyer may also determine its effectiveness. Information can be presented verbally, numerically or visually. Consumers often remember pictures better than words, and the combination of pictures and words further enhances learning.[8] Consequently, marketers pay great attention to the visual components of their advertising materials.

A successful information search yields a group of possible brand alternatives. This group of products is sometimes called the buyer's **evoked set**. For example, an evoked set of televisions might be those manufactured by Sony, LG, JVC and Philips.

evoked set
The group of products that a buyer views as possible alternatives after conducting an information search

Stage 3: Evaluation of alternatives

When evaluating the products in the evoked set, a buyer establishes criteria for comparing the products. These criteria are the characteristics or features that the buyer wants (or does not want). For example, one buyer may favour a smartphone whereas another may not require mobile office features but be keen to buy a model with an excellent quality camera. The buyer also assigns a certain **salience**, or level of importance, to each criterion; some features carry more weight than others. The salience of criteria varies from buyer to buyer. For example, when choosing a newspaper one buyer may consider the political stance of the editorial to be crucial, while another may place greater importance on the quality and coverage of sports. The criteria and their salience are used by the buyer to rank the brands in the evoked set. This involves comparing the brands with each other as well as with the criteria. If the evaluation stage does not yield a brand that the buyer wishes to buy, further information search may be necessary.

salience
The level of importance a buyer assigns to each criterion for comparing products

Marketers can influence consumers' evaluation by *framing* the alternatives – that is, by the manner in which the alternative and its attributes is described. Framing can make a characteristic seem more important and can facilitate its recall from memory. For example, by emphasizing whitening ingredients in toothpaste, manufacturers can encourage the consumer to consider this particular aspect to be important. Framing affects the decision processes of inexperienced buyers more than those of experienced ones. If the evaluation of alternatives yields one or more brands that the consumer is willing to buy, the consumer is ready to move on to the purchase stage.

Stage 4: Purchase

The purchase stage, when the consumer chooses which product or brand to buy, is mainly the outcome of the consumer's evaluation of alternatives, but other factors have an impact too. The closeness of alternative stores and product availability can both influence which brand is purchased. For example, if the brand the buyer ranked highest is not available locally, an alternative may be selected.

During this stage, the buyer also picks the seller from whom the product will be purchased and finalizes the terms of the sale. Other issues such as price, delivery, guarantees, service agreements, installation and credit arrangements are discussed and settled. Finally, provided the consumer does not terminate the buying decision process before then, the purchase is made.

Stage 5: Post-purchase evaluation

After the purchase has taken place, the buyer begins evaluating the product to check whether its actual performance meets expected levels. Many of the criteria used in evaluating alternatives are revisited during this stage. The outcome will determine whether the consumer is satisfied or dissatisfied, and will influence future behaviour. The level of satisfaction a consumer experiences will determine whether they make a complaint, communicate with other possible buyers or purchase the product again.[9] The extent to which consumers are angered by the outcome of a purchase also influences how they will behave in the future.[10] Figure 4.3 illustrates the types of action that dissatisfied consumers may take. The likelihood that consumers will stop buying a particular product will depend on a range of factors, including how much knowledge they have about alternatives.[11] Some marketing experts believe that increasing consumer assertiveness is a positive move, which illustrates industry's willingness to respond to feedback about products and services.[12] The impact of post-purchase evaluation is illustrated by the feedback loop in Figure 4.1.

cognitive dissonance
Doubts that occur as the buyer questions whether s/he made the right decision in purchasing the product or service

The evaluation that follows the purchase of some products, particularly expensive or important items, may result in **cognitive dissonance** – doubts that occur because the buyer questions whether the best purchase decision was made. For example, after buying a branded football shirt from a market stall, a consumer may worry about

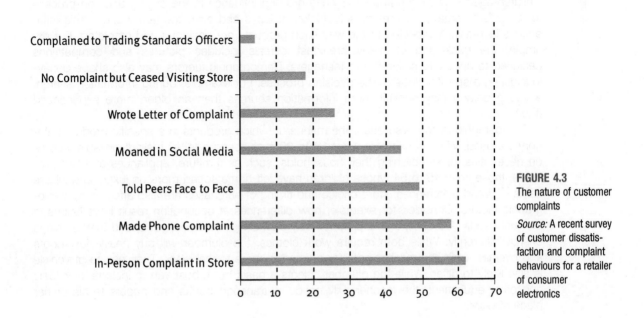

FIGURE 4.3
The nature of customer complaints

Source: A recent survey of customer dissatisfaction and complaint behaviours for a retailer of consumer electronics

whether the item is genuine. A buyer who experiences cognitive dissonance may attempt to return the product or may seek positive information about it to justify the choice. For example, motoring journalists often note with amusement that car shows and exhibitions are frequented by consumers who have recently purchased a new car.

As shown in Figure 4.1, three major categories of influence are believed to affect the consumer buying decision process: personal, psychological and social factors. These factors determine which particular instant coffee, shampoo, washing powder, DVD player, holiday, car or house a particular consumer will buy. Understanding these aspects helps marketers gain valuable insights into their customer base and can help ensure that a more suitable marketing mix is developed. The remainder of this chapter focuses on these factors. Although each major factor is discussed separately, it is a combination of their effects that influences the consumer buying decision process.

Personal factors influencing the buying decision process

personal influencing factors
Demographic, situational and level of involvement factors unique to a particular individual

Personal influencing factors are unique to a particular person. Many different personal factors can influence purchasing decisions. In this section, three types are considered: demographic factors, situational factors and level of involvement.

Demographic factors

demographic factors
Individual characteristics such as age, sex, race, ethnic origin, income, family life cycle and occupation

Demographic factors are individual characteristics such as age, sex, race, ethnic origin, income, family life cycle and occupation. (These and other characteristics are discussed in Chapter 6 as possible segmentation variables.) Given the potential impact of such features on buying requirements and behaviour, marketing professionals must develop a clear understanding of them.

Demographic factors have a bearing on who is involved in family decision-making. For example, UK, Germany and Turkey are some of the largest markets for children's toys and clothes in the EU, based on the number of children in the population. Children aged 6 to 17 are known to have growing influence in the buying decision process for breakfast cereals, ice cream, soft drinks, holidays and even the family car.[13] This influence is increasingly reflected in the way such products are designed and marketed. For example, the packaging of many breakfast cereals includes pictures and competitions designed to appeal to children and teenagers. Demographic factors may also shape behaviour during a specific stage of the decision process. For example, during information search, a young person may consult more information sources than an older, more experienced adult.

Demographic factors also affect the manner in which products in a specific product category are used. While consumers aged 18 to 30 may spend a lot of their disposable income on necessities for establishing their households, such as furniture, appliances and DIY products, those aged 45 to 54 whose children have left home spend more on luxury and leisure items.[14] Brand preferences, store choice and timing of purchases are also affected by demographic factors. Consider, for example, how differences in occupation result in variations in product needs. A teacher and a plumber may earn similar incomes, yet spend their earnings entirely differently. While both require work clothes, the plumber will buy heavy-duty boots and overalls, while the teacher opts for a smarter, more formal wear. Their choice of vehicle is also likely to differ. While the plumber selects a basic but robust van to include their tools and other equipment, the teacher only needs to transport books and papers to his or her place of work.

Situational factors

situational factors
External circumstances or conditions that exist when a consumer is making a purchase decision

Situational factors are the external circumstances or conditions that exist when a consumer is making a purchase decision. These factors can influence the buyer at any stage of the consumer buying decision process and may cause the individual to shorten, lengthen or terminate the process. For example, a nurse who usually commutes to work by car may be forced to travel by train while her car is being serviced.

Similarly, a family bowling trip or family holiday may have to be postponed if one of the family members is ill. The effects of situational factors can be felt throughout the buying decision process. Uncertainty about employment may sway a consumer against making a purchase. On the other hand, a conviction that the supply of a particular product is sharply limited may impel an individual to buy it. This explains why consumers have purchased and hoarded fuel, food products and even toilet tissue when these products were believed to be in short supply. These and other situational factors can change rapidly; their influence on purchase decisions is generally as sudden as it is short-lived.

The amount of time a consumer has available to make a decision strongly influences buying decisions. If there is little time for selecting and purchasing a product, an individual may quickly decide to buy a readily available brand. The time available also affects the way consumers process the information contained in advertisements[15] and the length of the stages within the decision process. For example, if a family is planning to redecorate its house, everyone may get together to collect and review a wide range of information from a variety of sources. They may read home and garden magazines, visit DIY outlets to collect paint charts and wallpaper samples, talk to friends and decorators, look at a number of advertisements and spend time comparing special offers in a number of stores. However, if the family has just moved to a new house that urgently needs renovating, the extent of the information search, the number of alternatives considered and the amount of comparative shopping may be more restricted.

Levels of involvement

level of involvement
The level of interest, emotional commitment and time spent searching for a product in a particular situation

Many aspects of consumer buying decisions are affected by the individual's **level of involvement**. This term refers to the level of interest, emotional commitment and time spent searching for a product in a particular situation. The level of involvement determines the extent to which a buyer is motivated to spend time seeking information about a particular product or brand. The extensiveness of the buying decision process therefore varies greatly with the consumer's level of involvement. The sequence of the steps in the process may also be altered. Low-involvement buyers may form an attitude towards a product – perhaps as a result of an advertising campaign – and evaluate its features after purchasing it rather than before.[16] Conversely, high-involvement buyers often spend a great deal of time and effort researching their purchase beforehand. For example, the purchase of a car is a high involvement decision.

The level of consumer involvement is linked to a number of factors. Consumers tend to be more involved in the purchase of high-priced goods and products that are visible to others, such as fashion items, electronic goods or cars. As levels of perceived risk associated with a purchase increase, involvement levels are likely to rise.

Enduring involvement Sometimes individuals experience enduring involvement with a product class. Enduring involvement is an ongoing interest in a product class because of personal relevance. For example, people often have enduring involvement with products associated with their leisure activities. These individuals engage in ongoing search and information gathering for these products over extensive periods of time, irrespective of whether or not a purchase is imminent. Football fans often watch the sport on television, attend their local club's games, read the football pages of the newspaper and may even buy their favourite team's football strip.

FIGURE 4.4

The purchase of a car is high involvement, particularly for those utilizing unfamiliar and innovative energy solutions

Source: Reproduced with permission from Toyota (GB) PLC.

Situational involvement Situational involvement is experienced by buyers as a result of the particular circumstance or environment in which they find themselves. This type of involvement, sometimes also called pre-purchase involvement, is temporary because the conditions that triggered this high involvement may change.[17] A man searching for an engagement ring for his prospective fiancée, for example, will probably experience a high level of involvement in the purchase decision. His information search and evaluation of alternatives may be lengthy. However, once the choice is made, an engagement ring is probably no longer personally relevant.

Low consumer involvement Many purchase decisions do not generate much consumer involvement. When the involvement level is low, as with routine response purchases, the buying is almost automatic, and the information search and evaluation of alternatives are extremely limited. Thus the purchase of floor cleaner is low involvement for many consumers; the product is chosen out of habit and with minimal effort.

Psychological factors influencing the buying decision process

psychological factors
Factors that influence consumer behaviour, including perception, motives, learning, attitudes and personality

Psychological factors operating within individuals partly determine people's general behaviour and thus influence their behaviour as consumers. The primary psychological influences on consumer behaviour are:

● perception

● motives

● learning

● attitudes

● personality.

Even though these psychological factors operate internally, it will become apparent later in this chapter that they are highly affected by social forces external to the individual.

Perception

Are the fish in Figure 4.5 changing into birds or are the birds changing into fish? It could be either depending on how you perceive the birds. People's perception of the same thing varies.

Similarly, the same individual at different times may perceive the same item in a number of ways. **Perception** involves a three-step process of selecting, organizing and interpreting information inputs to produce meaning.

Information inputs are the sensations received through sight, taste, hearing, smell and touch. Each time we see an advertisement, go online, visit shops or use a product, we receive information inputs.

The first step of the perceptual process is the selection of information. Individuals receive numerous pieces of information all the time, yet only a few of these reach awareness. Certain inputs are selected while others are ignored. **Selective exposure** occurs because consumers cannot be conscious of all inputs at the same time, and involves the selection of inputs that are to be exposed to awareness. A student typing a report may be unaware that the light is on, that the computer is making a humming sound, that there is background noise in the room or that other students are working at the same table. All of these inputs are being received, but the student will ignore them unless their attention is specifically drawn to them.

An input is more likely to reach awareness if it relates to an anticipated event or relates to current needs. If a violent storm has damaged the roof of a couple's house, they are much more likely to notice a local newspaper advertisement promoting a building and repairs service. Similarly, thirsty people are more likely to notice a billboard advertising a soft drink or a café that they pass than are those who are not thirsty.

Finally, an input is more likely to be noticed if its intensity changes significantly. Consumers are much more likely to notice if a furniture store cuts its prices by half than if the same store offers a much smaller reduction. The selective nature of perception leads to two other conditions: selective distortion and selective retention. **Selective distortion** is the changing or twisting of currently received information. This sometimes

perception
The process of selecting, organizing and interpreting information inputs to produce meaning

information inputs
The sensations received through sight, taste, hearing, smell and touch

selective exposure
The selection of inputs that people expose to their awareness

selective distortion
The changing or twisting of currently received information

FIGURE 4.5
Fish or birds? Do you see the fish changing into birds or the birds changing into fish?

Source: M.C. Escher's 'Sky and Water 1' © 2011 The M.C. Escher Company – Holland. All rights reserved www.mcescher.com

happens when someone receives information that is inconsistent with personal feelings or beliefs. For example, an individual who reads some favourable publicity about a company he or she dislikes is likely to distort the information to make it more consistent with personally held views. The publicity may therefore have greater impact on another consumer who views the same brand more positively. **Selective retention** means that an individual remembers information inputs that support personal feelings and beliefs, and forgets inputs that do not. After hearing a sales presentation and leaving the shop, a customer may forget many of the selling points if they contradict pre-existing beliefs. The information inputs that do reach awareness are not received in an organized form. For them to be meaningful, an individual must enter the second step of the perceptual process – organizing and integrating the new information with that already stored in the memory. Although this step is usually carried out quickly, it may take longer when the individual is considering an unfamiliar product area.

selective retention
The process of remembering information inputs that support personal feelings and beliefs, and of forgetting those that do not

Interpretation – the third step in the perceptual process – is the assignment of meaning to what has been organized. All consumers base their interpretation on what is familiar, on knowledge already stored in memory. For this reason, a company that changes a package design or logo can face major problems. Since people look for the product in the old, familiar package, they may not recognize it in the new one. Unless a package or logo change is accompanied by a promotional programme making people aware of the change, a company may lose sales. Even when such a programme is conducted, positive reaction from the consumer cannot be guaranteed. When Gap gave its logo a makeover, consumers were quick to respond, insisting that the old logo be reinstated. An online backlash on social networking sites quickly showed that the company had got it wrong. Initially Gap decided to use crowdsourcing to help solve its branding crisis, by seeking the consumers' views. Companies often try to get around this difficulty by making only small changes to their logo or brand identity. In practice, Gap quickly made the decision to return to the original logo only a week later.

Although marketers cannot control people's perceptions, they often try to influence them. This may be difficult to achieve for a number of reasons. First, a consumer's perceptual process may prevent the information from being received. Second, a buyer may receive the information but perceive it differently from the way that was intended. For example, when an anti-wrinkle face cream manufacturer advertises that '80 per cent of consumers using this product notice a reduction in wrinkles', a customer might infer that 20 per cent of the people who use the product have more wrinkles. Third, buyers who perceive information inputs to be inconsistent with their personally held beliefs tend to forget the information quickly. Sometimes consumers can be overwhelmed by the large number of information inputs they encounter, making it difficult to interpret the information.[18] For example, a student travelling by bus to college may pass more than 30 different advertising hoardings, but notice only one or two. In addition to perceptions about packages, products, brands and organizations, individuals also have self-perceptions. These perceptions are known as the **self-concept** or self-image. It seems likely that a person's self-concept affects purchase decisions and consumption behaviour. The results of some studies suggest that buyers purchase products that reflect and enhance their self-concepts. For instance, one man might buy an Armani suit to project a sophisticated and businesslike image, while another might buy an outfit from Republic to enhance acceptability within their peer group.

self-concept
A person's perception of himself or herself; self-image

Motives

motive
An internal, energy-giving force that directs a person's activities towards satisfying a need or achieving a goal

A **motive** is an internal, energy-giving force that directs an individual's activities towards satisfying a need or achieving a goal. Motivation is the set of mechanisms for controlling movement towards goals.[19] At any time a buyer's actions are affected by a set of motives rather than by just one. These motives are unique to the individual and to the situation. At any point in time some motives in the set will have priority. For example, someone's motives for stocking up on food may be particularly strong if a prolonged period of bad weather is forecast. Motivation affects the direction and intensity of behaviour, as individuals must choose which goals to pursue at a particular time. Motives influencing where a person regularly purchases products are called patronage motives. A buyer may use a particular shop because of **patronage motives** such as price, service, location, honesty, product variety or friendliness of sales staff. Marketers seeking to capitalize on these motives should determine why regular customers patronize a store and then emphasize these characteristics in the store's marketing mix. Motivation research can be used to analyze the major motives that influence whether consumers buy particular products. However, some of these motives are subconscious and people are therefore unaware of them. As a consequence, marketers cannot always elicit these motives through direct questioning. Most motivation research therefore relies on interviews or projective techniques (see Figure 4.6).

patronage motives
Those motives that influence where a person purchases products on a regular basis

Researchers using interviews to study motives may use individual **in-depth interviews**, focus groups or a combination of the two. In an in-depth interview, the researcher encourages the subject to talk freely about general topics before focusing the discussion on the areas of interest. In a process that may last for several hours, the interviewer can then probe the subject's answers for clarification. In a **focus group**, the moderator – through leadership that appears to be not highly structured – tries to generate discussion about one or several topics in a group of six to twelve people. Through what is said in the discussion, the moderator attempts to discover people's motives relating to some issue such as the use of a product. The researcher usually cannot probe as far in a focus group as in an in-depth interview, and some products may not be suitable for such group discussion. To determine successfully the subconscious motives reflected in the interviews, motivation researchers must have certain qualities: they must be perceived as non-threatening by members of the group, must be able to adopt a demeanour appropriate to the characteristics of those in the group and must be well trained in clinical psychology. The use of sound and video recordings can simplify the process of analysis. Both in-depth and focus group techniques can yield a variety of information. For example, they may help marketers discover why customers continue to buy and smoke cigarettes despite being aware of the profound health risks.

in-depth interview
The collection of data from an individual by interview

focus group
A semi-structured discussion involving six to twelve people, led by a moderator

Projective techniques are tests in which subjects are asked to perform specific tasks for particular reasons, while actually being evaluated for other purposes. Such tests are based on the assumption that subjects will unconsciously 'project' their motives through the tasks they perform. Researchers trained in projective techniques can analyze

projective techniques
Tests in which subjects are asked to perform specific tasks for particular reasons, while actually being evaluated for other purposes

FIGURE 4.6
Discussing the customers' buying decision making process, perceptions and attitudes is an important aspect of the marketer's role

Source: Shutterstock, © Yuri Arcurs

Word association tests

Subjects are asked to say what words come into their minds when a particular topic/product is mentioned.

Fresh foods are . . .	Frozen foods are . . .
Natural	Processed
Fresh	Quick
Healthy	Simple
Expensive	Convenient
Good for you	Preservatives
Real	Manufactured

Sentence completion tests

Subjects are asked to complete the sentences.

'People who use recycled toilet tissue . . .'
'People who look for the ingredients on packets before they buy them are . . .'
'People who buy Swatch watches . . .'

Bubble drawings

Subjects are asked to say what the man is thinking.

FIGURE 4.7
Common types of projective technique

the results and make predictions about the subject's subconscious motives. Common types of projective technique include word association tests, sentence completion tests and bubble drawings. These are illustrated in Figure 4.7. Such tests can be useful to marketers in a number of ways, such as helping to make advertising more effective.[20] The complexity of motivation research means that marketers wishing to research people's motives should employ the services of professional psychologists with specific skills in the area.[21]

Learning

learning
Changes in a person's behaviour caused by information and experience

Learning refers to changes in behaviour caused by information and experience. The consequences of behaviour strongly influence the learning process. Thus behaviour resulting in satisfying consequences tends to be repeated. For example, if a consumer buys a hair gel that he believes makes him appear trendy, he is more likely to buy the same brand next time. In fact, he may continue to purchase the brand until he is no longer satisfied with it. If the consumer's hair subsequently starts to look out of condition, he may switch allegiance to an alternative brand.

The ability of buyers to process information when making purchasing decisions varies. For example, when purchasing a computer, a well-educated potential buyer who has experience with computers may be able to read, comprehend and synthesize the considerable quantities of information found in the technical brochures for competing brands. On the other hand, a buyer with more limited abilities may be incapable of performing this task and will have to rely instead on information obtained from advertisements or from sales representatives.

knowledge
Familiarity with the product and expertise – the ability to apply the product

A critical aspect of an individual's ability to process information is knowledge. **Knowledge,** in this context, has two components: familiarity with the product, and expertise or the ability to apply the product.[22] The duration and intensity of the buying decision process depends on the buyer's familiarity with or prior experience in purchasing and using the product. The individual's knowledge influences his or her search for, recall and use of information.[23] Inexperienced buyers may use different types of information from more experienced shoppers when making purchasing decisions. Inexperienced buyers use price as an indicator of quality more frequently than buyers who are knowledgeable about a particular product category.[24] Thus two potential buyers of a pedigree dog may use quite different types of information in making their purchase decision. The more experienced buyer, wishing to take the animal to dog shows, may seek detailed information about the dog's pedigree; the less experienced buyer, looking for a loyal family pet, may judge the animal by how approachable and friendly it appears.

Consumers who lack expertise are more likely to seek advice from others when making a purchase. More experienced buyers have greater confidence; they also have more knowledge about the product or service, and can tell which features are reliable indicators of product quality. For example, consider two families choosing a long-haul holiday. Members of one family are unused to overseas travel, are unsure of the suitability of locations offered in travel brochures, and do not understand how to investigate flight options or medical and insurance requirements. Members of the other family have holidayed abroad on a regular basis. Although on this occasion they intend to visit a country that is new to them, they are sufficiently conversant with this type of travel to make their purchase without assistance and with confidence.

Consumers can gain the knowledge they need to make decisions from marketers or from other sources. Marketers sometimes help customers to learn about and gain experience of their products. Free samples encourage consumer trial and reduce purchase risk. In-store demonstrations help people acquire knowledge of product uses. Innovative technology company Dyson, well known for its bag-less vacuum cleaners and Airblade hand dryers, has videos on its website which explain how its Air Multiplier range of bladeless fans work.

However, consumers are increasingly turning to other consumers for information about different product offerings. As discussed later in this chapter, sharing of information on the Internet through social networking sites and other digital sources has provided a host of new opportunities for consumers gathering insights into product and services. A new website, Gransnet, aims to provide social networking for older people, but will also feature information about brands targeting this group.

In view of these trends, it is no surprise that marketers encounter problems in attracting and holding consumers' attention, providing the kinds of information that are important for making purchase decisions, and convincing consumers to try the product. These attempts are most likely to be successful when designed to appeal to a well-defined target market. In Figure 4.8, Walkers is striving for attention through strong and evocative images for its 'posh crisps'.

FIGURE 4.8
These advertisements for 'posh' crisps evidently play on consumers' aspirations to portray a certain image through the brands and products they select

Source: Courtesy of Kate Plumb, Abbot Mead Vickers. BBDO

Attitudes

attitude
An individual's enduring evaluation, feelings and behavioural tendencies towards an object or activity

An **attitude** is an individual's enduring evaluation, feelings and behavioural tendencies towards an object or activity. These objects or activities may be tangible or intangible, living or non-living. Some attitudes relate to things that have a major impact on our lives, while others are less important. For example, we have attitudes towards relationships, culture and politics, just as we do towards rock music, skiing and pizza. An individual learns attitudes through experience and interaction with others. Just as attitudes are learned, they can also be changed. Nevertheless, an individual's attitudes are generally quite stable and do not change from moment to moment. Likewise, at a particular point in time, some attitudes may be stronger than others. For example, a consumer who recently lost their driving licence and had their identity stolen, may have strong views about the need for consumer protection legislation in this area. An attitude consists of three major components: cognitive, affective and behavioural. The cognitive (or thinking) component is a person's knowledge and information about the object or idea, whereas the affective (or feeling) component comprises feelings and emotions towards the object or idea. The behavioural (or action) component consists of the action tendencies exhibited towards the object or idea. Changes in one of these components may or may not alter the other components. Thus consumers may become more knowledgeable about a specific brand without changing the affective or behavioural components of their attitude towards that brand.

Consumer attitudes towards a company and its products greatly influence the products individuals will buy, and therefore impact on the success or failure of the company's marketing strategy. When consumers are strongly negative towards aspects of a business's practices, they may stop using the business's product, and may urge relatives and friends to do the same. For example, BP's response to the Gulf of Mexico drilling disaster resulted in negative feeling towards the company and its brands, as well as a huge fall in share price and the departure of the CEO.

Since attitudes can play such an important part in determining consumer behaviour, marketers should measure consumer attitudes towards prices, package designs, company logos and brand names, advertisements, warranties, store design and location, features of existing or proposed products and social responsibility issues. Marketers can use a range of techniques to gauge these attitudes. One of the simplest ways is to question people directly. A marketing research agency carrying out attitude research for Rayban, for example, might question consumers about their opinions on the latest trends in eye wear. Sometimes marketers evaluate attitudes through attitude scales. An **attitude scale** usually consists of a series of adjectives, phrases or sentences about an object. Subjects are asked to indicate the intensity of their feelings towards the object by reacting to the adjectives, phrases or sentences in a certain way. For example, attitudes towards flexible mortgages might be measured by asking respondents to state the degree to which they agree or disagree with a number of statements, such as 'When I have spare money I would like the opportunity to pay more than my usual monthly repayment amount'.

attitude scale
A series of adjectives, phrases or sentences about an object used by a subject to indicate his or her feelings towards that object

If marketers identify particularly negative attitudes towards an aspect of a marketing mix, they may try to make consumer attitudes more favourable. This task is generally long, expensive, difficult and may require extensive promotional efforts. For example, in the UK, the Post Office embarked on a prolonged advertising campaign to draw customers' attention to the fact that local post offices offer a wide range of services. This publicity aimed to alter customers' attitude that the Post Office exists purely for mailing letters and parcels.

Personality

personality
All the internal traits and behaviours that make a person unique

Personality includes all the internal traits and behaviours that make a person unique. Each person's unique personality is both inherited and the result of personal experiences. Personalities are typically described as having one or more characteristics, such as compulsiveness, ambitiousness, gregariousness, dogmatism, authoritarianism, introversion, extroversion, aggressiveness and competitiveness. Many marketers believe that a consumer's personality does influence the types and brands of products purchased, and there has been a drive to increase research in this area.[25] For example, the type of make-up or clothing that people buy, as well as the social activities in which they engage, may reflect one or more personality characteristics. Perhaps surprisingly, marketing researchers who have tried to find relationships among such characteristics and buying behaviour have reported inconclusive results. However, some of these researchers see this apparently weak association between personality and buying behaviour as due to unreliable measures rather than because no such relationship exists.[26]

At times, marketers aim advertising campaigns at general types of personality. In doing so, they use positively valued personality characteristics, such as gregariousness, independence or competitiveness. Products promoted in this way include drinks, cars, cigarettes, clothing and computer games. For example, television advertising promoting the alcoholic beverage Lambrini is designed to appeal to young, outgoing women.

Social factors influencing the buying decision process

social factors
The forces other people exert on buying behaviour

The forces that other people exert on buying behaviour are called **social factors**. As shown in Figure 4.1, they can be grouped into four major areas:

1 roles and family
2 reference groups
3 social classes
4 culture and sub-cultures.

Roles and family

role
A set of actions and
activities that a person in
a particular position is
supposed to perform,
based on the
expectations of both the
individual and
surrounding people

All of us occupy positions within our family, social setting, organizations and institutions. Associated with each position is a **role** – a set of actions and activities that a person is supposed to perform, based on their own expectations and those of others around them. Because people occupy numerous positions, they also have many roles. For example, one woman may perform the roles of mother, wife, grandmother, daughter, sister, teacher, part-time youth club organizer and member of the local music society. Thus there are several sets of expectations for each person's behaviour.

An individual's roles influence both general behaviour and buying behaviour. The demands of different roles may be inconsistent and confusing. For example, assume that a man is thinking about buying a boat. While he wants a boat for fishing, his children want one suitable for water skiing. His wife wants him to delay the boat purchase until next year. A colleague at work insists that he should buy a particular brand, known for high performance. Thus an individual's buying behaviour may be partially affected by the opinions of family and friends.

Family roles relate directly to purchase decisions. The male head of household may be involved heavily in the purchase of products such as household insurance, garden equipment and alcohol. Although female roles have changed, women often still make buying decisions related to many household items, including healthcare products, washing products, household cleaners and food. Husbands and wives are often jointly involved in buying many durable goods, such as a washing machine or television set. Children are also increasingly involved in household purchase decisions that were traditionally made only by their parents. Some buying decisions, such as the purchase of a family holiday, are made by the whole family, with different family members playing different roles in the process. When two or more individuals participate in a purchase, their roles may dictate that each is responsible for performing certain tasks: initiating the idea, gathering information, deciding whether to buy the product or selecting the specific brand. The particular tasks performed depend on the types of product being considered. Marketers need to be aware of how roles affect buying behaviour. To develop a marketing mix that precisely meets the target market's needs, marketers must know not only who does the actual buying but also what other roles influence the purchase.

Reference groups

reference group
A group with which an
individual identifies so
much that he or she takes
on many of the values,
attitudes or behaviour of
group members

A group is referred to as a **reference group** when an individual identifies with it so much that he or she takes on many of the values, attitudes or behaviour of group members. Most people have several reference groups, such as families, friends, work colleagues and social, religious and professional organizations. Social media networks have added a new dimension to the notion of reference groups, with consumers sharing opinions and experiences about products, services and brands in contexts deemed relevant by many consumers. Sometimes such digital networks are created or encouraged by brands themselves, otherwise they are within people's Twitter or Facebook networks.

A group can be a negative reference group for an individual. Someone may have been a part of a specific group at one time but later have rejected its values and members, even taking specific action to avoid it.[27] However, in this discussion reference groups mean those that the individual involved views positively.

An individual may use a reference group as a point of comparison and a source of information, and may change their behaviour to be more in line with other group members. For example, a student may decide not to go to see a movie on the advice of a close friend. An individual may seek information from a reference group about the best brand to buy or about where to buy a certain product. Facebook and Twitter are now frequently turned to by consumers seeking advice and opinions.

The degree to which a reference group will affect a purchase decision depends on an individual's susceptibility to its influence, and the strength of his or her involvement with the group. Young people are often especially susceptible to this kind of influence. In general, the more conspicuous a product, the more likely the brand decision will be influenced by reference groups. A marketer sometimes tries to use reference group influence in marketing communications by suggesting that people in a specific group buy and are highly satisfied with a product. The marketer is hoping that people will accept the suggested group as a reference group and buy (or react more favourably to) the product as a result. Whether this kind of marketing communication succeeds depends on three factors:

1 how effectively the message is communicated

2 the type of product

3 the individual's susceptibility to reference group influence.

opinion leader
The member of a reference group who provides information about a specific sphere of interest to reference group participants seeking information

In most reference groups, one or more members stand out as opinion leaders. An **opinion leader** provides information about a specific sphere of interest to reference group participants who seek such information. Opinion leaders are viewed by other group members as being well informed about a particular area, and easily accessible. Such individuals often feel a responsibility to remain informed about the sphere of interest, and thus seek out websites, discussion groups, advertisements, manufacturers' brochures, sales people and other sources of information. The growing use of social media and associated consumer-to-consumer communication have radically disrupted how marketers perceived reference groups, putting consumers in touch with a far broader and larger number of peers who may influence their purchasing decisions.

Social classes

social class
An open group of individuals who have similar social rank

Within all societies, people rank others into higher or lower positions of respect. This ranking results in social classes. A **social class** is an open group of individuals who have similar social rank. A class is referred to as 'open' because people can move into and out of it. The criteria for grouping people into classes vary from one society to another. In the UK, as in other western countries, many factors are taken into account, including occupation, education, income, wealth, race, ethnic group and possessions. In Russia, wealth and income are less important in determining social class than education and occupation: although Russian doctors and scientists do not make a great deal of money, they are highly valued in Russian society. A person who is ranking someone does not necessarily apply all of a society's criteria. The number and importance of the factors chosen depend on the characteristics of the individual being ranked and the values of the person who is doing the ranking. For example, one individual may particularly respect status within a church or religious sect, while another may regard it as having little relevance.

To some degree, people within social classes develop and assume common patterns of behaviour. They may have similar attitudes, values, language patterns and possessions. Social class influences many aspects of people's lives. For example, it affects whom they marry, their likelihood of having children and the children's chances of surviving infancy. It influences childhood training, choice of religion, selection of occupation and the way in which people spend their time. Because social class has a bearing on so many aspects of a person's life, it also affects buying decisions. For example, upmarket fashion labels Fendi and Versace are popular among upper-class Europeans because they believe these brands symbolize their status, income and aspirations.

Social class affects the type, quality and quantity of products that a person buys and uses. Social class also affects an individual's shopping patterns and the types of store patronized. Advertisements are sometimes based on an appeal to a specific social class. Different countries often collate data about their populations based on social or socio-economic factors. For example, for many years the UK, like some other countries, used a relatively simple classification based on social status and occupation (see Table 4.1). However, in 2001, the UK's Office for

TABLE 4.1 Socio-economic classification

Social grade	Social status	Head of household's occupation
A	Upper middle class	Higher managerial, professional or administrative positions; often living in expensive accommodation in the best residential areas
B	Middle class	Middle managerial, professional or administrative jobs; good living standards, usually in good accommodation in reasonable areas
C_1	Lower middle class	Junior managerial, professional or administrative, supervisory or clerical jobs; sometimes referred to as 'white collar' workers
C_2	Skilled working class	Skilled manual workers, perhaps who have served some kind of apprenticeship to train
D	Manual workers	Semi-skilled and unskilled manual workers
E	Those at lowest levels of subsistence	Old age pensioners, widows, casual workers, the unemployed or those who are dependent on social security or have little in the way of independent means

See www.medialive.ie for more details of socio-economic groups.

National Statistics introduced a modified system known as NS SEC (National Statistics Socio-Economic Status). This approach is still based on occupation, but aims to more closely reflect consumers' purchasing power on the basis of their position in the labour market.[28] Table 4.2 describes the NS SEC social class categories.

Culture and sub-cultures

culture
All the things around us that are made by human beings: tangible items, such as food, furniture, buildings, clothing and tools; and intangible concepts, such as education, the legal system, healthcare and religion; plus values and behaviours

Culture consists of everything in our surroundings that is made by human beings. It includes tangible items, such as food, furniture, buildings, clothing and tools and intangible concepts, such as education, the legal system, healthcare and religion. Culture also includes the values and wide range of behaviours that are acceptable within a specific society. The concepts, values and behaviours that make up a culture are learned and passed on from one generation to the next.

Culture influences buying behaviour, determining what people wear and eat, how they socialize, where they live and travel. Society's interest in the health-related aspects of food has affected companies' approaches to developing and promoting their products. Recent concern about increasing levels of obesity and its impact on health has caused the food industry to question how it markets high-fat and high-sugar products.[29] Culture also influences how consumers buy and use products, and the satisfaction gained from them. For example, the consumption of packaged goods, and the usage and ownership of durable goods varies across cultures.[30] In many western cultures, shortage of time is a growing problem because of the increasing number of women who work and the current emphasis placed on physical and mental self-development. Many people buy convenience and labour-saving products to cope with this problem.[31]

Because culture partly determines how products are purchased and used, it also affects the development, promotion, distribution and pricing of products. Food marketers have needed to radically overhaul their marketing efforts to reflect day-to-day changes in how consumers live their lives. Some 40 years ago, most families ate at least two meals a day together, and the mother devoted four to six hours a day to preparing those meals. Today, more than 60 per cent of women aged 25 to 54 are employed outside the home, and average family incomes have risen considerably. These shifts, along with lack of time, have resulted in dramatic increases in per capita consumption of refrigerated readymeals ranges and shelf-stable foods such as microwavable rice and Pot Noodles. As a result of increasing demands from those wishing to 'eat on the move', many fuel stations now sell coffee and prepared snacks.

TABLE 4.2 NS SEC eight-class socio-economic classification

Class	Occupation groups
1	Higher managerial and professional occupations (ABs): e.g. business executives, doctors, vets, teachers
2	Lower managerial and professional occupations (C1s): e.g. nurses, police sergeants and constables, market researchers, junior managers
3	Intermediate occupations (C2s): e.g. secretaries, clerical staff, technicians and telephone engineers
4	Small employers and own-account workers: e.g. the self-employed and those employing fewer than 25 people
5	Lower supervisory and technical occupations: e.g. supervisors in factories
6	Semi-routine occupations: e.g. drivers, assembly-line workers, shop staff
7	Routine occupations: e.g. porters, labourers, domestic staff
8	Never worked or long-term unemployed

Source: adapted from Angela Donkin, Yuan Huang Lee and Barbara Toson, 'Implications of change in the UK social and occupational classifications in 2001 for vital statistics', *Population Trends*, 107, *National Statistics*, Spring 2002, pp. 23–9.

An increase in ethnic diversity in many societies has important implications for the way in which new products and services are developed and marketed. A key part of this process is ensuring the availability of good-quality data, so that the attitudes and behaviour of minority groups are properly understood. The Marketing Insight box shows how the need to better understand cultural diversity among ethnic minorities and its impact on consumer behaviour is spawning initiatives to drive forward best practice in marketing research. When marketers sell products overseas, they often see the tremendous impact that culture has on the purchase and use of products. International marketers find that people in other regions of the world have different attitudes, values and needs, which call for different methods of doing business. Some international marketers fail because they do not adjust to cultural differences. A culture can be divided into **sub-cultures** according to geographic regions or human characteristics, such as age or ethnic background. In any country, there are a number of different sub-cultures. Within these, there are even greater similarities in people's attitudes, values and actions than within the broader culture, resulting in stronger preferences for specific types of clothing, furniture or leisure activity. For example, the wearing of kilts tends to be confined to Scotland rather than England or Wales. Marketers must recognize that, even though their operations are confined to one country, state or city, sub-cultural differences may dictate considerable variations in what products people buy and how they make their purchases. To deal effectively with these differences, marketers may have to alter their product, promotion, distribution systems, price or people to satisfy members of particular sub-cultures.

sub-cultures
Sub-divisions of culture according to geographic regions or human characteristics, such as age or ethnic background

The impact of social media and consumer-to-consumer (C2C) communication

With the arrival of social networking sites and digital media such as blogs, consumers can connect with each other like never before. This is changing the way consumers learn about and evaluate products. Through these connections consumers can share information and experiences without company interferences, getting the 'real story' about a brand or company. In many ways the power of marketing practitioners to control and disperse information has been placed in the hands of the consumers. **Consumer-to-consumer communication (C2C)** refers to communication taking place between consumers through face to face, online or other electronic media. Today, blogs, wikis, podcasts, ratings and the like have the capability to publicise, praise or challenge the company.

consumer-to-consumer communication (C2C)
refers to communication taking place between consumers through face-to-face, online or other electronic media

Marketing to ethnic consumers

Building customer relationships

The UK population is truly multicultural with some estimates suggesting that one fifth will come from ethnic minorities by the middle of the twenty-first century. The commercial potential of ethnic consumers is huge. The Indian community alone currently numbers over one million and has huge spending power.

Recent research suggests that Asian and Black men account for an annual spend of over £30 billion. Professional marketers are facing increasing pressure to cater more effectively for the needs and buying requirements of these groups. Studies on culture illustrate the diversity of attitudes and behaviour across ethnic groups, showing that these differences are also reflected in product preferences and consumer buying behaviour. Tesco has led the way in creating 'ethnic stores' catering for the diversity of consumers in particular store catchments, Lloyds has launched banking products tailored to the Polish community in the UK, and Tilda has rice varieties targeted at separate ethnic communities.

Yet recent research findings suggest that not enough is being done to reflect these characteristics in product design and marketing.

For example, despite a recent rise in Bollywood-style advertisements, such as those for Peugeot and Walkers Crisps, the advertising industry has been accused of tokenism and ethnic stereotyping. Even though an analysis of television advertising reveals 13 per cent of actors used are non-white, a more systematic review shows that the vast majority of these are included in minor roles. According to a report by Mediaedge, cia, a large global player in media communications and part of the WPP Group, current advertising campaigns are still failing to reflect the cultural characteristics of Asian, African-Caribbean and other ethnic minorities.

So what needs to be done to ensure that cultural variety is better reflected in marketing practice? Industry experts suggest that the first challenge is to develop a fuller picture of ethnic diversity by collecting appropriate research data across the different communities. This raises challenges of its own, as agencies must equip themselves to overcome the cultural and religious barriers sometimes associated with such data-collection exercises. For example, some experts highlight the importance of including community leaders in the process; others suggest that researchers from the same ethnic groups as respondents must be used and that appropriate settings for the research must be chosen. Not surprisingly, the number of marketing research agencies specializing in researching ethnic minorities is on the increase and various initiatives have been established to improve the availability and quality of work in this area. For example, ethnic research experts ETHNOS uses a range of tailored research methods to gain insights into profile, attitudes, preferences, consumption patterns and identities of the main UK ethnic communities.

The potential benefits of research of this nature are readily apparent. When broadcaster Sky researched the viewing behaviour of the UK's South Asian population, it identified the importance this group attaches to Asian TV channels such as Zee TV and StarTV. According to the findings, 96 per cent of respondents from this group regarded these kinds of channel as essential. Yet only 54 per cent had the same view about ITV1. The analysis also revealed the level of Internet access among South Asians to be much higher than the UK norm.

The implications for advertisers and marketers seeking to target these individuals are readily apparent. Yet, even here, care is needed. The research also showed striking viewership patterns across the South Asian community, illustrating the danger of developing ethnic stereotypes. In the words of Saber Khan, the research director of Ethnic Focus, the specialist research company conducting the study:

> These channels reflect the heterogeneity of the Asian community. Marketers have had the will to reach communities. But what they sometimes need assistance with is to capture the diversity. It's more than just Bollywood or Caribbean – it's capturing the fusion.

Sources: **www.mediaedge.com**; Robert Gray, 'Ethnic insight', *Marketing*, 4 March 2004, pp. 25–6; 'Ethnic marketing: "a double edged sword"', **www.redhotcurry.com**, 3 March 2003; Tescoplc, 2007; BBC news, 2007; Tilda, 2007 and 2011. MRS; Ethnic Research Network, 2008; **www.ethnos. co.uk**.

Forrester Research, a technology and market research company, emphasises the importance of understanding these changing relationships between corporates and consumers. By grouping online customers into different segments based on how they use digital online media, marketers can gain a better understanding of the online influences on consumers.[32] As well as learning about how C2C is likely to affect their products, they can use these insights to influence consumers through their own marketing strategies. The Social Technographics Profile developed by Forrester Research groups the online community into six segments according to how they interact with new digital media. It is important to note that in this particular analysis some consumers can belong to multiple segments at the same time. Table 4.3 describes the six groups. *Creators* are consumers who create their own media outlets, such as blogs, podcasts, consumer-generated videos and wikis. Online marketers are recognizing the power of this C2C communication and are harnessing it as a conduit for addressing consumers directly. For instance, many marketers are now pitching public relationship products or stories to professional reporters and bloggers.

The second group of Internet users are the *Critics.* These are people who comment on blogs or post ratings or reviews. Anyone who has ever posted a product review or rated a bar or movie, has engaged in this activity. Critics need to be an important component in a company's digital marketing strategy, because the majority of online shoppers read ratings and reviews to aid in their purchasing decisions. Consumer-generated content like ratings and reviews tends to be viewed as more credible than corporate messages. Hence marketers must carefully monitor what consumers are saying about their products and address consumers concerns that may affect their corporate reputation.

Collectors are the most newly recognized group of the six. They gather information and organize content generated by Critics and Creators. The growing popularity of this segment is leading to the creation of social networking sites like Digg, del.icio.us, and RSS feeds. Such sites allow users to vote on the sites or stories that they like the best. Because collectors are active members in the online community, a company story or site that catches the eye of a collector is likely to be posted and discussed on collector sites.

TABLE 4.3 Social technographics

Creators	■ Publish a blog ■ Publish personal web pages ■ Upload original videos ■ Write articles or stories and post them
Critics	■ Post ratings/reviews of products or services ■ Comment on someone else's blog ■ Contribute to online forums ■ Contribute to/edit articles in a wiki
Collectors	■ Use RSS feeds ■ Add tags to web pages or photos ■ 'Vote' for websites online
Joiners	■ Maintain profile on a social networking site ■ Visit social networking sites
Spectators	■ Read blogs ■ Watch video from other users ■ Listen to podcasts ■ Read online forums ■ Read customer ratings/reviews
Inactives	■ None of the activities

Source: Charlene Li and Josh Bernoff, Groundswell (Boston: Harvard Business Review) 2008, p. 43.

Another technographic segment known as *Joiners* is growing dramatically. Anyone who becomes a member of MySpace, Twitter, Facebook or other social networking sites is a *Joiner*. These consumers are often members of more than one such site. Joiners join these sites to connect and network with other users. Marketers can also take significant advantage of these sites to connect with consumers and form customer relationships.

The last two segments are the *Spectators* and *Inactives.* Inactives are online users who do not participate in any digital online media, but as more and more people use computers as a resource, this number is dwindling. Spectators are the largest group in most countries. They are those consumers who read what other consumers produce but do not product any comment themselves.

Understanding consumer behaviour

Marketers try to understand consumer buying behaviour so that they can satisfy consumers more effectively. For example, consumer concerns about the exploitation of workers in less developed countries have encouraged supermarkets to stock more ethical products. An appreciation of how and why individuals buy products and services helps marketers design more appropriate and relevant marketing programmes.[33] For example, by understanding the browsing and readership habits of prospective digital camera buyers, companies such as Sony and Panasonic are able to make more informed decisions about their marketing communications strategy.

At a time when consumers are increasingly focused on maximizing the value of what they buy, it is more important than ever to keep abreast of trends in consumer behaviour. If marketers are to keep consumers satisfied, they must focus carefully on the marketing concept and on being consumer oriented. They must be equipped with a clear understanding of the process and motivations of consumer buying, and also of how changing use of media is altering how that process takes place.

The fact that it may be difficult to analyze consumer behaviour precisely, does not detract from the importance of doing so. Even though research on consumer buying behaviour has not supplied all the knowledge that marketers need, considerable progress has been made in recent years. Advances in technology and changing shopping habits are increasing the opportunities for capturing and managing information about consumers. For example, the increasing use of online banking has been made possible by the development of computer systems that can handle the full range of banking transactions in which consumers wish to engage. The same systems are enabling providers such as First Direct and ing.com to store and analyze a huge variety of information about customers' spending and savings patterns. When analyzed, this information provides vital insights into the needs and wants of different customer types. These insights can be used to develop and market new products and services. At a time when an increasingly competitive business environment is making it more difficult to develop an edge over rival organizations, the demands for such information are only likely to grow.

Summary

Buying behaviour comprises the decision processes and actions of people involved in buying and using products. *Consumer buying behaviour* refers to the buying behaviour of ultimate consumers – those who purchase products for personal or household use, not for business purposes. Analyzing consumer buying behaviour helps marketers to determine what satisfies customers, so that they can implement the marketing concept and better predict how consumers will respond to different marketing programmes.

Consumer decisions can be classified into three categories: routine response behaviour, limited decision-making and extensive decision-making. A consumer uses *routine response behaviour* when buying frequently purchased, low-cost, low-risk items that require very little search and decision effort. *Limited decision-making* is used for products purchased occasionally or when a buyer needs to acquire information about an unfamiliar brand in a familiar product category. *Extensive decision-making* is used when purchasing an unfamiliar, expensive, high-risk or infrequently bought product. *Impulse buying* is an unplanned buying behaviour involving a powerful, persistent urge to buy something immediately. The purchase of a certain product does not always elicit the same type of decision-making behaviour. Individuals differ in their response to purchase situations. Even the same individual may make a different decision in other circumstances.

The *consumer buying decision process* comprises five stages: problem recognition, information search, evaluation of alternatives, purchase and post-purchase evaluation. Decision processes do not always culminate in a purchase, and not all consumer decisions include all five stages. Problem recognition occurs when a buyer becomes aware that there is a difference between a desired state and an actual condition. After recognizing the problem, the buyer searches for product information that will help resolve the problem or satisfy the need. *Internal search* involves buyers searching their memory for information about products that might solve the problem. If insufficient information is retrieved in this way, additional information is sought through *external search*. A successful information search will yield a group of brands, called an *evoked set*, that are viewed as possible alternatives. The level of involvement, which is the amount of interest, emotion and activity expended on a purchase, affects the degree of the external search. To evaluate the products in the evoked set, a buyer establishes certain criteria and assigns each a certain *salience* – or level of importance – by which to compare, rate and rank the different products. During purchase, the consumer selects the product or brand on the basis of results from the evaluation stage and on other factors. The buyer also chooses the seller from whom to buy the product. After the purchase, the buyer evaluates the product's actual performance. Shortly after the purchase of an expensive product the post-purchase evaluation may provoke *cognitive dissonance* – dissatisfaction brought on by the consumer's doubts as to whether he or she should have bought the product in the first place. The results of the post-purchase evaluation will affect future buying behaviour.

Three major categories of influences are believed to affect the consumer buying decision process: personal, psychological and social factors. A *personal factor* is one that is unique to a particular person. Personal factors include demographic factors, situational factors and level of involvement. *Demographic factors* are individual characteristics such as age, sex, race, ethnic origin, income, family life cycle and occupation. *Situational factors* are the external circumstances or conditions that exist when a consumer is making a purchase decision, such as the time available. An individual's *level of involvement* – the level of interest, emotional commitment and time spent searching for a product in a particular situation – also affects the buying decision process. Enduring involvement is an ongoing interest in a product class because of personal relevance. Situational involvement is a temporary interest resulting from the particular circumstance or environment in which buyers find themselves.

Psychological factors partly determine people's general behaviour and thus influence their behaviour as consumers. The primary psychological influences on consumer behaviour are perception, motives, learning, attitudes and personality. *Perception* is the process of selecting, organizing and interpreting *information inputs* (the sensations received through sight, taste, hearing, smell and touch) to produce meaning. The first step in the perceptual process is the selection of information. *Selective exposure* is the phenomenon of people selecting the inputs that are to be exposed to their awareness; *selective distortion* is the changing or twisting of currently received information. *Selective retention* involves remembering information inputs that support personal feelings and beliefs, and forgetting those that do not. The second step of the perceptual process requires organizing and integrating the new information with that already stored in memory. Interpretation – the third step in the perceptual process – is the assignment of meaning to what has been organized. In addition to perceptions of packages, products, brands and organizations, individuals also have a *self-concept*, or self-image.

A *motive* is an internal, energy-giving force directing a person's activities towards satisfying a need or achieving a goal. *Patronage motives* influence where a person purchases products on a regular basis. To analyze the major motives that influence consumers to buy or not buy products, marketers conduct motivation research, using *in-depth interviews, focus groups* or *projective techniques*. Common types of projective technique include word association tests, bubble drawings and sentence completion tests.

Learning refers to changes in a person's behaviour caused by information and experience. *Knowledge*, in this context, has two components: familiarity with the product and expertise – the ability to apply the product.

Attitude refers to an individual's enduring evaluation, feelings and behavioural tendencies towards an object or activity. Consumer attitudes towards a company and its products greatly influence the success or failure of its marketing strategy. Marketers measure consumers' attitudes using *attitude scales*.

Personality comprises all the internal traits and behaviours that make a person unique. Though the results of many studies have been inconclusive, some marketers believe that personality does influence the types and brands of products purchased.

Social factors are the forces that other people exert on buying behaviour. They include the influence of roles and family, reference groups, social classes and culture and sub-cultures. We all occupy positions within groups, organizations and institutions. Each position has a *role* – a set of actions and activities that a person in a particular position is supposed to perform. A group is a *reference group* when an individual identifies with the group so much that he or she takes on many of the values, attitudes or behaviours of group members. In most reference groups, one or more members stand out as *opinion leaders*. A *social class* is an open group of individuals who have similar social rank. *Culture* is everything in our surroundings that is made by human beings, plus values and behaviours. A culture can be divided into *sub-cultures* on the basis of geographic regions or human characteristics, such as age or ethnic background. The arrival of social networking sites and digital media like blogs is changing the way consumers learn about and evaluate products. Through these connections consumers can share information and experiences without company interferences. This is putting more power to control and disperse information in the hands of consumers.

Marketers try to understand consumer buying behaviour so that they can offer consumers greater satisfaction. Improvements in technology and refinements in research methods are increasing opportunities to capture and manage data about consumers and their behaviour. The combination of the pressure of rising consumer expectations, combined with an increasingly competitive business environment, will spur marketers to seek a fuller understanding of consumer decision processes.

Key links

This chapter, about consumer buying behaviour, should be read in conjunction with Chapter 5, which examines buying behaviour in business markets.

- Without an understanding of customers' buying behaviour, it is difficult for marketers to develop effective marketing programmes, as discussed in Part Three.

- An understanding of customer buying behaviour is also essential for two core facets of marketing strategy: developing target market strategies (see Chapter 6); and creating powerful brand propositions (see Chapters 6 and 14).

Important terms

Buying behaviour
Consumer buying behaviour
Routine response behaviour
Limited decision-making
Impulse buying
Extensive decision-making
Consumer buying decision process
Internal search
External search
Involvement
Evoked set
Salience
Cognitive dissonance
Personal influencing factors
Demographic factors
Situational factors
Level of involvement
Psychological factors
Perception
Information inputs
Selective exposure
Selective distortion
Selective retention
Self-concept
Motive
Patronage motives
In-depth interview
Focus group
Projective techniques
Learning
Knowledge
Attitude
Attitude scale
Personality
Social factors
Role
Reference group
Opinion leader
Social class
Culture
Sub-cultures
Consumer-to-consumer (C2C) communication

Discussion and review questions

1   Name the types of buying behaviour consumers use. List some products that you have bought using each type of behaviour.

2   In what circumstances have you bought a product on impulse?

3   What are the five stages in the consumer buying decision process? Are all these stages used in all consumer purchase decisions?

4   What are the personal factors that affect the consumer buying decision process? How do they affect the process?

5   How does a consumer's level of involvement affect his or her purchase behaviour?

6   What is the function of time in a consumer's buying decision process?

7   What is selective exposure and what effect does it have on consumer buying?

8   How do marketers attempt to shape consumers' learning?

9   Why are marketers concerned about consumer attitudes?

10 Describe reference groups. How do they influence buying behaviour? Name some of your own reference groups.

11 In what ways does social class affect a person's purchase decisions?

12 What is culture? How does it affect a person's buying behaviour?

13 Describe the sub-cultures to which you belong. Identify buying behaviour that is unique to your sub-culture.

14 If consumers are dissatisfied with a particular purchase, what actions are open to them? What can marketers do to respond to these actions?

15 How is consumer-to-consumer communication changing the way consumers buy products?

Recommended readings

Blackwell, R. D., Engel, J. F. and Miniard, P. W., *Consumer Behaviour* (South-Western, 2005).

Evans, M.E., Foxall, G. and Jamal, A., *Consumer Behaviour* (John Wiley, 2009).

Jansson-Boyd, C.V., *Consumer Psychology* (Open University Press, 2010).

Foxall, G. R., *Understanding Consumer Choice* (Palgrave Macmillan, 2005).

Hanson, H., Schiffman, L.G. and Kanuk, L., *Consumer Behaviour* (FT/Prentice-Hall, 2011).

Solomon, M., Bamossy, G., Askegaard, S. and Hogg, M. K., *Consumer Behaviour* (FT/Prentice-Hall, 2009).

Internet exercise

Some mass-market or mainstream eCommerce sites, such as Amazon.co.uk, have extended the concept of customization to their customer base. Amazon has analyzed its customer data, then used its understanding of certain users' likes and dislikes to make recommendations to other users. Take a look at this online retailer at: www.amazon.co.uk or www.amazon.com. Focusing on the organization's bookselling activities, answer the following:

1 What might motivate some consumers to read a 'best-selling' list?

2 Is the consumer's level of involvement with online book purchase likely to be high or low?

3 Discuss the consumer buying decision process as it relates to a decision to purchase from Amazon.co.uk.

Applied mini-case

InterContinental Hotels Group is the world's largest hotel group, with 4 400 hotels and 652 000 guest rooms in over 100 countries, providing 146 million room nights per annum. The company has adopted a multi-segment strategy in order to address a variety of consumer requirements in the lodging industry. Its hotels include the upmarket InterContinental and Crown Plaza brands, boutique chain Hotel Indigo, Holiday Inn, budget brand Holiday Inn Express, as well as hotel operations Staybridge and Candlewood. In deriving its brand and target market strategies, InterContinental's marketers have considered a host of customer characteristics, requirements and behaviours, such as duration of stay, hotel location and proximity to other addresses, amenities and services sought or expected, desired luxury, value-for-money, hotel ambiance and feel, hotel usage, size of guest room, purpose of stay, booking/decision-making personnel and organizations, amongst other variables.

Sources: Sally Dibb and Lyndon Simkin, *Market Segmentation Success: Making It Happen!*, 2008, New York: The Haworth Press; **www.ichotelsgroup.com**; InterContinental Hotels Group marketing materials, 2011.

Question

A large company such as InterContinental Hotels Group is interested in finding out more about the factors that influence people buying hotel weekend breaks. Relating your answer to this example, review the different personal, psychological and social influences that might impact on someone seeking to make this kind of purchase.

Case study

Crayola promotes colouring in for all

While Nintendo and Playstation games, music videos, satellite TV cartoon channels and Web-based interactive gaming, have captured children's attention, Crayola Crayons have maintained a role in children's play and remained on store shelves. Crayola LLC, formerly Binney & Smith, fought back with a new marketing strategy and marketing plan for the venerable crayon. The company launched a huge MTV-style campaign, targeted at children rather than parents.

Traditionally, Crayola Crayons were targeted at parents, using educational themes. But after recognizing that children's purchasing power and influence on family purchases have increased in recent years, the company decided to change the crayon's image as an old fashioned toy to an exciting way for kids and teens to express themselves. To this end, the company developed new advertisements featuring rock music, 'hip' kids and soaring colours for showing during television programmes seen by children. In-store videos provided to toy stores and retailers of children's clothing followed up the theme.

After marketing research indicated that children prefer brighter colours, the company decided to retire blue grey, green blue, lemon yellow, maize, orange red, orange yellow, raw umber and violet blue to the Crayola Hall of Fame and to replace them with the more vivid cerulean, dandelion, fuchsia, jungle green, royal purple, teal blue, vivid tangerine and wild strawberry. This decision was controversial, however. The company was inundated with phone calls, letters and petitions from people who missed the old colours. Protesters marched on the company, carrying placards with slogans like 'We hate the new 8!' and 'They call it a retirement, I call it a burial'. RUMPS, the Raw Umber and Maize Preservation Society, finally got its way. The company issued a commemorative tin containing the 64 crayon box and a special pack of the eight colours dropped one year earlier. Even though children liked the new colours, parents liked the old eight colours. The company issued a statement saying that the old colours were revived partly because the company is in the business of providing what the consumer wants.

Along with new advertisements and colours, the company introduced ColourWorks, a line of erasable crayon sticks and retractable coloured pencils and pens. The company brought out Silver Swirls, crayons that have twirls of silver mixed in with the wax colours. Pictures coloured with Silver Swirls can be buffed to a high sheen with tissue. The new line was not only tested by children but also named by them. The company licensed its brand to Concord Cameras for a range of brightly coloured single use cameras aimed at children under 12. Several software companies have recognized the Crayola brand appeal: Micrografx offers the Crayola Amazing Art Adventure and the Crayola Art Studio – software games that encourage art and design a long way from the traditional wax crayon. IBM brought out Crayola Creation Corner to 'transform ordinary household items into toys, animals, jewellery, spaceships, greeting cards, stationery, party decorations and all sorts of other inventions'.

A full range of PC interactive software products emerged, still focusing on drawing and creativity, but not based purely on the familiar wax crayon. The latter remains the company's core line, though it now features as part of making kits – Badge Bonanza or Crayola Jewellery – and a whole host of design sets. Clearly, the Crayola brand is still very popular with children, parents and toy stores. More and more children are discovering the Crayola name, encouraged by Crayola's embracing of the Internet. The website **www.crayola.com** has a wealth to offer, with games, craft ideas and products aimed at three target audiences: parents, educators and 'Crayola kids'. The Cut and Colour pages have something for everyone – from dream catchers and chinese lanterns to Christmas decorations and remembrance poppies. The company has very effectively created an online community around its wax crayon brand.

Despite its new focus on children, the company has not forgotten who actually holds the purse strings. The company continues to target parents with advertisements in women's and parents' magazines, while new products or services – such as **www.crayola.com** – include educational and child development messages aimed at parents. However, the revised marketing strategy and accompanying marketing plan have led more children to reach for Crayola Crayons instead of the Nintendo joystick or LEGO bricks. Sales are up and shelf space in toy stores could not be better, despite stiff competition from a host of rival entertainment products and toys.

Sources: **www.crayola.com**, 2011; Ellen Neuborne, 'Crayola crayons have old colors back', *USA Today*, 2 October 1991, p. 2B; Ken Riddle, 'Crayola draws brighter lines in the market', *Marketing*, 21 January 1991, p. 4; Beefeater Restaurants, 1993; Toys 'R' Us, Leicester, 1996; Loretta Roach, 'Single use explosion', *Discount Merchandiser*, September 1995, pp. 28–30; Robyn Parets, 'Children's edutainment titles vie for shelf space', *Discount Store News*, 19 June 1995, pp. C6–C9; Binney & Smith UK, 1999; Toys 'R' Us, 1999, 2004, 2007, 2011; **www.crayola.com**, 2007.

Questions for discussion

1 Why did Crayola LLC have to update its marketing and change its strategy?

2 What are Crayola's target audiences? Why did the company need to approach them differently?

3 Why has the company embraced the Internet?

CHAPTER 5

Business markets and business buying behaviour

"Business customers are complex, demanding and require managing differently to consumers"

Objectives

- To become familiar with the various types of business market

- To identify the major characteristics of business buyers and transactions

- To understand several attributes of business demand

- To become familiar with the major components of a buying centre

- To understand relationship marketing and exchanges between industrial buyers and sellers

- To understand the stages of the business buying decision process and the factors that affect this process

- To learn how to select and analyze business target markets

- To appreciate some of the nuances of marketing business products

INTRODUCTION

Most readers of this book will have related the material in the previous chapter to their own purchasing experiences as consumers. Many marketers, though, do not address consumers. Instead, their target customers are other businesses or organizations. Or, they must develop marketing strategies for consumers and engage with them, while also managing trade channel relationships in order to reach their final customers. Either way, many marketers are involved with B2B (business-to-business) rather than B2C (business-to-consumer) marketing. This chapter addresses the nature of business-to-business marketing, known here as business marketing.

business market
The customers are not consumers, private individuals or households: instead the target customers are other businesses and organizations that purchase a specific type of product or service for resale, for use in making other products or for use in their daily operations

A **business market** is one in which the customer is not a consumer, a private individual or household. In business markets, the target customers are other businesses and organizations that purchase a specific type of product or service for resale, for use in making other products or for use in their daily operations. In older books, this used to be known as **industrial** or **organizational marketing**. More recently, the term **business-to-business marketing** has become popular. Now, this has been abbreviated to 'business marketing' or B2B. Whether known as industrial, organizational, business-to-business or simply business

industrial, organizational or business-to-business marketing
See business market

marketing, the emphasis is on other businesses and organizations as customers, rather than end-user consumers.

Nectar Business

Many consumers have a purse or wallet full of loyalty cards, such as Tesco Clubcard, AirMiles or Nectar. How often when filling up with fuel at a BP service station are you asked whether you have a Nectar card? It is not only consumers who receive loyalty cards. Businesses also are persuaded to sign up, in B2B deals with the major loyalty schemes. Nectar Business was launched in 2005 and now has around 600 000 SMEs as corporate members.

What is Nectar Business?

Collect Nectar points on your everyday business purchases and then spend them on rewards for your business and treats for you – it's that simple.

http://www.nectar.com/dynamic/business/
about-nectar

Nectar Business customers can collect reward points when they hire Hertz vehicles, purchase from Dulux Decorator Centres, consume snacks from Brakes, buy business insurance from Premierline or stationery from Viking. 'It's easy to collect points on the things you already buy for your business everyday – from stationery and insurance to specialist trade equipment or even food supplies', explains

more via BOC's or via the telephone'.

Nectar Business. Perhaps for some surprises, too … 'Collect Nectar points when you purchase quality industrial and refrigerant gases, equipment and much nationwide network of retail stores

Just as for any consumer product, Nectar Business's marketers must work hard to reflect customer views, refresh the proposition and communicate effectively to both new account prospects and to the 600 000 business customers already signed up. In particular, the company wanted to increase redemption rates of its reward points so that more personnel in its 600 000 SME customers were actively using the service. A piece of marketing research found that many potential users were too 'time-poor' to spend their points on the items included in Nectar's official rewards portfolio.

As a result of the survey findings, the redemption process was re-thought and simplified. A group of highest value collectors was offered a one-to-one concierge service that identified, sourced, secured and shipped the items on which they wanted to spend their points. Certain call centre staff were dedicated to the Silver Service concierge proposition. In addition, the categorization of rewards on offer was streamlined and made easier to navigate. Agency Crocodile developed a new campaign promoting the concierge service. Two mailings were developed, one for e-mail and one for direct mail. The e-mail response rate was 28 per cent with an 80 per cent increase in redemptions, while the direct mail approach enjoyed a response rate of 13 per cent and an uplift in people redeeming of 192 per cent. Further campaigns have since been run to support the Silver Service concept, resulting in good improvements in redemption rates and a growing number of active users.

Sources: **http://www.nectar.com/business/NectarHomeForward.nectar**, 22 March 2011; **http://www.nectar.com/dynamic/business/about-nectar**, 22 March 2011; **http://www.boconline.co.uk/how_to_buy/nectar_business.asp**, 22 March 2011; Meg Carter, 'Silver service', *The Marketer*, March 2011, pp. 20–22.

© Carolyn Jenkins / Alamy

Nectar Business provides a loyalty card scheme for members such as Hertz and Viking, targeting business users rather than consumers. This chapter explores what is meant by business marketing, before examining the characteristics of business buying and the nature of demand for business products. The chapter's focus is on the buying centre and the buying decision process as applied to business-to-business marketing. The chapter concludes by examining how marketers select and analyze business markets, and the ways in which marketers in business markets modify their use of the marketing toolkit. For example, in terms of branding, addressing customer needs, determining market segments, understanding competitive forces, undertaking marketing research and in constructing marketing programmes. Read in conjunction with the previous chapter, users of *Marketing Essentials* will have a sound appreciation of buying behaviour and also how marketing must differ between business and consumer markets.

Types of business market

There are four broad kinds of business markets: producers, resellers (retailers, wholesalers, distributors), public sector and governments, plus institutions. Some would argue that aspects of the

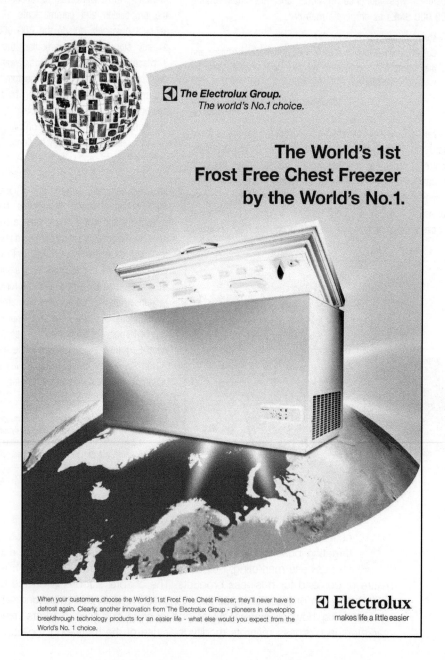

FIGURE 5.1
This Electrolux advertisement targets retailers stocking the manufacturer's range of freezers

Source: Courtesy of Electrolux Major Appliances (UK)

third sector warrant their own category. The following section describes the characteristics of the customers that make up these markets.

Producer markets

producer markets
Buyers of raw materials and semi-finished and finished items used to produce other products or in their own operations

Individuals and business organizations that purchase products to make a profit by using them to produce other products or by using them in their own operations are classified as **producer markets**. Producer markets include buyers of raw materials and semi-finished and finished items used to produce other products. For example, a manufacturer buys raw materials and component parts to use directly in the production of its products. Grocers and supermarkets are producer markets for numerous support products, such as paper and plastic bags, displays, scanners and floorcare products. Hotels are producer markets for food, cleaning equipment, laundry services and furniture. Figure 5.1 targets retailers stocking the manufacturer's range of freezers. Producer markets cover a broad array of industries, ranging from agriculture, forestry, fisheries and mining, to construction, transport, communications and public utilities.

Manufacturers tend to be geographically concentrated in certain industries, particularly if dependent on certain locally available raw materials, grants and financial inducements or skills. This concentration occurs in Europe too, with heavy industry centred on the Ruhr valley in Germany, and on the Midlands and the north-west in the UK. Sometimes an industrial marketer may be able to serve customers more efficiently as a result. Within certain areas, production in just a few industries may account for a sizeable proportion of total industrial output.

Reseller markets

reseller markets
Intermediaries, such as wholesalers and retailers, who buy finished goods and resell them to make a profit

Reseller markets consist of intermediaries, such as wholesalers and retailers, who buy finished goods and resell them to make a profit. These intermediaries are discussed in Chapter 11. Other than making minor alterations, resellers do not change the physical characteristics of the products they handle. Tesco stocks and sells Heinz or Tilda products without altering the branding, content or packaging. With the exception of items that producers sell directly to consumers, all products sold to consumer markets are first sold to reseller markets.

wholesalers
Intermediaries who purchase products for resale to retailers, other wholesalers and producers, governments and institutions

Wholesalers Wholesalers or distributors purchase products for resale to retailers, other wholesalers and producers, governments and institutions. Although some highly technical products are sold directly to end users, many products are sold through wholesalers/intermediaries, who in turn sell products to other companies in the distribution system. Thus wholesalers are very important in helping to get a producer's product to customers. Wholesalers often carry many products, perhaps as many as 250 000 items. From the reseller's point of view, having access to such an array of products from a single source makes it much simpler to buy a variety of items. When inventories are vast, the reordering of products is normally automated and the wholesaler's initial purchase decisions are made by professional buyers and buying committees.

retailers
Intermediaries that purchase products and resell them to final consumers

Retailers Retailers purchase products and resell them to final consumers. Some retailers carry a large number of items. Chemists, for example, may stock up to 12 000 items, and some supermarkets may handle in excess of 20 000 different products. In small, family-owned retail stores, the owner frequently makes purchasing decisions. Large department stores or supermarket retailers have one or more employees in each department who are responsible for buying products for that department. As for chain stores, a buyer or buying committee in the central office frequently decides whether a product will be made available for selection by store managers. For smaller businesses, local store managers make the actual buying decisions.

Factors considered by resellers When making purchase decisions, resellers consider several factors. They evaluate the level of demand for a product to determine in what quantity and at what prices it can be resold. They assess the amount of space required to handle a product relative to its potential profit. Sometimes resellers will put a product on trial for a fixed period, allowing them to judge customers' reactions and to make better-informed decisions about shelf space and positions as a result. Retailers, for example, sometimes evaluate products on the basis of sales per square metre of selling area or contribution to overall gross margin. Since customers often depend on a reseller to have a product when they need it, a reseller typically evaluates a supplier's ability to provide adequate quantities when and where wanted. Resellers also take into account the ease of placing orders, and the availability of technical assistance and training programmes from the producer.

More broadly, when resellers consider buying a product not previously carried, they try to determine whether the product competes with or complements the products the company is currently handling. These types of concern distinguish reseller markets from other markets. Sometimes resellers will start stocking a new line of products in response to specific requests from customers. Marketers dealing with reseller markets must recognize these needs and be able to serve them.

Government and public sector markets

government markets
Departments that buy goods and services to support their internal operations, and to provide the public with education, water, energy, national defence, road systems and healthcare

National and local governments make up **government markets** and contribute to **public sector markets**. They spend huge amounts annually for a variety of goods and services to support their internal operations and to provide the public with education, utilities (in some countries), national defence, road systems and healthcare. In Europe, the amount spent by local governments varies from country to country, depending on the level and cost of services provided. The types and quantities of products bought by government markets reflect social demands on various government agencies. As the public's needs for government services change, so do the government markets' demands for products.

public sector markets
Government and institutional not-for-profit customers and stakeholder groups

Because government agencies spend public funds to buy the products they need to provide services, they are accountable to the public. This accountability is responsible for a relatively complex set of buying procedures. Some organizations, unwilling to deal with so much red tape, do not even try to sell to government buyers, while others have learned to deal efficiently with government procedures. For certain companies, such as BAE, and for certain products, such as defence-related items, the government may be one of only a few customers.

Governments usually make their purchases through bids or negotiated contracts. To make a sale under the bid system, a company must apply and receive approval to be placed on a list of qualified bidders. When a government unit wants to buy, it sends out a detailed description of the products to these qualified bidders. Organizations that wish to sell such products then submit bids. The government unit is usually required to accept the lowest bid. When buying non-standard or highly complex products, a government unit often uses a negotiated contract. Under this procedure, the government unit selects only a few companies, negotiates specifications and terms, and eventually awards the contract to one of the negotiating companies. Most large defence contracts held by such companies as BAE or Thales are reached through negotiated contracts.

Although government markets have complicated requirements, they can also be very lucrative. When government departments modernize obsolete computer systems, for example, successful bidders can make high sales with attractive margins during the life of a contract, which may last for five years or more. Some companies have established separate departments to facilitate marketing to government units, while others specialize entirely in this area. The buying behaviour of governments is complex, though. A business such as Fujitsu sells IT services to banks, retailers, manufacturers and utility companies. Fujitsu is a leading supplier of IT services to central and local government and the health service: it has specialist management teams and sales and marketing specialists who focus purely on these public-sector clients owing to the specialized nature of their buying.

Institutional markets

institutional markets
Organizations with charitable, educational, community or other non-business goals

third sector
Includes charities, the voluntary sector, not-for-profit organizations and NGOs.

Organizations with charitable, educational, community or other non-business goals constitute **institutional markets**. Members of institutional markets include libraries, museums, universities, charitable organizations and some churches and hospitals. Some of these are also public-sector bodies, such as libraries and museums. Increasingly, government and institutional markets are being grouped together and referred to as public sector markets, although the term **third sector** has emerged to cover charities, the voluntary sector, not-for-profit organizations and NGOs.

Institutions purchase large amounts of products annually to provide goods, services and ideas to members, congregations, students and other stakeholder groups. For example, a library must buy new books for its readers; pay rent, fuel and water bills; fund the staffing and cleaning of its buildings; invest in IT facilities; and pay to produce publicity material about its services. Because such institutions often have different goals and fewer resources than other types of organization, marketers may use special marketing activities to serve these markets. Public sector markets consist of government and institutional not-for-profit customers and stakeholder groups: public sector marketing is a significant growth area within the marketing discipline. Within some of these activities, notably government bodies promoting health and wellbeing for the population and the planet, there is a role for social marketing (see Chapter 1), which has further extended marketing's contribution in this domain.

Dimensions of business buying

Having clarified the different types of business customer, the next step is to consider the dimensions of business-to-business buying. After first examining several characteristics of business transactions, this section then discusses various attributes of business buyers and some of their primary concerns when making purchase decisions. Next it looks at methods of business buying and the major types of purchase that organizations make. The section concludes with a discussion of how the demand for business products and services differs from the demand for consumer products and services.

Characteristics of business transactions

Although the marketing concept is equally applicable to business and consumer markets, there are several fundamental differences between the transactions that occur in each. Business buyers tend to order in much larger quantities than do individual consumers and often demand customized or tailored propositions. Suppliers must often sell their products in large quantities to make profits; consequently, they prefer not to sell to customers who place small orders.

Generally, business purchases are negotiated less frequently than consumer sales. Some purchases involve expensive items, such as machinery or office equipment, that are used for a number of years. Other products, such as raw materials and component items, are used continuously in production and may have to be supplied frequently. However, the contract regarding the terms of sale of these items is likely to be a long-term agreement, requiring periodic negotiations.

Negotiations in business sales may take much longer than those for consumer sales. Most consumers do not negotiate on prices paid, whereas many business customers never pay the list price. Purchasing decisions are often made by a committee; orders are frequently large, expensive and complex; and products may be custom built. There is a good chance that several people or departments in the purchasing organization will be involved. One department might express a need for a product; a second department might develop its specifications; a third might stipulate the maximum amount to be spent; and a fourth might actually place the order. This approach allows individuals with relevant expertise to be incorporated into the process when required. Sales personnel play an important role in negotiations with customers. The quality of the relationship that develops has been shown to impact on the outcome of such negotiations.

reciprocity
An arrangement unique to business-to-business marketing in which two organizations agree to buy from each other

One practice unique to business-to-business sales is **reciprocity**, an arrangement in which two organizations agree to buy from each other. In some countries, reciprocal agreements that threaten competition are illegal, and action may be taken to stop anti-competitive reciprocal practices. Nonetheless, a certain amount of reciprocal dealing occurs among small businesses and, to a lesser extent, among larger companies as well. Such companies often find that developing long-term relationships of this kind can be an effective competitive tool.[1] Reciprocity can create a problem because coercive measures may be used to enforce it or because reciprocity influences purchasing agents to deal only with certain suppliers.

Attributes of business buyers

Business buyers are usually thought of as being different from consumer buyers in their purchasing behaviour because they are better informed about the products they purchase and often deliberate/negotiate for longer. The viability of their employer's business and thereby their own careers may well depend on their purchasing decisions, so they must be well informed. To make purchasing decisions that fulfil an organization's needs, business buyers demand detailed information about a product's functional features and technical specifications.

Business buyers, however, also have personal goals that may influence their buying behaviour. Most buyers seek the psychological satisfaction that comes with promotion and financial rewards. In general, managers are most likely to achieve these personal goals when they consistently exhibit rational buying behaviour and perform their jobs in ways that help their companies achieve their organizational objectives. Suppose, though, that a business buyer develops a close friendship with a certain supplier. If the buyer values the friendship more than organizational promotion or financial rewards, s/he may behave irrationally from the company's point of view. Dealing exclusively with that supplier regardless of better prices, quality or service from competitors may indicate an unhealthy or unethical alliance between the buyer and seller. Companies have different ways of dealing with such problems. Some require more than one person to be involved in buying products, while others periodically review their use of suppliers.

Primary concerns of business buyers

When they make purchasing decisions, business customers take into account a variety of factors. For example, in the business advertisement in Figure 5.2 the range of product options and convenience are emphasized. Among their chief considerations are quality, delivery, service and price. Product range, innovation, reliability and logistical support may also be significant considerations. Increasingly, business buyers are concerned with service support levels and ongoing commitment from their selected suppliers. There is a growing view, too, that a supplier's personnel in terms of knowledge, motivation, attitude and passion for assisting the customer, are an integral part of the product proposition being 'consumed' by the business customer (see Chapter 8).

Business catering doesn't
have to be complicated

Tiffin box

10 people – £35

www.jagscatering.co.uk

JAGS

FIGURE 5.2
This business-to-business advertisement
for Jags Catering makes business catering
simple

Most business customers try to achieve and maintain a specific level of quality in the products they offer to their target markets. To accomplish this goal, they often buy their products on the basis of a set of expressed characteristics, commonly called specifications. These allow a business buyer to evaluate the quality of the products being considered according to particular features and thus to determine whether or not they meet the organization's needs.

Meeting specifications is extremely important to business customers. If a product fails to meet specifications and malfunctions for the ultimate consumer, that product's supplier may be dropped and an alternative sought. On the other hand, a business buyer is usually cautious about buying products that exceed specifications, because such products often cost more and thus increase production costs. Suppliers, therefore, need to design their products carefully to come as close as possible to their customers' specifications without incurring any unnecessary extras.

Business buyers also value service. The services offered by suppliers directly and indirectly influence their customers' costs, sales and profits. When tangible goods are the same or quite similar – as with most raw materials – they may have the same specifications and be sold at the same price in the same kind of containers. Under such conditions, the mix of services a business marketer provides to its customers represents its greatest opportunity to gain a competitive advantage. For example, bitumen supplier Nynas has a reputation for technical expertise, technical assistance and flexible logistics. Competitors may be able to offer a similar bitumen product, but few can emulate Nynas's ability to look after customers or offer bespoke solutions.

Among the most commonly expected services are market information, regulatory compliance support, inventory maintenance, on-time delivery, flexible ordering and logistical support, technical assistance, warranty back-up, repair services and credit facilities. Specific services vary in importance, however, and the mix of services that companies need is also affected by environmental conditions.

Market information Business buyers in general are likely to need technical product information, data regarding demand, information about general economic conditions or supply and delivery information. For example, when technology is changing rapidly, forcing companies to change their production machinery, the demand for consultancy support services and warranty assurances will be especially high.

Regulatory compliance In many markets, regulators and government agencies insist on certain product conformity, production and distribution practices, commercial practices and customer management, and customers may demand or welcome support in these regards from their suppliers.

Inventory maintenance It is critical for suppliers to maintain an adequate inventory in order to keep products accessible for when a business buyer needs them and to reduce the buyer's inventory requirements and costs.

On-time delivery Reliable, on-time delivery by suppliers also enables business customers to carry less inventory.

Warranty back-up Purchasers of machinery and high tech equipment are especially concerned about adequate warranties. They are also keen to obtain repair services and replacement parts quickly, because equipment that cannot be used is costly.

Credit facilities Suppliers can also give extra value to business buyers by offering credit. Credit helps to improve a business customer's cash flow, reduces the peaks and troughs of capital requirements and thus lowers the company's cost of capital. Although no single supplier can provide every possible service to its customers, a marketing-oriented supplier will try to create a service mix that satisfies the target market.

The importance of service quality

Service quality has become a critical issue because customer expectations of service have broadened. Marketers also need to strive for uniformity of service, simplicity, truthfulness and accuracy; to develop customer service objectives; and to monitor or audit their customer service programmes. Companies can monitor the quality of their service by formally surveying customers or calling on them informally to ask questions about the service they have received. Marketers with a strong customer service programme reap a reward: their customers keep coming back long after the first sale.[2] With customer expectations increasing, it is becoming more difficult for companies to achieve a differential advantage in these areas, and companies must take care to ensure that complaints are handled properly.[3] This reduces the likelihood that dissatisfied customers will give negative feedback to others in the marketplace.[4] One study found that boosting customer retention by 5 per cent could double a small company's profitability.[5] As explored in Chapter 11, some experts argue that service quality delivery is the most important aspect of marketing.

The importance of price

Price matters greatly to a business customer because it influences operating costs and costs of goods sold, and these costs affect the customer's selling price and profit margin. When purchasing major equipment, an industrial buyer views the price as the amount of investment necessary to obtain a certain level of return or savings. Such a purchaser is likely to compare the price of a machine with the value of the benefits that the machine will yield. A while ago, Caterpillar lost market share to foreign competitors because its prices were too high. A business buyer does not compare alternative products by price alone, though; other factors, such as product quality and supplier services, are also major elements in the purchase decision. For example, one study found that in the buying decision process for mainframe computer software operating systems, intangible attributes, such as the seller's credibility and understanding of the buyer's needs, were very important in the buyer's decision process.[6]

Methods of business buying

Although no two business buyers go about their jobs in the same way, most use one or more of the following purchase methods: description, inspection, sampling and negotiation.

Description When products being purchased are commonly standardized according to certain characteristics – such as size, shape, weight and colour – and graded using such standards, a business buyer may be able to purchase simply by describing or specifying quantity, grade and other attributes. Agricultural produce often falls into this category. In some cases a buyer may specify a particular brand or its equivalent when describing the desired product. Purchases on the basis of description are especially common between a buyer and seller who have established an ongoing relationship built on trust.

Inspection Certain products, such as large industrial machinery, used vehicles and buildings, have unique characteristics and are likely to vary in condition. For example, a transport depot may need its parking area to be resurfaced. Consequently, buyers and sellers of such products must base their purchase decisions on inspection.

Sampling In buying based on sampling, a sample of the product is taken from the lot and evaluated. It is assumed that the characteristics of this sample represent the entire lot. This method is appropriate when the product is homogeneous – for instance, grain – and examination of the entire lot is not physically or economically feasible.

Negotiation Some business purchasing relies on negotiated contracts. In certain instances, a business buyer describes exactly what is needed and then asks sellers to submit bids. The buyer may take the most attractive bids and negotiate with those suppliers. In other cases, the buyer may not be able to identify specifically what is to be purchased but can provide only a general description – as might be the case for a special piece of custom-made equipment. A buyer and seller may negotiate a contract that specifies a base price and contains provisions for the payment of additional costs and fees. These contracts are most likely to be used for one-off projects, such as buildings and capital equipment. For example, the prices that Orbital Sciences Corporation charges its customers for launching and placing satellites in orbit are determined through negotiated contracts.

Types of business purchase

Most business purchases are one of three types: new task purchase, modified re-buy purchase or straight re-buy purchase. The type of purchase affects the number of individuals involved and the length of the buying process.

new task purchase
An organization's initial purchase of an item to be used to perform a new job or to solve a new problem

New task purchase In a **new task purchase**, an organization makes an initial purchase of an item to be used to perform a new job or to solve a new problem. This may take a long time because it might require the development of product specifications, supplier specifications and procedures for future purchases. To make the initial purchase, the business buyer usually needs a good deal of information and may formally review a set of possible suppliers. A new task purchase is important to the supplier because it may lead to the sale of large quantities of the product over a period of years.

modified re-buy purchase
A new task purchase that is changed when it is reordered or when the requirements associated with a straight re-buy purchase are modified

Modified re-buy purchase In a **modified re-buy purchase**, a new task purchase is changed the second or third time it is ordered, or the requirements associated with a straight re-buy purchase are modified. For example, an organization might seek faster delivery, lower prices or a different quality of product specifications. When modified re-buying occurs, regular suppliers may become more competitive to keep the account. Competing suppliers may have the opportunity to obtain the business.

straight re-buy purchase
A routine repurchase of the same products under approximately the same terms of sale

Straight re-buy purchase A **straight re-buy purchase** occurs when a buyer re-purchases the same products routinely under approximately the same terms of sale. For example, when re-ordering photocopying paper, a buyer requires little additional information and can usually place the order relatively quickly, often using familiar suppliers that have provided satisfactory service and products in the past. These suppliers try to set up automatic re-ordering systems to make reordering easy and convenient for business buyers, and may even monitor the organization's inventory to indicate to the buyer what needs to be ordered.

Demand for business products

Products sold to business customers are called business products and, consequently, the demand for these products is called business demand. Unlike consumer demand, business demand – formerly known as industrial demand – is:

● derived

● inelastic

● joint, and

● more fluctuating.

derived demand
Demand for business products that arises from the demand for consumer products

Derived demand As business customers, especially producers, buy products to be used directly or indirectly in the production of goods and services to satisfy consumers' needs, the demand for business products arises from the demand for consumer products; it is, therefore, called **derived demand**. In fact, all business demand can in some way be traced to consumer demand. This occurs at a number of levels, with business sellers being affected in various ways. For instance, consumers today are more concerned with good health and nutrition than ever before, and as a result are purchasing food products containing less cholesterol, saturated fat, sugar and salt. When some consumers stopped buying high-cholesterol cooking fats and margarine, the demand for equipment used in manufacturing these products also dropped. Thus factors influencing consumer buying of various food products have ultimately affected food processors, equipment manufacturers, suppliers of raw materials and even fast-food restaurants, which have had to switch to lower-cholesterol oils for frying. Changes in derived demand result from a chain reaction. When consumer demand for a product changes, a wave is set in motion that affects demand for all of the items involved in the production of that consumer product.

inelastic demand
Demand that is not significantly affected by a price increase or decrease

Inelastic demand The demand for many business products at the industry level is **inelastic demand** – that is, a price increase or decrease will not significantly alter demand for the item. Because many business products contain a number of parts, price increases that affect only one or two parts of the product may yield only a slightly higher per-unit production cost. Of course, when a sizeable price increase for a component represents a large proportion of the total product's cost, demand may become more elastic, because the component price increase will cause the price at the consumer level to rise sharply. For example, if manufacturers of aircraft engines substantially increase the price of these engines, forcing Boeing in turn to raise the prices of its aircraft, the demand for aircraft may become more elastic as airlines reconsider whether they can afford them. An increase in the price of windscreens, however, is unlikely to affect greatly the price of the aircraft or the demand for them.

The characteristic of inelasticity applies only to industry demand for the business product, not to the demand curve faced by an individual company. For example, suppose that a car component company increases the price of rubber seals sold to car manufacturers, while its competitors retain their lower prices. The car component company would probably experience reduced unit sales because most of its customers would switch to the lower-priced brands. A specific organization is vulnerable to elastic demand, even though industry demand for a particular product is inelastic.

joint demand
Demand that occurs when two or more products are used in combination to produce another product

Joint demand The demand for certain business products, especially raw materials and components, is subject to joint demand. **Joint demand** occurs when two or more items are used in combination to produce a product. For example, a company that manufactures cork noticeboards for schools and colleges needs supplies of cork and wood to produce the item; these two products are demanded jointly. A shortage of cork will cause a drop in the production of wooden surrounds for noticeboards or a lack of chips will hinder computer manufacture.

Marketers selling many jointly demanded items must realize that when a customer begins purchasing one of the jointly demanded items, a good opportunity exists for selling related products. Similarly, when customers purchase a number of jointly demanded products, the producer must take care to avoid shortages of any one of them, because such shortages jeopardize sales of all the jointly demanded products. The susceptibility of producers to the shortage of a particular item is illustrated clearly when industrial action at companies producing microchips results in a halt in production at manufacturers of computers and related goods.

Fluctuating demand Because the demand for business products fluctuates according to consumer demand, when particular consumer products are in high demand, their producers buy large quantities of raw materials and components to ensure that they can meet long-run production requirements. Such producers may also expand their production capacity, which entails the acquisition of new equipment and machinery, more workers, a greater need for business services, and more raw materials and component parts.

Conversely, a decline in the demand for certain consumer goods significantly reduces the demand for business products used to produce those goods. When consumer demand is low, business customers cut their purchases of raw materials and components, and stop buying equipment and machinery, even for replacement purposes. This trend is especially pronounced during periods of recession.

A marketer of business products may notice changes in demand when its customers change their inventory policies, perhaps because of expectations about future demand. For example, if several dishwasher manufacturers who buy timers from one producer increase their inventory of timers from a two-week to a one-month supply, the timer producer will experience a significant immediate increase in demand.

Sometimes price changes can lead to surprising temporary changes in demand. A price increase for a business item may initially cause business customers to buy more of the item because they expect the price to rise further. Similarly, demand for a business product may be significantly lower following a price cut as buyers wait for further price reductions. Such behaviour is often observed in companies purchasing information technology. Fluctuations in demand can be significant in industries in which price changes occur frequently.

Business buying decisions

business (or business-to-business) buying behaviour
The purchase behaviour of producers, resellers, the public sector, government units and institutions

Business (or business-to-business) buying behaviour refers to the purchase behaviour of producers, resellers, the public sector, government units and institutions. Although several of the same factors that affect consumer buying behaviour (discussed in Chapter 4) also influence business buying behaviour, a number of factors are unique to the latter. This section first analyzes the buying centre to learn who participates in making business purchase decisions and then focuses on the stages of the buying decision process and the factors that affect this process.

The buying centre

buying centre
The group of people within an organization who are involved in making business-to-business purchase decisions

Most business-to-business purchase decisions are made by more than one person. The group of people within an organization who are involved in making business purchase decisions are usually referred to as the **buying centre**. These individuals include users, influencers, buyers, deciders and gatekeepers, although one person may perform several of these roles.[7] Participants in the buying process share the goals and risks associated with their decisions. Effective marketers strive to understand the constituents of risk, as perceived by their target customer personnel, so that they may tailor their messages and marketing propositions to reassure members of the buying centre. In this way, marketers hope to gain an advantage over those rivals that fail to understand these customer concerns and issues.

Users are those in the business who actually use the product being acquired. They frequently initiate the purchase process and/or generate the specifications for the purchase. After the purchase, they also evaluate the product's performance relative to the specifications. Although users do not ordinarily have sufficient power to make the final decision to buy, it is important that their views be considered. A user who is unhappy with a piece of equipment may not work efficiently. Influencers are often technical personnel, such as engineers, who help develop the specifications and evaluate alternative products. Technical personnel are especially important influencers when the products being considered involve new, advanced technology. For example, a chemicals manufacturer seeking to install new processing equipment may take advice from a wide range of technical experts.

Buyers are responsible for selecting suppliers and actually negotiating the terms of purchase. They may also become involved in developing specifications. Buyers are sometimes called purchasing agents or purchasing managers and in retailers, merchandisers. Their choices of suppliers and products, especially for new task purchases, are heavily influenced by individuals occupying other roles in the buying centre. For straight re-buy purchases, the buyer plays a major role in the selection of suppliers and in negotiations with them. Deciders actually choose the products and suppliers. Although buyers may be the deciders, it is not unusual for different people to occupy these roles. For routinely purchased items, buyers are commonly the deciders. However, a buyer may not be authorized to make purchases that exceed a certain monetary value, in which case higher-level management personnel are the deciders. Gatekeepers, such as secretaries and technical personnel, control the flow of information to and among others in the buying centre. The flow of information from supplier sales representatives to users and influencers is often controlled by buyers or other personnel in the purchasing department. Unfortunately, relations between members of the buying centre can become strained at times.

Practitioners' use of the buying behaviour theory: the Dibb/Simkin Buying Proforma

Marketing tools and techniques

Most practitioners do not want to read a 500-page text book about understanding customers, but equally they recognize that in order to fully appreciate a business customer's requirements or consumers' buying behaviour, they must be able to:

- profile the targeted customers/consumers – be like them!
- understand the composition of the buying centre
- identify their key customer values (KCVs) – customer/consumer needs and expectations
- determine how the customers/consumers buy – their buying process
- understand the influences at work on this process.

In order to devise effective marketing strategies and programmes, marketers must be able to answer three key questions.

1 What needs must be satisfied and for whom?

2 Where should marketers be active in the business customer (or consumer) buying process?

3 Which influencing factors can they in turn influence?

There are many approaches to addressing such an understanding of business customers or consumers, but one proposed by Dibb and Simkin has been widely adopted across consumer, business and service markets. Two examples are presented here in order to illustrate this approach.

Example 1

A leading supplier of herbicides, pesticides and seeds segmented the farmers – the customers – in Latin America, identifying 22 market segments (see Chapter 6). As an example, one segment is profiled below, illustrating the types of farmer in this segment, the nature of the buying centre and the very specific, ego-led customer needs. In order to operate successfully in this market segment, a supplier has to satisfy these needs but also tailor marketing campaigns to the characteristics of these farmers and the varied mix of professionals within

this buying centre. In developing a better understanding of the buying process, this agrichemicals business realized there were important influencing factors impacting on customer choice that it had previously ignored. Contact was made with organizers of the technical seminars and the trade association in order to gain an advantage over rivals.

Example 2

In common with most banks and building societies, the bank that conducted this research (see following page) marketed its products directly to the targeted consumers: first-time house buyers. Marketing research (see Chapter 7) identified the important influencing role played by the parents of these potential customers, and of independent financial advisers, estate agents and the bank's own staff involved in daily routine banking activities with such customers. Different marketing messages and campaigns were produced to appeal to these various target audiences. The real added value came from targeting information about its mortgage products to the parents of young adults aged in their 20s. It was quite straightforward for this bank to trawl through its customer database in order to identify customers with children in such an age range. Market share in this mortgage segment duly quadrupled in less than a year. This bank undertook a similar analysis across all of its segments in both consumer markets – as illustrated below – and in its business markets.

The Dibb/Simkin Buying Proforma:

- forces managers to 'think customer'!
- provides much more than just a description of 'who to sell to'
- identifies exactly what a company must provide/offer
- reveals the influences the company in turn must strive to influence
- provides a framework against which to compare competitors' moves and marketing programmes.

The Dibb/Simkin Buying Proforma is copyright Sally Dibb and Lyndon Simkin. A more extensive explanation of this technique is offered in either *The Market Segmentation Workbook* (Dibb and Simkin) or *The Marketing Planning Workbook* (Dibb, Simkin and Bradley), both originally published in 1996 by Thomson, London; or in the authors' newer titles *Market Segmentation Success: Making It Happen!* (The Haworth Press/Routledge, 2008) and *Marketing Planning* (Cengage Learning, 2008).

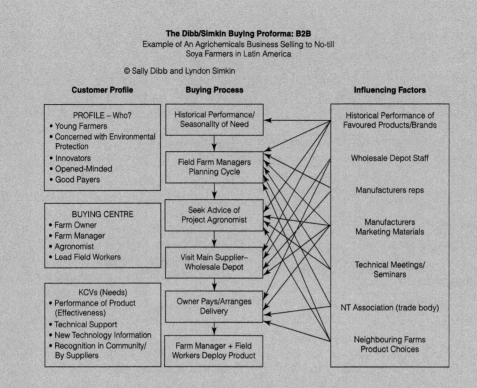

The Dibb/Simkin Buying Proforma: B2B
Example of An Agrichemicals Business Selling to No-till
Soya Farmers in Latin America

© Sally Dibb and Lyndon Simkin

Customer Profile

PROFILE – Who?
- Young Farmers
- Concerned with Environmental Protection
- Innovators
- Opened-Minded
- Good Payers

BUYING CENTRE
- Farm Owner
- Farm Manager
- Agronomist
- Lead Field Workers

KCVs (Needs)
- Performance of Product (Effectiveness)
- Technical Support
- New Technology Information
- Recognition in Community/ By Suppliers

Buying Process

Historical Performance/ Seasonality of Need

Field Farm Managers Planning Cycle

Seek Advice of Project Agronomist

Visit Main Supplier– Wholesale Depot

Owner Pays/Arranges Delivery

Farm Manager + Field Workers Deploy Product

Influencing Factors

Historical Performance of Favoured Products/Brands

Wholesale Depot Staff

Manufacturers reps

Manufacturers Marketing Materials

Technical Meetings/ Seminars

NT Association (trade body)

Neighbouring Farms Product Choices

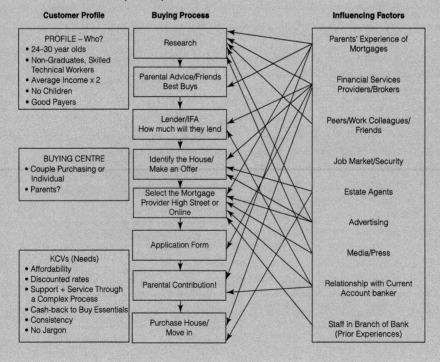

The Dibb/Simkin Buying Proforma:B2C
Example of a Bank Marketing Mortgages to
First-Time House Buyers, Non-Professionals in the UK

© Sally Dibb & Lyndon Simkin

Customer Profile

PROFILE – Who?
- 24–30 year olds
- Non-Graduates, Skilled Technical Workers
- Average Income x 2
- No Children
- Good Payers

BUYING CENTRE
- Couple Purchasing or Individual
- Parents?

KCVs (Needs)
- Affordability
- Discounted rates
- Support + Service Through a Complex Process
- Cash-back to Buy Essentials
- Consistency
- No Jargon

Buying Process

Research

Parental Advice/Friends Best Buys

Lender/IFA How much will they lend

Identify the House/ Make an Offer

Select the Mortgage Provider High Street or Online

Application Form

Parental Contribution!

Purchase House/ Move in

Influencing Factors

Parents' Experience of Mortgages

Financial Services Providers/Brokers

Peers/Work Colleagues/ Friends

Job Market/Security

Estate Agents

Advertising

Media/Press

Relationship with Current Account banker

Staff in Branch of Bank (Prior Experiences)

The size and characteristics of an organization's buying centre are affected by the number of its employees and its market position, the volume and types of products being purchased and the company's overall managerial philosophy regarding exactly who should be involved in purchase decisions. A marketer attempting to sell to a business customer needs to know who is in the buying centre, the types of decisions each individual makes and which individuals are the most influential in the decision process. The marketer should also strive to understand the respective needs of these members and how each perceives risk in terms of the proposed purchase: the marketer should then tailor messages to reassure the various members of the buying centre. Then the marketer will be in a position to contact those in the buying centre who have the most influence. Such an approach is detailed in the Marketing Tools and Techniques box above, which also explains how many organizations deploy the buying behaviour concepts presented in this chapter as they build up an understanding of their customers.

Relationship marketing and managing exchange relationships

The relationship that exists between a supplying organization and its customers is an important aspect of the buying process that deserves special consideration. In fact, marketing experts have become much more interested in marketing relationships in general.[8] The term **relationship marketing** has been used to express this particular development, as explained in Chapter 1. Instead of being concerned about individual transactions between suppliers and buyers, the relationship marketing approach emphasizes the importance of the whole relationship between the parties. Relationship marketing can, therefore, be regarded as all of the activities an organization uses to build, maintain and develop ongoing customer relations.[9] The intention is to nurture a mutually beneficial sustainable relationship and to maximize the 'share of wallet' from the customer over a period of time.

relationship marketing
All of the activities an organization uses to build, maintain and develop customer relations

Put simply, relationship marketing is concerned with acquiring and keeping customers by ensuring that an appropriate combination of marketing, customer service and quality is provided.[10] Underlying the relationship marketing concept is the idea that the relationship between a supplying organization and its buyers is essentially similar to the relationship between two individuals. For example, bitumen company Nynas, featured in the case at the end of this chapter, has achieved market leadership in many of its key markets through building ongoing relationships with a diversity of customers 24 hours a day and 365 days a year. Such relationships are conducted over a period of time through a series of meetings and interactions, which allow each party to get to know the other, to share information, to adapt to each other and generally to build trust and cooperation.[11]

As explained in Chapter 1, the concept of relationship marketing is changing the way in which marketers for both consumer and business markets are looking at marketing. However, it is also particularly pertinent to this chapter's discussion of the exchange relationships that develop between buyers and sellers.[12] When a company buys a product or service from another company, both organizations become involved in an exchange process. During the transaction, both buyer and seller will exchange items of value in return for something else. For example, when a software company provides a printing company with a desktop publishing package, it will provide the buyer with a package of benefits that include the software, regular updates, a helpline, on-site support, detailed users' guide, warranty details, a variety of payment options and the opportunity to attend a training course. In exchange, the printer will agree to pay the price negotiated with the manufacturer. Figure 5.3 shows the range of factors that can be exchanged during the purchase process.

It is often in the interests of both parties to develop long-term relationships. If buying and selling companies are used to dealing with each other, they are more likely to be able to adapt to each other's needs and to reach an agreement quickly and easily. Some research suggests that adaptation by suppliers happens more often than adaptation by buyers. However, long-term relationships are often attractive to both companies because they reduce the level of risk – financial

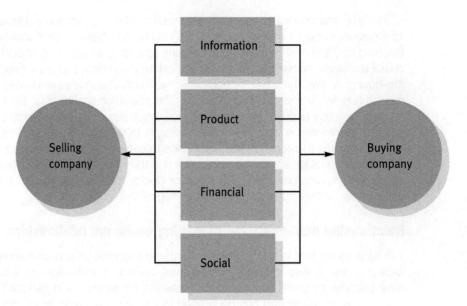

FIGURE 5.3
The exchange process in business buying

relationship management
The process of encouraging a match between the seller's competitive advantage and the buyer's requirements over an item's life cycle

and practical – associated with the purchase. The trend towards long-term relationships has resulted in the development of what is called **relationship management**.[13] This process encourages a match between the seller's competitive advantage and the buyer's requirements over the life cycle of the item being purchased. Larger customer accounts warrant close attention and bespoke customer support, nurturing an ongoing relationship and protecting sales. **Key account management** is practised by businesses with several very large and important customers, whose volume of business justifies one-to-one tailored handling.

Stages of the business buying decision process

key account management
Dedicated and close support for individual business customers whose volume of business is significant and warrants one-to-one handling

Like consumers, businesses follow a buying decision process. This process is summarized on the right-hand side of Figure 5.4.

Stage 1 In the first stage, one or more individuals recognize that a problem or need exists. Problem recognition may arise under a variety of circumstances, either from inside or outside the company. For example, a machine might reach the end of its working life and need to be replaced, the CEO may dictate the desirability of finding a supplier for an IT outsourcing agreement, a key customer might demand a new material be sourced, or changes in fire regulations might dictate the need for a new approach to manufacturing. Often, the problem recognized is simply the need to replenish stocks of raw materials or components. Individuals in the buying centre, such as users, influencers or buyers, may be involved in problem recognition, but this may be stimulated by external sources, such as sales representatives or customers.

Stage 2 The second stage of the process – development of product specifications – requires those involved to assess the problem or need, and to determine what is necessary to resolve or satisfy it. During this stage, users and influencers, such as technical personnel, production managers and engineers, often provide information and advice for developing product specifications. By assessing and describing needs, the organization should be able to establish product specifications.

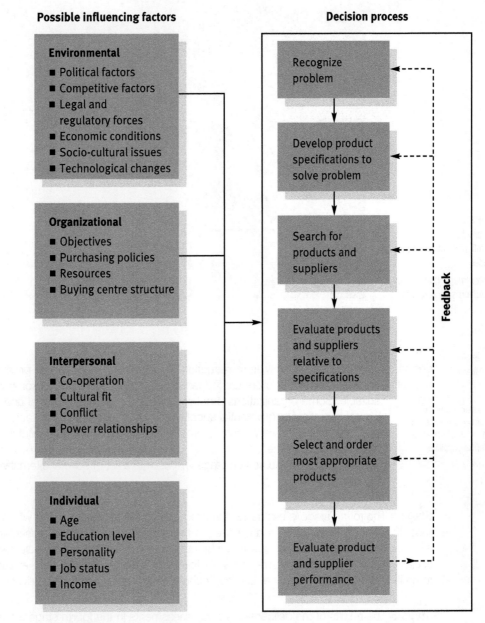

Possible influencing factors

Decision process

FIGURE 5.4
The business buying decision process and factors that may influence it

Source: Wind, Y., Webster, F.E. Jr, Organisational Buying Behaviour, Ist edition copyright © 1972, pp. 33-37. Adapted by permission of Pearson Education, Inc. Upper Saddle River, NJ.

Stage 3 Searching for possible products to solve the problem and then locating suitable suppliers is the third stage in the decision process. Search activities may involve surfing the Web, looking in company files and trade directories, contacting suppliers for information and networking, visiting trade shows, identifying suppliers used by rivals, soliciting proposals from known suppliers and examining catalogues and trade publications. Suppliers may be viewed as unacceptable because they are too small to supply the quantities needed, or because they do not have the necessary information technology systems to keep appropriate delivery records. In some instances, the product may not be available from any existing supplier and the buyer must then find an innovative company, that can design and build the product. During this search stage, some organizations engage in **value analysis**, which is an evaluation of each component of a potential purchase. Value analysis examines quality,

value analysis
An evaluation of each component of a potential purchase

FIGURE 5.5
DHL promotes the quality
and reliability of its courier
services

Source: Image Courtesy of
The Advertising Archives

designs, materials and possibly item reduction or deletion to acquire the product in the most
cost-effective way. Usually suppliers are judged against several criteria and some will be ruled un-
suitable. Some organizations practice **supplier analysis**, a formal and systematic appraisal of current and potential suppliers or vendors, focusing on factors such as price,
product quality, delivery service, product availability, reliability, reputation, client profile
and customer service.

supplier analysis
A formal and systematic
evaluation of current and
potential suppliers

If all goes well, the search stage will result in a list of several alternative products and
suppliers.

Stage 4 The fourth stage is evaluating the products on the list to determine which options (if any)
meet the product specifications developed in the second stage. The advertisement in Figure 5.5
stresses the particular product quality attributes that may help customers evaluate whether a particular offering meets their requirements. At this point, various suppliers are evaluated according
to multiple criteria, such as price, service, technical support and ability to deliver.

Stage 5 The results of the deliberations and assessments in the fourth stage are used during the
fifth stage, to select the most appropriate product and supplier. In some cases the buyer may
decide on several suppliers. In others, only one supplier is selected – a situation known as **sole
sourcing**. Sole sourcing has traditionally been discouraged except when a product is

sole sourcing
A buying process that
involves the selection of
only one supplier

available from only one company. In recent times sole sourcing has become more
popular, partly because such an arrangement means better communications between
buyer and supplier, stability and higher profits for the supplier and, often, lower prices
for the buyer. The popular manufacturing approach of just-in-time often requires sole
sourcing, in order to facilitate the logistical arrangements between buyer and supplier.
However, many organizations prefer to purchase goods and services from several
suppliers – **multiple sourcing** – to reduce the possibility of disruption caused by

multiple sourcing
A business's decision to
use several suppliers

strikes, shortages, quality problems, delivery glitches or bankruptcy. The actual product is ordered in this fifth stage and specific details regarding terms, credit arrangements, delivery dates and methods, and technical assistance are worked out.

Stage 6 During the sixth stage, the product's performance is evaluated by comparing it with specifications and customer expectations of the relationship. Sometimes, even though the product meets the specifications, its performance does not adequately solve the problem or satisfy the need recognized in the first stage. In such cases, the product specifications must be adjusted. The supplier's performance is also evaluated during this stage, and if it is found wanting, the buyer seeks corrective action from the supplier or searches for a new supplier. Buyers are increasingly concerned with obtaining high-quality service from suppliers and may formally set performance targets for them. The results of such performance evaluations become feedback for the other stages and influence future purchase decisions. In many business relationships, particularly long-term relationships, suppliers formally audit their customers' satisfaction levels in order to minimize any problems that may eventually lose a customer to a competitor.

Uses of the business buying decision process This business buying decision process is used in its entirety primarily for new task purchases. Several of the stages, but not necessarily all, are used for modified re-buying and straight re-buying, and fewer individuals are likely to be involved in these decisions. If a buyer–supplier relationship is working well, there may be no consideration of alternative suppliers, for example. Indeed, customers may work with such well-regarded suppliers when specifying their next product or purchasing needs. There is a desire in many business markets, particularly in supplier–manufacturer relationships, to create mutually beneficial ongoing partnerships, with customers and suppliers openly sharing market data, knowledge of product or competitor developments, and future plans.

Influences on business buying

Figure 5.4 also lists the four major categories of factors that influence business buying decisions: environmental, organizational, interpersonal and individual. In the Marketing Insight box (see page 172), insurance broker Willis's SME clients reflect in their customer engagement the influencing factors that impact on their corporate customers' decision-making.

environmental factors
Uncontrollable forces such as politics, competitive and economic factors, legal and regulatory issues, technological changes and socio-cultural issues

Environmental factors Chapter 3 explained that **environmental factors** are uncontrollable forces such as politics, laws, regulations and regulatory agencies, activities of interest groups, changes in the economy, competitors' actions and technological changes. These forces generate a considerable amount of uncertainty for an organization, which can make individuals in the buying centre apprehensive about certain types of purchase. Changes in one or more environmental forces can create new purchasing opportunities. For example, changes in competition and technology can make buying decisions difficult in the case of products such as computers, a field in which competition is increasingly affected by new cooperative strategies between companies. Compaq Computers, for instance, grew into a billion-dollar company by competing only against IBM and developing cooperative relationships with all other potential competitors, ultimately tying up with HP.[14]

organizational factors
Include the buyer's objectives, purchasing policies and resources, as well as the size and composition of its buying centre

Organizational factors **Organizational factors** influencing the buying decision process include the buyer's objectives, purchasing policies and resources, as well as the size and composition of its buying centre. An organization may have certain buying policies to which buying centre participants must conform. For instance, a company's policies may require long-term contracts, perhaps longer than most sellers desire. The nature of an organization's financial resources may require special credit arrangements. Any of these conditions could affect purchase decision processes.

interpersonal factors
The relationships among the people in the buying centre

Interpersonal factors **Interpersonal factors** are the relationships among the people in the buying centre, where the use of power and the level of conflict significantly influence organizational buying decisions. Certain managers in the buying centre may be better communicators than others and thus more persuasive. Often these interpersonal dynamics are hidden, making them difficult for business marketers and key account managers to appraise. There are also interpersonal factors to consider between supplier and customer personnel. While a customer may be purchasing a particular product, the supplier's personnel involved with placing the order, offering technical assistance or customer service, and in logistical arrangements, become a very important concern for the customer's managers. No matter how good the product may be, if the supplier's personnel are not regarded in a good light by the customer's managers, there is unlikely to be a high level of customer satisfaction. Suppliers must select, train, motivate and reward, control and orientate their customer-facing personnel very carefully. The individual factors pertinent to particular managers are, therefore, important.

individual factors
The personal characteristics of individuals in the buying centre, such as age, education, personality, position in the organization and income level

Individual factors Individual factors are the personal characteristics of individuals in the buying centre, such as age, education, personality, position in the organization and income level. For example, a 60-year-old manager who left school at 16 and has been with the organization ever since may affect the decisions of the buying centre differently from a 30 year old with a two-year employment history, who left university with a business studies degree and an MBA. How influential these factors will be depends on the buying situation, the type of product being purchased and whether the purchase is new task, modified re-buy or straight re-buy. The negotiating styles of individuals will undoubtedly vary within an organization and from one organization to another. To be effective, a marketer needs to know customers well enough to be aware of these individual factors and the effects they may have on purchase decisions.

Topical insight

Insurance brokers reflect influences on clients' decision-making

Willis is a global leading Anglo-American insurance broker serving many large commercial clients. In order to look after the SME market, Willis established the innovative Willis Network and its sister N². Independent insurance brokers can sign up to become a member of the Willis Network and receive the support, market insight, products and negotiating power with the large insurers that normally would only be available to large scale insurance firms. Members are guaranteed a regional monopoly within the Willis Network.

> The Willis Networks offer independent regional insurance brokers The Best of Both Worlds through the Willis Commercial Network and Willis N².
>
> Our regional broker network members can access Willis' resources to help them to flourish and grow in a dynamic market.

Member broker firms in the network serve many private and commercial customers. One key market is the insurance cover provided to corporate SME clients to cover their commercial activities. For example, the insurance cover required by a manufacturing business with turnover of around £5m and employing 80 workers. The cover generally is provided by the major insurers, such as Allianz, AXA, RSA or Zurich, but is purchased via an intermediary which is the local broker. The purchasing power and scale of Willis enable the company to negotiate preferential terms and customer service on behalf of network member local brokers, who in turn may deliver improved deals and service to their corporate clients.

Marketing research identified SME client needs for commercial combined insurance to be value, credibility of the package and supplier, well-specified products, incentives, customer service, supportive advice and peace of mind. The proposition offered and the way in which it is conveyed by the broker must reflect these B2B client requirements. While the product and service package is a key determining factor in gaining client interest, members of the Willis Network must reflect other research findings in their sales and marketing practices. For example, these corporate customers seek value for money but also reassurance that the provided insurance cover will be fit for purpose and give them peace of mind. The personal relationship and degree of empathy between the boss of the SME client and the broker's staff are essential requisites for success and for giving such peace of mind.

One of the most important influences upon these companies' selection of preferred broker and the purchase of the specific insurance package relates as much to peer comments as to the overt activities of the broker's staff. If the bosses of other SMEs speak highly about Willis Networks' local broker, there is likely to be a sales opportunity for the broker. As a result, the broker must identify and then engage with clients' networks and business circles, ensuring positive reinforcement for its brand reputation, service and products from the trusted contacts of the prospective SME's owner. This networking and reputation building often involves many afternoons on the golf course, business lunches, sponsoring local business gatherings and gaining coverage in the business pages of the local press. The importance of understanding such influencing forces and the various roles within the purchase decision-making process is essential for marketers in this challenging and very competitive sector.

Sources: **http://www.willisnetworks.co.uk/why-willis-networks/gateway-to-willis**, 22 March 2011; **http://www.willis.com/About_Willis**, 22 March 2011, Willis Networks, February and September, 2012.

Selection and analysis of business markets

business marketing
Activities directed towards facilitating and expediting exchanges between businesses

Marketing research is becoming more important in business markets. Most of the marketing research techniques discussed in Chapter 7 can be applied to **business marketing**. This section focuses on important and unique approaches to selecting and analyzing business markets.

Many business marketers have easy access to a considerable amount of information about potential customers, particularly in industrial or manufacturing markets, for much of this information appears in government and industry publications. Even though marketers may use different procedures to isolate and analyze target markets, most follow a similar pattern:

1 determining who potential customers are and what they require

2 deciding how many and locating where they are

3 estimating their purchase potential and likelihood of ongoing loyalty

4 identifying how to engage with them.

Identifying potential customers

Standard Industrial Classification (SIC) system
A system that provides information on different industries and products, and classifies economic characteristics of industrial, commercial, financial and service organizations

All marketers must determine who are potential customers.

The Standard Industrial Classification system Much information about business customers is based on the **Standard Industrial Classification (SIC) system**, which provides information on different industries and products, and was developed to classify selected economic characteristics of industrial, commercial, financial and service organizations. In the UK, this system is administered by the Office for National Statistics. Table 5.1 shows how the SIC system can be used to categorize products.

The most recent SIC manual contains ten broad divisions, each denoted by a single digit from 0 to 9. These are sub-divided into classes (each denoted by the addition of a

TABLE 5.1 The Standard Industrial Classification (SIC) system for categorizing industrial consumers

0	Agriculture, forestry and fishing
1	Energy and water supply industries
2	Extraction of minerals and ores other than fuels; manufacture of metals, mineral products and chemicals
3	Metal goods, engineering and vehicles
4	Other manufacturing industries
5	Construction
6	Distribution, hotels and catering; repairs
7	Transport and communication
8	Banking, finance, insurance, business services and leasing
9	Other services

TABLE 5.2 Types of government information available about industrial markets (based on SIC categories)

Value of industry shipments
Number of establishments
Number of employees
Exports as a percentage of shipments
Imports as a percentage of apparent consumption
Compound annual average rate of growth
Major producing areas

second digit), the classes are divided into groups (three digits) and the groups into activity headings (four more digits). There are ten divisions, 60 classes, 222 groups and 334 activity headings. For example, Division 4 (see Table 5.1), 'Other manufacturing industries', has eight classes, 50 groups and 91 activity headings. The numbering system follows that of NACE (Nomenclature Générale des Activités Économiques dans les Communautés Européennes) as far as possible.[15] To categorize manufacturers in more detail, the *Census of Distribution* further sub-divides manufacturers.

Data are available for each SIC category through various government publications and departments. Table 5.2 shows the types of information that can be obtained from government sources. Some data are available by town, county and metropolitan area. Business market data also appear in such non-government sources as Dun & Bradstreet's *Market Identifiers.*

The SIC system is a ready-made tool that allows business marketers to allocate industrial organizations to market segments based mainly on the type of product manufactured or handled. Although the SIC system is a vehicle for segmentation – identifying groupings of customers (see Chapter 6) – it must be used in conjunction with other types of data to enable a business marketer to determine exactly which customers he or she can reach and how many of them can be targeted. The SIC system is a convenient grouping categorization, but it does not negate the need to fully explore customer buying behaviour, as depicted in the Marketing Tools and Techniques box on pages 165–166, in order to properly consider target market priorities.

Input–output analysis Input–output analysis works well in conjunction with the SIC system. This type of analysis is based on the assumption that the output or sales of one industry are the input or purchases of other industries. For example, component manufacturers provide products that

input–output data
Information on what types of industries purchase the products of a particular industry

form an input for manufacturers of white goods such as washing machines, dishwashers and fridges. **Input–output data** tell what types of industries purchase the products of a particular industry.

After discovering which industries purchase the major portion of an industry's output, the next step is to find the SIC numbers for those industries. Because organizations are grouped differently in the input–output tables and the SIC system, ascertaining SIC numbers can be difficult. However, the Office for National Statistics does provide some limited conversion tables with the input–output data. These tables can assist business marketers in assigning SIC numbers to the industry categories used in the input–output analysis. Having determined the SIC numbers of the industries that buy the company's output, a business marketer is in a position to ascertain the number of establishments that are potential buyers nationally, by town and by county. Government publications report the number of establishments within SIC classifications, along with other types of data, such as those shown in Table 5.2.

Identifying and locating potential customers Once business marketers have achieved this level of information, they can identify and locate potential customers using the Internet or business directories such as *Kompass* and *Kellysearch*. These sources contain information about a company such as its name, SIC number, address, phone number and annual sales, allowing organizations to develop lists of potential customers by area.

A second approach, which is more expedient but also more expensive, is to use one of the many marketing services businesses. For example, Market Location and Experian are able to provide lists of organizations that fall into particular SIC groups. Information can include name, location, sales volume, number of employees, types of product handled and names of chief executives. Business marketers can then decide which companies on the list to pursue. This will usually involve an assessment of attractiveness and purchase potential. As described in Chapters 6 and 9, there are also many techniques that assist marketers in assessing the relative attractiveness of customers and market segments, such as the directional policy matrix and 'ABC sales: contribution' analysis, explained later in *Marketing Essentials*.

In business marketing, situation-specific variables may be more relevant in segmenting markets than general customer characteristics. Business customers concentrate on benefits sought; therefore, understanding the end use of the product is more important than the psychology of decisions or socio-economic characteristics. Segmenting by benefits rather than by customer characteristics can provide insight into the structure of the market and opportunities for new customers.[16]

FIGURE 5.6
Networking, discussing and engaging with prospective business customers is an important part of identifying likely sales leads and honing an appropriate marketing proposition

Source: iStock, 12-14-07 © Dmitriy Shironosov

To estimate the purchase potential of business customers or groups of customers, a marketer must find a relationship between the size of potential customers' purchases and a variable available in SIC data, such as the number of employees. For example, a fabric manufacturer might attempt to determine the average number of metres of different materials purchased by a specific type of potential clothing manufacturer relative to the number of people employed. If the marketer has no previous experience in this market segment, it will probably be necessary to survey a random sample of potential customers in order to establish a relationship between purchase sizes and numbers of people employed. Once this relationship has been established, it can be applied to potential customer segments to estimate their purchases. After deriving these estimates, the marketer selects the customers to be included in the target market.

More and more businesses are adopting segmentation schemes that are based on the needs, buying behaviour and characteristics of their customers, rather than on simple trade categories or SIC codes. Such segmentation demands a thorough understanding of the nature of purchasing, the buying decision-making process and influencing factors, as described in this chapter. The next chapter *of Marketing Essentials* explores the ways in which business marketers derive market segments and establish target market strategies.

Marketing's variations in business markets

Business marketers often have to address the needs of business customers within a marketing channel and the needs of their intended business customers. Some business marketers must also serve the needs of consumers. Marketers of consumer goods often manage many products and deal with perhaps thousands of customers. Mostly, although not always, such consumer products pass through a marketing channel so that a manufacturer's marketing managers deal primarily with channel member business customers. So for example, the marketers handling Snickers or Mars bars are concerned with understanding and satisfying their retail customers, such as the large cash-and-carry groups and the supermarkets. However, these marketers are also developing the marketing programmes targeting the end user consumers – Mars' marketers also handle the company's marketing activity aimed at the individual consumer. While a manufacturer's marketers often have to address dual audiences – channel member customers and consumers – it is more likely that their focus will be on the business (trade) customer.

Many business marketers handle a relatively small number of clients and the need to tailor marketing propositions to these customers' wishes is arguably more important than in consumer markets. While all marketers must properly understand buying behaviour and purchasers' characteristics, it is absolutely crucial in business marketing for marketers to develop such an understanding. Sales staff play a central role in building this understanding. Their relationships with customers can be leveraged to gain a particularly in-depth appreciation of customers' needs. Not surprisingly, the sales and marketing personnel in many business-to-business companies work together very closely.

There are other nuances, too, that it is worth mentioning. Most advertisements shown on television over the course of an evening are for consumer goods and services: they are eye-catching, emotive and highly persuasive. This style of advertising reflects the emotive brand positionings developed for many consumer goods, such as Nike or Guinness. While business marketers also strive to create strong brands (see Chapter 14) that are distinctive and attractive, much business branding lacks the emotion of consumer branding and suffers from a relative paucity of investment in supportive marketing communications activity and spending. Business branding tends to be more simplistic, focusing on identification and product differentiation. There are, of course, exceptions, with some business-to-business brands such as IBM or JCB being just as powerful as consumer brands.

The role of competition is different, too. It is unlikely that arch-rivals Tesco, Sainsbury's and ASDA would ever cooperate and work together. Similarly, why would KP and Walkers ever unite? Many brands between which a consumer may choose are unlikely ever to cooperate and work in harmony with each other. Indeed, the Competition Commission and EU regulators would probably be unimpressed if they did. In many business situations, though, individual companies pool their expertise and resources in order to win contracts with customers. For example, to offer retailers a viable chip-and-pin payment service, IT services company Fujitsu joined forces with Barclaycard Merchant Services (payment transactions), Box (hardware) and Cybertill (installation and maintenance) as a partnership. However, partners in one market segment may in fact be arch-rivals in another. Fujitsu may compete with CapGemini, BT or IBM in one segment, but partner such companies in order to serve the needs of business customers in another. The implication is that the understanding of competitive forces is often more complex and intriguing in many business markets and rivals cannot always be treated as the enemy!

Target market strategies are important to all marketers, irrespective of product or market. In order to develop a target market strategy, marketers must be able to allocate a market's customers into groups or market segments. The consumer marketer may use lifestyles, socio-economic information or consumers' perceived benefits to create market segments or groups of like-minded consumers. The business marketer, however, may fall back on more simple criteria, such as SIC codes or the trade sectors of their customers, in order to determine market segments. This very important aspect of marketing strategy is explored in Chapter 6. Until an understanding of business customers' buying behaviour has been developed, as described in this chapter, it is not possible to produce a market segmentation scheme.

If consumer marketers feel they have an inadequate appreciation of consumers' issues and buying behaviour, it is relatively straightforward to embark on suitable marketing research activities in order to rectify this deficiency. As described in Chapter 7, undertaking observations or surveys of consumers is fairly routine. However, busy executives and decision-makers inside business customers rarely offer to attend focus groups, they discard questionnaires and are not easy to access for interviews. Apart from access problems, business customers may well use any surveying to lobby. For example, they may feedback to the supplier's marketers behind the survey, the apparent importance of a better pricing option or improved customer service systems, rather than objectively and openly engage in the marketing research activity. Consumer products are readily visible on retailers' shelves; their prices, marketing communications campaigns, product features or attributes, and their channels to market are there to be seen by competitors' marketers. In most business markets, it is not easy to gain access to rivals' products or services, and the marketing programmes are not so readily visible.

The marketing mix is the set of tactical ingredients manipulated by marketers in marketing programmes designed to implement a target market strategy. As described in Part Three of *Marketing Essentials*, all marketers manipulate the marketing mix in order to reflect the nature of their market, customer buying behaviour, the activities of competitors, organizational capabilities and corporate objectives. Compared with consumer marketers, those tasked with marketing business products have to make certain adjustments to their marketing mix programmes.

The overall implication is that business marketers must modify their use of the marketing toolkit to reflect the nature of their markets and the characteristics of their business customers. The overall marketing process and the toolkit apply irrespective of the marketplace, but it is evident that business marketers, consumer goods marketers and the marketers of services need to make certain modifications.

Business marketers often have to address the needs of customers within a marketing channel as well as the needs of their intended customers. Some business marketers must also serve the needs of consumers. Many business marketers handle a relatively small number of customers and must tailor marketing propositions to these customers' specific wishes. The sales and marketing personnel in many business-to-business companies work together very closely.

Summary

Business marketing or B2B marketing used to be known as *organizational, industrial* or *business-to-business marketing.* Business markets consist of individuals or groups that purchase a specific kind of product for resale, for direct use in producing other products, or for use in their day-to-day operations. *Producer markets* include those individuals and business organizations that purchase products for the purpose of making a profit by using them either to produce other products or in their own operations. Classified as reseller *markets* are intermediaries, such as *wholesalers*, distributors and *retailers*, who buy finished products and resell them for the purpose of making a profit. *Government markets* consist of national and local governments, which spend huge amounts annually on goods and services to support their internal operations and provide citizens with needed services. Many businesses refer to government, local government and institutions collectively as the public sector, and the *public sector market* is a growing area of activity within the marketing discipline. Organizations that seek to achieve charitable, educational, community or other non-business goals constitute *institutional markets*. Aspects of government and much of institutional marketing today are described as the third sector, with social marketing addressing their customers.

Business-to-business transactions differ from consumer transactions in several ways. The transactions tend to be larger, and negotiations occur less frequently, though they are often lengthy. Business transactions sometimes involve more than one person or one department in the purchasing organization. They may also involve *reciprocity*, an arrangement in which two organizations agree to buy from each other, although some countries have strict rules governing such agreements. Business customers are usually viewed as more rational and more likely to seek information about a product's features and technical specifications than are ultimate consumers.

When purchasing products, business customers must be particularly concerned about quality, delivery, service and price. Quality is important because it directly affects the quality of the organizational buyer's ultimate product. To achieve an exact standard, organizations often buy their products on the basis of a set of expressed characteristics, called specifications. Reliable and fast delivery is crucial to many organizations, whose production lines must be fed with a continuous supply of component parts and raw materials. Because services can have a direct influence on a company's costs, sales and profits, such matters as market information, on-time delivery and availability of parts can be crucial to a business buyer. Although a business customer does not decide which products to purchase solely by their price, cost is of prime concern because it directly influences a company's profitability. Product range, regulatory compliance, innovation, reliability and logistical support may also be significant considerations. Increasingly, business buyers are concerned with service support levels and the ongoing commitment from their selected suppliers. There is a view that a supplier's personnel in terms of knowledge, motivation, attitude and passion for assisting the customer, are an integral part of the product proposition being 'consumed' by the business customer.

Business buyers use several purchasing methods, including description, inspection, sampling and negotiation. Most business purchases are new task, modified re-buy or straight re-buy. In a *new task purchase*, an organization makes an initial purchase of an item to be used to perform a new job or to solve a new problem. In a *modified re-buy purchase,* a new task purchase is changed the second or third time it is ordered, or the requirements associated with a straight re-buy purchase are modified. A *straight re-buy purchase* occurs when a buyer repurchases the same products routinely under approximately the same terms of sale.

Business demand differs from consumer demand along several dimensions. *Derived demand* is the demand for business products that arises from the demand for consumer products. At the industry level, *inelastic demand* is a demand that is not significantly affected by a price increase or decrease. If the price of an industrial item changes, demand for the product will not change proportionally. Some business products are subject to *joint demand*, which occurs when two or more items are used in combination to make a product. Finally, because business demand ultimately derives from consumer demand, the demand for business products can fluctuate widely.

Business (or business-to-business) buying behaviour refers to the purchase behaviour of producers, resellers, government units and institutions. Business purchase decisions are made through a *buying centre* – the group of people who are involved in making organizational purchase decisions. Users are those in the organization that actually use the product. Influencers help develop the specifications and evaluate alternative products for possible use. Buyers are responsible for selecting the suppliers and negotiating the terms of the purchases. Deciders choose the products and suppliers. Gatekeepers control the flow of information to and among people who occupy the other roles in the buying centre.

When a company buys a product or service from another company, both organizations enter into a process during which items of value are exchanged in return for something else. This exchange process may lead to a long-term relationship between buyer and seller. *Relationship marketing* is the term used to explain the special attention being given to this area and is defined as the activities an organization uses to build, maintain and develop customer relations (for both business and consumer markets). The trend toward long-term relationships has resulted in *relationship management,* increased *value analysis* and the more systematic evaluation of suppliers in *supplier analysis. Key account management* is an associated development.

The stages of the business buying decision process are (1) problem recognition, (2) development of product specifications to solve the problem, (3) search for products and suppliers, (4) evaluation of products relative to specifications, (5) selection and ordering of the most appropriate product and (6) evaluation of the product's and the supplier's performance. The evaluation of product and suppliers will directly affect future purchasing decisions. *Sole sourcing*, the process of selecting only one supplier, is becoming more popular, particularly where manufacturers are practising just-in-time production. Many organizations still opt to practise *multiple sourcing*.

Four categories of factors influence business buying decisions: environmental, organizational, interpersonal and individual. *Environmental factors* include politics, laws and regulations, economic conditions, competitive forces and technological changes. *Organizational factors* include the buyer's objectives, purchasing policies and resources, as well as the size and composition of its buying centre. *Interpersonal factors* refer to the relationships among the people in the buying centre, and relationships between supplier and customer personnel. *Individual factors* refer to the personal characteristics of individuals in the buying centre, such as age, education, personality, position in the organization, and income.

Business marketing is a set of activities directed at facilitating and expediting exchanges between organizations rather than with consumers.

Business marketers have a considerable amount of information available to them for use in planning their marketing strategies and for identifying sales potential. Much of this information is based on the *Standard Industrial Classification (SIC) system*, which classifies businesses into major industry divisions, classes, groups and activities. The SIC system provides business marketers with information needed to identify market leads. It can best be used for this purpose in conjunction with other information, such as *input–output data*. After identifying target industries, the marketer can locate potential customers by using the Internet or directories, or by employing a marketing services business. The marketer must then estimate the potential purchases of business customers.

Business-to-business branding tends to be more simplistic than is the case with consumer brands, focusing on identification and product differentiation. In many business situations, individual companies pool their expertise and resources in order to win contracts with customers. However, partners in one market segment may in fact be arch-rivals in another. The implication is that the understanding of competitive forces is often more complex and intriguing in business markets and rivals cannot always be treated as 'the enemy'.

Although SIC codes and industry trade categories are often used by business marketers, increasingly the approaches deployed by consumer marketers in creating market segments are being deployed in business markets. The next chapter explores market segmentation and target marketing in more detail. Undertaking marketing research in business markets is quite different from researching consumers. Compared with consumer markets, those tasked with marketing business products have to reflect certain market nuances when developing their marketing mix programmes.

Key links

● This chapter must be read in conjunction with Chapter 4, which details the buying behaviour of consumers. A popular examination question is to compare and contrast the buying behaviour models in consumer and business markets.

● In strategic marketing, a key use of an understanding of customer behaviour is the construction of market segments, as discussed in Chapter 6.

● The marketing mix should reflect the nuances of the market in question, as described throughout *Marketing Essentials* and the strategic cases ending each Part.

Important terms

Business market
Industrial, organizational or business-to-business market
Producer markets
Reseller markets
Wholesalers
Retailers
Government markets
Public sector markets
Institutional markets
Third sector
Reciprocity
New task purchase
Modified re-buy purchase
Straight re-buy purchase
Derived demand
Inelastic demand
Joint demand
Business (or business-to-business) buying behaviour
Buying centre
Relationship marketing
Relationship management
Key account management
Value analysis
Supplier analysis
Sole sourcing
Multiple sourcing
Environmental factors
Organizational factors
Interpersonal factors
Individual factors
Business marketing
Standard Industrial Classification (SIC) system
Input–output data

Discussion and review questions

1 Identify, describe and give examples of four major types of business market.

2 Why are business buyers generally considered more rational in regard to their purchasing behaviour than consumers?

3 What are the primary concerns of business customers?

4 List several characteristics that differentiate business transactions from consumer ones.

5 What are the commonly used methods of business buying?

6 Why do buyers involved in a straight re-buy purchase require less information than those making a new task purchase?

7 How does industrial/business demand differ from consumer demand?

8 What are the major components of a buying centre?

9 What elements may be exchanged by a buyer and seller when a purchase transaction takes place?

10 Why has relationship management attracted so much interest in business markets?

11 Identify the stages of the business buying decision process. How is this decision process used when making straight re-buys?

12 What impact does the evaluation of a particular purchase have on future buying decisions?

13 How do environmental, organizational, interpersonal and individual factors affect business purchases?

14 What function does the SIC system help business marketers perform?

15 List some sources that a business marketer can use to determine the names and addresses of potential customers.

16 In what ways do business marketers have to reflect the nuances of business markets when deploying the marketing toolkit?

Recommended readings

Brennan, R., Canning, L. and McDowell, R., *Business-to-Business Marketing* (Sage, 2010).

Ellis, N., *Business-to-Business Marketing: Relationships, Networks and Strategies* (OUP, 2010).

Gillin, P. and Schwartzman, E., *Social Marketing to Business Customers: Listen To Your B2B Market, Generate Major Account Leads and Build Client Relationships* (Wiley, 2011).

Hakansson, H., Ford, D., Gadd, L.-E., Snehota, I. and Waluszewski, A., *Business in Networks* (Wiley, 2009).

Hutt, M.D. and Speh, T.W., *Business Marketing Management: B2B* (South Western Educational, 2009).

Webster, F.E., *Industrial Marketing Strategy* (Wiley, 1995).

Internet exercise

Log onto Dell's website. Ignore the sections aimed at consumers. Instead, go to *Business* products. This section details Dell's business-to-business products, services and upcoming events. There are sections offering solutions to small business, public sector and large enterprises. Visit Dell's website at: http://www1.euro.dell.com or http://www.dell.com.

1   In what ways do Dell's web pages for business products reflect the requirements of business customers?

2   How have the messages been tailored to reflect the buying behaviour of Dell's business customers?

Applied mini-case

According to *The Marketer* magazine, B2B opportunities from social media are blossoming. American Express's B2B networking site *Openforum.com* is accessible to both new business customers and current Open Card members. It provides small and medium sized enterprises (SMEs) access to a wealth of advice and insight, including the views of Richard Branson and Seth Godin. Growing at 350 per cent year on year, the site quickly reached 10 000 Twitter followers. Intel's blog network allows readers to 'dig' or recommend its blogs on news sharing site Digg. Some Intel staff blogs have been recommended by over a thousand Digg users, providing a valuable platform for shaping opinion in Intel's markets, building reputation, and conveying a point of view favourable to supporting the company's marketing strategy. In a separate development, it is expected that many B2B social media gated communities will emerge, providing confidential business or issue 'chat rooms' for professionals in certain industries, similar to VuMedi for registered doctors. Social media applications are no longer only of interest to marketers addressing consumers.

Question

As the marketing director of a business-to-business organization, why might you be excited by the potential of communicating on social networking sites?

Case study

Nynas: in the black and leading

For most people, oil is evident as a fuel for cars, heating and the generation of electricity, or as the basis for the plastics industry. What about the black surfaces of pavements, roads, driveways, car parks and school playgrounds? Bitumen is an oil-based product most of us take for granted, but it is a major part of the revenue for companies such as Shell, BP, Esso, Total, Colas or Lanfina. The leading bitumen player in the UK, Scandinavia and much of western Europe is Stockholm-based Nynas. In the UK, this relatively small player in the petrochemicals industry has overall market leadership in the bitumen market and is renowned for its innovative product development with polymer formulations.

Bitumen is one of the most ubiquitous materials made by industry, underfoot almost everywhere as a core ingredient of the macadams and asphalts in roads and pavements. There are numerous specialist applications too, such as the backing for carpet tiles, roofing felts, sealants for mighty dams and waterproofing for bridge decks. Inevitably this results in a diverse customer base for an organization such as Nynas. In a market with competitors as large as Esso or Shell, Nynas's leadership has not occurred by accident. Nynas has established its enviable position by astutely utilizing the resources required to develop innovative products, customer service schemes and flexible delivery capabilities in order to ensure customer satisfaction. At the heart of its business strategy is a desire to innovate, listen to customers and develop services that genuinely enable customers to be served properly.

Nynas believes it has several important edges over its rivals, as described below.

Customer dialogue

As a major producer with significant R&D technical support, Nynas's laboratories can determine a product formulation for most bitumen-based applications. Whether the customer is a local authority requiring a cost-effective thin surfacing for a housing estate's ageing pavements; a contractor such as Tarmac requiring 24-hour supply of high-quality, state-of-the-art bitumen for the construction of a new motorway; or a builder buying polymer-enhanced mastic asphalts to act as a waterproofing membrane for regency mews properties, Nynas can develop a quality bitumen-based product.

Consistent quality and innovative product development

Refineries in Belgium, Sweden and the UK, supported by a network of terminals and research laboratories across Europe, enable Nynas to continually improve its products and their performance. Customers do not want to have to resurface major roads or busy shopping centre pavements on a frequent basis. Specialist applications such as waterproofing dams or houses are time consuming, costly and inconvenient remedial activities that clients do not want to repeat in a hurry. Nynas has access to high-grade Venezuelan bitumen, not readily available to its major competitors, which gives it added flexibility in producing high-quality bitumen grades for specific applications. Whether it is for a routine commodity bulk job such as a school playground surface or an unusual requirement for waterproofing a royal building, Nynas has developed a reputation as being a leading supplier.

Logistical support

Users of bitumen often require deliveries at very short notice, in specific quantities and to guaranteed quality levels. These deliveries may be anywhere at any time. A contractor repairing a busy commuter route out of daylight hours needs on-time delivery of ready-to-use bitumen products. Repairs to a remote bridge still require guaranteed on-time delivery. Nynas's depots operate around the clock despatching computer monitored deliveries by tanker to clients as and when the customer has specified. Twenty-four hours a day, 365 days

a year, Nynas prides itself on its high levels of responsiveness and reliability of delivery.

Nynas's composition of customers is varied. A major new road-building scheme will involve formal tendering and guarantees with penalties for inferior product or missed deliveries. The buying process of such customers will be highly formal, involving numerous managers, and functions as diverse as purchasing, technical support, construction, finance and logistical support. On both sides – customer and Nynas – cross-functional teams of scientists, engineers, managers and the field force will spend many months agreeing on the product requirements, contractual obligations, delivery requirements and application techniques. For other customers, the purchase is perhaps more of a routine re-buy, with only limited interaction and discussion between Nynas and the customer. On other occasions, the Nynas helpline may receive a midnight telephone call from a highways agency surveyor who has just discovered cracks in the surface of a major road and requires immediate assistance in both identifying the cause of the problem and rectifying the situation before commuters awake the next morning.

For a rather bland-looking substance such as bitumen, the market is diverse and challenging. Nynas has established its successful position in the European market for bitumen-based products by practising the best principles of marketing. The company strives to understand its customers' needs and to offer reliable products supported with effective customer service, round the clock. Product innovation is at the forefront of the company's strategy and, coupled with constantly improving ways of offering peace of mind to customers, provides an edge over rivals. Shrewd marketing analysis constantly monitors product changes, customers' expectations, competitors' activities and those aspects of the marketing environment – notably technological and regulatory forces – that will impact on the business's fortunes. Resources are allocated to match this thorough assessment of market opportunities and marketing requirements.

Questions for discussion

1 Who are Nynas's customers?

2 What types of business markets – as classified in this chapter – purchase the products made by Nynas?

3 Would most purchases of Nynas's products be new task, modified re-buy or straight re-buy?

Sources: Siobhan McKelvey and Willie Hunter, Nynas UK; Network magazine; the Nynas Annual Review.

CHAPTER 6

Segmenting markets, targeting and positioning

"Strategy requires trade-offs and agreed priorities... segmentation shapes a target market strategy"

Objectives

- To understand the definition of a market

- To recognize different types of market

- To appreciate what is meant by market segmentation

- To know the most commonly adopted bases for segmenting markets

- To understand the role of customer relationship management

- To discover how marketers prioritize between markets and segments

- To learn about strategies for positioning

INTRODUCTION

As explained in Chapter 2, marketing strategy revolves around the choice of which opportunities should be pursued and the specification of an appropriate target market strategy. Market segmentation is a fundamental part of marketing strategy, assisting organizations to deal with the fact that not all consumers or business customers share identical needs, buying behaviour or product requirements. Customer relationship management (CRM) helps marketers build beneficial relationships with important customers within the target market segment(s).

Limited resources generally result in organizations being unable to serve all of the needs in the market, and marketers must make trade-off choices based on the relative merits of different market segments in determining which groups to prioritize. The consumers or business customers in those market segments deemed to be priorities for a company must be communicated with in a manner that emphasizes their importance to the company: this is the positioning task.

The market segmentation process, therefore, has a number of stages: segmenting, targeting and positioning. Many marketers believe these aspects of marketing are the most important decisions made by marketers.

Rice … not all grains seem the same

Do you enjoy rice? Which brand and variety do you buy? In the rice isle of the supermarkets there are many brands, several of which offer similar varieties such as basmati or long grain, brown or white. However most households have a preference and purchase their favourite brand each time they require more rice. This is partly because of the branding adopted by the leading players, sometimes owing to the promo price deal, but often it stems from the segmentation strategies adopted by the leading brands.

Market leader Uncle Ben's, part of the Mars family of companies within Masterfoods, has been producing good tasting rice since the 1940s, but very much targeted at families or couples who are either in a hurry or needing the convenience of pre-prepared easy-to-cook rice in a variety of guises and cooking styles. Uncle Ben's brought rice to the attention of many consumers in the 1960s and 1970s, with generations now having grown up enjoying simple-cook rice out of the familiar orange packaging.

Recently Indian business Veetee launched its Dine In range of innovative plastic trays packed to show off the ready-cooked range of enticing rices: basmati, pilau, long grain, Thai jasmine, basmati and wild, Thai lime and herb and wholegrain; all ready to eat in two-minutes. Not aimed at scratch cooks or those prepared to boil on the hob, this range is targeting 'food cheats' who want an easy-to-prepare good looking product in no time at all so as to get on with their evening.

Further up the rice fixture will be found premium-priced Tilda, from another Indian food group based in the UK. While Tilda also has a microwave range, the bulk of its business is from dry rice, predominantly top-end dry basmati. Priced way above competitors, Tilda enjoys a strong market share and has legions of loyal users who are convinced they can discern a taste premium from the perfect looking aromatic basmati grains. Although far from complicated to cook, Tilda's appeal is more to scratch cooks and those who enjoy both cooking and consuming great tasting food. Not that Uncle Ben's or Veetee do not taste good, but their appeal is to consumers in a hurry or who are less confident cooks, seeking a value for money reliable rice.

Each of these leading rice brands has managed to differentiate what in many parts of the world is a basic commodity … grains of rice. Each company, through recipes, packaging, product formulations, cooking methods, pricing and branding, has managed to appeal to a distinctive set of consumers. While they compete with retailers' own label rice ranges and with each other for many of the same consumers, each rice company has adopted a segmented approach to guide its product innovation, proposition development, marketing messages and consumer engagement programmes. Even in an apparent commodity market such as rice, segmentation has become firmly entrenched to direct the major players' strategies.

Source: © Elena Elisseeva, iStock.com

This chapter begins by considering the nature of markets, first defining the term and then describing the different types. The market segmentation concept is then explained and the rationale for its use explored. Not only rice companies apply the concept of market segmentation. Management consultancies, manufacturers, healthcare providers, leisure operators and universities all practise market segmentation. The segmenting, targeting and positioning stages of the segmentation process are explored in turn. The explanation of segmenting focuses on the variables used to segment consumer and business markets. An understanding of customer needs and buying behaviour, as described in Chapters 4 and 5, is essential for developing market segments.

The targeting and positioning decisions within segmentation and target market strategy are explored in the second part of this chapter. Customer relationship management is explained, as this is a part of managing ongoing relationships, with the most important customers within the market segments identified to be priorities.

What are markets?

The word 'market' has various meanings. It used to refer primarily to the place where goods were bought and sold. It can also refer to a large geographic area. In some cases, the word is used to describe the relationship between the demand and supply of a specific product. For instance, 'What is the state of the market for copper?' Sometimes, 'market' is used to mean the act of selling something. The dictionary defines 'market' as an occasion on which goods are publicly exposed for sale, a place in which goods are exposed for sale, or to offer for sale. In marketing terms, a market is defined in terms of customers, their need for a product, and their ability to purchase or consume.

market
An aggregate of people who, as individuals or within organizations, have a need for certain products and the ability, willingness and authority to purchase such products

In *Marketing Essentials*, a **market** is defined as a group of people who, as consumers or as part of organizations, need and have the ability, willingness and authority to purchase products in a product class. In general use, the term 'market' sometimes refers to the total population, or mass market, that buys products. However, the definition used here is more specific, referring to individuals seeking products in a specific product category. For example, students are part of the market for textbooks, as well as being markets for calculators, laptops, pens and pencils, paper, food, music and other products. Obviously, there are many different markets in any economy. In this section, the requirements for markets are considered in conjunction with these different types.

Requirements for a market

For a group of people to be a market, the members of the group must meet the following four requirements:

- They must need or want a particular product or service.
- They must have the ability to purchase the product or service. Ability to purchase is related to buying power, which consists of resources such as money, goods and services that can be traded in an exchange situation.
- They must be willing to use their buying power.
- They must have the authority to buy the specific products or services.

consumer market
Purchasers or individuals in their households who personally consume or benefit from the purchased products and do not buy products primarily to make a profit

Individuals sometimes have the desire, the buying power and the willingness to purchase certain products but may not be authorized to do so. For example, secondary school students may want, have the money for and be willing to buy alcoholic drinks, but a brewer does not consider them a market until they are legally old enough to buy alcohol. An aggregate of people that lacks any one of the four requirements thus does not constitute a market.

Types of market

Markets can be divided into two categories: consumer markets and business markets. A **consumer market** consists of purchasers and/or individuals in their households who personally consume or benefit from the purchased products and who do not buy products primarily to make a profit. Each of us belongs to numerous consumer markets for such products as housing, cars, appliances, furniture, clothing, food, financial services and leisure activities. Consumer markets are discussed in more detail in Chapter 4 of *Marketing Essentials*.

business market
Individuals or groups that purchase a specific kind of product to resell, use directly in producing other products or use in general daily operations

A **business market** – also referred to as an *organizational or business-to-business market* – consists of individuals or groups that purchase a specific kind of product for one of three purposes: resale, direct use in producing other products or use in general daily operations. The four categories of business market – producer, reseller, government and institutional – are discussed in Chapter 5. The so-termed Third Sector of non-profit markets generally feature within this category, although some authors now believe they warrant separate classification.

What is market segmentation?

Chapter 1 explained that at the heart of marketing strategy are the decisions about which opportunities to pursue and which markets to target. Segmentation is a popular approach to identifying target markets. As will be explained later in this chapter, organizations sometimes decide to target the total market, using an **undifferentiated (or total market) approach**. However, it is much more usual for a differentiated approach using market segmentation to be followed.

undifferentiated (or total market) approach
An approach which assumes that all customers have similar needs and wants, and can be served with a single marketing mix

Defining market segmentation

The varying characteristics, needs, wants and interests of customers mean that there are few markets where a single product or service is satisfactory for all. The extensive array of goods on supermarket shelves reflects basic differences in customers' requirements. The trend, it seems, is away from a mass-marketing approach. Even markets that were traditionally undifferentiated have undergone change, with an ever increasing number of products on offer. For instance, the market for food seasoning used to be dominated by salt. Now, low-sodium substitutes are being offered as alternatives for the increasingly health-conscious consumer.

heterogeneous markets
Markets in which all customers have different requirements

Markets in which all customers have different requirements are termed **heterogeneous markets**. For example, the market for wrist watches is quite diverse. Swatch designs relatively low-priced watches for the fashion-conscious customer; Rotary markets much more conservative and expensive designs for an older customer group. In completely heterogeneous markets the only way to satisfy everyone is by offering tailor-made or bespoke products. This situation is more prevalent in business-to-business markets, where, for example, plant machinery is designed for a specific task and situation. However, while it may not be feasible to offer every customer a tailor-made product, it is often possible to aggregate customers into groups with similar product needs and wants.

market segmentation
The process of grouping customers in markets with some heterogeneity into smaller, more similar or homogeneous segments. The identification of target customer groups in which customers are aggregated into groups with similar requirements and buying characteristics

Market segmentation is the process by which customers in markets with some heterogeneity can be grouped into smaller, more similar or homogeneous segments. A **market segment** is therefore a group of individuals, groups or organizations sharing one or more similar characteristics that cause them to have relatively similar product needs and buying characteristics. Market segmentation involves identifying such groups, so that marketers are better able to develop product or service benefits that are appropriate for them (see Figure 6.1). They do this by designing products and brands to appeal to particular target segments and to be supported by an appropriate promotional campaign, relevant customer service, and suitable pricing and place/distribution strategies. For example, clothing sold through Top Shop or New Look is manufactured for youthful female consumers; this is reflected in both the product styling and the promotional campaign.

market segment
A group of individuals, groups or organizations sharing one or more similar characteristics that cause them to have relatively similar product needs and buying characteristics

Once market segments have been identified, marketers decide which, if any, they intend to enter. A marketing programme covering all elements of the marketing mix can then be designed to suit the particular requirements of the segments targeted. German-owned BMW previously concentrated on selling premium-priced luxury vehicles aimed at the luxury and executive segments of the car market. In order to appeal to

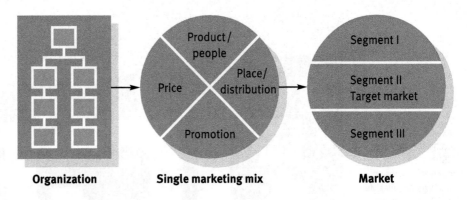

FIGURE 6.1
Market segmentation approach

Organization   **Single marketing mix**   **Market**

a younger age group, during the 1990s BMW introduced the Compact version of its popular 3 Series. This had the desired effect of attracting buyers who previously could not afford this aspirational marque. Now BMW has gone further, with the launch of the 1 Series, aiming to further broaden the appeal of its brand – to young professionals. The 4 × 4 X3 and X5 appeal to other customers.

Reasons for using market segmentation

Companies have turned to market segmentation with good reason.[1] Whitbread, Diner's Club and Bird's Eye have all demonstrated that success can follow the effective implementation of market segmentation strategies. For example, the variety of offerings in the market for frozen, ready-to-eat meals illustrates the spread of customer needs: healthy options, quick snacks, gourmet selections. Careful segmentation, and the customer understanding underlying it, can make it easier for companies to identify and exploit different market opportunities. For example, segmentation can help minor players in the market achieve a foothold in a particular niche, perhaps by identifying an opportunity not directly exploited by market leaders. Figure 6.2 relates to construction equipment manufacturer JCB's entry into clothing, travel mugs, and other merchandise.

Segmentation is seen to offer businesses a number of advantages that make it easier to develop and capitalize on opportunities available to them. These advantages can be considered at the customer level, in relation to the competition or in terms of the effectiveness of resource allocation and strategic planning.[2]

Customer analysis Segmenting markets facilitates a better understanding of customers' needs, wants and other characteristics. The sharper focus that segmentation offers, allows those personal, situational and behavioural factors that characterize customers in a particular segment to be considered. In short, questions about how, why and what customers buy can be addressed. By being closely in touch with segments, marketers can respond quickly to even slight changes in what target customers want. For example, by monitoring the trends towards healthier eating and lifestyles, McDonald's was able to respond by introducing a wider range of salads and healthy eating options – including grilled chicken, fruit and yoghurt – on to its menus.

Competitor analysis Most markets are characterized by intense competition. Within this environment, companies need to understand the nature of the competition they face. Who are their main competitors? At which segments are they targeting their products? Answering these questions allows marketers to make decisions about the most appropriate segments to target and the kind of competitive advantage to seek. For example, before opening a new café outlet, Costa needs to build a picture of the existing café, restaurant and other outlets offering a comparable

FIGURE 6.2
Appreciation for JCB products goes far beyond the machines JCB is traditionally known for. Licensing the image and lifestyle of JCB, the company has been able to successfully transfer its image into licenced merchandise including footwear and clothing, and other target markets.

Source: © Tim Scrivener / Alamy

service in the location. The company must also appraise the extent to which the needs of the consumers it aims to target are already served by what is currently available. Companies that do not understand their competitive environment risk encountering competition they had not envisaged or putting resources into unattractive areas of the market.

Effective resource allocation   All companies have limited resources. To target the whole of the market is usually unrealistic. The effectiveness of personnel and material resources can be greatly improved when they are more narrowly focused on a particular segment of customers. With limited resources, Saab and Porsche target only a few market segments compared with Ford or Toyota. Segmentation enables Mazda and Porsche to identify homogeneous groups of customers at whom the Mazda 5 or Porsche 911 models can be targeted. This maximizes these companies' use of resources and marketing mix activities.

Strategic marketing planning   Companies operating in a number of segments are unlikely to follow the same strategic plans in them all. Dividing up markets allows marketers to develop plans that give special consideration to the particular needs and requirements of customers in different segments. The timescale covered by the strategic plan can also be structured accordingly, because some segments change more rapidly than others. The market for recorded music is a typical example. While tastes in classical music remain fairly steady, tastes in pop music change very rapidly. Companies like EMI and Columbia clearly need to consider this factor when developing corporate plans.

Segmenting, targeting and positioning

There are three stages to carrying out market segmentation: segmentation, targeting and positioning. Figure 6.3 gives an overview of these stages.

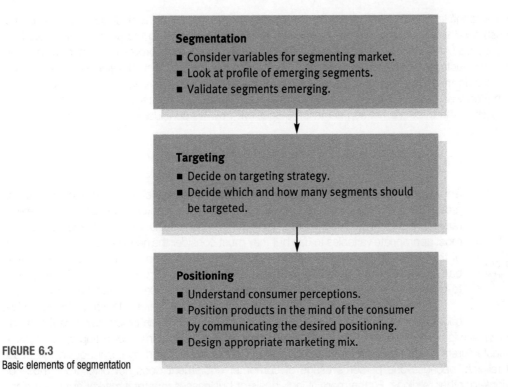

FIGURE 6.3
Basic elements of segmentation

Segmenting the market

There are many ways in which customers can be grouped and markets segmented. In different markets, the variables that are appropriate change. The key is to understand which are the most suitable for distinguishing between different product requirements. Understanding as much as possible about the customers in the segments is also important, as marketers who 'know' their targets are more likely to design an appropriate marketing mix for them. For example, the Post Office has reintroduced savings stamps after an absence of 40 years to help people who struggle to balance their finances. They are aimed at people who have regular outgoings such as household bills; in particular, they are targeted at the five million people in the UK who do not have any kind of bank account.

Targeting strategy

Once segments have been identified, decisions about which and how many customer groups to target can be made. There are several options:

- adopt an undifferentiated approach, focusing on the total market
- concentrate on a single segment with one product and marketing programme
- offer one product and marketing programme to a number of segments
- target a different product and marketing programme at each of a number of segments.

The choices companies make should take resource implications into consideration and the organization's stated mission and strategic vision (see Chapter 2).

Positioning the product

Companies must decide precisely how and where within the targeted segments to aim a product or products, brand or brands. The needs and wants of targeted customers must be translated into a tangible mix of product/service, personnel, price, promotion and place/distribution. The consumers' view of the product and where it is positioned relative to the competition is particularly critical. After all, the paying public does not always perceive a product or brand in the way the manufacturer would like. For example, to the dismay of those who developed it, the Sinclair C5 electric trike was perceived as an object of ridicule. Apple's move into Sony's MP3 territory with iPod was based on a very shrewd targeting and positioning strategy.

Each of the three market segmentation stages will now be considered.

Segmentation variables

segmentation variables or bases
The dimensions or characteristics of individuals, groups or businesses that are used for dividing a total market into segments

Segmentation variables or bases are the dimensions or characteristics of individuals, groups or businesses that are used for dividing a total market into segments.[3] There is rarely one best way to segment a market. Companies must make choices about the most appropriate variables to use but they must consider the needs and buying behaviour of their intended customers, as discussed in Chapters 4 and 5. In consumer markets, background characteristics like age, sex and occupation are widely used. In business-to-business markets, customer size, location and product use are often the focus.

The choice of segmentation variables is based on several factors. The variables chosen should relate to customers' needs for, uses of or behaviour towards the product or service. The selected bases should be usable and easy to measure. Laptop computer manufacturers might segment the market on the basis of income and age, but not on the basis of religion, because one person's usage of computer equipment does not differ from those of people of other religions. Furthermore, if individuals or businesses in a total market are to be classified accurately, the segmentation variable must be measurable. For example, segmenting a market on the basis of intelligence or moral standards would be quite difficult because these attributes are hard to measure accurately.

Creativity is also a factor; sometimes organizations benefit from moving away from a traditionally popular segmentation approach. For example, First Direct led the way in telephone banking, by responding to the fact that some customers' needs were not being met by existing banking operations. By developing a better understanding of the demographics, lifestyle and needs of these customers, the bank was able to develop a new kind of service. Later in this chapter there is a more detailed review of segmentation effectiveness, which focuses on some of these issues.

Selecting appropriate variables

Selecting appropriate variables for market segmentation is an important marketing management decision, because the variable is the primary factor in defining the target market.[4] In some cases, segmentation is based on more than one variable. Decisions about the number of segmentation variables used are partly based on a company's resources and capabilities. The type of product and degree of variation in customers' needs also dictate the number and size of segments targeted.

In general, as developments in information technology make it easier to capture and manage customer information, the move is towards more complex segmentation schemes. Many organizations now have databases providing a wider range of segmentation variables than was previously possible.[5] One outcome is that there is, increasingly, a tendency to use multivariable segmentation rather than single-variable segmentation.[6] Indeed, technological advance means that it is now technically feasible to capture information about and respond to the needs and wants of smaller and smaller segments.[7] Taken to its extreme, this means that instead of dealing at the mass-market or segment level, it is even possible to develop relationships with *individual* customers. This principle has been variously referred to as 'customer-centric marketing'[8] or 'one-to-one marketing'.[9] **One-to-one marketing** involves developing long-term relationships with individual customers in

one-to-one marketing
Involves developing long-term relationships with individual customers in order to understand and satisfy their needs

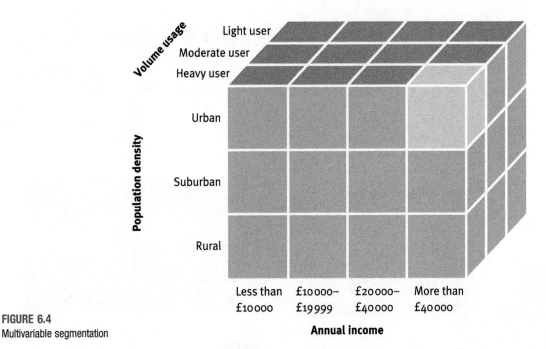

FIGURE 6.4
Multivariable segmentation

order to understand and satisfy their needs.[10] However, despite the attention these new ideas have attracted, it is widely recognized that one-to-one segmentation involves a substantial injection of resources, raising concerns about whether the returns are sufficiently high to justify the required investment.

single variable segmentation
Segmentation achieved by using only one variable, the simplest type of segmentation to perform

Single variable segmentation **Single variable segmentation**, which is the simplest to perform, is achieved by using only one variable – for example, country. However, the sales of one product in different countries will differ and the numbers of relevant consumers in each country will vary. A single characteristic gives marketers only moderate precision in designing a marketing mix to satisfy individuals in a specific segment.

multivariable segmentation
Segmentation using more than one characteristic to divide a total market

Multivariable segmentation To achieve **multivariable segmentation**, more than one characteristic is used to divide a total market (see Figure 6.4). Notice in the figure that the market is segmented by three variables: annual income, population density and volume usage. The people in the highlighted segment earn more than £40 000, are urban dwellers and heavy users. Multivariable segmentation provides more information about the individuals in each segment, which may enable a company to develop a marketing mix that will satisfy customers in a given segment more precisely.

The major disadvantage of multivariable segmentation is that the more variables used, the greater the number of segments likely to be identified. This proliferation reduces the sales potential of many of the segments. It may also be more complicated to resource and manage the proliferation of segments that result. A marketing manager must therefore consider whether additional variables will actually help improve the company's marketing mix. Where many variables are deployed, it may be prudent to utilize multivariate statistical techniques – such as cluster analysis[11] – to assist in the grouping of customers into market segments.

Variables for segmenting consumer markets

Companies developing their strategy for segmentation can choose one or several variables or bases from a wide range of choices. As Figure 6.5 shows, segmentation variables can be grouped into four categories: demographic, geographic, psychographic and behaviouristic.

Demographic variables

- Age
- Gender
- Race
- Ethnicity
- Income
- Education
- Occupation
- Family size
- Family life cycle
- Religion
- Social class

Geographic variables

- Population
- Region
- Urban, suburban, rural
- City size
- Market density
- Climate

Psychographic variables

- Personality attributes
- Motives
- Lifestyles

Behaviouristic variables

- Volume usage
- End use
- Benefit expectations
- Brand loyalty
- Price sensitivity

FIGURE 6.5
Segmentation variables for consumer markets

Targeting fashion

Marketing insight

Venture into a branch of White Stuff and the consumers tend to be between thirty and fifty, seeking well produced and stylish casual clothing for home or office. They will often be from the leafy suburbs and professional families, educated to degree level and with children. The ambiance in-store is quiet but visually stimulating, the stores packed with vibrant designs and helpful sales assistants. While not retailing the latest cat-walk fashions with four-figure pricing, White Stuff targets an upmarket and discerning independent consumer.

By contrast, a New Look store will be packed to the rafters with the latest look sought by sixth formers and ladies in their twenties. Little customer service is desired or offered. The stores are functional and simply fitted out. Price points offer value for money. Although targeting many of the same consumers, River Island offers larger and more vibrant stores, fitted out more expensively to provide more of a buzz than New Look. On the face of it, both New Look and River Island target many of the same consumers, but in practice some of the consumers in the intended demographic target audience prefer the vibrance and energy of River Island, while others prefer the size, feel and pricing of New Look.

Republic also targets price-conscious shoppers in their late teens and twenties, but has adopted a different approach to either River Island or New Look. Its mall-located or out of town stores are very large, jam-packed with the latest season's styles, with little customer service sought. The big difference is that Republic has developed a selection of its own branded ranges, which many consumers assume to be manufacturer brands. Highly sought-after, these brands have created a loyal following amongst some of Republic's consumers. In addition, Republic stocks a selection of well-established proprietary brands, such as Bench and Diesel, targeted at the under-25s who visit Republic stores. In this way, Republic offers a one-stop shop showcasing many brand collections, including its own well-managed portfolio of brands. Adopting the fashion editor's positioning – the premise is that Republic selects the best from its stocked ranges and brands – to guide its fashion-conscious young shoppers, Republic duly appeals to a different buying behaviour than River Island or New Look and to consumers expecting a different in-store or online experience.

Whether White Stuff, New Look, River Island or Republic, each company has identified a core set of consumers to target from within the overall clothes-buying population, honing their locations, store sizes and ambiance, specifying their customer service and pricing, and managing their brands accordingly. Segmentation and brand positioning drive the propositions and marketing for these well-known clothing companies.

Sources: New Look Leamington, Republic Leeds, River Island Leamington and White Stuff Stratford, 2011/2012.

Demographic variables Demographers study aggregate population characteristics such as the distribution of age and gender, fertility rates, migration patterns and mortality rates. Demographic characteristics that marketers commonly use in segmenting markets include age, gender, race, ethnicity, income, education, occupation, family size, family life cycle, religion and social class. Marketers rely on these demographic characteristics because they are often closely linked to customers' needs and purchasing behaviour, and can readily be measured.

Manufacturers of tea bags, such as PG and Twinings, offer their products in packages of different sizes to satisfy the needs of consumers ranging from singles to large families. Financial institutions such as banks and building societies attempt to interest children in their products by offering free gifts such as book vouchers. Meanwhile, retired customers are targeted with products designed for a leisure-oriented lifestyle. The emphasis is on tailoring the service package to suit particular needs.

Age is a commonly used segmentation variable. Population statistics help marketers to understand and keep track of changing age profiles. As the population of western Europe continues to increase, the numbers in the 0- to 19-year-old age band is falling, while the number of those over 60 continues to rise. This has ramifications for marketers, who must increasingly cater for an ageing population. Given the relative affluence of this particular group, many companies (particularly those in leisure and service industries) have benefited from this demographic change. Marketers are also recognizing the purchasing influence of children and are targeting their marketing efforts at them. Numerous products are aimed specifically at children: toys, clothing, food, drinks, video games and entertainment. In addition, children profoundly influence certain purchasing decisions made by their parents.[12] For example, in households with only one parent or in which both parents work, children often take on additional responsibilities such as cooking, cleaning and food shopping, and thus influence the products and brands that are purchased.

Gender is another demographic variable commonly used to segment markets, including the markets for clothing, alcoholic drinks, books, magazines, non-prescription drugs and even cigarettes. EU statistics show that women and girls outnumber men and boys by just over 1 per cent in the population.

The confectionery market did not traditionally segment its market on the basis of gender. Chocolate manufacturers, including Cadbury, tried to change this by developing assortments aimed primarily at men. In general, despite the care taken in each product's design, packaging and promotion, these were not successful. However, efforts by manufacturers of skincare products to develop lines specifically aimed at men have been more successful.

The way in which marketers treat ethnicity varies in different parts of the world. For instance, in the USA, where a quarter of the population is made up of ethnic minorities, ethnicity is widely used as a means of segmenting markets for goods and services of all kinds. The US Hispanic population, comprising people of Mexican, Cuban, Puerto Rican, and Central and South American heritage, is growing five times faster than the general population. Consequently, it is being

FIGURE 6.6
Many brands such as Bratz dolls develop specific marketing programmes targeting children
© picturesbyrob/Alamy

targeted by more and more companies, including Campbell Soup Co., Nabisco and Procter & Gamble. However, targeting Hispanic customers is not an easy task. For example, although marketers have long believed that Hispanic consumers are exceptionally brand loyal and prefer Spanish-language media, research does not support these assumptions. Not only do advertisers disagree about the merits of using Spanish-language media, they also question whether it is appropriate to advertise to Mexicans, Puerto Ricans and Cubans using a common Spanish language.[13] In other areas the proportion of ethnic minorities is much lower than in the USA, affecting the level of marketing attention they receive. In the UK, the percentage of the population from ethnic minorities increased from 3.9 per cent in 1980 to 7.4 per cent in 2001: it is now estimated at 11 per cent. Marketers are now looking for new ways to connect with the needs of these particular groups.

Product and service needs also vary according to marital status, and the number and age of children. These factors are collectively taken into consideration by the 'family life cycle' concept. Some of the more obvious markets in which the impact of different life cycles is seen are tourism, housing and financial services. The family life cycle has been broken down in several different ways. Table 6.1 illustrates one such scheme.

The scheme presented in Table 6.1 assumes that individuals at different life cycle stages have varying product needs. Marketers can respond to this by targeting such groups with marketing mixes designed to capitalize on these differences. For example, parents whose children have grown up and left home ('empty nesters') tend to have more disposable income than those with young children, and tend to spend more on the home, holidays and new cars. Banks and financial institutions in particular are getting better at gearing their marketing efforts to life cycle changes. Critics of the life cycle concept point out that it can be difficult to decide to which categories families belong. Some households, such as single-parent families and older married couples who have never had children, do not appear to fit in at all.

Obviously, this discussion of demographic variables is not exhaustive. However, the variables described above probably represent the most widely used demographics. Other examples of the use of demographics include segmenting the cosmetic and haircare markets on the basis of race and directing certain types of food and clothing towards people of specific religious sects.

Socio-economic variables include income, occupation, education and social class. Some marketing academics and practitioners include certain of these variables under the 'demographics' label. Income can be a very useful way of dividing markets because it strongly influences people's product needs. It affects their ability to buy (as discussed in Chapter 2) and their aspirations for a certain style of living. Obvious products in this category include housing, furniture, clothing, cars, food, certain kinds of sporting goods and leisure activities.

TABLE 6.1 The Wells and Gubar life cycle stages

Bachelor stage (young single people not living with parents)
Newly married couples without children
Full nest I (youngest child under six)
Full nest II (youngest child six or over)
Full nest III (older married couple with dependent children)
Empty nest I (no children living at home, family head working)
Empty nest II (family head retired)
Solitary survivor (working)
Solitary survivor (retired)

Source: Copyright © ESOMAR® 2000. Permission for using this material has been granted by ESOMAR®, Amsterdam, the Netherlands
http://www.esomar.org/

The occupations of the members of the household are known to have an impact on the types of products and services that are purchased. The type of housing individuals and families own or rent, is strongly linked to this variable. It is obvious, for example, that sales of products for refurbishment and decoration, such as paints, fabrics and wallpapers, will occur predominantly among those professions that have owner-occupier status. Occupation is also known to affect the types of sporting and leisure activities people prefer. For example, professionals may be active with walking, swimming, cycling and jogging, but not so involved with darts or football. Intermediate managers enjoy walking, swimming and keep fit/yoga. Unskilled manual workers are not particularly active in sports and physical activities.

Other socio-economic variables that may be used to segment markets include education level and social class.

Geographic variables   The needs of consumers in different geographic locations may be affected by their local climate, terrain, natural resources and population density. Markets may be divided into regions because one or more geographic variables may cause customers' needs to differ from one region to another. A company that sells products throughout the EU will, for example, need to take the different languages spoken into account when labelling its goods.

City size can be an important segmentation variable. For example, one franchised restaurant organization will not locate in cities of fewer than 100 000 people because experience shows that a smaller population base could make the operation unprofitable. The same company may add a second, or even a third, restaurant once the city reaches a certain size. Other businesses, however, seek out opportunities in smaller towns. The major petroleum retailers, such as Esso and Shell, have traffic density thresholds, below which they perceive a local market as unviable. It is, therefore, quite common – particularly in villages and small towns in rural areas – for petroleum retailing to be dominated by independent garage owners and the smaller petroleum companies.

market density
The number of potential customers within a unit of land area

Market density refers to the number of potential customers within a unit of land area, such as a square kilometre. Although market density is generally related to population density, the correlation is not exact. For example, in two different geographic markets of approximately equal size and population, the market density for office supplies might be much higher in the first than in the second if the first contains a significantly greater proportion of business customers. Market density may be a useful segmentation variable because low-density markets often require different sales, advertising and distribution activities from high-density markets.

In Europe, climate can be used as a geographic segmentation variable. Companies entering new markets in Europe increasingly need to consider the impact of climate on their customer base. For example, washing machines sold in Italy do not require such fast spin speeds as those sold in Germany because the Italian climate is much sunnier. Other markets affected by climate include air conditioning and heating equipment, clothing, gardening equipment, recreational products and building materials.

geodemographic segmentation
Clustering people according to postcode areas and census data

Marketers are increasingly using geodemographic segmentation. **Geodemographic segmentation** clusters people according to postcode areas. For example, ACORN (A Classification Of Residential Neighbourhoods) uses information taken from census data and allows people to be grouped according to a number of factors, including geography, socio-economics, culture and lifestyle. All 1.9 million UK postcodes have been described using over 125 demographic statistics and 287 lifestyle variables. The underlying concept is that customers living in different residential neighbourhoods have different profiles in respect of these variables. Their product needs in terms of styling and features, therefore, also vary. Consumers can be classified under ACORN on the basis of the postcode of their home address and then allocated to one of the groups in Table 6.2. These categories further sub-divide to give a total of 17 groups and 56 neighbourhood types. For example, Wealthy

TABLE 6.2 The ACORN categorization of UK consumers

Category	Group	Type
Wealthy Achievers	Wealthy Executives	01 Affluent mature professionals, large houses 02 Affluent working families with mortgages 03 Villages with wealthy commuters 04 Well-off managers, larger houses
	Affluent Greys	05 Older affluent professionals 06 Farming communities 07 Old people, detached houses 08 Mature couples, smaller detached houses
	Flourishing Families	09 Larger families, prosperous suburbs 10 Well-off working families with mortgages 11 Well-off managers, detached houses 12 Large families and houses in rural areas
Urban Prosperity	Prosperous Professionals	13 Well-off professionals, larger houses and converted flats 14 Older professionals in detached houses and apartments
	Educated Urbanites	15 Affluent urban professionals, flats 16 Prosperous young professionals, flats 17 Young educated workers, flats 18 Multi-ethnic young, converted flats 19 Suburban privately renting professionals
	Aspiring Singles	20 Student flats and cosmopolitan sharers 21 Singles and sharers, multi-ethnic areas 22 Low-income singles, small rented flats 23 Student terraces
Comfortably Off	Starting Out	24 Young couples, flats and terraces 25 White collar singles/sharers, terraces
	Secure Families	26 Younger white-collar couples with mortgages 27 Middle income, home-owning areas 28 Working families with mortgages 29 Mature families in suburban semis 30 Established home-owning workers 31 Home-owning Asian family areas
	Settled Suburbia	32 Retired home owners 33 Middle income, older couples 34 Lower income people, semis
	Prudent Pensioners	35 Elderly singles, purpose-built flats 36 Older people, flats
Moderate Means	Asian Communities	37 Crowded Asian terraces 38 Low-income Asian families
	Post-industrial Families	39 Skilled older family terraces 40 Young family workers
	Blue-collar Roots	41 Skilled workers, semis and terraces 42 Home-owning, terraces 43 Older rented terraces
Hard-pressed	Struggling Families	44 Low-income larger families, semis 45 Older people, low income, small semis 46 Low income, routine jobs, unemployment 47 Low-rise terraced estates of poorly-off workers 48 Low incomes, high unemployment, single parents 49 Large families, many children, poorly educated

Category	Group	Type
	Burdened Singles	50 Council flats, single elderly people
		51 Council terraces, unemployment, many singles
		52 Council flats, single parents, unemployment
Hard-pressed	High-rise Hardship	53 Old people in high rise flats
		54 Singles and single parents, high rise estates
	Inner-city Adversity	55 Multi-ethnic purpose-built estates
		56 Multi-ethnic, crowded flats

Source: CACI, June 2011. Reproduced by permission.

Achievers includes several groups, such as *Wealthy Executives, Affluent Greys* and *Flourishing Families*. The *Wealthy Executives* group then sub-divides into several types, such as *Affluent Working Families with Mortgages, Villages with Wealthy Commuters,* or *Well-off Managers in Larger Houses*.

Psychographic variables Marketers sometimes use psychographic variables such as personality characteristics, motives and lifestyles to segment markets. A psychographic dimension can be used by itself or combined with other types of segmentation variables.

Personality characteristics are useful when a product is similar to many competing products and when consumers' needs are not significantly affected by other segmentation variables. However, segmenting a market according to personality characteristics can be problematic. Although marketing practitioners have long believed that consumer choice and product use should vary with personality and lifestyle, marketing research has shown only weak relationships. However, the weakness of such relationships may be due to the difficulty of accurately measuring personality traits, because most existing personality tests were developed for clinical use, not for segmentation purposes. As the reliability of more recent measurement instruments increases, a greater association between personality and consumer behaviour has been demonstrated.[14] For example, it has been shown that personality sometimes influences the clothes, make-up and hairstyles that individuals adopt.

When motives are used to segment a market, it is divided on the basis of consumers' reasons for making a purchase. Product durability, value for money, concern for the environment, convenience and status are all motives affecting the types of product purchased and the choice of stores in which they are bought. For example, one consumer may be motivated to purchase recycled kitchen paper out of concern for the environment. Another may travel to a large supermarket in order to buy the most absorbent, high-quality brand of kitchen towel.

Individuals are grouped by lifestyle segmentation according to how they live and spend their time, the importance of items in their surroundings (their homes or their jobs, for example), their beliefs about themselves and broad issues, and some socio-economic characteristics, such as income and education.[15] Lifestyle analysis provides a broad view of buyers because it encompasses numerous characteristics related to people's activities, interests and opinions (see Table 6.3). It can be thought of as going beyond a simple understanding of personality.

The use of lifestyle as a segmentation variable is problematic, because it is so difficult to measure accurately compared with other types of segmentation variable. In addition, the relationships between psychographic variables and consumers' needs are sometimes obscure and unproven, and the segments that result from psychographic segmentation may not be reachable.[16] For example, a marketer may determine that highly compulsive individuals want a certain type of clothing. However, no specific stores or particular media – such as television or radio programmes, newspapers or magazines – appeal precisely to this group and this group alone. Psychographic

TABLE 6.3 Characteristics related to activities, interests and opinions

Activities	Interests	Opinions
Work	Family	Themselves
Hobbies	Home	Social issues
Social events	Job	Politics
Holidays	Community	Business
Entertainment	Recreation	Economics
Club membership	Fashion	Education
Community	Food	Products
Shopping	Media	Future
Sports	Achievements	Culture

Source: 'The concept and application of life style segmentation' by Joseph Plummer, Journal of Marketing, January 1974, p. 34. Published by the American Marketing Association. Adapted and reprinted with permission.

variables can sometimes offer a more useful way of understanding segments that have been defined using other base variables.

One of the more popular programmes studying lifestyles is conducted by the Stanford Research Institute's Value and Lifestyle Programme (VALS). This programme surveys consumers to select groups with identifiable values and lifestyles. Initially, VALS identified three broad consumer groups: Outer-directed, Inner-directed and Need-driven consumers. The current VALS classification categorizes consumers into eight basic lifestyle groups: Innovators, Thinkers, Achievers, Experiencers, Believers, Strivers, Makers and Survivors. The VALS studies have been used to create products as well as to segment markets.

Behaviouristic variables Marketers can also segment markets on the basis of an aspect of consumers' behaviour towards the product. This might relate to the way the particular product is used or purchased, or perhaps to the benefits consumers require from it.

Purchase behaviour can be a useful way of distinguishing between groups of customers, giving marketers insight into the most appropriate marketing mix. For example, brand-loyal customers may require a different kind of treatment from those who switch between brands. On-pack sales promotions are often geared towards building loyalty in brand switchers.

The occasion on which customers buy a particular product may impact upon product choice because in different sets of circumstances different product selection criteria may be applied. For instance, a customer who replaces a car tyre in an emergency will probably be less concerned about price than one who is routinely maintaining his or her car. **Benefit segmentation** is the division of a market according to the benefits consumers want from the product.[17] Although most types of market segmentation are based on the assumption that there is a relationship between the variable and customers' needs, benefit segmentation is different in that the benefits the customers seek are their product needs. By determining the benefits desired, marketers may be able to divide people into groups seeking certain sets of benefits.

benefit segmentation
The division of a market according to the benefits consumers want from the product

The effectiveness of benefit segmentation depends on several conditions. First, the benefits people seek must be identifiable. Second, using these benefits, marketers must be able to divide people into recognizable segments. Finally, one or more of the resulting segments must be accessible to the companies' marketing efforts.

Product usage is another method marketers sometimes use to segment their customers. Individuals can be divided into users and non-users of a particular product. Users can then be classified further as heavy, moderate or light. To satisfy a specific user group, marketers some-times create a distinctive product, set special prices or initiate special promotion and distribution activities. Thus airlines such as British Airways and KLM offer frequent-flier programmes to re-ward their regular customers with free trips and discounts for car hire and hotel accommodation. Light users or non-users of products often receive little attention from companies. There is a ten-dency sometimes to dismiss these groups when developing a marketing programme. For exam-ple, research in the holiday industry tends to focus on feedback from current customers, often forgetting to question why non-users failed to buy.

How customers apply the product may also determine segmentation. To satisfy customers who use a product in a certain way, some feature – say, packaging, size, texture or colour – may have to be designed with special care to make the product easier to use, more convenient or more environmentally friendly. For instance, Unilever and Procter & Gamble are focusing more and more on the development of refill packs of detergents and other household products, to cater for increasing consumer concerns about the environment.

The varying attitude of customers towards products constitutes another set of variables that can be used to segment markets. Clothing retailers like River Island and Benetton are particularly conscious of this. While one customer seeks outfits that are practical and comfortable, another is concerned with achieving a highly fashionable image.

As this brief discussion shows, consumer markets can be divided according to numerous characteristics. Ultimately, the choices marketers make will depend on a host of market and company factors.

Variables for segmenting business markets

Like consumer markets, business (organizational) markets are often segmented. Here the mar-keter's aim is to satisfy the needs of businesses for products. Marketers may segment business markets according to company demographics, operating variables, purchasing approach, situa-tional factors or the personal characteristics of buyers.

Marketers attempting to segment business markets may face various problems.[18] The partic-ular characteristics of the market or the distribution structure in place may restrict the types of segment bases that can be used. For example, many European car manufacturers are depen-dent upon the fleet car market. This market tends to be structured on the basis of car engine and vehicle size, with companies providing their more senior managers with more powerful, larger and expensive vehicles. It is likely that customers would resist a move away from this ac-cepted structure by the car manufacturers, who are therefore not in a position to use possibly contradictory segmentation approaches. Various segmentation approaches have been developed to try to make it easier for companies to deal with these kinds of constraints.[19]

Whatever the approach adopted, just as in consumer markets, some segment bases are eas-ier to measure and apply than others.[20] For example, it is much more straightforward to segment on the basis of company size, which is a measurable and visible characteristic, than on the basis of buying centre structure (see Chapter 5), which may be much more difficult to appraise. Table 6.4 provides an overview of the variables for segmenting business markets, and illustrates the relative ease with which they can be measured. Variables at the base of the table are easier to measure and more objective than those at the top.

Company demographics Variables relating to the type of business or industry, geographic lo-cation, company age and size are probably the most widely used segmentation variables in busi-ness markets.

A company sometimes segments a market by the types of business within that market, per-haps on the basis of industry area or SIC code (see Chapter 5). Different types of organization often require different product features, distribution systems, price structures and selling stra-tegies. Given these variables, a company may either concentrate on a single segment with one marketing mix (concentration strategy) or focus on several groups with multiple mixes

TABLE 6.4 Variables for segmenting business markets

Personal characteristics of buyers
Just as in consumer markets, the demographics, personality and lifestyle of those individuals in the buying centre impact upon purchasing decisions, practices, attitudes towards risk and loyalty to suppliers.
Situational factors
The urgency of purchase, size of order or product application can play an important role in the choices that are made.
Purchasing approach
Buying centre structure (centralized/decentralized), buying policies (sealed bidding, service contracts, leasing), nature of existing relationships (focus on new or existing customers), balance of power among decision-makers and buying criteria (quality, delivery, service, price, product range, innovation) may shape an organization's purchase decisions.
Operating variables
The technologies applied by an organization, the manner in which products are used or customer capabilities can fundamentally affect purchase choice.
Demographics
Company age, location, industry (SIC code) and size are likely to alter product requirements.

(multi-segment strategy). A paint manufacturer could segment customers into several groups, such as paint wholesalers, do-it-yourself retail outlets, vehicle manufacturers, decorators and housing developers.

The demand for some consumer products can vary considerably by geographic area because of differences in climate, terrain, customer preference or similar factors. Demand for business-to-business products also varies according to geographic location. For example, the producers of certain types of timber divide their markets geographically because their customers' needs vary regionally. Geographic segmentation may be especially appropriate for reaching industries that are concentrated in certain locations, for example, textiles in West Yorkshire, information technology (IT) along the M4 corridor in England or financial services in London. Examples of such concentration in Europe include heavy industry around Lille or in the Ruhr Valley, and banking in Zurich.

Operating variables Customer requirements can be affected in a range of ways by different operating variables such as the technology applied by the buying organization or the product types used. Certain products, especially raw materials such as steel, petrol, plastics and timber, are used in numerous ways. Sometimes the technology used by a company will play an important role. How a company uses products affects the types and amounts it purchases, as well as the method of making the purchase.[21] For example, computers are used for engineering purposes, basic scientific research, business operations such as word processing and book-keeping, as well as Internet access and games in the home. A computer manufacturer may segment the computer market by types of use because organizations' needs for computer hardware and software depend on the purpose for which the products are purchased.

Purchasing approach Although it may be difficult for a company to appraise the buying approach of its customers, this is nonetheless sometimes an appropriate way for business markets to be segmented. The characteristics of the buying centre, including its structure (where the balance of buying power lies), and the nature of any buying policies can all affect the product requirements of customers. For example, suppliers of building materials must organize their sales efforts to satisfy a wide array of customer types who organize their buying activities in vastly different ways. While dealing with large buyers, such as Carillion or Tarmac, will require an understanding of a relatively complex buying structure, small local builders may be perfectly satisfied with a much simpler supply arrangement.

Situational factors Sometimes it is appropriate to segment a business market on the basis of situational factors such as the urgency or size of an order. How urgently the order is required may have an impact on the importance a customer attaches to particular product features. For example, if a robot on a car production line has broken down, bringing the entire production process to a standstill, the price of replacement parts to fix it may be less important than their availability. However, if the same part is being replaced as part of a routine service, price may be the most important factor. The size and frequency of different orders can be effective segmentation variables because they have ramifications concerning the way the customer relationship is handled. For example, a university that regularly orders vast amounts of stationery would expect a different level of service to that of a small business that only infrequently buys small quantities of paper and envelopes.

Personal characteristics Although individuals involved in business buying may not have as much control over the products and services selected as when they are making purchases for personal or family use, their individual characteristics still play a role in the preferences they demonstrate. For this reason it is sometimes appropriate to segment business markets on the basis of the characteristics of individuals within the buying centre. For example, the demographics, personality and lifestyle of managers tasked with buying a selection of new office furniture will influence the preferred designs. If power in the buying centre rests with one senior manager who strongly dislikes modern designs, say, this will influence the final selection of products.

Profiling market segments

Whatever the variable, or combination of variables, used to group customers, a more comprehensive understanding of the characteristics of individuals is likely to be required. For example, a company that segments the market for energy drinks on the basis of age, focusing on customers in their late teens, would do well to understand as much as possible about its particular target group in other respects. What reference groups influence them? Where do they live? Where and when do they socialize? What social background are they from? What motivates them? The more comprehensive the image developed, the better the opportunity to develop an effective marketing mix with maximum appeal.

profiling
The task of building up a fuller picture of the target segments

descriptors
Variables used to profile or build a fuller picture of target segments brand's desired stature

Profiling is the task of building up a fuller picture of target segments, and the variables being used in the description are termed **descriptors**. The types of descriptors available to marketers are broadly the same as the variables used to segment markets in the first place – that is, demographics, socio-economics and so on. This is sometimes a cause of confusion for students, who struggle to remember whether they are dealing with base or descriptor variables. It helps to note that while base variables should discriminate between customer needs, descriptors are simply used to enrich the picture, to help summarize what else can be gleaned about the customers in a particular segment. This gives added inspiration to the creative team developing the product and promotional material, and helps to fine-tune decisions on price and distribution.

Overall, profiling segments in this way ensures that the impact of the marketing mix on the customer is maximized. If segments are not properly profiled, it is unlikely sales personnel, advertising agency staff or senior managers will fully comprehend the proposed segmentation scheme. Therefore its effective implementation may be jeopardized.

Segmentation effectiveness

As Table 6.5 illustrates, segmentation analysis invariably involves several stages. Marketers must be aware that whatever the approach followed and whichever base variables are used,

TABLE 6.5 Stages in segmentation analysis

Objectives
Marketers must know the purpose of the exercise and have clear objectives.
Data
Required information must be specified and collected. This may encompass a qualitative phase to develop a robust view of consumer or customer attitudes, motives, behaviour and perceptions, and a quantitative phase involving larger samples and statistical analysis of questionnaire responses (see Chapter 7).
Analysis
Various statistical packages, such as SPSS, can be used. Factor analysis, conjoint analysis and cluster analysis are commonly used techniques for analyzing the collected data. Multidimensional scaling (MDS) is widely used in product positioning studies. Such techniques should not be applied by those without the necessary statistical skills, if inappropriate solutions are to be avoided.[22]
Interpretation
Marketers must interpret the proposed solutions to ensure any adopted segmentation scheme is statistically valid (complies with the relevant statistical significance tests) and managerially or intuitively valid, and that it presents market segments that are effective. Ultimately, the analysis should comply with statistical validity tests. Any recommendations must also be sensible in the view of managers.[23]
Recommendation
The final proposed solution must first be presented internally to senior and line managers expected to approve the segments, and then actioned for the external audience of distributors and customers.

Sources[24, 25, 26]

haphazard implementation can lead to ineffective market segmentation, missed opportunities and inappropriate investment. To avoid such difficulties marketers should take note of the following criteria. The first is that there must be real differences in the needs of consumers for the product or service. There is no value in segmenting a homogeneous market. Equally, dissimilar consumers in terms of their needs and purchasing behaviour must not be grouped together in the same market segment. In addition, the segments revealed must be:

● *measurable* – easy to identify and measure; some basis must be found for effectively separating individuals into groups or segments with relatively homogeneous product or service needs

● *substantial* – large enough to be sufficiently profitable to justify developing and maintaining a specific marketing mix

● *accessible* – easy to reach with the marketing mix developed – for example, the promotional effort should target the relevant consumers

● *stable* – the question of segment stability over time is not often addressed; if companies are to make strategic decisions on the basis of revealed segments, they need to be reasonably certain that those segments will be around long enough for action to be taken

● *useful* – the selected segments must be meaningful to the managers tasked with operationalizing them and be likely to enable the company to better satisfy its target market.

Using market segmentation also requires a good deal of common sense. It is often difficult for companies to implement totally new segmentation schemes because they would be at odds with the existing marketing structures and ways of doing things. In such cases companies sometimes choose to make minor changes to what is already in place.

CRM

Having divided a market into segments a company must decide which segments should be pursued as priorities in terms of its marketing programmes and budget allocation. Once a company has determined its target markets, it should strive to exploit relationships with its customers in these segments. Customer relationship management (CRM) is the term used to describe the processes for managing such relationships, with the aim of maintaining the interest and support of the most worthwhile and valuable customers. Technology enables such approaches and today most companies operate some form of a CRM system. Even smaller businesses can afford off-the-shelf systems for handling customer data, building profiles of purchasing and behaviours, and regularly communicating with selected customers.

customer relationship management (CRM)
The identification of the most worthwhile and valuable customers within targeted segments and the development of ongoing relationships to foster loyalty and repeat purchasing.

Customer relationship management (CRM) aims to increase profitability by identifying the best customers within targeted segments, developing ongoing relationships and satisfying their needs in order to encourage these customers to remain loyal and to keep returning.[27] The aim is to enhance the life time value to a company of a particular customer.[28] CRM provides a framework for achieving coordination between marketing, customer service and quality programmes.

CRM hinges on the notion that pursuing long-term relationships with customers, instead of a one-off transaction-oriented approach, is more profitable for marketers. The idea that detecting and collecting data about customers could help them acquire and retain profitable customers through learning-based and evolving relationships is key to CRM. Through interaction and ongoing dialogues with customers, marketers are able to monitor and learn about their customers' needs, enabling them to make changes – both internal to the organization as well as in external communications – to suit the needs of the customers. Amazon was a forerunner, building up a profile of customers' reading habits and preferences, tailoring subsequent offers and suggested reading lists accordingly. Florists and gift companies remember birthdays of relatives or friends for which a customer has previously purchased a gift, so as to be able to prompt the customer in advance of such a date next year. This 'reminder service' will be deemed helpful by the customer and may well lead to a new order and sale.

There are two broad areas of CRM:[29] operational CRM that focuses on the IT-related processing which affects day-to-day operations and an analytical CRM that focuses on the strategic planning of how a company may build customer relationships and enhance their value base. Emphasis must be put on learning relationships – a key factor for success in CRM. Developing **learning relationships** (understanding better a customer's needs and behaviours) has many benefits for marketers, including repeat purchases, increased purchases, cross-selling opportunities, up-selling, reduced costs, free word of mouth communications between customers, added customer life-time value and possibly less attention to price.

learning relationships
understanding better a customer's needs and behaviours

Technology is essential, as without adequate data capture and analysis, CRM is not possible. The Internet is increasingly integral to CRM systems, which is partly to blame for the growth of spyware monitoring customers' online behaviours and purchasing records. How often does your web browser apparently spontaneously show adverts for brands and products you happen to frequently use or view online? This is not accidental. With recent advancement in CRM applications, the communication directed towards potential buyers can now be customized at an individual level through e-mails and social media, such as Facebook pages, Twitter, YouTube, fora and blogs. Such interactions between buyer and seller should be stored in a CRM database system. The marketer must track and store customer information, in order to customize and personalize offerings to suit individual customer needs and desires. Knowledge management is a key tool here. Learning-based relationships are a way for companies to evolve and modify their behaviour.

Essential requirements for effective CRM include:[30]

● A focus on customer needs;
● Interaction, ongoing dialogue and transparent communication;
● Learning relationships and customer involvement/integration;
● Customization, personalization, individualization, one-to-one;
● Adoption of technological advancements and applications;

- Monitoring, tracking and use of data and ability to make sense of information;
- Use of customer databases and CRM tools;
- Ability to create value added through positive experiences;
- Understanding buyer–seller relationships which involve the psychology of trust, commitment, satisfaction, symmetry, dependence, fairness and morality.

Effective CRM requires a growth of value so that both buyer and seller are better off. However, marketers must recognize consumers' and the public's concerns linked to monitoring and managing customer data. Inappropriate and incomplete use of CRM may jeopardize the reputation of a brand and alienate intended customers. In addition, marketers must beware of alienating some of their customers. CRM enables marketers to identify their most desirable customers and to give them preferential attention – more frequent communications, tailored propositions, deals and so forth – but inevitably this is at the expense of certain other customers who are not deemed quite so valuable or desirable. When these disadvantaged customers find out, they may be less than happy. Research has shown that such favouritism and differential treatment of customers may cause perceptions of unfairness.[31]

One of the real advantages of CRM is that marketers obtain other measures and information that are of strategic value, including information about customers' lifetime value or acquisition and retention costs, all of which can contribute to the value creation process. Recent developments in CRM are increasingly sophisticated, with methods to understand consumer behaviours and needs through brain scanning, the ability for machines to have 'eyes' so they can recognize customers individually and monitor their shopping patterns, targeted advertising on Facebook, intelligent billboards capable of recognizing customers, and even customized adverts based on an individual customer's appearance (e.g. age, gender, hair, style, etc.).

Segmentation targeting strategies

segmentation targeting
The decision about which market segment(s) an organization decides to prioritize for its sales and marketing efforts

Segmentation targeting involves marketers in decisions about which market segment(s) an organization should prioritize for its sales and marketing efforts. As Figure 6.7 shows the three basic targeting strategies are: undifferentiated, concentrated and differentiated. The decision made on the targeting strategy to follow must be based on a clear understanding of a company's capabilities and resources, the nature of the competition, the product or service in question and the characteristics of the market.

Undifferentiated strategy

undifferentiated targeting strategy
When a company targets an entire market for a product with a single marketing mix

An organization sometimes defines an entire market for a particular product as its target market. When a company designs a single marketing mix and directs it at the entire market for a particular product, it is using an **undifferentiated targeting strategy**. For example, a one-product soft drink business targeting all consumers in the overall market for soft drinks. This is a strategy in which an organization defines an entire market for a particular product as its target market, designs a single marketing mix, and directs it at that market. The strategy assumes that all customers in the target market for a specific kind of product have similar needs, and thus the organization can satisfy most customers with a single marketing mix. This mix consists of one type of product with little or no variation, one price, one promotional programme aimed at everybody and one distribution system to reach most customers in the total market. Products marketed successfully through the undifferentiated strategy include staple food items, such as sugar and salt, and certain kinds of farm produce. However, there are relatively few companies opting to follow this targeting approach, because of the risk that better honed or tailored propositions from rivals appeal much more strongly to specific sub-groups of consumers in the market.

The undifferentiated targeting strategy is effective under two conditions. First, a large proportion of customers in a total market must have similar needs for the product, a situation termed a 'homogeneous market'. A marketer using a single marketing mix for a total market of customers with a variety of needs would find that the marketing mix satisfies very few people. A 'universal car' meant to satisfy everyone would satisfy very few customers' needs for cars because it would not provide the specific attributes a particular person wants. Second, the organization must be able to develop and maintain a single marketing mix that satisfies customers' needs. The company must be able to identify a set of needs common to most customers in a total market and have the resources and managerial skills to reach a sizeable portion of that market.

Although customers may have similar needs for a few products, for most products their needs are quite different. In such instances, a company should use a concentrated or a differentiated strategy.

Concentrated strategy

concentration strategy
A process by which an organization directs its marketing effort towards a single market segment through one marketing mix

When an organization directs its marketing efforts towards a single market segment by creating and maintaining one marketing mix, it is employing a **concentration strategy**. The fashion house Chanel targets the exclusive fashion segment, directing its marketing effort towards high-income customers who want to own the most chic apparel. The cross Pen Company aims its products at the upmarket gift segment of the pen market and does not compete with Bic, which focuses on the inexpensive, disposable pen segment.

The chief advantage of the concentration strategy is that it allows a company to specialize. The company can analyze the characteristics and needs of a distinct customer group and then focus all of its energies on satisfying that group's needs.

A company may be able to generate a large sales volume by reaching a single segment. In some cases, concentrating on a single segment permits a company with limited resources to compete with much larger organizations, which may have overlooked some smaller segments.

Concentrating on one segment also means that a company puts 'all its eggs in one basket' – clearly a disadvantage. If a company's sales depend on a single segment and the segment's demand for the product declines, the company's financial strength declines as well. When the North American sports coupé market declined in the late 1980s, Porsche found itself in severe trouble as it had no exposure to other parts of the car market. More recently, several mobile phone producers failed to spot the emergence of smart phones, led by the iPhone, Blackberry and Samsung. Motorola and Nokia were big losers, focusing on a product category for which consumers switched user behaviours and opted for the alternative smartphones. Moreover, when a company penetrates one segment and becomes well entrenched, its popularity may keep it from moving into other segments. For example, it is hard to imagine that Rolex would start producing low-cost watches, or that Swatch might compete at the high end of the luxury watch segment. This might have been true for Moto and Nokia initially, because Moto and Nokia still had high-selling ranges of existing mobile phones when smartphones and mobile e-mail/social media took off, and may have been reluctant to switch over to the competing smartphones.

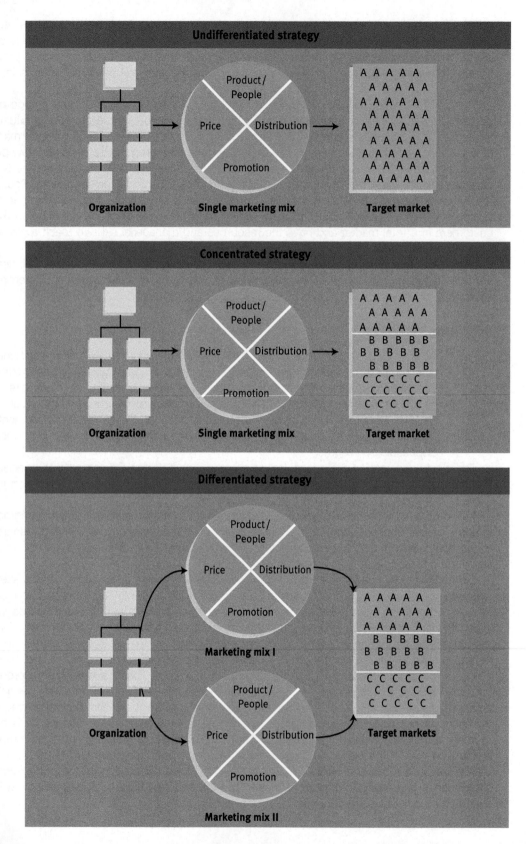

FIGURE 6.7

Targeting Strategies. The letters in each target market represent potential customers. Customers with the same letters have similar characteristics and similar product needs

FIGURE 6.8
The contents of this store retailing wargames miniatures has been selected for a narrowly defined group of shoppers in a concentration strategy
Source: © Robert Convery / Alamy

Differentiated strategy

differentiated strategy
A strategy by which an organization directs its marketing efforts towards two or more market segments by developing a marketing mix for each

With a **differentiated strategy** (see Figure 6.7), an organization directs its marketing efforts at two or more market segments by developing a marketing mix for each segment selected. Sometimes this is a natural progression from the successful application of a concentration strategy in one market segment. For example, Jockey underwear has traditionally been aimed at one segment: men. However, the company has expanded its efforts and now markets underwear for women and children as well. The marketing mixes used for a differentiated strategy may vary as to product/service differences, place/distribution methods, promotion methods and prices. The majority of users of Gatwick Airport near London are packaged holiday travellers. A significant minority, however, are business users, so the airport now has various marketing programmes targeting different segments. Most brand-led mainstream businesses today adopt a differentiated multi-segment targeting strategy, with a portfolio of propositions and marketing programmes targeting a set of segments in order to pursue a selection of opportunities.

An organization can usually increase its sales in the aggregate market through a differentiated strategy because its marketing mixes are aimed at more people. For example, Gap, which established its retail clothes reputation by targeting people under 25, now targets several age groups, from infants to people over 60. A company with excess production capacity may find a differentiated strategy advantageous because the sale of products to additional segments may absorb this excess capacity. On the other hand, a differentiated strategy often demands a greater number of production processes, materials and people. Thus production and marketing costs may be higher than with a concentration strategy.

Factors affecting choice of a segmentation targeting strategy

Irrespective of the type of targeting strategy an organization chooses to adopt when faced with the decision about whether or not to enter a new segment, it must consider a number of issues. These issues include:

1 the nature of the needs and wants of end users
2 the size, structure and future potential of the segment

3 the availability of company resources

4 the intensity of the competition

5 the size of the company's existing market share, and

6 the possibility of any production/marketing scale economies.

Figure 6.9 sums up the core factors affecting the choice of targeting strategy. A company may recognize that a fit between its products or capabilities and target customer needs is stronger and more 'marketable' in one market segment than in another. In some cases a decision may be made to expand into a new area, market or territory where the fit between customer needs and the product and marketing proposition is poor, with the intention of rectifying such short-comings. Certain markets' size or value makes them attractive, as does a company's existing or potential sizeable market share. There may be economies of scale available in targeting a particular market segment alongside related ones, so that certain aspects of the production, sales and marketing activity may be shared. Of course, if truly homogeneous market segments have been identified, then each segment will require certain unique aspects of sales and marketing activity. If two segments really can be treated identically in terms of marketing mix programmes, then they are probably really one segment! Highly intensive and well-established competition may to some companies be something of a 'turn-off', whereas others may take such competitor activity to be indicative of extensive market growth and business opportunity. Finally, even a company the size of Ford or GM does not have the time, people or financial resources to develop a marketing mix for every single segment in the vehicle market. Available resources play a significant role in management's target market decisions.

There are many factors considered by companies determining which markets to target and which target market strategy to deploy. Figure 6.9 is nevertheless a useful summary of the core factors. Marketing planning expert, Malcolm McDonald, suggests[32] a variety of issues to consider when determining which and how many target market segments to prioritize. These include

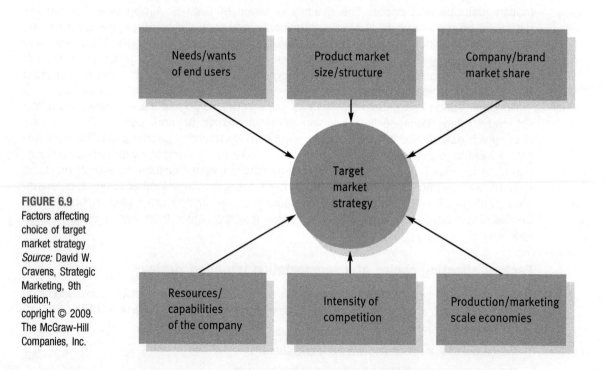

FIGURE 6.9
Factors affecting choice of target market strategy
Source: David W. Cravens, Strategic Marketing, 9th edition, copright © 2009. The McGraw-Hill Companies, Inc.

Innocent goes mumsy

Building customer relationships

Innocent Smoothies transformed the category into big business for retail stockists and Innocent alike. What started as a small venture by three friends has become a major brand, now part-owned by Coca-Cola. Innocent promotes the health and nutritional values of its fruit smoothie drinks, but in a fun and 'huggy' style which proves very popular with its users. The company has diversified into Veg Pots, a children's range, and to other areas of the market. The brand has wide appeal, largely to health and taste-conscious consumers and few readers will be unfamiliar with its range. The launch of its Kids range was supported with advertising and sales promotions targeting children and their parents, so a recent link with Mumsnet is not too surprising.

Mumsnet is a social network which claims 1.25 million regular users and over 30 million monthly page impressions. Politicians and brands, including Ford and Asda, have turned to the site in order to convey their messages but also to learn about their targeted audiences. According to Mumsnet, 'The idea was to create a website where parents could swap advice about holidays, pushchairs and last night's TV. Our aim is to make parents' lives easier by pooling knowledge, advice and support. We try, as far as possible to let the conversation flow and not to over-moderate. Mumsnet is a site for grown-ups'.

Mumsnet offers product reviews and advice, but has created a panel of mums which brands may use in order to glean insights into the behaviours and attitudes of parents and their children. Innocent plans to improve the appeal of its ranges to children and their parents by benefiting from the feedback provided by Mumsnet's panel of expert mothers and also from the 1.25 million users of the web site. Innocent is using the channel to promote the health of its range, too, but it fully expects to learn from consumers, so as to modify its appeal and family-focused messages. Immediately there were benefits for Innocent's team, as they explained to Mumsnet users on the web site:

> When we decided to make a recipe book all about healthy, tasty, no-fuss food that the whole family could enjoy (and that didn't take ages to make), we thought it'd be a good idea to get as many mums, dads and kids as possible to test the recipes first.
>
> So thanks to a group of Mumsnetters, who very kindly took the time to test, taste and tell us what they thought of a selection of the recipes, the result is a book that's got the thumbs up from parents and kids alike.
>
> Filled with over 100 delicious, simple, healthy recipes (from two-minute breakfasts to proper Sunday lunches) and with 85 per cent of recipes containing at least one of your five-a-day, there are also loads of tips, distractions and ways of getting everyone involved in cooking, making and eating.
>
> We couldn't have done it without you. So thank you very much.
>
> **www.mumsnet.com**, June 2011

Innocent still targets adult users and households without any children, adopting different campaigns for its 'grown up' audiences. In this instance, however, the company is explicitly developing products and marketing programmes targeted at children and their parents.

Sources: 'Innocent to Fine-Tune Range with Mumsnet', Russell Parsons, *Marketing Week*, February 3 2011, p. 4; Innocent, 2011; **www.Mumsnet.com**, June 2011.

market, competition, financial and economic, technological, socio-political and regulatory factors – the forces of the marketing environment (see Chapter 3) and core market trends, as outlined below:

- *Market factors* – size (money, units or both); growth rate per annum; diversity of the market; sensitivity to price, service features and external factors; cyclicality; seasonality; bargaining power of upstream and downstream suppliers.
- *Competition* – types of competitor; degree of concentration; changes in type and mix; entries and exits; changes in market share; substitution by new technology; degrees and types of integration.
- *Financial and economic* – contribution margins; leveraging factors such as economies of scale and experience; barriers to entry or exit; capacity utilization.

- *Technology* – maturity and volatility; complexity; differentiation; patents and copyrights; manufacturing process technology required.

- *Socio-political and regulatory* – social attitudes and trends; influence with pressure groups, government and regulatory bodies; laws, government and EU regulations; human factors such as unionization and community acceptance.

Target market attractiveness and opportunity selection

In practice, every organization has its own preferences for which variables to consider when assessing the relative attractiveness of markets or opportunities to serve. Unfortunately, some corporate leaders only assess profitability as their measure of attractiveness. A survey[33] of marketing practices in the largest UK companies revealed an interesting set of variables utilized in determining target market attractiveness (see Table 6.6). This study revealed the extent to which UK businesses are overly restricted by the City's short-termism, and the emphasis placed by financial journalists and pundits on performance only in terms of profitability in the most recent few months. US, German and South-east Asian financial markets tend not to be quite so short-termist in their thinking.[34] Outside the UK, organizations worry about market share and profitability, not just for today and tomorrow, but for a few years to come. It is desirable to adopt a balanced set of variables or criteria with which to judge the relative merits of possible opportunities and target markets.

A market may well be targeted because of its future potential, not just because of current sales. For-profit businesses inevitably will be driven by likely financial rewards, but often these result from other factors, such as competitor intensity, customer salience and the ability to achieve differentiation. Success should be construed in terms of both today's performance and longer-term potential. The UK survey had some good news: it is reassuring to see customer satisfaction, sustainable differential/competitive advantage and likely product differentiation well up the

TABLE 6.6 Market attractiveness factors adopted by UK companies

Companies' market attractiveness criteria	
First tier:	• Market share
• Profitability	• Relative strength/key functions
Second tier:	• Customers' price sensitivity
• Market growth	• Customer image of company
• Market size	
• Likely customer satisfaction	**Fourth tier:**
• Sales volume	• Technological factors
Third tier:	• Fit with business strategy
• Likelihood of a sustainable differential advantage over rivals	• Stability of market
	• Environmental factors
• Ease of access for the business	• Threat of substitutes
• Opportunities in the industry	• Barriers to entry
• Product differentiation	• Negotiating power of buyers
• Competitive rivalry	• Ease of profiling customers
	• Supplier power

Source: Sally Dibb and Lyndon Simkin

list of factors considered in the UK. Chapter 1 explained the importance in marketing of satisfying customers, outpacing competitors and developing differentiation. It is not so good to note that the marketing environment and issues relating to non-direct competitor activity are so low down the list. Organizations really should adopt a balanced list of criteria, mixing short-term and longer-term issues and internal and external factors such as financial considerations and market characteristics.

Understanding what is worthwhile or attractive is not restricted to the selection of target markets and which segments to pursue. Marketers must also identify worthwhile opportunities for their organizations to pursue. Often, the same criteria used to select between segments are used to prioritize opportunities to go after. Therefore, this section of *Marketing Essentials* considers the selection of opportunities, before the chapter returns to examine target market selection.

Identifying and selecting opportunities

Most businesses have a set of corporate objectives guiding their strategic thinking (see Chapter 2). Some companies may have a strategy of consolidation or survival, but even they will face trade-offs between resourcing and supporting viable or growing markets against markets facing declining fortunes. Driven by shareholders' and investors' financial desires, most leadership teams seek growth. Accordingly, a marketing strategy is expected to identify parts of the market likely to generate growing sales or where the company's brand and capabilities will generate commercial opportunities. Two very frequently posed questions by senior executives are:

1 Where is big growth likely?
2 Have we assessed all possible opportunities?

Armed with topical insights from the market, knowledge of customers' expectations, and awareness of competitors' developments, marketers should be well placed to answer such questions and assist in their organizations' strategy creation. They should also address these questions in their annual marketing planning activity, as described later in Chapter 15 of *Marketing Essentials*.

As explored in Chapter 9, the DPM assessment of attractiveness may be applied to selecting which brands or product groups to support, which opportunities to pursue, or which markets to target: it increasingly is used within the targeting phase of market segmentation to decide which segments to pursue.

When using the directional policy matrix to select between opportunities or market segments, there are nine steps:

1 Select a 'balanced' set of attractiveness variables, not only expected profitability. These should include financial criteria, but also market-facing criteria such as the ability to satisfy the customers in question, the likelihood of achieving differentiation versus competitors, the longevity and growth prospects and so forth.

2 Select a set of business strength or capability variables, pertinent to the industry in question, with which it is possible to compare strengths against the strongest competitor. Each industry tends to have certain unique capabilities, appropriate for comparisons between competitors in terms of their strengths and weaknesses for achieving success with consumers or business customers in opposition to their strongest rivals.

3 For both sets of variables – market attractiveness and business strengths – the selected variables should be weighted, because some matter more than others. Typically this involves allocating 100 points across the market attractiveness variables (as in the above list for the telecomms business) and 100 points across the business strength variables.

4 These two sets of variables and their respective weightings should be held constant over time, so that progress quarter by quarter or year by year of the opportunities or market segments being assessed, may be observed.

5 Each opportunity or individual market segment, depending on the unit of analysis for the study, should then be judged variable by variable. If the specific opportunity or segment performs well against a selected variable, it should be scored '1'; if it performs only 'so-so' it should be scored '0.5', while if it performs poorly it should be scored '0'.

6 For each variable, the weighting (out of 100) multiplied by the score ('1', '0.5' or '0') will result in a value for the variable.

7 In both lists separately – market attractiveness and business strengths – the summation of these values will provide total values between 0 and 100: one total for the market attractiveness dimension and one total for business strengths.

directional policy matrix
A market attractiveness and business strength/ capability assessment tool ideal for trade-off analyses for identifying resourcing priorities

8 These total values enable the relative position of each opportunity being assessed or each market segment under examination to be plotted on the **Directional policy matrix.**

9 Those opportunities or market segments plotted upper left on the DPM are more desirable than anything plotted towards the lower right. See Chapter 9 for an illustration.

Whether assessing opportunities, market segments or target markets to prioritize, marketers must be able to determine the best ones to pursue because they will never have permission or resources to go after them all. Life is about trade-off choices, and this is very much the case when creating a target market strategy or business opportunity pursuit list. The tools originally designed to assist in resourcing decisions for brands and products, as explored in Chapter 9, such as the market attractiveness – business capability directional policy matrix – are very useful in the targeting stage of creating a marketing strategy or market segmentation strategy. The main lesson is to adopt a balanced set of attractiveness criteria, which includes financial worth but additionally looks to more market-facing criteria. More is stated about this in Chapter 9 of *Marketing Essentials*. Under-pinning any such assessment about investment, budget allocations and strategy priorities must be a robust set of marketing analyses. Analyses of current performance, market trends and the forces of the marketing environment, capabilities, competitors and consumer/business customer behaviour must provide a robust and topical foundation for selecting priorities and developing the marketing strategy.

Evaluating markets and forecasting sales

Whatever segmentation choices organizations make, measuring the sales potential of the chosen target market or markets is crucial. Moreover, a marketing manager must determine the portion or share of the selected market that the company can capture relative to its objectives, resources and managerial skills, as well as to those of its competitors. Unless this is assessed, financial returns cannot be calculated and no judgement is possible about the desirability of the necessary marketing spend.

sales potential
The amount of sales possible for a particular brand or product in the context of market conditions in a specific period of time

Sales potential is the amount of sales possible for a particular brand or product in the context of market conditions in a specific period of time. This assessment should reflect the attributes of the brand or product, likely customer interest, the nature of competitors' propositions, and market trends. For example, in the current depressed economic climate, the sales potential for some upmarket lines has decreased. Following the terrible 2011 Japanese nuclear power station incidents, the potential for more nuclear installations globally has declined but sales potential for competing energy generating technologies rose, reflecting consumer, regulator and government concerns about civil nuclear safety.

market share
The company's brand or product share of total sales in a particular target market or market segment, versus competing brands

Market share is a long-standing measure of marketing success: if market share rises in a particular time period, the view would be that a marketing strategy is achieving some of its goals. Market share is the company's brand or product share of total sales in a particular target market or market segment, versus competing brands. Arguably, were more organizations equally focused on driving up market share and profitability, as opposed to only profitability, they would be more successful and secure in the longer term. The pursuit of increased market share in priority target markets should be a key success metric for marketers, as explored in Chapter 15.

value share
The proportion of total market monetary sales attracted by an individual brand or product within a particular market

Some businesses, particularly those producing fast moving consumer goods (FMCG), such as those products retailed in supermarkets, examine **value share** as a performance metric. Value share is the proportion of total market monetary sales attracted by an individual brand or product within a particular market. Market share may be 6 per cent while value share is 9 per cent for a premium-priced brand. For longer-term security, it is important that market share rises as well as value share: it is possible for a short-term rise in value share to satisfy directors and improve necessary cash flow, but only market share will safeguard future fortunes.

Developing and maintaining a marketing mix consumes a considerable amount of a company's resources. Thus the target market or markets selected must have enough sales potential to justify the costs of developing and maintaining one or more marketing mixes. Arguably, to be an attractive target market, there must be the propensity for growing market share and value share. As part of developing an effective target market strategy, it is necessary for marketers to calculate and assess market size and sales potential, along with achievable market share and value share. Some or all of these variables often feature in companies' directional policy matrix trade-off assessments.

The potential for sales can be measured along several dimensions, including product, geographic area, time and level of competition.[35] With respect to product, potential sales can be estimated for a specific product item (for example, Diet Coke) or an entire product line (for example, Coca-Cola, Coca-Cola Classic, Diet Coke, Diet Caffeine-Free Coke and Cherry Coca-Cola are one product line). A manager must also determine the geographic area to be included in the estimate. In relation to time, sales potential estimates can be: short range, one year or under; medium range, one to five years; or long range, longer than five years. The competitive level specifies whether sales are being estimated for a single company or for an entire industry. Marketers measure sales potential both for the entire market and for their own companies, and then develop a sales forecast. A target market strategy is incomplete without an appraisal of the likely sales potential and expected levels of sales within the prioritized target market segments, with assessment of the implications for market share and value share.

Marketing programmes

The final stage of the marketing process is the execution of marketing programmes utilizing the ingredients of the marketing mix. These product, people, place, pricing and promotion decisions are in effect the final phase of the creation and operationalization of a target market strategy. These aspects of an effective marketing programme are covered at length in the following Part of *Marketing Essentials*. Before they are specified and executed, marketing analyses must have identified the opportunities to pursue, market segments to target and a compelling proposition to take to market. This analysis phase will have included customers, competitors, market trends and the forces of the marketing environment, along with internal capabilities, resources and performance.

For the selected opportunities and target markets, marketers must decide a positioning strategy. The desired positioning should be agreed before marketing programmes and their marketing mixes are created. The adopted positioning must reflect the expectations of targeted consumers or business customers, the nature of competitors' propositions, and the characteristics of the product or service in question. Positioning is the final component of the so-termed STP process of market segmentation: segmentation, targeting and positioning. Effective positioning is fundamental to the success of a marketing strategy.

Positioning

Figure 6.3 illustrated the link between market segmentation, targeting and positioning. Having identified the segments in a market and decided on which segment (or segments) to target, a company must position its product, service or idea. A product's positioning has been described as the place occupied in a particular market, as perceived by the customer segment at which that product is targeted.[36] Another definition suggests that the positioning of a product is the sum of those attributes normally ascribed to it by the consumers – its standing, its quality, the type of people who use it, its strengths, its weaknesses, any other unusual or memorable characteristics it may possess, its price and the value it represents.[37]

positioning
The process of creating an image for a product in the minds of target customers

Positioning starts with a product, a piece of merchandise, a service, a company, an institution or even a person. **Positioning** is not what is done to the product, it is what image is created in the minds of the targeted consumers or business customers. The product is positioned in the minds of these customers and is given an image.[38] There may be a few cosmetic changes to the product, to its name, price, packaging, styling or channel of distribution, but these are to facilitate the successful promotion of the image desired by the target customers. Targeted consumers or business customers must perceive the product to have a distinct and desirable image and positioning vis-à-vis its competitors. Product differentiation is widely viewed as the key to successful marketing; the product must stand out and have a clearly defined positioning.

Determining a positioning

Positioning is based on customers' perceptions and is therefore only partly within the control of marketers. Positionings are essentially selected by customers, based on variables and within parameters that are important to them. Word of mouth and social media consumer-to-consumer communication are increasingly able to shape a company's brand positioning. Brand managers no longer control communications about their products and brands, so consumers also help shape a brand positioning with both positive and negative observations.

Price may be the key in grocery shopping, service level and trust in selecting a bank, quality and reliability in buying computer hardware, value for money and speed of access in choosing which theme park to visit. In-depth qualitative marketing research (commonly using depth interviews or focus group discussions) is required if customer motivations and expectations in a particular market are to be fully understood. Management's intuition is not always sufficient. For example, research for a major furniture retailer revealed that consumers often have to decide between replacement living room or dining room furniture and a family holiday abroad. Managers at most leading furniture retailers perceived other furniture retailers to be their competitors, when in reality they were competing for a consumer's disposable income and attention against other product areas, such as holidays or the timing of replacing the family car. In addition, in the budget-conscious sector of the furniture buying market, retailers believed only price to be important. In-depth research proved that value for money, a concept that includes product quality and durability in addition to price, was perceived to be the main purchase consideration.

Consumers generally assign positionings to a company or a product that is the market leader – and probably has the highest profile or greatest familiarity – and the limited number of competitors they can recollect are oriented to this market leader. For example, in the market for tomato ketchup, perceptions of brands are oriented towards market leader Heinz. Occasionally the brand consumers regard as the market leader may not be the genuine market leader in terms of market share, but simply the one most visible at that time, possibly because of heavy promotional exposure. Customers respond to the attributes of a product and to its promotional imagery, but the product's positioning as perceived by its target customers is affected by the reputation and image of the company, coupled with its other products, and by the activities of its competitors. For example, bad publicity such as that experienced by British Airways following the opening of Terminal 5 at Heathrow damaged BA's image and transitory iPhone quality issues impacted briefly on Apple.

In-depth marketing research leads to an understanding of how consumers perceive different brands and companies, which marketing variables they believe to be most important and by

perceptual mapping
A tool used by marketers and marketing researchers to visually depict consumer perceptions and prioritising of brands and their perceived attributes

what magnitude. **Perceptual mapping** is a tool commonly adopted by marketers and marketing researchers to visually depict such consumer perceptions and prioritizing of brands and their perceived attributes. Figure 6.10 illustrates a hypothetical example in which consumers thought product range width and price – the two axes – were the key characteristics of the market. On the chart, a cross marks the ideal positioning, with high product range width and above average price (typical of high-quality shopping goods such as cameras or hi-fi systems). Brands (or companies) A and C are perceived as being relatively close to the ideal – their pricing policy does not fully match the image required – but brand (or company) B is viewed as being too cheap, with inadequate product range width.

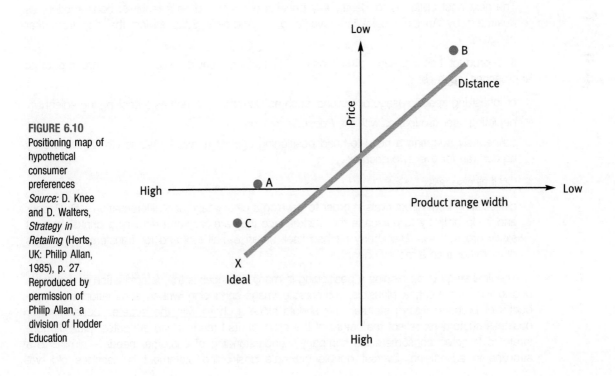

FIGURE 6.10
Positioning map of hypothetical consumer preferences
Source: D. Knee and D. Walters, *Strategy in Retailing* (Herts, UK: Philip Allan, 1985), p. 27. Reproduced by permission of Philip Allan, a division of Hodder Education

Although customers' perceptions play an important role in positioning, the role of marketers is also crucial. A simple step-by-step approach can be used for establishing a clear positioning plan for a product. This process commences with the identification of target market priorities, as outlined below:

1 Define the segments in a particular market.

2 Decide which segment(s) to target.

3 Understand what the target segment's consumers or business customers expect and believe to be the most important considerations when deciding on the purchase.

4 Develop a product or products catering specifically for these needs and expectations.

5 Evaluate the positioning and images, as perceived by the target customers, of competing products in the selected market segment or segments.

6 Select an image that sets the product or products apart from the competing products, thus ensuring that the chosen image matches the aspirations of the target customers. The selected positioning and imagery must be credible: consumers would not believe Kia or Skoda if they promoted their cars in the same manner as Porsche or Aston Martin.

7 Inform target consumers about the product. Although this is primarily a task for marketing communications, it is also vital that the product is made readily available at the right price, through the development of the full marketing mix.

There are various options when determining a positioning strategy:

1 The approach most plausible in terms of the consumer and the most defensible against competitors' marketing ploys is to identify product attributes or features that are superior to competitors, but which also are desirable to targeted customers. Better still if these features are matched by few or no rivals. This is at the heart of the positioning deployed by Bang & Olufsen, BMW and Bosch, which all emphasize product features and attributes providing superiority over rivals.

2 The next best option is to identify key benefits encountered as a result of consumption, as illustrated by Anadin's painkiller advertising or Andrew's Salts saving the day from *that* hangover.

If a product has no such distinctions or is lagging behind major rivals, there are other approaches, such as:

3 emphasizing specific usage occasions, such as Campbell's soups as a cooking ingredient

4 depicting user groups, as with the *Pepsi Generation*

5 deliberately adopting a head-to-head positioning against a rival – 'Avis is No. 2, but we try harder' ran for over two decades.

Or, if all else fails:

6 dissociating from direct rivals in order to develop a clear image and differentiation – Dr Pepper and 7 Up both try to persuade the marketplace they are fizzy and refreshing drinks, but not sickly brown colas. Blackberry pitched itself as an e-mail tool and for transferring business data, rather than a mobile phone.

The final stage in developing a positioning in many instances is the determination of a suitable positioning statement, a plausible, memorable image-enhancing written summation of a product's or brand's desired stature. This should strike a chord with the targeted consumers or business customers; reflect the nature of the product, its branding and attributes; plus demonstrate to targeted consumers the company's understanding of customer needs – similar to a strapline in advertising. Everest double glazing's positioning statement is decades old, yet instantly recognizable: 'Fit the best, fit Everest'. 'The ultimate driving machine' can only be BMW; 'Because I'm worth it' is L'Oréal; and 'We try harder' is still used by car rental company Avis. Ultimately, a product or brand positioning must be memorable, plausible and relevant to the target market's perceptions. The intention is to develop a distinctive image for the product or service and, through a well-honed positioning statement, to establish a platform for its effective communication.

Summary

A *market* is defined as a group of people who, as consumers or as part of organizations, need and have the ability, willingness and authority to purchase products in a product class. A *consumer market* consists of purchasers and/or those in their households who intend to consume or benefit from the purchased products and who do not buy products for the main purpose of making a profit. A *business market* consists of people and groups who purchase a product for resale, direct use in producing other products or for general day-to-day operations. Because products are classified according to use, the same product may be classified as both a consumer product and an industrial product.

At the heart of marketing strategy are the decisions about which opportunities to pursue and which market segments to target. The varying characteristics, needs, wants and interests of customers mean that there are few markets where a single product or service is satisfactory for all.

Markets made up of individuals with different needs are called *heterogeneous markets*. The *market segmentation* approach divides the total market into smaller groups of customers who have similar product needs and buying characteristics. A *market segment* is a group of individuals, groups or organizations sharing one or more similar characteristics that cause them to have relatively similar product needs.

Segmentation and the customer understanding underlying it can make it easier for companies to identify and exploit different market opportunities. The approach offers businesses a number of advantages at the customer level, in relation to the competition or in terms of the effectiveness of resource allocation and strategic planning.

There are three stages to carrying out market segmentation: segmentation, targeting and positioning. Segmentation uses one or more base variables to group similar customers into segments. *Targeting* involves decisions about which and how many customer groups – segments – to target. *Positioning* involves deciding precisely how and where within the targeted segments to aim a product or products, brand or brands.

Marketers must decide how many segmentation variables to use. *Single variable segmentation* involves only one variable, but in *multivariable segmentation*, more than one characteristic is used to divide a total market. The latter is often more meaningful. One-to-one *marketing* involves developing long-term relationships with individual customers in order to understand and satisfy their needs. Although technological advances are making it easier for companies to achieve this goal, this approach involves considerable investment.

Segmentation variables or bases are the dimensions or characteristics of individuals, groups or businesses that are used for dividing a total market into segments. The segmentation variable should be related to customers' needs for, uses of or behaviour towards the product. Consumer segmentation variables can be grouped into four categories: demographics (age, gender, race, ethnicity, income, education, occupation, family size, family life cycle, religion and social class), geographic (population, *market density*, climate), psychographic (personality traits, motives, lifestyles) and behaviouristic (volume usage, end use, expected benefits, brand loyalty, price sensitivity). *Geodemographic segmentation*, which combines geographic and demographic factors, involves clustering people according to postcode areas. Variables for segmenting business markets include demographic factors, operating variables, purchasing approach, situational factors and the personal characteristics of buyers. *Benefit segmentation* is the division of a market according to the benefits consumers want from the product.

Certain conditions must exist for market segmentation to be effective. First, consumers' needs for the product should be heterogeneous. Second, the segments of the market should be measurable so that the segments can be compared with respect to estimated sales potential, costs and profits. Third, at least one segment must be substantial enough to have the profit potential to justify developing and maintaining a special marketing mix for that segment. Fourth, the company must be able to access the chosen segment with a particular marketing mix. Fifth, the segment should be reasonably stable over time. Sixth, the resulting segmentation scheme must be managerially useful. Customers with dissimilar needs and buying behaviour must not be grouped together in the same market segment.

Profiling segments using *descriptor* variables can help the marketer build up a fuller picture and design a marketing mix (or mixes) that more precisely matches the needs of people in a selected market segment (or segments).

Once a company has determined its target markets, it should strive to exploit relationships with its customers in these segments. *Customer relationship management* (CRM) is the term used to describe the processes for managing such relationships, with the aim of maintaining the ongoing interest and support of the most worthwhile and valuable customers.

No organization has the resources or will to pursue all possible opportunities or target markets: there must be trade-off choices. These need to be informed by topical and robust market analyses. *Targeting* is the task of prioritizing which markets and market segment(s) to address. When a company designs a single marketing mix and directs it at the entire market for a particular product, it is using an *undifferentiated (or total market)* approach as its targeting strategy. Although customers may have similar needs for a few products, for most products their needs are very different. In such instances, a company should use a concentrated or a differentiated strategy. In the *concentration strategy*, an organization directs its marketing efforts towards a single market segment through one marketing mix. In the *differentiated strategy*, an organization develops different marketing mixes for two or more market segments. The decisions about which segment or segments to enter are linked to considerations about company resources, expertise and the nature of customers and competitors.

Marketers have a responsibility to identify opportunities and target markets which provide growth potential for their companies. Marketers routinely achieve this during their annual marketing planning activity, but many companies have intervening strategy requirements which benefit from insights into marketing environment trends, *SWOT* analyses, *Ansoff*-inspired assessments of new opportunities, customer-led developments and knowledge of competitors' intentions.

Inevitably, companies are faced with far many more opportunities, market segments and target market options than they have the resources, desire or aptitude to pursue. There must be informed trade-off choices which take into account more than only short-term profitability levels. Many approaches prove useful, but none more than the *directional policy matrix* or market attractiveness–business strength model. This approach identifies and weights two sets of criteria: variables with which to judge the relative attractiveness of whatever is under consideration and variables with which to evaluate business strengths against the capabilities of strong competitors. The desire is to avoid the 'who shouts loudest' solution to executive decision-making in terms of selecting priorities and budget allocation.

Measuring the sales potential of the chosen target market or markets is crucial, as a target market strategy is incomplete without an appraisal of the likely sales potential and expected levels of sales within the prioritized target market segments. This can be measured along several dimensions, including product, geographic area, time and level of competition, as well as at segment level.

Sales potential is the amount of sales possible for a particular brand or product in the context of market conditions in a specific period of time. Market share is a long-standing measure of marketing success. Market share is the company's brand or product share of total sales in a particular target market or market segment, versus competing brands. *Value share* is the proportion of total market income attracted by an individual brand or product within a particular market.

Developing and maintaining a marketing mix consumes a considerable amount of a company's resources. The target market or markets selected must have enough sales potential to justify the costs of developing and maintaining one or more marketing mixes. As part of developing an effective target market strategy, it is necessary for marketers to calculate and assess market size and sales potential, along with achievable market share and value share.

Having decided which segment or segments to target, the marketer must position the product in order to create a clearly defined image in the minds of its target consumers, which is the *positioning* aspect of marketing strategy and market segmentation. The product's positioning must be perceived by its consumers to be different from the positionings of competing products. *Perceptual maps* assist marketers in graphically depicting the relative positionings of the products in a particular market. Although a product's attributes and styling, along with its pricing, service levels and channel of distribution, contribute to how consumers perceive the product, a marketer uses mainly promotion to establish a product's positioning. The final stage in developing a positioning is the *positioning statement*, a plausible and memorable written summation of a product's or brand's desired stature.

Key links

This chapter has explained a core aspect of marketing strategy: market segmentation, targeting and positioning. It has also over-viewed CRM. It should be read in conjunction with:

- Chapter 2's overview of marketing strategy
- The requirement to understand consumers and business customers, as described in Chapters 4 and 5
- Chapter 14's explanation of effective branding
- The analytical tools – notably the directional policy matrix – used for choosing priority target markets, as presented in Chapter 9

Important terms

Market
Business market
Consumer market
Undifferentiated or total market approach
Heterogeneous markets
Market segmentation
Market segment
Segmentation variables or bases
One-to-one marketing
Single variable segmentation
Multivariable segmentation
Market density
Geodemographic segmentation
Benefit segmentation
Profiling
Descriptors
Customer relationship management

Segmentation targeting
Concentration strategy
Differentiated strategy
Directional policy matrix
Sales potential
Market share
Value share
Positioning
Perceptual mapping
Positioning statement

Discussion and review questions

1   What is the market segmentation approach? What are the three main stages of the market segmentation process?

2   What is a market segment? Identify several examples of market segments.

3   Describe the basic conditions required for effective segmentation.

4   Identify and describe four basic categories of base variables used to segment consumer markets. Give examples of product markets often segmented by each category.

5   What dimensions tend to be used to segment business markets?

6   How do marketers decide whether to use single variable or multivariable segmentation? Give examples of product markets that are divided using multivariable segmentation.

7   What is customer relationship management?

8   In what ways does customer relationship management benefit an organisation?

9   In what ways do CRM and segmentation co-exist?

10 Are there situations in which segmentation is not appropriate to use?

Recommended readings

Baran, R.J. and Glaka, R., *Principles of Customer Relationship Management* (Routledge, 2012).

Buttle, F., *Customer Relationship Management* (Butterworth-Heinemann, 2008).

Dibb, S. and Simkin, L., *Market Segmentation Success: Making It Happen!* (The Haworth Press/Routledge, 2008).

Dibb, S. and Simkin, L., *The Market Segmentation Workbook* (Thomson, 1996).

Hooley, G., Piercy, N.F. and Nicoulaud, B., *Marketing Strategy and Competitive Positioning* (FT/Prentice-Hall, 2011).

Hutt, M.D. and Speh, T.W., *Business Marketing Management: B2B* (South Western, 2009).

McDonald, M. and Dunbar, I., *Market Segmentation* (Goodfellow Publishers, 2010).

Ries, A. and Trout, J., *Positioning: The Battle for Your Mind* (McGraw-Hill, 2001).

Tsiptsis, K. and Chorianopoulos, A., *Data Mining Techniques in CRM: Inside Customer Segmentation* (Wiley-Blackwell, 2010).

Webber, H., *Divide and Conquer: Target your Customer through Market Segmentation* (Wiley, 1998).

Weinstein, A., *Handbook of Market Segmentation: Strategic Targeting for Business and Technology Firms* (The Haworth Press/Routledge, 2004).

Internet exercise

Voyage is an Internet company that offers a variety of travel and adventure products. Learn more about its goods, services and travel advice through its website at: www.voyageconcepts.co.uk

1 Based on the information provided at the website, what are some of Voyage's basic products?

2 What market segments does Voyage appear to be targeting with its website?

3 What segmentation variables is the company using to segment these markets?

Applied mini-case

Most readers of *Marketing Essentials* will have a Facebook account and be used to social media networking. Business executives and professionals often are on LinkedIn, which explains:

Over 100 million professionals use LinkedIn to exchange information, ideas and opportunities:

> Stay informed about your contacts and industry
> Find the people and knowledge you need to achieve your goals
> Control your professional identity online

Get the most from your professional network:

> Re-connect
>> Find past and present colleagues and classmates quickly. LinkedIn makes staying in touch simple.
>
> Power your career
>> Discover inside connections when you're looking for a job or new business opportunity.
>
> Get answers
>> Your network is full of industry experts willing to share advice. Have a question? Just ask.

Source: **www.linkedin.com**, June, 2011.

Question

What is the brand positioning proposition at the heart of LinkedIn's proposition? Explain how this relates to the apparent target market strategy for LinkedIn.

Marriott: getting down to business with business travellers

Imagine marketing more than 3 000 hotels and resorts under 16 brands in 68 countries which is the challenge facing Marriott, a multinational marketer that provides lodging services to millions of customers every day. The company, founded by J. Willard Marriott in 1927, started with a single root-beer stand and the 'spirit to serve'. Today, it achieves $11 billion in global sales from guest room revenue, meals, meeting and special-events and other services.

Each of Marriott's brands has its own positioning. The flagship Marriott brand stands for full service: properties have restaurants, meeting rooms, fitness centres, and other facilities. The JW Marriott brand is more up-market and the Ritz-Carlton brand is known for top quality service. Marriott's newest hotel brand is Edition, a chain of stylish luxury hotels. TownePlace Suites are mid-priced suite hotels for customers who plan an extended stay away from home. Fairfield Inn & Suites are for businesspeople and vacationers seeking value-priced accommodation.

Sluggish economic conditions have only intensified rivalry within the hyper-competitive hotel industry. Major hotel companies such as Accor, Hilton, Hyatt, InterContinental and Starwood all offer a wide range of hotel and resort brands for different customers' needs and tastes. In addition, local hotels and regional chains compete on the basis of location, ambience, price, amenities and other elements. To compete effectively in this pressured environment, Marriott is relying on extensive marketing research, expert segmentation and careful targeting.

Marriott uses a variety of research techniques to find out about customer needs and behaviour, including focus groups, online surveys and in-room questionnaires. For example, when it conducted focus groups with customers who had stayed at its Marriott and Renaissance properties, it discovered some interesting differences. Renaissance customers said they like to open the curtains and look out of the window when they first enter their rooms. In contrast, Marriott guests said they get unpacked quickly and get right to work in their rooms. 'That's when we started making connections about the individual personalities that gravitate toward the Marriott brand', says the vice president of marketing strategy. With this research in hand, marketers for the Marriott hotel brand targeted a segment they call 'achievers'; business travellers who feel driven to get a lot done in a short time. They created an advertising campaign to communicate that Marriott is about productivity and performance. The print and online adverts featured

interviews with six real customers, who discussed their drive to accomplish personal and professional goals.

When Marriott looked at visitors who prefer SpringHill Suites, one of its suite hotel brands, it found a slightly different profile. These are business people who travel often and see a suite hotel as a place to spread out, feel refreshed and take a break from the stress of being on the road. These customers are also heavy users of technology, especially mobile communication devices such as smartphones. In reaching out to this target market, Marriott uses mobile marketing as well as traditional media to get its message across. It invites business travellers to download its iPhone *app* and runs adverts designed especially for viewing on smartphone screens. Customers can click on the mobile advert to check room availability online or to speak with the reservations department.

Marriott also targets companies that need hotel space to hold meetings and seminars. In most cases, these companies bring in attendees from outside the immediate location, which means Marriott can fill more guest rooms during meetings. Meetings usually involve additional purchases, such as snacks or meals, another profitable reason to target businesses. Sales reps at major Marriott properties are ready to help companies plan employee workshops, supplier and distributor events and other meetings, for a handful to a ballroom full of people.

Studying the needs and buying patterns of companies that hold business meetings, Marriott's marketers have found that a growing number are interested in videoconferencing and other high-tech extras. To appeal to this segment, Marriott has equipped many of its meeting rooms with the latest in recording and communications technology. It has also partnered with AT&T and Cisco to offer 'virtual meeting' capabilities in its Marriott, JW Marriott, and Renaissance Hotels. This teleconferencing technology allows a group gathered in one of Marriott's hotel meeting rooms to collaborate with colleagues, clients or others anywhere in the world.

The segment of consumers and business travellers who care about the environment is sizable these days, and Marriott wants its share of this growing market. The company has developed prototype green hotels for several of its brands, designing the public space and guest rooms with an eye toward conserving both water and energy. Marriott will build hundreds of these green hotels during the next decade. Thanks to the company's emphasis on saving power, 275 of its hotels already qualify for the US Environmental Protection Agency's Energy Star designation. Marriott is also going green by working with suppliers that operate in environmentally friendly ways. It provides pads made from recycled paper for attendees of business meetings held at its properties and buys key cards made from recycled plastic. Even the pillows in the guest rooms are made from recycled plastic bottles.

Marriott set up a central database to capture details such as how long customers stay and what they purchase and when they stay at any of its hotels or resorts. It also stores demographic data and tracks individual preferences so it can better serve customers. By analyzing the information in this huge database, Marriott discovered that many of its customers visit more than one of its brands. Therefore, the company created sophisticated statistical models to target customers for future marketing offers based on their history with Marriott. In one campaign, Marriott sent out three million e-mail messages customized according to each recipient's unique history with the company. Because of its database capabilities, Marriott was able to track whether recipients returned to one of its properties after this campaign – and actual sales results exceeded corporate expectations. This database technology has paid for itself many times over with improved targeting efficiency and higher response rates.

Questions for discussion

1 How is Marriott segmenting the market for hotel services?

2 Which of the targeting strategies is Marriott using? Explain your answer.

3 What specific types of data should Marriott have in its customer database for segmentation purposes?

CHAPTER 7

Marketing research

Marketers have a responsibility to understand and to find out … research

Objectives

- To understand the importance of marketing research in marketing decision-making

- To distinguish between research and intuition in solving marketing problems

- To learn the five basic steps of the marketing research process

- To understand the fundamental methods of gathering data for marketing research

- To gain a sense of the relative advantages and disadvantages of marketing research tools

- To understand how tools such as databases, decision support systems and the Internet facilitate marketing research

- To identify key ethical considerations in marketing research

INTRODUCTION

As the preceding chapters have explained, effective marketing is contingent upon marketers having a clear understanding of customers, competitors, market trends and aspects of the marketing environment. **Marketing research** is the systematic design, collection, interpretation and reporting of information to help marketers solve particular problems or take advantage of marketing opportunities. As the word 'research' implies, it is the process of gathering information not currently available to decision-makers. The purpose of marketing research is to inform an organization about customers' needs and desires, marketing opportunities for particular goods and services, and changing attitudes and purchase patterns. Detecting shifts in buyers' behaviour and attitudes helps companies stay in touch with the ever-changing marketplace, which often necessitates marketing research.

marketing research
The process of gathering, interpreting and reporting information to help marketers solve specific marketing problems or take advantage of marketing opportunities

Marketing research goes digital

Have you ever wondered how marketers ensure that the products they develop are suitable for their customers, or how they decide on the best marketing programmes? Marketing research provides much of the insight which businesses need to make these decisions. Now digital advances and changes in how different media are used are altering how such information is gathered. With a host of new research techniques available to practitioners, deciding which method to use seems more complex than ever.

Marketers can now use digital platforms to run online surveys, set up focus groups, create online panels and use Twitter feeds to capture instant responses to burning questions about their products and how they are marketed. Members of the public can be invited to supplement their opinions by keeping online diaries, or uploading photographs, or engaging in conversation about products and services with others in the online community. In the words of one research manager: 'This mass of information can give researchers unprecedented insight into a person's life – trends, feedback, suggestions – without the need for proactive survey. We can access instant feedback about our services – from a student's tweet about their lunch at college, to a fan at a rugby ground updating his Facebook status about the corporate hospitality he enjoyed at the stadium'.

Perhaps more significant is the rising popularity of product review sites like TripAdvisor, where consumers themselves generate content based on their reviews of different market offerings. Many shoppers now rely heavily on such reviews when deciding which brands to buy. This move away from businesses being in sole charge of researching customer reaction means that the reputation of brands is now more firmly in the hands of customers.

The immediacy of the information available to market researchers using new media, together with the ready access to a geographically dispersed and demographically divergent population has obvious attractions for practitioners keen to learn more about their target markets. However, as the table below reveals, there are also drawbacks, not least because it can be difficult to control the process or to ensure that sufficiently tailored information is obtained. Consequently, marketing research experts urge maintaining a careful balance between traditional and digital approaches for undertaking research.

Pros and cons of online qualitative research

Pros	Cons
Speed of response	Risk of participants being more 'playful' or even dishonest
Lack of geographical limitations	
Gets around mobility issues	Harder – or impossible – to interpret body language
Prevents louder, pushier types dominating proceedings	Social network bonds may lead to respondents influencing one another more than in a face-to-face setting
Anonymity can trigger candour	
Subjects can be explored at own pace in a non-confrontational way	
Longer timespans present greater opportunities	Potential overload of untargeted data that are costly to analyze
	Arguably only for the tech-savvy

Source: Adapted from R. Gray, How to do 'qual' research, *The Marketer*, June 2010.

☉☉ tripadvisor.co.uk The world's largest travel review site

Sources: R. Gray, How to do 'qual' research, *The Marketer*, June 2010, pp. 35–38; L. Cooper, How the consumer has become judge and jury, *Marketing Week*, 11 November 2010, pp. 22–23.

Marketing research of all kinds, whether collected from product review sites or from specifically designed consumer studies, provides much needed insights into the characteristics, needs and desires of target market customers. When used effectively, such information facilitates the relationship with the customers, by helping organizations focus their efforts on meeting, and even anticipating, the needs of their customers.

This chapter begins by defining marketing research and examining its importance. It then analyzes the five basic steps of the marketing research process, including various methods of collecting data. This is followed by a review of how technology aids in collecting, organizing and interpreting marketing research data. Finally, the ethical aspects of marketing research are considered.

The importance of marketing research

Building an understanding of customers, competitors, market trends and the marketing environment requires that marketers have access to information and marketing intelligence.[1] Sometimes the available information will be judged inadequate to tackle a specific decision or marketing task, in which case marketing research may provide the additional insights required. Such research is generally conducted on a project-by-project basis, with research methods being adapted to the context and problems being studied.

Marketing research involves collecting and analyzing data concerning the characteristics, attitudes, behaviour of individuals, customers or organizations. As the Market Research Society explains:

> Research is one of the most useful tools in business, any business. It is the way in which organizations find out what their customers and potential customers need, want and care about. The key elements in obtaining good research material are that researchers talk to a few people to the views of many, and that it only works if they talk to the right number of people, ask the right questions and interpret the results correctly.

[http://www.mrs.org.uk/media/quanda.htm, sourced on 22 February 2011]

The purpose of marketing research is to provide information about customers' needs and desires, marketing opportunities for particular goods and services, and the changing attitudes and purchase patterns of customers. Marketing planning requires marketing research to facilitate the process of assessing opportunities and threats. Marketing research can help a company better understand market opportunities, ascertain the potential for success of new products and determine the feasibility of a particular marketing strategy. Pizza Hut, for example, conducted research to learn more about its most profitable group of customers: school and college students. The research involved asking a carefully chosen group of 350 students to refrain from eating pizza products for 30 days and record their cravings for pizza and feelings about 'going without' during the study period. One objective was to help better understand the effects of 'pizza deprivation', food cravings and food desires among this attractive market, which may lead to modifications in its marketing strategy.[2]

marketing intelligence
The composite of all data and ideas available within an organization, which assists in decision-making

quantitative research
Research aimed at producing data that can be statistically analyzed and whose results can be expressed numerically

All organizations have some marketing intelligence **Marketing intelligence** is the composite of all data and ideas available within an organization – for example, a company or a marketing department that assists in decision-making. Often the available information is deemed inadequate, which may lead to the commissioning of marketing research. There are, broadly, two types of marketing research: quantitative and qualitative.[3] **Quantitative research** uses techniques and sample sizes leading to the collection of data that can be statistically analyzed and whose results can be expressed numerically. These data tend to come from large surveys, sales data or market forecasts (see Figure 7.1).

qualitative research
Research that deals with information too difficult or expensive to quantify, such as subjective opinions and value judgements, typically unearthed during interviews or discussion groups

Qualitative research deals with information that is too difficult or expensive to quantify: subjective opinions and value judgements that are not amenable to statistical analysis and quantification,[4] typically unearthed during in-depth interviews or discussion groups, but also now increasingly collected in online forums.

While some organizations continue to handle their own information needs, others buy in help from outside agencies that specialize in market research. According to ESOMAR's figures, by 2008 the total worldwide market for market research had reached a massive US$28 billion. North America is responsible for 34 per cent of this figure, with Europe accounting for 45 per cent (**http://www.mrs.org.uk/media/quanda.htm**). Recent growth in the industry highlights marketing research's status as a management tool. Some experts suggest that this is also because the marketing research agencies have worked hard to quantify the effects of their work on business performance.[5]

The Marketing Insight box on page 227 reveals how global business P&G uses direct observation methods to gain a better understanding of how customers really use its products. The insights which are generated about the characteristics, needs and desires of target market customers help marketers to design more suitable marketing.

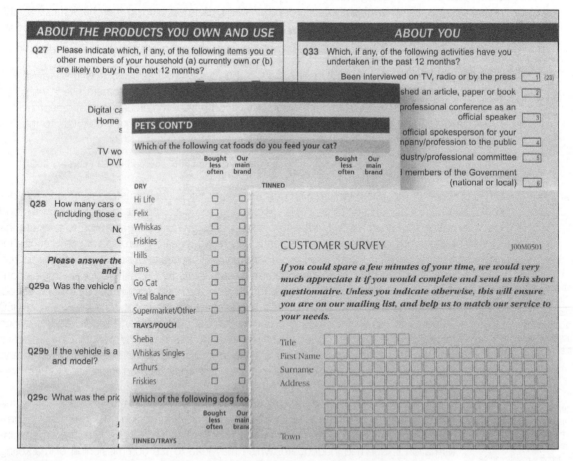

FIGURE 7.1
Questionnaires are an integral part of marketing research, often but not exclusively for quantitative studies
Photo: Copyright © Karen Beaulah

P&G keeps a close eye on its customers

Building customer relationships

Imagine waking up in the morning, stumbling to the bathroom wash basin, putting Crest toothpaste on your toothbrush and looking up to see the fuzzy reflection of a video camera in the mirror. Maybe you think that you might have signed up for a reality TV show? No, it's just the Procter & Gamble (P&G) research crew you allowed into your home to observe how you perform your daily activities. Although marketing research has traditionally focused on problems that consumers generally recognize, P&G researchers hope this direct observation approach will help them identify and address problems that consumers do not even know they have.

Globally, around one-third of consumers buy products made by US-based P&G. With sales growth of just a few per cent each year, the company hopes to boost its revenues by capitalizing on growth opportunities in its overseas markets. To achieve this goal, much of P&G's marketing research effort is now targeted in international markets such as the UK, Italy, Germany and China.

Compared with other research methods, direct observation of consumers provides several benefits. Video clips can be placed on a secure website for viewing by 150 P&G employees. A bigger audience gives the company greater potential for valuable feedback. More problems can be identified and solutions found to address those issues. Direct observation can also generate information that participants might normally forget or choose not to disclose when being interviewed or surveyed. For example, many people say they brush their teeth twice a day because they believe this is the correct and expected response. But the reality is that many people do not brush twice daily. Direct observation of consumers can uncover such information. Another advantage of this approach is that it contributes to the insights gained through the coordinated and integrated research studies it conducts annually or to its existing database of 50 000 studies. Finally, P&G gets global perspectives on the wants and needs of its target market.

This new form of research also has some drawbacks, however – especially in terms of concerns about privacy. Although participants in these studies willingly allow themselves to be videotaped, the company must be careful about what it records, inform any unsuspecting visitors about the recording, and guarantee the videos will only be viewed internally for research purposes. Another issue is reactivity, which occurs when participants modify normal behaviours because they know they are being watched. For example, a participant might increase his or her daily intake of vegetables during the observation period to appear more in line with social norms or expectations. Another drawback is that it is not practical to pore through hours of videotape for just a few clues about human behaviour. Although the information gained may be interesting, not all of it will be relevant. Finally, such research does not guarantee than any product innovation or improved marketing programme will result.

All kinds of organizations use marketing research to help them develop marketing programmes that match the needs of customers or to find out more about their stakeholders' views. The CEO of a large marketing research business recently generalized the categories in which his company received requests for research help. For quantitative studies, these included customer satisfaction surveys, advertising tracking analyses, evaluations of new or modified products, brand awareness studies and customer attitude surveys. For qualitative research, the main categories were customer attitude and satisfaction studies, followed by concept testing (new products or new brand identities). After these came the testing of advertisements, packaging concepts and promotional offers.

intuition
The personal knowledge and past experience on which marketing managers may base decisions

As managers recognize the benefits of marketing research, they assign it a much greater role in decision-making. For example, Japanese managers, who traditionally put greater faith in information they get directly from wholesalers and retailers, are now grasping the importance of consumer surveys and scientific methods of marketing research as they seek ways to diversify their companies.[6]

scientific decision-making
An orderly and logical approach to gathering information

The increase in marketing research activities represents a transition from intuitive to scientific problem-solving. In relying on **intuition**, marketing managers base decisions on personal knowledge and past experience. However, in **scientific decision-making**,

TABLE 7.1 Distinctions between research and intuition in marketing decision-making

	Research	**Intuition**
Nature	Formal planning, predicting based on a scientific approach	Preference based on personal feelings or 'gut instinct'
Methods	Logic, systematic methods, statistical inference	Experience and demonstration
Contributions	General hypotheses for making predictions, classifying relevant variables, carrying out systematic description and classification	Minor problems solved quickly through consideration of experience, practical consequences
Situation	High risk decision-making involving high costs, investment, strategic change or long-term effects	Low-risk problem solving and decision-making

managers take an orderly and logical approach to gathering information. They seek facts on a systematic basis, and they apply methods other than trial and error or generalization from experience. This does not mean that intuition has no value in marketing decision-making; successful decisions blend both research and intuition. Consider an extreme example. A marketing research study conducted for Xerox Corporation in the late 1950s indicated a very limited market for an automatic photocopier. Xerox management judged that the researchers had drawn the wrong conclusions from the study, and they decided to launch the product anyway. That product, the Xerox 914 copier, was an instant success. An immediate backlog of orders developed, and the rest is history. Although the Xerox example is certainly an extreme one, by and large a proper blend of research and intuition offers the best formula for a correct decision. Table 7.1 distinguishes between the roles of research and intuition in decision-making.

Despite the obvious value of formal research, marketing decisions are often made without it. Certainly, minor, low-risk problems that must be dealt with at once can and should be handled on the basis of personal judgement and common sense. If good decisions can be made with the help of currently available information, costly formal research may be superfluous. However, as the financial, social or ethical risks increase or the possible courses of action multiply, full-scale research as a prerequisite for marketing decision-making becomes both desirable and rewarding.

Marketing research improves a marketer's ability to make decisions. Marketers should treat information in the same manner as other resources utilized by the company, and they must weigh the costs of obtaining information against the benefits derived. Information is worthwhile if it results in marketing activities that better satisfy the needs of the company's target markets, leads to increased sales and profits, or helps the company achieve some other goal.

The marketing research process

To maintain the control needed for obtaining accurate information, marketers approach marketing research in logical steps, as follows (see Figure 7.2):

1 locating and defining problems or research issues
2 designing the research
3 collecting data
4 analyzing and interpreting research findings
5 reporting research findings.

These five steps should be viewed as an overall approach to conducting research rather than a rigid set of rules to be followed in each project. In planning research projects, marketers must think about each of the steps and how they can best be adjusted for each particular problem.

| 1 Locating and defining issues or problems | 2 Designing the research | 3 Collecting data | 4 Interpreting research findings | 5 Reporting research findings |

FIGURE 7.2
The five steps of the marketing research process

Step 1: locating and defining problems or research issues

problem definition
The process of uncovering the nature and boundaries of a situation or question

The first step in launching a research study is **problem definition**, which focuses on uncovering the nature and boundaries of a situation or question related to marketing strategy or implementation. The first sign of a problem is usually a departure from some normal function, such as failures to attain objectives. If a company's objective is a 12 per cent return on investment and the current return is 6 per cent, this discrepancy should be analyzed to help guide future marketing strategies. Decreasing sales, increasing expenses or decreasing profits also signal problems. Conversely, when an organization experiences a dramatic rise in sales, or some other positive event, it may conduct marketing research to discover the reasons and maximize the opportunities stemming from them.

To pin down the specific boundaries of a problem or an issue through research, marketers must define the nature and scope of the problem in a way that requires probing beneath the superficial symptoms. The interaction between the marketing manager and the marketing researcher should yield a clear definition of the problem. Researchers and decision-makers should remain in the problem definition stage until they have determined precisely what they want from the research and how they will use it. Deciding how to refine a broad, indefinite problem into a clearly defined and researchable statement is a prerequisite for the next step in planning the research: the design phase.

FIGURE 7.3
Many marketing research agencies, data analysis houses and marketing services businesses support marketers

Source: Image courtesey Metro Research

Step 2: designing the research

research design
An overall plan for obtaining the information needed to address a research problem or issue

Once the problem or issue has been defined, the next step is **research design**, an overall plan for obtaining the information needed to address it. This step requires detailed research objectives or hypotheses to be formulated, and the most appropriate type of research to be designed to ensure that the results are reliable and valid.

Developing research objectives and hypotheses

research objective
The desired outcome from the marketing research project being undertaken

hypothesis
An informed guess or assumption about a certain problem or set of circumstances

A clear statement of research objectives plays an important part in guiding a research project. A **research objective** is the desired outcome from the marketing research project being undertaken. Sometimes researchers develop hypotheses that may be drawn both from previous research and expected research findings. A **hypothesis** is an informed guess or assumption about a certain problem or set of circumstances. It is based on all the insight and knowledge available about the problem from previous research studies and other sources. As information is gathered, a researcher can test the hypothesis. For example, toy manufacturer Lego might propose the hypothesis that children today are more interested in product lines relating to characters featured in their favourite movies or television programmes than previous generations. A marketing researcher would then gather data, perhaps through surveys of children and their parents, and draw conclusions as to whether or not the hypothesis was correct.

Supermarkets worried about shoplifting would be interested in the findings of research showing that 40 per cent of supermarket managers surveyed reported cigarettes and alcohol as their most frequently shoplifted items. If a supermarket manager had hypothesized that other products, such as confectionery, were more susceptible to shoplifting, the research would lead this individual to reject that hypothesis. Sometimes several hypotheses are developed during the actual study; the hypotheses that are accepted or rejected become the study's chief conclusions.

Types of research

exploratory research
Deliberately flexible data gathering used to discover the general nature of a problem and the factors that relate to it

The research objectives and any hypotheses being tested determine the approach to be used for gathering data. When marketers need more information about a problem or want to make a tentative hypothesis more specific, they may conduct **exploratory research**. Exploratory studies discover the general nature of a problem and the factors that relate to it. The design is deliberately flexible.[7] For instance, this kind of research may involve reviewing the information in the company's own records or examining publicly available data. Questioning knowledgeable people inside and outside the organization may also yield new insights into the problem. Information available on the Internet about industry trends or demographics may also be an excellent source for exploratory research. For example, information on the buying power of different ethnic groups is readily available through this source.

descriptive research
Data collection that focuses on providing an accurate description of the variables in a situation

If marketers need to understand the characteristics of certain phenomena to solve a particular problem, **descriptive research** can aid them. Descriptive studies focus on providing an accurate description of the variables in a situation. Such studies may range from general surveys of consumers' education, occupation or age to specifics on how many pairs of sports shoes individuals purchase each year. For example, if Nike and Reebok wanted to target more young women, they might ask 15–34-year-old females how often they work out, how often they buy sports footwear and whether they wear them for casual use. Descriptive studies generally demand much prior knowledge and assume that the problem is clearly defined. The marketers' major task is to choose adequate methods of collecting and measuring data.

TABLE 7.2 Comparison of data-gathering approaches

Project component	Exploratory studies	Descriptive or causal studies
Purpose	Provide general insights	Confirm insights, verify hypotheses
Data sources	Ill-defined	Well defined
Collection form	Open-ended	Structured
Sample	Small	Large
Collection procedure	Flexible	Rigid
Data analysis	Informal	Formal
Recommendations	Tentative	Conclusive

Source: *Marketing Research*, p. 122, ©1986. Reprinted by permission by Professor A. Parasuraman.

causal research
Data collection that assumes that a particular variable *X* causes a variable *Y*

Hypotheses about causal relationships call for a more complex approach than a descriptive study. In **causal research**, it is assumed that a particular variable *X* causes a variable *Y*. Marketers must plan the research so that the data collected prove or disprove that *X* causes *Y*. To do so, marketers must try to hold constant all variables except *X* and *Y*. For example, to find out whether new carpeting, curtains and ceiling fans increase the leasing rate in a block of flats, marketers need to keep all variables constant except the new furnishings and the leasing rate. Table 7.2 compares the features of these types of research study.

Research reliability and validity

reliability
The quality of producing almost identical results in successive repeated trials

validity
A condition that exists when an instrument measures what it is supposed to measure

In designing research, marketing researchers must ensure that their research techniques are both reliable and valid. A research technique has **reliability** if it produces almost identical results in successive repeated trials. But a reliable technique is not necessarily valid. To have **validity**, the method must measure what it is supposed to measure, not something else. A valid research method provides data that can be used to test the hypothesis being investigated. For example, although a group of customers may express the same level of satisfaction based on a rating scale, the individuals may not exhibit the same repurchase behaviour because of different personal characteristics. This result might cause the researcher to question the validity of the satisfaction scale if the purpose of rating satisfaction was to estimate repurchase behaviour.[8]

Step 3: collecting data

primary data
Information gathered by observing phenomena or surveying respondents

The next step in the marketing research process is collecting data to satisfy research objectives and to help prove (or disprove) research hypotheses. The research design must specify what types of data to collect and how they will be collected.

Types of data

secondary data
Information compiled inside or outside the organization for some purpose other than the current investigation

Marketing researchers have two types of data at their disposal. **Primary data** are observed and recorded or collected directly from respondents. This type of data must be gathered by observing phenomena or surveying respondents. **Secondary data** are compiled inside or outside the organization for some purpose other than the current investigation. Secondary data include general reports supplied to an enterprise by various data services. Such reports might concern market share, retail inventory levels

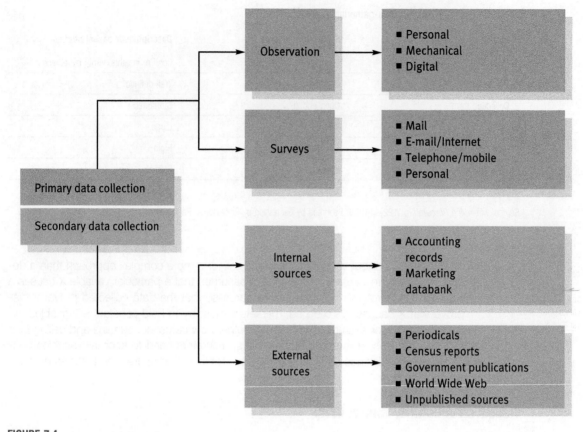

FIGURE 7.4
Approaches to collecting data

and consumer buying behaviour. Figure 7.4 illustrates how primary and secondary sources differ. Secondary data are generally already available in private or public reports, or have been collected and stored by the organization itself. Because secondary data are already available – 'second hand' – to save time and money they should be examined prior to the collection of any primary data. Clearly, primary data collection is bespoke and therefore both time-consuming and costly. For relatively straightforward problems, secondary data may prove adequate. More complex or risky situations may require specific primary data collection. Figure 7.5 reveals how market research companies promote their data analysis services.

Sources of secondary data

Marketers often begin the marketing research process by gathering secondary data. They may use available reports and other information from both internal and external sources to study a marketing problem.

Internal sources of secondary data can contribute tremendously to research. An organization's own databases may contain information about past marketing activities, such as sales records and research reports, that can be used to test hypotheses and pinpoint problems. From sales reports, for example, a company may be able to determine not only which product sold best at certain times of the year, but also which colours and sizes were preferred. Such information may have been gathered for management or financial purposes.[9] Table 7.3 reveals some commonly available internal company information that may be useful for marketing research purposes.

FIGURE 7.5
A business-to-business advertisement for JRA's marketing research services
Source: Image courtesey of JRA Research

TABLE 7.3 Internal sources of secondary data

Sales data taken from periodic sales reports	The frequency with which this information is updated will vary for different organizations and industry sectors. However, the increasing use of technology to monitor sales is leading to improvements in the quality and availabiliy of such data.
Customer feedback gathered by the salesforce, marketers or services functions	In addition to sales information, the salesforce is in a position to provide other data on customer views and preferences. The service functions of many organizations also have access to a range of customer feedback. Marketers capture customer views. Organizations with systems in place for capturing and managing these data are more likely to be able to take advantage of such insights.
Accounting information	This can include detailed data on sales, expenses and profit levels in different product categories.
Competitive information collected by the salesforce or marketers	Through contact with customers and by attending sales-related events, such as trade shows, the salesforce is often in a position to accumulate information about competitors, their product portfolios and strategies.

An organization's accounting records and feedback available from any service function are excellent sources of data that are often overlooked. This is partly because the volumes of data that these departments collect may not automatically flow to the marketing area. As a result, detailed information about costs, sales, customer accounts or profits by product

TABLE 7.4 Guide to external sources of secondary data

Trade journals	Virtually every industry or type of business has a trade journal. These journals give a feel for the industry – its size, degree of competition, range of companies involved and problems. To find trade journals in the field of interest, check *The Source Book*, a reference book that lists periodicals by subject.
Trade associations	Almost every industry, product category and profession has its own association. Depending on the strength of each group, they often conduct research, publish journals, conduct training sessions and hold conferences. A telephone call or e-mail to the association may yield information not available in published sources.
International sources	Periodical indices, such as *Anbar*, are particularly useful for overseas product or company information. More general sources include the *United Nations Statistical Yearbook* and the *International Labour Organization's Yearbook of Labour Statistics*.
Commercial sources	Market survey/report organizations produce many sector reports and analyses of companies or brands, for example, *Verdict, Mintel, Kompass, The Times 1000, Key British Enterprises*.
Governments	Governments, through their various departments and agencies, collect, analyze and publish statistics on practically everything. Government documents also have their own set of indices. A useful index for government generated information in the UK is the government's weekly *British Business*.
Books in Print (BIP)	*BIP* is a several volume reference book found in most libraries. All books issued by publishers and currently in print are listed by subject, title and author.
Periodical indices	Library reference sections contain indices on virtually every discipline. *ABI Inform (Pro-Quest)*, for example, indexes each article in all major periodicals.
Computerized literature retrieval databases	Literature retrieval databases are periodical indices stored on computer disks. Books and dissertations are also included. Key words (such as the name of a subject) are used to search a database and generate references. Examples include *Textline, Harvest* and *Pro-Quest*.
Internet	Many companies have established 'home pages' on the Internet's World Wide Web for disseminating information on their products and activities.

category may not be part of the marketing information system (MIS). This situation occurs particularly in organizations that do not store marketing information on a systematic basis.

External sources of secondary data include periodicals, census reports, government publications, the Internet and unpublished sources. Periodicals such as *Investors' Chronicle, Marketing, Campaign, Marketing Week, The Wall Street Journal* and *Fortune* print general information that is helpful for defining problems and developing hypotheses. *Business Monitor* contains sales data for major industries. Mintel publishes sector reports. Many research companies publish reports on markets, consumers, trends and products. Table 7.4 summarizes the major external sources of secondary data, excluding syndicated services.

syndicated data services
Organizations that collect general information and sell it to clients

Syndicated data services periodically collect general information, which they sell to clients. BARB, for example, supplies television stations and media buyers with estimates of the number of viewers at specific times. Globescan furnishes monthly information that describes market shares for specific sectors. ACNielsen provides retail tracking and other data. This information includes total sales in a product category, sales of clients' own brands and sales of important competing brands.

Another type of secondary data, which is available for a fee, is demographic analysis. Companies, such as CACI or Experian, that specialize in demographic databanks have special knowledge and sophisticated computer systems to work with the very complex census databanks. These were explored in Chapter 6. As a result, they are able to respond to specialized requests. Such information may be valuable in tracking demographic changes that have implications for consumer behaviour and the targeting of products.[10]

Primary data collection methods

The collection of primary data is a more lengthy, expensive and complex process than the collection of secondary data. To gather primary data, researchers use sampling procedures, survey methods, observation and experimentation. These efforts can be handled in-house by the company's own research personnel or contracted out to private research businesses such as Taylor Nelson Sofres, Millward Brown UK or Research International.

Sampling Because the time and resources available for research are limited, it is almost impossible to investigate all the members of a target market or other population. A **population**, or 'universe', comprises all elements, units or individuals that are of interest to researchers for a specific study. A **sample** is a limited number of units chosen to represent the characteristics of a total population. For example, if a Gallup poll is designed to predict the results of an election, all the registered voters in the country would constitute the population. A representative national sample of several thousand registered voters would be selected in the Gallup poll to project the probable voting outcome. The projection would be based on the assumption that no major political events would occur before the election. The objective of **sampling** in marketing research, therefore, is to select representative units from a total population. Sampling procedures allow marketers to predict buyer behaviour fairly accurately on the basis of responses from the representative portion of the population of interest. Most types of marketing research employ sampling techniques.

There are two basic types of sampling: probability sampling and non-probability sampling. With **probability sampling**, every element in the population being studied has a known chance of being selected for study. Random sampling is basic probability sampling. When marketers employ **random sampling**, all the units in a population have an equal chance of appearing in the sample. The various events that can occur have an equal or known chance of taking place. For example, a specific playing card in a pack has a 1/52 probability of being drawn at any one time. Sample units are ordinarily chosen by selecting from a table of random numbers which have been statistically generated so that each digit, from zero to nine, will have an equal probability of occurring in each position in the sequence. The sequentially numbered elements of a population are sampled randomly by selecting the units whose numbers appear in the table of random numbers.

Another kind of probability sampling is **stratified sampling**, in which the population of interest is divided into groups according to a common characteristic or attribute, and a probability sampling is then conducted within each group. Employing a stratified sample may reduce some of the error that could occur as a result of using a simple random sample. By ensuring that each major group or segment of the population receives its proportionate share of sample units, investigators avoid including too many or too few sample units from each stratum. Usually, samples are stratified when researchers believe that there may be variations among different types of respondent. For example, many political opinion surveys are stratified by sex, race and age.

Area sampling, a variation of stratified sampling, involves two stages:

1 selecting a probability sample of geographic areas, such as streets, census tracts or census enumeration districts

2 selecting units or individuals within the selected geographic areas for the sample.

To select the units or individuals within the geographic areas, researchers may choose every n^{th} house or unit, or they may adopt random selection procedures to pick out a given number of units or individuals from a total listing within the selected geographic areas. Area sampling may be used when a complete list of the population is not available.

population
All elements, units or individuals that are of interest to researchers for a specific study

sample
A limited number of units chosen to represent the characteristics of a total population

sampling
The selection of representative units from a total population

probability sampling
Every element in the population has a known chance of being selected for study

random sampling
A sampling method in which all the units in a population have an equal chance of appearing in the sample

stratified sampling
A sampling method in which the population of interest is divided according to a common characteristic or attribute; a probability sampling is then conducted within each group

area sampling
A sampling method that involves selecting a probability sample of geographic areas and selecting units or individuals within the selected areas for the sample

quota sampling
A sampling method in
which the final choice of
respondents is left to the
interviewers, who base
their choices on two or
three variables (such as
age, sex and education)

In **quota sampling**, researchers divide the population into groups and then arbitrarily choose participants from each group. A study of consumers who are diabetic for an organization seeking to market snacks to this group, for example, may be conducted by interviewing any person who has diabetes. In quota sampling, there are some controls – usually limited to two or three variables such as age, sex and education – over the selection of respondents. The controls attempt to ensure that representative categories of respondents are interviewed. Because quota samples are not probability samples, not everyone has an equal chance of being selected and sampling error therefore cannot be measured statistically. Quota samples are used most often in exploratory studies, in which hypotheses are being developed. Often a small quota sample will not be projected to the total population, although the findings may provide valuable insights into a problem. A probability sample used to study people allergic to cats would be highly inefficient.

survey methods
Interviews by mail,
telephone, web and
personal interviews

Survey methods   Marketing researchers often employ sampling to collect primary data through mail, telephone, online or personal interview surveys. Selection of a **survey method** depends on the nature of the problem, the data needed to satisfy the research objectives and any hypotheses, and the resources, such as funding and personnel, that are available to the researcher. Table 7.5 illustrates the current breakdown of research budgets across the different techniques in Great Britain.

TABLE 7.5 Breakdown of research budgets across the different techniques in the UK

Expenditure on market research					
Estimated value of commercially available research in the UK:					
	2003	**2004**	**2005**	**2006**	**2007**
£m	1222	1288	1321	1353	1800[1]
Yr-on-yr % change	2.8	5.4	2.5	2.4	2.3[2]

Total revenue by client sector, 2007			
	% of total		**% of total**
Other FMCG	17.7	Business goods and services	7.3
Government and public services	15.2	Non-OTC pharmaceutical	6.6
IT/telecoms and consumer tech.	10.9	Other consumer goods and services	5.6
Food and beverages	9.3	Transport, travel and tourism	3.8
Media	9.1	Retailing (incl. mail order)	3.8
Financial services	7.4		

Quantitative revenue by data collection method, 2007			
	%[2]		**%**
Face-to-face	24.2	Other quantative data collection method	8.6
Telephone	19.4	Other web/Internet	6.2
Continuous panel (non-Internet)	13.6	Mystery customer/observation	3.6
Internet based access panel	11.9	Continuous panel (Internet based)	2.4
Postal/other paper self-completion	9.5	Non-Internet access panel	0.5

Notes: [1] Following comprehensive re-assessment of market size.
        [2] Like-for-like growth.

Sources: MRS *Annual Survey of UK Market Research Industry*, published with permission from MRS (The Market Research Society);
The Marketing Pocket Book 2009, published by the World Advertising Research Centre, Henley-on-Thames, 2008.

Gathering information through surveys is increasingly difficult because respondent rates are declining. Many people believe that responding to surveys takes too long and have become fatigued by the frequency with which they are asked to become involved in such studies. The unethical use of 'sugging' ('selling under the guise of marketing research', i.e. sales techniques disguised as market surveys) has also contributed to decreased respondent cooperation, while Internet surveys have been affected by concerns about spam (junk e-mails).

mail surveys
Questionnaires sent by mail to respondents, who are encouraged to complete and return them

In a **mail survey**, questionnaires are sent by mail to respondents, who are encouraged to complete and return them. Mail surveys are used most often when the individuals chosen for questioning are spread over a wide area and funds for the survey are limited. A mail survey is the least expensive survey method as long as the response rate is high enough to produce reliable results. The main disadvantages of mail surveys are the possibility of a low response rate or of misleading results, if respondents are significantly different from the population being sampled.

Researchers can boost response rates in mail surveys by offering respondents an incentive to return the questionnaire. Incentives and follow-ups have consistently been found to increase response rates. On the other hand, promises of anonymity, special appeals for cooperation and questionnaire length have no apparent impact on the response rate. Other techniques for increasing the response rate, such as advance notification, personalization of survey materials, type of postage, corporate or university sponsorship, or foot-in-the-door techniques, have had mixed results, varying according to the population surveyed.[11] Although such techniques may help increase the response rates, they can introduce sample composition bias, or non-response bias, which results when those responding to a survey differ in some important respect from those not responding to the survey. In other words, response-enhancing techniques may alienate some people in the sample and appeal to others, making the results non-representative of the population of interest. Organizations devote relatively little funding to mail surveys.

mail panels
Groups of consumers selected to represent a market or market segment, who agree to be interviewed regularly by mail

Premiums or incentives encouraging respondents to return questionnaires have been effective in developing panels of respondents who are interviewed by mail on a regular basis. **Mail panels** of consumers selected to represent a market or market segment are especially useful for evaluating new products, providing general information about consumers and providing records of consumers' purchases. While many companies use consumer mail panels; others use **consumer purchase diaries**. These surveys are similar to mail panels, but consumers keep track of purchases only. Consumer mail panels and consumer purchase diaries are much more widely used than mail surveys, but they do have shortcomings. Research indicates that the people who take the time to fill out a consumer purchase diary have a higher income and are better educated than the general population. If researchers include less well-educated consumers in the panel, they must risk poorer response rates.[12] Web panels are now very popular.

consumer purchase diaries
A marketing research tool in which consumers record their purchases

telephone surveys
Surveys in which respondents' answers to a questionnaire are recorded by interviewers on the phone

Telephone surveys, where respondents' answers to a questionnaire are recorded by interviewers on the phone, are widely used by businesses. A telephone survey has some advantages over a mail survey. The rate of response is higher because it takes less effort to answer the telephone and talk than to fill out a questionnaire and return it. If there are enough interviewers, telephone surveys can be conducted very quickly. Thus they can be used by political candidates or organizations seeking an immediate reaction to an event. In addition, this survey technique permits interviewers to develop a rapport with respondents and ask some probing questions.

Telephone interviews also have drawbacks, especially as a large proportion of the population is becoming increasingly unwilling to become involved. Furthermore, these interviews are limited to oral communication; visual aids or observation cannot be included. Interpreters of results must make adjustments for subjects who are not at home or who do not have telephones. Many households are excluded from the telephone directory. Others use answering machines, voicemail or caller ID to screen or block calls. Researchers seeking business respondents can also face non-response problems, particularly as secretaries frequently 'gate-keep' calls, preventing researchers from talking to their targets.

Overall, reliance on panels of various kinds is increasing. Telephone surveys, like mail and personal interview surveys, are sometimes used to develop panels of respondents who can be interviewed repeatedly to measure changes in attitudes or behaviour. Increasingly such panels are also being run through digital media, including in the online environment. An advantage of the online setting is that it enables an ongoing dialogue with panel members to be achieved.

computer-assisted telephone interviewing
A survey method that integrates questionnaire, data collection and tabulations, and provides data to aid decision-makers in the shortest time possible

Computer-assisted telephone interviewing integrates questionnaire, data collection and tabulations, and provides data to aid decision-makers in the shortest time possible. Questionnaire responses are entered on a terminal keyboard, or the interviewer can use a light-pen (a pen-shaped torch) to record a response on a light-sensitive screen. On the most advanced devices, the interviewer merely points to the appropriate response on a touch-sensitive screen with his or her finger. Open-ended responses can be typed on the keyboard or recorded with paper and pencil. This kind of interviewing saves time and facilitates monitoring the progress of interviews. Because data are available as soon as they are entered into the system, interim results can be retrieved quickly. With some systems, a mobile computer may be taken to off-site locations for use in data analysis. Some researchers believe that computer-assisted telephone interviewing is less expensive than conventional paper and pencil methods.[13]

online survey
Questionnaires that are sent to an individual's e-mail account or that are available over the Internet or via a website

Online surveys have evolved as an alternative to telephone surveys. In an **online survey** questionnaires can be transmitted to respondents who have agreed to be contacted and have provided their e-mail addresses. Because e-mail is semi-interactive, recipients can ask for clarification of specific questions or pose questions of their own. The fact that the data are instantly available in electronic format also eases the process of data entry. The potential advantages of e-mail surveys are quick response and lower costs than traditional mail and telephone surveys. However, these advantages cannot yet be fully realized because of limited access to some respondents. In general, though, the opportunities for using e-mail and the Internet to collect data are increasing significantly, especially as companies are pooling their e-contact lists and some are selling their e-lists to third parties. There has also been a growth in surveying by SMS via people's mobile phones. Tapping into social media networks has proved very fruitful.

personal interview survey
Face-to-face situation in which the researcher meets the consumer and questions him or her about a specific topic

In a **personal interview survey**, participants respond to questions face to face.[14] Various audio-visual aids – pictures, products, diagrams or pre-recorded advertising copy – can be incorporated into a personal interview. Rapport gained through direct interaction usually permits more in-depth interviewing, including probes, follow-up questions or psychological tests. In addition, because personal interviews can be longer, they can yield more information. Finally, respondents can be selected more carefully, and reasons for non-response can be explored. A **depth interview** is a lengthy, one-to-one structured interview examining a consumer's views about a product in detail.

depth interview
A lengthy, one-to-one structured interview, examining in detail a consumer's views about a product

focus group interview
A survey method that aims to observe group interaction when members are exposed to an idea or concept

The object of a **focus group interview** is to observe group interaction when members are exposed to an idea or concept. Focus groups are frequently held in viewing facilities, as illustrated in Figure 7.6. Often these interviews are conducted informally, without a structured questionnaire, in small groups of 8 to 12 people. Consumer attitudes, behaviour, lifestyles, needs and desires can be explored in a flexible and creative manner through this widely used technique (see Chapter 4). Questions are open-ended and stimulate consumers to answer in their own words. Researchers can ask probing questions to clarify something they do not fully understand, or something unexpected and interesting that may help to explain consumer behaviour.

When Cadbury used information obtained from focus groups to change its advertising and to test product concepts, the new advertisements and product launches pushed up sales.[15] The case study at the end of this chapter describes focus group research. Focus group discussions usually start with a general chat, which will be led

FIGURE 7.6
Viewing facilities are often used for experiments or for conducting focus group interviews

Source: Image courtesey of West Midlands Viewing Facility

by a researcher or moderator. The conversation is then narrowed during the course of the session, enabling the moderator to home in on a specific brand, product or advertisement – hence the term 'focus' group.

quali-depth interviews
25- to 30-minute intercept interviews that incorporate some of the in-depth advantages of focus group interviews with the speed and flexibility of shopping mall/pavement intercept interviews

Quali-depth interviews are 25- to 30-minute intercept interviews that incorporate some of the in-depth advantages of focus group interviews with the speed and flexibility of shopping mall/pavement intercept interviews (see below). Typically, intercepted consumers are taken to a nearby hall or café and asked more probing and searching questions than is possible in a three- to four-minute shopping mall/pavement intercept interview. They can also be shown a greater variety of stimulus material. This is a useful approach for sensitive issues that people might not wish to discuss in a group – gambling and drugs, for example.

Another research technique is the **in-home interview**. Because it may be desirable to eliminate group influence, the in-home interview offers a clear advantage when thoroughness of self-disclosure is important. In an in-depth interview of 45 to 90 minutes, respondents can be probed to reveal their real motivations, feelings, behaviours and aspirations. In-depth interviews permit the discovery of emotional 'hot buttons' that provide psychological insights.[16] Door-to-door interviews last only a few minutes and are similar to pavement intercepts.

in-home interview
45- to 90-minute interview in which the researcher visits the respondent in his or her home

The nature of personal interviews has changed. In the past, most personal interviews, which were based on random sampling or pre-arranged appointments, were conducted in the respondent's home. Today, most personal interviews are conducted in shopping centres or malls, or on pavements. **Shopping mall/pavement intercept interviews** involve interviewing a percentage of people who pass by certain 'intercept' points in a shopping centre or pavement. Like any face-to-face interviewing method, shopping mall/pavement intercept interviewing has many advantages. The interviewer is in a position to recognize and react to respondents' non-verbal indications of confusion. Respondents can be shown product prototypes, videotapes of advertisements and the like, and reactions can be sought. The environment lets the researcher deal with complex situations. For example, in taste tests, researchers know that all the respondents are reacting to the same product, which can be prepared and monitored from the shopping centre's test kitchen or some other facility. In addition, lower cost, greater control and the ability to conduct tests requiring bulky equipment make shopping mall/pavement intercept interviews popular.

shopping mall/ pavement intercept interviews
Personal interviewing of a percentage of individuals who pass by certain 'intercept' points in a shopping centre or on a pavement

Research indicates that given a comparable sample of respondents, shopping mall/pavement intercept interviewing is a suitable substitute for telephone interviewing.[17] In addition, there seem to be no significant differences in the completeness of consumer responses between telephone interviewing and shopping mall/pavement intercept interviewing. In fact, for questions dealing with socially desirable behaviour, shopping mall/pavement intercept respondents appear to be more honest about their past behaviour.[18]

on-site computer interviewing
A survey method that requires respondents to complete a self-administered questionnaire displayed on a computer monitor

In **on-site computer interviewing**, a variation of the shopping mall/pavement intercept interview, respondents complete a self-administered questionnaire displayed on a computer monitor. A computer software package can be used to conduct such interviews in shopping centres or transport termini. After a brief lesson on how to operate the software, respondents can go through the survey at their own pace. Questionnaires can be adapted so that respondents see only those items that may provide useful information about their attitudes.[19]

Questionnaire construction   A carefully constructed questionnaire is essential to the success of any survey. A **questionnaire** is a base document for research purposes that provides the questions and the structure for an interview or self-completion, and has provision for respondents' answers.[20] Questions must be designed to elicit information that meets the study's data requirements. These questions must be clear, easy to understand and directed towards a specific objective. Researchers need to define the objective before trying to develop a questionnaire because the objective determines the substance of the questions and the amount of detail. A common mistake in constructing questionnaires is to ask questions that interest the researchers but do not yield information useful in deciding whether to accept or reject a hypothesis. Finally, the most important rule in composing questions is to maintain impartiality.

questionnaire
Base document for research purposes, providing the questions and structure for an interview or self-completion, and providing space for respondents' answers

The questions are usually of four kinds:

1 open-ended
2 dichotomous
3 multiple choice
4 Likert scale.

Here are some examples.

1 OPEN-ENDED QUESTION
   What is your general opinion of broadband Internet access for your computer?

   _____

   _____

   _____

2 DICHOTOMOUS QUESTION
   Do you presently have broadband access at home?
   Yes ____   Provider's identity ____
   No ____

3 MULTIPLE-CHOICE QUESTION
   What age group are you in?
   Under 20   ____
   20–29   ____
   30–39   ____
   40–49   ____
   50–59   ____
   60 and over ____

4 LIKERT SCALE QUESTION
   To what extent do you expect to use the Internet for buying travel products (flights, hotel accommodation) in the near future?

   Not at |___|___|___|___|___| A great
   all   1   2   3   4   5   deal

The design of questionnaires is extremely important because it affects the validity and usefulness of the results. Testing a questionnaire on a few respondents before conducting a full survey helps to eliminate such difficulties. There are also certain guidelines that should be followed when undertaking questionnaire design. The questions must relate to the research objectives. The layout of the questionnaire must not be off-putting to respondents or to the researchers conducting the work. This is particularly pertinent given that technological advances mean that carefully laid-out questionnaires can be read (scanned) and analyzed by computers. This can save researchers a great deal of time. Question type is also an important factor. Open-ended questions can be the most revealing, but are time-consuming – and therefore off-putting – for respondents, as well as difficult to analyze. Dichotomous questions are straightforward but not very revealing. Multiple-choice questions are popular, but care must be exercised in the choice of categories. Likert scale questions are very popular and can enable batches or strings of questions to be listed together in a space-saving style that can be time-saving for the respondent. They allow respondents to express degrees of a positive or negative response, rather than give an absolute yes or no. There is also the option to give a 'neutral' ('3') answer. Most questionnaires include a mix of question styles.

Sometimes respondent fatigue can affect the quality of questionnaire responses. This may result in answers being rushed, or the questionnaire being abandoned altogether. For example, sometimes when faced with a long list of Likert scale questions, respondents move through the questions ticking the same point in the scale, rather than taking time to reflect on their answers. The wording of questions is also critical. Researchers must ensure that personal questions, such as those about income or educational attainment, are worded in as inoffensive a manner as possible. These types of question are often placed towards the end of the questionnaire, because it is believed that they are more likely to be answered once the respondent has invested time in the research instrument.

observation methods
Methods by which researchers record respondents' overt behaviour and take note of physical conditions and events

Observation methods In using **observation methods**, researchers record respondents' overt behaviour, taking note of physical conditions and events. Direct contact with respondents is avoided; instead, their actions are examined and noted systematically. For example, researchers might use observation methods to answer the question, 'How long do shoppers in computer game stores such as Game, typically spend browsing?'. As the Marketing Insight earlier in this chapter demonstrates, observation may include the use of ethnographic techniques, such as watching customers interact with a product in a real-world environment. Ethnography is increasingly being used by many marketing research agencies to gain greater insights into consumer lifestyles. Indeed, in a recent survey of the marketing research industry, 27 per cent of respondents giving an opinion about the most exciting developments mentioned ethnographic research.[21]

Observation may also be combined with interviews. For example, during a personal interview, the condition of a respondent's home or other possessions may be observed and recorded, and demographic information such as ethnic origin, approximate age and sex can be confirmed. Some forms of 'observation' are now common on e-shopping sites, with businesses monitoring the amount of time consumers spend browsing and even whether they complete the purchase process once they have started. Observation is also not confined to consumers; shops and service establishments can also be observed, through 'mystery shopper' research, as the Marketing Tools and Techniques box below explains.

Data gathered through observation can sometimes be biased if the respondent is aware of the observation process. An observer can be placed in a natural market environment, such as a grocery store, without biasing or influencing shoppers' actions. However, if the presence of a human observer is likely to bias the outcome or if human sensory abilities are inadequate, mechanical means may be used to record behaviour. **Mechanical observation devices** include cameras, recorders, counting machines and other equipment that records physiological changes in individuals. For instance, a special camera can be used to record the eye movements of respondents looking at an advertisement, and to detect the sequence of reading and the parts of the advertisement that receive greatest

mechanical observation devices
Cameras, recorders, counting machines and other equipment that records physiological changes in individuals

The intrigues of 'mystery shopper' research programmes

Marketing tools and techniques

Retailers and providers of services depend increasingly not only on the products they sell or deliver but also on the ability, attitude and quality of their personnel and the internal environment of their branch outlets. The regional directors and head office managers who check such standards all too often enter through the staff door at the rear of the branch, focusing primarily on operations and not on customer concerns. The branch's customers enter from the front, having first seen the exterior of the branch. They deal with all levels of personnel, not just the manager or manageress to whom the visiting director talks. These customers are not wrapped up in the company's products and operations; they seek help and advice. They expect courtesy and professionalism.

Customers buy a company's products; quite often the company's management never does, instead requesting items direct from storage at staff discount rates without ever visiting shops or showrooms. Car manufacturers give their senior management vehicles and offer all employees highly attractive deals. The result is that few senior managers ever visit a showroom or dealer – even their servicing is taken care of – so they never see the 'sharp end', their dealers, as customers do.

One car producer instigated a programme of 'mystery shopper' surveys. This programme involved visits by bogus potential car buyers to dealers to rate the upkeep and appearance of showrooms, technical knowledge and attitude of personnel, quality of displays, negotiating criteria and adherence to company policies. Dealers did not know who the bogus buyers were, or when they were to visit. Service reception staff were similarly targeted. A favourite ploy by the researchers was to book a car service by telephone and then phone again to cancel, judging the receptionist's response to the lost business. As a result of these frequent but anonymous visits, the car producer was able to improve the standards of its dealers, the attitude of its personnel and ultimately the quality of its service and customer satisfaction.

This form of marketing research – 'mystery shopper' – is one of the fastest-growing areas in the industry. It is defined by MSPA (the Mystery Shoppers Providers Association), is valuable because:

⊠ Most customers who have unsatisfactory experiences will not complain ... they will just never come back.

⊠ Dissatisfied customers are likely to tell many others about their experience, who in turn probably will avoid doing business with the offending merchant.

⊠ The use of mystery shopping to provide independent and impartial feedback reduces any perception of favoritism in incentive programs.

⊠ Mystery shopping helps determine whether customers' actual experiences are as intended.

⊠ Shopping programs can identify areas of training which need improvement and can identify areas of training that are working particularly well.

(Source http://www.mspa-eu.org/en/what-is-ms.html, accessed on March 8th 2011)

Even so, market research companies such as GfK, which offers mystery shopping services, must take care that staff are trained to a high standard and must also ensure that they behave in an ethical manner. Employees must be trained to evaluate how customers are greeted, how stores that they visit look and whether shop assistants understand the products on sale. They are also expected to be able to blend in inconspicuously in the settings they visit.

Recently concerns have been expressed about the use of mystery shopper researcher by organizations such as the European Society for Opinion and Marketing Research (ESOMAR), over worries that employees might be tricked into handling awkward customers in an inappropriate way and that this might have future consequences for those individuals jobs. In other forms of research, those involved have the opportunity to withdraw from the process, but this opportunity is not provided to those being inspected by mystery shoppers. Another concern is that in most forms of ethical marketing research, the respondent is guaranteed anonymity, but if mystery shopper research is deployed to check up on staff or to develop 'league tables' of branch performance, it is difficult for the research findings not to identify the personnel in question.

Some marketing research firms that use mystery shopping are trying to address these concerns by ensuring that they comply with the guidelines laid down by organizations such as ESOMAR and the Market Research Society. Others have joined the MSPA, an association of organizations providing mystery shopping services. MSPA is a membership organization which aims to 'improve the acceptance, performance, reputation and use of mystery shopping services' Its members must be able to demonstrate that have at least two years' experience, have a reputation for excellence, and agree to abide by the Association's codes of professional ethics and standards (http://www.mspa-eu.org/en/what-is-ms.html, sourced on March 8th 2011).

Sources: *Marketing Guides: Market Research*, 13 June 1996; **http://www.mystery-shoppers.co.uk**; **www.mspa-eu.org**; **http://www.gfkmysteryshopping.co.uk**, March 2011.

attention. Electronic scanners in supermarkets can provide accurate data on sales and consumers' purchase patterns, and marketing researchers may buy such data from the supermarket company.

Observation is straightforward and avoids a central problem of survey methods: motivating respondents to state their true feelings or opinions. However, observation tends to be descriptive. When it is the only method of data collection, it may not provide insights into causal relationships. Another drawback is that analyses based on observation are subject to the biases of the observer or the limitations of the mechanical device.

experimentation
Data collection that involves maintaining certain variables as constant so that the effects of the experimental variables can be measured

Experimentation **Experimentation** can be used to determine which variable or variables caused an event to occur. It involves keeping certain variables constant so that the effects of the experimental variables can be measured. For instance, if an online fashion vendor wishes to examine the effect of a price reduction on sales, all other marketing variables should be held constant except the change in price.

In experimentation, an **independent variable** (a variable not influenced by or dependent on other variables) is manipulated and the resulting changes measured in a **dependent variable** (a variable contingent on, or restricted to, one value or a set of values assumed by the independent variable). Figure 7.7 illustrates the relationship between these variables. For example, when Coca Cola introduces a new variant of its carbonated soft drink, it may want to estimate the number of each variant that could be sold at various levels of advertising expenditure and price. The dependent variable would be sales, the independent variables would be advertising expenditure and price. Researchers would design the experiment to control other independent variables that might influence sales, such as distribution and variations of the product.

independent variable
A variable not influenced by or dependent on other variables in experiments

dependent variable
A variable that is contingent on, or restricted to, one value or a set of values assumed by the independent variable

Experiments may be conducted in the laboratory or in the field; each research setting has advantages and disadvantages. In **laboratory settings**, participants or respondents are invited to a central location to react or respond to experimental stimuli. In such an isolated setting it is possible to control independent variables that might influence the outcome of an experiment. The features of laboratory settings might include a taste kitchen, video equipment, projection facilities, digital recorders, Internet hook-ups, one-way mirrors, central telephone banks and interview rooms. In an experiment to determine the influence of price (independent variable) on sales of a new line

laboratory settings
Central locations at which participants or respondents are invited to react or respond to experimental stimuli

of microwave ready meals (dependent variable), respondents would be invited to a laboratory – a room with table, chairs and sample ready meals – before the product was available in stores. The ready meal would be placed on a table with competing products. Analysts would then question respondents about their reactions to the ready meal at various prices. One problem with a laboratory setting is its isolation from the real world, making it difficult, or impossible, to duplicate all the conditions that affect choices in the marketplace.

field settings
'Real world' environments in which experiments take place

The experimental approach can also be used in **field settings**, which are 'real world' environments. A taste test of regional cheeses conducted in a supermarket is one example of an experiment in a field setting. Field settings can allow a more direct

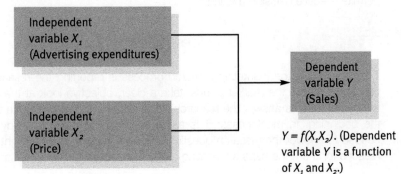

FIGURE 7.7
Relationship between independent and dependent variables

home placements
Experiments in which a product is used in a home setting

diary tests
Experiments in which households log their weekly purchases and consumption patterns

test of marketing decisions than laboratory settings. However, these experiments also have their drawbacks. It may be difficult to encourage respondents to cooperate with the experiment, or the findings may be influenced or biased by unexpected events, such as the weather or major economic news. Sometimes the experiment itself can cause bias. For example, in **home placements** (when a product is used in the home in a real setting) or **diary tests** (when households log their weekly purchases and consumption patterns), people may become artificially involved with the product. They might sniff items they would not normally sniff, or ask for their children's opinions about a food item when, normally, they would just give their children the meal and expect them to eat it.[22]

Step 4: analyzing and interpreting research findings

After collecting data to test their hypotheses, marketers analyze and interpret the research findings. Interpretation is easier if marketers plan their data analysis methods carefully and early in the research process. All too often, when data collection has been completed, it is discovered that different wording of questions or ordering of the sections in a questionnaire could have simplified the analysis. Marketers should also allow for continual evaluation of the data during the entire collection period. They can then gain valuable insight into areas that ought to be probed during the formal interpretation.

The first step in drawing conclusions from most research is displaying the data in table format. If marketers intend to apply the results to individual categories of the things or people being studied, cross-tabulation may be quite useful, especially in tabulating joint occurrences. For example, a cross-tabulation of data using the two variables 'gender' and 'purchase rates of car tyres' would show differences in how men and women purchase this product.

statistical interpretation
An analysis of data that focuses on what is typical or what deviates from the average

After the data are tabulated, they must be analyzed. **Statistical interpretation** focuses on what is typical or what deviates from the average. It indicates how widely responses vary and how they are distributed in relation to the variable being measured. This interpretation is another facet of marketing research that relies on marketers' judgement or intuition. Moreover, when they interpret statistics, marketers must take into account estimates of expected error or deviation from the true values of the population. The analysis of data helps researchers to achieve their research objectives and may lead to the hypothesis being studied being accepted or rejected.[23]

Data require careful interpretation by the marketer. If the results of a study are valid, the decision-maker should take action; however, if it is discovered that a question has been worded incorrectly, the results should be ignored. For example, if a study by a restaurant chain reveals that 50 per cent of its customers believe that its waiting staff are efficient, is that finding good, bad or indifferent? Two important benchmarks help interpret the result: how the 50 per cent figure compares with that for competitors and how it compares with a previous time period. The point is that managers must understand the research results and relate them to a context that permits effective decision-making.[24]

Step 5: reporting research findings

The final step in the marketing research process is reporting the research findings. Before preparing the report, the marketer must take a clear, objective look at the findings to see how well the gathered facts answer the research question, or support or negate the hypotheses posed in the beginning. In most cases, it is extremely doubtful that the study can provide everything needed to answer the research question. Thus the report must highlight the deficiencies and the reasons for them, perhaps suggesting areas that require further investigation.

The report presenting the results is usually a formal, written document. Researchers must allow time for the writing task when they plan and schedule the project. Since the report is a means of communicating with the decision-makers who will use the research findings, researchers need to determine beforehand how much detail and supporting data to include. They should keep in mind that corporate executives prefer reports that are short, clear and simply expressed. Often researchers will give their summary and recommendations first, especially if decision-makers do not have time to study how the results were obtained. Such summary findings tend to be presented via a face-to-face audio-visual presentation or possibly via a virtual webinar. A technical report allows its users to analyze data and interpret recommendations because it describes the research methods/procedures and the most important data gathered. Thus researchers must recognize the needs and expectations of the report user and adapt to them.

When marketing decision-makers have a firm grasp of research methods and procedures, they are better able to integrate reported findings and personal experience. If marketers can spot limitations in research from reading a report, their personal experience assumes additional importance in the decision-making process. Marketers who cannot understand basic statistical assumptions and data gathering procedures may misuse research findings. Consequently, report writers should be aware of the backgrounds and research abilities of those who will rely on the report in making decisions. Clear explanations presented in plain language make it easier for decision-makers to apply the findings and less likely that a report will be misused or ignored. Talking to potential research users before writing a report can help researchers supply information that will improve decision-making.

Care must be taken when writing the report to avoid bias and distortion. Marketing researchers want to find out about behaviour and opinions, and they need accurate data for making decisions. Reliable marketing research and marketing information systems provide a clearer understanding of dynamics in the marketplace and are more likely to be used by managers in decision-making.

Using technology to improve marketing information gathering and analysis

Marketing information systems

marketing information system (MIS)
The framework for the day-to-day management and structuring of information gathered from sources both inside and outside an organization

A **marketing information system (MIS)** is a framework for the day-to-day management and structuring of information gathered regularly from sources both inside and outside an organization. As such, an MIS provides a continuous flow of information about prices, advertising expenditure, sales, competition and distribution expenses.[25] Kraft Foods, for example, operates one of the largest marketing information systems in the food industry, maintaining, using and sharing information with others to increase the value of what the company offers customers. Kraft seeks to develop a dialogue with customers through a variety of means including via its own Facebook page. As Kraft explains:

> We've started this page to share company news; our community involvement and sustainability efforts; health and wellness updates and a look back at our history. Feel free to jump in with your own perspectives too.

http://www.kraftfoodscompany.com/About/who-we-are/facebook_final.aspx,
accessed on 23 February 2011

The main focus of the marketing information system is on data storage and retrieval. Regular reports of sales by product or market category, data on inventory levels and records of sales people's activities are all examples of information that is useful in making marketing decisions. In the MIS, the means of gathering data receive less attention than do the procedures for

FIGURE 7.8
CACI market themselves as an unrivalled range of marketing solutions and information systems, to a number of businesses from all industry sectors

Logo courtesy of CACI

expediting the flow of information. Figure 7.8 illustrates the chief components of an MIS. The inputs into a marketing information system include the information sources inside and outside the organization assumed to be useful for future decision-making. An effective marketing information system starts by determining the objective of the information – that is, by identifying decision needs that require certain information. The business can then specify an information system for continuous monitoring to provide regular, pertinent information on both the external and internal environment.

Databases

Most marketing information systems include internal databases. A database is a collection of information arranged for easy access and retrieval. Databases allow marketers to tap into an abundance of information useful in making marketing decisions: internal sales reports, newspaper articles, company press releases, government economic reports, bibliographies and more, often accessed through a computer system. Information technology has made it possible to develop databases to guide strategic planning and help improve customer services. Wal-Mart, for example, maintains one of the largest company databases, with data on sales and inventory levels, as well as data mined from customer receipts in its stores. These data help Wal-Mart pinpoint purchasing patterns, which helps the company manage inventory levels and determine effective product placement. Frequent-flier programmes permit airlines to ask loyal customers to participate in surveys about their needs and desires, allowing the airlines to track their best customers' flight patterns by time of day, week, month and year. Supermarkets, such as Tesco and Sainsbury's, gain a substantial amount of data through checkout scanners tied to loyalty cards.

Marketing researchers can also use commercial databases developed by information research organizations to obtain useful information for marketing decisions. Many of these commercial databases are accessible online for a fee. In most commercial databases, the user typically does a computer search by key word, topic or company, and the database service generates abstracts, articles or reports that can be printed out. Accessing multiple reports or a complete article may cost extra. Information provided by a single company – for example, on household demographics, purchases, television viewing behaviour and responses to promotions such as coupons or loyalty schemes, is called **single-source data**.[26] For example, CACI provides demographic and lifestyle information on people living in different UK neighbourhoods; see Figure 7.8.

single-source data
Information provided by a single marketing research company

The Internet and online information services

The Internet has evolved as a powerful communication medium, linking customers and companies around the world via computer networks with e-mail, forums, web pages and more.

Growth of the Internet has launched an entire industry that is working to make market information easily accessible both to marketing organizations and customers.

Companies can also mine their own websites for useful information. Amazon, for example, has built a relationship with its customers by tracking the types of books and music they purchase. Each time a customer logs on to its website, Amazon can offer recommendations based on the customer's previous purchases. Such a marketing system helps the company track the changing desires and buying habits of its most valued customers.

Marketing researchers can use a range of Internet sites set up to support their data collection activities. Some sites, such as SurveyMonkey (www.surveymonkey.com), provide the means to design research instruments and collect data in a format that can be readily analyzed. With millions of customers around the world, organizations ranging from charities such as the National Multiple Sclerosis Society (NMSS) to corporates such as Samsung have used this service to acquire insights they need. Other organizations, such as Lightspeed and Populus have created online market research panels, providing their clients with ready access to consumers around the world who can answer questions about the products and services they prefer, their purchase behaviour and lifestyles, or even their views about global events. Marketers can also subscribe to 'mailing lists' that periodically deliver electronic newsletters to their computer screens and they can participate in on-screen discussions with thousands of network users. This enhanced communication with a business's customers, suppliers and employees provides a high-speed link that boosts the capabilities of the business's marketing information system.

While most web pages are open to anyone with Internet access, big organizations like Cisco Systems also maintain internal 'intranets', that allow employees to access such internal data as customer profiles and product inventory – information once hidden in databases only technicians could unlock. Such sensitive company information can be protected from outside users of the Internet by special security software called firewalls. Marketers who get into the habit of accessing their companies' internal web pages often move on to seek information externally as well, via the rest of the World Wide Web.

The importance of ethical marketing research

Marketing managers and other professionals are relying more and more on marketing research, marketing information systems and new technologies to make better decisions. It is therefore essential that professional standards are established by which to judge the reliability of this research. Such standards are necessary because of the ethical and legal issues that develop in gathering marketing research data. In addition, the relationships between research suppliers, such as marketing research agencies, and the marketing managers who make strategy decisions, require ethical behaviour. Without such clear standards, ethical conflict can lead to mistrust and questionable research results.[27] Attempts to stamp out shoddy practices and establish generally accepted procedures for conducting research are important developments in marketing research. Other issues of great concern relate to researchers' honesty, manipulation of research techniques, data manipulation, invasion of privacy and failure to disclose the purpose or sponsorship of a study in some situations. Too often, respondents are unfairly manipulated and research clients are not told about flaws in data. For example, one dubious practice that damages the image of marketing research is 'sugging', as mentioned earlier in the chapter. More recently, direct marketers have disguised their selling mailings with questionnaires, adding to respondents' confusion and dislike of honest marketing research.[28]

All kinds of organizations involved in research have developed codes of conduct and guidelines to promote ethical marketing research.[29] These include professional associations, academic research funders, as well as government bodies, commercial organizations and universities. To be effective, such guidelines must instruct those who participate in marketing research on how to avoid misconduct. Table 7.6 compares the principles driving the ethics codes of professional association, the Market Research Society (MRS), and academic research funding body, the Economic and Social Science Research Council (ESRC).

Marketing research is essential in planning and developing marketing strategies. Information about target markets provides vital input in planning the marketing mix and in controlling marketing activities. It is no secret that companies can use information technology as a key to gaining an advantage over the competition.[30] In short, the marketing concept – the marketing philosophy of customer orientation – can be implemented better when adequate information about customers, competition and trends is available.

TABLE 7.6 The principles of the MRS and ESRC code of conduct

MRS principles	ESRC principles
1 Researchers shall ensure that participation in their activities is based on voluntary informed consent.	1 Research should be designed, reviewed and undertaken to ensure integrity, quality and transparency.
2 Researchers shall be straightforward and honest in all their professional and business relationships.	2 Research staff and participants must normally be informed fully about the purpose, methods and intended possible uses of the research, what their participation in the research entails and what risks, if any, are involved.
3 Researchers shall be transparent as to the subject and purpose of data collection.	
4 Researchers shall respect the confidentiality of information collected in their professional activities.	3 The confidentiality of information supplied by research participants and the anonymity of respondents must be respected.
5 Researchers shall respect the rights and well-being of all individuals.	
6 Researchers shall ensure that respondents are not harmed or adversely affected by their professional activities.	4 Research participants must take part voluntarily, free from coercion.
7 Researchers shall balance the needs of individuals, clients and their professional activities.	5 Harm to research participants must be avoided in all instances.
8 Researchers shall exercise independent professional judgement in the design, conduct and reporting of their professional activities.	6 The independence of research must be clear, and any conflicts of interests or partiality must be explicit.
9 Researchers shall ensure that their professional activities are conducted by persons with appropriate training, qualifications and experience.	
10 Researchers shall protect the reputation and integrity of the profession.	

Source: **http://www.mrs.org.uk/standards/codeconduct.htm**, accessed on 22 February 2011; ESRC Frame for Research Ethics, **http://www.esrc.ac.uk/**, accessed on 22 February 2011.

Summary

Effective marketing is contingent on marketers having information about the characteristics, needs and wants of their target markets. Marketing research and information systems that furnish practical, unbiased information help companies avoid the assumptions and misunderstandings that could lead to poor marketing performance.

Marketing research is the systematic design, collection, interpretation and reporting of information to help marketers solve specific marketing problems or take advantage of marketing opportunities. Marketing research projects are adapted to the context and problems under study.

All organizations have some *marketing intelligence*, which is the composite of all data and ideas available within the organization. Often the information is inadequate, leading to the commissioning of marketing research.

Quantitative marketing research leads to findings that can be quantified and statistically analyzed. *Qualitative research* examines subjective opinions and value judgements.

The increase in marketing research activities represents a transition from intuitive to scientific problem-solving. Intuitive decisions are made on the basis of personal knowledge and past experience. *Scientific decision-making* is an orderly, logical and systematic approach to gathering information. Minor, non-recurring low-risk problems can be handled successfully by *intuition.* As the amount of risk and alternative solutions increases, the use of research becomes more desirable and rewarding.

The five basic steps of planning marketing research are: (1) locating and defining problems or research issues; (2) designing the research; (3) collecting data; (4) analyzing and interpreting research findings; (5) reporting research findings.

The first step towards finding a solution or launching a research study means uncovering the nature and boundaries of a negative, or positive, situation or question. Researchers and decision-makers should remain in the *problem definition* stage until they have determined precisely what they want from the research and how they will use it.

Careful *research design* is of vital importance as a clear statement of research objectives guides a research project. Sometimes hypotheses – or informed guesses or assumptions about a certain problem or set of circumstances – are formulated. The *research objectives* and *any hypotheses* determine the approach for gathering data: *exploratory research, descriptive research or causal research.* Researchers need to be concerned about issues of reliability and validity: techniques are *reliable* if they produce almost identical results in successive repeated trials; they have *validity* if they measure what they are supposed to measure and not something else.

Collecting data is the third step of the research process. *Secondary data* are compiled inside or outside the organization for some purpose other than the current investigation. Secondary data may be collected from an organization's databank and other internal sources; from periodicals, census reports, government publications, the Internet and unpublished sources; and from *syndicated data services,* which collect general information and sell it to clients. Secondary data 'pre-exists' and should be examined prior to the collection of any primary data.

To gather *primary data,* researchers use sampling procedures, survey methods, observation and experimentation. *Sampling* involves selecting a limited number of representative units, or a *sample,* from a total *population.* There are two basic types of sampling: probability and non-probability. In *probability sampling,* every element of the population has a known chance of being selected. In *random sampling,* all the units in a population have an equal chance of appearing in the sample. In *stratified sampling,* the population of interest is divided into groups according to a common characteristic or attribute, and then a probability sampling is conducted within each group. *Area sampling* involves selecting a probability sample of geographic areas such as streets, census tracts or census enumeration districts, and selecting units or individuals within the selected geographic areas for the sample. *Quota sampling* differs from other forms of sampling in that it is judgemental (or non-probability).

Survey methods include *mail surveys* and *mail and online panels*, e-mail and Internet surveys (*online surveys*), *consumer purchase diaries, telephone surveys, computer assisted telephone interviewing and personal interview surveys*, such as *depth interviews, shopping mall/pavement intercept interviews, on-site computer interviewing, focus group interviews, quali-depth interviews and in-home interviews. Questionnaires* are instruments used to obtain information from respondents and to record observations; they should be unbiased and objective. Observation methods including ethnographic techniques that involve researchers recording respondents' overt behaviour and taking note of physical conditions and events. Observation may be facilitated by *mechanical observation devices.*

Experimentation involves maintaining as constants those factors that are related to or may affect the variables under investigation, so that the effects of the experimental variables can be measured. Marketing experimentation is a set of rules and procedures according to which the task of data gathering is organized so as to expedite analysis and interpretation. In experimentation, an *independent variable* is manipulated and the resulting changes are measured in a *dependent variable.*

Experiments may take place in *laboratory settings*, which provide maximum control over influential factors, or in *field settings*, which are preferred when marketers want experimentation to take place in 'real world' environments, such as with *home placements* and *diary tests.*

To apply research findings to decision-making, marketers must tabulate, analyze and interpret their findings properly. *Statistical interpretation* is analysis of data that focuses on what is typical or what deviates from the average. After interpreting their research findings, researchers must prepare a report of the findings that the decision-makers can use and understand. Information provided by a single firm is called *single-source data.*

The *marketing information system (MIS)* is a framework for the day-to-day managing and structuring of information regularly gathered from sources both inside and outside an organization. The inputs into a marketing information system include the information sources inside and outside the organization considered useful for future decision-making. They may include internal databases. Processing information involves classifying it and developing categories for meaningful storage and retrieval. Marketing decision-makers then determine which information – the output – is useful for making marketing decisions. Feedback enables those who are responsible for gathering internal and external data to adjust the information inputs systematically.

Growth of the Internet has launched an entire industry that is working to make market information easily accessible to both organizations and customers. Companies can also mine their own websites for useful information, subscribe to online services and join 'mailing lists' that periodically deliver electronic newsletters to their computer screens so that they can participate in on-screen discussions with thousands of network users.

Marketing managers and other professionals are relying more and more on marketing research, marketing information systems and new technologies to make better decisions. Professional standards are needed to judge the reliability of such research. These enable ethical and legal issues associated with data gathering to be handled.

Key links

This chapter has concentrated on the marketing research tools available to capture information about markets and customers. It should be read in conjunction with:

☒ Chapter 2's examination of the nature of opportunity analysis and the importance of analyzing competitors

☒ Chapters 4 and 5, reviewing the required insights into buying behaviour

☒ Chapters 4, 6 and 14, discussing how to create market segments from an understanding of customers, and how best to develop a brand positioning strategy.

Important terms

Marketing research
Marketing intelligence
Quantitative research
Qualitative research
Intuition
Scientific decision-making
Problem definition
Research design
Research objective
Hypothesis
Exploratory research
Descriptive research
Causal research
Reliability
Validity
Primary data
Secondary data
Syndicated data services
Population
Sample
Sampling
Probability sampling
Random sampling
Stratified sampling
Area sampling
Quota sampling
Survey methods
Mail surveys
Mail panels
Consumer purchase diaries
Telephone surveys
Computer-assisted telephone interviewing
Online survey

Personal interview survey
Depth interview
Focus group interview
Quali-depth interviews
In-home interview
Shopping mall/pavement intercept interviews
On-site computer interviewing
Questionnaire
Observation methods
Mechanical observation devices
Experimentation
Independent variable
Dependent variable
Laboratory settings
Field settings
Home placements
Diary tests
Statistical interpretation
Marketing information system (MIS)
Single-source data

Discussion and review questions

1 What is the marketing information system (MIS) of a small organization likely to include?

2 What are the differences between quantitative and qualitative marketing research?

3 How do the benefits of decisions guided by marketing research compare with those of intuitive decision-making? How do marketing decision-makers know when it will be worthwhile to conduct research?

4 Give specific examples of situations in which intuitive decision-making would probably be more appropriate than marketing research.

5 What are the differences between exploratory, descriptive and causal research?

6 What are the major limitations of using secondary data to solve marketing problems?

7 List some of the problems of conducting a laboratory experiment on respondents' reactions to the taste of different brands of beer. How would these problems differ from those of a field study of beer taste preferences?

8 In what situation would it be best to use random sampling? Quota sampling? Stratified or area sampling?

9 Suggest some ways to encourage respondents to cooperate in mail surveys.

10 What are the benefits of the focus group technique?

11 How has the growth of the Internet increased the opportunities for collecting information?

12 Give some examples of marketing problems that could be solved through information gained from observation.

13 Why is questionnaire design important? Why should questionnaires be tested?

14 What is 'sugging'? Why is it damaging to the marketing research industry?

15 Why are ethics so important in conducting marketing research?

Recommended readings

Aaker, D., Kumar, V. and Day, G., *Marketing Research* (John Wiley & Sons, 2010).

Bradley, N., *Marketing Research: Tools and Techniques* (Oxford University Press, 2011)

Chisnall, P.M., *Marketing Research* (McGraw-Hill, 2004).

McQuarrie, E.F., *The Market Research Toolbox: A Concise Guide for Beginners* (Sage, 2005).

Malhotra, N.K. and Birks, D.F., *Marketing Research: An Applied Approach* (FT Prentice Hall, 2006).

Internet exercise

The World Association of Opinion and Marketing Research Professionals (ESOMAR, founded as the European Society for Opinion and Marketing Research in 1948) is a non-profit association for marketing research professionals. ESOMAR promotes the use of opinion and marketing research to improve marketing decisions in companies worldwide and works to protect personal privacy in the research process. Visit the association's website at: **http://www.esomar.org/**

1 How can ESOMAR help marketing professionals conduct research to guide marketing strategy?

2 How can ESOMAR help marketers protect the privacy of research subjects when conducting marketing research in other countries?

3 ESOMAR introduced the first professional code of conduct for marketing research professionals in 1948. The association continues to update this document to address new technology and other changes in the marketing environment. According to ESOMAR's code, what are the specific professional responsibilities of marketing researchers?

Applied mini-case

Advances in information technology, especially in terms of data storage and processing capacity, have made available an ever-growing quantity of data about customer buying behaviour. To extract from this mound of data potentially useful information to guide marketing decisions, marketers are developing methods of mining data. Data mining refers to the discovery of patterns hidden in databases that have the potential to contribute to marketers' understanding of customers and their needs. Data mining employs computer technology to extract data from internal and external sources; translate and format the data; analyze, substantiate and assign meaning to data; organize databases; and build and implement support systems to make data mining results accessible to decision-makers.

Question

Adopt the role of a retail analyst who is helping a large retail group to organize its databases. You have been asked to help guide the process by providing a list of the kinds of information helpful to a company when making decisions about marketing strategy.

Focus group interviewing: in-depth views from group discussions

Focus group interviews, which are generally informal group discussions about marketing ideas or concepts conducted by a marketer or marketing research company, are used by most major organizations in developing marketing or business plans. In the 1980s, focus group interviewing became one of the most widely practised types of marketing research, expanding from the packaged goods industry into financial services and industrial applications.

However, the function of focus group interviewing is expected to change. Traditionally, companies have relied on focus group interviews to define the input going into quantitative studies, but a new trend is to conduct focus group interviews after tabulating research results, to provide insight into why the results were achieved. The trend is also towards higher costs (the average today is £2500 for 90 minutes and £3000 for an extended, video-recorded group lasting two and a half hours).

Other changes pertain to moderator guides and their reports. The moderator guides will be expected to involve clients in the development process. Their reports will concentrate on providing conclusions that interpret the findings and on making recommendations for action by the client. The reports will also contain fewer actual quotations from individual focus group participants. The post-focus group debriefing techniques are also being altered. The shift is towards disciplined debriefing that asks participants their reactions to the group session. Such debriefing can provide the link between concept development and application, and can serve as a rough check on validity and reliability.

Another new development in focus group interviewing is the use of electronics to offer three-way capabilities. Computerized decision-making software can supplement research findings and consolidate opinions from three different audiences. For example, in healthcare research in a hospital setting, the three audiences would be former patients, medics and employees. The advantages of using electronics include easier scheduling of participating groups and more interaction among the three audiences.

A major UK service retailer was faced with declining sales and two new competitors. In order to re-establish itself as the dominant force in its market, it decided to undertake some in-depth qualitative marketing research using focus groups. The retailer's new competitors were opening stores at the rate of six per month, and the company realized it had to act quickly to defend its position. However, it had not conducted any consumer research for many years and was uncertain why its customers preferred its stores, how competitors were perceived and what types of people constituted its customer profile. Before modifying its marketing mix and launching an advertising campaign to combat its new competitors, the company had to gain a better understanding of its target market. For approximately £14 000 (1989), using a specialist consumer qualitative agency, in just three weeks the company managed to get a good 'feel' for its standing in its core trading area, as perceived by customers. The table shows that the information resulted from a fairly 'standard' programme of focus groups.

Each group had eight consumers, four of whom were shoppers in the retailer's stores and four of whom shopped in competitors' stores. Each group session lasted three hours, and a free merchandise voucher and buffet meal was provided for participants. The same moderator ran all eight groups to maintain consistency. Each session was tape recorded, the tapes being transcribed later into a report and presentation to the retailer's board of directors. Two sessions were video recorded, and several were 'secretly viewed' by the company's marketing executives.

Group composition	Social class	Location
1 Male 25–39, white-collar commuters[†]	A, B	Eastcheap
2 Male 40–55, white-collar commuters	A, B	Hitchin
3 Female 25–44, executives/Pas	A, B, C1	Bristol
4 Female 25–44, semi-skilled	C2	Woking
5 Female 35–40 'housewives'[†]	A, B	Leamington
6 Female 25–34, 'housewives'	C1, C2	Sheffield
7 Male 18–29, young earners[†]	C1, C2	Ealing
8 Female 18–29, young earners	C1, C2	Telford

Note: [†]Held in branches after hours

Sources: Lynne Cunningham, 'Electronic focus groups offer 3-way capability', *Marketing News*, 8 January 1990, pp. 22, 39; Thomas L. Greenbaum, 'Focus group spurt predicted for the '90s', *Marketing News*, 8 January 1990, pp. 21, 22; Nino DeNicola, 'Debriefing sessions: the missing link in focus groups', *Marketing News*, 8 January 1990, pp. 20, 22; Peter Jackson, *Adsearch*, Richmond, 1989, 2007, 2011.

Questions for discussion

1 What are the strengths and benefits of focus group marketing research?

2 This retailer chose to commission a programme of focus groups. Given the aims of the company's research, what other research tools might the company have used? Explain your selection.

PART THREE
Developing Marketing Programmes

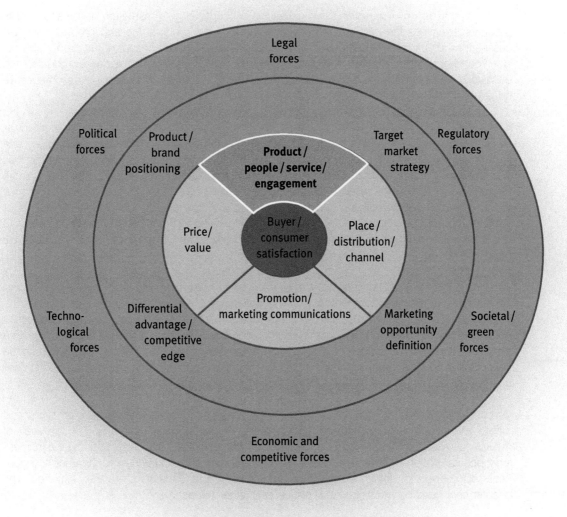

Legal
forces

Political
forces

Product /
brand
positioning

Product /
people / service /
engagement

Target
market
strategy

Regulatory
forces

Price /
value

Buyer /
consumer
satisfaction

Place /
distribution /
channel

Promotion /
marketing communications

Techno-
logical
forces

Differential
advantage /
competitive
edge

Marketing
opportunity
definition

Societal /
green
forces

Economic and
competitive forces

I n Chapter 1 of *Marketing Essentials*, marketing was said to involve marketing opportunity analysis, target market selection and the development of a marketing mix for each target market. The marketing mix is the set of marketing programme activities deployed by marketing managers in order to implement an organization's agreed target market strategy. The marketing mix centres on the '5Ps' of product, people, place (distribution), promotion and pricing decisions.

The marketing mix must endeavour to match the identified needs of targeted business customers or consumers in order to satisfy these customers' requirements. It must also communicate the desired brand or product positioning and emphasise any differential advantage held by an organization and its products or services over its rivals. As explained in Chapters 1 and 2, marketers should first analyze the forces of the marketing environment, customer buying behaviour, competitors' strategies and their own organizational capabilities before developing their marketing strategies. The marketing mix for a specific target market should only be specified once the marketing strategy has been formulated and agreed by senior management.

Part III of *Marketing Essentials* examines the product and people ingredients of the marketing mix, the integral issues of branding and customer service, as well as the important concepts of the product life cycle and the management of product portfolios. Also explored are marketing communications (promotion), marketing channel selection (place) and pricing strategies.

Chapter 8, 'Product Decisions', introduces the concepts of how marketers define and classify products; examines the differences between product item, product line and product mix; discusses the various levels of a product, and explores the important concept of the product life cycle. The chapter then discusses organizational structures available to manage products, and concludes by examining the importance of the levels of a product in determining a competitive edge over rivals' products.

Chapter 9, 'Developing Products and Managing Product Portfolios', outlines the organizational alternatives for managing products, explains how an organization develops a product idea into a commercial product, and analyses the role of product development in the marketing mix. The chapter includes a discussion of how products should be managed during the various stages of a product's life cycle. It discusses how existing products can be modified and how product deletion can sometimes benefit a marketing mix. The chapter concludes with a look at some of the related analytical tools associated with the planning of a product portfolio: the BCG product portfolio analysis, the market attractiveness-business position model or directional policy matrix (DPM) and the ABC sales: contribution analysis.

Chapter 10, 'The Marketing of Services', explores how services differ from tangible goods and considers the implications for marketers. The chapter begins by explaining the nature and characteristics of services, classifying services and the development of marketing strategies for services. It goes on to discuss the significant problems encountered in developing a differential advantage for a service and also addresses the crucial concept of service quality. The chapter then explores the concept of marketing in non-business situations, the development of marketing strategies in non-business organizations and methods for controlling non-business marketing activities.

Chapter 11, 'Marketing Channels', explains the marketing channel concept, the functions and different types of marketing channels. The chapter considers channel integration and the levels of market coverage, and then examines the selection of distribution channels, including the increasingly popular option of direct marketing. Behavioural aspects of channels, particularly the concepts of co-operation and relationship building, conflict and leadership, are then explored. The chapter concludes by examining legal issues in channel management.

Chapter 12, 'Pricing', explains the characteristics and role of price in marketing, outlines the differences between price and non-price competition, examines different pricing objectives and explores key factors that affect marketers' pricing decisions. The chapter then discusses perceived value for money, before turning to the complex aspect of pricing in business-to-business markets. Having examined the concept of economic value to the customer, the chapter concludes with an overview of the major stages in the process used to establish prices.

Chapter 13, 'An Overview of Marketing Communications', discusses the role of promotion in the marketing mix, the process of communication *per se*, the nature of marketing communications and the way in which the concept of the product adoption process relates to promotional activity. The chapter goes on to explain the aims of promotion and the elements of the promotional mix. The chapter concludes by examining the factors that influence the selection of promotional mix ingredients. Throughout the chapter, the notion of integrated marketing communications (IMC) is discussed, along with the growth of digital marketing and the role of social media.

Chapter 14, 'Branding and Packaging', recognizes the fundamental importance of brands and brand equity in marketing, and looks at different types of brands, their benefits, selection, naming, protection and licensing. In most organizations, marketers are the champions of the brand: the chapter presents the key concepts for creating strong and effective brands. The chapter goes on to discuss the functions of packaging, design considerations and the role of packaging in marketing strategy.

By the conclusion of Part III of *Marketing Essentials*, readers should understand the core decisions that must be made in determining a marketing mix, including products; people and service delivery issues; the management of product life cycles and portfolios of products; marketing of services; the selection of marketing channels; pricing; marketing communications; branding, and packaging.

The Marketects

1. What excites me most about marketing?

The power of ideas. Marketing demands that the left brain (analysis and insights) informs the right brain (imaginative product and communication concepts), to create a competitive advantage for your brand and business.

Excellent marketing is both a catalyst and accelerator of organic growth. Marketing is essentially results driven – you can see the fruits of your inputs immediately. There is no problem, brand, business or scenario where intelligent marketing solutions cannot help growth.

2. What are the biggest challenges for marketing?

Within a context of reduced resources – physical, financial and human – marketing has to focus even more on delivering sustained growth, fast and efficiently. It has to look towards ever smarter business insights as well as stimulate innovation and unlock performance from deeper analysis of customer metrics; this is the new trinity. Not only this, but marketing has to embrace the ongoing digital media and social marketing revolutions.

3. What does marketing contribute?

In short, profitable brand growth ... through intelligent and insightful analysis leading to an efficient management of the imagination. Marketing fuels brands. And the ethos of competition within any sector. It is the life blood of any branded product or service.

JOHN WRINGE
FORMER MD OF PUBLICIS/RED CELL,
NOW MANAGING PARTNER OF THE MARKETECTS

Tata's Nano steers into low pricing

How can a car sell for less than $3000? That's the price Tata Motors set for its Nano, a four-door, four-seat subcompact designed specifically for India and introduced in 2009. With a rear-mounted motor, this tiny car initially included absolutely no extras – no radio, no reclining seats, certainly no aircon or electric windows. What the Nano does have, however, is an ultra-low price tag. And that is what makes it very attractive to millions of potential buyers in India. Now 'someone who never even dreamed of a car finds it within reach,' says Tata's CEO. The range today is more extensive, with various engine options and specifications, but still retails between 140 000 to 210 000 Indian rupees (£2000 or $3300 to £2900 or $4700).

Racing to develop and market the world's cheapest car has been a challenge, even for a car manufacturer with as much experience as Mumbai-based Tata, which is India's largest automaker and owner of Jaguar and Land Rover in the UK. The company began working on the Nano in 2003, with the goal of creating a functional yet eye-pleasing design that would fit buyers' lifestyles and tight budgets and, at the same time, be profitable to manufacture and sell. The most essential ingredient was keeping costs in line to keep the car ultra-affordable.

Low price, low costs

The first step in developing the Nano was to establish an upper level for the car's price: roughly one lakh (100 000 Indian rupees), the equivalent of less than £1400. To sell a car at this price, 'you have to cut costs on everything – seats, materials, components – the whole package', says a Tata official. That's exactly what Tata did, using expertise gained from its years of marketing trucks, cars and buses for markets in India, Europe, South America, Southeast Asia, and the Middle East. For instance, Tata sells its Indica compact car for $8500 in eastern Europe.

The 330 horsepower engine of the Nano may not win any races, but it can get the car to a top speed of about 80 miles per hour. Thanks to low cost parts and manufacturing, the cost of each engine is only about $700. In contrast, an engine made in the West can be twice as much. By shaving the cost of each part and component, streamlining assembly methods, and offering only a stripped-down basic model, Tata has been able to achieve its low price goal.

What's driving the market?

India's healthy economy is propelling millions of consumers into the middle class and accelerating demand for affordable transportation. As many as 65 million people currently drive small motor scooters in India, often carrying family members

Strategic case

on the back. Some of these drivers will be able to trade up to a new car if the price is right.

In fact, sales of small cars are projected to reach 1 million units by 2016. Small wonder that Tata designed its Nano with four doors to appeal to buyers who often have family members and friends riding along. Finally, India's population skews young, with a median age under 25. If Tata can attract young first-time buyers with a low priced model and maintain their loyalty as they trade up to higher priced cars in the years ahead, the company will profit in the long term.

Competition on the roads of India

Competition is fierce at the low end of the car market. Maruti Suzuki India, which sells small cars starting at about $5000, is the market leader. With its nationwide service network, high brand recognition, and new production facilities in the works, Maruti Suzuki is a formidable competitor.

Other rivals are also expanding to take advantage of this fast-growing segment of the market. Hyundai India, for instance, is opening a global centre for small car manufacturing and adding manufacturing space. Its Santro, which offers both air conditioning and power steering as standard features, sells for about $6300. Volkswagen's Skoda division offers the low priced Fabia model, among others, in India.

Toyota is designing a no-frills car that will sell in India and other emerging nations for under $7500. In the process, the company expects to develop new technology that will help it cut costs on other vehicles in its global product mix. Honda has a plant in India and is opening a second plant to support its marketing initiatives in the area. Meanwhile, US carmakers are looking at how they might enter the market in the near future.

Renault-Nissan, working with Indian motorcycle manufacturer Bajaj, is developing a car to be priced around $3 000. The company knows a lot about low cost, low priced cars because since 2004 it has produced its popular $7000 Logan four-door saloon in Romania and Russia. Nearly half a million Logans are already on the roads of Europe, and even though Renault-Nissan's two plants are operating at full capacity all day and every day, the firm is still struggling to meet ever-growing demand.

To shave costs, Renault-Nissan limited the number of parts that go into the Logan and avoided expensive electronics. To speed development and eliminate the high costs of building prototypes, the company proceeded from digital design directly to production. This alone saved $40 million and is one reason for the CEO's confidence that Renault-Nissan can succeed in the worldwide ultra-low-price segment. 'With the Logan, we have the product and we have the lead', he says.

Environmental and safety concerns

As enthusiastic as Tata and other car manufacturers may be about marketing millions of tiny cars with tiny price tags, the car has generated both environmental and safety concerns. Some critics fear that broadening the base of car ownership will only add to the pollution problems in India's largest cities. Where national and local regulations do not require anti-pollution devices, manufacturers are unlikely to install them because of the added costs.

Safety is an issue because more cars on the road mean more traffic congestion and more opportunity for accidents. Cars made by Tata and its competitors comply with all of India's safety standards, but those standards do not require equipment, such as air bags and antilock brakes. Safety advocates worry that people travelling in the smallest, lightest cars will be more vulnerable to serious injury if involved in a traffic accident. For now, the automakers are moving ahead as they monitor the issues and stay alert for possible changes in government regulations.

Getting in gear

Buyers have responded to the Nano's low price tag. Tata received more than 200 000 orders during the 12 months after the car's introduction. Because of limited production capabilities, it has to use a lottery system to select the first 100 000 buyers. Recently, Tata opened a second factory that can produce 250 000 Nanos per year, in an effort to keep up with the expected surge in demand as the Indian economy grows and consumers continue to trade up from motorcycles to cars.

Tata has a long history of good marketing management and above-average profitability. Being based in India gives Tata the advantage of being close to its customers and understanding their needs. Tata's engineers and designers have found creative ways of containing costs to keep the new car ultra-affordable. With increased competition in the super-budget segment, however, Tata will have to get in gear to keep the Nano ahead of the pack.

Questions for discussion

1 Explain which factors seem to have the greatest influence on Tata's decision about pricing its Nano.

2 What would be the most appropriate way to communicate the Nano's brand proposition to its intended target audiences?

3 What options for distribution are open to Tata as it enters additional markets/territories with the Nano?

http://www.tatanano.com/home.htm, July 2011. William M. Pride and O.C. Ferrell, *Marketing 2012* (Cengage Learning, 2012).

CHAPTER 8
Product decisions

"Marketers must have ever-evolving products and suitable support in order to satisfy customers and fend off competitors"

Objectives

- To learn how marketers define products
- To define product levels
- To understand how to classify products
- To become familiar with the concepts of product item, product line and product mix
- To understand the concept of product life cycle
- To understand the types of organizational structure used to manage products
- To grasp the importance of the levels of a product in determining a competitive edge

INTRODUCTION

The product is defined as everything that is received in an exchange, whether favourable or unfavourable. It is a complexity of tangible and intangible attributes, including functional, social and psychological utilities or benefits.[1] A product can be a physical good, a service, an idea or any combination of these three. This definition also covers supporting services that go with goods, such as installation, guarantees, product information and promises of repair or maintenance. In other words, the product is everything the consumer or business customer receives.

The product is a key element of the marketing mix and is central to a company's marketing proposition. Without the 'right' product it is unlikely that marketers will be able to satisfy their customers and persuade them to become repeat buyers. As will be explored in this chapter, there is much more to the product component of the marketing mix than the actual tangible product or the service supplied to a customer.

A successful product will not remain so indefinitely. Marketers must judge when to modify their products, launch new ones and delete existing – perhaps once highly successful – products. While identifying a new product that will prove successful is challenging for marketers, knowing when to cut a product and walk away from it, is often harder.

Smelly fabrics!

Ambrosia, Apple, Bouquet, Coffee, Cola, Eau de Cologne, Fiji, Forest, Lavender, Lemon, Lime, Orange, Peppermint, Pineapple, Pizza, Rose, Strawberry, Tropical Paradise, Vanilla, Wild Flowers, Floral Bouquet, Jasmine and Banana.

What is the connection between these exotic-sounding names? Foods? Paint colours? Brand names? No, the connection is that they are all odours! Courtaulds Textiles, part of PD Enterprise (Hong Kong), developed an innovative range of Fragrance Fabrics. The 'micro-encapsulated' scent is 'glued' to the fabric via an acrylic polymer and applied in solution to the fabric during its final production process (known as the 'stenter run'). When the fabric is rubbed, the scent 'capsules' are broken, releasing the fragrance. Staggeringly, after over 30 washes at 40°C, the fragrance is still evident.

The Japanese producers of the micro-capsules have carried out extensive skin-sensitivity tests at the Japanese Laboratory for Cutaneous (Skin) Health. Courtaulds Jersey Underwear Ltd found ways of 'sticking' the fragrance to 150g cotton single jersey and to 150g cotton/Lycra fabrics. The following are the core fragrances in demand.

- *Lemon* – a refreshing scent, with characteristic uplifting properties, associated with cleansing and the ability to revive the skin.

Source: iStock, 07-24-10 © Isabella Pfenninger

- *Orange* – a slightly sweet scent, known for its calming qualities.

- *Rose* – the 'queen' of essential oils, associated with beauty, femininity and purity, as well as a relaxed state of mind.

- *Vanilla* – commonly linked with taste, a distinctive smell that is obtained from the pods of a beautiful tropical orchid.

- *Lavender* – a beautiful scent with endearing qualities, encourages restful sleep and has balancing properties; widely used in perfumery and with an oil base to ease muscular aches and pains.

- *Apple and strawberry* – fresh and fruity fragrances that are the essence of a sunny summer.

- *Forest and wild flowers* – mirroring the scents of woodland, two fragrances that combine tranquillity and freshness.

So why the excitement? Well, in fabric development, innovations tend to be based around texture and durability – for example, the stretchy Lycra phenomenon. New product development has rarely been so innovative in this market, and for Courtaulds the result has been a competitive edge over rivals. The main target market is currently users of sportswear: using this new technology, such clothing emits a pleasant odour when the wearer gets hot and sweaty on the squash court or in the gym. However, it's not only overheated sports enthusiasts for whom this new product technology has appeal – it can also be used in the creation of 'intelligent' fabrics, which can detect, for example, when a women is menstruating, and will then release soothing lavender or rose fragrances.

Many clothing applications will make use of these micro-encapsulated scents. The task for fabric manufacturers' marketers is to promote these attributes to the garment makers, whose marketers will need to entice retailers to stock these new lines and consumers to trial these fragrant products.

Sources: *Fragrance Fabrics and Essential Oils and Their 'Well Being' Qualities,* Courtaulds Jersey Underwear; Courtaulds Textiles, Nottingham.

P roducts such as the Fragrance Fabrics devised by Courtaulds, are among a company's most crucial and visible contacts with buyers. If a company's products do not meet its customers' desires and needs, the company will have to adjust its offering in order to survive. Developing a successful **product** requires knowledge of fundamental marketing and product concepts. Courtaulds' range of Fragrance Fabrics needs to appeal both to garment makers and consumers if it is to achieve long-term success. This chapter starts by introducing and defining the concepts that help clarify what a product is, and looks at how buyers view products. The next section examines the concepts of product mix and product line as an introduction to product planning. The chapter then explores the stages of the product life cycle. Each life-cycle stage generally requires a specific marketing strategy, operates within a certain competitive environment and has its own sales and profit pattern. The final section discusses the elements that make up a product.

product
Everything, both favourable and unfavourable, tangible and intangible, received in an exchange of an idea, service or good

What is a product?

good
A tangible physical entity

service
The application of human and mechanical efforts to people or objects in order to provide intangible benefits to customers

ideas
Concepts, philosophies, images or issues that provide the psychological stimulus to solve problems or adjust to the environment

A **good** is a tangible physical entity, such as a bottle of Pantene shampoo, a loaf of Hovis bread, a Muse CD or an iPad. A **service**, by contrast, is intangible; it is the result of the application of human and mechanical efforts to people or objects. Examples of services include hairdressing, tennis tuition and medical treatment. (Chapter 10 provides a detailed discussion of services marketing.) **Ideas** are concepts, philosophies, images or issues. They provide the psychological stimulus to solve problems. For example, Oxfam provides famine relief and attempts to improve the long-term prospects of people in hunger-stricken countries by raising awareness of their issues.

When buyers purchase a product, they are really buying the benefits and satisfaction they think the product will provide. A pair of Adidas Predator football boots, for example, is purchased for status and image, not just to protect the feet. Services, in particular, are bought on the basis of promises of satisfaction. Promises, with the images and appearances of symbols, help consumers make judgements about tangible and intangible products.[2] Symbols and cues are often used to make intangible products more tangible to the consumer. Intel's famous Blue Men imagery personalized computer chips and differentiated Intel very effectively from rival chip producers.

Classifying products

consumer products
Items purchased to satisfy personal or family needs

industrial or **business products**
Items bought for use in a company's operations or to make other products

Products fall into one of two general categories. **Consumer products** are purchased to satisfy personal and family needs. **Industrial** or **business products** are bought for use in a company's operations or to make other products. The same item can be both a consumer product and an industrial product. For example, when consumers purchase light bulbs for their homes, they are classified as consumer products. However, when a large company purchases light bulbs to provide lighting in a factory or office the same goods are considered industrial products. Thus the buyer's intent, or the ultimate use of the product, determines whether an item is classified as a consumer or an industrial/business-to-business product. It is common for more people to be involved in buying an industrial product than in a consumer purchase. Chapters 4 and 5 explained the differences in buying and decision-making for consumer and business-to-business products.

It is important to know about product classifications because different classes of product are aimed at particular target markets, and classification affects distribution, promotion and pricing decisions. Furthermore, the types of marketing activity and effort needed – in short, the entire marketing mix – differ according to how a product is classified. This section examines the characteristics of consumer and industrial products and explores the marketing activities associated with some of them.

Consumer products

The most widely accepted approach to classifying consumer products relies on the common characteristics of consumer buying behaviour. It divides products into four categories: convenience, shopping, speciality and unsought products. However, not all buyers behave in the same way when purchasing a specific type of product. Thus, a single product can fit into more than one category. To minimize this problem, marketers think in terms of how buyers *generally* behave when purchasing a specific item. In addition, they recognize that the 'correct' classification can be determined only by considering a particular company's intended target market.

convenience products
Inexpensive, frequently purchased and rapidly consumed items that demand only minimal purchasing effort

Convenience products Relatively inexpensive, frequently purchased and rapidly consumed items on which buyers exert only minimal purchasing effort are called **convenience products** They range from chocolate, magazines and chewing gum to petrol and soft drinks. The buyer spends little time planning the purchase or comparing available brands or sellers. Even a buyer who prefers a specific brand will readily choose a substitute if the preferred brand is not conveniently available.

Classifying a product as a convenience product has several implications for a company's marketing strategy. A convenience product is normally marketed through many retail outlets. Because sellers experience high inventory turnover, the per unit gross margins can be relatively low. Producers of convenience products such as PG Tips tea and Domestos bleach expect little promotional effort at the retail level and so must provide their own through advertising, sales promotion and the item's packaging. The package may have an especially important role to play, because many convenience items are available only on a self-service basis at the retail level. The use of on-pack sales promotion and point-of-sale displays are ways to maximize the impact of the package. Such products are known as low-involvement products because, as explored in Chapter 4, consumers spend very little time considering their purchase and there is little opportunity for marketers to persuade consumers to examine alternatives ... except for price discounting and prominent point of sale offers.

shopping products
Items chosen more carefully than convenience products; consumers will expend effort in planning and purchasing these items

Shopping products Items that are chosen more carefully than convenience products are called **shopping products**. They are purchased infrequently and are expected to last a long time. Buyers are willing to expend effort in planning and purchasing these items. They allocate time for comparing stores and brands with respect to prices, credit, product features, qualities, services and perhaps guarantees. Appliances, furniture, bicycles, stereos, jewellery and cameras are examples of shopping products. Even though shopping products are more expensive than convenience products, few buyers of shopping products are particularly brand loyal. If they were, they would be unwilling to shop and compare brands.

Marketers seeking to market shopping products effectively must consider that they require fewer retail outlets than convenience products. Because they are purchased less frequently, inventory (stock) turnover is lower and middlemen (retailers) expect to receive higher gross margins. Although large sums of money may be required to advertise shopping products, an even larger proportion of resources is likely to be used for personal selling. Indeed, the quality of the service may be a factor in the consumer's choice of outlet. Thus, a couple that buys a new dishwasher might expect sales personnel in the chosen retail outlet to explain the advantages and features of competing brands. In many cases, the producer and the middlemen also expect some cooperation from one another with respect to providing parts and repair services, and performing promotional activities.

Speciality products Products that possess one or more unique characteristics and which a significant group of buyers is willing to expend considerable effort to obtain are called **speciality products**. Buyers plan the purchase of a speciality product carefully; they know exactly what they want and will not accept a substitute. An example of a speciality product is a painting by L.S. Lowry or a Cartier watch. When searching for speciality products, buyers do not compare alternatives; they are concerned primarily with finding an outlet that has a pre-selected product available.

speciality products
Items that possess one or more unique characteristics; consumers of speciality products plan their purchases and will expend considerable effort to obtain them

The marketing of a speciality product is very distinctive. The exclusivity of the product is accentuated by the fact that speciality products are often distributed through a limited number of retail outlets. Some companies go to considerable lengths to control this aspect of their distribution. Like shopping goods, speciality products are purchased infrequently, causing lower inventory turnover and thus requiring relatively high gross margins.

unsought products
Items that are purchased when a sudden problem arises or when aggressive selling is used to obtain a sale that would not otherwise take place

Unsought products Products that are purchased when a sudden problem arises, or when aggressive selling obtains a sale that otherwise would not take place, are called **unsought products**. The consumer does not usually expect to buy these products regularly. Emergency windscreen replacement services and graveyard headstones are examples of unsought products. Life insurance is an example of an unsought product that often needs aggressive personal selling.

Business products

Business products are usually purchased on the basis of a company's goals and objectives. The functional aspects of these products are usually more important than the psychological rewards sometimes associated with consumer products. Business products can be classified into seven categories according to their characteristics and intended uses:

1 raw materials
2 major equipment
3 accessory equipment
4 component parts
5 process materials
6 consumable supplies
7 industrial/business services.[3]

raw materials
The basic materials that become part of physical products

Raw materials The basic materials that become part of physical products are **raw materials**. These include minerals, chemicals, agricultural products and materials

FIGURE 8.1
Confectionery brands are convenience products
© JoeFox / Alamy

from forests and oceans. They are usually bought and sold in relatively large quantities according to grades and specifications.

Major equipment Large tools and machines used for production purposes, such as cranes and spray painting machinery, are types of **major equipment**. Major equipment is often expensive, may be used in a production process for a considerable length of time and is often custom-made to perform specific functions. For example, Alsthom manufactures purpose-built large gears and turbines. Other items are more standardized, performing similar tasks for many types of company. Because major equipment is so expensive, purchase decisions are often long and complex and may be made by senior management. Marketers of major equipment are frequently called upon to provide a variety of services, including installation, training, repair, maintenance assistance and financing. This may lead to long-term relationships being developed between suppliers of major equipment and their customers.

major equipment
Large tools and machines used for production purposes

Accessory equipment Equipment that does not become a part of the final physical product, but is used in production or office activities is referred to as **accessory equipment**. Examples include telephone systems, stationery supplies, fractional horsepower motors and tools. Compared with major equipment, accessory items are usually much cheaper, are purchased routinely with less negotiation and are treated as expenditure items rather than capital items because they are not expected to last long. More outlets are required for distributing accessory equipment than for major equipment, but sellers do not have to provide the multitude of services expected of major equipment marketers.

accessory equipment
Tools and equipment used in production or office activities that do not become part of the final physical product

component parts
Parts that become a part of the physical product and are either finished items ready for assembly or products that need little processing before assembly

Component parts Parts that become part of the physical product and are either finished items ready for assembly or products that need little processing before assembly are called **component parts**. Although they become part of a larger product, component parts can often be easily identified and distinguished. Tyres, spark plugs, gears, lighting units, screws and wires are all component parts of a delivery van. Buyers purchase such items according to their own specifications or industry standards. They expect the parts to be of specified quality and delivered on time so that production is not slowed or stopped. Producers that are primarily assemblers, such as most washing machine or lawnmower manufacturers, depend heavily on suppliers of component parts.

process materials
Materials used directly in the production of other products, but not readily identifiable

Process materials Materials that are used directly in the production of other products are called process materials. Unlike component parts, however, **process materials** are not readily identifiable. For example, Reichhold Chemicals markets a treated fibre product: a phenolicresin, sheet-moulding compound used in the production of flight deck instrument panels and aircraft cabin interiors. Although the material is not identifiable in the finished aircraft, it retards burning, smoke and formation of toxic gas when subjected to fire or high temperatures.

consumable supplies
Supplies that facilitate production and operations but do not become part of the finished product

Consumable supplies Supplies that facilitate production and operations but do not become part of the finished product are referred to as **consumable supplies**. Paper, print cartridges, pencils, oils, cleaning agents and paints are in this category. They are purchased by many different types of business. Consumable supplies are purchased routinely and sold through numerous outlets. To ensure that supplies are available when needed, buyers often deal with more than one seller. Consumable supplies can be divided into three subcategories – maintenance, repair and operating (or overhaul) supplies – and are sometimes called **MRO items**.

MRO items
Consumable supplies in the subcategories of maintenance, repair and operating (or overhaul) supplies

industrial/business services
The intangible products that many organizations use in their operations, including financial, legal, marketing research, computer programming and operation, caretaking and printing services

Industrial/business services Industrial/business services are the intangible products that many organizations use in their operations. They include financial, legal, marketing research, computer programming and operation, caretaking and printing services for business. Some companies decide to provide their own services internally, while others outsource them. This decision depends largely on the costs associated with each alternative and the frequency with which the services are needed.

The three levels of product

core product
The level of a product that provides the perceived or real core benefit or service

The product may appear obvious – a carton of fresh orange juice or a designer handbag – but generally the purchaser is buying much more than a drink or a means of carrying personal items. To be motivated to make the purchase, the product must have a perceived or real core benefit or service. This level of product, termed the **core product**, is illustrated in Figure 8.2. The **actual product** is a composite of several factors: the features and capabilities offered, quality and durability, design and product styling, packaging and, often of great importance, the brand name.

actual product
A composite of the features and capabilities offered in a product, quality and durability, design and product styling, packaging and brand name

In order to make the purchase, the consumer often needs the assistance of sales personnel; there may be delivery and payment credit requirements and, for bulky or very technical products, advice regarding installation. The level of warranty back-up and after-sales support, particularly for innovative, highly technical or high value goods, will be of concern to most consumers. Increasingly, the overall level of customer service constitutes part of the purchase criteria, and in many markets it is deemed integral to the product on offer. These 'support' issues form what is termed the **augmented product** (see Figure 8.2).

augmented product
Support aspects of a product, including customer service, warranty, delivery and credit, personnel, installation and after-sales support

When a £35 000 BMW 3 Series executive car is purchased, the vehicle's performance specification and design may have encouraged the sale. Speed of delivery and credit payment terms may have been essential to the conclusion of the deal. The brand's image, particularly in the case of a car costing £35 000, will also have

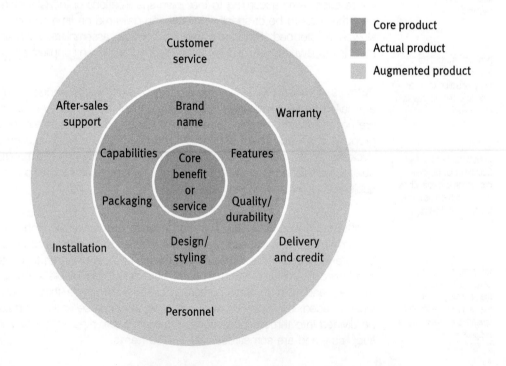

FIGURE 8.2
The three levels of product: core, actual and augmented

influenced the sale. Once behind the wheel of the BMW, its new owner will expect reliability and efficient, friendly, convenient service in the course of maintenance being required. The purchase might have been lost at the outset had the salesperson mishandled the initial enquiry. Repeat servicing business and the subsequent sale of another new car may be ruled out if the owner encounters incompetent, unhelpful service engineers. The core benefit may have been a car to facilitate journeys to work, transport for the family or the acquisition of a recognized status symbol. Customer satisfaction will depend on the product's actual performance and also on service aspects of the augmented product. This example is not unusual. For most consumer or business products and services, the consumer is influenced by the three levels of the product: core, actual and augmented. Marketers need to take this into consideration when developing product offers. Careful consideration of all levels of the product can provide the basis for a competitive edge. Indeed, often it is aspects of the augmented product which make or break the relationship with the customer and can create differentiation vis-à-vis competing propositions.

Many marketers now recognize the important role that personnel play in product exchanges. People are responsible for the design, production, marketing, sale and distribution of products. As will be explained in Chapter 10, personnel are especially important in the sale and delivery of services. Thus, a financial services adviser must have considerable expertise in the sector to give good advice. Similarly, a good-quality haircut can only be delivered by a skilled hairdresser. As consumers, people make decisions and ultimately adopt products for use and consumption. When deciding which products to adopt and use, people now pay considerable attention to the skills, attitudes and motivations of personnel involved in the marketing channel. As explained in Chapter 1, personnel also constitute an essential ingredient of the marketing mix for consumer and business goods.

product item
A specific version of a product that can be designated as a distinct offering among a business's products

product line
A group of closely related product items that are considered a unit because of marketing, technical or end-use considerations

Product line and product mix

Marketers must understand the relationships between all their organization's products if they are to coordinate their marketing. The following concepts describe the relationships between an organization's products. A **product item** is a specific version of a product that can be designated as a distinct offering among a business's products – for example, Procter & Gamble's Pantene shampoo. A **product line** includes a group of closely related product items that are considered a unit because of marketing, technical or end-use considerations. All the shampoos manufactured by Procter & Gamble constitute one of its product lines. Figure 8.3 illustrates the product line for Tilda. The Marketing Insight box explains how manufacturers of nicotine replacement products

FIGURE 8.3
This advertisement for leading rice brand Tilda makes clear that the Tilda line includes a wide range of rice types
Source: Image courtesey of Tilda

Laundry detergents	Toothpastes/ dental	Bar soaps	Deodorants	Shampoos	Tissue/towel
Ivory Snow 1930	Gleem 1952	Ivory 1879	Old Spice 1948	Head & Shoulders 1961	Charmin 1928
Dreft 1933	Crest 1955	Camay 1926	Secret 1956	Pantene Pro 1965	Puffs 1960
Tide 1946	Oral-B 2005	Zest 1952	Sure 1972	Vidal Sassoon 1974	Bounty 1965
Cheer 1950	Scope	Safeguard 1963		Pert Plus 1979	Royale 1996
Bold 1965		Olay 1993		Ivory 1983	
Gain 1966					
Era 1972					
Febreze 1998					

Product line depth (vertical axis, left)

Product mix width (horizontal axis)

FIGURE 8.4

The concepts of width of product mix and depth of product line applied to selected Procter & Gamble products

Source: Reproduced with permission from The Procter & Gamble Company

are expanding their product line to allow them to capitalize on the opportunities this market provides. To come up with the optimum product line, marketers must understand buyers' goals.[4] Specific items in a product line reflect the desires of different target markets or the different needs of consumers.

product mix
The composite group of products that a company makes available to customers

A **product mix** is the composite, or total, group of products that a company makes available to customers. For example, all the personal care products, laundry detergent products and other products that Procter & Gamble manufactures constitute its product mix. The **depth** of a product mix is measured by the number of different products offered in each product line. The **width** of a product mix is measured by the number of product lines a company offers. Figure 8.4 shows the width of the product mix and the depth of each product line for selected Procter & Gamble products in the USA. Procter & Gamble is known for using distinctive technology, branding, packaging and consumer advertising to promote individual items in its detergent product line. Tide, Bold and Cheer – all Procter & Gamble detergents – share similar distribution channels and manufacturing facilities. Yet due to variations in product formula and attributes, each is promoted as being distinct, adding depth to the product line.

depth (of product mix)
The number of different products offered in each product line

width (of product mix)
The number of product lines a company offers

Product life cycles

product life cycle
The four major stages through which products move: introduction, growth, maturity and decline

Just as biological cycles progress through growth and decline, so too do **product life cycles**. A new product is introduced into the marketplace; it grows; it matures; and when it loses appeal and sales decline, it is terminated.[5] As explained in Chapter 9, different marketing strategies are appropriate at different stages in the product life cycle. Thus, packaging, branding and labelling techniques can be used to help create or modify products that have reached different points in their life.

As Figure 8.5 shows, a product life cycle has four major stages:

1 introduction
2 growth
3 maturity
4 decline

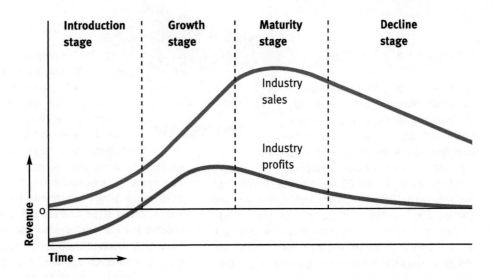

FIGURE 8.5
The four stages of the product life cycle

When a product moves through its cycle, the strategies relating to competition, promotion, place/distribution, pricing and market information must be evaluated periodically and possibly changed. Astute marketing managers use the life-cycle concept to make sure that the introduction, alteration and termination of a product are timed and executed properly. By understanding the typical life-cycle pattern, marketers are better able to maintain profitable products and drop unprofitable ones.

Introduction

introduction stage
A product's first appearance in the marketplace, before any sales or profits have been made

The **introduction stage** of the life cycle begins at a product's first appearance in the marketplace, when sales are zero and profits are negative. Profits are below zero because a new product incurs development costs, initial revenues are low, and at the same time a company must generally incur the significant expenses incurred during promotion and distribution. As time passes, sales should move upwards from zero and profits should build up from the negative position (see Figure 8.5).[6]

Because of cost, very few product introductions represent major inventions. Developing and introducing a new product can mean an outlay of many millions of pounds. The failure rate for new products is quite high, ranging from 60 to 90 per cent depending on the industry and on how product failure is defined. For example, in the food and drinks industry, 80 per cent of all new products fail. Typically, product introductions involve a new style of deodorant, a new type of vacuum cleaner or a new leisure concept rather than a major product innovation. In general, the more marketing-oriented the company, the more likely it will be to launch innovative products that are new to the market.[7]

New product ideas are more likely to be successful when senior management is involved in product development and launch. In addition, research shows that a clear, stable vision, flexibility and improvization, information exchange and collaboration are also key ingredients in new product success.[8]

Potential buyers must be made aware of the new product's features, uses and advantages. Two difficulties may arise at this point. Only a few sellers may have the resources, technological knowledge and marketing know-how to launch the product successfully; and the initial product price may have to be high in order to recoup expensive marketing research or development costs. Given these difficulties, it is not surprising that many products never get beyond the introduction stage; indeed many are never launched commercially at all.

Crave life not cigarettes

Topical insight

Patch, lozenge or gum, Nicotinell 'can double your chances of quitting compared to willpower alone', claims Novartis. Nicotine replacement therapy (NRT) fights nicotine dependence and relieves the symptoms of withdrawal in smokers who are trying to give up the habit. Leading brands include Nicotinell, NiQuitin CQ and Nicorette. Novartis, the company behind Nicotinell nicotine replacement gum and patches, also launched food products designed to help smokers quit the habit. Many consumers are already familiar with the Nicotinell brand. As smoking becomes increasingly socially unacceptable, the company now believes that there are a variety of new product development opportunities for its brand. Novartis launched a nicotine replacement lozenge that, when sucked, provides a continual, low-level boost of nicotine for relatively light smokers. Other initiatives include the possible development of nicotine-enhanced food and a detoxification programme for ex-smokers. Supportive counselling services are viewed as a key part of the therapy, and most of the leading players have examined how to offer such services alongside their patches, gums, pills and lozenges.

It is not difficult to understand the attractions of the nicotine replacement therapy market and to appreciate why Novartis is seeking to extend its product offerings. As millions seek to leave their smoking habit behind, the market for nicotine replacement products is growing rapidly. Indications also show that 1 in 20 of those attempting to 'kick the habit' will use some form of nicotine replacement therapy. Not surprisingly, Novartis is not alone in seeking to develop its product range. Since NRT products were first launched in the UK more than two decades ago, several companies have dominated the market: Novartis, with its Nicotinell patch and gum; Pharmacia & Upjohn (P&U), with its Nicorette gum, inhalator and patches; and Boots, with its own-label patches and gum. Recent developments include Boots' inhalator and competing brand Nicorette's launch of its micro-tab, a kind of nicotine pill that, when placed under the tongue, takes half an hour to dissolve.

Perhaps the most aggressive challenge to the market has come from pharmaceutical giant SmithKline Beecham (SKB), which spent £12 million on the UK launch of NiQuitin CQ (CQ stands for 'committed quitters'). SKB claimed this to have been the largest ever over-the-counter launch in the UK. Clearly the company expected the brand, already the best-seller in the USA, to claim a large slice of the UK market. Company representatives suggested that this was achieved by the unique 'personalized literature pack' included with the NiQuitin CQ product. This pack includes a questionnaire for smokers to fill in, detailing the circumstances in which they are most vulnerable to lighting up. Advice is then offered that is tailored to match the answers provided in the questionnaire. According to Elaine MacFarlane, SKB's director of consumer healthcare communications, this represented a unique approach in the NRT market. She explains, 'When these products first launched, they were positioned as a magic bullet – "take this and you won't want to smoke". Now with all the noise from the political, health and economic perspectives, you know it doesn't make sense to smoke any more, and we felt the time was right for a more mature consideration of people's motivation.'

In such a volatile market, future trends are difficult to predict. When NRT products were first launched in the UK in 1993, they were met with considerable consumer excitement. However, following an initial growth in sales, consumer confidence in the capabilities of the products declined. Today, with the products widely available in supermarkets as well as pharmacies, and governments throughout the EU considering further anti-smoking measures, the key players are looking for innovative ways to ensure that their products play a major role in the continued fight against smoking. New product development is likely to be just part of the solution, with manufacturers also seeking a fresh and more realistic promotional stance. For Novartis, with its original slogan 'Helps you stop smoking', this involves repositioning the brand to stress its role in harm reduction and Nicotinell's role in supporting the quitter's willpower and resolve to stop smoking, while making the product desirable. An advertising strapline required little explanation, accompanying images of a leather-clad attractive female biker: *Lose the Smoke. Keep The Fire!* With smokers over 30 years old as the key target, and the biggest increase in new smokers among those in their early teens and twenties, the market potential is considerable. Time will tell whether Novartis and the other players continue to meet the challenge.

Sources: Novartis Consumer Healthcare, 2004–12; Neil Denny, 'Smokers may be offered nicotine food to help quit', *Marketing*, 28 January 1999, p. 1; Sue Beenstock, 'Queuing up to quit', *Marketing*, 28 January 1999, p. 1; **www. Nicotinell.com**, June 2004, November 2007 and March 2011; 'Crave Life Not Cigarettes', **http://nicotinell.co.uk/**, 5 March 2011. **www.mypharma cy.co.uk/medicines/topics/n/nicotine_replacement_therapy**, June 2004; Boots, November 2007 and March 2011; **http://nicotinell.co.uk/** 26 November, 2007.

Growth

growth stage
The stage at which a product's sales rise rapidly and profits reach a peak, before levelling off into maturity

During the **growth stage**, sales rise rapidly, and profits reach a peak and then start to decline (see Figure 8.5). The growth stage is critical to a product's survival because competitive reactions to its success during this period will affect the product's life expectancy. For example, Mars successfully launched Ice Cream Mars, the first ice-cream version of an established confectionery product. Today the product competes with more than a dozen other brands. Some of the competing brands failed quickly and others followed. Profits decline late in the growth stage as more competitors enter the market, driving prices down and creating the need for heavy promotional expenses. At this point a typical marketing strategy encourages strong brand loyalty, perhaps using sales promotion, and competes with aggressive emulators of the product. During the growth stage, a company tries to strengthen its market share and develop a competitive position by emphasizing the product's benefits. This is what the various smartphone providers are currently striving to achieve.

Aggressive promotional pricing, including price cuts, is typical during the growth stage. The smartphone industry is now well into its growth stage, and many competitors have entered the market. Companies like Samsung and Blackberry must battle hard to maintain their existing positions in this competitive arena.

Maturity

maturity stage
The stage during which a product's sales curve peaks and starts to decline, and profits continue to decline

During the **maturity stage**, the sales curve peaks and starts to decline, and profits continue to decline (see Figure 8.5). This stage is characterized by severe competition, with many brands in the market. Competitors emphasize improvements and differences in their versions of the product. Inevitably, during the maturity stage, some weaker competitors are squeezed out or switch their attention to other products. For example, some Internet service providers are perishing or being acquired by rivals now that the product is in its maturity stage.

During the maturity stage, the producers who remain in the market must make fresh promotional and distribution efforts. These efforts must focus on dealers as much as on consumers to ensure that brand visibility is maintained at the point of sale. Advertising and dealer-oriented promotions are typical during this stage of the product life cycle. The promoters must also take into account the fact that, as the product reaches maturity, buyers' knowledge of it attains a high level. Consumers of the product are no longer inexperienced generalists, but rather experienced specialists.

Decline

decline stage
The last stage of a product's life cycle, during which sales fall rapidly

During the **decline stage**, sales fall rapidly (see Figure 8.5). New technology or a new social trend may cause product sales to take a sharp downturn. For example, iPods have reduced CD sales and green concerns have damaged the sales volumes of certain models of vehicles. When this happens, the marketer must consider pruning items from the product line to eliminate those not earning a profit. Sony surprised the market by announcing it would be pulling out of selling PDAs. The decision came because Sony believed that technology changes are signalling a move away from handheld organizers towards multifunctional mobile phones.[9] At this time, too, the marketer may cut promotion efforts, eliminate marginal distributors and, finally, plan to phase out the product.

Because most businesses have a product mix consisting of multiple products, a company's destiny is rarely tied to one product. A composite of life-cycle patterns is formed when various products in the mix are at different stages in the cycle. As one product is declining, other products are in the introduction, growth or maturity stage. Marketers must deal with the dual problems of prolonging the life of existing products and introducing new products to meet sales goals. More details of this kind of portfolio management activity are given in Chapter 9, which also explores the development of new products and considers how they can be managed in their various life-cycle stages.

Why some products fail and others succeed

Thousands of new products are introduced each year and many of them fail. Some estimates put the product failure rate as high as 60 to 90 per cent. Failure and success rates vary in different industries and from company to company. Figures suggest that consumer products are more likely to fail than those directed at business markets. Being one of the first brands launched in a product category is no guarantee of success. One study found that in 50 product categories, only half of the pioneers survived.[10]

Products fail for many reasons. One of the most common is the company's failure to match product offerings to customer needs. When products do not offer value and lack the features customers want, they fail in the marketplace. Ineffective or inconsistent branding has also been blamed for product failures. Other reasons often given for new product failure include technical or design problems, poor timing, overestimation of market size, ineffective promotion and inefficient distribution. The problems leading to the downfall of Coca-Cola's UK launch of bottled water Dasani were widely debated in the press. Technical difficulties led to bromide contamination at the company's plant. At a time when consumers were already concerned about the purity of tap water, the withdrawal of the product was inevitable.[11] For Cadbury Trebor Bassett's 24-7 chewing gum, failure was blamed on distribution problems and lack of in-store support.[12]

Degrees of product failure

It is important to distinguish between degrees of product failure. Absolute failure occurs when a company loses money on a new product because it is unable to recover development, production and marketing costs. Such a product is usually deleted from the product mix. Relative product failure occurs when a product returns a profit but does not meet a company's profit or market share objectives. If a relative product failure is repositioned or improved, it may become a successful member of the product line. Some products experience relative product failure after years of success. Drinks business Diageo stepped in to stem declining sales of Guinness stout. Part of this effort involved reformulating the canned version of the drink, to make its taste closer to that of draught Guinness. The cans were also redesigned to appeal to a younger segment of drinkers.

The ingredients for success

Despite this gloomy picture of product failure, some new products are very successful. Perhaps the most important ingredient for success is the product's ability to provide a significant and perceivable benefit to a sizeable number of customers. New products with an observable advantage over similar available products – such as more features, ease of operation or improved technology – have a greater chance of success, such as the iphone or ipad.

Tangible and intangible product characteristics

When developing products, marketers make many decisions. Some of these involve the tangible, or physical, characteristics of the product; others focus on less tangible support services that are very much a part of the total product.

Physical characteristics and product quality

quality
The core product's ability to achieve the basic functional requirements expected of it

The question of how much **quality** to build into the product is crucial for marketers. In the core product, quality constitutes the product's ability to achieve the basic functional requirements expected of it. A major dimension of quality is durability. Higher quality often demands better materials and more expensive processing, which increases production costs and, ultimately, the product's price. How much the target market is prepared to pay will affect the level of quality specified. The concepts of quality and value are related. A consumer may be happy to pay a premium for a hard-wearing paint, because they perceive it as better value than competing offerings. In general, a company should set consistent quality levels for all products with a similar brand. The quality of competing brands is also an important consideration. As explained in Chapter 7, marketing research plays an important role in determining the optimum physical features – such as quality – of a product.

Upgrading service for competitive advantage

Building customer relationships

Many consumers of high tech products, such as computers and home entertainment systems, will have visited retailers only to find little more product information or advice available than already printed in the manufacturers' brochures or in online product reviews. It is a frustrating experience to encounter a sales person with no more insight into the products on display than the naïve customer already has. Those days may be drawing to a close, if long-standing retailer Dixons Stores Group has its way. Trading as PC World, Currys and Dixons, the company has a large share of the market for electrical goods, appliances and high technology products.

Now the store-led retailers are fighting back against online retailers by providing enhanced customer service. Under its *Knowhow* programme, Dixons wants to be recognized by consumers for knowledge and service, rather than only the brands it stocks. Marketing Director Katie Bickerstaffe's goal is for her customers to state they chose Dixons ahead of rivals because of the know-how of its staff and the reassurance provided. This is partly also a reaction to the entry in Europe of America's Best Buy, known for its high levels of customer service and customer satisfaction, and domestic competitor Comet's ongoing and high profile strategy of emphasizing customer service and its staff.

Comet has promoted in-store ambiance and advice extensively, but has also joined forces with magazines *stuff* and *What Hi-Fi?* to produce the highly supportive *PluggedIn* web resource for consumers seeking reviews and advice pre-purchase and offering tips for how to maximize their post-purchase experiences. America's Best Buy has won many plaudits in its homeland for looking after customers and its UK website makes it very clear that Best Buy aims to support its customers:

'We don't just offer an extensive range of the latest technology, we also promise a new level of advice and support.'

For Dixons, the stated aim is to remove the 'wheel of uncertainty' for consumers purchasing technology products, often for large sums of money and which will be in the home for many years. Such high involvement purchases are often perceived as risky by consumers. For many such consumers, the point of purchase advice and the nature of aftercare are as important as the actual computer or flatscreen TV brought home.

Dixons' *Knowhow* brings much aftercare in-house and away from erratic subcontractors, consolidates the practices of the company's call centres, and boosts delivery and installation provision, and even recycling of old products no longer wanted by customers. The aims are to (a) help customers at point of purchase, (b) install and set up products, (c) repair and upgrade products and (d) help when anything goes wrong. The company has invested heavily in upgrading these service aspects of its operation so that consumers may purchase well-known brands with more certainty and confidence. The likes of Sony, HP or Whirlpool may well design and produce very attractive and reliable products, but for Dixons, the expectation is that the wrap-around service component of its product offering will provide an edge over rivals and bolster consumer satisfaction.

Sources: 'Dixons upgrades service levels with a little Knowhow', Rosie Baker, *Marketing Week*, 25 November 2010, p. 11; 'Dixons sets up new technical support service Knowhow', Andrew Clark, *The Observer*, 21 November 2010; http://www.dsgiplc.com, March 2011; http://www.dixons.co.uk, 7 March 2011; www.comet.co.uk, 8 March 2011; www.pluggedin.co.uk, March 2011; http://www.bestbuy.co.uk/category/services.aspx, 8 March 2011.

Supportive product-related services

All products possess intangible features. When prospective customers are unable to experience the product in advance, they are making decisions based on promises of satisfaction.[13] A woman buying lingerie over the Internet hopes that when the garments she ordered arrive, they will meet her expectations of quality, look and fit. Should she be disappointed, she will expect to be able to return the items. Arrangements for product returns are just one of many product-related services. Others include product guarantees, credit and repair facilities. Although these product features may be less tangible than the product itself, they are often a strong influence on the choices that customers make. Can you imagine buying an expensive watch with no guarantee, or a technology product that cannot be repaired? As the Marketing Insight explains, Dixons has turned to aspects of the augmented product in order to gain competitive advantage.

The type of guarantee a company provides can be critical for buyers, especially when expensive, technically complex goods such as appliances are involved. A **guarantee** specifies what the producer or supplier will do if the product malfunctions. Some photographic processors offer free processing on prints not ready within 24 hours. A leading hotel group will not charge for room service meals if there is a long delay on the order being delivered to the hotel guest. Guarantors are legally required to state more simply and specifically the terms and conditions under which the company will take action. For example, changes in EU law now require electrical items to carry a two-year guarantee. Marketers are now using guarantees more aggressively as tools to give their brands a competitive advantage.

guarantee
An agreement specifying what the producer or supplier will do if the product malfunctions

An effective guarantee should be unconditional, easy to understand and communicate, meaningful, easy to invoke and quick and easy to act on. The customer should be able to return a product and get a replacement, a refund or a credit for the returned item. Such guarantees are beneficial because they generate feedback from customers and help build customer loyalty and sales.[14] Although it is more difficult to provide guarantees for services than for goods, some service marketers do guarantee customer satisfaction. For example, some opticians offering a one hour turnaround for new lenses or frames do not charge customers who have to wait longer than this time.

Establishing a system to provide replacement parts and repair services is an essential support service for complex and expensive consumer or business products. For example, builders expect construction machinery manufacturers like Caterpillar to be able to provide replacement parts quickly and without fuss. Sometimes these services are provided directly to buyers, in other cases regional service centres or middlemen are used.

Finally, a company must sometimes provide credit services to customers. Even though credit services place a financial burden on a business, they can be beneficial. For instance, a company may acquire and maintain a stable market share. Many major oil companies, for example, have competed effectively against petrol discounters by providing credit services. For marketers of relatively expensive items, such as cars or soft furnishings, offering credit services enables a larger number of people to buy the product, thus enlarging the market for the item.

Summary

A *product* is everything, both favourable and unfavourable, that is received in an exchange. It is a complex set of tangible and intangible attributes, including functional, social and psychological utilities or benefits. A product can be a good, a service, an idea or any combination of these three. Customers buy the benefits and satisfaction they think the product will provide.

Products can be classified on the basis of the buyer's intentions. *Consumer products* are purchased to satisfy personal and family needs. *Industrial* or *business products* are purchased for use in a company's operations or to make other products. The same product may be classified as both a consumer product and a business product. Consumer products can be subdivided into *convenience, shopping, speciality* and *unsought products.* Business products can be divided into *raw materials, major equipment, accessory equipment, component parts, process materials, consumable supplies (MRO items)* and *business services.*

It is important to remember that a product has three levels: core, actual and augmented. The purchaser buys a core benefit or service (the *core product*) in addition to the product's brand name, features, capabilities, quality, packaging and design (the *actual product*). Increasingly, aspects of the *augmented product* are important considerations for purchasers of consumer goods, services and business goods. Warranties, delivery and credit, personnel, installation, after-sales support and customer service are integral to the actual product's appeal and perceived benefits. The role of personnel in particular is of fundamental concern to marketers; people and customer service now form a central part of the marketing mix.

A *product item* is a specific version of a product that can be designated as a distinct offering among a business's products. A product line is a group of closely related product items that are a unit because of marketing, technical or end-use considerations. A company's total group of products is called the *product mix.* The *depth* of a product mix is measured by the number of different products offered in each product line. The *width* of the product mix is measured by the number of product lines a company offers.

The *product life cycle* describes how product items in an industry move through four major stages: (1) *introduction stage,* (2) *growth stage,* (3) *maturity stage* and (4) *decline stage.* The life-cycle concept is used to make sure that the introduction, alteration and termination of a product are timed and executed properly. The sales curve is at zero on introduction, rises at an increasing rate during growth, peaks at maturity and then declines. Profits peak towards the end of the growth stage of the product life cycle. The life expectancy of a product is based on buyers' wants, the availability of competing products and other environmental conditions. Most businesses have a composite of life-cycle patterns for various products. It is important to manage existing products and develop new ones to keep the overall sales performance at the desired level.

Thousands of new products are introduced each year and many of them fail. Some estimates put the product failure rate as high as 60 to 90 per cent. Failure and success rates vary in different industries and from company to company. Products fail for many reasons: because of a failure to match product offerings to customer needs, ineffective or inconsistent branding, technical or design problems, poor timing, over-estimation of market size, ineffective promotion and inefficient distribution.

It is important to distinguish between degrees of product failure. Absolute failure occurs when a company loses money on a new product because it is unable to recover development, production and marketing costs. Relative product failure occurs when a product returns a profit but does not meet a company's profit or market share objectives.

Despite this gloomy picture of new product failure, some new products are very successful. Perhaps the most important ingredient for success is the product's ability to provide a significant and perceivable benefit to a sizeable number of customers.

When creating products, marketers must take into account other product-related considerations, such as physical characteristics and less tangible support services. Specific physical product characteristics that require attention are the level of quality and product features, such as textures, colours and sizes. Support services that may be viewed as part of the total product include guarantees, repairs/replacements and credit.

Key links

This chapter has given an overview of the product element of the marketing mix.

- It must be read in conjunction with Chapter 9, which examines how marketers manage portfolios of products.

- For those involved in marketing services, there are additional considerations, as discussed in Chapter 10.

Important terms

Product
Good
Service
Ideas
Consumer products
Industrial or business products
Convenience products
Shopping products
Speciality products
Unsought products
Raw materials
Major equipment
Accessory equipment
Component parts
Process materials
Consumable supplies
MRO items
Industrial/business services
Core product
Actual product
Augmented product
Product item
Product line
Product mix
Depth
Width
Product life cycle
Introduction stage
Growth stage
Maturity stage
Decline stage
Quality
Guarantee

Discussion and review questions

1 List the tangible and intangible attributes of a spiral notebook. Compare the benefits of the spiral notebook with those of an intangible product such as life insurance.

2 A product has been referred to as a 'psychological bundle of satisfaction'. Is this a good definition of a product?

3 Is a roll of carpet in a shop a consumer product or a business product? Defend your answer.

4 How do convenience products and shopping products differ? What are the distinguishing characteristics of each type of product?

5 Would a music system that sells for £750 be a convenience, shopping or speciality product?

6 In the category of business products, how do component parts differ from process materials?

7 How does a company's product mix relate to its development of a product line? When should a company add depth to its product lines rather than width to its product mix?

8 How do industry profits change as a product moves through the four stages of its life cycle?

9 What is the relationship between the concepts of product mix and product life cycle?

10 What factors must marketers consider when deciding what quality level to build in to a product? What support services can be offered to back up product quality?

11 What are aspects of the augmented product for a new car?

12 Why is the augmented product increasingly important when determining a differential advantage?

Recommended readings

Baker, M. and Hart, S., *Product Strategy and Management* (Pearson/FT, 2007).

Crawford, C.M. and Di Benedetto, C.A., *New Products Management* (McGraw-Hill, 2011).

Lehmann, D. and Winer, R., *Product Management* (McGraw-Hill, 2004).

Loch, C. and Kavadias, S., *Handbook of Product Management* (Butterworth-Heinemann, 2008).

Rifkin, G., 'Product development: the myth of short life cycles', *Harvard Business Review*, vol. 72, no. 4, 1994, p. 11.

Wind, Y.J., *Product Policy: Concepts, Methods and Strategy* (Addison-Wesley, 1982).

Internet exercise

Goodyear Tyres

In addition to providing information about the company's products, Goodyear's website helps customers find the exact products they want and will even direct them to the nearest Goodyear retailer. Visit the Goodyear site at: http://www.goodyear.eu/uk_en/homepage.jsp

1 How does Goodyear use its website to communicate information about the quality of its tyres?

2 How does Goodyear's website demonstrate product design and features?

3 Based on what you learned at the website, describe what Goodyear has done to position its tyres.

Applied mini-case

'Just when you thought our legendary hatchback couldn't get any better, along comes the stunning new Golf', stated the VW website. The Volkswagen Golf is over 40! Yet VW is celebrating the launch of the latest generation of the model, which seems to have defied middle age and maintained its status as a trendy brand. The motoring magazines commented about its advantages 'brushing the others aside' (*What Car?*) and 'quieter, plusher and completely redecorated' (*Car Magazine*). These plaudits and sales figures vindicate VW's decision to continually upgrade the Golf, rather than replace it with a different model.

Source: **http://www.volkswagen.co.uk/#/new/golf-vi**, 5 March 2011.

Question

Several years from now you have secured a job as brand manager for the Golf. Assume that VW is about to make a decision about whether to launch a new generation of the Golf or replace it with a new model with a new name. Prepare a report arguing in support of one of these options. You should explore the arguments for and against each option.

Case study

Heineken's portfolio of brands

Heineken is Europe's largest brewer, having acquired part of the UK's Scottish & Newcastle. While over 60 per cent of its sales are European, worldwide Heineken is one of the biggest beer businesses. Heineken beer is recognized around the globe. With a presence in more than 170 countries and more than 85 per cent of sales originating outside the domestic Dutch market, Heineken has been described as the most international beer brand. However, there is more to the company than the single Heineken brand. While some rivals have tackled the global market with a strategy of focusing only on international premium beer brands, Heineken has adopted a tiered approach, with strong international premium brands such as Amstel and Heineken, alongside numerous local or regional brands. Heineken brews and sells more than 200 international premium, regional, local and specialty beers and ciders, including Primus, Birra Moretti, Sagres, Cruzcampo, Foster's, Strongbow, Bulmer, Newcastle Brown Ale, Zywiec, Ochota, Kingfisher, Tiger, Star, Dos Equis, Tecate and Sol (**http://www. heinekeninternational.com/aboutheineken.aspx**).

Despite its activities in the USA, Latin America, Africa, South-east Asia and Asia, Heineken recognizes the significance of its strength in Europe – a particularly important market, which accounts for over 40 per cent of world beer sales. Many acquisitions over the past decade have cemented the company's number one status in Europe. Here, despite the mass appeal of the Heineken brand, to stay ahead of the competition the company has to adjust its product mix to suit the needs of different countries, fitting in with local cultures and tastes.

In general, Heineken achieves this goal by offering a portfolio of three core brands in each European country:

1 a local brand, aimed at the standard and largest market segment. In Italy this is Dreher, in France '33' and in Spain Aguila Pilsener

2 a brand targeted at the 'upper' end of the market; sometimes this is a locally produced brand, such as the Spanish Aguila Master, in other cases Amstel is preferred

3 the eponymous Heineken brand itself, aimed at the premium market segment; the beer offered may be manufactured locally or it may be exported from the Netherlands; either way, the Dutch head office works hard to maintain product quality and brand image.

As the company explains,

'The consistent growth of our brands requires solid creative brand management, which we coordinate centrally. By carefully balancing our brands portfolios and achieving optimal distribution and coverage, we aim to build and sustain strong positions in local markets. For the Heineken and Amstel brands, we develop and maintain central guidelines and standards for brand style, brand value and brand development.'

Currently, significant growth is evident in the company's sales in Africa and the Middle, Asia Pacific, Mexico, India and South Africa, reflecting the company's global footprint. Sales of Heineken in the premium segment are rising at around 3.4 per cent per annum. No other brewer has secured strong market positions in as many countries, Heineken is proud to state, and no individual beer brand is as successful in as many countries as the Heineken brand. Heineken is market leader in Austria, Romania, Hungary, Poland, Slovakia, Bulgaria and Macedonia, illustrating the company's identification some time ago of the growing commercial opportunities in eastern Europe, where there have been many acquisitions of local brewers.

Sources: **www.Heineken.com**, 2004–2011; **http://www.heinekeninternational. com/aboutheineken.aspx**, 26 November, 2007; **http://www. heinekeninternational.com**, 5 March 2011; **www.heineken.co.uk**, 2010/11.

Questions for discussion

1 Why does Heineken opt for a mix of internationally known brands marketed alongside local beers?

2 In what ways is Heineken continuously updating its product portfolio and its marketing mix?

3 What problems are likely for Heineken from trading such a large portfolio of beer brands?

CHAPTER 9

Developing products and managing product portfolios

" Success depends on great new products but also the courage to drop products from the portfolio when the time is right "

Objectives

- To become aware of organizational alternatives for managing products

- To understand how organizations develop a product idea into a commercial product

- To understand the importance and role of product development in the marketing mix

- To acquire knowledge of the management of products during the various stages of a product's life cycle

- To become aware of how existing products can be modified

- To learn how product deletion can be used to improve product mixes

- To examine tools for the strategic planning of product or market portfolios

INTRODUCTION

Companies have to create new ideas for products and turn some of these into marketable product or service propositions. Such a process is far from easy, with more new product launches failing than succeeding. As additional products are included in a company's portfolio, it becomes increasingly difficult to identify on which of them investment and sales/marketing resources should be focused. A range of tools, known as product portfolio techniques, exists to assist marketers in such decision making. A related and important concept is that of product life cycle management: the logic being that products are launched and – if successful – they grow, then mature, before going into decline. Marketers must be aware of the relative standings of their respective products and brands. These are the themes of this chapter of *Marketing Essentials*.

Virgin Money: is innovation enough?

Richard Branson's Virgin brand is known to consumers across a range of products and services, from airlines to entertainment to mobile phones. In 1995, Virgin launched its financial services arm with Virgin Direct. At a time when major retailers such as Marks & Spencer and Tesco were entering many sectors of financial services, from banking to insurance, the entry of Virgin Direct made many of the traditional businesses in the financial services sector very anxious. Branson's reputation among consumers for 'taking on faceless corporations' gave Virgin Direct a head start.

Virgin Direct, replicating the activities of Virgin in other sectors, intended to be seen as an innovator that always strives to offer a value-for-money proposition that strongly benefits the consumer. Virgin launched a tracker fund that tracked shares across the entire stock market rather than across only a limited selection. This innovation was subsequently copied by many rivals. Then Virgin lobbied the government to launch stakeholder pensions. Although successful, it is widely accepted that the eventual appearance of stakeholder pensions has been far from a success story for the industry. Virgin also led the way with off-set mortgages, with the Virgin One account. Virgin found this complex proposition difficult to market to consumers, without face-to-face contact via branches. In 2001, the One Account was handed over to Royal Bank of Scotland, which did have a suitable branch network and has been able to sell this mortgage product to consumers.

Despite such teething problems, Virgin Money – as the company is now known – is profitable and thanks largely to its tie-up with card provider MBNA, has a growing credit card business, too. The business now also offers pensions, insurance, mortgages, savings and investments, in conjunction with partners, such as Santander, Friends Provident and MBNA. The philosophy is simple: Virgin Money intends to introduce more interesting propositions, rather than simply churning out new products. The company has a focus on being customer-led, rather than product-led, explaining that:

> **We are aiming to make everyone better off**
> Like all Virgin companies, Virgin Money was launched to give customers a better deal. We aim to offer you a wide range of great value financial products that are easy to understand and sort out. In today's busy world our customers tell us it's why they choose to deal with Virgin rather than anyone else.
>
> http://uk.virginmoney.com/virgin/about

The Virgin-branded financial services products are always innovative and place an emphasis on addressing consumer needs and consumer concerns about the sprawling global financial services corporations. Value for money, simplicity, ease of setting up and the Virgin brand have proved irresistible propositions for thousands of consumers who perceive Virgin and Branson to represent a desirable alternative to large, faceless corporations. As a result of this approach, Virgin Money has won countless industry awards in recent years, notably for its credit card operation, car insurance, pet insurance and pensions. With ownership now of Northern Rock's high street outlets, now branded under Virgin, many more consumers are set to encounter the proposition that is Virgin Money.

Source: Image courtesy of Virgin

Sources: Virgin Money; David Benady, 'Virgin Money pushes for its renaissance', *Marketing Week*, 6 May 2004, pp. 20–1; virginmoney.com, January, 2008; http://uk.virginmoney.com, 5 March 2011, Virgin Money, 2012.

To compete effectively and achieve their goals, companies must develop products that reflect consumer needs and preferences, while seeking to be different from competitors. They also must recognize that customer expectations, competitors and market trends do not stand still, so product portfolios must be constantly appraised and uprated. This is certainly the approach adopted by Virgin Money. A company often has to modify existing products, introduce new products or eliminate products that were successful perhaps only a few years ago. Sometimes, product alterations are required to keep pace with changing consumer demographics and new technologies. Whatever the reasons for altering products, the product mix must be managed and kept fresh, reflecting customer expectations, changing market trends and competitors' products. It may be appropriate to expand a company's product mix to take advantage of excess marketing and production capacity.

The product portfolio approach tries to create specific marketing strategies to achieve a balanced mix of products that will maximize a company's longer-term profits. This chapter begins by considering how businesses are organized to develop and manage products. Next, several ways to improve a company's product mix, including new product development from idea generation to commercialization, are reviewed. The chapter then considers issues and decisions associated with managing a product through the growth, maturity and declining stages of its life cycle. Different types of product modification are also examined. The deletion of weak products from the product mix, often one of the hardest decisions for a marketer, is examined. The chapter concludes with a look at some of the related analytical tools associated with the planning of product portfolio: the Boston Consulting Group (BCG) product portfolio analysis, the market attractiveness – business position model or directional policy matrix (DPM), and the ABC sales: contribution analysis.

Organizing to manage products

A company must often manage a complex set of products, markets or both. Often, it finds that the traditional functional form of organization – in which managers specialize in business functions such as advertising, sales and distribution – does not fit its needs. Consequently, management must find an organizational approach that accomplishes the tasks necessary to develop and manage products. Alternatives to functional organization include the product or brand manager approach, the marketing manager approach and the venture or project team approach.

product manager
The person responsible for a product, a product line or several distinct products that make up an interrelated group within a multi-product organization

The product or brand manager approach A **product manager** is responsible for a product, a product line or several distinct products that make up an interrelated group within a multi-product organization. A **brand manager**, on the other hand, is responsible for a single brand, for example Dove or Dairy Milk. A product or brand manager operates cross-functionally to coordinate the activities, information and strategies involved in marketing an assigned product. Product managers and brand managers plan marketing activities to achieve objectives by coordinating a mix of place/distribution, promotion – especially sales promotion, advertising and digital comms – and price. They must consider packaging and branding decisions, and work closely with research and development, engineering and production departments. The product manager or brand manager approach is used by many large, multi-product companies in the consumer goods sector. Increasingly it is a popular approach adopted by marketers responsible for services brands and business-to-business markets.

brand manager
The person responsible for a single brand

marketing manager
The person responsible for managing the marketing activities that serve a particular group or class of customers

The marketing manager approach A **marketing manager** is responsible for managing the marketing activities that serve a particular group or class of customers. This organizational approach is particularly effective when a company engages in different types of marketing activity to provide products to diverse customer groups. For example, a company may have one marketing manager for business markets and another for consumer markets. These broad market categories may be broken down into more limited market responsibilities. IT services company Fujitsu has identified core target market sectors, such as government customers, retail, financial services, utilities and so forth. There is a separate marketing manager responsible for each sector, all reporting to the central marketing director. Each Fujitsu marketing manager handles the implementation of marketing programmes bespoke to his or her clients, but is also tasked with developing new products or services relevant to their category of clients.

venture or project team
The group that creates entirely new products, perhaps aimed at new markets, and is responsible for all aspects of the products' development

The venture or project team approach A **venture or project team** is designed to create entirely new products that may be aimed at new markets. Unlike a product or marketing manager, a venture team is responsible for all aspects of a product's development: research and development, production and engineering, finance and accounting, and marketing. Venture teams work outside established divisions to create inventive approaches to new products and markets. As a result of this flexibility, new products can be developed to take advantage of opportunities in highly segmented markets. Fujitsu has a separate team of marketers and new product development specialists working outside any specific client sectors, who are also striving to develop the next generation of attractive IT services but are not focused on a particular client sector, which is the role of the marketing managers. For example, their cloud computing offering has relevance to most of the company's client markets.

The members of a venture team come from different functional areas of an organization. Companies are increasingly using such cross-functional teams for product development in an effort to boost product quality. Quality may be positively related to information integration within the team, customers' influence on the product development process, and a quality orientation within the business.[1] When the commercial potential of a new product has been demonstrated, the members may return to their functional areas, or they may join a new or existing division to manage the product. The new product may be turned over to an existing division, a marketing manager or a product manager. Innovative organizational forms such as venture teams are especially important for well-established companies operating in mature markets. These companies must take a dual approach to marketing organization. They must accommodate the management of mature products and also encourage the development of new ones.[2]

New product development

Developing and introducing new products is frequently expensive and risky. The development of Gillette's Sensor razor took over eight years and resulted in a £150 million investment.[3] Thousands of new consumer products are introduced annually, and anywhere from 60 to 90 per cent of them fail. Lack of research, technical problems in design or production, and errors in timing the product's introduction are all causes of failure. Although developing new products is risky, so is failing to introduce new products. For example, the makers of Timex watches gained a large share of the watch market through effective marketing strategies during the 1960s and early 1970s. By 1983, Timex's market share had slipped considerably, in part because the company had failed to introduce new products. Timex has since regained market share by introducing a number of new products, but in the meantime competitors such as Swatch established their brands and stole significant market share from Timex.

The term 'new product' can have more than one meaning. It may refer to a genuinely new product – such as digital cameras – offering innovative benefits. But products that are merely different and distinctly better are also often viewed as new, such as lighter-weight wireless laptops. The following items, listed in no particular order, are product innovations of the last 30 or 40 years: Post-it notes, birth-control pills, personal computers, felt-tip pens, anti-ulcer drugs, Viagra, VCRs, DVDs, deep-fat fryers, compact disc players, mobile phones, e-mail, soft contact lenses, wireless data networks, hybrid cars and telephone banking. Thus, a new product can be an innovative variation of an existing product, as in the example shown in Figure 9.1.

A radically new product such as the Kindle involves a complex development process, including an extensive business analysis to determine the possibility of success.[4] It can also be a product that a given company has not marketed previously, although similar products may be available from other companies. The first company to introduce a DVD player was clearly launching a new product, yet if Boeing introduced its own brand of DVD player, this would also be viewed as a new product for Boeing, because it has not previously marketed such products.

FIGURE 9.1

Building on the popularity of crisps and savoury snacks, Ryvita launched rye-based 'Ryvita Minis', promoting the product's low calorie content

Source: Image courtesy of Advertising Archives

Managers in companies trying something new are often highly excited by sales prospects, yet the targeted consumers have probably been able to purchase similar products from a variety of other suppliers for some time; so, to be successful, the new entrant must have a visible and desirable competitive edge.

Before a product is introduced, it goes through the seven phases of **new product development** shown in Figure 9.2:

new product development
The process a product goes through before introduction, involving seven phases: idea generation, screening ideas, concept testing, business analysis, product development, test marketing and commercialization

1 idea generation

2 screening ideas

3 concept testing

4 business analysis

5 product development

6 test marketing

7 commercialization.

A product may be dropped, and many are, at any of these stages of development. This section examines the process through which products are developed from the inception of an idea to a product offered for sale. Table 9.1 shows how companies can improve their new product success rate.

idea generation
The process by which companies and other organizations seek product ideas that will help them achieve their objectives

Idea generation **Idea generation** involves companies and other organizations seeking product ideas that will help them achieve their objectives. This task is difficult because only a few ideas are good enough to be commercially successful. Although some organizations get their ideas almost by chance, companies trying to manage their product mixes effectively usually develop systematic approaches for generating new product ideas. Indeed, there is a relationship between the amount of market information gathered and the number of ideas generated by work groups in organizations.[5]

At the heart of innovation is a purposeful, focused effort to identify new ways to serve a market. Unexpected occurrences, incongruities, new needs, industry and market changes and demographic changes may all indicate new opportunities.[6] The forces of the marketing environment (see Chapter 3) often create new opportunities, as well as threats to combat.

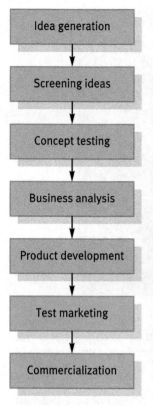

FIGURE 9.2
Phases of new product development

screening ideas
The process by which a company assesses whether product ideas match its organizational objectives and resources

New product ideas can come from several sources. They may come from internal sources: marketing managers, researchers, sales personnel, engineers or other organizational personnel. Brainstorming and incentives or rewards for good ideas are typical intra-organization devices for stimulating the development of ideas. The company 3M is well known for encouraging the generation of new ideas. The idea for 3M's Post-it adhesive-backed yellow notes came from an employee. As a church choir member, he used slips of paper for marking songs in his hymn book. Because the pieces of paper fell out, he suggested developing an adhesive-backed note. Hewlett-Packard keeps its labs open to engineers 24 hours a day to help generate ideas; it also encourages its researchers to devote 10 per cent of company time to exploring their own ideas for new products.[7] Company suggestion boxes for employees' ideas provide many of the stimuli for BMW's automotive innovations.

New product ideas may also arise from sources outside the company – for example, customers, competitors, advertising agencies, management consultants and private research organizations. Johnson & Johnson, for example, acquired the technology for its clear orthodontic braces through a joint venture with Saphikon, the developer of the technology behind the braces. Developing new product alliances with other businesses has also been found to enhance the acquisition and use of information helpful for creating new product ideas.[8] Sometimes ideas come from potential buyers of a product. Asking weekend fishermen what they wanted in a sonar fish finder led Techsonic to develop its LCR (liquid crystal recorder) fish finder.[9] For example, Chapter 3 outlined how companies such as Fujitsu discuss with clients their marketing environment drivers so that they can develop new products and services that reflect these client issues. In some markets, it is particularly important for new ideas to stem from customers. For example, many defence programmes take ten years to instigate, and the big defence equipment manufacturers are led by the stated buying plans and budgets of government defence departments.

Screening ideas **Screening ideas** involves first assessing whether they match organizational objectives and resources, and then choosing the best ideas for further review. Next, the company's overall ability to produce and market the product is analyzed. Other aspects of an idea that should be weighed are the nature and

TABLE 9.1 How to improve new product success

1	Talk with consumers and observe them; don't introduce a product just because you have the technology to make it.
2	Set realistic sales goals. Unrealistic goals can result in potentially successful products being terminated.
3	Make all parts of the company (research, manufacturing, marketing and distribution) work together for customer orientation.
4	At each stage of development, the product should have consumer acceptance, the ability to be manufactured at an acceptable cost and sales support.
5	Test market a product long enough to get an accurate assessment. Some products fail because consumers buy them early as a novelty only.
6	Carefully evaluate all product failures to provide information for future product introductions.
7	Monitor competitor developments: a new product must not merely replicate a rival.
8	Keep internal colleagues up-to-date and explain new developments to them.

Source: Adapted from Christopher P. Power, Kathleen Kerwin, Ronald Grover, Keith Alexander and Robert D. Hof, 'Flops: too many new products fail. Here's why – and how to do better', from *Business Week*, 16 August 1993, pp. 78–9.

wants of buyers, and possible marketing environment changes. More new product ideas are rejected during the idea-screening phase than during any other phase.

Sometimes a checklist of new product requirements is used to ensure that the screening process is as systematic as possible. If a critical factor on the checklist remains unclear, the type of formal marketing research described in Chapter 7 may be needed. To screen ideas properly, it may be necessary to test product concepts; a product concept and its benefits can be described or shown to consumers or business customers. Several product concepts may be tested to discover which might appeal most to a particular target market.

concept testing
Seeking potential buyers'responses to a product idea

Concept testing **Concept testing** is a phase in which a small sample of potential buyers is presented with a product idea, often in focus groups, through a written or oral description and perhaps a few drawings – to determine their attitudes and initial buying intentions regarding the product. For a single product idea, an organization can test one or several concepts of the same product. Concept testing is a low-cost procedure that lets a company determine customers' initial reactions to a product idea before it invests considerable resources in research and development. The results of concept testing can be used by product development personnel to better understand which product attributes and benefits are most important to potential customers.

business analysis
A company's evaluation of a product idea to determine its potential contribution to the company's sales, costs and profits

Business analysis During the **business analysis** phase, the product idea is evaluated to determine its potential contribution to the company's sales, costs and profits. In the course of a business analysis, evaluators ask a variety of questions:

● Does the product fit in with the company's existing product mix? Does the company have the right expertise to develop the new product?

● Is demand strong enough to justify entering the market and will the demand endure?

● What types of environmental and competitive changes can be expected, and how will these changes affect the product's future sales, costs and profits?

● Are the organization's research, development, engineering and production capabilities adequate?

● If new facilities must be constructed, how quickly can they be built and how much will they cost?

● If additional staff are required, when will they be in post?

● Is the necessary financing for development and commercialization on hand or obtainable at terms consistent with a favourable return on investment?

● Will the new product or idea benefit the company's existing portfolio of products?

● Is there any danger that existing products or services will be cannibalized?

In the business analysis stage, companies seek market information. The results of consumer surveys, along with secondary data, supply the specifics needed for estimating potential sales, costs and profits. At this point, a research budget should explore the financial objectives and related considerations for the new product.

product development
The phase in which the organization determines if it is technically and financially feasible to produce a new product

Product development **Product development** is the phase in which the organization determines if it is technically feasible to produce the product and if it can be produced at costs low enough to make the final price reasonable. To test its acceptability, the idea or concept is converted into a prototype, or working model. Concept cars are used in the development of new vehicles. The prototype should reveal tangible and intangible attributes associated with the product in consumers' minds. The product's design, mechanical features and intangible aspects must be linked to wants in the marketplace. This includes the service aspects of the product, which are a vital component of many products. Failure to determine how consumers feel about the product and how they would use it may lead to the product's failure. For example, the Sinclair C5 electric buggy was developed as a serious on-road, single-seater car for city or country use. However, drivers felt unsafe in the buggy, and campus students ended up using the remaining stocks as on-pavement runabouts.

The development phase of a new product is frequently lengthy and expensive; thus a relatively small number of product ideas are put into development. If the product appears sufficiently successful during this phase to merit testing, then during the latter part of the development phase marketers begin to make decisions regarding branding, packaging, labelling, pricing and promotion for use in the test marketing phase.[10]

Test marketing The limited introduction of a product in geographic areas or a marketing channel chosen to represent the intended market is called **test marketing**. Its aim is to determine the reactions of probable buyers. For example, after McDonald's developed fried chicken products for its fast-food menu, it test marketed the idea in certain McDonald's restaurants to find out how those customers felt about eating chicken at McDonald's. The company followed a similar strategy for test marketing its range of salads and pizza. Test marketing is not an extension of the development phase – it is a sample launching of the entire marketing mix, and should be conducted only after the product has gone through development and after initial plans regarding the other marketing mix variables have been made.

test marketing
The limited introduction of a product in geographic areas or a channel chosen to represent the intended market

Companies of all sizes use test marketing to reduce the risk of product failure. The dangers of introducing an untested product include undercutting already profitable products and, should the new product fail, loss of credibility with distributors and customers. Test marketing provides several benefits. It lets marketers expose a product to a natural marketing environment to gauge its sales performance. While the product is being marketed in a limited area, the company can seek to identify weaknesses in the product or in other parts of the marketing mix. Corrections can be made more cheaply than if the product had already been introduced nationwide. Test marketing also allows marketers to experiment with variations in advertising, price and packaging in different test areas and to measure the extent of brand awareness, brand switching and repeat purchases that result from alterations in the marketing mix.

The accuracy of test marketing results often hinges on where the tests are conducted. The selection of appropriate test areas is very important. The validity of test marketing results depends heavily on selecting test sites that provide an accurate representation of the intended target market. The criteria used for choosing test cities or television regions depend on the product's characteristics, the target market's characteristics and the company's objectives and resources.

Test marketing can be risky because it is expensive and a company's competitors may try to interfere. This is common in the confectionery market. A competitor may invalidate test results in an attempt to 'jam' the test programme by increasing advertising or promotions, lowering prices or offering special incentives – all to combat the recognition and purchase of a new brand. Sometimes, too, competitors copy the product in the testing stage and rush to introduce a similar product. It is therefore desirable to move quickly and commercialize as soon as possible after testing. When the product introduction is delayed to the point where the public begins to doubt its existence, such products may become known as 'vapourware', particularly in the computer software industry.[11]

To avoid these risks, companies may use alternative methods to gauge consumer preferences. One such method is simulated test marketing. Typically, consumers at shopping centres are asked to view an advertisement for a new product and are given a free sample to take home. These consumers are subsequently interviewed and asked to rate the product. The major advantages of simulated test marketing are lower costs, tighter security and, consequently, a reduction in the flow of information to competitors, and the elimination of jamming. Scanner-based test marketing is another, more sophisticated version of the traditional test marketing method. Some marketing research companies, such as ACNielsen, offer test marketing services to help provide independent assessment of products.

commercialization
The process of refining and settling plans for full-scale manufacturing and marketing

Commercialization During the **commercialization** phase, plans for full-scale manufacturing and marketing must be refined and settled, and budgets for the project must be prepared. Early in the commercialization phase, marketing management analyzes the results of test marketing to find out what changes in the marketing mix are needed before the product is introduced. For example, the results of test marketing may tell the marketers to change one or more of the product's physical attributes, modify the distribution plans to include more retail outlets, alter promotional efforts or change the product's price. During this phase, the company also has to gear up for production and may therefore face sizeable capital expenditure and personnel costs.

The product enters the market during the commercialization phase. One study indicates that only 8 per cent of new product projects started by major companies reach this stage.[12] When introducing a product, marketers often spend enormous sums of money on advertising, personal selling and other types of promotion. These expenses, together with capital outlays, can make commercialization extremely costly; such expenditures may not be recovered for several years. For example, when Ford introduced its new Focus model, the company spent millions of pounds on advertising to communicate the new car's attributes. Commercialization is easier when customers accept the product rapidly, which they are more likely to do if marketers can make them aware of its benefits.

Line extensions

line extension
A product that is closely related to existing products in the line, but meets different customer needs

A **line extension** is the development of a product that is closely related to one or more products in the existing product line but is designed specifically to meet the somewhat different needs of customers. For example, Fairy Liquid washing-up detergent was used as a springboard for various detergent-based Fairy products including washing powder for automatic washing machines. Many of the so-called new products introduced each year by organizations are in fact line extensions. Line extensions are more common than radically new products because they are a less expensive, lower-risk alternative for increasing sales. A line extension may focus on a different market segment or may be an attempt to increase sales within the same market segment by more precisely satisfying the needs of people in that segment. For example, Nestlé launched an extra-strong variant of its Polo mints, Supermints, aimed at lovers of strong peppermints. However, one side-effect of employing a line extension is that it may result in a more negative evaluation of the core product.[13] It has been suggested that the success of line extensions is partly affected by consumer perceptions of how well the extension fits with the core brand.[14]

Product adoption process

product adoption process
The stages buyers go through in accepting a product: awareness, interest, evaluation, trial and adoption

The following stages of the **product adoption process** are generally recognized as those that buyers go through in accepting a product, from gaining awareness of it to buying the product.

1 *Awareness* the buyer becomes aware of the product.

2 *Interest* the buyer seeks information and is generally receptive to learning about the product.

3 *Evaluation* the buyer considers the product's benefits and determines whether to try it.

4 *Trial* the buyer examines, tests or tries the product to determine its usefulness relative to his or her needs.

5 *Adoption* the buyer purchases the product and can be expected to use it when the need for this general type of product arises again.[15]

In the first stage, when individuals become aware that the product exists, they have little information about the product and are not concerned about obtaining more. Consumers enter the interest stage when they are motivated to obtain information about the product's features, uses, advantages, disadvantages, price or location. During the evaluation stage, individuals consider whether the product will satisfy certain criteria that are crucial for meeting their specific needs. In the trial stage, they use or experience the product for the first time, possibly by purchasing a small quantity, by taking advantage of a free sample or demonstration, or by borrowing the product from someone. Supermarkets, for instance, frequently offer special promotions to encourage consumers to taste products. During this stage, potential adopters determine the usefulness of the product under the specific conditions for which they need it.

Individuals move into the adoption stage by choosing the specific product when they need a product of that general type. However, the fact that a person enters the adoption process does not mean that she or he will eventually adopt the new product. Rejection may occur at any stage, including adoption. Both product adoption and product rejection can be temporary or permanent. Just because a consumer or business customer adopts a particular product once, does not guarantee future loyalty to the product or brand. Marketers must work hard to achieve a customer's ongoing loyalty and repeat purchasing.

This adoption process model has several implications for the commercialization phase. First, the company must promote the product to create widespread awareness of its existence and its benefits. Samples or simulated trials should be arranged to help buyers make initial purchase decisions. Marketers should also emphasize quality control and provide solid guarantees to reinforce buyer opinion during the evaluation stage. Finally, production and physical distribution must be linked to patterns of adoption and repeat purchase. The product adoption process is also discussed in Chapter 13, as marketing communications are not only important for achieving awareness, but also for informing and persuading customers right through the product adoption process. When launching a new product, companies must realize that buyers differ in the speed with which they adopt a product. Identifying buyers who are most open to new products can help expedite this process.

Consumers do not always pass through all the stages of the product adoption process as formally as this overview may have implied. A minor upgrade to a familiar brand may not cause consumers much concern, whereas an innovative product launched by an unknown supplier will give rise to much more extensive consumer decision-making. Business customers making routine rebuys or consumers making routine response purchases – see Chapters 4 and 5 – already have awareness of a particular product and are interested in it. Previously, they have tried and adopted the product, so their limited decision-making does not require them to pass through the product adoption process in this manner. On the whole, though, marketers would do well to remember the importance of all five stages in this important concept. Consumers and business-to-business customers must be aware of, have interest in, and be prepared to evaluate and try out a product or service if they are to adopt it: that is, to buy and consume it. The marketing task does not end with first-time adoption, however. The ongoing requirement for marketers is to ensure customer loyalty and repeat purchase.

Products are not usually launched nationwide overnight but are introduced through a process called a roll-out. In a roll-out, a product is introduced in stages, starting in a set of geographic areas and gradually expanding into adjacent areas. Thus, Cadbury's Wispa bar appeared initially in the north-east of England. It may take several years to market a product nationally. Sometimes the test cities are used as initial marketing areas, and the introduction becomes a natural extension of test marketing. Gradual product introduction reduces the risks of introducing a new product. If the product fails, the company will experience smaller losses. Furthermore, it may take some time for a company to develop a suitable distribution network. Also, the number of units needed to satisfy the national demand for a successful product can be enormous, and a company cannot usually produce the required quantities in a short time.

Despite the good reasons for introducing a product gradually, marketers realize that this approach creates some competitive problems. A gradual introduction allows competitors to observe what a company is doing and to monitor results, just as the company's own marketers are doing. If competitors see that the newly introduced product is successful, they may enter the same target market quickly with similar products. Avoiding competition is critical when a company introduces a brand into a market in which it already has one or more brands. Marketers usually want to avoid cannibalizing sales of their existing brands, unless the new brand generates substantially larger profits. When KP introduces a new snack brand, it must take care to ensure that sales of other KP brands do not suffer.

If a product has been planned properly, its attributes and brand image will give it the distinctive appeal needed. Style, shape, construction, quality of work and colour help create the image and the appeal. Of course buyers are more likely to purchase the product if they can easily identify the benefits. When the new product does not offer some preferred attributes, there is room for another new product or for repositioning of an existing product.[16] Methods of positioning are discussed in the final part of Chapter 6.

Product life cycle management

Most new products start off slowly and seldom generate enough sales to produce profits immediately. As buyers learn about the new product, marketers should be looking out for any weaknesses and be ready to make corrections quickly, in order to prevent the product's early demise. Computer software companies expect to modify 'bugs' when launching new software products. Consumers must be informed quickly and efficiently of any difficulties if damage to the brand image is to be avoided. Marketing strategy should be designed to attract the segment that is most interested in, and has the fewest objections to, the product. If any of these factors need adjustment, this action, too, must be taken quickly to sustain demand. As the sales curve moves upwards and the break-even point is reached, the growth stage begins. See Figure 8.5 in Chapter 8 for an explanation of the product life cycle concept, which assumes a path from introduction to growth, into maturity and then decline, mimicking the human life cycle from birth to death.

Marketing strategy in the growth stage

As sales increase, management must support the momentum by adjusting the marketing strategy. The goal is to establish the product's positioning and to fortify it by encouraging brand loyalty. As profits increase, the company must brace itself for the entrance of aggressive competitors, who may make specialized appeals to selected market segments.

During the growth stage, product offerings may have to be expanded. To achieve greater penetration of an overall market, segmentation may have to be used more intensely. That would require developing product variations to satisfy the needs of customers in several different market segments. Marketers should analyze the product positioning regarding competing products, and correct weak or omitted attributes. Further quality, functional or style modifications may be required.

Gaps in the marketing channels should be filled during the growth period. Once a product has won acceptance, new distribution outlets may be easier to obtain. Sometimes marketers tend to

exclusive distribution
Market coverage in which only one outlet is used in a geographic area

selective distribution
Market coverage in which only some available outlets in an area are chosen to distribute a product

intensive distribution
Market coverage in which all available outlets are used for distributing a product

move from **exclusive distribution** or **selective distribution** to a more **intensive distribution** of dealers to achieve greater market penetration. Marketers must also make sure that the physical distribution system is running efficiently and delivering supplies to distributors before their inventories are exhausted. Because competition increases during the growth period, good service and an effective mechanism for handling complaints are important.

Advertising expenditure may be lowered slightly from the high level of the introductory stage but still needs to be quite substantial. As sales increase, promotion costs should drop as a percentage of total sales. A falling ratio between promotion expenditure and sales should contribute significantly to increased profits. The advertising messages should aim to stress brand benefits and emphasize the product's positioning. Coupons and samples may be used to increase market share.

After recovering development costs, an organization may be able to lower prices. As sales volume increases, efficiencies in production can result in lower costs. These savings may be passed on to buyers. If demand remains strong and there are few competitive threats, prices tend to remain stable. If price cuts are feasible, they can improve price competition and discourage new competitors from entering the market. For example, when compact disc players were introduced in the early 1980s, they carried an £800 price tag. Primarily because of the price, the product was positioned as a 'toy for audiophiles' – a very small market segment. To generate mass-market demand, compact disc player manufacturers dropped their prices to around £150, and the cost of discs also dropped. The price was at a point where the margin was low but the turnover was high. However, with most homes having a CD player, sales volumes inevitably diminished. A similar pattern has emerged in the sale of smart phones and home PCs, as unit prices have plummeted. Widescreen home entertainment systems are now following this pattern, as margins reduce but volumes increase. CD player sales are being replaced for manufacturers such as Sony with the growth in MP3 players, smartphones and multi-media PCs which play music and tablets. In other words, sales of other products compensate for declining sales of CD players, which is why the management of product portfolios – examined later in this Chapter – is so important.

Marketing strategy for mature products

As many products are in the maturity stage of their life cycles, marketers must always be ready to improve the product and marketing mix. During maturity, the competitive situation stabilizes and some of the weaker competitors drop out. It has been suggested that as a product matures, its customers become more experienced and their requirements more diverse, so that market segmentation opportunities increase. As customers' needs change, new marketing strategies for mature products may be called for.[17] For example, in the wake of competition from Eurotunnel, car ferry operators stressed excellent on-board shopping, catering facilities and spacious accommodation in their advertising. Marketers may also need to modify the product. Symptoms of a mature product include price cutting, increased competitive action and shifting from a product orientation to a non-product orientation (price, promotion and place/distribution adaptation); in addition, market growth slows.[18]

product modification
The alteration of one or more characteristics of a company's product

Product modification means changing one or more characteristics of a company's product. This strategy is most likely to be used in the maturity stage of the product life cycle to give a company's existing brand a competitive edge. Even well-established brands such as Sellotape must be modified from time to time, with innovative dispensers or versions with 'Happy Birthday' or suchlike printed along the tape. Altering a product mix in this way entails less risk than developing a new product because the product is already established in the market.

If certain conditions are met, product modification can improve a company's product mix. First, the product must be modifiable. Second, existing customers must be able to perceive that a modification has been made, assuming that the modified item is still aimed at them. Third, the

Topical insight

eBanking, telebanking, texts, TV banking and now banking apps: What next?

Marketers must constantly look at ways to keep their products 'fresh' and up to date, modifying existing products as appropriate or bringing out new ones. Personal banking has gone through many phases. Many readers will remember the days when high-street banks were open only until mid-afternoon Monday to Friday, and there were no ATMs for easy cash withdrawals. Queuing at ageing tills in austere branches was the primary means of operating current bank accounts. Direct debits and standing orders helped, but the real revolution came in the late 1970s with the growth of ATMs (cash dispensers) and then in the early 1990s as most leading banks extended their opening hours and range of services aimed at private customers.

Technology has emerged as a driving force for change via other banking services in addition to ATMs. HSBC's First Direct broke ranks by launching as a telephone-only, 365-days-a-year, 24-hour full-service personal banking provider. The rapid take-off of first direct encouraged its traditional high-street competitors to offer their own 24-hour telephone banking services such as Barclays' BarclayCall, based on heavy investment in call centres.

Internet banking and now mobile technology are changing the way in which many customers interact with their banks. It is not only the major high-street banking giants that have turned to technology. The Prudential also turned to eBanking

with the Egg brand of eCommerce financial services; 65 000 people enquired about this intriguing product departure in the first five days after its launch, more than double the number anticipated by the Prudential. Now many customers prefer eBanking.

Another departure from the traditional high-street bank branch is the launch of TV banking. NatWest joined with Microsoft to provide an interactive banking service on Microsoft's WebTV network. The service included information about mortgages, travel insurance, currency rates, plus standard current account banking, based on NatWest's PC banking package already established online. Smartphone apps, telephones, Internet-hooked home PCs, even TVs with set-top boxes, are all emerging as means by which personal bankers can avoid traipsing into their local branch in order to execute financial transactions and manage their accounts.

First direct offers mobile phone users texting access to their banking details. Most banks now have apps for smartphone users. As more people use their web browsers on their mobile phones, there is an increase in accessing bank accounts via mobiles on the go: a far cry from the queues in fuddy-duddy branches. No doubt other technological solutions will emerge. To banking customers, such product developments are revolutionizing their banking habits and access to financial services.

Sources: NatWest, first direct and Barclays websites, 2000–12.

---

modification should make the product more consistent with customers' desires so that it provides greater satisfaction. If these conditions are not met, it is unlikely that the product modification, however innovative, will be successful. The Marketing Insight box describes several successful modifications to personal banking that have been developed due to emerging technology. Product modifications fall into three major categories: quality, functional and style modifications.

quality modifications
Changes that affect a product's dependability and durability

Quality modifications Changes concerning a product's dependability and durability are called **quality modifications**. Usually, they are executed by altering the materials or the production process. Reducing a product's quality may allow a company to lower its price and direct the item at a larger target market.

By contrast, increasing the quality of a product may give a company an advantage over competing brands. During the last 30 years, marketers have been forced by increased global competition, technological change and more demanding customers to improve product integrity.[19] Higher quality may enable a company to charge a higher price by creating customer loyalty and by lowering customer sensitivity to price. However, higher quality may require the use of more expensive components, less standardized production processes, and other manufacturing and management techniques that force a company to charge higher prices.[20]

Functional modifications Changes that affect a product's versatility, effectiveness, convenience or safety are called **functional modifications**; they usually require the product to be redesigned. Typical product categories that have undergone considerable functional modifications include home computers, audio equipment and cleaning products. Functional modifications can make a product useful to more people, thus enlarging its market, or improve the product's competitive position by providing benefits that competing items do not offer. Functional modifications can also help a company achieve and maintain a progressive image. For example, washing machine manufacturers such as Whirlpool or AEG have developed appliances that use less heat and water. In Figure 9.3 well known washing liquid brand Fairy has opted to promote additional ways of washing your clothes efficiently and easily by using dissolvable casings. At times, too, functional modifications are made to reduce the possibility of product liability claims.

> **functional modifications**
> Changes that affect a product's versatility, effectiveness, convenience or safety

FIGURE 9.3
Fairy Liquitabs modification focused on unique 'liquitabs' as a new laundry method
Source: © Errol Rait / Alamy

Style modifications **Style modifications** change the sensory appeal of a product by altering its taste, texture, sound, smell or visual characteristics. Such modifications can be important, because when making a purchase decision, a buyer is swayed by how a product looks, smells, tastes, feels or sounds.

> **style modifications**
> Changes that alter a product's sensory appeal – taste, texture, sound, smell or visual characteristics

Although style modifications can be used by a company to differentiate its product from competing brands, their major drawback is that their value is highly subjective. A company may strive to improve the product's style, but customers may actually find the modified product less appealing. Some companies try to minimize these problems by altering product style in subtle ways. For example, Mattel's Barbie doll has gradually changed over the years in terms of career and lifestyle to reflect changing fashions.

During the maturity stage of the cycle, marketers actively encourage dealers to support the product, perhaps by offering promotional assistance or help in lowering their inventory costs. In general, marketers go to great lengths to serve dealers and to provide incentives for selling the manufacturer's brand, partly because own-label or retailer brands are a threat at this time. Own-label brands are both an opportunity and a threat to manufacturers, who may be able to sell their products through recognized own-label or retailer brand names as well as their own. However, own-label or retailer brands frequently undermine manufacturers' brands.

Maintaining market share during the maturity stage requires moderate and sometimes heavy advertising expenditure. Advertising messages focus on differentiating a brand from numerous competitors, and sales promotion efforts are aimed at both consumers and resellers.

A greater mixture of pricing strategies is used during the maturity stage. In some cases, strong price competition occurs and price wars may break out. Sometimes marketers develop price flexibility to differentiate offerings in product lines. Mark-downs and price incentives are more common, but prices may rise if distribution and production costs increase. Marketers of mature products also often alter packaging and even positioning strategies. For example, in the USA, Heinz repackaged and repositioned its vinegar as an all-natural cleaning product.

Marketing strategy for declining products

As a product's sales curve turns downwards, industry profits continue to fall. A business can justify maintaining a product as long as it contributes to profits or enhances the overall effectiveness of a product mix. In this stage of the product life cycle, marketers must determine whether to eliminate the product or seek to reposition it in an attempt to extend its life. Usually, a declining product has lost its distinctiveness because similar competing products have been introduced. Competition engenders increased substitution and brand switching as buyers become insensitive to minor product differences. For these reasons, marketers do little to change a product's style, design or other attributes during its decline. New technology, product substitutes or environmental considerations may also indicate that the time has come to delete a product. Digital broadcasting has forced manufacturers to drop analogue TVs, for example.

During a product's decline, outlets with strong sales volumes are maintained and unprofitable outlets are weeded out. An entire marketing channel may be eliminated if it does not contribute adequately to profits. Sometimes a new marketing channel, such as a factory outlet, will be used to liquidate remaining inventory of an obsolete product. Advertising expenditure is at a minimum. Advertising or special offers may slow the rate of decline. Sales promotions, such as coupons and premiums, may temporarily regain buyers' attention. As the product continues to decline, the sales staff shifts its emphasis to more profitable products. The strategy pursued depends heavily on the nature of the portfolio. Sony could downgrade the role of CD players and switch its focus to downloadable music players. However, CD and DVD retailer HMV faces a tough challenge, as consumers move to downloads from purchasing software and increasingly have no need to visit an HMV store.

To have a product return a profit may be more important to a company than to maintain a certain market share. To squeeze out all possible remaining profits, marketers may maintain the price despite declining sales and competitive pressures. Prices may even be increased as costs rise if a loyal core market still wants the product, such as those consumers preferring turntables to CD or MP3 players. In other situations, the price may be cut to reduce existing inventory so that the product can be deleted. Severe price reductions may be required if a new product is making an existing product obsolete.

Deleting products

product deletion
The process of eliminating a product that no longer satisfies a sufficient number of customers

Product deletion is the process of eliminating a product that no longer satisfies a sufficient number of customers. Products cannot usually contribute to an organization's goals indefinitely, and a declining product reduces a company's profitability, draining resources that could be used to modify other products or develop new ones. A marginal product may require shorter production runs, which can increase per unit production costs. Finally, when a dying product completely loses favour with customers, the negative feelings may transfer to some of the company's other products.

Most companies find it difficult to delete a product or a brand. It was probably a hard decision for Sony to cease producing Clio handhelds, for HP to drop the well-known Palm brand or for Thomas Cook to drop the long-standing Going Places chain of travel agents. Many observers felt Motorola's failure to drop its hugely successful but long-in-the-tooth Razr line of mobile phones permitted rivals to leapfrog with enhanced technology and so steal much of Moto's market share. The company is now fighting back with new ranges. A decision to drop a product may be opposed by management and other employees who feel that the product is necessary in the product mix, or by sales people who still have some loyal customers. Considerable resources and effort are sometimes spent in trying to improve the product's marketing mix enough to increase sales and thus avoid having to delete it.

Some companies delete products only after they have become heavy financial burdens. A better approach is to institute some form of systematic review to evaluate each product and monitor its impact on the overall effectiveness of the company's product mix. Such a review should analyze a product's contribution to the company's sales for a given period and should include estimates of future sales, costs and profits associated with the product. It should also gauge the value of making changes in the marketing strategy to improve the product's performance. A systematic review allows a company to improve product performance and to ascertain when to delete products. Although many companies do systematically review their product mixes, one research study found that few companies have formal, written policies concerning the process of deleting products. The study also found that most companies base their decisions to delete weak products on poor sales and profit potential, low compatibility with the company's business strategies, unfavourable market outlook and historical declines in profitability.[21]

Basically, there are three ways to delete a product, either (see Figure 9.4):

phase out
An approach that lets the product decline without a change in marketing strategy

1 phase it out

2 run it out

3 drop it immediately.

run out
A policy that exploits any strengths left in the product

A **phase out** approach allows the product to decline without a change in the marketing strategy. No attempt is made to give the product new life. A **run out** policy exploits any strengths left in the product. Intensifying marketing efforts in core markets or eliminating some marketing expenditures, such as advertising, may cause a sudden profit increase. This approach is commonly taken for technologically obsolete products, such as older models of camcorders or computers, and is often accompanied by a price reduction. Some car manufacturers use a run out approach to dispose of certain models just before a new launch. The third option, an **immediate drop** of an unprofitable product, is the best strategy when losses are too great to prolong the product's life.

immediate drop
An option that drops an unprofitable product immediately

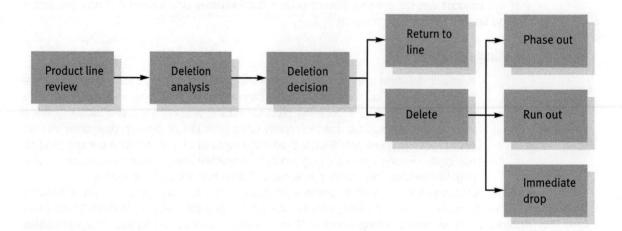

FIGURE 9.4
Product deletion process

Source: Martin L. Bell, *Marketing: Concepts and Strategies*, 3rd edn, p. 267; copyright © 1979, Houghton Mifflin Company.

Tools for managing product portfolios

A number of tools have been developed to aid marketing managers in their planning efforts. Based on ideas used in the management of financial portfolios, several models that classify an organization's product portfolio have been proposed. These models allow strategic business units (SBUs) or products to be classified and visually displayed both according to the attractiveness of various markets and a business's relative market share within those markets. Three of these tools are the Boston Consulting Group (BCG) product portfolio analysis, the market attractiveness – business position model, and the ABC sales: contribution analysis. In addition, the product life cycle concept explored in Chapter 8 is an important tool often utilized in determining future strategies for brands and products. This assessment – based on the notion of the introduction, growth, maturity and decline stages in the life of a product or market – is useful in recommending a marketing strategy. As described above, the options are quite different for marketers facing growth or mature stages, and markedly so for the introduction versus the decline stages. The Boston Consulting Group matrix, described next, builds on this suggestion.

The Boston Consulting Group (BCG) product portfolio analysis

Just as financial investors have different investments with varying risks and rates of return, businesses have a portfolio of products characterized by different market growth rates and relative market shares. **Product portfolio analysis**, the Boston Consulting Group approach, is based on the philosophy that a product's market growth rate and its relative market share are important considerations in determining its marketing strategy. All the company's products should be integrated into a single, overall matrix and evaluated to determine appropriate strategies for individual SBUs and the overall portfolio strategies. However, a balanced product portfolio matrix is the end result of a number of actions, not just the analysis alone. Portfolio models can be created on the basis of present and projected market growth rates and proposed market share strategies. These strategies include four options:

product portfolio analysis
A strategic planning tool that takes a product's market growth rate and its relative market share into consideration in determining a marketing strategy

1 build share

2 maintain share

3 harvest share

4 divest business.

Managers can use these models to determine and classify each product's expected future cash contributions and future cash requirements.

Generally, managers who use a portfolio model must examine the competitive position of a product – or product line – and the opportunities for improving that product's contribution to profitability and cash flow.[22] The BCG analytical approach is more of a diagnostic tool than a guide for making strategy prescriptions.

stars
Products with a dominant share of the market and good prospects for growth

Figure 9.5, which is based on work by the BCG, enables the marketing manager to classify a company's products into four basic types: stars, cash cows, dogs and problem children.[23]

- **Stars** are products with a dominant share of the market and good prospects for growth. However, they use more cash than they generate to finance growth, add capacity and increase market share.

cash cows
Products with a dominant share of the market but low prospects for growth

- **Cash cows** have a dominant share of the market but low prospects for growth. Typically, they generate more cash than is required to maintain market share. Cash cows generate much needed funds to support the stars and problem children.

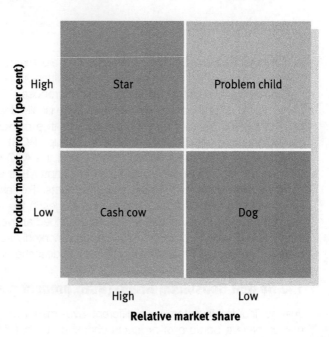

FIGURE 9.5
Illustrative growth-share matrix developed by the Boston Consulting Group

Source: The BCG Portfolio Matrix from the Product Portfolio Matrix, © 1970, The Boston Consulting Group

dogs
Products that have a subordinate share of the market and low prospects for growth

problem children
Products that have a small share of a growing market, generally requiring a large amount of cash to build share

- **Dogs** have a subordinate share of the market and low prospects for growth. These are struggling products. They are frequently found in mature markets and often should be phased out or withdrawn immediately.

- **Problem children** sometimes called 'question marks', have a small share of a growing market and generally require a large amount of cash to build share. The question is, are they capable of becoming star products or are they destined to be dogs?

The product portfolio growth-share matrix in Figure 9.5 can be expanded to show a company's whole portfolio by providing for each product:

- its cash sales volume, illustrated by the size of a circle on the matrix
- its market share *relative* to competition, represented by the horizontal position of the product on the matrix
- the growth rate of the market, indicated by the position of the product in the vertical direction.

It should be noted that relative market share is a company's own market share relative to the biggest competitor's. Figure 9.6 suggests marketing strategies appropriate for cash cows, stars, dogs and problem children. By following these guiding philosophies, an organization can make strategic decisions based on the diagnosis of the BCG product portfolio growth-share matrix.

The long-term health of an organization depends on having some products that generate cash and provide acceptable profits, plus others that use cash to support growth. Among the indicators of overall health are the size and vulnerability of the cash cows, the prospects for the stars, if any, and the number of problem children and dogs. Particular attention must be paid to those products with large cash appetites. Unless the company has an abundant cash flow, it cannot afford to sponsor many such products at one time. If resources, including debt capacity, are spread too thinly, the company will end up with too many marginal products and will be unable to finance promising new product entries or acquisitions in the future.

Product market growth (per cent) High	**Stars** Characteristics ■ Market leaders ■ Fast growing ■ Substantial profits ■ Require large investment to finance growth Strategies ■ Protect existing share ■ Re-invest earnings in the form of price reductions, product improvements, providing better market coverage, production efficiency and so on ■ Obtain a large share of the new users	**Problem children** Characteristics ■ Rapid growth areas ■ Poor profit margins ■ Enormous demand for cash Strategies ■ Invest heavily to get a disproportionate share of new sales ■ Buy existing market shares by acquiring competitors ■ Divestment (see Dogs) ■ Harvesting (see Dogs) ■ Abandonment (see Dogs) ■ Focus on a definable niche where dominance can be achieved
Low	**Cash cows** Characteristics ■ Profitable products ■ Generate more cash than needed to maintain market share Strategies ■ Maintain market dominance ■ Invest in process improvements and technological leadership ■ Maintain price leadership ■ Use excess cash to suppport research and growth elsewhere in the company	**Dogs** Characteristics ■ Greatest number of products fall in this category ■ Operate at a cost disadvantage ■ Few opportunities for growth at a reasonable cost ■ Markets are not growing; therefore, little new business Strategies ■ Focus on a specialized segment of the market that can be dominated and protected from competitive inroads ■ Harvesting—cut back all support costs to a minimum level; support cash flow over the product's remaining life ■ Divestment—sale of a growing concern ■ Abandonment—deletion from the product line
	High	Low

Relative market share

FIGURE 9.6

Characteristics and strategies for the four basic product types in the growth-share matrix

Source: 'Diagnosing the product portfolio' by George S. Day, *Journal of Marketing*, April 1977, pp. 30-31. Published by the American Marketing Association. Adapted and reprinted with permission

Although a popular tool in the 1980s, the BCG growth-share matrix is not commonly deployed these days. Many marketers believe that market attractiveness equates to more than simply the growth rate of a market and a product's – or – brand's respective market share. As marketers have sought more complex approaches, utilizing many variables, the market attractiveness – business position model has grown in popularity.

Market attractiveness – business position model

market attractiveness – business position model
A two-dimensional matrix that helps determine which SBUs have an opportunity to grow and which should be divested

The **market attractiveness – business position model**, illustrated in Figure 9.7, is another two-dimensional matrix, often known as the directional policy matrix or DPM. However, rather than using single measures to define the vertical and horizontal dimensions of the matrix, the model employs multiple measurements and observations. It is an increasingly popular tool, particularly in businesses producing detailed annual marketing plans. The vertical dimension – market attractiveness – includes all the issues that relate to the market. For example, seasonality, economies of scale, competitive intensity, industry sales and the overall cost and feasibility of entering the market. The horizontal axis – business position – is a composite of factors – for example, sales, relative market share, research and development, price competitiveness, product quality and market knowledge. These are only examples, because each set of marketers will select variables as they relate to the product and particular market. Each company deploying this tool selects its own criteria, but uses these same ones over time to analyze changes. A slight variation of this matrix is called General Electric's Strategic Business Planning Grid because General Electric is credited with extending the product portfolio planning tool to examine market attractiveness and business strength.

The best situation for a company is to have a strong business position in an attractive market. The upper-left area in Figure 9.7 represents the opportunity for an invest/grow strategy, but the matrix does not indicate how to implement this strategy. The purpose of the model is to serve as a diagnostic tool to highlight SBUs that have an opportunity to grow or that should be divested or approached selectively.[24] SBUs that occupy the invest/grow position can lose their position through faulty marketing strategies.

Decisions on allocating resources to SBUs of medium overall attractiveness should be arrived at on a basis relative to other SBUs that are either more or less attractive. The lower-right area of the matrix is a low-growth harvest/divest area. Harvesting is a gradual withdrawal of marketing

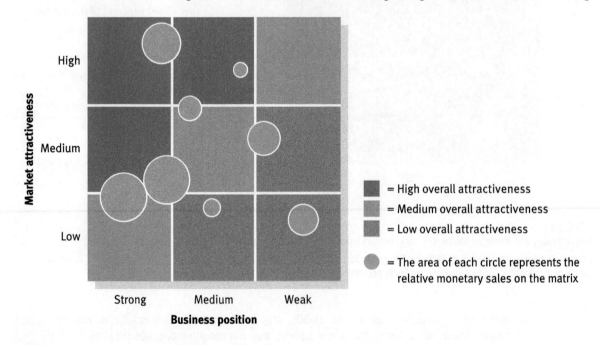

FIGURE 9.7
Market attractiveness – business position model

Source: adapted from Derek F. Abell and John S. Hammond, *Strategic Market Planning: Problems and Analytical Approaches* (Englewood Cliffs, NJ: Prentice-Hall, 1979), p. 213. Used by permission

Practitioners' use of the directional policy matrix (DPM)

Marketing tools and techniques

Most organizations have more than one product and operate in several markets. This results in the need to prioritize in which markets to focus resources, particularly in terms of sales and marketing activities. Often the 'who shouts the loudest' approach to management meetings wins, or else historical successes with specific clients, products or markets colour the judgement of decision-makers irrespective of current business performance. One effective approach to ensuring that objectivity has an input into such prioritization is the directional policy matrix (DPM) or GE grid.

Along with the PEST analysis described in Chapter 3, the directional policy matrix is a pivotal tool in strategic business planning. The DPM is useful to marketers as a means for identifying the relative merits of apparently attractive opportunities. Suggested worthwhile opportunities may be benchmarked against a company's existing activities to judge the value of supporting the new ideas. The tool can be used to evaluate the relative merits of individual products or product groups.

The DPM is useful, too, in selecting between market segments (see Chapter 6). The market attractiveness criteria identified for the DPM can easily be utilized to assess the relative merits of market segments.

So, how is a DPM produced? Occasionally, a strategic planner or marketing director may produce such an analysis, but often the variables to be used in order to construct the DPM are selected and weighted by a team of senior decision makers, often the directors or leadership team, supplemented by marketing managers and analysts who understand the trends and dynamics of individual markets. The steps are as follows.

1 Identify a set of opportunity or market attractiveness criteria. These should be a mix of short-term variables (e.g. sales volumes and current profitability) and longer-term variables (e.g. market growth prospects or ability to sustain a differential advantage). In addition, some variables should be internal-facing (e.g. profitability) and some variables must be market-facing (e.g. customer satisfaction or intensity of competition). The aim is to have a balanced set of criteria.

2 Allocate 100 points across the selected variables in order to weight them in terms of their relative importance. If a team of managers is involved, each should 'vote' with 100 points, then the whole team's votes should be aggregated.

3 Identify business strength variables and as – with market attractiveness – allocate 100 points between these business strength variables for their weighting.

4 Then the main task. Score each major product group, market segment or marketing opportunity (given the specific context of the analysis). To score, a simple three-category scoring system is usually adequate: $n \times 1 =$ strong/good; $n \times 0.5 =$ 'so-so'/average; $n \times 0 =$ low/weak/poor (where $n =$ the selected variable). When scoring, business strength variables are usually taken as being relative to the dominant player(s) in the market, while market attractiveness scoring is usually one market segment versus 'the others' in the company's portfolio.

5 Weight $\times$ score $=$ total to be plotted. Each product group, segment or opportunity is, therefore, allocated a value between 0 and 100 for market attractiveness and for business strength, so its position may be plotted on the DPM grid. The Y axis represents market attractiveness (0–100), while the X axis represents business strength (0–100).

In the real B2B example depicted on page 300, the company identified 11 market attractiveness criteria and ten business strength criteria. Each market segment was in turn judged against all 21 variables, warranting 1, 0.5 or 0. For example, market segment 'A' scored 0.5 for 'long-term prospects with the client' ($14 \times 0.5 = 7$) and 0.5 for 'current presence in the client' ($8 \times 0.5 = 4$), and so forth. However, segment 'B' scored 1 for the first variable ($14 \times 1 = 14$). The result is depicted in the DPM chart on page 300.

Having assessed each of its many market segments, this company plotted them on a DPM. In addition, the management team predicted where the segments would head over the following three years. The circle size represents the proportionate income to the company from each market segment.

Further details may be found in the authors' titles *Market Segmentation Success: Making It Happen!* (The Haworth Press, 2008) and *Marketing Planning* (Cengage Learning, 2009).

Marketing attractiveness	*weighting*	Business strengths	*weighting*
Long-term prospects with the client	14	Clarity and cohesion of message	19
Profitability	14	Thought leadership	16
Strategic fit	12	Easy to do business with/flexibility	15
Size of the opportunity	12	Right people/right support/right milieu	14
(Right) relationship	9	Perceived quality of delivery	12
Ability to deliver the necessary solution	9	Understanding of the market sector	10
How well the opportunity can be defined/realized	8	Referenceability	7
Current presence in the client	8	Price competitive	3.6
Nature of competition	6	Winning business/closure mindset	5
Risk	5	Breadth and depth	2.4
Whether the task can be replicated or referenced	3		

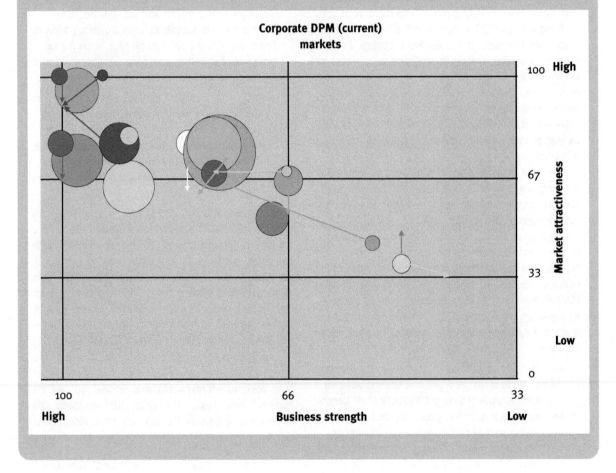

Corporate DPM (current)
markets

FIGURE 9.8
The White Company has a reputation for retailing superior products, a theme emphasized in this shop window
Source: © Alamy/Mark Richardson

resources on the assumption that sales will decline at a slow rate but profits will still be significant at a lower sales volume. Harvesting and divesting, even abandonment, or deletion from the product line – may be appropriate strategies for SBUs characterized by low overall attractiveness.

Marketers proficient in this technique often use the agreed variables and weightings to evaluate market segments in order to determine investment priorities: certain segments will be more attractive than others, while the organization's strengths will vary between segments (see Chapter 6). The matrix can also be used for mapping a company's products or brands.

directional policy matrix (DPM)
A more commonly used name for the market attractiveness – business position model

The Marketing Tools and Techniques box on page 299 offers a step-by-step example of one company's use of the **directional policy matrix (DPM)**, in this instance examining the relative performance of different market segments. The same approach could be deployed to examine SBUs' products, rather than market segments.

ABC sales: contribution analysis
An approach that examines the financial worth to a company of its products, product groups or customers

The ABC sales: contribution analysis

The **ABC sales: contribution analysis** can be conducted at product group or product line level; for the total market, territories or sub-markets; for customer groups/ market segments; or for individual customer accounts. In other words, whatever the unit of analysis, the ABC sales: contribution analysis is revealing. In the context of this chapter, individual products or product groups may be plotted. Sales managers focusing on key accounts may plot individual key customer accounts, instead of products, while marketers developing target market strategies may well plot different market segments in order to understand their relative performance better (see Chapter 6).

The aim of this analysis is to show both the amount of sales and the financial contribution from these sales – that is, the financial worth – to the company's fortunes. Financial success, after all, is not confined to sales volume figures; a company must have an adequate level of contribution – sales revenue minus all variable costs – from its sales. This analysis helps companies to identify the relative value of different products, markets or even individual customer accounts, assisting with the allocation of resources.

An example of an ABC sales: contribution analysis chart is shown in Figure 9.9. The 45-degree diagonal line from bottom left to top right is the optimum. It is a straightforward rule, not a regression line. Ideally, the dots plotted on the chart would be located on the line – having both good sales and contribution – and be at the top right of the graph, with high sales and high contribution. These 'sell a lot, make a lot' plots to the top right, are the 'A' class. Typically, however, this is not the case: often the majority of products, customers or markets – depending on the selected unit of analysis – fall to the bottom left of the graph. Here, they are low sales and low contribution (the 'C' class) or they have average sales and average contribution (the 'B' class).

Three important conclusions can be drawn from an ABC analysis:

1 The analysis can identify highly attractive customers, markets or products (depending on the chosen unit of analysis) in terms of the associated contributions, but where sales are relatively low. For such accounts, an increase in sales, no matter how slight, with associated high prices and good financial returns, will be highly rewarding.

2 The analysis can determine accounts with high sales figures but low or pitiful contributions. Cash flow may be good, but the company's profitability is not helped. Even a slight increase in contribution is most desirable and will greatly assist the company's overall fortunes.

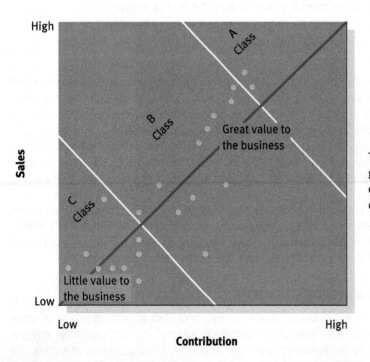

The dots could be products, product groups, market territories, segments or even individual customer accounts depending on the chosen level of analysis

FIGURE 9.9
Example of an ABC sales: contribution chart

3 The analysis can challenge the historical perspective that often clouds judgement as to what constitutes a good product, market or customer. Every organization has its historically most rewarding customers and products that in reality are no longer performing in terms of sales, contribution or both. Often, managers still believe the historical rhetoric rather than recognize that the situation has moved on; new priorities must benefit from the available resources and marketing effort. The ABC analysis generally unearths a few such instances and identifies the rump of unrewarding accounts or customers that are not worth pursuing.

The approaches presented here provide an overview of the most popular analytical methods used in strategic market planning. This chapter has focused on the management of product portfolios, but as has been explained, techniques such as the directional policy matrix (DPM) and the ABC sales: contribution analysis are extremely helpful in evaluating the relative merits of market segments or even individual customer accounts.

The Boston Consulting Group's portfolio analysis, the market attractiveness – business position model, the ABC sales: contribution analysis and the product life cycle concept are used not only to diagnose problem areas or to recognize opportunities, but also to facilitate the allocation of resources among business units. They are not intended to serve as formulae for success or prescriptive guides, which lay out specific strategic action plans.[25] These approaches are supplements to, not substitutes for, the marketing manager's own judgement. The real test of each approach, or any integrated approach, is how well it helps management diagnose the company's strengths and weaknesses and prescribe strategic actions for maintaining or improving performance. The emphasis should be on making sound decisions with the aid of these analytical tools.[26]

Summary

To maximize the effectiveness of a product mix, a company usually has to alter its mix through the modification of existing products, deletion of a product or new product development. Developing and managing products is critical to a company's survival and growth. The various approaches available for organizing product management share common activities, functions and decisions necessary to guide a product through its life cycle. A *product manager* is responsible for a product, a product line or several distinct products that make up an interrelated group within a multi-product organization. A *brand manager* is responsible for a single brand. *Marketing managers* are responsible for managing the marketing activities that serve a particular group or class of customers. A *venture or project team* is sometimes used to create and develop entirely new products that may be aimed at new markets.

A new product may be an innovation that has never been sold by any organization; or it can be a product that a given company has not marketed previously, although similar products have been available from other organizations. Before a product is introduced, it goes through the seven phases of *new product development.* (1) In the *idea generation* phase, new product ideas may come from internal or external sources. (2) In the process of *screening ideas,* those with the greatest potential are selected for further review. (3) *Concept testing* presents a small number of potential buyers with the concept idea in order to ascertain early approval indicators. (4) During the *business analysis* stage, the product idea is evaluated to determine its potential contribution to the company's sales, costs and profits. (5) *Product development* is the phase in which the organization determines if it is technically feasible to produce the product and if it can be produced at costs low enough for the final price to be reasonable. (6) *Test marketing* is a limited introduction of a product in geographic areas or channels chosen to represent the intended market. (7) The decision to enter the *commercialization* phase means that full-scale production of the product begins and a complete marketing strategy is developed.

Not all 'new' products are genuinely new! Many product introductions are in fact a *line extension* the development of a product that is closely related to products in the existing product line, but designed to meet different customer needs. The *product adoption process* that buyers go through in accepting a product includes awareness, interest, evaluation, trial and adoption.

As a product moves through its life cycle, marketing strategies will require continual adaptation. In the growth stage, it is important to develop brand loyalty and a market position. Marketers may move from an *exclusive distribution* or *selective distribution* to a more *intensive distribution* of dealers. In the maturity stage, a product may be modified or new market segments may be developed to rejuvenate its sales.

Product modification involves changing one or more characteristics of a company's product. This approach to altering a product mix can be effective when the product is modifiable, when customers can perceive the change and when customers want the modification. *Quality modifications* are changes that relate to a product's dependability and durability. Changes that affect a product's versatility, effectiveness, convenience or safety are called *functional modifications. Style modifications* change the sensory appeal of a product.

A product that is declining may be maintained as long as it makes a contribution to profits or enhances the product mix. Marketers must determine whether to eliminate the declining product or to reposition it to extend its life.

Product deletion is the process of eliminating a product that is unprofitable, consumes too many resources and no longer satisfies a sufficient number of customers. *Phase out, run out* and *immediate drop* are three ways to delete a product. A product mix should be systematically reviewed to determine when to delete products.

A number of tools have been developed to aid marketing managers in their portfolio planning efforts; these include the Boston Consulting Group (BCG) *product portfolio analysis,* the market attractiveness – business position model, and the ABC sales: contribution analysis. The product life cycle concept is also important in determining marketing strategies. The BCG approach is based on the philosophy that a product's market growth rate and its relative market share are key factors influencing marketing strategy. All the company's products are integrated into a single, overall matrix – including *stars, cash cows, dogs* and *problem children* – and are evaluated to determine appropriate strategies for individual SBUs and the overall portfolio strategies.

The *market attractiveness – business position model* is a two-dimensional matrix, often known as the *directional policy matrix (DPM).* The market attractiveness dimension includes variables that relate to the attractiveness of the market or product opportunity, such as seasonality, economies of scale, competitive intensity, industry sales and the cost of competing. The business position axis measures variables that relate to a business's strengths and capabilities, such as sales levels, relative market share, research and development expertise, and other factors that support building market share for a product. Each set of marketers will select variables pertinent to the respective company and industry.

The *ABC sales: contribution analysis* examines the financial worth to a company of its products, product groups or customers. The analysis highlights areas in which to avoid or limit further investment and sales and marketing activity. It also reveals specific targets for financial contribution improvement or sales volume improvement.

Tools for portfolio planning are used only to diagnose problem areas or recognize opportunities. They are supplements to, not substitutes for, the marketing manager's own judgement. The real test of each approach, or any integrated approach, is how well it helps management diagnose the company's strengths and weaknesses, and prescribe strategic actions for maintaining or improving performance.

The portfolio planning approaches presented here provide an overview of the most popular analytical methods used in strategic market planning. This chapter has focused on the management of product portfolios, but techniques such as the market attractiveness – business position model more commonly now known as the directional policy matrix (DPM) – and the ABC sales: contribution analysis are extremely helpful in evaluating the relative merits of market segments or even individual customer accounts.

Key links

- This chapter has examined the development of products and the first part should be read in conjunction with Chapter 8, on product decisions.

- The management of products should be considered in harmony with the material presented in Chapter 14, on branding.

- The product portfolio techniques explained in this chapter, particularly the directional policy matrix and ABC sales: contribution analysis, are often deployed by marketers making trade-off decisions between emerging opportunities or various market segments. These techniques are useful when reading about targeting in Chapter 6's discussion of market segmentation.

Important terms

Product manager
Brand manager
Marketing manager
Venture or project team
New product development
Idea generation
Screening ideas
Concept testing
Business analysis
Product development
Test marketing
Commercialization
Line extension
Product adoption process
Exclusive distribution
Selective distribution
Intensive distribution
Product modification
Quality modifications
Functional modifications
Style modifications
Product deletion
Phase out
Run out
Immediate drop
Product portfolio analysis
Stars
Cash cows

Dogs
Problem children
Market attractiveness – business position model
Directional policy matrix (DPM)
ABC sales: contribution analysis

Discussion and review questions

1 What organizational alternatives are available to a company with two product lines, each consisting of four product items?

2 When is it more appropriate to use a product manager than a marketing manager?

3 What type of company might use a venture team to develop new products? What are the advantages and disadvantages of such a team?

4 Do small companies that manufacture one or two products need to be concerned about developing and managing products? Why or why not?

5 Why is product development a cross-functional activity within an organization? That is, why must finance, engineering, manufacturing and other functional areas be involved?

6 Develop a list of information sources for new product ideas for the car industry.

7 What are the advantages and disadvantages of test marketing?

8 Compare and contrast three ways of modifying a product.

9 What are the stages of the product adoption process, and how do they affect the commercialization phase?

10 Detail the key stages of the product life cycle.

11 How can a company prolong the life of a mature product? What actions should be taken to try to stem the product's decline?

12 Give several reasons why a company might be unable to eliminate an unprofitable product.

13 In what ways do the stages of the product life cycle impact on a company's management of its product portfolio?

14 What are the major considerations in developing the BCG product portfolio matrix? Define and explain the four basic types of product suggested by the Boston Consulting Group.

15 What are the advantages of the directional policy matrix (DPM) over the BCG product portfolio matrix?

16 What are the diagnostic capabilities of the ABC sales: contribution analysis?

Recommended readings

Baker, M. and Hart, S., *Product Strategy and Management* (Pearson/FT, 2007).

Crawford, C.M. and Di Benedetto, C.A., *New Products Management* (McGraw-Hill, 2011).

Day, G.S., *Analysis for Strategic Marketing Decisions* (St Paul, Minnesota: West, 1986).

Lehmann, D. and Winer, R., *Product Management* (McGraw-Hill, 2004).

Loch, C. and Kavadias, S., *Handbook of Product Management* (Butterworth-Heinemann, 2008).

Trott, P., *Innovation Management and New Product Development* (Harlow: Pearson/FT, 2004).

Wind, Y.J., *Product Policy: Concepts, Methods and Strategy* (Reading, Mass.: Addison-Wesley, 1982).

Internet exercise

The success of BMW's Mini has been phenomenal. Despite a limited range of cars, each one on the road appears unique, and research reveals that Mini owners feel they have the power to tailor their car to suit their specific tastes and driving styles. BMW and Mini have incorporated this individualization, of what in reality is far from a bespoke one-to-one product, in their product development process and in their commercialization of this product. Take a look at either: www.mini.co.uk or www.mini.com and in particular the section detailing accessories and *Design Your Own Mini*.

1   What product features and characteristics are portrayed on the Mini website?

2   To what extent does Mini's commercialization enable customers to individualize or personalize their cars?

Applied mini-case

People visit cinemas to watch a film for many reasons: to catch the latest release; because friends are going; to be entertained; to go on a date; to occupy the children; to escape from the children; to be with people; to have an emotional experience; to kill time; to have a rest, or 'just because it's somewhere to go'. The choice of which film to see may often be the first decision, but these days, with the growth of multiplexes and record cinema attendances, the choice may be which multiplex: Odeon, Cineworld, Gaiety or National Amusements' Showcase? For rival operators, the 'augmented' product is becoming increasingly important as they seek to develop a competitive edge and to encourage customer loyalty. For example, Showcase strongly emphasizes many once secondary or minor features in an attempt to add to the appeal of its cinemas:

- state-of-the-art film projection
- acres of free, illuminated car parking
- best seats in town – exclusive rocking loungers
- bargain matinees daily
- freshly popped popcorn
- cinema hire and special group rates
- on main coach/bus routes
- Dolby stereo-equipped auditoria
- air conditioning
- excellent facilities for the disabled
- late-night shows every Friday and Saturday
- efficient, courteous service
- gift certificates always available
- art gallery with prints for sale.

For many companies, not only Showcase, the augmented product is an increasingly important element in the marketing strategy and the search for customer satisfaction. The new product development process increasingly includes the required customer service attributes desired by targeted customers to accompany the purchased product.

Source: National Amusements/Showcase Cinema, Coventry; **http://www. showcasecinemas.co.uk,** January, 2008 and March, 2012.

Question

As a marketing manager, to what extent does inclusion of the augmented product simplify or complicate the new product development process?

Sellotape or adhesive tape? increasing market penetration – a classic tale

Case study

Just as JCB is a generic term for backhoe diggers in the construction industry, Hoover for vacuum cleaners, Post-it for those useful sticky stationery tags, and Bic for disposable pens, for many decades Sellotape has been the term applied to sticky transparent tape. It is even cited in the Oxford Dictionary. Over the years, however, many other brands and suppliers have entered the market and eaten away Sellotape's once dominant market share. So where was Sellotape to seek growth?

At the end of 1995, following nearly two years of research and planning, Sellotape enjoyed a £2 million relaunch. This represented the 'most significant change in the brand's 60 year history', according to Neil Ashley executive director of the company renamed the Sellotape Company. The name Sellotape had been the company's core marketing asset for many decades, with nine out of ten consumers familiar with the brand. However, the company had for some time sold a wider range of products than its sticky tape association implies. Michael Peters of the branding specialist Identica, responsible for the Sellotape rethink, was more fervent in his view: 'while it is a very famous trademark, it's a grey one'. Qualitative marketing research revealed that, although well known, hardly any consumer asked for Sellotape by name. Worse, they readily accepted other brands because they could see no obvious product or brand features that gave Sellotape a competitive edge or differentiation over rival products.

The relaunch aimed to address the inherent weakness in becoming a generic name for a product by re-establishing a new brand identity alongside existing core brand values. Rival products not using cellulose are cheaper, so alongside its traditional tape, the Sellotape Company now offers a range of tape made from other source materials. Elephant Tape, for example, is a heavy-duty fabric tape that is targeted at the do-it-yourself (DIY) market.

Under the sub-brand Sellotape Office, a range of products aimed at office use was launched. Ranges were also targeted at the children's market and the home security market. The view that there were three distinct markets – retail, DIY and office – led to the development of novel product applications and totally separate ranges.

The key problem to overcome was 'the Colman's mustard dilemma'. Colman's, the market leader in mustards, had tremendously high brand awareness, and consumers perceived its mustards to be of high quality. Unfortunately these consumers usually bought only one type of mustard, English; and that one jar lasted for years! Colman's had to increase usage. It achieved this by both:

1 demonstrating in advertisements and cookery supplements that mustard could be used in a variety of ways, particularly as an additional ingredient in many sauces, just like a herb or spice

2 bringing out a range of different mustards, each with unique strengths, flavours and applications, French, Italian and American mustards, along with the traditional English.

Consumers were encouraged to have several jars in their cupboards and to consume greater quantities.

For Sellotape, research showed that most customers bought only one roll of sticky tape each year, often around Christmas. The launch of ranges designed for different target audiences – retail, DIY and office – and for various applications children's – activities and home security uses – emulated the brand extension principles so well deployed by Colman's.

Sellotape's strong brand awareness and identity meant that the company did not need to advertise heavily. Instead, the Sellotape Company relied on direct marketing and point-of-sale promotion to create awareness of its new sub-brands and their applications. A core task for the company had been to break down the traditional views of the product and its customers held by employees, and to establish additional channels of distribution through toy shops and garden centres to reflect the extended and additional product ranges. If the Sellotape Company can, like Colman's, encourage its customers to buy two products annually instead of just one and to look for its branded products by name, the heritage of the brand and the reorganization of the company will have reaped significant rewards. Today, owned by global adhesives giant Henkel, this strategy is proving very successful for Sellotape.

Sources: 'Sellotape acts to avoid getting stuck in a rut', *Independent on Sunday*, 26 November, 1995, IB8; the Sellotape Company, 1996; B&Q, 1996; Sainsbury's Homebase, 1996, 2004. With grateful thanks to Meg Carter; January, 2008; 'Welcome to Sellotape', 5 March 2011; **http://www.henkel. com/brands-and-solution/adhesives-sealants-surface-treatments-12123. htm**, 2011.

Questions for discussion

1   At what stages in their product life cycle are the different Sellotape products, and what are the management implications?

2   Why was it necessary for the Sellotape Company to relaunch its Sellotape range?

3   How might new lines help Sellotape develop its competitive position in this market?

CHAPTER 10

The marketing of services

"Nebulous and difficult to differentiate, for services, quality and effective delivery are paramount"

INTRODUCTION

As discussed in Chapter 8, all products – goods, services and ideas – possess a certain amount of intangibility. For services, intangibility is often all-embracing. A **service** is an intangible product involving a deed, a performance or an effort that cannot physically be possessed.[1]

service
An intangible product involving a deed, a performance or an effort that cannot physically be possessed

This chapter presents concepts that apply specifically to the marketing of services. Services marketing involves marketing in non-profit organizations such as education, healthcare, charities and government, as well as for-profit making areas such as entertainment, tourism, finance, personal services and professional services. The characteristics of services and the markets for services demand important adaptation of the marketing toolkit and warrant specific discussion of the nuances of the service 'product'.

Marketing a solution to today's stresses

In a world that is increasingly demanding, Champneys is committed to providing a world of relaxation and calm to enhance a more balanced lifestyle.

At Champneys, we believe that true beauty can only come through health and wellbeing. Synonymous with quality and luxury, our heritage ensures exceptionally high standards of both service and care, across all our resorts, Day Spas and products.

Our philosophy is to help people who visit Champneys to detoxify their mind and body. Whether you want to change the way you feel, the way you look or the way you live, we have the know-how to help you improve your lifestyle and wellbeing, through pampering treatments, healthy food and fitness.

Our spa therapists are trained to world-class standards and deliver treatments that address every aspect of your body's needs, from skincare to aching limbs. Using only the finest products from prestige beauty brands, as well as Champneys' own exclusive range, you'll discover the most indulgent spa therapies.

Our fitness facilities are second to none, with a vast range of activities on offer and something to suit every ability. Our fitness teams can provide personal training, as well as health appraisals, body composition analysis and cholesterol checks.

Our head chefs select only the freshest ingredients and our menus are carefully planned, relying on the principle of moderation, balance and variety, but definitely not starvation.

**http://www.champneys.com/About-Champneys/
Our-Philosophy**

Source: Image courtesy of www.champneys.com

Champneys is but one of dozens of spa businesses to emerge during the past two decades, responding to the stresses of modern living and hectic business lives, as consumers seek solace from the rigours of daily life, either for routine 'pick-me-ups' or special occasion pampering. There are plenty of tangible aspects to a typical spa, from treatment beds to invigorating spa pools, but for most consumers it is the experience that they seek, supplemented with an appropriate ambience and attentive staff. The marketing concept is just as relevant for such experiential and nebulous products as for the marketers of well-known grocery products found in a major supermarket. However, the execution of the marketing process has rather important characteristics unique to services, as suggested by the sentiments of Champneys' proposition.

The health and wellbeing products offered by Champneys are services rather than tangible goods: they are experiential. This chapter presents concepts that apply specifically to products that are services. The organizations that market service products include: for-profit businesses, such as those offering financial, personal and professional services; and non-profit organizations, such as educational institutions, religious groups, charities and governments. The activities of the so-termed third sector lie within these realms. The practices of social marketing are directly applicable for many non-profit services.

The chapter begins by considering the contribution of service industries to the economy. It then addresses the unique characteristics of services and the problems they present to marketers: these traits often form the basis for examination questions and they explain why marketers of services have to manipulate an extended marketing mix, devote extensive resources to branding and often struggle to create a differential advantage over rivals. Next, the chapter presents various classification schemes that can help services marketers develop marketing strategies. Then a variety of marketing mix considerations are discussed, along with the associated problems of creating and sustaining a differential advantage. The important concept of service quality is then explored. Finally, the chapter defines non-profit marketing and examines the development of non-profit marketing strategies and the control of non-profit marketing activities.

The nature and importance of services

Few products can be classified as a pure good or a pure service. Consider, for example, the purchase of a laptop computer. When consumers buy a laptop, they take ownership of a physical item which they might use at work and at home, but the maintenance contract linked with the purchase and providing reassurance is a service. Similarly, a helpline facility offering software support is providing a service. Most products, such as computers and other high tech goods, contain both tangible and intangible components. An airline provides a service, yet offers tangible items such as lounges and comfortable seats; hotels require tangible items such as pools, beds, bar tables, yet fundamentally provide a service … somewhere to stay. One component, however, will dominate, and it is this dominant component that leads to the classification of goods, services and ideas.

Figure 10.1 illustrates the tangibility concept by placing a variety of 'products' on a continuum of tangibility and intangibility. Tangible dominant products are typically classified as goods, and intangible dominant products are typically considered services. A restaurant meal or taxi cab may be tangible and physical, but the restaurant or taxi operator is providing a service: refreshment or transportation. Thus, as defined in Chapter 8, services are intangible dominant products that involve the application of human and mechanical efforts to people or objects.

Growth of services

consumer services
Services such as education, healthcare, leisure, catering, tourism, financial, entertainment, home maintenance and other services to help consumers

business services
Services such as repairs and maintenance, consulting and professional advice, installation, equipment leasing, marketing research, advertising, temporary office personnel and caretaking services

In Europe, as in the United States, the importance of services in the economy is increasing, with nearly two-thirds of the EU workforce employed in the sector. Service industries encompass trade, communications, transport, leisure, food and accommodation, financial and medical services, education, government and technical services. There are services intended for consumers – **consumer services** – and those designed to satisfy businesses – **business services**.

Economic prosperity has been a major catalyst for consumer services growth, leading to an increase in financial services, travel, entertainment and personal care. Lifestyle changes have also encouraged expansion of the service sector. Smaller families result in more free time and relatively higher disposable income. Consumers are keener than ever to 'buy in' outside services. With the growth of households in which both adults are working, many consumers want to avoid tasks such as meal preparation, house cleaning, home maintenance and preparation of tax returns, so they buy-in such service provision or assistance. Furthermore, Europeans have become more fitness and recreation oriented and, with greater leisure time, the demand for fitness and recreational facilities has escalated. In terms of demographics, the population is growing older, and this change has promoted tremendous expansion of healthcare services.

Goods
(tangible)

Bananas Jewellery TV Cars/maintenance Fast-food restaurants Airlines Beauty salons Financial services Telephone services Education

Services
(intangible)

FIGURE 10.1
A continuum of product tangibility and intangibility

Finally, the number and complexity of goods needing servicing have spurred demand for repair services.

Not only have consumer services grown in the economy, business services have prospered as well. Business or industrial services include repairs and maintenance, consulting and professional advice, installation, equipment leasing, marketing research, advertising, temporary office personnel and caretaking services. Expenditures for business and industrial services have risen even faster than expenditures for consumer services. This growth has been attributed to the increasingly complex, specialized and competitive business environment.[2]

There are three key reasons behind the growth of business-to-business services:

1 Specialization – the delegation of non-care tasks, such as advertising, executive recruitment and car fleet management.

2 Technology – the increase in sophistication leading to the 'buying in' of expert knowledge and skills, such as IT computing consultants or manufacturing design.

3 Flexibility – the need in many organizations to avoid fixed overhead costs; for example, marketing research, catering, maintenance and cleaning are frequently brought in only on an *ad hoc* basis or out-sourced.

Characteristics of services

The marketing of services is distinct from goods marketing.[3] To understand the nature of services marketing, it is necessary to appreciate the particular characteristics of services. Services have for a long time been viewed in marketing circles as 'being different' to goods, because of four fundamental distinguishing characteristics:

1 intangibility

2 inseparability of production and consumption

3 perishability

4 heterogeneity.[4]

Table 10.1 summarizes these characteristics and the resulting marketing challenges.

intangibility
An inherent quality of services that are performed and therefore cannot be tasted, touched, seen, smelled or possessed

search qualities
Tangible attributes of a service that can be viewed prior to purchase

experience qualities
Attributes that can be assessed only after purchase and consumption, including satisfaction and courtesy

credence qualities
Attributes that cannot be assessed even after purchase and consumption

Intangibility The characteristic of **intangibility** stems from the fact that services are performances. They cannot be seen, touched, tasted or smelled, nor can they be possessed. Intangibility also relates to the difficulty that consumers may have in understanding service offerings.[5] Services have a few tangible attributes, called **search qualities**, which can be viewed prior to purchase, such as the décor in a restaurant or the facilities in a care home. Independent wholesaler hair products company Capital Hair and Beauty offer clients an extensive range of tangible hair products to use in their own hair and beauty business (see Figure 10.2), which offers personal service. When consumers cannot examine a service product in advance, they may not understand exactly what is being offered. Even when consumers do gain sufficient knowledge about service offerings, they may not be able to evaluate the possible choices. On the other hand, services are rich in experience and credence qualities. **Experience qualities** are those qualities that can be assessed only after purchase and consumption (satisfaction, courtesy, pleasure). Leisure centres and holidays are examples of services that are high in experience qualities. **Credence qualities** are those qualities that cannot be assessed even after purchase and consumption.[6] A medical operation, car repairs, consulting and legal representation are examples of services high in credence qualities. How many consumers are knowledgeable enough to assess the quality of an appendectomy, even after the surgery has been performed?

TABLE 10.1 Service marketing challenges

Service characteristics	Resulting marketing challenges
Intangibility	Difficult for customer to evaluate
	Customer does not take physical possession
	Difficult to advertise and display
	Difficult to set and justify prices
	Service process is not usually defended by patents
Inseparability of production and consumption	Service provider cannot mass-produce services
	Customer must participate and comply in production
	Other consumers affect service outcomes
	Services are difficult to distribute and replicate
Perishability	Services cannot be stored
	Very difficult to balance supply and demand
	Unused capacity is lost forever
	Demand may be very time-sensitive
Heterogeneity	Service quality is difficult to control
	Difficult to standardize service delivery
Client-based relationships	Success depends on satisfying and keeping customers over the long term
	Generating repeat business is challenging
	Relationship building becomes critical
Customer contact	Service providers are critical to delivery
	Requires high levels of service employee training and motivation
	Changing a high-contact service into a low-contact service to achieve lower costs without reducing customer satisfaction

Sources: Adapted from the ideas of K. Douglas Hoffman and John E.G. Bateson, *Essentials of Services Marketing* (Fort Worth, TX: Dryden Press, 1997), pp. 25–38; Valarie A. Zeithaml, A. Parasuraman and Leonard L. Berry, *Delivering Quality Service: Balancing Customer Perceptions and Expectations* (New York: Free Press, 1990); Leonard L. Berry and A. Parasuraman, *Marketing Services: Competing through Quality* (New York Free Press, 1991), p. 5.

A Renault car can be test-driven before being purchased. It can be viewed in the dealer's showroom and on the streets. It can, to an extent, be consumed (tested) prior to purchase. The same is not true of a beauty treatment or an opera seat. The beauty treatment and the opera may fail to live up to expectations, but by the time this disappointment is recognized it is too late – the service has been partially consumed and paid for and the opportunity cost long gone.

inseparability
In relation to production and consumption, a characteristic of services that means they are produced at the same time as they are consumed

Inseparability Related to intangibility, therefore, is **inseparability** of production and consumption. Services are normally produced at the same time as they are consumed. A medical examination is an example of simultaneous production and consumption. In fact, the doctor cannot possibly perform the service without the patient's presence, and the consumer is actually involved in the production process. With other services, such as taking tennis lessons, consumers are simultaneously involved in production. Because of high consumer involvement in most services, standardization and control are difficult to maintain. The Marketing Insight box on page 315 illustrates how students may be as much to blame for a poor lecture as their tutor.

FIGURE 10.2
Many services are targeted at business customers. Here wholesalers Capital Hair and Beauty attempt to entice new clients for its services, via a wide range of products
Source: Image courtesy of Capital Hair

perishability
A characteristic of services whereby unused capacity on one occasion cannot be stockpiled or inventoried for future occasions

Perishability As production and consumption are simultaneous, services are also characterized by **perishability**. The consumer of a service generally has to be present and directly involved in the consumption of the service at the time of its production. This means that unused capacity in one time period cannot be stockpiled or inventoried for future time periods. This is a problem that airline operators face every day. Each operator engages in an ongoing struggle to maintain seat occupancy levels. Empty seats mean lost business. Many operators offer 'last-minute' cut-price deals to reduce the numbers of empty seats. In many cases it is not possible to change the flight on which the seat is booked and monies paid are generally not refunded in the event of cancellation. This example illustrates how service perishability presents problems very different from the supply and demand problems encountered in the marketing of goods.[7] While an empty airline seat on a flight is a sale lost for ever, cans of soup remaining on the supermarket shelf at the close of business will be available for sale the following day.

heterogeneity
Variability in the quality of service because services are provided by people, and people perform inconsistently

Heterogeneity Most services are labour intensive, they are susceptible to **heterogeneity**. For the service to be provided and consumed, the client generally meets and deals directly with the service provider's personnel. Direct contact and interaction are distinguishing features of services. However, the people delivering services do not always perform consistently. There may be variation from one service to another within the same organization or variation in the service that a single individual provides from day to day and from customer to customer. A good branch manager is crucial for a restaurant chain such as Pizza Express or a coffee shop like Starbucks. Poor customer reaction and branch performance can often be traced back to a poor branch manager.[8] Waiting times in either outlet can vary greatly, often due to teamwork, speed and efficiency variations between branches. This may result in varying levels of customer satisfaction – for example, between one Starbucks and another. Thus standardization and quality are extremely difficult to control. However, it is also true that the characteristics of services themselves may make it possible for marketers to customize their offerings to consumers. In such cases, services marketers often face a dilemma: how to provide efficient, standardized service at an acceptable level of quality, while simultaneously treating each customer as a unique person.

Building customer relationships

People's performance is inconsistent ... good lecture?

How often have you seen a truly awesome lecturer perform consistently session to session without a drop in her or his performance? Just as actors have an 'off performance', so do your lecturers. It is unlikely they left home with the express intention of disappointing you, failing to provide you with value for money, or not helping you with your studies ... and yet they might fail to deliver to their normally high standards.

More likely, an e-mail rant from a colleague, a worrying situation for a student under their care, rejection from the editor of a journal for a hard-crafted research paper, or a problem at home has distracted your tutor. Academics have been known to deliver back-to-back lectures with identical visual aids and script to ostensibly identical cohorts of students in terms of their profiles and motivations for attending the lecture. Nevertheless, rarely are such sessions delivered in identical fashion or to similar levels of acclaim ... one lecture zings while the other in the supposed matching pair falls flat. Not only because of the tutor's service delivery, but perhaps the students in the first were more participative, upbeat and prepared, so played their parts more effectively than the 'customers' in the second session.

Universities do a great deal to maintain the consistency and quality of delivery. Training of staff, systems for reviewing teaching materials, peer reviews, student evaluation processes seeking feedback and formal staff appraisals, are just some of the devices employed. Nevertheless, an outstandingly engaging and informative lecture may well be followed with one not so strong or well received.

You might have found a reassuring and sympathetic dentist who seems capable, courteous and attentive. Unfortunately, your next appointment occurs after your dental practitioner has been awake all night looking after a poorly toddler, or while s/he is still seething following a morning row with their spouse, or your dentist might be distracted having learned of a relative's illness. Your experience is in no way similar to your previous visit and you feel somewhat let down and possibly very annoyed. Unfortunately, service delivery often is erratic and is inextricably linked to the mood, skills, behaviour and engagement of the person delivering it.

Occasionally, you may encounter a pleasant surprise: the car dealer's service personnel listen attentively to your concerns, locate the problem promptly, fix it soon after and the cost is considerably less than you feared. Their attentive, smiling and engaging manner has left you with an all-round good feeling of your experience. As a result, you feel more positive about the dealership, the brand of car you are driving and your experience of customer service. The problem is that you suspect it will not be such a good experience next time you visit. The challenges for marketers are to maintain consistency in the customer's experience and to ensure the level of satisfaction is high. These desires will not be achieved by accident. They must be planned, monitored, controlled and modified.

---

client-based relationships
Interactions that result in satisfied customers who use a service repeatedly over time

Client-based relationships The success of many services depends on creating and maintaining **client-based relationships**, interactions with customers that result in satisfied customers who use a service repeatedly over time.[9] In fact, some service providers, such as solicitors, accountants and financial advisers, call their customers 'clients' and often develop and maintain close, long-term relationships with them. Customers are generally more satisfied in relational exchanges than they are with exchanges based on single transactions. Indeed, research suggests that customer loyalty and re-patronage behaviour can be encouraged through this approach.[10] The building of such relationships has also been shown to be important in non-profit contexts.[11] It seems that services businesses are successful only to the degree to which they can maintain a group of clients who use their services on an ongoing basis. For example, a dentist may serve a family for many years. If the family members are confident in the dentist and think he or she offers a good service, they are likely to recommend the dentist to friends. If this positive word-of-mouth communication continues, the dentist may acquire a large number of clients through this route. To ensure that client-based relationships are created and maintained, a service provider must take action to build trust, demonstrate customer commitment, and satisfy customers so well that they become very loyal to the provider and unlikely to switch to competitors.

customer contact
The level of interaction between the provider and customer needed to deliver the service

Customer contact Not all services require a high degree of **customer contact**, but many do. Customer contact refers to the level of interaction between the service provider and the customer that is necessary to deliver the service. High-contact services include healthcare, real estate, and hair and beauty services. Examples of low-contact services are car repairs and dry cleaning. As the following section explains, the level of customer contact is sometimes used as the basis for classifying services.

Classification of services

Services are a very diverse group of products, and an organization may provide more than one kind. Examples of services include car hire, maintenance services, healthcare, hairdressing, health centres, childcare, domestic services, legal advice, banking, insurance, air travel, education, entertainment, catering, business consulting, dry cleaning and accounting. Nevertheless, services can be meaningfully analyzed using a **five-category classification** scheme:

five-category classification
A method of analyzing services according to five criteria: type of market, degree of labour intensiveness, degree of customer contact, skill of the service provider and goal of the service provider

1 type of market
2 degree of labour intensiveness
3 degree of customer contact
4 skill of the service provider, and
5 goal of the service provider.

Table 10.2 summarizes this scheme.

Type of market Services can be viewed in terms of the market or type of customer they serve – consumer or business.[12] The implications of this distinction are very similar to those for all products and do not require detailed discussion here.

TABLE 10.2 Classification of services

Category	Examples
Type of market	
Consumer	Childcare, legal advice, entertainment
Business	Consulting, caretaking services, installation
Degree of labour intensiveness	
Labour based	Education, haircuts, dentistry
Equipment based	Telecommunications, fitness centres, public transport
Degree of customer contact	
High	Healthcare, hotels, air travel
Low	Home deliveries, postal service
Skill of the service provider	
Professional	Legal advice, healthcare, accountancy
Non-professional	Domestic services, dry cleaning, public transport
Goal of the service provider	
Profit	Financial services, insurance, tourism
Non-profit	Some healthcare, education, government

Degree of labour intensiveness A second way to classify services is by degree of labour intensiveness. Many services – such as domestic cleaning, education and medical care – rely heavily on human labour. Other services – such as telecommunications, fitness centres and public transport – are more equipment intensive.

Labour-based (that is, people-based) services are more susceptible to heterogeneity than most equipment-based services. Marketers of people-based services must recognize that the service providers are often viewed as the service itself. Therefore, strategies relating to selecting, training, motivating and controlling employees are crucial to the success of most service businesses. A bad attitude from Ryanair's ground staff would colour the customer's view not just of the employee concerned but also of the company, the brand and all of its service products. A customer who has flown quite happily with Ryanair for many years may, so prompted, consider taking his or her custom to a rival company.

Degree of customer contact The third way in which services can be classified is by degree of customer contact. High-contact services include healthcare, hotels, property agents and restaurants; low contact services include home deliveries, theatres, dry cleaning and spectator sports.[13] High contact services generally involve actions that are directed towards individuals. Because these services are directed at people, the consumer must be present during production. Sometimes – for example, in the case of a car valeting service – it is possible for the service provider to go to the consumer. However, high-contact services typically require that the consumer goes to the production facility. Consequently, the physical appearance and ambience of the facility may be a major component of the consumer's overall evaluation of the service. The enjoyment of a visit to a health spa stems not just from the quality of the beauty treatments, or the suitability of the dietary or fitness programmes on offer, but also from the décor and furnishings, general ambience, and the abilities and attitude of the staff. Because the consumer must be present during production of a high-contact service, the process of production may be just as important as its final outcome. For example, open-plan banks, quick queue systems and ATM facilities aim to improve the transaction process and make the service more enjoyable for the consumer.

Low-contact service, in contrast, commonly involves actions directed at things. Although consumers may not need to be present during service delivery, their presence may be required to initiate or terminate the service. The Post Office maintains a network of branches, sorting offices and vehicles. The process of sending a parcel from Edinburgh to Cardiff or Lille is lengthy. Yet consumers only need to be present to initiate the service. The appearance of the production facilities and the interpersonal skills of actual service providers are thus not as critical in low-contact services as they are in high-contact services.[14]

Skill of the service provider Skill of the service provider is a fourth way to classify services. Professional services tend to be more complex and more highly regulated than non-professional services. In the case of legal advice, for example, the final product is situation specific. As a result, consumers often do not know what the actual service will involve or how much it will cost until the service is completed.

Goal of the service provider Finally, services can be classified according to whether they are profit or non-profit. The second half of this chapter examines non-profit (not-for-profit) marketing, such as that present in the public sector and charities. Most non-profit organizations provide services rather than goods.

Developing marketing strategies for services

Strategic considerations

In developing marketing strategies, the marketer must first understand what benefits the customer wants, how the company's service offer and brand are perceived relative to the competition and what services consumers buy.[15] In other words, the marketer must develop the right service for the right people at the right price, in the right place with the right positioning and image. The marketer must then communicate with consumers so that they are aware of the need-satisfying services available to them. The key aspects of effective target marketing – as explained in Chapter 6 – and of managing the implementation of the determined marketing strategy apply strongly to the marketing of services.[16]

One of the unique challenges service marketers face is matching supply and demand. Price can be used to help smooth out demand for a service. There are also other ways in which marketers can alter the marketing mix to deal with the problem of fluctuating demand. Through price incentives, advertising and other promotional efforts, marketers can remind consumers of busy times and encourage them to come for service during slack periods. Additionally, the product itself can be altered to cope with fluctuating demand. Restaurants, for example, may change their menus, vary their lighting and décor, open or close the bar, and change the entertainment on offer. A historical tourist destination may stage theatrical events and firework displays to attract customers out of season. Finally, distribution can be modified to reflect changes in demand. For example, some libraries have mobile units that travel to different locations during slack periods.[17]

The strategies that services marketers implement are contingent upon a good understanding of the pattern and determinants of demand. Does the level of demand follow a cycle? What are the causes of this cycle? Are the changes random?[18] An attempt to use price decreases to shift demand for public transport to off-peak periods would achieve only limited success because of the cause of the cyclical demand for public transport. Employees have little control over their working hours and are therefore unable to take advantage of pricing incentives.

Table 10.3 summarizes a range of marketing and non-marketing strategies that service businesses may use to deal with fluctuating demand. Non-marketing strategies essentially involve internal, employee-related actions.[19] They may be the only choices available when fluctuations in demand are random. For example, a strike or natural disaster may cause fluctuations in consumer demand for public transport.

differential advantage
Something desired by the customer that only one company – not its rivals – can offer

Creating a differential advantage in services

The aim of marketing is to satisfy customers, achieving product or brand differentiation with an advantage over competitors' products. This **differential advantage**,

TABLE 10.3 Strategies for coping with fluctuations in demand for services

Marketing strategies	Non-marketing strategies
Use different pricing	Hire extra staff/lay off employees
Alter product	Work employees overtime/part time
Change place/distribution	Cross-train employees
Use promotional efforts	Use employees to perform non-vital tasks during slack times
Modify customer service levels	Subcontract work/seek subcontract work
Alter branding and positioning	Slow the pace of work
Focus on a niche segment	Turn away business

TABLE 10.4 Difficulties in creating a differential advantage in services

Intangibility minimizes product differentiation
No – or little – patent protection exists
Few barriers to entry enable competitors to set up and copy successful initiatives
The interface with customers is difficult to control
Growth is hard to achieve, particularly since key personnel can only be spread so far
Service quality is irregular
It is difficult to improve productivity and lower the cost to the consumer
Innovation leads to imitation
Restrictive regulations abound, particularly in the professions

sometimes termed a 'competitive edge', is determined by customers' perceptions. A differential advantage is something desired by the customer that only one company can offer, as explained in Chapter 2. If the targeted customers do not perceive an advantage, in marketing terms the product offers no benefit over rival products.

For any product, achieving and sustaining a differential advantage is difficult, but for services the challenge is even greater. The intangibility of the service product and the central role of people in its delivery are the prime causes of this difficulty, but, as Table 10.4 shows, there are others, such as difficulties ensuring consistent service quality delivery and the fact that the interface with the customer may be difficult to control.

The difficulty encountered in creating a differential advantage in services makes it even more important that marketing activities are carried out in a systematic and appropriate manner. Thus, services marketers must ensure that the needs of targeted markets are well understood in order to bring service products and the marketing mix into line with customers' exact requirements. There must be a clear appreciation of competitors' service offerings and marketing programmes, and regular efforts are needed to research customers' satisfaction levels. Branding, supported with well-constructed promotional campaigns, is even more central to the reinforcement and communication of any differential advantage for services.

The extended marketing mix for services

The standard marketing mix comprises the '4Ps':

- product
- promotion
- price
- place/distribution.

The discussion about the classification of services has emphasized the importance of three additional elements:

extended marketing mix for services
In addition to the standard '4Ps' marketing mix – product, promotion, price and place/distribution – there are 3Ps: process, physical evidence (ambience) and people

- process
- physical evidence (ambience)
- people.

Collectively, these seven elements, which are sometimes called the '7Ps', form what is termed the **extended marketing mix for services** (see Figure 10.3). It is essential for services marketers to recognize the importance of these additional '3Ps'.

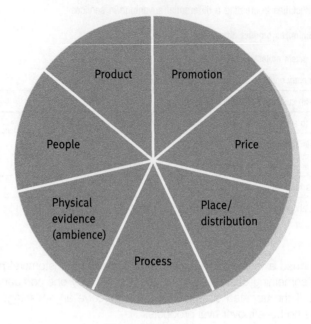

FIGURE 10.3
The extended marketing mix for services

Service quality

The delivery of high-quality services is one of the most important and difficult tasks that any service organization faces. Because of their unique characteristics, services are very difficult to evaluate. Hence customers must look closely at service quality when comparing services. **Service quality** is defined as customers' perception of how well a service meets or exceeds their expectations.[20] Service quality is judged by customers, not the organization. This distinction is critical because it forces services marketers to examine their quality from the customer's viewpoint. For example, a dental surgery may view service quality as having friendly and knowledgeable employees. However, the customers may be more concerned with waiting time, cleanliness and the effectiveness of patient pain relief. Thus it is important for service organizations to determine what customers expect and then develop service products that meet or exceed those expectations.

service quality
Customers' perception of how well a service meets or exceeds their expectations

Customer evaluation of service quality

The biggest obstacle for customers in evaluating service quality is the intangible nature of the service. How can customers evaluate something they cannot see, feel, taste, smell or hear? The evaluation of a good is much easier because all goods possess 'search qualities' in the form of tangible attributes, such as colour, style, size, feel or fit, that can be evaluated prior to purchase. Trying on a new coat and taking a car for a test drive are examples of how customers evaluate search qualities. Services, on the other hand, have very few search qualities; instead, they abound in experience and credence qualities. Experience qualities, such as taste, satisfaction or pleasure, are attributes that can be assessed only during the purchase and consumption of a service. Restaurants and holidays are examples of services high in experience qualities. Credence qualities are attributes that customers may be unable to evaluate even after the purchase and consumption the service. Examples of services high in credence qualities are surgical operations, vehicle repairs, consulting and legal representation. Most consumers lack the knowledge or skills to evaluate the quality of these types of service. Consequently they must place a great deal of faith in the integrity and competence of the service provider.

Despite the difficulties in evaluating quality, service quality may be the only way customers can choose one service over another. For this reason, service marketers live or die by understanding how consumers judge service quality. This is one reason behind many retail banks now returning staff to their branches and refocusing on their branches as a key part of their customer relationship building, as described in the Marketing Insight box on page 322. Table 10.5 defines five dimensions consumers use when evaluating service quality:

1 tangibles

2 reliability

3 responsiveness

4 assurance

5 empathy.

Note that all of these dimensions have links to employee performance. Of the five, reliability is the most important in determining customer evaluations of service quality.[21]

Services marketers pay a great deal of attention to the tangibles dimension of service quality. Tangible attributes, or search qualities, such as the appearance of facilities and employees, are often the only aspects of a service that can be viewed before purchases and consumption. Therefore, services marketers must ensure that these tangible elements are consistent with the overall image of the service product.

Except for the tangibles dimension, the criteria that customers use to judge service quality are intangible. For instance, how does a customer judge reliability? Since dimensions such as reliability cannot be examined with the senses, consumers must rely on other ways of judging service criteria. One of the most important factors in customer judgements of service quality is **service expectations.** These are influenced by past experiences with the service, word-of-mouth communication from other customers and the service company's own advertising. For example, customers are usually eager to try a new restaurant, especially when friends recommend it. These same customers may also have seen advertisements placed by the restaurant. As a result, these customers have an idea of what to expect when they visit the restaurant for the first time. When they finally dine at the restaurant, the quality they experience will change the expectations they have for their next visit and affect their own comments to friends. That is why providing consistently high service quality is important. If the quality of a restaurant, or any services marketer, begins to deteriorate, customers will alter their own expectations and word-of-mouth communication to others accordingly.

service expectations
A factor used in judging service quality involving impressions from past experiences, word-of-mouth communication and the company's advertising

Delivering exceptional service quality

Providing high-quality service on a consistent basis is very difficult. All consumers have experienced examples of poor service: long queues at retail checkouts, trains and buses that are late or rude cinema employees. Obviously, it is impossible for a service organization to ensure exceptional service quality 100 per cent of the time. However, there are many steps that can be taken to increase the likelihood of providing high-quality service. First, though, the service company must understand the four **service quality factors**. As shown in Table 10.5, they are:

service quality factors
Factors that increase the likelihood of providing high-quality service: understanding customer expectations, service quality specifications, employee performance, managing service expectations

1 analysis of customer expectations

2 service quality specifications

3 employee performance

4 managing service expectations.[22]

We're committed to helping you: banks remember customer service

Building customer relationships

A trend for close to 20 years has been for banks to close rural branches and reduce the number of town-centre branches. Many Victorian banks, with their large chambers, grand facades and prime locations, have been turned into bars or restaurants. TV viewers in the UK will have seen a well-known retail bank advertising the last of its branches being turned into wine bars: instead it was decided that branches were to be kept open. A separate advertisement revealed that customers would once again be able to talk directly to staff in their local branch, rather than only to anonymous personnel in a far-flung faceless call centre. In 2010, NatWest went even further, announcing its *Customer Charter* and stating that it intended to be the UK's most helpful bank by 2011, to be verified via independent research, with a focus on in-branch customer service. So, why the about-turn in these policies?

For some time pundits had forecast the demise of the bank branch, as first telephone banking and then the Internet enabled customers to conduct their transactions and make enquiries via telecommunications. The era of the call centre permitted banks to make further cost savings by directing apparently local calls to regional call centres rather than into branches. This also reduced the number of personnel in branches and often removed mortgage, investment and insurance specialists altogether. In effect, for many customers, this had the impact of further reducing or downgrading the appeal of visiting branches. Mergers and acquisitions in the banking sector have also encouraged a reduction in branch numbers, as newly merged chains close and relocate branches in order to reduce duplication and operating costs. From 1999 to 2003, over 1700 UK bank branches closed.

There is little doubt that telephone, e-banking and now mobile apps have become increasingly popular. Nevertheless, there is talk of an end to the culling of bank branches. This is because marketing research reveals that not all customers wish to deal with call centres or to conduct their business via a PC or smartphone. Many customers find face-to-face contact reassuring, and only the bank branch environment provides this direct interaction.

The role of the branch may be rejuvenated even further. Leading consultants Booz Allen Hamilton produced a report pointedly entitled 'Implementing the Customer-centric Bank – the Rebirth of the Forgotten Branch'. The report concluded that 90 per cent of customer relationships are made – and lost – in branches. Even customers utilizing e-banking often need to visit branches, and the vast majority of customers still believe that complex enquiries or topics perceived as risky by the consumer are better handled face to face, inside a bank branch. Unfortunately, the removal of specialist staff from many branches and the downgrading of the majority of branches to simple transaction-processing points, have led to a growing level of customer dissatisfaction with bank branches.

Now, in a strategy shift, the leading high-street banking brands are acknowledging that they must reinvest in their bank branches: more and better trained staff, improved IT enabling speedy processing of enquiries and creating more opportunities for the cross-selling of products, plus enhanced interior designs. As part of this shift in emphasis, different staff – with a greater customer orientation – are required. NatWest announced that it planned to invest in additional members of branch staff. Barclays, Santander and the other leading brands quickly followed suit.

While efficiency and reducing operating costs are still important to the boards of these companies, there is an acceptance that customers expect improved service and that many prefer the bank branch as the setting for interactions with, it is hoped, more customer-oriented personnel.

Sources: NatWest 2003–12; Barclays, 2004–12; 'Back to the branch', *Marketing*, 26 May 2004, pp. 30–2; Fujitsu Services, 2003–8; Box Technologies, 2007; **http://www.natwest.com/personal.ashx**, 8 March 2011; **http://www.natwest.com/global/customer-charter.ashx**, March 2011.

Analysis of customer expectations Providers need to understand customer expectations when designing a service to meet or exceed those expectations. Only then can they deliver good service. Customers usually have two levels of expectations: desired and acceptable. The desired level of expectations is what the customer really wants. If this level of expectations is provided, the customer would be very satisfied. The acceptable level is viewed as a reasonable level of

TABLE 10.5 Dimensions of service quality

Dimension	Evaluation criteria	Examples
Tangibles Physical evidence of the service	Appearance of physical facilities Appearance of service personnel Tools or equipment used to provide the service	A clean and professional-looking doctor's office A clean and neatly dressed repair person The appearance of food in a restaurant The equipment used in a medical examination
Reliability Consistency and dependability in performing the service	Accuracy of billing or recordkeeping Performing services when promised	An accurate bank statement A confirmed hotel reservation An airline flight departing and arriving on time
Responsiveness Willingness or readiness of employees to provide the service	Returning customer phone calls Providing prompt service Handling urgent requests	A server refilling a customer's cup of tea without being asked An ambulance arriving within three minutes
Assurance Knowledge/competence of employees and ability to convey trust and confidence	Knowledge and skills of employees Company name and reputation Personal characteristics of employees	A highly trained financial adviser A known and respected service provider A doctor's bedside manner
Empathy Caring and individual attention provided by employees	Listening to customer needs Caring about customers' interests Providing personalized attention	A store employee listening to and trying to understand a customer's complaint A nurse counselling a heart patient

Sources: Adapted from Leonard L. Berry and A. Parasuraman, *Marketing Services: Competing through Quality* (New York: Free Press, 1991); Valarie A. Zeithaml, A. Parasuraman and Leonard L. Berry, *Delivering Quality Service: Balancing Customer Perceptions and Expectations* (New York: Free Press, 1990); A. Parasuraman, Leonard L. Berry and Valarie A. Zeithaml, 'An empirical examination of relationships in an extended service quality model', *Marketing Science Institute Working Paper Series*, report no. 90–112 (Cambridge, MA: Marketing Science Institute, 1990), p. 29.

customer's zone of tolerance
The difference between the customer's desired level of expectations and the customer's acceptable level of expectations

performance that the customer considers as being adequate. The difference between these two levels of expectations is called the **customer's zone of tolerance**.[23]

Service marketers sometimes use marketing research, such as surveys and focus groups, as a means of discovering customer needs and expectations. Other services companies, such as hotel chains, seek customer feedback using comment cards. Another approach is to ask employees. Because customer-contact employees interact daily with customers, they often know what customers want from the company. Service managers should interact regularly with their employees to ensure that they remain in touch with this useful source of information.

Service quality specifications Once an organization understands its customers' needs, it must establish goals to help ensure good service delivery. These goals, or service specifications, are typically set in terms of employee or machine performance. For example, a bank may require its employees to conform to a dress code. The same bank may insist that all incoming phone calls are answered by the third ring. Specifications like these can be very important in providing quality service as long as they are linked to customer needs.

Service managers who are visibly committed to service quality become role models for all employees in the organization.[24] Such commitment motivates personnel at all levels in the organization, from customer-contact employees through to senior managers, to comply with service specifications.

Employee performance Once an organization sets service quality standards and managers are committed to them, the organization must find ways to ensure that customer contact employees perform their jobs well. Contact employees in many service industries – bank tellers, flight cabin crew, waiters, sales assistants – are often the least trained and lowest-paid members of the organization. Yet these individuals represent the most important link to the customer, and thus their performance is critical to customer perceptions of service quality.[25] Well-managed recruitment and training are essential if employees are to understand properly how to do their jobs. Providing information about customers, service specifications and the organization itself, during the training promotes this understanding.[26]

The use of evaluation and remuneration systems plays a part in employee performance. Many service employees are evaluated and rewarded on the basis of output measures such as sales volume for car salespeople, or lack of errors during work for data-input administrators. Such systems may overlook certain key aspects of job performance: friendliness, teamwork, effort and customer satisfaction. As the importance of customer relationship building comes more to the fore, companies are increasingly considering that customer-oriented measures of performance may be a better basis for evaluation and reward. For example, Dun & Bradstreet has tied employee commissions to customer satisfaction surveys rather than sales volume.[27] This type of system stimulates employees to take care of customer needs rather than focus solely on sales or profits.

Managing service expectations Because expectations are so significant in customer evaluations of service quality, service companies recognize that they must set realistic expectations about the service they can provide. These expectations can be set through advertising and good internal communication. In their advertisements, service companies make promises about the kind of service they will deliver. In fact, a service company is forced to make promises since the intangibility of services prevents it from showing them in the advertisement. However, the advertiser should not promise more than it can deliver; doing otherwise may mean disappointed customers.

To deliver on promises made, a company needs to have good internal communication among its departments – especially management, advertising and operations. Assume, for example, that a supermarket's advertising guarantees that shoppers will not have to queue at the checkout for more than ten minutes. In order to meet this promise, the retailer will need to ensure that its operations and staff levels can support such a guarantee. Failure to do so may result in customers' service expectations not being met, with a consequent loss of credibility for the company.

Word-of-mouth and digital communication from other customers also shape customer expectations. However, service companies cannot manage this 'advertising' directly. The best way to ensure positive word-of-mouth communication is to provide exceptional service quality. It has been estimated that customers tell four times as many people about bad service as they do about good service. Consequently, services marketers must provide four good service experiences for every bad experience just to break even. Social media in this digital area have speeded up the likelihood of consumers informing others about a specific brand.

The dominance of relationships and service

Many marketers argue that services are now more important than goods, with services marketing forming 'a new dominant logic for marketing, one in which service provision rather than goods is fundamental to economic exchange'. Vargo and Lusch (2006) have popularized this notion in recent years, suggesting that marketing has moved from a goods-dominant view, in which tangible output and discrete transactions were central, to a service-dominant view, in which intangibility, exchange processes, and relationships are central. Certainly the growth of interest in maintaining ongoing relationships (see Chapter 1) with customers and building the augmented product (see Chapter 8) support this contention.

Non-profit marketing

Marketing was broadly defined earlier as a set of individual and organizational activities aimed at facilitating and expediting satisfying exchanges in a dynamic environment through the creation, distribution, promotion and pricing of goods, services and ideas. Most of the concepts and approaches to managing marketing activities discussed above also apply to non-profit situations such as the public sector and charities. This is largely why **social marketing** has emerged as a sub-set of the marketing discipline. Of special relevance is the material offered in the first half of this chapter, because many non-profit organizations provide services. As a discipline, marketing is becoming increasingly important in the non-profit sector. Social marketing uses tools and techniques from commercial marketing to encourage positive behavioural changes, such as quitting smoking, reducing alcohol consumption, minimizing anti-social behaviours, reducing carbon footprint and to raise awareness of important social issues. The health and wellbeing of individuals, society and the planet are at the core of social marketing.

Non-profit marketing includes marketing activities conducted by individuals and organizations to achieve some goal other than the ordinary business goals of profit, market share or return on investment. Charities, the voluntary sector, not-for-profit organizations and NGOs form the third sector and many utilize the marketing concept and toolkit. Although a non-profit organization has primary goals that are non-economic, it may be required to become involved in 'profit making' in order to achieve those goals.[28] Thus a charity, such as the Red Cross, must raise funds to support its charitable work. Non-profit marketing can be divided into two categories: non-profit organization marketing and social marketing. Non-profit organization marketing is the application of marketing concepts and techniques to organizations such as hospitals and colleges. Social marketing is the development of programmes designed to influence the acceptability of social ideas, such as getting people to recycle more newspapers, plastics and aluminium, or promoting the regeneration of a deprived inner-city area.[29] **Cause-related marketing** is the linking of an organization's products to a particular social cause, Body Shop-style, on an ongoing or short term basis.

As discussed in Chapter 1, an exchange situation exists when individuals, groups or organizations possess something that they are willing to give up in an exchange. In non-profit marketing, the objects of the exchange may not be specified in financial terms. Usually, such exchanges are facilitated through **negotiation** – mutual discussion or communication of terms and methods – and **persuasion** – convincing and prevailing upon by argument. Often, negotiation and persuasion are conducted without reference to, or awareness of, marketing's role in transactions. The discussion here concerns the non-profit performance of marketing activities, whether exchange takes place or not.

The rest of this chapter first examines the concept of non-profit marketing to determine how it differs from marketing activities in commercial organizations. Next it explores the overall objectives of non-profit organizations, their marketing objectives and the development of their marketing strategies. The discussion closes by illustrating how a marketing audit can control marketing activities and promote marketing awareness in a non-profit organization.

social marketing
Social marketing uses tools and techniques from commercial marketing to encourage positive behavioural changes, such as quitting smoking, reducing alcohol consumption, minimizing anti-social behaviours or reducing carbon footprint. The health and wellbeing of individuals, society and the planet are at the core of social marketing

non-profit marketing
Activities conducted by individuals and organizations to achieve some goal other than the ordinary business goals of profit, market share or return on investment

cause-related marketing
The linking of an organization's products to a particular social cause on a short-term or ongoing basis

negotiation
Mutual discussion or communication of terms and methods in an exchange situation

persuasion
The act of prevailing upon someone by argument to facilitate an exchange

Why is non-profit marketing different?

Traditionally and mistakenly, people have not thought of non-profit exchange activities as marketing; but consider the following example. Warwick Business School used to promote its degree courses solely through the University of Warwick's prospectuses. In the early 1980s, its main programmes received small advertising budgets. As courses were improved, the wider use of advertising increased awareness of the school and its programmes. The school is not commercially driven in the context of seeking profits for stakeholders: any income from fees, training and consultancy is reinvested into its degree programmes and facilities. A new corporate identity was developed by Coley Porter Bell of London, and each degree programme, led by the MBA, developed its own full marketing mix and more extensive promotional strategy – all in line with the school's new mission statement. Even when the corporate identity was updated, the school continued to ensure a good fit between the marketing mixes for its different programmes and its overall strategy. As the school moved into the twenty-first century, it became a budget holder within the university and managed its own budgets. This move facilitated the appointment of a marketing director, public relations manager and external affairs manager. These personnel developed target market strategies, updated the school's marketing programmes and monitored the performance of these marketing activities, just as marketers in a for-profit company would do. Many university departments and state-maintained schools are now engaging in developing a marketing strategy and associated marketing programmes.

Many non-profit organizations strive for effective marketing activities. Charitable organizations and supporters of social causes are major non-profit marketers. Political parties, unions, religious groups and student organizations also perform marketing activities, yet they are not considered businesses. Whereas the chief beneficiary of a business enterprise is whoever owns or holds shares in it, the main beneficiaries of a non-profit organization are its clients, its members or the public at large.

Non-profit organizations have a greater opportunity for creativity than most business organizations, but trustees or board members of these organizations may find it harder to evaluate the performance of doctors, lecturers or social workers than it is for sales managers to evaluate the performance of salespeople in a for-profit organization.

Another way in which non-profit marketing differs from for-profit marketing is that non-profit organizations are sometimes quite controversial. Amnesty International, the RSPCA and Greenpeace spend lavishly on lobbying efforts to persuade government and even the courts to support their interests, in part because acceptance of their aims is not always guaranteed. Although marketing aims to provide a body of knowledge to further an organization's goals, it does not attempt to judge their appropriateness. It is for individuals to decide whether they approve of an organization's goal orientation. Most marketers would agree that profit and consumer satisfaction are appropriate goals for business enterprises, but there may be considerable disagreement about the goals of a controversial non-profit organization.

Non-profit marketing objectives

The basic aim of non-profit organizations is to obtain a desired response from a target market. The use of social marketing principles is directly pertinent to third sector non-profit organizations, as they seek to target and convey their messages. The response could be a change in values, a financial contribution, the donation of services or some other type of exchange. Non-profit marketing objectives are shaped by the nature of the exchange and the goals of the organization. BBC-sponsored Children in Need and Comic Relief telethons have raised millions of pounds. Telethons have three specific marketing objectives:

1 to raise funds to support programmes
2 to plead a case on behalf of disadvantaged groups
3 to inform the public about the organization's programmes and services.

Tactically, telethons have received support by choosing good causes; generating extensive grass-roots support; portraying disadvantaged people in a positive and dignified way; developing national, regional and local support; and providing quality entertainment.[30] Figure 10.4 illustrates how the exchanges and the purpose of the organization can influence marketing objectives. These objectives are used as examples and may or may not apply to specific organizations.

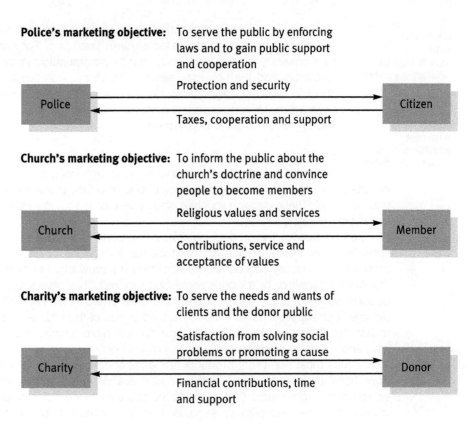

Police's marketing objective: To serve the public by enforcing laws and to gain public support and cooperation

Police — Protection and security → Citizen
Police ← Taxes, cooperation and support — Citizen

Church's marketing objective: To inform the public about the church's doctrine and convince people to become members

Church — Religious values and services → Member
Church ← Contributions, service and acceptance of values — Member

Charity's marketing objective: To serve the needs and wants of clients and the donor public

Charity — Satisfaction from solving social problems or promoting a cause → Donor
Charity ← Financial contributions, time and support — Donor

FIGURE 10.4
Examples of marketing objectives for different types of exchange

Source: Philip Kotler 'Examples of marketing objectives for different types of exchange' from *Marketing for Non-profit Organisations*, 2nd edition, copyright © 1982, p. 38. Reprinted by permission of Pearson Education, Inc., Upper Saddle River, NJ.

Non-profit marketing objectives should state the rationale for an organization's existence. An organization that defines its marketing objective merely in terms of providing a product can be left without a purpose if the product becomes obsolete. However, serving and adapting to the perceived needs and wants of a target public or market, enhances an organization's chances of surviving and achieving its goals.

Developing non-profit marketing strategies

Non-profit organizations must also develop marketing strategies by defining and analyzing a target market, and creating and maintaining a marketing mix that appeals to that market. They practice the techniques promoted by social marketing (see Chapter 1), as described in this chapter's concluding case study, and apply many of the concepts routinely deployed by commercial marketers in for-profit businesses.

target public
A collective of individuals who have an interest in or concern about an organization, a product or a social cause

Target markets The concept of target markets needs to be revised slightly to apply to non-profit organizations. Whereas a business is supposed to have target groups that are potential purchasers of its product, a non-profit organization may attempt to serve many diverse groups. A **target public** is broadly defined as a collective of individuals who have an interest in or concern about an organization, a product or a social cause. The terms target market and target public are difficult to distinguish for many non-profit organizations. The target public for campaigns promoting healthy eating is adults and teenagers of all ages. However, the target market for many of the advertisements may be individuals currently suffering from a weight problem. When an organization is concerned about changing values or obtaining a response from the public, it views the public as a market.[31]

client publics
In non-profit organizations, direct consumers of a product

general publics
In non-profit organizations, indirect consumers of a product

In non-profit organizations, direct consumers of a product are called **client publics** and indirect consumers are called **general publics**.[32] For example, the client public for a university is its student body, and its general public includes parents, graduates, employers and the university senate. The client public usually receives most of the attention when an organization develops a marketing strategy. The techniques and approaches to segmenting and defining target markets discussed in Chapters 6 also apply to non-profit target markets.

Developing a marketing mix A marketing mix strategy limits choices and directs marketing activities towards achieving organizational goals. The strategy should outline or develop a blueprint for making decisions about product, place/distribution, promotion, price and personnel. These decision variables should be blended to serve the target market as specified in the marketing strategy.

When considering the product variable, it is important to recognize that non-profit organizations deal more often with ideas and services than with goods. This means it is crucial for organizations to have clearly defined exactly what they are providing. For example, what products do the Women's Institute or a work's social club provide? They offer a forum for social gatherings, courses, outings and a sense of cooperation. Their products are more difficult to define than the average business product. As indicated in the first part of this chapter, the intangibility of services means that the marketing of ideas and concepts is more abstract than the marketing of tangibles, and it requires considerable effort to present benefits.

Because most non-profit products are ideas and services, distribution decisions relate to how these ideas and services will be made available to clients. If the product is an idea, selecting the right media (the promotional strategy) to communicate the idea will facilitate distribution. The availability of services is closely related to product decisions. By nature, services consist of assistance, convenience and availability. Availability is part of the total service. For example, making a product such as health services available on the high street calls for knowledge of such retailing concepts as site location analysis and logistics management.

Developing a channel of distribution to coordinate and facilitate the flow of non-profit products to clients is a necessary task, but in a non-profit setting the traditional concept of the marketing channel may need to be reviewed. The independent wholesalers available to a business enterprise do not exist in most non-profit situations. Instead, a very short channel – non-profit organization to client – is prevalent, because production and consumption of ideas and services are often simultaneous. For example, local government departments often deal directly with householders. Charities generally pitch their fundraising activities directly to their target customers/householders/donors.

Making promotional decisions may be the first sign that non-profit organizations are performing marketing activities. Non-profit organizations use advertising and publicity to communicate with clients and the public. As the Case Study at the end of this chapter explains, direct mail remains the primary means of fundraising for services such as those provided by Christian Aid and UNICEF. In addition to direct mail, organizations such as these use press advertising, public relations and sponsorship. Many non-profit organizations now have websites to promote their causes. Face-to-face selling is also used by non-profit organizations, although it may be called something else. Churches and charities rely on personal selling when they send volunteers to recruit new members or request donations. The armed forces use personal selling when recruiting officers and when attempting to persuade men and women to enlist. Special events to obtain funds, communicate ideas or provide services are sales promotion activities. Competitions, entertainment and prizes offered to attract donations resemble the sales promotion activities of business enterprises. Amnesty International, for example, has held worldwide concert tours, featuring artists such as Sting and Phil Collins, to raise funds and increase public awareness of political prisoners around the world.

The number of advertising agencies that are donating their time for public service announcements (PSAs) or public information films is increasing, and the quality of print PSAs is improving. Not-for-profit groups are becoming more interested in the impact of advertising on their organizations, and they realize that second-rate PSAs can cause a credibility loss.[33] For example, each year the UK government's 'Don't drink and drive' campaign, usually timed to coincide with the Christmas and New Year period, is a high-spending, hard-hitting programme of advertisements designed to attract as much attention as possible.

Although product and promotion techniques may require only slight modification when applied to non-profit organizations, the pricing structure is generally quite different and the decision-making more complex. The different pricing concepts that the non-profit organization faces include pricing in user and donor markets. There are two types of monetary pricing: fixed and variable. Membership fees, such as the amount paid to become a member of an amateur operatic society, represent a fixed approach to pricing, whereas fundraising activities that lead to donations that help with the society's running costs represent a variable pricing structure.[34]

The broadest definition of price (valuation) must be used when considering non-profit products or services. Financial price, an exact monetary value, may or may not be charged for a non-profit product. Economists recognize the giving up of alternatives as a cost. **Opportunity cost** is the value of the benefit that is given up by selecting one alternative rather than another. This traditional economic view of price means that if a non-profit organization can persuade someone to donate time to a cause, or to change his or her behaviour, the alternatives given up are a cost to – or a price paid by – the individual. Volunteers who answer phones for a university counselling service or suicide hotline, for example, give up the time they could have spent studying or doing other things, as well as the income they might have earned from working in a business organization.

opportunity cost
The value of the benefit that is given up by selecting one alternative instead of another

For other non-profit organizations, financial price is an important part of the marketing mix. Non-profit organizations today are raising money by increasing the prices of their services or starting to charge for services if they have not done so before. For example, many museums and art galleries, which traditionally allowed free entry to their exhibits, are now charging nominal entrance fees. Organizations like these often use marketing research to determine for what kinds of product people will pay.[35] The pricing strategies of non-profit organizations often stress public and client welfare over equalization of costs and revenues. If additional funds are needed to cover costs, then donations, contributions or grants may be solicited.

The additional elements of the marketing mix for services are also important in non-profit marketing. The physical environment quite often poses problems: subscribers and donors want an organization with the appearance of business-like efficiency without any extravagance. It is important that funds do not appear to have been wasted on luxuries. The process for transactions is increasingly important: regular donors are offered direct debits, automatic payment methods, and regular information packs or leaflets detailing the recipient organization's activities, expenditures and plans. People, too, are important: capable administrators, sympathetic helpers, trustworthy fundraisers – they, too, must project a caring yet efficient image to the client and general publics.

Controlling non-profit marketing activities

To control marketing activities in non-profit organizations, managers use information obtained in the marketing audit to make sure that goals are achieved. Table 10.6 lists several summary statistics that are useful for both planning and control. Control is designed to check that the activities outlined in the marketing strategy have taken place and to take corrective action where any deviations are found. The purpose of control is not only to point out errors but to revise organizational goals and marketing objectives as necessary. One way to measure the impact of an advertisement is to audit the number of requests for information or applications, such as those received by Amnesty International, the Army or the WWF. Hits on an organization's website via leading search engines are also counted (see Figure 10.5).

TABLE 10.6 Examples of data useful in controlling non-business marketing activities

1 Product mix offerings
  A Types of product or services
  B Number of organizations offering the product or service
	1 By organization
	  2 Total industry wide
	C Number of volunteers
	  1 By organization
	  2 Total industry wide

2 Financial resources
  A Types of funding used
    1 Local government grants
    2 Government grants
    3 Foundations
    4 Public appeals
    5 Fees/charges
  B Number using each type of funding
  C Number using combinations of funding sources
	D Number of customers/users serviced
	  1 By type of service
	  2 By organization
	  3 Total industry wide
	4 Facilities
	  A Number and type
	    1 By organization
	    2 Total industry wide

3 Size
  A Budget (cash flows)
  B Number of employees
	B Location
	    1 By address
	    2 By postcode

Source: Adapted from Philip D. Cooper and George E. McIlvain, 'Factors influencing marketing's ability to assist non-profit organizations', John H. Summey and Ronald D. Taylor, eds, 'Evolving Marketing Thought for 1980', *Proceedings of the Southern Marketing Association* (19–22 November 1980), p. 315. Used by permission.

Many potential contributors decide which charities to support based on the amount of money actually used for charitable purposes. Charities are more aggressively examining their own performance and effectiveness. For example, compared with other charities, the Salvation Army contributes the majority of every pound (£) it receives to the needy; its employees are largely volunteers, who work for almost nothing. Charities are making internal changes to increase their effectiveness, and many are hiring professional managers and fundraisers to help with strategic planning in developing short-term and long-range goals, marketing strategies and promotional plans.

To control non-profit marketing activities, managers must make a proper inventory of activities performed, and be prepared to adjust or correct deviations from standards. Knowing where and how to look for deviations and knowing what types of deviation to expect are especially important in non-profit situations. Because non-profit marketing activities may not be perceived as marketing, managers must define clearly what activity is being examined and how it should function.

It may be difficult to control non-profit marketing activities, because it is often hard to determine whether goals are being achieved. A support group for victims of childhood abuse that wants to inform community members of its services may not be able to find out whether it is communicating with those people who need assistance. Surveying to discover the percentage of the population that is aware of the assistance the group offers can show whether the awareness objective has been achieved, but it fails to indicate what percentage of victims of abuse has been assisted. The detection and correction of deviations from standards are certainly major purposes of control, but standards must support the organization's overall goals. Managers can refine goals by examining the results that are being achieved and analyzing the ramifications of those results.

Techniques for controlling overall marketing performance must be compatible with the nature of an organization's operations. Obviously, it is necessary to control the marketing budget in most non-profit organizations, but budgetary control is not tied to standards of profit and loss; responsible management of funds is the objective. Central control responsibility can facilitate

FIGURE 10.5
Many non-business organizations judge the effectiveness of their marketing in terms of hits on their websites and requests for information
Source: Logo courtesy of Google

orderly, efficient administration and planning. For example, most universities evaluate graduating students' progress to control and improve the quality of education provided. The audit phase typically relies on questionnaires sent to students and eventual employers. The employer completes a questionnaire to indicate the former student's progress; the graduate completes a questionnaire to indicate what additional concepts or skills were needed to perform duties. In addition, a number of faculty members may interview certain employers and former students to obtain information for control purposes. Results of the audit are used to develop corrective action if university standards have not been met. Corrective action could include an evaluation of the deficiency and a revision of the curriculum.

Summary

Services are experiential, intangible, dominant products that cannot physically be possessed, the result of applying human or mechanical efforts to people or objects. The importance of services in the economy is increasing. There are *consumer services* and *business services.*

Services have a number of distinguishing characteristics: *intangibility, inseparability* of production and consumption, *perishability, heterogeneity, client-based relationships* and *customer contact.* Intangibility places greater importance on *search, experience* and *credence qualities.* Services can be viewed in terms of a *five-category classification:* type of market, degree of labour intensiveness, degree of customer contact, skill of the service provider and goal of the service provider.

Fluctuating demand is a major problem for most service organizations. Marketing strategies and the marketing mix as well as non-marketing strategies and primarily internal, employee-based actions can be used to deal with the problem. Before attempting to undertake any such strategies, however, services marketers must understand the patterns and determinants of demand. The intangibility of the service product, together with the importance of the people component of the extended marketing mix for services, leads to significant difficulties in creating and sustaining a *differential advantage.*

The basic marketing mix is augmented for services through the addition of people, physical evidence (ambience) and the process of transaction in order to produce the '7Ps' or the *extended marketing mix for services.*

Service quality is the perception of how well a service meets or exceeds customers' *service expectations.* The intangibility of services makes service quality very difficult for customers to evaluate. When competing services are very similar, service quality may be the only way for customers to distinguish between them. It is crucial for marketers to comprehend the four *service quality factors:* (1) understanding customer expectations, (2) service quality specifications, (3) employee performance and (4) managing service expectations. To achieve customer satisfaction, a service must fall within the *customer's zone of tolerance.*

Non-profit marketing includes marketing activities conducted by individuals and organizations to achieve goals other than normal business goals. The chief beneficiary of a business enterprise is whoever owns or holds shares in the business, but the beneficiary of a non-profit enterprise should be its clients, its members or its public at large. The goals of a non-profit organization reflect its unique philosophy or mission. Some non-profit organizations have very controversial goals, but many organizations exist to further generally accepted social causes.

The marketing objective of non-profit organizations is to obtain a desired response from a target market, often through *negotiation* or *persuasion*. Developing a non-profit marketing strategy consists of defining and analyzing a target market, and creating and maintaining a marketing mix. *Target, client* and *general publics* must all be identified. In non-profit marketing, the product is usually an idea or service. Distribution is involved not so much with the movement of goods as with the communication of ideas and the delivery of services, which results in a very short marketing channel. Promotion is very important in non-profit marketing; personal selling, sales promotion, advertising and publicity are all used to communicate ideas and inform people about services. Price is more difficult to define in non-profit marketing because of *opportunity costs* and the difficulty of quantifying the values exchanged.

It is important to control marketing strategies in non-profit situations. Control is designed to identify what activities have occurred in conformity with marketing strategy and to take corrective action where deviations are found. The standards against which performance is measured must support the non-profit organization's overall goals.

Key links

This chapter about marketing services should be read in conjunction with:

● Chapter 8, the overview of the product ingredient of the marketing mix.

● Chapter 9, exploring the management of product portfolios.

● Chapter 6, which examines the creation of target market strategy.

Important terms

Service
Consumer services
Business services
Intangibility
Search qualities
Experience qualities
Credence qualities
Inseparability
Perishability
Heterogeneity
Client-based relationships
Customer contact
Five-category classification
Differential advantage
Extended marketing mix for services
Service quality
Service expectations
Service quality factors
Customer's zone of tolerance

Social marketing
Non-profit marketing
Cause-related marketing
Negotiation
Persuasion
Target public
Client publics
General publics
Opportunity cost

Discussion and review questions

1 Identify and discuss the distinguishing characteristics of services. What problems do these characteristics present to marketers?

2 What is the significance of 'tangibles' in service industries?

3 Use the five-category classification scheme (page 316) to analyze a car valeting service, and discuss the implications for marketing mix development.

4 How do search, experience and credence qualities affect the way consumers view and evaluate services?

5 What additional elements must be included in the marketing mix for services? Why?

6 Why is it difficult to create and maintain a differential advantage in many service organizations?

7 Analyze the demand for the hire of sunbeds and discuss ways to cope with fluctuating demand.

8 What is the most important dimension in determining customer evaluation of service quality?

9 Compare and contrast the controversial aspects of non-profit versus business marketing.

10 Relate the concepts of product, place/distribution, promotion and price to a marketing strategy aimed at preventing drug abuse.

11 What are the differences between clients, publics and consumers? What is the difference between a target public and a target market?

12 Discuss the development of a marketing strategy for a university. What marketing decisions should be made in developing this strategy?

13 Why is the concept of market segmentation relevant here?

Recommended readings

Berry, L., *On Great Service* (The Free Press, 1995).

Gilmore, A., *Services Marketing and Management* (Sage, 2003).

Grönroos, C., *Service Management and Marketing* (Wiley, 2007).

Kasper, H., van Helsdingen, P. and de Vries Jr, W., *Services Marketing Management: An International Perspective* (Wiley, 1999).

Lovelock, C.H. and Wirtz, J., *Services Marketing* (Pearson Education, 2010).

Lusch, R. and Vargo, S., *The Service-Dominant Logic of Marketing* (Sharpe, 2006).

Palmer, A., *Principles of Services Marketing* (McGraw-Hill, 2011).

Zeithaml, V., Bitner, M. and Gremler, D., *Services Marketing* (McGraw-Hill, 2012).

Internet exercise

As Internet usage rises, the number of people using this method to communicate with friends, family and colleagues is also increasing. The founders of the Friends Reunited website spotted an opportunity to provide a service that helped people to get back in touch with friends and acquaintances. Since its launch, its range of services and coverage have increased significantly. Take a look at this online organization at: **www. friendsreunited.co.uk**

1 Classify Friends Reunited's product in terms of its position on the service continuum.

2 How does Friends Reunited enhance customer service and foster its relationship with customers through its Internet marketing efforts?

3 Discuss the degree to which experience and credence qualities exist in the services offered by Friends Reunited.

Applied mini-case

Express carriers such as TNT, UPS and Federal Express do much more than provide a swift delivery service for letters and packages. As the sector has become more competitive and eShopping increases the numbers of packages delivered each day, the expectations of clients have also risen. The home delivery service for many well-known brands is subcontracted to the major carriers, which in effect impact through their reliability and service levels on their clients' brand reputation and customer satisfaction. Inventory handling, assistance with customs clearance, barcoded tracking that can be monitored over the Web and the provision of a responsive customer services function, are just some of the extra services that are now expected as part of the product offering. Some clients even require their carriers to play a role in the packing process in their pursuit of a delivery solution that eases the movement of packages from the point of dispatch to the point of receipt.

Question

Assume the role of a management consultant who has been retained by one of the express carriers to undertake an analysis of service quality. Prepare a report that outlines the key dimensions of service quality.

Social marketing for charities

Case study

Marketing is not an activity that consumers automatically associate with charities. Instead they link advertising and sales promotion with big brands such as Coca-Cola, McDonald's and Virgin. In reality, while commercial organizations such as these seek high returns and profits, charities must find ways to increase their revenues to fund their good causes. In recent years, the fundraising activities of charities have become characterized by an increasing professionalism, often involving the appointment of marketing managers, strategists and public relations executives. This has resulted in a greater variety of fundraising methods than ever before, including the use of viral campaigns, creative affinity tie-ups, e-marketing and Internet-based approaches. For example, the Multiple Sclerosis Trust and the Multiple Sclerosis Society backed a joint fundraising initiative with shoe retailers. Known as MyShoes, the innovative scheme involved a partnership with footwear retailers, who donated a fixed amount to the MS charities for every pair of shoes they sold. MyShoes provided participating retailers with point-of-sales material that educated shoppers about MS (there are 85 000 MS sufferers in the UK).

Research shows that nearly 90 per cent of UK adults have participated in charitable activities in the past 12 months. Most are involved in giving money, but a third of these have taken part in a special charity activity or event. Others have been involved in organizing events or have worked for a charity. Face-to-face fundraising remains the most popular way to give, with 67 per cent of all those donating using this approach. There has, however, been a trend away from traditional tin-rattling and towards the use of 'chugging' or face-to-face recruitment, designed to encourage would-be donors to agree to regular direct debit or covenant arrangements. More than ever, charities are recognizing that fundraising activities should be targeted particularly at those in the population who are prepared to become committed donors. In some cases this means attracting a new generation of people prepared to donate regularly. A NOP survey suggested that just 15 per cent of fundraising revenue is accrued from long-term donors, with human rights charities the biggest winners, and good causes supporting the young or elderly gaining least from this means.

Even though many consumers dislike the use of direct marketing methods such as direct mail and telephone calls to solicit funds, the second most important channel for donations is by post. This approach has proved particularly popular with human rights and wildlife causes. However, relatively few supporters of children's charities and those supporting the elderly choose this method. Indeed, it seems that traditional personal approaches to collecting funds, such as the use of collecting tins in shopping malls and high streets, are declining in effectiveness. Instead, the public's imagination has been captured by a host of media-based activities. For example, specially organized events, and television appeals and programmes have been shown to be particularly effective ways of attracting funds. The use of high-profile individuals in such appeals, such as royalty, television personalities, and well-known actors or sports stars, is particularly popular. In a survey, 80 per cent of consumers questioned also supported the use of commercial and promotional schemes, such as the sale of products through gift shops and catalogues. A similar percentage stated that they like to buy products that involve the manufacturer making a contribution to charity.

Evidence of increasing professionalism in fundraising is readily apparent across the charity sector. Cancer Research overhauled its marketing strategy to focus afresh on fundraising. This followed a period when the charity concentrated on brand building, following its creation out of the merger of Imperial Cancer Research and the Cancer Research Campaign. Social marketing techniques have been embraced by most leading charities, while web-based communications have now enabled many to target and reach their audiences more effectively than in the past.

Many charities practising social marketing are utilizing the Web to good effect. Dog's Trust focuses on dog welfare and has used its social media networks to convey messages about re-homing, neutering and microchipping. Mainstream TV commercials also regularly appear, but the social media messages arguably are harder hitting and more outspoken than the TV broadcasters or viewing public will tolerate. A recent debate on Facebook was deliberately timed to coincide with a lobbying campaign aimed at MPs regarding microchipping of pets. Bullying UK, the anti-bullying charity, used social media to foster word-of-mouth communication of its core messages. The charity's posters have a mobile download version which can then be shared easily by readers amongst their social media contacts. Children's charity Barnardo's is using the Web as a means of recruiting and communicating with its younger donors. In the age of television, the Internet and the smartphone, it seems that charities such as these must be ready, willing and able to use the full range of media-based approaches available as they enact their social marketing strategies.

Sources: **http://www.bullying.co.uk/index.php/make-a-poster.html**, 8 March, 2011; **www.barnardos.org.uk**, 8 March 2011; Emily Rogers, 'MS charity initiative to roll out brand identity', *Marketing*, 1 April 2004, p. 10; Ben Bold, 'Cancer Research £10m work goes to Ogilvy Group', *Marketing*, 8 April 2004, p. 3; Caroline Parry, 'Factfile: it's a matter of give and take', *Marketing Week*, 19 February 2004, pp. 36–7; Mark Sweney, 'Barnardo's focuses fundraising on web', *Marketing*, 1 April 2004, p. 8; 'Charities unite in donor appeal', *Marketing*, 14 January 1999, p. 4; 'Spotlight: charity', *Marketing Week*, 17 December 1998, pp. 28–9; Tony Lees, NOP Research Group; **www. wspa.org.uk**; Ross McCulloch of Third Sector Lab, 'How four charities got the social marketing mix right', **http://www.mycustomer.com**, 8 March 2011; **http://www.dogstrust.org.uk/**, 8 March 2011.

Questions for discussion

1 Why are charities such as Barnardo's and Cancer Research UK turning more to the marketing approaches deployed by consumer goods companies?

2 To what kinds of donor must charities appeal? How might collection methods vary for these different groups?

3 How might the marketing strategy vary according to whether a charity is targeting consumers or corporate donors?

CHAPTER 11

Marketing channels

"Channel selection and multi-channel management drive products to market"

Objectives

- To understand the marketing channel concept and the nature of marketing channels

- To discuss the functions of marketing channels

- To examine different types of channel

- To examine channel integration and levels of market coverage

- To consider the selection of distribution channels and the emergence of direct marketing

- To explore the behavioural aspects of channels, especially the concepts of cooperation, relationship building, conflict and leadership

- To examine legal issues in channel management

INTRODUCTION

Distribution involves activities that make products available to customers when and where they want to purchase them. It is sometimes referred to as the 'place' element in the marketing mix of the 5Ps: product, place/distribution, promotion, price and people. Choosing which channels of distribution to use is a major decision in the development of marketing strategies, particularly with the advances in digital options. High customer service levels may require heavy investment in distribution and the shrewd identification of channel members with which to work. There has to be a compromise between adequate responsiveness to customers' needs and expectations and delivering to their requirements in a cost-effective manner.

This chapter focuses on the description and analysis of marketing channels, first discussing the nature of channels and their functions, and then explaining the main types of channel and their structures. These sections are followed by a review of several forms of channel integration. Consideration is given to how marketers determine the appropriate intensity of market coverage for a product and to the factors that are considered when selecting suitable channels of distribution. After examining behavioural patterns within marketing channels, and the relationships that develop between channel members, the chapter concludes by looking at several legal issues affecting channel management.

BA's focus on eCommerce

Not too many years ago, the bulk of BA flights were booked either via travel agents or over the telephone by passengers. BA introduced e-tickets, rather than sending out traditional books of travel coupon tickets, and passengers could print off their own documentation. Soon, even such behaviour was passé, as a simple booking reference sufficed and paperless travel had arrived. Passengers either inserted their credit card into a ticket dispenser at the airport or told a customer service agent their allocated booking reference code in order for the agent to allocate a seat and boarding pass. No paper was necessary. Now, most travellers simply scan a passport or insert a credit card into self-serve kiosks in order to self-check in. Even access to a boarding card has changed, as increasing numbers of passengers simply downloading a booking barcode onto their smartphones to be scanned at airport security for totally paperless transactions and boarding.

In late 2003, BA made a radical decision. Its 24-hour telephone booking service ceased: night-time tele-booking or changes to travel itineraries became a thing of the past, too. Although partly driven by a cost-saving strategy, the reduction in call centres also reflected the growth in the airline's e-booking service. 'If you choose to complete your booking by phone, you will incur a £15 off-line service fee per passenger', greeted customers dialling 0870 8507850 intending to book seats by phone, as BA steered customers towards its web-based operation. While passengers wishing to book at night could no longer speak over the telephone to a BA customer service agent, they could go online 24 hours a day in order to make or change a booking.

Prior to the opening of Heathrow's Terminal 5, BA's new hub, marketing researchers probed consumers' buy-in to e-tickets and self check-in. The result was the opening of a very different passenger experience, with numerous self-check kiosks, bag drop-off points and few queues at old-style check-in counters.

The BA website reflects this shift in emphasis, suggesting special offers, linking to customer support and providing Web users with corporate information, but focusing on:

- *Flights and Holidays*
- *Manage My Booking*
- *Information*
- *Executive Club*

The primary focus on the home page, though, is on a *Create a Trip* menu-driven system providing speedy access to BA's network and timetable. *Create a Trip* enables users to check for routes, suitable times, prices and seat availability in seconds, or to place a confirmed booking in under a minute. The company launched a set of related mobile services, with timetables, booking, check-in and now boarding enabled digitally and remotely. The airline has fully embraced eCommerce and mobile as a channel to market.

Source: Image courtesy of British Airways

Sources: **www.BA.com**, May 2004; BA, BAA, January, 2008; **www.ba.com**, January, 2008; **www.britishairways.com**, June, 2011 and May, 2012.

A s in the example of BA's move to focus on eCommerce and mobile, changes in the manner in which products are distributed have a major impact on customers. For example, moves by food retailers to sell petrol from sites adjacent to their supermarkets have affected the UK petrol market in a number of important ways. Reducing petrol prices and increasing promotional activity are damaging margins to a point where profitability is severely threatened. In the long term this may force small suppliers out of business, thus reducing consumer choice. Internet retailing is a new channel that, for some products and services, increasingly cuts out the need for wholesalers and retail stores. In some markets, such as music sales and banking transactions, there has been a huge shift to online transactions away from music stores and bank branches. Such direct marketing negates the need for high-street shops and bank branches, and changes the nature of the proposition being marketed. All products and services pass through a distribution channel or supply chain. The selection of the type most applicable to a particular target market is an important choice for marketers. This chapter focuses on the nature of marketing channels and their functions, types of channel and their structures. The factors relevant in selecting a channel of distribution are discussed, along with the nature of relationships within the marketing channel.

The nature of marketing channels and supply chain management

channel of distribution (or marketing channel)
A group of individuals and organizations that direct the flow of products from producers to customers

A **channel of distribution** (sometimes called a **marketing channel**) is a group of individuals and organizations that direct the flow of products from producers to customers. Providing customer satisfaction should be the driving force behind all marketing channel activities. Buyers' needs and behaviour are, therefore, important concerns of channel members. Channels of distribution make products available at the right time, in the right place and in the right quantity by providing such product-enhancing functions as transport and storage.[1]

The basic premise is simple. A manufacturer of a particular product could sell directly to the intended ultimate consumers, or the manufacturer could utilize the services of wholesalers, retailers or other channel members, rather than bear the hassle and costs of dealing with many end-user consumers directly. Alternatively, the manufacturer could opt to use a mix of routes to convey its products to the ultimate consumers: some direct selling, links with wholesalers and retailers, and possibly alliances with the selling activities of other manufacturers. There has to be a balance between optimizing customer satisfaction and making an adequate return on investment. These are the challenges of channel management for marketers. Challenges significantly complicated with the onset of eChannels and often an associated new set of competitors given access to markets previously ignored or unattainable.

marketing intermediary
A middleman who links producers to other middlemen or to those who ultimately use the products

Most, but not all, channels of distribution have marketing intermediaries, although there is currently a growth in direct marketing, with some suppliers interacting with consumers without the use of intermediaries. A **marketing intermediary**, or middleman, links producers to other middlemen or to those who ultimately use the products. Marketing intermediaries perform the activities described in Table 11.1. There are two major types of intermediary: merchants and functional middlemen – agents and brokers. **Merchants** take title to products and resell them, whereas **functional middlemen** do not take title to products. Both types facilitate the movement of goods and services from producers to consumers.

merchants
Intermediaries who take title to products and resell them

Both retailers and wholesalers are intermediaries. Retailers purchase products for the purpose of reselling them to users. Merchant wholesalers resell products to other wholesalers and to retailers. Functional wholesalers, such as agents and brokers, expedite exchanges among producers and resellers, and are compensated by fees or

functional middlemen
Intermediaries who do not take title to products

TABLE 11.1 Marketing channel activities performed by intermediaries

Category of marketing activities	Possible activities required
Marketing information and market insight	Collect and analyze information such as sales data; perform or commission marketing research studies
Marketing management	Establish objectives; plan activities; manage and coordinate financing, personnel and risk taking; evaluate and control channel activities
Facilitating exchange	Choose and stock product assortments that match the needs of buyers
Promotion	Set promotional objectives; coordinate advertising, personal selling, web activity, sales promotion, publicity, sponsorship, direct mail and packaging
Price	Establish pricing policies and terms of sales
Physical distribution	Manage transport, warehousing, materials handling, inventory control and communication
Customer service	Provide channels for advice, technical support, after sales back-up and warranty provision
Relationships	Facilitate communication, products and parts, financial support and credit, inventory levels, after-market needs, on-time delivery and customer service to maintain relationships with other marketing intermediaries and between suppliers and their targeted customers

commissions. For purposes of discussion in this chapter, all wholesalers are considered merchant middlemen unless otherwise specified.

Channel members share certain significant characteristics. Each member has different responsibilities within the overall structure of the distribution system, but mutual profit and success can be attained only if channel members cooperate in delivering products to the market. The area of relationship management has received a great deal of attention in marketing circles. This is increasingly important in delivering adequate customer service to target market customers. A supplier desires an ongoing and lucrative relationship with its customers: it recognizes the importance of the various channel members in maintaining this relationship and strives for mutually beneficial relationships with its channel intermediaries.

Although distribution decisions need not precede other marketing decisions, they do exercise a powerful influence on the rest of the marketing mix. Channel decisions are critical because they determine a product's market presence and buyers' accessibility to the product. They also affect customers' overall satisfaction with the product or service provider.[2] At a time when organizations increasingly offer their products through multiple channels, the challenge of maintaining quality of delivery irrespective of the channel used, is very much to the fore. The strategic significance of channel decisions is further heightened by the fact that they often entail long-term commitments. For example, it is much easier for a company to change prices or packaging than to change existing distribution systems.

It may be necessary for companies to use different distribution paths in different countries, for different target market segments or for the various products in its portfolio. Some companies, particularly clothing retailers, have stores and a Web proposition in their home country but only a Web presence overseas. The links in any channel, however, are the merchants – including producers – and agents who oversee the movement of products through that channel. Marketing channels are commonly classified into channels for consumer products/services or channels for industrial, business-to-business products/services.

Increasingly, an important function of the marketing channel is the joint effort of all channel members to create a supply chain: a total distribution system that serves customers and creates a competitive advantage. **Supply chain management** refers to long-term partnerships among marketing channel members that reduce inefficiencies, costs and redundancies in the marketing channel and develop innovative approaches

supply chain management
Long-term partnerships among marketing channel members that reduce inefficiencies, costs and redundancies in the marketing channel and develop innovative approaches to satisfying targeted customers

to satisfying targeted customers. The goal is still to provide customers with the product or service demanded, in line with their expectations, but in a more coordinated way that builds on the combined strengths of the members of the distribution channel. Key tasks in supply chain management include: planning and coordination of marketing channel partnerships; sourcing necessary resources, goods and services to support the supply chain; facilitating delivery; and relationship building in order to nurture ongoing customer relationships.

Functions of marketing channels

Marketing channels serve many functions. Although some of these functions may be performed by a single channel member, most are accomplished through both the independent and joint efforts of channel members. These functions include creating utility, facilitating exchange efficiencies, alleviating discrepancies, standardizing transactions and providing customer service.

Creating utility

Marketing channels create four types of utility: time, place, possession and form.

1 Time utility is having products available when the customer wants them.
2 Place utility is created by making products available in locations where customers wish to purchase them.
3 Possession utility is created by giving the customer access to the product to use or to store for future use. Possession utility can occur through ownership or through arrangements such as lease or rental agreements that give the customer the right to use the product.
4 Channel members sometimes create form utility by assembling, preparing or otherwise refining the product to suit individual customer needs.

Facilitating exchange efficiencies

Marketing intermediaries can reduce the costs of exchanges by performing certain services or functions efficiently. Even if producers and buyers are located in the same city, there are costs associated with exchanges. As Figure 11.1 shows, when four buyers seek products from four producers, sixteen transactions are possible. If one intermediary serves both producers and buyers, the number of transactions can be reduced to eight. Intermediaries are specialists in facilitating exchanges. They provide valuable assistance because of their access to, and control over, important resources used in the proper functioning of marketing channels.

Nevertheless, the press, consumers, public officials and other marketers freely criticize intermediaries, especially wholesalers – retail wholesalers, dealers, distributors. In a US survey of the general public, 74 per cent believed that 'wholesalers frequently make high profits, which significantly increase prices that consumers pay'.[3] Critics accuse wholesalers of being inefficient and parasitic. Consumers often wish to make the distribution channel as short as possible, assuming that the fewer the intermediaries, the lower the price. For example, Virgin's financial services operation or Direct Line insurance aim to offer competitive prices by cutting out brokers. Because suggestions to eliminate them come from both ends of the marketing channel, wholesalers must be careful to perform only those marketing activities that are truly desired. To survive, they must be more efficient and more customer focused than alternative marketing institutions.

Critics who suggest that eliminating wholesalers would lower consumer prices do not recognize that doing so would not remove the need for services that wholesalers provide. Although wholesalers can be eliminated, in many markets the functions they perform cannot. Other channel members would have to perform those functions, and customers would still have to fund

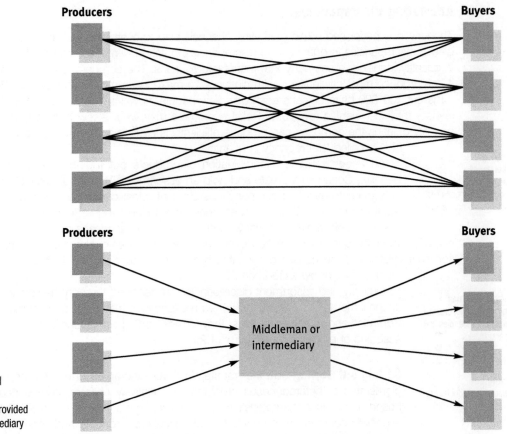

FIGURE 11.1
Efficiency in
exchanges provided
by an intermediary

them. In addition, all producers would have to deal directly with retailers or consumers, so that every producer would have to keep voluminous records and hire enough personnel to deal with a multitude of customers. Customers might end up paying a great deal more for products because prices would reflect the costs of less efficient channel members.

Direct customer–supplier marketing is possible in some markets. For instance, telesales-led Direct Line has a successful direct relationship with its insurance-buying customers. JCB, on the other hand, would find it difficult to sell directly and depends on its dealers for parts and maintenance provision to its construction equipment customers. Heinz, Kellogg's, Sony, Ford and BA all utilize channel members – retailers, dealers or travel agents – in order to sell their products and services. These companies may well use direct mail and the Web to contact their existing or potential customers, but channel members play an important role in some of their marketing programmes.

To illustrate wholesalers' efficient services, assume that all wholesalers have been eliminated. Because there are millions of retailers, a widely purchased consumer product – say, toilet paper – would require an extraordinary number of sales contacts, possibly more than a million, to maintain the current level of product exposure. For example, Scott would have to deliver its paper products, establish warehouses all over Europe and maintain fleets of trucks. Selling and distribution costs for Scott's products would rocket. Instead of a few contacts with food brokers, large retail businesses and merchant wholesalers, such manufacturers would face thousands of expensive contacts with, and shipments to, smaller retailers. Such an operation would be highly inefficient, and costs would be passed on to consumers. Wholesalers are often more efficient and less expensive.

Alleviating discrepancies

The functions performed within marketing channels help to overcome two major distribution problems: discrepancies in quantity and discrepancies in assortment. With respect to discrepancies in quantity, consider a company that manufactures jeans. The company specializes in the goods it can produce most efficiently: denim clothing. To make jeans most economically, the producer turns out 100 000 pairs of jeans each day. Few people, however, want to buy 100 000 pairs of jeans – they just want a few pairs. Retail customers may want a few hundred pairs. Thus the quantity of jeans the company can produce efficiently is more than the average customer wants. This is called 'discrepancy in quantity'.

assortment
A combination of products put together to provide customer benefits

An **assortment** is a combination of products put together to provide customer benefits. Consumers create and hold an assortment. The set of products made available to customers is a company's assortment. Most consumers want a broad assortment of products. Besides jeans, they want to buy shoes, food, cars, entertainment systems, soft drinks and many other products. Yet the jeans manufacturer has a narrow assortment because it only makes jeans and a few other denim clothes. A discrepancy in assortment exists because consumers want a broad assortment, but an individual manufacturer produces a narrow assortment.

sorting activities
Functions that let channel members divide roles and separate tasks

Quantity and assortment discrepancies are resolved through the sorting activities of channel members. **Sorting activities** are functions that allow channel members to divide roles and to separate tasks; they include sorting out, accumulation, allocation and assorting of products (see Figure 11.2).[4]

sorting out
Separating products into uniform, homogeneous groups

Sorting out Sorting out, the first step in developing an assortment, is separating conglomerates of heterogeneous products into relatively uniform, homogeneous groups based on product characteristics such as size, shape, weight or colour. Sorting out is especially common in the marketing of agricultural products and other raw materials, which vary widely in size, grade and quality, and would be largely unusable in an undifferentiated mass. A grape crop, for example, must be sorted into grapes suitable for making wine, those best for turning into grape juice and those to be sold by food retailers.

accumulation
The development of a bank of homogeneous products with similar production or demand requirements

Accumulation Accumulation is the development of a bank, or inventory, of homogeneous products with similar production or demand requirements. Farmers who grow relatively small quantities of grapes, for example, transport their sorted grapes to central collection points, where they are accumulated in large lots for movement into the next level of the channel. Accumulation lets producers continually use up stocks and replenish them, thus minimizing losses from interruptions in the supply of materials.

allocation
The breaking down of large homogeneous inventories into smaller lots

Allocation Allocation is the breaking down of large homogeneous inventories into smaller lots. This process, which addresses discrepancies in quantity, enables wholesalers to buy efficiently in lorry loads or railway car loads, and apportion products by

FIGURE 11.2
Sorting activities conducted by channel members

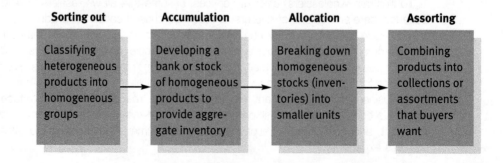

Sorting out	Accumulation	Allocation	Assorting
Classifying heterogeneous products into homogeneous groups	Developing a bank or stock of homogeneous products to provide aggregate inventory	Breaking down homogeneous stocks (inventories) into smaller units	Combining products into collections or assortments that buyers want

Tesco's multi-channel approach to market leadership

Building customer relationships

The Internet has changed the way in which consumers shop. In the past, those seeking to replenish their kitchen cupboards, fridges and freezers would usually visit their local supermarket or hypermarket. Now, these same consumers can visit the Internet and order their groceries for direct delivery to their homes. The concept is seen to be particularly attractive to professional, high-earning, ABC1 men and women who work long hours and have limited leisure time, but many other consumers increasingly buy their groceries online. Indeed, the most visited websites each week are those operated by Tesco, Asda, Sainsbury's and Ocado. **Tesco.com** is one service that allows customers to buy their groceries direct over the Internet. Consumers can access the Tesco website at **Tesco.com** and select their purchase items. Their orders are then compiled by a team of in-store sales assistants for delivery to consumers' homes at a time of their choosing. So large is the Internet part of the grocery market that many supermarket retailers now operate fully 'dark stores', where no consumers visit and only teams of staff operate picking online orders for home delivery. Assorting within such stores into clusters or product categories is particularly important for operations staff, just as it is within normal stores for consumers requiring similar products to be grouped together.

Initially, the **Tesco.com** concept was trialled in 11 stores in two major UK cities. The company's preliminary research showed that around 200 000 consumers were using the service offered by these 11 stores and that this was increasing by 10 000 every week. Before long, the obvious popularity of Internet shopping prompted Tesco to roll out **Tesco.com** to other parts of the UK. By the end of the first year, the company offered the service from 100 Tesco stores. Careful consideration has been given to the marketing of the Internet shopping service. The sight of the **Tesco.com** logo displayed by the company's delivery vans has become familiar to those living in the areas where the service is offered. In addition, the retailer is using a combination of local poster and in-store advertising, direct mail and an

Internet campaign to promote the **Tesco.com** operation. Today, Tesco is the most used website of all e-tailers.

Increasing familiarity with shopping on the Internet looks set to increase the demand for services like **Tesco.com**. A whole generation of young adults is emerging that has grown up with the convenience and reassurance of web-based shopping. How substantial a part of Tesco's business the service will become remains to be seen. However, Tesco management clearly understands that retaining its market-leading position means being ready to respond to changing shopping needs. There had been concerns in certain quarters that the large retailers would reduce investment in their stores and the in-store customer experience, but such fears seem unfounded. At the moment, the largest supermarket companies are opening new stores faster than ever before in their history. Another concern expressed by the pundits was that a substantial shift in grocery shopping from the supermarkets to the Internet could damage scale advantages and affect profitability. In fact, for Tesco, online retailing is supporting its portfolio of stores.

In common with many retailers, Tesco has a multi-channel operation. Tesco Extra is an edge-of-town hypermarket business offering mixed merchandise on top of groceries and Tesco Superstores are large grocery-led supermarkets, often on edge-of-town retail parks. The town centre and suburbs are not ignored in Tesco's multi-channel strategy: Tesco Express is a large chain of C-stores (convenience stores) often mini-marts in the suburbs and Tesco Metro are town centre supermarkets focusing on groceries. These store-based propositions are joined by **Tesco.com**, providing home deliveries of everything found in a Tesco Extra hypermarket and more. Some consumers may prefer just one of these options, while others will use a mix of Tesco stores depending on their whereabouts, the occasion and time of shopping, and may prefer the web and **Tesco.com**. Tesco's management must understand the different customer profiles that its concepts attract and engage accordingly with these consumers in order to build loyalty.

Sources: *Marketing: Concepts and Strategies*, 5th edition and Tesco, 2011.

cases to other members. A food wholesaler, for instance, serves as a depot, allocating products according to market demand. The wholesaler may divide a single lorry load of Del Monte canned tomatoes among several retail food stores.

assorting
The grouping of products that buyers want to have available in one place

Assorting Assorting is the process of combining products into collections or assortments that buyers want to have available in one place. Assorting eliminates discrepancies in assortment by grouping products in ways that satisfy buyers. Assorting is especially important to retailers, for they strive to create assortments matching the demands of consumers who visit their stores. Although no single customer is likely to buy one of everything in the store, retailers must anticipate the probability of purchase and provide a satisfactory range of product choices. For example, the same food wholesaler that supplies supermarkets with Del Monte tomato products may also buy canned goods from competing food processors so that the grocery store can choose from a wide assortment of canned fruit and vegetables. The Marketing Insight box on page 343 outlines Tesco's multi-channel strategy and the importance of assorting.

Standardizing transactions

Marketing channels help to standardize the transactions associated with numerous products. In many purchase situations, the price is not negotiable; it is predetermined. Although there may be some variation in units of measurement, package sizes, delivery schedules and location of the exchange, marketing channel members tend to limit customer options with respect to these types of issue. When a customer goes to a supermarket to purchase a loaf of bread, it is unlikely that the individual will be able to buy half a loaf of bread, buy a loaf sliced lengthwise, negotiate the price, obtain a written warranty or return an unused portion of the loaf. Many of the details associated with the purchase of a loaf of bread are standardized.

Providing customer service

Channel members participate in providing customer service. Retailers of durable goods are expected to provide in-store advice and demonstrations, technical know-how, delivery, installation, repair services, parts and perhaps instruction or training. Channel members above the retailers are responsible for supporting retailers' efforts to provide end-user service and satisfaction, even though they may not come into direct contact with ultimate customers. To gain and maintain a differential advantage, channel members make decisions and take actions to provide excellent customer service and support.

In mature markets with relatively little product differentiation between rival brands – such as packaged holidays, audio/hi-fi systems, conference venues or replacement car exhausts/tyres – and in newly emerging markets with innovative products and inexperienced consumers, it is often the customer service provided through the distribution channel that provides marketers with an edge over their competitors. In many markets – from cars and financial services to grocery retailing and PCs – it is the service provided by channel members that maintains an ongoing, mutually satisfactory relationship between supplier and consumer, and that may be responsible for maintaining brand loyalty.

Types of channel

Because marketing channels appropriate for one product may be less suitable for others, many different distribution paths have been developed. The various marketing channels can be classified generally as channels for consumer products and services, or channels for industrial, business-to-business products and services.

Channels for consumer products or services

Figure 11.3 illustrates several channels used in the distribution of consumer products or services. Besides the channels listed, a manufacturer may use sales branches or sales offices.

Channel A Channel A describes the direct movement of goods from producer to consumers. Customers who pick their own fruit from commercial orchards or buy cosmetics from door-to-door sales people are acquiring products through a direct channel. A producer who sells goods directly from the factory to end users and ultimate consumers is using a direct marketing channel; for example, Direct Line's teleselling of car insurance. Although this channel is the simplest, it is not necessarily the cheapest or the most efficient method of distribution. **eCommerce** – the use of the Internet for marketing communications, selling and purchasing – has in recent years led to a growth in direct marketing for a variety of products, notably travel tickets, music downloads, financial services and merchandise retailed by the traditional mail-order catalogue operators. Channel A, the direct approach, certainly is no longer the preserve of farm shops and factory outlets.

eCommerce
The use of the Internet for marketing communications, selling and purchasing

Channel B Channel B, which moves goods from producer to retailers and then to consumers, is often used by large retailers that can buy in quantity from a manufacturer. Such retailers as Marks & Spencer, Sainsbury's, Aldi and Carrefour, for example, sell clothing, food and many other items they have purchased directly from the producers. Cars are also commonly sold through this type of marketing channel.

Channel C A long-standing distribution channel, especially for consumer products, channel C takes goods from producer to wholesalers, then to retailers and finally to consumers. This option is very practical for a producer who sells to hundreds of thousands of consumers through thousands of retailers. A single producer finds it hard to do business directly with thousands

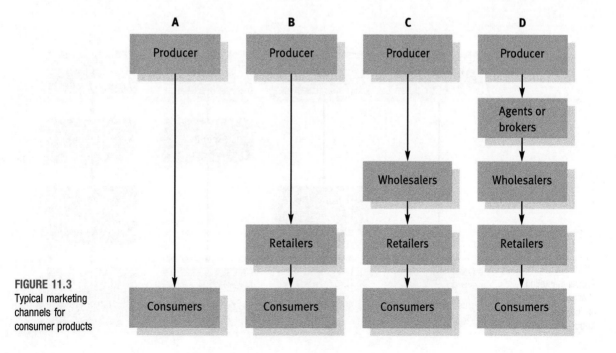

FIGURE 11.3
Typical marketing channels for consumer products

of retailers. For example, consider the number of retailers that stock Coca-Cola. It would be extremely difficult, if not impossible, for Coca-Cola to deal directly with all the retailers that sell its brand of soft drink. Manufacturers of tobacco products, confectionery, some home appliances, hardware and many convenience goods sell their products to wholesalers, who then sell to retailers, who in turn do business with individual consumers.

Channel D Channel D – through which goods pass from producer to agents to wholesalers to retailers, and only then to consumers – is frequently used for products intended for mass distribution, such as processed food. For example, to place its biscuit line in specific retail outlets, a food processor may hire an agent (or a food broker) to sell the biscuits to wholesalers. The wholesalers then sell the biscuits to supermarkets, vending machine operators and other retail outlets.

Benefits of a long channel Contrary to popular opinion, a long channel may be the most efficient distribution channel for certain consumer goods. When several channel intermediaries are available to perform specialized functions, costs may be lower than if one channel member is responsible for all the functions in all territories. Some manufacturers opt for all or most of these four channels in order to cater for the needs and buying processes of the different customers that make up their various targeted market segments.

Channels for industrial or business-to-business products or services

Figure 11.4 shows four of the most common channels for industrial or business products and services. Like their consumer products' counterparts, manufacturers of industrial or business products sometimes work with more than one level of wholesalers.

Channel E Channel E illustrates the direct channel for industrial or business products. In contrast to consumer goods, many business products – especially expensive equipment, such as steam generators, aircraft and mainframe computers – are sold directly to the buyers. For example, Air-

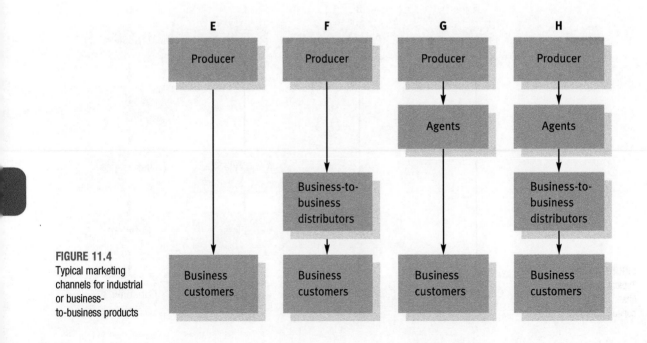

FIGURE 11.4
Typical marketing channels for industrial or business-to-business products

bus Industries sells aircraft direct to airlines such as British Airways and Air France. The direct channel is most feasible for many manufacturers of business goods because they have fewer customers, and those customers may be clustered geographically, as explained in Chapter 5. Buyers of complex industrial products can also receive technical assistance from the manufacturer more easily in a direct channel. In some cases the provision of such information may continue for the lifetime of the product. As with consumer markets, eCommerce and the desire to develop one-to-one direct relationships have led to a growth in the use of channel E.

Channel F If a particular line of business products is aimed at a larger number of customers, the manufacturer may use a marketing channel that includes **industrial distributors**, merchants who take title to products and carry inventory (channel F). Construction products made by Case or JCB, for example, are sold through industrial or business-to-business distributors, as are building materials, operating supplies and air-conditioning equipment. Industrial distributors are carrying an increasing percentage of business products. Due to mergers and acquisitions, they have become larger and more powerful.[5] Industrial distributors can be most effectively used when a product has broad market appeal, is easily stocked and serviced, is sold in small quantities and is needed rapidly to avoid high losses.[6]

> **industrial distributor**
> An independent business that takes title to industrial products and carries inventories.

Channel G Channel G – from producer to agents to industrial or business buyers – may be chosen when a manufacturer without a marketing department needs market information, when a company is too small to field its own salesforce or when a company wants to introduce a new product or to enter a new market without using its own sales people. Thus a large soya bean producer might sell its product to animal food processors through an agent.

Channel H Channel H is a variation of channel G: goods move from producer to agents to industrial distributors and then to business customers. A manufacturer without a salesforce may rely on this channel if its business customers purchase products in small quantities or if they must be re-supplied frequently and therefore need access to decentralized inventories. Japanese manufacturers of electronic components, for example, work through export agents who sell to industrial distributors serving small producers or dealers overseas.

Multiple marketing channels

When aiming at diverse target markets, it may be appropriate for a manufacturer to use several marketing channels simultaneously, with each channel involving a different group of intermediaries. For example, a manufacturer turns to multiple channels when the same product is directed to both consumers and business customers. When Procter & Gamble sells cleaning products for household use, the products are sold to supermarkets through grocery wholesalers or, in some cases, directly to the larger retailers, whereas the cleaning products going to restaurants or institutions follow a different distribution channel. In some instances, a producer may prefer **dual distribution**: the use of two marketing channels for distributing the same products. Villeroy & Boch is a respected supplier of fine china and glassware to households across the world. The company also has ranges for the catering industry, sold and promoted through a separate marketing channel.

> **dual distribution**
> A channel practice whereby a producer distributes the same products through two different channels

A **strategic channel alliance** exists when the products of one organization are distributed through the marketing channels of another. The products are often similar with respect to target markets or product uses, but they are not direct competitors. For example, a brand of bottled water might be distributed through a marketing channel for soft drinks, or a US cereal producer could form a strategic channel alliance with

> **strategic channel alliance**
> Arrangement for distributing the products of one organization through the marketing channels of another

a European food processor. Alliances can provide benefits both for the organization that owns the marketing channel and for the company whose brand is being distributed through the channel. An example of this is the 'chip and pin' system, which has replaced signatures on credit card slips. Barclaycard Merchant Services provides the banking/payment service, while IT company Fujitsu supplies the technology, through a partnership with IT installers and service engineers. In a joint venture, each company markets the same service to its respective clients – in retailing, catering and entertainment establishments.

multi-channel marketing
The decision to reach target consumers or business customers through more than one channel

Multi-channel marketing is the decision to reach target consumers or business customers through more than one channel. Increasingly, companies opt to serve their target markets via online channels and more traditional channels side by side. For example, Sony products are available online or in-store, while many business-to-business products and services now can be sourced online as well as from industrial distributors, brokers or other middle players.

Channel integration

Channel functions may be transferred among intermediaries, to producers and even to customers. This section examines how channel members can either combine and control most activities or pass them on to another channel member. Remember, though, that the channel member cannot eliminate functions; unless buyers themselves perform the functions, they must pay for the labour and resources needed for the functions to be performed. The statement that, 'you can eliminate middlemen but you can't eliminate their functions', is an accepted principle of marketing.

Many marketing channels are determined by consensus. Producers and intermediaries co-ordinate their efforts for mutual benefit. Some marketing channels, however, are organized and controlled by a single leader, which can be a producer, a wholesaler or a retailer, depending on the industry. The channel leader may establish channel policies and coordinate the development of the marketing mix. Marks & Spencer and IKEA, for example, are channel leaders for several of the many products they sell, exerting significant pressure on suppliers to adhere to their production, delivery and pricing standards. The various links or stages of the channel may be combined under the management of a channel leader, either horizontally or vertically. Integration may stabilize supply, reduce costs and increase coordination of channel members.

Vertical channel integration

vertical channel integration
The combination of two or more stages of the channel under one management

Combining two or more stages of the channel under one management is **vertical channel integration**. One member of a marketing channel may purchase the operations of another member or simply perform the functions of the other member, eliminating the need for that intermediary as a separate entity. For example, changes in the regulations controlling the UK electricity industry have led to an increase in vertical channel integration, as some companies controlling the generation and distribution of electricity have merged. Total vertical integration encompasses all functions from production to ultimate buyer; it is exemplified by oil companies such as BP or Shell, which own oil wells, pipelines, refineries, terminals and service station forecourts.

Whereas members of conventional channel systems work independently and seldom cooperate, participants in vertical channel integration coordinate their efforts to reach a desired target market.[7] This more progressive approach to distribution enables channel members to regard other members as extensions of their own operations. Vertically integrated channels are often more effective against competition because they result in increased bargaining power, the ability to inhibit competitors, and the sharing of information and responsibilities.[8] At one end of an integrated channel, for example, a manufacturer might provide advertising and training assistance, and the retailer at the other end would buy the manufacturer's products in quantity and actively promote them.

In the past, integration has been successfully institutionalized in marketing channels called vertical marketing systems. A **vertical marketing system (VMS)** is a marketing channel in which a single channel member coordinates or manages channel activities to achieve efficient, low-cost distribution aimed at satisfying target market customers. Because the efforts of individual channel members are combined in a VMS, marketing activities can be coordinated for maximum effectiveness and economy, without duplication of services. Vertical marketing systems are also competitive, accounting for a growing share of retail sales in consumer goods. Most vertical marketing systems today take one of three forms: corporate, administered or contractual.

vertical marketing system (VMS)
Marketing channel in which a single channel member coordinates or manages channel activities to achieve efficient, low-cost distribution aimed at satisfying target market customers

The corporate VMS The corporate VMS combines all stages of the marketing channel, from producers to consumers, under a single ownership. Supermarket chains that own food-processing plants, and large retailers that purchase wholesaling and production facilities, are examples of corporate VMSs. Figure 11.5 contrasts a conventional marketing channel with a VMS, which consolidates marketing functions and roles.

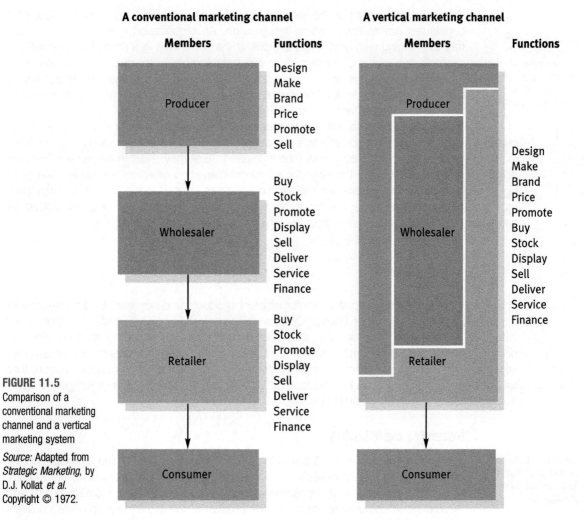

FIGURE 11.5
Comparison of a conventional marketing channel and a vertical marketing system

Source: Adapted from *Strategic Marketing*, by D.J. Kollat *et al.* Copyright © 1972.

The administered VMS In an administered VMS, channel members are independent, but a high level of inter-organizational management is achieved by informal coordination. Members of an administered VMS may agree, for example, to adopt uniform accounting and ordering procedures, and to cooperate in promotional activities. Although individual channel members maintain their autonomy, as in conventional marketing channels, one channel member – such as the producer or a large retailer – dominates the administered VMS, so that distribution decisions take into account the system as a whole. Because of its size and power as a retailer, Marks & Spencer exercises a strong influence over the independent manufacturers in its marketing channels, as do Kellogg's (cereals) and BMW (cars).

The contractual VMS Under a contractual VMS, the most popular type of vertical marketing system, inter-organizational relationships are formalized through contracts. Channel members are linked by legal agreements that spell out each member's rights and obligations. For instance, franchise organizations such as McDonald's and KFC are contractual VMSs. Other contractual VMSs include wholesaler-sponsored groups such as SPAR, Mace or IGA (Independent Grocers' Alliance) stores, in which independent retailers band together under the contractual leadership of a wholesaler.

Horizontal channel integration

horizontal channel integration
The combination of institutions at the same level of channel operation under one management

Combining institutions at the same level of channel operation under one management constitutes **horizontal channel integration**. An organization may integrate horizontally by merging with other organizations at the same level in a marketing channel. For example, the owner of a bistro chain may buy another bistro or a bar chain and then rebrand it in the same way as the existing business and merge the two chains' supply channels. Horizontal integration may enable an organization to generate sufficient sales revenue to integrate vertically as well.

Although horizontal integration permits efficiencies and economies of scale in purchasing, marketing research, advertising and specialized personnel, it is not always the most effective method of improving distribution. The increase in size may result in decreased flexibility, difficulties in coordination, and the need for additional marketing research and large-scale planning. Unless distribution functions for the various units can be performed more efficiently under unified management than under the previously separate managements, horizontal integration will not reduce costs or improve the competitive position of the integrating company.

Different levels of market coverage

The kind of coverage that is appropriate for different products is determined by the characteristics and behaviour patterns of buyers. Chapter 8 divided consumer products into four broad categories – convenience products, shopping products, speciality products and unsought products – according to how the purchase is made. In considering products to buy, consumers take into account replacement rate, product adjustment (services), duration of consumption, time required to find the product and similar factors.[9] Three major levels of market coverage are intensive, selective and exclusive distribution.

Intensive distribution

intensive distribution
The use of all available outlets for distributing a product

In **intensive distribution**, all available outlets are used for distributing a product. Intensive distribution is appropriate for convenience products such as bread, chewing gum, beer and newspapers. To consumers, availability means a store located nearby and minimal time necessary to search for the product at the store. Sales may have a direct relationship to availability. The successful sale of bread and milk at service stations or of petrol at convenience grocery stores has shown that the availability of these products is more important than the nature of the outlet. Convenience products have a high replacement rate and require almost no service. To meet these demands, intensive distribution is necessary, and multiple channels may be used to sell through all possible outlets.

Producers of packaged consumer items rely on intensive distribution. In fact, intensive distribution is one of L'Oreal's key strengths: L'Oreal shampoo and its other products such as make-up, skin care, sun screen and perfume, are expected to be readily and intensively available by consumers.

FIGURE 11.6
L'Oreal hair products are intensively distributed

Source: © Lou Linwei/ Alamy

Selective distribution

selective distribution
The use of only some available outlets in an area to distribute a product

In **selective distribution**, only some available outlets in an area are chosen to distribute a product. Selective distribution is appropriate for shopping products. Durable goods such as electrical appliances and exclusive fragrances usually fall into this category. Such products are more expensive than convenience goods. Consumers are willing to spend more time searching: visiting several retail outlets to compare prices, designs, styles and other features.

Selective distribution is desirable when a special effort – such as customer service from a channel member – is important. Shopping products require differentiation at the point of purchase. To motivate retailers to provide adequate pre-sale service, selective distribution and company-owned stores are often used. Many business products are sold on a selective basis to maintain a certain degree of control over the distribution process. For example, agricultural herbicides are distributed on a selective basis because dealers must offer services to buyers, such as instructions about how to apply the herbicides safely, or offer the option of having the dealer apply the herbicide.

exclusive distribution
The use of only one outlet in a relatively large geographic area to distribute a product

Exclusive distribution

In **exclusive distribution**, only one outlet is used in a relatively large geographic area. Exclusive distribution is suitable for speciality products that are purchased rather infrequently, consumed over a long period of time, or require service or information to fit them to buyers' needs. Exclusive distribution is not appropriate for convenience products and many shopping products. It is often used as an incentive to sellers when only a limited market is available for products. For example, cars such as the Rolls-Royce are sold on an exclusive basis. Royal Copenhagen's premium china is retailed through carefully selected, exclusive retail outlets. A producer who uses exclusive distribution generally expects a dealer to be very cooperative with respect to carrying a complete inventory, sending personnel for sales and service training, participating in promotional programmes and providing excellent customer service. Exclusive distribution gives a company tighter image control because the types of distributors and retailers that distribute the product are monitored closely.[10]

Choosing distribution channels

Choosing the most appropriate distribution channels for a product can be a complex affair. Some well-known store-based retailers still are reluctant to lose in-store impact by switching to the Web, which may frustrate some consumers interested in IKEA or Selfridges, but these companies perceive their store-based offering to be their core appeal. The Marketing Insight box on page 353 outlines the multi-channel strategy developed by Games Workshop. Producers must choose specific intermediaries carefully, evaluating their sales and profit levels, performance records, other products carried, clientele, availability and so forth. In addition, producers must examine other factors that influence distribution channel selection, including organizational objectives and resources, market characteristics, buying behaviour, product attributes and environmental forces. In some markets, such as the distribution of insurance products, these factors may indicate that multiple channels should be used.[11]

Organizational objectives and resources

Producers must consider carefully their objectives and the cost of achieving them in the marketplace. A company's objectives may be broad – such as higher profits, increased market share and greater responsiveness to customers – or narrow, such as replacing an intermediary that has left the channel. The organization may possess sufficient financial and marketing muscle to control its distribution channels – for example, by engaging in direct marketing or by operating its own fleet of lorries. On the other hand, an organization may have no interest in performing distribution services or may be forced by lack of resources and experience to depend on middlemen.

Companies must also consider how effective their past distribution relationships and methods have been, and question their appropriateness with regard to current objectives. One organization might decide to maintain its basic channel structure but add members for increased coverage in new territories. Another company might alter its distribution channel so as to provide same-day delivery on all orders.

Market characteristics

Beyond the basic division between consumer markets and business markets, several market variables influence the design of distribution channels. Geography is one factor; in most cases, the greater the distance between the producer and its markets, the less expensive is distribution through intermediaries rather than through direct sales. Market density must also be considered; when customers tend to be clustered in several locations, the producer may be able to eliminate middlemen.

Games workshop: the best model soldiers in the world!

Building customer relationships

As its name suggests, Games Workshop manufactures and sells games, but these are no ordinary games and this is no ordinary business. Games Workshop is 'the largest and most successful tabletop fantasy and futuristic battle-games company in the world'. With a turnover of over £126 million, the company employs more than 2000 people and has over 380 retail outlets in Australia, Canada, France, Germany, Hong Kong, Spain, the USA and the UK, with growing South American, Asian and Eastern European markets. 70 per cent of sales now come from outside the UK. The fantasy games produced by Games Workshop take place in one of two settings:

1 a fantasy world filled with Dwarves, Elves, rat-like Scaven, green Orcs and Goblins

2 the future of a war-torn universe in the forty-first millennium – a setting occupied by the enigmatic Eldar, genetically enhanced Space Marines and an alien race called the Tyranids, who are all battling for survival.

In addition, the company has the franchise for a range linked to *The Lord of The Rings* movies.

Games Workshop enthusiasts can buy from a range of boxed games, containing the rule book, charts and templates, dice and miniature figures needed to begin their fantasy battle. The basics can then be added to from the extensive range of Games Workshop troops, special squads and war machines. As enthusiasts develop their armies and paint them in colours of their choice, they begin to build their own personalized version of their game of choice. The success of Peter Jackson's *The Lord of the Rings* films has added a new dimension, as Games Workshop holds a global licence for a game based on this award-winning trilogy.

For those unfamiliar with the fantasy game concept, the uncharted territory of the retail outlets can itself feel like alien territory. Wall space is stacked high with numerous games, figures, paints, magazines, books and T-shirts. In the centre is a gaming table, which is usually covered with the remains of an ongoing battle. At other times, the shops are full of teenagers and children, conducting a closely fought Warhammer contest. On some days the outlets resemble a crèche for big kids, with staff carefully orchestrating activities. The battles organized in-store are an important part of the weekly itinerary. The featured game varies on different days, so that enthusiasts of Warhammer, Warhammer 40 000, Necromunda and the other Games Workshop products can all get their turn. These games induct newcomers into the gaming experience, while for 'old hands' they showcase new product launches.

The shop staff, always Games Workshop enthusiasts, are vital to the success of the retail outlets. They must be able to maintain an enthusiasm for the brand, keeping up to date with all of the latest new product launches. The ability to handle customers of all ages and backgrounds – from the young teenagers who regularly hang out at the stores to the uninitiated visiting the outlets for the first time – is also essential. Nonplussed parents clutching 'Christmas lists' or birthday present suggestions experience a friendly welcome from staff, who will happily search among the reams of Games Workshop packaging to retrieve some bizarrely named item.

As well as its network of retail stores, Games Workshop has agencies – typically specialist modelling and hobbyist shops – distributing its figures and games, while even the likes of Toys 'Я' Us has been known to stock the popular gaming sets. In total, more than 3700 independent shops retail the company's ranges. In addition, there is a mail-order operation that can be accessed through the retail stores as well as directly by telephone or the Web. The online operation has grown significantly recently. This £40 million mail-order operation has 40 staff and a growing database of contacts. The aim is to provide a fast and efficient service, despatching all orders within 24 hours. This facility handles up to a thousand calls daily and can deal with enquiries in a range of languages. While the stores are an integral feature of the Games Workshop 'experience', the company has been quick to recognize the value of adopting a mix of distribution channels to support its rapid expansion plans: online sales and mail order contribute significantly to the company's sales. The company believes its destiny is in its own hands, saying, 'Games Workshop remains a vertically integrated company, retaining control over every aspect of design, manufacture, distribution and retail of our models and rulebooks'.

Sources: Jervis Johnson and Chris Prentice of Games Workshop; Games Workshop website, **www.games-workshop.co.uk**; James Dibb-Simkin; Sally Dibb and Lyndon Simkin, *The Marketing Casebook*, 2nd edn (London: ITBP, 2001); May, 2004; **http://investor.games-workshop.com/about_us.aspx**, January, 2008; **www.games-workshop.com**, June, 2011; Games Workshop Leamington Spa, July, 2011.

With over 500 cameras and camcorders online,
you're sure to focus on one.

FIGURE 11.7

Leading supermarket retailer Tesco now operates
a successful on-line catalogue operation called Tesco
Direct, offering a wide range of products from furniture
to cameras to home accessories

Source: copyright © Tesco

Transport, storage, communication and negotiation are specific functions performed more efficiently in high-density markets. Market size – measured by the number of potential customers in a consumer or business market – is yet another variable. Direct sales may be effective if a producer has relatively few buyers for a product, but for larger markets the services of middlemen may be required.[12] eCommerce is encouraging many suppliers to deal directly with customers, even when they are geographically spread or diverse in nature. There is no doubt that the growing popularity of direct marketing and web-based marketing is forcing marketers to reappraise their market characteristics and deployment of channel intermediaries. This results in direct customer–supplier relationships in those channels where wholesaler/retailer channel members once dominated, such as music, books, holidays, clothing and financial services. Figure 11.7 shows supermarket store Tesco's home delivery operation.

Buying behaviour

Buying behaviour is a crucial consideration in selecting distribution channels. To be able to match intermediaries with customers, the producer must have specific, current information about customers who are buying the product, and how, when and where they are buying it.[13] A manufacturer may find direct selling economically feasible for large-volume sales but inappropriate for small orders.

The producer must also understand how buyer specifications vary according to whether buyers perceive products as convenience, shopping or speciality items (see Chapters 4 and 8). Customers for magazines, for example, are likely to buy the product frequently – even impulsively – from a variety of outlets. Buyers of home computers, however, carefully evaluate product features, dealers, prices and after-sales services.

Buyers may be reached most effectively when producers are creative in opening up new distribution channels. In the UK, effective distribution, the essential tool in the highly competitive soft drinks sector, is forcing brand leaders Coca-Cola and Schweppes Beverages to find creative ways of extending distribution. Schweppes launched a company, Vendleader, to increase penetration of sales through vending machines.

Product attributes

Another variable in the selection of distribution channels is the product itself. Because producers of complex industrial products must often provide technical services to buyers both before and after the sale, these products are usually shipped directly to buyers. Perishable or highly fashionable consumer products with short shelf lives are also marketed through short channels. In other cases, distribution patterns are influenced by the product's value; the lower the price per unit, the longer the distribution chain. Additional factors to consider are the weight, bulkiness and relative ease of handling the products. Producers may find wholesalers and retailers reluctant to carry items that create storage or display problems.[14] For example, manufacturers of breakfast cereals, such as Kellogg's, must use packaging that retailers find easy to handle and display.

Marketing environmental forces

Finally, producers making decisions about distribution channels must consider the broader forces in the total marketing environment – that is, the political, legal, regulatory, societal/Green, technological, economic and competitive forces. Technology, for example, has made possible electronic scanners, computerized inventory systems such as EPoS (electronic point-of-sale) and electronic shopping devices, all of which are altering present distribution systems and making it harder for technologically unsophisticated companies to remain competitive. Internet access has led to a growth in home shopping and direct marketing. Changing family patterns and the emergence of important minority consumer groups are driving producers to seek new distribution methods for reaching market segments. Interest rates, inflation and other economic variables affect members of distribution channels at every level. Marketing environmental forces are numerous and complex, and must be taken into consideration if distribution efforts are to be appropriate, efficient and effective (see Chapter 3).

Behaviour of channel members

The marketing channel is a social system with its own conventions and behaviour patterns. Each channel member performs a different role in the system and agrees – implicitly or explicitly – to accept certain rights, responsibilities, rewards and sanctions for non-conformity. Channel members have certain expectations of other channel members. Retailers, for instance, expect wholesalers and manufacturers to maintain adequate inventories and to deliver goods on time. For their part, wholesalers expect retailers to honour payment agreements and to keep them informed of inventory needs. This section discusses several issues related to channel member behaviour, including cooperation and relationship building, conflict and leadership. Marketers need to understand these behavioural issues in order to make effective channel decisions, and to maintain relationships with facilitating channel members and loyal customers.

Channel cooperation and relationship building

Channel cooperation is vital if each member is to gain something from other members.[15] Without cooperation, neither overall channel goals nor member goals can be realized. Policies must be developed that support all essential channel members, otherwise failure of one link in the chain could destroy the channel.

There are several ways to improve channel cooperation. A marketing channel should consider itself a unified system, competing with other systems. This way, individual members will be less likely to take actions that would create disadvantages for other members. Similarly, channel members should agree to direct their efforts towards a common target market so that channel roles can be structured for maximum marketing effectiveness, which in turn can help members achieve their individual objectives.

Heineken, for example, was having difficulty with its 450 distributors; at one point, the time between order and delivery stretched to 12 weeks. A cooperative system of supply chain management, with web-based communications, decreased the lead time from order to delivery to four weeks, and Heineken's sales increased 24 per cent.[16] It is crucial to define precisely the tasks that each member of the channel is to perform. This definition provides a basis for reviewing the intermediaries' performance and helps reduce conflicts because each channel member knows exactly what is expected. It is often in the interests of channel members to build long-term relationships. These relationships can improve channel cooperation and help individual channel members adapt better to the needs of the others.[17]

Channel conflict

Although all channel members work towards the same general goal – distributing goods and services profitably and efficiently – members may sometimes disagree about the best methods for attaining this goal.[18] Each channel member wants to maximize its own profits while maintaining as much autonomy as possible.[19] However, if this self-interest leads to misunderstanding about role expectations, the end result is frustration and conflict for the whole channel. For individual organizations to function together in a single social system, each channel member must communicate clearly and understand role expectations, especially as channel conflict often arises when a channel member does not conduct itself in the manner expected by the other channel members. Communication difficulties are a particular form of channel conflict and can lead to frustration, misunderstandings and poorly coordinated strategies.

The increased use of multiple channels of distribution, driven partly by new technology, has increased the potential for conflict between manufacturers and intermediaries. For example, Hewlett-Packard makes products available directly to consumers through its website (**www. hewlett.packard.com**), thereby directly competing with existing distributors and retailers.[20] SonyStyle sells Sony products online directly to consumers, competing with the large number of independent stores and major retail chains stocking Sony's products.

Channel conflicts also arise when dealers over-emphasize competing products or diversify into product lines traditionally handled by other, more specialized intermediaries. In some cases, conflict develops because producers strive to increase efficiency by circumventing intermediaries, as is happening in marketing channels for microcomputer software and video games. Many software-only stores are establishing direct relationships with software producers, bypassing wholesale distributors altogether. Some dishonest retailers also pirate software and make unauthorized copies, thus cheating other channel members of their due compensation. Consequently, suspicion and mistrust may heighten tensions in software marketing channels.

Although there is no single method for resolving conflict, an atmosphere of cooperation can be re-established if two conditions are met. First, the role of each channel member must be specified. To minimize misunderstanding, all members must be able to expect unambiguous, agreed-on levels of performance from one another. Second, channel members must institute certain measures of channel coordination, a task that requires leadership and the benevolent exercise of control.[21] To prevent channel conflict, producers or other channel members may provide competing resellers with different brands, allocate markets among resellers, define direct sales policies to clarify potential conflict over large accounts, negotiate territorial issues between regional distributors and provide recognition to certain resellers for the importance of their role in distributing to others. Hallmark, for example, distributes its Ambassador greetings card line in discount stores and its name brand Hallmark line in upmarket department and specialist card stores, thus limiting the amount of competition among retailers carrying its products.[22]

Channel leadership

channel power
The ability to influence another channel member's goal achievement

The effectiveness of marketing channels hinges on channel leadership, which may be assumed by producers, retailers or wholesalers. To become a leader, a channel member must want to influence and direct overall channel performance. Furthermore, to attain desired objectives, the leader must possess **channel power**, which is the ability to influence another channel member's goal achievement. As Figure 11.8 shows, the channel leader derives power from seven sources, two of them economic and five non-economic.

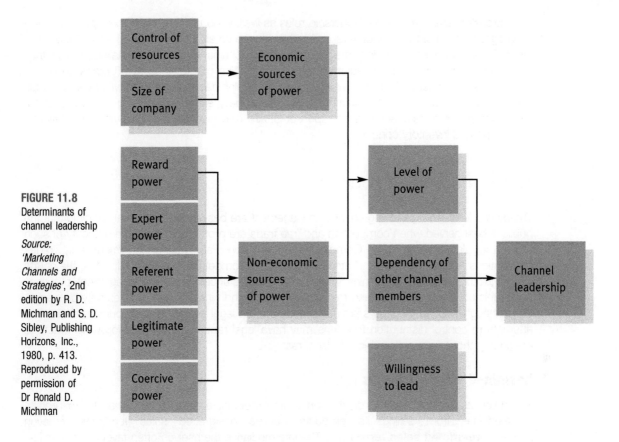

FIGURE 11.8
Determinants of
channel leadership

Source:
'*Marketing
Channels and
Strategies*', 2nd
edition by R. D.
Michman and S. D.
Sibley, Publishing
Horizons, Inc.,
1980, p. 413.
Reproduced by
permission of
Dr Ronald D.
Michman

The five non-economic sources of power – reward, expert, referent, legitimate and coercive –
are crucial for establishing leadership.

1 A channel leader gains *reward* power by providing financial benefits.
2 *Expert* power exists when other channel members believe that the leader provides special
expertise required for the channel to function properly.
3 *Referent* power emerges when other members identify strongly with and emulate the leader.
4 *Legitimate* power is based on a superior–subordinate relationship.
5 *Coercive* power is a function of the leader's ability to punish other channel members.[23]

In many countries, producers assume the leadership role in marketing channels. A
manufacturer – whose large-scale production efficiency demands increasing sales volume – may
exercise power by giving channel members financing, business advice, ordering assistance,
advertising and support materials.[24] For example, BMW and Mercedes-Benz control their dealers
totally, specifying showroom design and layout, discount levels and quotas of models. Coercion,
though, causes dealer dissatisfaction that is stronger than any impact from rewards, so the use
of coercive power can be a major cause of channel conflict.[25]

Retailers can also function as channel leaders, and with the domination of national chains and
own-label merchandise they are increasingly doing so. For example, Sainsbury's challenged
Coca-Cola with its own-label cola, whose packaging bore a strong resemblance to that of the
market leader. Small retailers, too, may share in the leadership role when they command particular consumer respect and patronage in local or regional markets. Among large retailers, Carrefour, IKEA, Marks & Spencer and Tesco base their channel leadership on wide public exposure
to their products. These retailers control many brands and sometimes replace uncooperative
producers. IKEA exercises power by dictating manufacturing techniques, lead times, quality levels and product specifications.

Wholesalers assume channel leadership roles as well, although they were more powerful decades ago, when most manufacturers and retailers were small, under-financed and widely scattered. Today, wholesaler leaders may form voluntary chains with several retailers, which they supply with bulk buying or management services or which market their own brands. In return, the retailers shift most of their purchasing to the wholesaler leader. In Scandinavia, buying groups act as wholesalers, with bulk ordering price advantages, expert advertising and purchasing. Other wholesaler leaders, such as Intersport or SPAR, may also help retailers with store layouts, accounting and inventory control.

Legal issues in channel management

The multitude of laws governing channel management are based on the general principle that the public is best served when competition and free trade are protected. Under the authority of such national legislation as the UK's Competition Commission, Fair Trading Act, Prices Act, Trades Descriptions Act and Consumer Protection Act, or EU Competition Laws and dictates, the courts and regulatory agencies determine under what circumstances channel management practices violate this underlying principle and must be restricted, and when these practices may be permitted. Although channel managers are not expected to be legal experts, they should be aware that attempts to control distribution functions may have legal repercussions. The following practices are among those frequently subject to legal restraint.

Restricted sales territories

To tighten its control over the distribution of its products, a manufacturer may try to prohibit intermediaries from selling its products outside designated sales territories, creating **restricted sales territories**. The intermediaries themselves often favour this practice, because it lets them avoid competition for the producer's brands within their own territories. Many companies have long followed the policy of restricting sales in this fashion. In recent years, the courts have adopted conflicting positions with regard to restricted sales territories. Although they have deemed restricted sales territories a restraint of trade among intermediaries handling the same brands – except for small or newly established companies – the courts have also held that exclusive territories can actually promote competition among dealers handling different brands. At present, the producer's intent in establishing restricted territories and the overall effect of doing so on the market must be evaluated for each individual case.

restricted sales territories
System by which a manufacturer tries to prohibit intermediaries from selling its products outside designated sales territories

Tying contract

When a supplier – usually a manufacturer or franchiser – furnishes a product to a channel member with the stipulation that the channel member must purchase other products as well, a **tying contract** exists. Suppliers, for instance, may institute tying arrangements to move weaker products along with more popular items. To use another example, a franchiser may tie the purchase of equipment and supplies to the sale of franchises, justifying the policy as necessary for quality control and protection of the franchiser's reputation. A related practice is full-line forcing. In this situation, a supplier requires that channel members purchase the supplier's entire line to obtain any of the products. Manufacturers sometimes use full-line forcing to ensure that intermediaries accept new products and that a suitable range of products is available to customers. The courts accept tying contracts when the supplier alone can provide products of a certain quality, when the intermediary is free to carry competing products as well, and when a company has just entered the market. Most other tying contracts are considered illegal.

tying contract
Arrangement whereby a supplier (usually a manufacturer or franchiser) furnishes a product to a channel member with the stipulation that the channel member must purchase other products as well

Exclusive dealing

exclusive dealing
System by which a manufacturer forbids an intermediary to carry the products of competing manufacturers

When a manufacturer forbids an intermediary to carry the products of competing manufacturers, the arrangement is called **exclusive dealing**. A manufacturer receives considerable market protection in an exclusive dealing arrangement and may cut off shipments to an intermediary that violates such an agreement. An exclusive dealing contract is generally legally permitted if dealers and customers in a given market have access to similar products or if the exclusive dealing contract strengthens an otherwise weak competitor.

Refusal to deal

refusal to deal
Situation in which suppliers will not do business with wholesalers or dealers simply because these wholesalers or dealers have resisted policies that are anti-competitive or in restraint of trade

Producers have the right to choose the channel members with whom they will do business and the right not to choose others. Within existing distribution channels, however, suppliers may not refuse to deal with wholesalers or dealers just because these wholesalers or dealers have resisted policies that are anti-competitive or in restraint of trade. Suppliers are further prohibited from organizing some channel members in **refusal to deal** actions against other members who choose not to comply with illegal policies. Recently several supermarket chains, such as ASDA and Tesco, have sought designer clothing from manufacturers such as Levi's. Following the manufacturers' refusal to supply those retailers – as they expected them to discount their lines – the retailers instead acquired the branded leisure wear on the 'grey market', often in eastern Europe or South East Asia. Several court cases have ensued, with the manufacturers arguing their case for being entitled to select which types of retailer to supply.

Summary

Distribution refers to activities that make products available to customers when and where they want to purchase them. A *channel of distribution* (or *marketing channel*) is a group of individuals and organizations that direct the flow of products from producers to customers. In most channels of distribution, producers and customers are linked by *marketing intermediaries* or middlemen, called *merchants* if they take title to products and *functional middlemen* if they do not take title. Channel structure reflects the division of responsibilities among members. Ongoing relationships with customers are seen as increasingly important via relationship marketing. Effective distribution channels and the deployment of channel intermediaries are central to the development of mutually satisfactory ongoing relationships between intermediaries, and between producers and their customers. Most businesses today distribute through more than one channel, with multi-channel selection and management a significant activity for marketers.

Supply chain management is the creation of long-term partnerships among marketing channel members that reduce inefficiencies, costs and redundancies in the marketing channel and develop innovative approaches to satisfying targeted customers. The goal is still to provide customers with the product or service demanded, in line with their expectations, but in a more coordinated way that builds on the combined strengths of the members of the distribution channel. Key tasks in supply chain management include planning, sourcing, facilitating delivery and relationship building to nurture ongoing customer relationships.

Marketing channels serve many functions that may be performed by a single channel member but are mostly accomplished through both the independent and joint efforts of channel members. These functions include creating utility, facilitating exchange efficiencies, alleviating discrepancies, standardizing transactions and providing customer service. Although intermediaries can be eliminated, their functions are vital and cannot be dropped; these activities must be performed by someone in the marketing channel or passed on to customers. Because intermediaries serve both producers and buyers, they reduce the total number of transactions that would otherwise be needed to move products from producer to ultimate users. Intermediaries' specialized functions also help keep down costs.

An *assortment* is a combination of products assembled to provide customer benefits. Intermediaries perform *sorting activities* essential to the development of product assortments. Sorting activities allow channel members to divide roles and separate tasks. Through the basic tasks of *sorting out, accumulation, allocation* and *assorting* products for buyers, intermediaries resolve discrepancies in quantity and assortment. The number and characteristics of intermediaries are determined by the assortments and the expertise needed to perform distribution activities.

Direct marketing, aided by *eCommerce,* has recently encouraged many marketers to cut out channel intermediaries in both consumer and business-to-business transactions.

Channels of distribution are broadly classified as channels for consumer products or channels for business products. Within these two broad categories, different marketing channels are used for different products. Although some consumer goods move directly from producer to consumers, consumer product channels that include wholesalers and retailers are usually more economical and efficient. Business goods move directly from producer to end users more frequently than do consumer goods. Channels for business products may also include agents, *industrial distributors* or both. Most producers use *dual distribution* or multiple channels so that the distribution system can be adjusted for various target markets. Sometimes *strategic channel alliances* are used so that the products of one organization can be distributed through the marketing channels of another. *Multi-channel marketing* is the decision to reach target consumers or business customers through more than one channel. Consumer brands may be retailed in store and via websites, while business products pass through dealers and directly via web-selling.

Integration of marketing channels brings various activities under the management of one channel member. *Vertical channel integration* combines two or more stages of the channel under one management. In the *vertical marketing system (VMS)* a single channel member coordinates or manages channel activity for the mutual benefit of all channel members. Vertical marketing systems may be corporate, administered or contractual. *Horizontal channel integration* combines institutions at the same level of channel operation under a single management.

A marketing channel is managed so that products receive appropriate market coverage. In *intensive distribution,* producers distribute a product using all available outlets. In *selective distribution,* outlets are screened to use those most qualified for exposing a product properly. *Exclusive distribution* usually uses one outlet to distribute a product in a large geographic area when there is a limited market for the product.

When selecting distribution channels for products, manufacturers evaluate potential channel members carefully. Producers consider the organization's objectives and available resources; the location, density and size of a market; buying behaviour in the target market; product attributes; and external forces in the marketing environment. Technology, notably eCommerce, has recently played a major role in certain markets in the selection of distribution channels.

A marketing channel is a social system in which individuals and organizations are linked by a common goal: the profitable and efficient distribution of goods and services. The positions or roles of channel members are associated with rights, responsibilities and rewards, as well as sanctions for non-conformity. Channels function most efficiently when members cooperate; when they deviate from their roles, channel conflict can arise. Effective marketing channels are usually a result of channel leadership and of relationship building between channel members.

Channel leaders can facilitate or hinder other channel members' goal achievement, deriving this *channel power* from seven sources, two of them economic and five non-economic. Producers are in an excellent position to structure channel policy and to use technical expertise and consumer acceptance to influence other channel members. Retailers gain channel control through consumer confidence, wide product mixes and intimate knowledge of consumers. Wholesalers and buying groups become channel leaders when they have expertise that other channel members value and when they can coordinate functions to match supply with demand.

Channel management is governed by a variety of legal issues. These are based on the principle that the public is best served when competition and free trade are protected. Various practices may be subject to legal restraint. To tighten their distribution control, manufacturers may try to operate *restricted sales territories,* where intermediaries are barred from selling products outside designated areas. A *tying contract* occurs when a supplier stipulates that another channel member must purchase other products in addition to the one originally supplied. *Exclusive dealing* occurs when a manufacturer forbids an intermediary to carry the products of competing manufacturers. *Refusal to deal* means that a producer will not do business with a wholesaler or dealer that has resisted policies that are anti-competitive or in restraint of trade.

Key links

The choice of marketing channel is critical to the success of a marketing strategy, as explored in this chapter, and channel selection is very much a part of the marketing remit. This chapter should be read in conjunction with:

- Chapter 2, the overview of marketing strategy.
- Chapter 8, the explanation of the product element of the marketing mix.

Important terms

Channel of distribution (or marketing channel)
Marketing intermediary
Merchants
Functional middlemen
Supply chain management
Assortment
Sorting activities
Sorting out
Accumulation
Allocation
Assorting
eCommerce
Industrial distributor
Dual distribution
Strategic channel alliance
Multi-channel marketing
Vertical channel integration
Vertical marketing system (VMS)
Horizontal channel integration
Intensive distribution
Selective distribution
Exclusive distribution
Channel power

Restricted sales territories
Exclusive dealing
Tying contract
Refusal to deal

Discussion and review questions

1 Compare and contrast the four major types of marketing channel for consumer products. Through which type of channel is each of the following products most likely to be distributed: (a) new cars, (b) cheese biscuits, (c) cut-your-own Christmas trees, (d) new textbooks, (e) sofas, (f) soft drinks?

2 'Shorter channels are usually a more direct means of distribution and therefore are more efficient.' Comment on this statement.

3 Describe an industrial distributor. What types of product are marketed through industrial distributors?

4 Why might a producer choose to use more than one marketing channel?

5 Why do consumers often blame intermediaries for distribution inefficiencies? List several reasons.

6 How do the major functions that intermediaries perform help resolve discrepancies in assortment and in quantity?

7 How does the number of intermediaries in the channel relate to the assortments retailers need?

8 Can one channel member perform all channel functions?

9 Identify and explain the major factors that influence decision-makers' selection of marketing channels.

10 Name and describe companies that use (a) vertical integration and (b) horizontal integration in their marketing channels.

11 Explain the major characteristics of each of the three types of vertical marketing system (VMS).

12 Explain the differences among intensive, selective and exclusive methods of distribution.

13 What impact has the growing popularity of eCommerce had on marketing channels?

14 'Channel cooperation requires that members support the overall channel goals to achieve individual goals.' Comment on this statement.

15 How do power bases within the channel influence the selection of the channel leader?

16 Why is multi-channel marketing increasingly the norm?

17 What considerations should influence multi-channel selection?

Recommended readings

Arikan, A., *Multichannel Marketing: Metrics and Methods for On and Offline Success* (Wiley, 2008).

Christopher, M., *Logistics and Supply Chain Management* (FT/Prentice-Hall, 2010).

Gattorna, J., ed., *Strategic Supply Chain Alignment: Best Practices in Supply Chain Management* (Gower, 2005).

Harrison, A. and van Hoek, R., *Logistics Management and Strategy: Competing Through the Supply Chain* (FT/Prentice-Hall, 2010).

Rosenbloom, B., *Marketing Channels: A Management View* (South Western, 2012).

Rushton, A., Croucher, P., Oxley J., and Baker, P., *The Handbook of Logistics and Distribution Management* (Kogan Page, 2010).

Internet exercise

The fortunes of many manufacturers depend on their dealer network, particularly producers of construction equipment. Take a look at two such companies' websites, and examine what they say about their dealer network and parts/service support: **www.caterpillar.com** and **www.jcb.com**

1 In the context of these websites, how important to these businesses is the chosen route to market: the dealer network?

2 In terms of delivering customer service, what is the role in the marketing channel of these dealerships?

Applied mini-case

Most recorded music used to be purchased by consumers from music stores or mail-order catalogues. First the Internet enabled e-selling from retailers' catalogues, and now it has permitted the instant downloading of a fan's favourite tracks. Not only are bands cutting out traditional distribution channels by offering new material directly to their fans via the Web, often via viral campaigns, but mainstream labels are also side-tracking the music store as a response to this growing trend.

It is not only artists and record labels that have embraced the Internet. Non-music brands wishing to appeal to youthful target markets have also sought to do so by making music available online to their customers. For example, Sony – wanting to sell more entertainment systems – has various downloads under *myplay*, *Vevo*, *Icon Collectibles* and *Aviama*; Coke launched *Music on Coke Zone*; Starbucks has developed an in-store music service called *Hear Music* to let coffee drinkers download tracks and provides downloads from its online StarbucksStore site; and T-Mobile has created a mobile phone-based music download service, *Mobile Jukebox*, designed to appeal to its younger mobile phone users.

Question

How can music store operators, such as HMV and Fopp, strive to maintain a strong customer base in the face of such substitute competition from e-downloads and even non-music stores providing music downloads?

First direct's innovative banking channels

Case study

With our 1st Account you'll get £100 for switching and a £250 interest-free overdraft comes as standard. Discover how simple our Easyswitch team make moving your account and just how refreshing it is to talk to *real people* 24 7 365. We're sure you'll love us.

www.firstdirect.com, Jun 2011

Most consumers have a bank cheque account from which cash is drawn, bills are paid and cheques written, and into which salaries, pensions or student loan cheques are paid. For many consumers, the bank is a high-street or shopping-centre office – imposing, formal and often intimidating. Whether it's NatWest, Barclays or Lloyds TSB in the UK or ABN AMRO or Rabobank in the Netherlands, each high-street bank is fairly alike, with similar products and services, personnel, branch layouts, locations and opening hours. Differentiation has been difficult to achieve and generally impossible to maintain over any length of time as competitors have copied rivals' moves. Promotional strategy and brand image have been the focus for most banking organizations, supported with more minor tactical changes in, for example, opening hours or service charges. For many bank account holders, however, the branch – with its restricted openings, formal ambience and congested town-centre location – is the only point of contact for the bulk of transactions.

First direct, owned by HSBC but managed separately, broke the mould in 1989. Launched with a then massive £6 million promotional campaign, first direct bypassed the traditional marketing channel. First direct has no branches and no branch overhead and operating costs. It provides free banking, unlike its high-street competitors with their systems of bank charges combined with interest paid on positive balances. First direct is a telephone and online banking service that offers full banking, mortgage, loan, investment/saving, insurance, foreign currency and credit card services, plus ATM 'hole in the wall' cash cards through HSBC's international service-till network. All normal banking transactions can be completed over the telephone or online.

Initial reactions were positive, with many non-HSBC account holders switching to the innovative new style of banking. The more traditional consumer – who equates the marbled halls of the Victorian branches with heritage, security and traditional values – has been less easily converted. For the targeted, more financially aware and independent income earner, first direct is proving very popular. Research shows that first direct is the most recommended bank with the most satisfied customers.

First direct's services and products are not new, but the chosen marketing channels are innovative: no branches, only telephone call centres, online banking and texting. Customers no longer have to reach inaccessible, parked-up, town-centre branches with queues and restricted opening hours. The company is fast to adopt evolving technologies and opportunities to interact with its customers digitally:

We're always trying to figure out new ways to make our customers' lives easier so as you'd expect, we're at the forefront of new technologies. We offer you *Mobile Banking*, *Text Message Banking*, award-winning online *Podcasts and Vodcasts* and on top of all that we create online spaces for you to communicate with us and other customers, inviting you to become part of our community and give voice to your thoughts. Check out *Little Black Book*, *Talking Point* and *Social Media Newsroom*.

www.firstdirect.com, Jun 2011

First direct has introduced a service, alien to some more traditional tastes perhaps, that is more readily available and with fewer costs. Hundreds of thousands of consumers have welcomed the launch of this new option, but millions have preferred to bank the traditional way. For HSBC, this is fine: its HSBC proposition caters for those consumers preferring the more traditional banking format, while first direct caters for the new breed of telephone, online and texting customers.

Sources: **www.firstdirect.com**, Jun 2011; *Marketing: Concepts and Strategies*, 5th edition, firstdirect, May 2012.

Questions for discussion

1 Why is innovation in marketing channels generally difficult to achieve?

2 Why was first direct different from its rivals? What gave it differentiation when it first launched?

3 Why might some potential customers of first direct have reservations about the innovative nature of the service?

CHAPTER 12

Pricing

"Pricing causes many arguments amongst senior management teams because it makes or breaks the business model and generally is hugely important to the customer"

Objectives

- To understand the characteristics and role of price

- To be aware of the differences between price and non-price competition

- To explore key factors that affect pricing decisions

- To examine different pricing objectives

- To consider issues unique to the pricing of products for business markets

- To analyze the concept of economic value to the customer

- To understand the eight major stages of the process used to establish prices

- To learn about demand for a product and to analyze the relationships between demand, costs and profits

- To explore the selection of a pricing strategy and to understand how to determine a specific price

INTRODUCTION

price
The value placed on what is exchanged

To a buyer, **price** is the value placed on what is exchanged.[1] Something of value – usually buying power – is exchanged for satisfaction or utility. In most marketing situations, the price is very evident, and buyer and seller are aware of the amount of value each must give up to complete the exchange.[2] As described in Chapter 3, buying power depends on a buyer's income, credit and wealth. Because buyers have limited resources they must weigh up the usefulness of a product or the satisfaction derived from it against its cost to decide whether the exchange is worthwhile. **Financial**

financial price
The basis of market exchanges; the quantified value of what is exchanged

price is most usually the basis of market exchanges. This can be used to quantify almost anything of value that is exchanged, including ideas, services, rights and goods. Thus, the financial value of a Paris penthouse might be 1.5 million euros. Yet price does not always have to have a financial basis. Barter, the trading of products, is the oldest form of exchange.

Price impacts strongly on how businesses fare competitively, so marketers need to give careful consideration to pricing issues. Price is critical to the marketing mix because it affects directly how much revenue is generated. As it can be changed very quickly, price is more flexible than other marketing mix elements. Businesses must avoid seeing price purely in terms of setting monetary price points. Because of the psychological impact of price on customers, price also has a symbolic value. A broader view of pricing is therefore needed which takes into account issues such as target customers' perceptions of value for money and requirements for easy payment terms.

There are essential stages for establishing prices, which involve taking into consideration a wide range of factors. Economic conditions, fluctuations in market growth and levels of competition all affect the price that customers are prepared to pay. Careful judgement is needed to ensure that these factors are taken into consideration when setting prices so that customers believe they are getting reasonable value for money.

Talk is not always cheap

From very high to very low, Nokia has a cell phone handset priced to fit wallets in every market. Headquartered in Finland, the company is the global leader in cell phones and rings up net sales of 42 billion Euros.

Nokia's strategy of marketing a full range of products, priced appropriately for each target market, has helped the company cope with intense competition from strong rivals like Samsung, Motorola, Research in Motion (maker of Blackberry), and Apple.

At the top of the pricing range, Nokia's status-symbol Vertu phones carry price tags starting at around £3500. Vertu phones are made of titanium, stainless steel, gold or platinum, and many are decorated with diamonds and other super-luxury touches. Special edition versions can sell for more than £200 000. Even the ringtone is distinctive and customers can enjoy a host of exclusive and expensive accessories; further signs that Vertu is not just another cell phone.

At the low end of the pricing range are basic phones geared to first-time buyers in developing countries. The company sells millions of inexpensive cell phones in China and India, which are by far its two highest volume markets. In those countries, it is also profiting from increased demand for its mid-priced smartphones that allow users to check e-mail, send and receive text messages, browse the web, participate in social media, download music, and play games.

For business customers, Nokia has introduced full keyboard, multifunction smartphones that can access corporate e-mail systems. Thanks to its economics of scale, Nokia can keep costs low and set affordable prices to encourage switching from Blackberry smartphones, a favourite among corporate users. Looking ahead, Nokia continues to research the communication needs and priorities of consumers and businesspeople, with an eye towards fine-tuning its pricing strategy and achieving its worldwide profit and market-share objectives.

Source: © Misha Gorden/Alamy

All companies, irrespective of whether their products are costly or cheap, use price along with other elements to distinguish their products from competitive brands. For these companies, as for most businesses, pricing is a crucial element in the marketing mix. However, as this chapter's 'Opener' clearly illustrates, a variety of factors impact upon pricing decisions. How much mobile phone buyers are prepared to pay is linked into their motives for buying and the services they wish to receive. The range of factors which affect pricing are considered later in this chapter.

This chapter begins by explaining what is meant by price and considers its importance to marketing practitioners. It then explores pricing objectives and the various factors affecting pricing decisions. The notion of perceived value for money is considered next. The chapter then examines pricing in business markets and the concept of economic value to the customer, and concludes by over-viewing the essential stages for establishing prices.

The characteristics and role of price

Terms used to describe price

Price is expressed differently in various exchanges. For instance, insurance companies charge a *premium* to holidaymakers requiring protection against the cost of illness or injury. A police officer who stops a motorist for speeding writes a ticket that requires a *fine* to be paid. In London, a congestion *charge* is levied on motorists travelling in central areas. An accountant charges a *fee,* and a *fare* is charged for travelling by plane, railway or taxi. A *toll* is sometimes charged for the use of motorway bridges. *Rent* is paid for the use of equipment or for a flat. An estate agent receives a *commission* on the sale of a property. A *deposit* is made to reserve merchandise. A *tip* helps pay waitresses or waiters for their services. *Interest* is charged for loans, and *taxes* are paid for government services. The value of many products is called *price.*

Although price may be expressed in a variety of ways, it is important to remember that the purpose of this concept is to quantify and express the value of the items in a marketing exchange.

The importance of price to marketers

As pointed out in Chapter 9, developing a product may be a lengthy process. It takes time to plan promotion and to communicate benefits. Distribution usually requires a long-term commitment to dealers who will handle the product. Often price and customer service levels are the only aspects a marketer can change quickly to respond to changes in demand or to the actions of competitors. However, as customers may be alienated by significant price changes, this does not mean that price is flexible in all situations.

Price is also a key element in the marketing mix because it relates directly to the generation of total revenue.[3] The following equation is an important one for the entire organization:

Profits = total revenues – total costs

or

Profits = (price × quantities sold) – total costs

Prices can have a dramatic impact on a company's profits. Price affects the profit equation in several ways. It directly influences the equation because it is a major component. It has an indirect impact because it can be a major determinant of the quantities sold. As will be explained, for many products an increase in price leads to a reduction of numbers sold. Even more indirectly, price influences total costs through its impact on quantities sold. Consequently, even a relatively small reduction in prices can cause profits to fall, sometimes dramatically. The relationship illustrates the difficulties faced by businesses attempting to build a differential advantage based on low prices. Marketers need to be fully aware of these stark relationships when setting prices, and the knock on ramifications for their organization's financial stability and corporate objectives.

Because price has a psychological impact on customers, marketers can use it symbolically. By raising a price, they can emphasize the quality of a product and try to increase the status associated with its ownership. The declining fortunes of Chevas Royal Scotch whisky were reversed following a substantial price rise! Lowering a price can also have a dramatic impact on demand, attracting bargain-hunting customers who are prepared to spend extra time and effort to save a small amount.

Price and non-price competition

A product offering can compete on either a price or a non-price basis. The choice will affect not only pricing decisions and activities but also those associated with other marketing mix decision variables.

Price competition

price competition
A policy whereby a marketer emphasizes price as an issue, and matches or beats the prices of competitors

When **price competition** is used, a marketer emphasizes price as an issue, and matches or beats competitors' prices. Budget airline easyJet engages in price competition and stresses its low prices in its advertisements. To compete effectively on a price basis, a company should be the low-cost producer of the product. If all companies producing goods in an industry charge the same, the company with the lowest costs is the most profitable. Companies that stress low price as a key element in the marketing mix tend to produce standardized products. For example, suppliers of fuel oils use price competition. Sellers using this approach may be prepared and able to change prices frequently, particularly in response to competitors altering their prices. In many parts of the world, the postal service and UPS or DHL engage in direct price competition in their pricing of overnight express-delivery services.

Price competition gives a marketer flexibility. Prices can be altered to account for changes in the company's costs or in demand for the product, or when competitors cut prices. However, a major drawback of price competition is that competitors may also have the flexibility to adjust their prices to match or beat another company's price cuts. If so, a price war may result. Furthermore, if a user of price competition is forced to raise prices, competing companies may decide not to do the same. The supermarket giants sometimes seem to be locked into a spiral of price competition. Waitrose has 1000 popular lines visibly price-aligned in-store on-fixture to Tesco, often perceived to provide lower prices compared to upmarket Waitrose. Companies like Procter & Gamble have attempted to strengthen consumer loyalty

FIGURE 12.1
Retailers' prominent use of 'sales' is a well known example of price competition

Source: © Mark Richardson / Alamy

by cutting the prices of key brands permanently. The first two categories to benefit were the core markets of washing-up liquids, such as Fairy Liquid, and disposable nappies, such as Pampers.

Non-price competition

non-price competition
A policy in which a seller elects not to focus on price but to emphasize other factors instead

In **non-price competition**, a seller elects not to focus on price but instead emphasizes distinctive product features, service, product quality, promotion, packaging or other factors to distinguish the product from competing brands, for example Figure 12.2. Organizations that use non-price competition aim to increase unit sales in other ways. For example, Louis Vuitton stresses the exclusivity, quality and fashionability

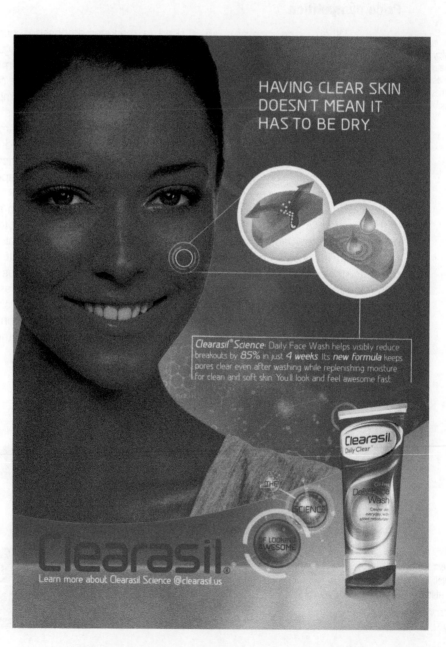

FIGURE 12.2
Although priced to be competitive with rival brands, Clearasil promotes functional product benefits

Source: Image courtesy of The Advertising Archives

of its handbags, rather than competitive price. A company can use non-price competition to build customer loyalty towards its brand. If customers prefer a brand or store because of non-price issues, they may not easily be lured away by competing offers. Indeed, such customers might become confused or irritated if price cuts are offered. Buyers of Chanel clothing, perfume or accessories enjoy the exclusivity associated with the high price. The implication is that price is not the most durable factor in terms of maintaining customer loyalty. However, when price is the primary reason that customers buy a particular brand, the competition can attract such customers through price cuts.

Non-price competition is workable under the right conditions. A company must be able to distinguish its brand through unique product features, higher quality, customer service, promotion, packaging and the like (see Figure 12.2). The brand's distinguishing features should be difficult, if not impossible, for a competitor to copy. Buyers must not only be able to perceive these distinguishing characteristics but must also view them as desirable. Finally, the organization must promote the distinguishing characteristics of the brand extensively in order to establish its superiority and to set it apart from competitors in the minds of buyers.

Many European companies put less emphasis on price than do their American counterparts. They look for a competitive edge by concentrating on promotion, research and development, marketing research and marketing channel considerations. In a study of pricing strategy, many companies stated specifically that they emphasize research and development and technological superiority; competition based on price was seldom a major marketing consideration.[4]

A marketer attempting to compete on a non-price basis must still consider competitors' prices. The business must be aware of competitors' prices and will probably price its brand near, or slightly above, competing brands. As an example, Sony sells flat screen televisions and Blu-ray players in a highly competitive market and charges higher prices than other manufacturers for them. Sony can achieve this because its emphasis on high product quality distinguishes it from its competitors and allows it to set higher prices.

Factors affecting pricing decisions

Pricing decisions are affected by many factors. Often, there is considerable uncertainty about reactions to price on the part of buyers, channel members, competitors and others. Price is also an important consideration in marketing planning, market analysis and sales forecasting. It is a major issue when assessing a brand's positioning relative to competing brands. Most factors that affect pricing decisions can be grouped into one of the nine categories shown in Figure 12.3. This section explores how each of these nine groups of factors enters into price decision-making.

Organizational and marketing objectives

Marketers should set prices that are consistent with the organization's goals and mission. For example, cosmetic brands such as Helena Rubenstein and Givenchy are positioned at the exclusive end of the market, and have high price tags to match. Marketers in these organizations know that discounting prices on these brands would not be in line with the overall organizational goal.

Decision-makers should also make pricing decisions that are compatible with the organization's marketing objectives. Say, for instance, that one of a producer's marketing objectives is a 12 per cent increase in unit sales by the end of the next year. Assuming that buyers are price sensitive, increasing the price or setting a price above the average market price would not be in line with the company's sales objective. A case in point: GM (Vauxhall) has introduced high-performance, well-specified model variants to the top of each of its model ranges – for example,

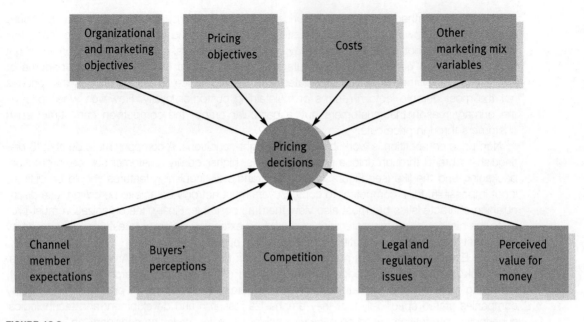

FIGURE 12.3
Factors that affect pricing decisions

the £19 000 Corsa 1.6 V6 VXR and the £34 000 Insignia 2.8T V6 VXR. Such prices ensure that these particular models have only limited appeal. GM's stated objective, however, is to be market leader in terms of sales volume. The company, therefore, is careful to price the great majority of its cars in line with the price expectations of the bulk of the car buying public and fleet operators – far below these £19 000 Corsa and £34 000 Insignia levels.

Pricing objectives

pricing objectives
Overall goals that describe what a company wants to achieve through its pricing efforts

Pricing objectives are overall goals that describe what a company wants to achieve through its pricing efforts. The type of pricing objective a marketer uses will have considerable bearing on the determination of prices.[5] Marketers often use multiple pricing objectives, including those that emphasize survival, profit, return on investment, market share, cash flow, status quo or product quality (see Table 12.1). Thus, a market share pricing objective usually causes a company to price a product below competing brands of similar quality to attract competitors' customers to the company's brand. This type of pricing can lead to lower profits, but may be used temporarily in the hope of gaining market share. By contrast, a cash flow pricing objective may involve setting a relatively high price, which can place the product at a competitive disadvantage. Paradoxically, a cash flow pricing objective sometimes results in a low price sustained in the long term. However, this type of objective is more likely to be addressed by using temporary price reductions, such as sales, refunds and special discounts.

Because pricing objectives influence decisions in most functional areas – including finance, accounting and production – the objectives must be consistent with the company's overall mission and purpose (see Chapter 2). Insurance is an area where pricing is a major concern. As competition has intensified, insurance executives have realized that their products must be priced to meet both short-term profit goals and long-term strategic objectives. Changes in the pricing objectives that companies use can occur for various reasons. For example, the objective of

TABLE 12.1 Different types of pricing objective

Survival
A fundamental pricing objective is survival. Most businesses will tolerate difficulties such as short-run losses and internal upheaval if they are necessary for survival. Because price is a flexible and convenient variable to adjust, it is sometimes used to increase sales volume to levels that match the company's expenses.
Profit
Although businesses often claim they aim to maximize profits, in practice this objective is difficult to measure. As a result, profit objectives tend to be set at satisfactory levels. Specific profit objectives may be stated in terms of actual monetary amounts or in terms of percentage change relative to previous profits.
Return on investment
Pricing to attain a specified rate of return on the company's investment is a profit-related pricing objective. Most pricing objectives based on return on investment (ROI) are achieved by trial and error, because not all cost and revenue data needed to project the return on investment are available when prices are set.
Market share
Many companies establish pricing objectives to maintain or increase a product's market share in relation to total industry sales. For example, car companies such as Volkswagen have been known to cut prices on existing models when introducing new ones, to boost share of the car market. Maintaining or increasing market share need not depend on growth in industry sales. A company can increase its market share even though sales for the total industry are decreasing. On the other hand, if the overall market is growing, a business's sales volume may actually increase as its market share decreases.
Cash flow
Some companies set prices to recover cash as fast as possible, especially when a short product life cycle (PLC) is anticipated or the capital spent to develop products needs to be recovered quickly. However, the use of cash flow and recovery as an objective oversimplifies the value of price in contributing to profits. A disadvantage of this pricing objective could be high prices, which might allow competitors with lower prices to gain a large share of the market.
Status quo
In some cases, a business may be in a favourable position and may simply wish to maintain the status quo. Such objectives can focus on maintaining a certain market share, meeting (but not beating) competitors' prices, achieving price stability or maintaining a favourable public image. Such an approach can reduce a company's risks by helping to stabilize demand for its products. The use of status quo pricing objectives sometimes leads to a climate of non-price competition in an industry.
Product quality
A company might have the objective of product quality leadership in the industry. For example, the construction equipment manufacturer JCB aims to be ranked as one of the leading companies in its industry in terms of product quality and customer satisfaction. This normally dictates a relatively high price to cover the high product quality and/or the high cost of research and development.

return on investment may be used less as managers and marketers in diversified companies stress the creation of shareholder value. When shareholder value is used as a performance objective, strategies – including those involving price – are evaluated according to their impact on the value investors perceive in the company.[6]

Costs

Obviously, costs must be an issue when establishing price. A business may temporarily sell products below cost to match the competition, to generate cash flow or even to increase market share; but in the long run it cannot survive by adopting this approach. A marketer should be careful to analyze all costs so that they can be included in the total costing for a product. Marketers must also take into account the costs that a particular product shares with other products in the product line, particularly the costs of research and development, production and distribution. Services are especially subject to cost sharing. For example, the costs of a bank building are spread over the costs of all services the bank offers.[7] Most marketers view a product's cost as a minimum, or floor, below which the product cannot be priced.

Other marketing mix variables

All marketing mix variables are closely interrelated. Pricing decisions can influence decisions and activities associated with product, place/distribution, promotion and customer service variables. A product's price frequently affects the demand for the item. A high price, for instance, may result in low unit sales, which in turn may lead to higher production costs per unit. Conversely, lower per-unit production costs may result from a low price. For many products, buyers associate better product quality with a high price and poorer product quality with a low price. This perceived price-quality relationship influences customers' overall image of products or brands. Thus consumers may be prepared to pay a high price for Rayban sunglasses because they believe they are a high-status item.

Pricing decisions influence the number of competing brands in a product category. When a company introduces a product, sets a relatively high price and achieves high unit sales, competitors may be attracted to this product category. If a company fixes a low price, the low profit margin may be unattractive to potential competition.

The price of a product is linked to several dimensions of its distribution. Premium-priced products are often marketed through selective or exclusive distribution; lower-priced products in the same product category may be sold through intensive distribution. For example, Montblanc pens are distributed through selective distribution and Bic pens through intensive distribution. The way in which a product is stored and transported may also be associated with its price. As Figure 12.4 shows, when deciding about a product's price, a producer must consider the profit margins of marketing channel members such as wholesalers and retailers. This way, channel members can be adequately compensated for the functions they perform.

The way a product is promoted can be affected by its price. Bargain prices are often included in advertisements, whereas premium prices are less likely to be mentioned. However, the exclusivity associated with a premium price is sometimes included in advertisements for upmarket items, such as luxury holidays or exclusive jewellery. Higher-priced products are more likely to require personal selling efforts than lower-priced ones. Indeed, there may be an expectation that a high price is accompanied by enhanced levels of customer service. A customer may purchase an inexpensive watch in a self-service environment but hesitate to buy an expensive watch in the same store, even if it is available there.

The price structure can affect a salesperson's relationship with customers. A complex pricing structure takes longer to explain to customers, is more likely to confuse the buyer and may cause misunderstandings that result in long-term customer dissatisfaction. For example, the pricing structure used by many hotels is complex and can confuse potential guests.

Channel member expectations

When making price decisions, a producer must consider what distribution channel members (such as wholesalers, retailers and dealers) expect. A channel member certainly expects to receive a profit for the functions performed. The amount of profit expected depends on the amount of time and resources expended, and on an assessment of what would be gained by handling a competing product instead.

Channel members often expect producers to provide discounts for large orders and quick payment. Discounts are discussed later in this chapter. At times, resellers expect producers to provide support activities, such as sales training, repair advisory services, cooperative advertising, sales promotions and perhaps a programme for returning unsold merchandise to the producer. These support activities clearly incur costs, so a producer must consider these costs when determining prices.

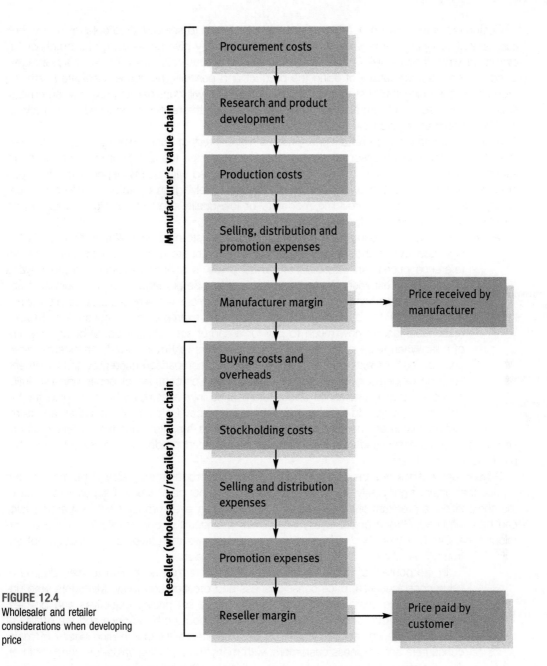

FIGURE 12.4
Wholesaler and retailer considerations when developing price

Buyers' perceptions

When making pricing decisions, marketers should be concerned with two vital questions.

1 How will customers interpret prices and respond to them? Interpretation in this context refers to what the price means or what it communicates to customers. Does the price mean 'high quality' or 'low quality', or 'great deal', 'fair price' or 'rip-off'?

2 How will customers respond to the price? Customer response refers to whether the price will move customers closer to the purchase of the product and the degree to which the price enhances their satisfaction with the purchase experience and with the product after purchase.

Customers' interpretation of and response to a price are to some degree determined by their assessment of what they receive compared with what they give up to make the purchase. In evaluating what they receive, customers will consider product attributes, benefits, advantages, disadvantages, the probability of using the product and possibly the status associated with the product. In assessing the cost of the product, customers will consider its price, the amount of time and effort required to obtain the product and perhaps the resources required to maintain or use the product after purchase.

At times, customers interpret a higher price as higher product quality. They are especially likely to make this price-quality association when they cannot judge the quality of the product themselves. This is not always the case: whether price is equated with quality depends on the types of customer and product involved. Obviously, marketers relying on customers making a price-quality association who are providing moderate or low-quality products at high prices, will be unable to build long-term customer relationships.

internal reference price
A price developed in the buyer's mind through experience with the product

When interpreting and responding to prices, how do customers determine if the price is too high, too low or about right? In general, they compare prices with internal or external reference prices. An **internal reference price** is a price developed in the buyer's mind through experience with the product. It is a belief that a product should cost approximately a certain amount. As consumers, previous experiences provide internal reference prices for a number of products. For example, most consumers have a reasonable idea of how much to pay for a can of soft drink, a loaf of bread or a litre of milk. When there is less experience, consumers rely more heavily on external reference prices.[8] An **external reference price** is a comparison price provided by others, such as retailers or manufacturers.[9] Customers' perceptions of prices are also influenced by their expectations about future price increases, by what they paid for the product recently, and by what they would like to pay for the product. Other factors affecting customers' perception of whether the price is right include time or financial constraints, the costs associated with searching for lower-priced products, and expectations that products will go on sale.

external reference price
A comparison price provided by others

Buyers' perceptions of a product relative to competing products may allow a business to set a price that differs significantly from rivals' prices. If the product is deemed superior to most of the competition, a premium price may be feasible. However, even products with superior quality can be overpriced. Strong brand loyalty sometimes provides the opportunity to charge a premium price. On the other hand, if buyers view a product less than favourably – though not extremely negatively – a lower price may generate sales.

value-conscious consumers
Those concerned about price and quality of a product

In the context of price, buyers can be characterized according to their degree of value consciousness, price consciousness and prestige-sensitivity. Marketers who understand these characteristics are better able to set pricing objectives and policies. **Value-conscious consumers** are concerned about both the price and the quality of a product. Recent economic difficulties have altered the purchasing habits of many consumers and business customers, with many more placing value-for-money high on their list of key customer values when making purchasing decisions. **Price-conscious consumers** strive to pay low prices. **Prestige-sensitive consumers** focus on purchasing products that signify prominence and status. For example, the Porsche Cayenne, one of the highest-priced sports utility vehicles ever marketed, created record sales and profits for Porsche. Only 18 per cent of Cayenne buyers had previously owned a Porsche; many of the rest were attracted to the vehicle by the prestige associated with the Porsche name. On the other hand, some consumers vary in their degree of value, price and prestige consciousness. In some segments, consumers are still 'trading up' to more status-conscious products despite the credit crunch and economic turmoil of recent years: this occurs with cars, electrical appliances, restaurants and even pet food. This trend has benefited companies such as Starbucks and BMW, which can charge premium prices for high-quality, prestige products.

price-conscious consumers
Those striving to pay low prices

prestige-sensitive consumers
Individuals drawn to products that signify prominence and status

Competition

A marketer needs to know competitors' prices so that a company can adjust its own prices accordingly.[10] This does not mean that a company will necessarily match competitors' prices; it may set its price above or below theirs. It is also important for marketers to assess how competitors will respond to price adjustments. Will they change their prices (some may not) and, if so, will they raise or lower them? For example, when motor insurance providers stress their keen pricing, competitors often do the same.

Chapter 3 describes several types of competitive market structure that impact upon price setting. When a company operates as a monopoly and is unregulated, it can set whatever prices the market will bear. However, the company may avoid adopting the highest possible pricing for fear of inviting government regulation or because it wants to penetrate a market by using a lower price. If the monopoly is regulated, it normally has less pricing flexibility; the regulatory body lets it set prices that generate a reasonable, but not excessive, return. A government-owned monopoly may price products below cost to make them accessible to people who could not otherwise afford them. However, government-owned monopolies sometimes charge higher prices to control demand.

In an oligopoly, only a few sellers operate, and there are high barriers to competitive entry. A business in such an industry – for example, telecommunications, drugs or steel – can raise its price, hoping that its competitors will do the same. Very little can be gained through price cuts because other companies are likely to follow suit when an organization cuts its price to gain a competitive edge.

A market structure characterized by monopolistic competition means numerous sellers with differentiated product offerings. The products are differentiated by physical characteristics, features, quality and brand image. The distinguishing characteristics of its product may allow a company to set a different price from its competitors. However, businesses engaged in a monopolistic competitive market structure are likely to practise non-price competition, as discussed earlier in this chapter.

Under conditions of perfect competition, there are many sellers. Buyers view all sellers' products as the same. All companies sell their products at the going market price and so there is no flexibility in setting prices.

Legal and regulatory issues

At times, government action sways marketers' pricing decisions. To curb inflation, the government may invoke price controls, 'freeze' prices at certain levels or determine the rates at which prices can be increased. Following the privatization of public utilities, the UK government set up regulatory bodies such as Ofwat for water, Ofgem for gas and electricity and Ofcom for the communications industry, which police pricing and billing, often establishing maximum and minimum charges.

Many regulations and laws affect pricing decisions and activities. Not only must marketers refrain from fixing prices, they must also develop independent pricing policies and set prices in ways that do not involve collusion. Over the years, legislation has been established to safeguard consumers and businesses from pricing sharp practices. In the UK, the Competition Commission prevents the creation of monopolistic situations. The consumer is protected by the Trade Descriptions Act, the Fair Trading Act, the Consumer Protection Act and many others. All countries have similar legislation, and the European Union legislates to protect consumers within the community.

perceived value for money
The benefit consumers perceive to be inherent in a product or service, weighed against the price demanded

Perceived value

Most discussions about pricing revolve around the actual monetary value – the price – to be charged for the good or service. However, the **perceived value for money** to consumers is also vital. This is the benefit consumers see as inherent in a product or service, weighed against the price demanded. Sometimes, particularly in consumer markets, these benefits are real and measurable, in other cases they are more psychological. For instance, interest-free credit, maintenance contracts and extended warranties are all features that may affect a consumer's perception of value for money. Consumers will not pay more than they value the benefit inherent in a product or service. Consumers balance the price demanded, typically in monetary terms, against the anticipated level of use and satisfaction to be gained from buying and using the specific product. This assessment is influenced by the consumers' previous experience of the brand and similar products, the perceived quality of the product in question, its brand image, purpose, anticipated usage, overall appeal and the nature of competing offers. These emotive issues are often difficult to quantify, but through qualitative marketing research, most businesses are able to assess their target market's views of value.

Pricing for business markets

As explored in Chapter 5, business markets consist of individuals and businesses that purchase products for resale, for use in their own operations or for producing other products. Establishing prices for this category of business-to-business buyer sometimes differs from setting prices for consumers. Differences in the size of purchases, geographic factors and transport considerations require sellers to adjust prices. This section discusses several issues unique to the pricing of industrial products and business markets including discounts, geographic pricing, transfer pricing and price discrimination. The section concludes by considering the concept of economic value to the customer (EVC).

Price discounting

Producers commonly provide intermediaries with discounts from list prices. Although there are many types of discount, they usually fall into one of five categories (see Table 12.2):

1 trade
2 quantity

TABLE 12.2 Discounts used for business markets

Type	Reason for use	Practical examples
Trade (functional)	To attract and keep resellers by compensating them for certain functions, such as transportation, warehousing, selling and providing credit	A university bookstore pays about a third less for a new textbook than the retail price paid by a student
Quantity	To encourage customers to buy large quantities and, in the case of cumulative discounts, to encourage customer loyalty	Large chains of tyre and exhaust outlets purchase parts at lower prices than individually owned outlets
Cash	To reduce expenses associated with accounts receivable by encouraging prompt payment	Companies operating in business markets often offer a discount for prompt payment
Seasonal	To allow resources to be used more efficiently by stimulating sales during off-peak periods	Hotels in large cities offer companies discounted accommodation for sales and other conferences during off-peak periods
Allowance	For trade-in allowances, the buyer is assisted in making the purchase by getting money back on used equipment; for promotional allowances, dealers are able to participate in advertising and sales support programmes	Companies such as Nestlé or Masterfoods pay promotional allowances to supermarkets for setting up and maintaining end-of-aisle displays to push their products

trade or functional discount
A reduction off the list price given by a producer to an intermediary for performing certain functions

quantity discounts
Reductions off the list price that reflect the economies of purchasing in large quantities

cumulative discounts
Quantity discounts aggregated over a stated period of time

non-cumulative discounts
One-off quantity discounts

cash discount
A simple price reduction given to a buyer for prompt payment or payment in cash

seasonal discount
A price reduction given to buyers who purchase goods or services out of season

allowance
A concession in price to achieve a desired goal

geographic pricing
Pricing that involves reductions for transport costs or other costs associated with the physical distance between the buyer and the seller

3 cash discounts

4 seasonal discounts

5 allowances.

Trade discounts A reduction off the list price given by a producer to an intermediary for performing certain functions is called a **trade or functional discount**. The functions for which intermediaries are compensated may include selling, transporting, storing, final processing and perhaps providing credit services. The level of discount can vary considerably from one industry to another.

Quantity discounts Reductions from the list price that reflect the economies of purchasing in large quantities are called **quantity discounts**. Cost savings usually occur in four areas. Fewer but larger orders reduce per-unit selling costs; fixed costs, such as invoicing, remain the same or go down; raw materials costs are lower, because quantity discounts may be available; longer production runs mean no increases in holding costs.[11] In addition, a large purchase may shift some of the storage, finance and risk-taking functions to the buyer.

Quantity discounts can be either cumulative or non-cumulative. **Cumulative discounts** are aggregated over a stated period of time. Purchases of £10 000 (€15 000) in a three-month period, for example, might entitle the buyer to a 5 per cent, or £500 (€750), rebate. Such discounts are supposed to reflect economies in selling and encourage the buyer to purchase from one seller. **Non-cumulative discounts** are one-off reductions in prices based on the number of units purchased, the monetary value of the order or the product mix purchased.

Cash discounts A **cash discount**, or simple price reduction, is given for prompt payment or payment in cash. A policy to encourage prompt payment is a popular practice in setting prices. For example, '2/10 net 30' means that a 2 per cent discount will be allowed if the account is paid within ten days. However, if the buyer does not pay within the ten-day period, the entire balance is due within 30 days without a discount. If the account is not paid within 30 days, interest may be charged.

Seasonal discounts A price reduction given to buyers who purchase goods or services out of season is a **seasonal discount**. These discounts let the seller maintain steadier production during the year. For example, hotels in holiday resorts offer seasonal discounts for business companies at times of year when the weather is poor.

Allowances Another type of reduction from the list price is an **allowance** – a concession in price to achieve a desired goal. Trade-in allowances are price reductions granted for handing in a used item when purchasing a new one. This type of allowance is popular in the aircraft industry. Another example is promotional allowances, which are price reductions granted to dealers for participating in advertising and sales support programmes intended to increase sales.

Geographic pricing

Geographic pricing involves reductions for transport costs or other costs associated with the physical distance between the buyer and the seller. Prices may be quoted as

FOB factory price
The price of the merchandise at the factory before it is loaded on to the carrier vehicle, which must be paid by the buyer

being FOB (free-on-board) factory or destination. An **FOB factory price** indicates the price of the merchandise at the factory before it is loaded on to the carrier vehicle; it thus excludes transport costs. The buyer must pay for shipping. An **FOB destination price** means the producer absorbs the costs of shipping the merchandise to customers.

To avoid the problems involved in charging different prices to each customer, **uniform geographic pricing**, sometimes called postage stamp pricing, may be used. The same price is charged to all customers regardless of geographic location, and the price is based on average shipping costs for all customers. Petrol, paper products and office equipment are often priced on a uniform basis.

FOB destination price
A price quotation indicating that the producer absorbs the costs of shipping the merchandise

Zone prices are regional prices that take advantage of a uniform pricing system; prices are adjusted for major geographic zones as the transport costs increase. For example, the prices of a manufacturer located in the northern French town of Lille may be higher for buyers in the south of France than for buyers in Paris.

uniform geographic pricing
Pricing in which the same price is charged to all customers regardless of geographic location

Base point pricing is a geographic pricing policy that includes the price at the factory, plus freight charges from the base point nearest the buyer. This policy, which is now rarely used, can result in all buyers paying freight charges from one location, regardless of where the product was manufactured!

When the seller absorbs all or part of the actual freight costs, **freight absorption pricing** is being used. The seller might choose this method because it wishes to do business with a particular customer or to get more business; more business will cause the average cost to fall and counter-balance the extra freight cost. This strategy is used to improve market penetration and to retain a hold in an increasingly competitive market.

zone prices
Regional prices that take advantage of a uniform pricing system

base point pricing
A geographic pricing policy that includes the price at the factory, plus freight charges from the base point nearest the buyer

Transfer pricing

When one unit in a company sells a product to another unit within the same company, **transfer pricing** occurs. The price is determined by one of the following methods.

freight absorption pricing
A pricing policy in which the seller absorbs all or part of the actual freight costs

- *Actual full cost* – calculated by dividing all fixed and variable expenses for a period into the number of units produced.
- *Standard full cost* – calculated on what it would cost to produce the goods at full plant capacity.
- *Cost plus investment* – calculated as full cost, plus the cost of a portion of the selling unit's assets used for internal needs.
- *Market based cost* – calculated at the market price less a small discount to reflect the lack of sales effort and other expenses.

transfer pricing
The type of pricing used when one unit in a company sells a product to another unit within the same company

The choice of transfer pricing method depends on the company's management strategy and the nature of the units' interaction. The company might initially choose to determine price by the actual full cost method but later move to an alternative method.[12]

Price discrimination

price discrimination
A policy in which different prices are charged in order to give a particular group of buyers a competitive edge

A policy of **price discrimination** results in different prices being charged to give a group of buyers a competitive edge. Some forms of price discrimination are illegal in the EU. Price differentiation is a form of market segmentation that companies use to provide a marketing mix that satisfies different segments. Because different market segments perceive the value of a particular product differently, depending on the product's importance and value to the business buyer, marketers may charge different prices to different market segments. Price discrimination can also be used to modify demand patterns, support sales of other products, dispose of obsolete goods or excessive inventories, fill excess production capacity and respond to competitors' activities in particular markets.[13]

Various conditions must be satisfied for price discrimination to be feasible. It must be possible to segment the market and the costs associated with doing so must not exceed the additional revenue generated. The practice should not break the law or breed customer discontent. Finally, the segment that is charged the higher price should not be vulnerable to competitor attack.

Economic value to the customer

The relationship between price and profitability was considered briefly at the start of this chapter. It is already clear that the ability to charge a higher price can have a major impact on profitability. It is also apparent that in order to achieve higher prices, businesses must be able to offer the customer some kind of differential advantage. In business markets, this advantage must usually

economic value to the customer (EVC)
The underlying principle that a premium price can be charged while still offering the customer better value than the competition

be measurable in economic terms because businesses are driven by the need to reduce costs and increase revenue. Thus, a manufacturer of switch gears may be prepared to change to a more expensive supplier of fork-lift trucks if the products supplied have lower running costs. The concept of economic value to the customer encapsulates this notion and is a useful aid to determining prices in business markets. The underlying principle of **economic value to the customer (EVC)** is that a premium price can be charged while still offering the customer better value than the competition.

Marketing tools and techniques

Business-to-business pricing using EVC analysis

Analyzing economic value to the customer (EVC) is a useful aid to setting prices for business-to-business organizations. This example concerns the pricing of panel presses, which are supplied to the car parts business. The analysis focuses on the market leader and two other competitors.

The analysis begins by considering a reference product against which the costs of competing products are compared.

In this case, the market leader is used as the reference product. In this example, a car parts company buying the panel press from the market leader would expect to pay the following costs. The purchase price of the press is £60 000. Start-up costs, such as installation charges, staff training and lost production during installation, are £20 000, and post-purchase costs, including operating costs such as labour, servicing/maintenance and power, are £130 000.

This means that, over its life cycle, the panel press will cost the car parts company a total of £210 000.

Companies competing with the market leader present the customer with a different profile of costs. Company A has, by

incorporating a number of new design features, managed to cut the start-up costs for a comparable panel press to £10 000 and reduced post-purchase costs to £105 000. This means that the total costs for the press are £35 000 less than those for the market leader. The result is that Company A's press offers the customer an EVC of £210 000 less £115 000, which equals £95 000. Assuming that Company A charged a purchase price of £95 000 for the panel press, the customer would face total life-cycle costs that were equivalent to the market leading product. If, however, Company A decided to offer the panel press at a purchase price of only £80 000, the lower life-cycle costs of the product would give the customer a considerable financial incentive to buy.

Consider the position of a second competitor, Company B, with similar start-up and post-purchase costs to the market leader. This company has, through certain technological advances, increased the rate at which the press can be operated, potentially increasing productivity and therefore revenue for the customer. As a result, the press has the potential to offer an additional £50 000 profit contribution over the presses of the market leader and Company A. The EVC associated with this is £110 000, because this is the highest price the customer may be expected to pay.

There are various reasons why a costly product may provide good economic value to the customer, including lower set-up or running costs, the provision of superior servicing or other after-sales support, or a better warranty deal. It is even possible that the life of the product may be longer or that its productivity may be greater than that of lower-priced alternatives. Whatever the reason behind the value on offer, if EVC is to be demonstrated, the initial high price of the product must be justified by an overall lower lifetime cost. The Marketing Tools and Techniques box below provides a worked example of how EVC works in practice.

Stages for establishing prices

When going through the stages for establishing prices, marketers must be able to grasp target customers' evaluation of price and perceived value for money, as well as understand market trends and competitors' pricing moves.[14] The 'economics' of pricing – demand curves and price elasticity, plus the relationship in the market in question between demand, costs and profits – must also be addressed. The marketer must ultimately choose from a variety of pricing approaches and specific pricing strategies. Figure 12.5 outlines the eight stages for establishing prices. These stages are explained far more extensively in the authors' sister title *Marketing: Concepts and Strategies*.

The first stage, selecting pricing objectives, is critical because pricing objectives are the foundation on which the decisions of subsequent stages are based. Businesses may use numerous short and long term pricing objectives. The second stage in establishing prices is an assessment of the target market's evaluation of price and its ability to buy. This shows how much emphasis to place on price and may help determine how far above the competition prices can be set. Understanding customers' buying power and the importance of a product to them in comparison with other products helps the target market's evaluation of price to be accurately assessed. In the third stage, a business must determine the demand for its product. The classic demand curve is a graph of the quantity of products expected to be sold at various prices, if other factors are held constant. It illustrates that, as price falls, the quantity demanded usually increases. However, for prestige products, there is a direct positive relationship between price and quantity demanded: up to a certain point demand increases as price increases. Next, price elasticity of

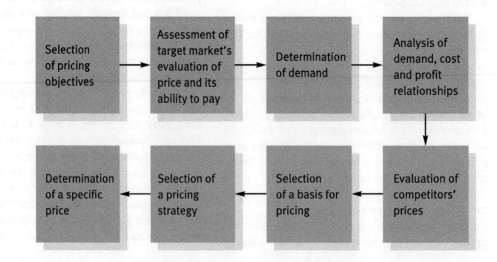

FIGURE 12.5
Stages for
establishing prices

cost-based pricing
A pricing approach whereby a monetary amount or percentage is added to the cost of a product

demand-based pricing
A pricing approach based on the level of demand for a product, resulting in a high price when demand is strong and a low price when demand is weak

price differentiation
A pricing strategy involving charging different prices to different buyers for the same quality and quantity of product

competition-based pricing
A pricing approach whereby an organization considers costs and revenue to be secondary to competitors' prices

marketing-oriented pricing
A pricing approach whereby a company takes into account a wide range of factors including marketing strategy, competition, value to the customer, price – quality relationships, explicability, costs, product line pricing, negotiating margins, political factors and effect on distributors/retailers

pricing strategy
An approach to influencing and determining pricing decisions

price skimming
A pricing strategy whereby a company charges the highest possible price that buyers who most desire the product will pay

demand – the percentage change in quantity demanded relative to a given percentage change in price – must be determined. If demand is elastic, a change in price causes an opposite change in total revenue. Inelastic demand results in a change in the same direction in total revenue when a product's price is changed.

Analysis of demand, cost and profit relationships – the fourth stage of the process – can be accomplished through marginal analysis or break-even analysis. Marginal analysis is the examination of what happens to a company's costs and revenues when production (or sales volume) is changed by one unit. Marginal analysis combines the demand curve with a company's costs to develop an optimum price for maximum profit. The optimum price is the point at which marginal cost equals marginal revenue. Marginal analysis offers little help in pricing new products before costs and revenues are established. Break-even analysis involves determining the number of units necessary to break even. The point at which the costs of producing a product equal the revenue made from selling the product is the break-even point. To use break even analysis effectively, a marketer should determine the break-even point for each of several alternative prices, so that the effects on total revenue, total cost and the break-even point for each price can be considered. However, this approach assumes that the quantity demanded is basically fixed and that the major task is to set prices to recover costs.

A marketer needs to be aware of the prices charged for competing brands – the fifth stage. This allows a company to keep its prices the same as competitors' prices when non-price competition is used. If a company uses price as a competitive tool, it can price its brand or product below competing brands or products.

The sixth stage is the selection of a basis for pricing. The three major dimensions on which prices can be based are cost, demand and competition. In using **cost-based pricing**, a company determines price by adding a monetary amount or percentage to the cost of the product. Two common cost-based pricing approaches are known as cost plus pricing and mark-up pricing. **Demand-based pricing** is based on the level of demand for a product and requires marketers to estimate the amounts of a product that buyers will demand at different prices, particularly if the company wishes to use **price differentiation** for a specific product. Demand-based pricing results in a high price when demand for a product is strong and a low price when demand is weak. In the case of **competition-based pricing**, costs and revenues are secondary to competitors' prices. Competition-based pricing and cost approaches may be combined to arrive at price levels necessary to generate a profit. The increasingly popular **marketing-oriented pricing** involves a company taking account of a wide range of factors including marketing strategy, competition, value to the customer, price-quality relationships, explicability, costs, product line pricing, negotiating margins, political factors and the effect on distributors/retailers.

A **pricing strategy** – stage seven – is an approach designed to achieve pricing and marketing objectives. The most common pricing strategies are differential pricing, new-product pricing, product-line pricing, psychological pricing, professional pricing, and promotional pricing. Using differential pricing involve charging different prices for the same quality or quantity of product. Negotiated pricing, secondary market discounting, periodic discounting and random discounting are forms of differential pricing. Establishing the final price through bargaining between seller and customer is negotiated pricing. Secondary market pricing involves setting one price for the primary target market and a different price for another market. Marketers employ a strategy of periodic discounting when they temporarily lower their prices on a systematic basis. Random discounting occurs on an unsystematic basis. Two strategies used in new product pricing are price skimming and penetration pricing. With **price skimming**, a company charges the highest price that buyers who most

penetration pricing
A pricing strategy of setting a price below the prices of competing brands in order to penetrate a market and produce a larger unit sales volume

psychological pricing
A pricing strategy designed to encourage purchases that are based on emotional rather than rational responses

promotional pricing
Pricing related to the short-term promotion of a particular product

desire the product will pay. **Penetration pricing** sets a price below the prices of competing brands in order to penetrate the market and produce a larger unit sales volume. Product line pricing establishes and adjusts the prices of multiple products within a product line. This strategy includes captive pricing, in which the marketer prices the basic product in a product line low but prices related items at a higher level; premium pricing, in which prices on a higher-quality or more versatile products are set higher than those on other models in the product line; bait pricing, in which the marketer tries to attract customers by pricing an item in the product line low with the intention of selling a higher-priced item in the line; and price lining, in which the organization sets a limited number of prices for selected groups or lines of merchandise.

Psychological pricing, encourages purchases that are based on emotional rather than rational responses. In referencing pricing marketers price a product at a moderate level and position it next to a more expensive model or brand. Bundle pricing is packaging together two or more complementary products that are sold for a single price. In multiple unit pricing, two or more identical products are packaged together and sold for a single price. Everyday low prices are employed by some companies to set a low price for products on a consistent basis. When using odd-even pricing marketers try to influence buyers' perceptions of the prices of the product by ending the price with certain numbers. Customary pricing is based on traditional prices. With prestige pricing, prices are set at an artificially high level to project a quality image. Professional pricing, is used by people who have great skill or experience in a particular field. **Promotional pricing** is a pricing approach in which pricing is related to the short term promotion of

Pricing an experience

Topical insights

How do you price an experience? This is the challenge Virgin faces as it sets prices for a diverse range of 'experiences' offered via its website **www.virginexperiencedays. co.uk** and in-store in participating retailers. Targeting consumers and business clients alike, those seeking a relaxing, exciting, indulgent experience for themselves, or looking for a 'different' gift for friends, family, colleagues or customers, can choose from a wide variety of options.

The gifts fall into a number of different categories: Gourmet, Pamper, Fly, Drive, Culture, Famous Venues, Racing Weekends, Hotel Breaks and so forth. The variety behind these titles is considerable. Perhaps your best friend has always wanted to discover scuba diving, learn circus skills or spend the day training border collies. Maybe your young sister fancies laying down a track at a recording studio, having a star named after her or just can't resist the 'I Love Chocolate Hamper'. All of these and many more activities and treats are available.

The diversity of experiences on offer is clearly illustrated by the *Drive* category, which includes the following:

- Supercars
- Rally Driving
- Motor Racing
- Off Road and Quads
- Tanks and Trucks
- Skills and Thrills
- Motorbikes

For customers finding it hard to make a decision, Virgin Experience Options Vouchers are available. Ranging in price from the Amber Collection (£50), Indigo Collection (£75) and Scarlett Collection (£100), these vouchers enable the holder to choose the experience they would like to get involved in. The colour of the voucher determines its value and also the experiences available to its holders. For example, the Scarlett Collection, priced at £100, can be exchanged for a bungee jump, Aston Martin thrill, face your phobia, garden design or llama trekking, amongst dozens of other options.

In setting the price of these vouchers and deciding for which experiences they can be swapped, Virgin is making a judgement about the value that customers attach to indulging themselves or others, and spending their time in a new and interesting way.

Sources: **www.virginexperiencedays.co.uk**, June 2011; Virgin marketing materials.

a particular product. Price leaders, special event pricing and comparison discounting are examples of promotional pricing. Misleading pricing – in which consumers are intentionally misled about the true cost or value of a product or service – is increasingly monitored and tackled through consumer protection legislation.

The final stage in establishing a price is to determine the specific price to be asked for from customers. The basis for a price and the pricing strategy should direct and structure the selection of a final price. For the most part, pricing remains a flexible and convenient way to adjust the marketing mix. Pragmatism may require the marketer to revise pricing on an *ad hoc* basis in response to market developments. While such reactions are to some extent inevitable, marketers must never lose sight of the longer term implications for the brand or the fundamental relationship between demand, costs and profits.

Summary

Price is the value placed on what is exchanged. The buyer exchanges buying power – which depends on the buyer's income, credit and wealth – for satisfaction or utility. *Financial price* is the basis of market exchanges – the quantified value of what is exchanged. However, price does not always involve a financial exchange; barter, the trading of products, is the oldest form of exchange.

Price is a key element in the marketing mix because it relates directly to the generation of total revenue. The profit factor can be determined mathematically by first multiplying price by quantities sold to calculate total revenues and then subtracting total costs. Price is often the only variable in the marketing mix that can be adjusted quickly and easily to respond to changes in the external environment.

A product offering can compete on either a price or a non-price basis. *Price competition* emphasizes price as the product differential. Prices fluctuate frequently, and sellers must respond to competitors changing their prices. *Non-price competition* emphasizes product differentiation through distinctive product features, services, product quality or other factors. Establishing brand loyalty by using non-price competition works best when the product can be physically differentiated and these distinguishing characteristics are viewed as desirable.

Pricing objectives are overall goals that describe what a company wants to achieve through its pricing efforts. The most fundamental pricing objective is the business's survival. Price can easily be adjusted to increase sales volume to levels that match the company's expenses. Profit objectives, which are usually stated in terms of actual monetary amounts or percentage change, are normally set at a satisfactory level rather than at a level designed for profit maximization. Pricing for return on investment (ROI) sets a specified rate of return as its objective. A pricing objective to maintain or increase market share is established in relation to total industry sales. Other types of pricing objective include cash flow, status quo and product quality.

Nine factors affect pricing decisions:

(1) organizational and marketing objectives, (2) pricing objectives, (3) costs, (4) other marketing mix variables, (5) channel member expectations, (6) buyers' perceptions, (7) competition, (8) legal and regulatory issues and (9) perceived value. Thus, pricing decisions should be consistent with the organization's goals and mission. Pricing objectives heavily influence price-setting decisions.

When interpreting and responding to prices, customers compare prices with internal or external reference prices. An *internal reference price* is a price developed in the buyer's mind through experience with the product. When there is less experience, consumers rely more heavily on external reference prices. An *external reference price* is a comparison price provided by others, such as retailers, manufacturers or competing products. In the context of price, buyers can be characterized according to their degree of value consciousness, price consciousness and prestige-sensitivity. *Value-conscious consumers* are concerned about both the price and the quality of a product. *Price-conscious consumers* strive to pay low prices. *Prestige-sensitive consumers* focus on purchasing products that signify prominence and status.

Most marketers view a product's cost as the floor below which a product cannot be priced. Due to the interrelationship of the marketing mix variables, price can affect product, promotion, place/distribution and service-level decisions. The revenue that channel members expect for the functions they perform must also be considered when making price decisions.

Buyers' perceptions of price vary so a marketer needs to be aware of these issues when determining the price. Knowledge of the prices charged for competing brands is essential so that a company can adjust its prices relative to those of competitors. Government regulations and legislation can also influence pricing decisions through laws to enhance competition and by invoking price controls – for example, to curb inflation.

Perceived value for money is an important consideration when setting prices. Consumers do not regard price purely as the monetary value being demanded in exchange for a good or a service. The quality of the item, its brand image, purpose, usage and overall appeal – along with the consumer's previous experiences and certain tangible benefits such as interest-free credit and warranties – dictate the consumer's view of value for money.

Unlike consumers, industrial or business buyers purchase products to use in their own operations or for producing other products. When adjusting prices, business sellers take into consideration the size of the purchase, geographic factors and transport requirements. Producers commonly provide *trade* or *functional discounts* off list prices to intermediaries. The five categories of discount include (1) trade, (2) quantity, (3) cash discounts, (4) seasonal discounts and (5) allowances.

Geographic pricing involves reductions for transport costs or other costs associated with the physical distance between the buyer and the seller. An *FOB factory price* means that the buyer pays for shipping from the factory; an *FOB destination price* means that the producer pays for shipping the merchandise. When the seller charges a fixed average cost for transport, the practice is known as *uniform geographic pricing*. *Zone prices* take advantage of a uniform pricing system adjusted for major geographic zones as the transport costs increase. *Base point pricing* involves prices being adjusted for shipping expenses incurred by the seller from the base point nearest the buyer. A seller who absorbs all or part of the freight costs is using *freight absorption pricing*. *Transfer pricing* occurs when one company unit sells a product to another unit within the same company.

When a *price discrimination* policy is adopted, different prices are charged in order to give a group of buyers a competitive edge. In some countries, price differentials are legal only in circumstances where competition is not damaged.

The concept of *economic value to the customer (EVC)* is sometimes used in business markets to aid price setting. The underlying principle is that a premium price can be charged while still offering better value than the competition.

The eight stages in the process of establishing prices are: (1) selecting pricing objectives; (2) assessing the target market's evaluation of price and its ability to buy; (3) determining demand; (4) analyzing demand, cost and profit relationships; (5) evaluating competitors' prices; (6) selecting a basis for pricing; (7) developing a pricing strategy; and (8) determining a specific price.

The three major dimensions on which prices can be based are cost, demand and competition. In using cost-based pricing, a company determines price by adding a monetary amount or percentage to the cost of the product. Demand-based pricing is based on the level of demand for a product and requires marketers to estimate the amounts of a product that buyers will demand at different prices, particularly if the company wishes to use price differentiation for a specific product. With competition- based pricing, costs and revenues are secondary to competitors' prices. The fourth dimension, which is increasingly popular, is marketing-oriented pricing, where a company takes account of a wide range of factors including marketing strategy, competition, value to the customer, price-quality relationships, explicability, costs, product line pricing, negotiating margins, political factors and the effect on distributors/retailers.

A pricing strategy is an approach designed to achieve pricing and marketing objectives. The most common pricing strategies are differential pricing, new-product pricing, product-line pricing, psychological pricing, professional pricing, and promotional pricing. Two strategies used in new product pricing are price skimming and penetration pricing. With price skimming, a company charges the highest price that buyers who most desire the product will pay. Penetration pricing sets a price below the prices of competing brands in order to penetrate the market and produce a larger unit sales volume.

Key links

- Price impacts strongly on how businesses fare competitively. The concepts of competitive strategy and the competitive environment are explored in Chapters 2 and 3.

- Price is a key element of the marketing mix, because it directly affects how much revenue is generated. Understanding pricing concepts is critical to the development of effective marketing programmes, as discussed in Part Three.

- Pricing impacts significantly on a brand's positioning, as described in Chapter 6.

Important terms

Price
Financial price
Price competition
Non-price competition
Pricing objectives
Internal reference price
External reference price
Value-conscious consumers
Price-conscious consumers
Prestige-sensitive consumers
Perceived value for money
Trade or functional discount
Quantity discounts
Cumulative discounts
Non-cumulative discounts
Cash discount
Seasonal discount
Allowance
Geographic pricing

FOB factory price
FOB destination price
Uniform geographic pricing
Zone prices
Base point pricing
Freight absorption pricing
Transfer pricing
Price discrimination
Economic value to the customer (EVC)
Cost-based pricing
Demand-based pricing
Competition-based pricing
Marketing-oriented pricing
Pricing strategy
Differential pricing
Price skimming
Penetration pricing
Psychological pricing
Promotional pricing

Discussion and review questions

1 Why are pricing decisions so important to a business?

2 Compare and contrast price and non-price competition. Describe the conditions under which each form works best.

3 How does a pricing objective of return on investment (ROI) differ from a pricing objective to increase market share?

4 Why is it crucial to consider both marketing objectives and pricing objectives when making pricing decisions?

5 In what ways do other marketing mix variables affect pricing decisions?

6 What types of expectation may channel members have about producers' prices, and how do these expectations affect pricing decisions?

7 How do legal and regulatory forces influence pricing decisions?

8 Why must marketers consider consumers' perceptions of value for money when setting prices?

9 What is the difference between a price discount and price discrimination?

10 Why is the concept of EVC (economic value to the customer) important when setting prices in business-to-business markets?

11 Identify the eight stages that make up the process of establishing prices.

Recommended readings

Baker, R.J., *Pricing on Purpose: Creating and Capturing Value* (Wiley, 2006).

Cram, T., *Smarter Pricing* (FT/Prentice-Hall, 2006).

Harvard Business Review, *Harvard Business Review on Pricing* (Harvard Business Press, 2008).

Nagle, T., Hogan, J. and Zale, J., *The Strategy and Tactics of Pricing* (Prentice-Hall, 2010).

Macdivitt, H. and Wilkinson, M., *Value-Based Pricing: Drive Sales and Boost Your Bottom Line by Creating, Communicating and Capturing Customer Value* (McGraw-Hill Professional, 2011).

Smith, T., *Pricing Strategy: Setting Price Levels, Managing Price Discounts and Establishing Price Structures* (South-Western, 2011).

Internet exercise

Whether interested in buying a used or a new car, buying it outright, on credit terms or by leasing, www.buyacar.co.uk offers car buyers a comprehensive website. Take a look at this online retailer at: www.buyacar.co.uk.

1 Find the lowest-priced VW Golf available today and list its features.

2 If you wanted to purchase this VW, what is the lowest monthly payment you could make and what would it cost if you were to buy this model outright?

3 Compare and contrast the relative benefits of leasing and buying this car outright.

Applied mini-case

Consumers can pay just 20 pence to write with a disposable biro, yet fancy fountain pens have become a common sight in the hands of influential businesspeople. Such pens have high price tags and are much more difficult to maintain than ballpoints, felt-tip pens or roller-ball pens. However, recent sales figures indicate that the semi-obsolete fountain pen is making a comeback as the writing instrument of choice for status-minded individuals. Of the premium-priced fountain pens, those produced by Montblanc are probably the most prestigious. Named after the highest mountain in Europe, these German-made fountain pens cost from about £100 to £5000 (for a solid-gold one). The most popular model costs about £300. Prestige pricing has worked well for Montblanc, placing the pen in the same category as Rolex watches, BMW cars and Gucci luggage.

Question

A company competing in the same sector as Montblanc has asked you to prepare a report explaining the factors that influence the pricing decisions they should make for a new range of pens. What areas should your report include?

Case study

Order just about anything from Amazon at a reasonable price

Online retail pioneer **Amazon.com** has built a profitable $24.5 billion business by paying close attention to pricing details. Founded as a web-based bookstore with discount prices, Amazon has since expanded into dozens of product categories and countries. The company never stops investing in technology to upgrade its sites, systems and offerings. Although hefty high-tech costs are a drag on profit margins, they are essential to Amazon's strategy of attracting customers, and keeping them loyal by making the shopping experience easy, fast and fun.

One hallmark of Amazon's pricing is its long-running offer of free delivery. For UK shoppers, many items can be delivered free to UK addresses under the so-called Super Saver Delivery. This free of charge delivery is also available for orders that are shipped to many other locations, providing the spend is £25 or more. This gives some shoppers an incentive to keep spending until they reach the £25 threshhold. Free shipping has helped Amazon build sales over the years, but it has also added to the company's costs and cut into profits.

Amazon is earning significant profits from serving as an online storefront for other marketers (and consumers) to sell their products. Every time a customer buys something from a seller participating in the Amazon Marketplace, Amazon collects a fee. The margins are especially attractive in this fast-growing part of the business because Amazon does not pay to buy or store any inventory, and the costs of posting items for other sellers is extremely low now that the electronic storefront is up and running.

All-digital products like electronic books, music, movies and games are lucrative because they entail no inventory or shipping costs. This is why Amazon is moving aggressively into digital content and related products. Its popular Kindle, first introduced in 2007, is an e-book reader that wirelessly connects to the Internet so customers can download an electronic book, newspaper or magazine in seconds. Initially, Amazon priced the Kindle higher than the Sony Reader, its main competitor at the time. Despite the high price, demand outstripped supply for a time and Amazon struggled to increase output. As other retailers began offering their own e-book readers, Amazon lowered the price and poured on the promotion to keep up the Kindle's sales momentum.

The Kindle also created a controversy over e-book pricing. When Amazon first launched the Kindle, it priced best-selling e-books at less than £10 each, with a few priced even lower. Publishers fumed, because the hard-cover price of these books was considerably higher. The situation changed in early 2010, as Apple prepared to debut its iPad tablet computer. Apple was trumpeting the iPad's capabilities as an e-book reader and making deals with publishers to carry downloadable digital content. Under pressure from the publishers and faced with a new level of competition from Apple's much-anticipated device, Amazon took a step back from its digital discounting. It listened to the publishers and raised the retail price of many digital best-sellers. However, today some books are available free and many others are offered at a few pounds or less via the bestseller list.

Today, Kindle customers can buy and instantly download more than 700 000 books. 'Our vision is to have every book that has ever been in print available in less than 60 seconds', says Amazon founder Jeff Bezos. The Kindle has become Amazon's best-selling product and dramatically increased sales of electronic books, magazines, and similar products. In fact, when Amazon offers the same book in printed and digital format, it sells six digital downloads for every ten physical units. Multiply the savings in shipping costs alone, and it's easy to see why Amazon has put so much emphasis on electronic delivery of books and other content.

Looking ahead, Amazon will be paying close attention to the pricing of rival gadgets and the way digital content is being priced. Although it's now the undisputed leader in electronic book sales, that market share is likely to erode little by little as more customers are offered the opportunity to buy and download more books from additional sources.

Questions for discussion

1 Are Amazon's delivery costs variable or fixed? How is the company's profitability likely to be affected if Amazon stopped offering free delivery?

2 Why would publishers be so concerned about the difference in price between a hard-cover best-seller and the digital version? Explain your answer in terms of this chapter's pricing concepts.

3 Do you think Amazon should be concerned about losing market share in e-book retailing? What are the implications for its pricing decisions?

CHAPTER 13

An overview of marketing communications

"If consumers or business customers are unaware or not seduced, they won't try, buy or return for more"

Objectives

- To understand the role of promotion in the marketing mix

- To examine the process of communication

- To understand the product adoption process and its implications for promotional efforts

- To understand the aims of promotion

- To explore the elements of the promotional mix

- To appreciate the nature of integrated marketing communications (IMC)

- To acquire an overview of the major methods of promotion

- To explore the factors that influence the selection of promotional mix ingredients

- To appreciate the role of marketing communications

INTRODUCTION

Marketers spend large sums of money and significant amounts of time developing advertising campaigns, PR programmes, sales promotions, websites and mobile comms, to list only some of the activities grouped under promotional activity within the marketing mix. As discussed in Chapter 1 of *Marketing Essentials* many lay people consider there to be little more to the role of marketing than the management of a company's marketing communications. In fact, there is much more to strategic marketing – as described in Chapters 1 and 2 – but the creation, execution and control of a company's marketing communications is indeed a significant task, occupying the time of many marketers and using up their budgets.

Communication is a sharing of meaning through the transmission of information. Marketing communication is the transmission of persuasive information about a good, service or an idea, targeted at key stakeholders and consumers within the target market segment. Not only commercial products and services require effective programmes of marketing communications … the growth of social marketing causes and messages which must be conveyed effectively by third sector bodies to their target audiences is huge. Marketing communications centre on the promotional mix, which comprises advertising, public relations, personal selling, sales promotion, direct mail, sponsorship and the Internet. Until relatively recently, each of these specialist areas was handled disparately within many companies. Integrated marketing communications (IMC) emerged to coordinate and integrate all marketing communication tools, avenues and sources within a company into a seamless programme that maximizes the impact on consumers and other end users, at minimal cost.

The 'target audience' is the marketing communications practitioner's term for those within the target market segment intended as the principal recipients of the promotional message. The product adoption process is awareness, interest, evaluation, trial and adoption; marketing communications play a key role in enticing customers to progress from awareness to adoption – consumption – of a product. In this context, there are five 'communications effects': category need, brand awareness, brand attitude, brand purchase intention and purchase facilitation. Marketers must be clear about their promotional objectives, and realistic about the likely returns.

There must be synergy with the specified segmentation or target market strategy, brand positioning and brand strategy. There should be strong associations between the executed marcomms and the understanding of consumers' or customers' buying behaviour, market trends and drivers, competitors' propositions and activities and the apparent capabilities of the product or brand being promoted: marketing communications must be informed by the core marketing analyzes explored in Parts One and Two of this book.

Cruelty to children must stop. FULL STOP.

The National Society for the Prevention of Cruelty to Children (NSPCC) exists to end cruelty to children. FULL STOP. The NSPCC wants you to join to fight to end cruelty to children. FULL STOP. 'Be the Full Stop ... Join.' Child abuse happens in many situations: in the home, at school and sports facilities and in residential care and on vacations. The NSPCC's strategy is to protect children in all areas of their lives, through action programmes such as ChildLine, community projects, advising professionals and children, researching the issues around child abuse and of course campaigning. Someone to turn to is a key part of these programmes, collectively termed the 'Full Stop' campaign.

In the run up to the last UK General Election, the *I Stand for Children* campaign encouraged people in England, Northern Ireland, Scotland and Wales to lobby their Parliamentary candidates to pledge, 'I Stand for Children'. As a result, over 900 election candidates committed themselves to child protection measures, raising the profile of such issues as required child protection reforms in the wake of the Baby Peter tragedy, funding of helpline services, tackling domestic violence from the child's perspective, making the Internet safer for children, strengthening the role of the Children's Commissioner and providing therapeutic services for children who have experienced abuse.

The *Child's Voice Appeal* commenced in 2008 and within its first three years had raised £45 million. The aim is to fund and further develop the ChildLine helpline, offering any child in need of help, or concerned about a friend, access to a support network and experts able to suggest a way forward. Until the *Child's Voice Appeal*, the charity could answer only two-thirds of calls to ChildLine and three-quarters of calls to its NSPCC-branded helpline, which is targeted at adults suspecting cases of abuse. The success of this campaign has enabled better coverage and timely response to calls, but also the addition of an online counselling service. Via phone, text and online, the NSPCC is now well placed to engage with children in need using media relevant to them and their lifestyles.

The charity's *Making The Internet Safer For Children* campaign intended to block the sharing online of images of abuse and to support children who have been abused and whose images are now online. The underlying thrust was,

Source: Image courtesy of Advertising Archives

'to ensure children are able to get the most from the Internet without stumbling into areas which might harm them'. This is only one example of how the charity's work has evolved to reflect the environment in which children find themselves at risk. As a result of this campaign, a petition of 30 000 names was submitted to Downing Street by musician and chef Levi

Roots. This was only one aspect of the campaign, aimed at putting children's safety and wellbeing high on the political agenda. Effective targeting and communication of strong messages central to the work of the NSPCC.

Source: **www.nspcc.org.uk**.

Organizations use various promotional approaches to communicate with target markets, and not only for-profit businesses harness the power of effective marketing communications, as evidenced with the NSPCC and its Full Stop message and various campaigns. Practitioners generally refer to the use of the promotion ingredient of the marketing mix as 'marketing communications' or 'MarComms'. It is important not to confuse the promotion ingredient of the marketing mix with either sales promotion or price offer promotions. Promotion in the marketing mix incorporates all aspects of the promotional mix, including advertising, public relations, sponsorship, direct mail, sales promotion, personal selling and the use of the Internet to communicate with an organization's target audiences. Increasingly, these elements of the promotional mix are coordinated in the guise of integrated marketing communications (IMC).

This chapter looks at the general dimensions of promotion, defining it in the context of marketing and examining the roles it plays. Next, to understand how promotion works, the chapter analyzes the meaning and process of communication, as well as promotion's role within the product adoption process. The remainder of the chapter discusses the major types of promotional method and the factors that influence an organization's decision to use specific methods of promotion: advertising, personal selling, publicity and public relations, sales promotion, sponsorship, direct mail, the Internet and direct marketing. The chapter includes an explanation of integrated marketing communications.

The role of promotion

The nature of promotion in the marketing mix has altered radically in recent years. First, the Web enabled communication to customers and potential users with virtually instant responses and follow-up possible along with tailored one-to-one messages not previously possible with mass media communications. Second, the take-off of social media networking removed the power of communication about products, services, brands, companies and those behind these, enabling easy customer-to-customer communication about products, brands and experiences, as explored in Chapter 4. Few marketers would disagree that Facebook, YouTube, Twitter and the like have presented significant challenges, opportunities and also threats. As a result, many people's views about product or brand communications have changed.

People's attitudes towards promotion anyway vary. Some hold that promotional activities, particularly advertising and personal selling, paint a distorted picture of reality because they provide the customer with only selected information.[1] Proponents of this view often suggest that promotional activities are unnecessary and wasteful, and that promotion costs are too high, resulting in higher prices. They may also argue that too much promotion has caused changes in social values, such as increased materialism. Others take a positive view. Some welcome the potential to communicate wellbeing and social cause messages. Others believe that advertising messages often project wholesome values – such as affection, generosity or patriotism[2] – or that advertising, as a powerful economic force, can free countries from poverty by communicating information.[3] It has also been argued that the advertising of consumer products was a factor in the decline of communism and the move towards a free enterprise system in eastern Europe. However, none of these impressions is completely accurate.

promotion
Communication with individuals, groups or organizations in order to facilitate exchanges by informing and persuading audiences to accept a company's products

The role of **promotion** in a company is to communicate with individuals, groups or organizations, with the aim of directly or indirectly facilitating exchanges by informing and persuading one or more of the audiences to accept the company's products.[4] Marketers try to communicate with selected audiences about their company and its goods, services and ideas in order to facilitate exchanges.

Exchanges are facilitated by marketers ensuring that information is targeted at appropriate individuals and groups: potential customers, special interest groups such as environmental and consumer groups, current and potential investors and regulatory agencies. Some marketers use **cause-related marketing**, which links the purchase of their products to philanthropic efforts for a particular cause. Cause-related marketing often helps a marketer boost sales and generate goodwill through contributions to causes that members of its target markets want to support. For example, Procter & Gamble has tied promotional efforts for some of its products to a campaign to promote cleaner water for children in developing countries so as to help 300 million children, by reducing illness and saving 20 000 lives each year with purer water in these communities.

cause-related marketing
Links the purchase of a product to philanthropic efforts for a particular 'good' cause

Viewed from this wider perspective, promotion can play a comprehensive communications role.[5] Some promotional activities, such as publicity and public relations, can be directed towards helping a company justify its existence and maintain positive, healthy relationships between itself and various groups.

Although a company can direct a single type of communication – such as an advertisement – towards numerous audiences, marketers often design a communication precisely for a specific target market. A company frequently communicates several different messages concurrently, each to a different group. For example, McDonald's may direct one communication towards customers for its Big Mac, a second message about its salads towards health-concerned consumers, a third message towards investors about the company's stable growth, and a fourth communication towards society in general regarding the company's Ronald McDonald Houses, which provide support to families of children suffering from cancer.

To gain maximum benefit from promotional efforts, marketers must make every effort to properly plan, implement, coordinate and control communications. As is explained later, the concept of integrated marketing communications helps to harmonize and coordinate an organization's promotional activities. Effective promotional activities are based on information from the marketing environment (see Chapter 3) and the company's market insights. How effectively marketers can use promotion to maintain positive relationships depends largely on the quantity and quality of information an organization takes in. For example, concerns about genetically modified (GM) foods have led certain supermarkets to improve in-store labelling, so that consumers are better informed about those products affected.

The basic role of promotion is to communicate, so it is important to analyze what communication is and how the communication process works.

The communication process

Communication can be viewed as the transmission of information.[6] For communication to take place, however, both the sender and the receiver of the information must share some common ground. They must share an understanding of the symbols used to transmit information, usually pictures or words. For instance, an individual transmitting the following message may believe he or she is communicating with readers of *Marketing Essentials*.

在工廠吾人製造化粧品，在商店吾人銷售希望。

communication
A sharing of meaning through the transmission of information

marketing communication
The transmission of persuasive information about a product, service or an idea, targeted at key stakeholders and consumers within the target market segment

source
A person, group or organization that has an intended meaning it attempts to share with an audience

receiver
An individual, group or organization that decodes a coded message

receiving audience
Two or more receivers who decode a message

coding process
The process of converting meaning into a series of signs that represent ideas or concepts; also called encoding

However, communication has not taken place, because few readers understand the intended message.[7] Thus **communication** is defined here as a sharing of meaning.[8] Implicit in this definition is the notion of transmission of information, because sharing necessitates transmission. Communication, therefore, is a sharing of meaning through the transmission of information. **Marketing communication** is the transmission of persuasive information about a product, service or an idea, targeted at key stakeholders and consumers within the target market segment. Marketing communications centre on the promotional mix, which comprises advertising, public relations, personal selling, sales promotion, direct mail, sponsorship and the Internet.

As Figure 13.1 shows, communication begins with a source. A **source** is a person, group or organization that has an intended meaning it attempts to share with an audience. For example, a source could be a political party wishing to recruit new members or an organization that wants to send a message to thousands of consumers through an advertisement. Developing a strategy can enhance the effectiveness of the source's communication. For example, a strategy in which a sales person attempts to influence a customer's decision by eliminating competitive products from consideration has been found to be effective.[9] A **receiver** is the individual, group or organization that decodes a coded message. A **receiving audience** is two or more receivers who decode a message. The intended receivers, or audience, of an advertisement for MBA courses might be business executives wishing to broaden their managerial skills. The source may be a European business school, such as INSEAD.

To transmit meaning, a source must convert that meaning into a series of signs that represent ideas or concepts. This is called the **coding process**, or encoding. When encoding meaning into a message, a source must take into account certain characteristics of the receiver or receiving audience. First, to share meaning, the source should use signs that are familiar to the receiver or receiving audience. Marketers who understand this fact realize how important it is to know their target market and to make sure that an advertisement, for example, is written in language that the target market can understand. Thus, when Unilever advertises its Persil washing powder, it makes no attempt to explain the chemical reactions involved when the product removes dirt and grease, because this would not be meaningful to consumers. There have been some notable problems in the language translation of advertisements. For example, Budweiser has been advertised in Spain as the 'Queen of Beers' and the Chinese have been encouraged to 'eat their fingers off' when receiving KFC's slogan 'Finger-Lickin' Good'.[10]

Second, when encoding a meaning, a source should try to use signs that the receiver or receiving audience uses for referring to the concepts the source intends. Marketers should generally avoid signs that can have several meanings for an audience. For example, an international advertiser of soft drinks should avoid using the word soda as a general term for

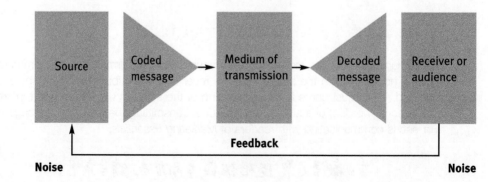

FIGURE 13.1
The communication process

soft drinks. Although in some places soda is taken to mean 'soft drink', in others it may connote bicarbonate of soda, an ice cream drink or something to mix with Scotch whisky.

medium of transmission
The tool used to carry the coded message from the source to the receiver or receiving audience

To share a coded meaning with the receiver or receiving audience, a source must select and use a medium of transmission. A **medium of transmission** carries the coded message from the source to the receiver or receiving audience. Transmission media include ink on paper, vibrations of air waves produced by vocal cords, chalk marks on a chalkboard and electronically produced communication, as in radio, television, mobile phones and the Internet.

Sometimes a source chooses an inappropriate medium of transmission. A coded message may reach some receivers, but not the right ones. For example, suppose a local theatre group spends most of its advertising budget on radio advertisements. If theatre-goers depend mainly on newspapers for information about local drama, then the theatre group will not reach its intended target audience. Coded messages may also reach intended receivers in an incomplete form because the intensity of the transmission is weak. For example, radio signals can be received effectively over a limited range that may vary depending on climatic conditions. Members of the target audience who live on the fringe of the broadcasting area may receive only a weak signal.

decoding process
The process in which signs are converted into concepts and ideas

In the **decoding process**, signs are converted into concepts and ideas. Seldom does a receiver decode exactly the same meaning that a source encoded. When the result of decoding is different from what was encoded, **noise** exists. Noise has many sources and may affect any or all parts of the communication process. When a source selects a medium of transmission through which an audience does not expect to receive a message, noise is likely to occur. Noise sometimes arises within the medium of transmission itself. Radio static, faulty printing processes and laryngitis are sources of noise. Interference on viewers' television sets during an advertisement is noise and reduces the impact of the message. Noise also occurs when a source uses a sign that is unfamiliar to the receiver or that has a different meaning from the one the source intended. Noise may also originate in the receiver. As Chapter 4 discussed, a receiver may be unaware of a coded message because his or her perceptual processes block it out or because the coded message is too obscure.

noise
A condition that exists when the decoded message is different from that which was encoded

feedback
The receiver's response to a message

The receiver's response to a message is **feedback** to the source. The source usually expects and normally receives feedback, although it may not be immediate. During feedback, the receiver or receiving audience is the source of a message that is directed towards the original source, which then becomes a receiver. Feedback is encoded, sent through a medium of transmission – for example, a survey questionnaire – and then decoded by the receiver, the source of the original communication. It is logical to think of communication as a circular process.

During face-to-face communication, such as in personal selling or product sampling, both verbal and non-verbal feedback can be immediate. Instant feedback enables communicators to adjust their messages quickly to improve the effectiveness of their communication. For example, when a sales person realizes through feedback that a customer does not understand a sales presentation, he or she adapts the presentation to make it more meaningful to the customer. This may be why face-to-face sales presentations create higher behavioural intentions to purchase services than do telemarketing sales contacts.[11] In interpersonal communication, feedback occurs through talking, touching, smiling, nodding, eye movements and other body movements and postures.

When mass communication such as advertising is used, feedback is often slow and difficult to recognize in terms of impact on sales or even buy-in to a brand proposition. If Disneyland Paris increased its advertising in order to raise the number of visitors, it might be 6 to 18 months before the theme park could recognize the effects of the expanded advertising. Although it is harder to recognize, feedback does exist for mass communication. Advertisers do obtain feedback in the form of changes in sales volume or in consumers' attitudes and awareness levels, monitored

FIGURE 13.2

This direct response advertisement provides an opportunity for feedback based on the coupon redemption rate

Source: Courtesy of Nestlé, Cheerios

through tracking research. The coupon redemption rate for the advertisement in Figure 13.2 provides an opportunity for feedback. It should be noted that web-based comms provide much more instant feedback; response to web-based advertising and other online tools is much more rapidly apparent.

channel capacity
The limit on the volume of information that a particular communication channel can handle effectively

Each communication channel has a limit on the volume of information it can handle effectively. This limit, called **channel capacity**, is determined by the least efficient component of the communication process. Communications that depend on vocal speech provide a good illustration of this. An individual source can talk only so fast, and there is a limit to how much an individual receiver can take in aurally. Beyond that point, additional messages cannot be decoded; thus meaning cannot be shared. Although a radio announcer can read several hundred words a minute, a one-minute advertising message should not exceed 150 words because most announcers cannot articulate the words into understandable messages at a rate beyond 150 words per minute. This figure is the limit for both source and receiver, and marketers should keep this in mind when developing radio advertisements. At times, a company creates a television advertisement that contains several types of visual material and several forms of audio message, all transmitted to viewers at the same time. Such communication may not be totally effective, because receivers cannot decode all the messages simultaneously.[12] Researchers believe that Generation Y consumers devote less than ten seconds to viewing a web message, TV advertisement or paragraph of a text document, so advertisers targeting younger consumers must tailor their approach accordingly, as in effect this attention span presents a capacity restraint.

Now that the basic communication process has been explored, it is worth considering more specifically how promotion is used in marketing communications to influence individuals, groups or organizations to accept or adopt a company's products. Although the product adoption process was touched upon briefly in Chapter 8, it is discussed more fully in the following section in order to provide a better understanding of the conditions under which promotion occurs.

Promotion and the product adoption process

Marketers do not promote simply to inform, educate and entertain; they communicate to facilitate satisfying exchanges – products or services for money or donations. One long-run purpose of promotion is to influence and encourage buyers to accept or adopt goods, services and ideas. At times, an advertisement may be informative or entertaining, yet it may fail to entice the audience to purchase the product. For example, some advertisements seem to be weak in communicating benefits – they focus instead on getting customers to feel good about the product. The ultimate effectiveness of promotion is determined by the degree to which it affects product adoption among potential buyers or increases the frequency of current buyers' purchases.

To establish realistic expectations about what promotion can do, product adoption should not be viewed as a one-step process. Rarely can a single promotional activity cause an individual to buy a previously unfamiliar product. The acceptance of a product involves many steps. Although there are several ways to look at the **product adoption process**, it is commonly divided into five stages, as depicted in Figure 13.3 and explored in Chapter 8:

product adoption process
A series of five stages in the acceptance of a product: awareness, interest, evaluation, trial and adoption

1 awareness

2 interest

3 evaluation

4 trial

5 adoption.[13]

awareness stage
The beginning of the product adoption process, when individuals become aware that the product exists but have little information about it

In the **awareness stage**, individuals become aware that the product exists, but they have little information about it and are not concerned about obtaining more. When Barclays launched b2 financial services, it used a provocative b2 flash teaser advertisement. Later, longer advertisements fully detailed the new portfolio of products. In Figure 13.4 Big Brother's teaser advertisement did not reveal full details of the forthcoming TV series, but later adverts did.

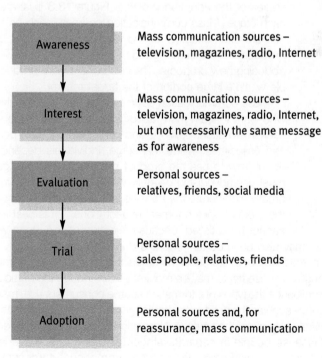

FIGURE 13.3
Effective promotional tools for reaching consumers in various stages of the product adoption process

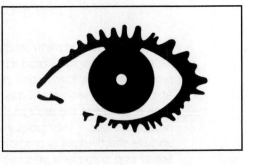

FIGURE 13.4
Building awareness. Channel 4 launched its Big Brother
new series initially with this teaser advertisement before running
the second advertisement, which revealed the actual product

Source: Channel 4 for the Big Brother eye logo,
copyright © Channel 4

interest stage
The stage of the product adoption process when customers are motivated to obtain information about the product's features, uses, advantages, disadvantages, price or location

evaluation stage
The stage of the product adoption process when customers decide whether the product will satisfy certain criteria that are crucial for meeting their specific needs

trial stage
The stage of the product adoption process when individuals use or experience the product for the first time

adoption stage
The final stage of product acceptance, when customers choose a specific product

Consumers enter the **interest stage** when they are motivated to obtain information about the product's features, uses, advantages, disadvantages, price or location. During the **evaluation stage**, individuals consider whether the product will satisfy certain criteria that are crucial for meeting their specific needs. In the **trial stage**, they use or experience the product for the first time, possibly by purchasing a small quantity, by taking advantage of a free sample or demonstration, or by borrowing the product from someone. Supermarkets, for example, frequently offer special promotions to encourage consumers to taste products such as cheese, cooked meats, snacks or pizza. During this stage, potential adopters determine the usefulness or desirability of the product under the specific conditions for which they need it.

Individuals move into the **adoption stage** by choosing the specific product when they need a product of that general type. It cannot be assumed, however, that because a person enters the adoption process she or he will eventually adopt the new product. Rejection may occur at any stage, including adoption. Both product adoption and product rejection can be temporary or permanent. Even if adoption occurs, as explored in Chapter 4, there is no guarantee of brand loyalty. Marketers must work hard to ensure repeat buying and an ongoing relationship.

For the most part, people respond to different information sources at different stages of the adoption process. Figure 13.3 illustrates the most effective sources for each stage. Mass communication sources, such as television advertising or the Internet, are often effective for moving large numbers of people into the awareness stage. Producers of consumer goods commonly use massive advertising campaigns when introducing new products. They do so to create product awareness as quickly as possible within a large portion of the target market.

Mass communication sources may also be effective for people in the interest stage who want to learn more about a product. During the evaluation stage, individuals often seek information, opinions and reinforcement from personal sources – relatives, friends and associates. In the trial stage, individuals depend on sales people for information about how to use the product properly in order to gain the most out of it. Marketers must use advertising carefully when consumers are in the trial stage. If advertisements greatly exaggerate the benefits of a product, the consumer may be disappointed when the product does not meet expectations.[14] It is best to avoid creating expectations that cannot be satisfied, because rejection at this stage will prevent adoption. Friends and peers may also be important sources during the trial stage. By the time the adoption stage has been reached, both personal communication from sales personnel and mass communication through advertisements may be required. Even though the particular stage of the adoption process may influence the types of information source consumers use, marketers must remember that other factors – such as the product's characteristics, price and uses, as well as the characteristics of customers – also affect the types of information source that buyers desire and believe.

Because people in separate stages of the adoption process often require different types of information, marketers designing a promotional campaign must determine what stage of the adoption process a particular target audience is in before they can develop the message. Potential adopters in the interest stage will need different information from people who have already reached the trial stage. Often a campaign will include several different advertisements and promotional mix tools in order to appeal simultaneously to different consumers who are at different stages in the product adoption process.

When a company introduces a new product, people do not all begin the adoption process at the same time and they do not move through the process at the same speed. Of those people who eventually adopt the product, some enter the adoption process rather quickly, whereas others start considerably later. For most products, too, there is a group of non-adopters who never begin the process.

Product adopter categories

Depending on the length of time it takes them to adopt a new product, people can be divided into five major **adopter categories**: innovators, early adopters, early majority, late majority and laggards.[15] Figure 13.5 shows each adopter category and indicates the percentage of total adopters that it typically represents.

Innovators are the first to adopt a new product. They enjoy trying new products and tend to be venturesome. **Early adopters** choose new products carefully and are viewed as 'the people to check with' by those in the remaining adopter categories. People in the **early majority** adopt just prior to the average person; they are deliberate and cautious in trying new products. **Late majority** people, who are quite sceptical about new products, eventually adopt them because of economic necessity or social pressure. **Laggards**, the last to adopt a new product, are oriented towards the past. They are suspicious of new products or unable to afford them easily, and when they finally adopt the innovation, it may already have been replaced by a newer product. When microwave ovens first appeared, only 'technocrats' or 'food boffins' – the innovators – bought them. Then 'trend setters' – the early adopters – came into the market. After several years and prompted by many frozen food manufacturers' new product launches, many more consumers – the early majority – decided to adopt the microwave oven. Eventually, the rest of the masses – the late majority – decided that they, too, should have a microwave oven 'given that most people have one now'. There are, though, some households only now deciding to buy one – the laggards; and some – the non-adopters – never will. Smartphones and eReaders more recently have followed a similar pattern, but with the late majority still to buy-in. When developing promotional efforts, a marketer should bear in mind that people in different adopter categories often need different forms of communication and different types of information or message.

adopter categories
Five groups into which customers can be divided according to the length of time it takes them to adopt a product: innovators, early adopters, early majority, late majority and laggards

innovators
The first people to adopt a new product

early adopters
People who choose new products carefully and are often consulted by people from the remaining adopter categories

early majority
People who adopt products just prior to the average person

late majority
People who are quite sceptical about new products but eventually adopt them because of economic necessity or social pressure

laggards
The last people to adopt a new product, suspicious of new products and oriented towards the past

FIGURE 13.5
Distribution of product adopter categories

Source: reprinted with the permission of The Free Press, a division of Simon & Schuster, Inc., from *Diffusion of Innovations*, 3rd edn, by Everett M. Rogers. Copyright © 1962, 1971, 1983 by The Free Press

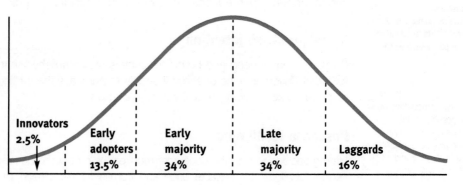

Aims of promotion

five communication effects
Communication aims that include category need, brand awareness, brand attitude, brand purchase intention and purchase facilitation

Product adoption is a major focus for any promotional activity. There are, though, five basic communications aims, known as the **five communication effects**. These are:[16]

1 category need
2 brand awareness
3 brand attitude
4 brand purchase intention
5 purchase facilitation.

Category need

category need
The consumer's perception of his or her need for a product in a certain category

The consumer must realize he or she wants a particular product – particularly for inno- vative new category product launches – and must perceive a **category need** in order to be motivated even to consider a product. When compact disc players were launched, many consumers had perfectly adequate album and/or cassette based hi-fi systems and did not see any need to purchase a compact disc player. CD producers had to create a category need. Mobile phone networks have persuaded many users of the need for built-in cameras, web browsing or music downloads: eye-catching advertising com- municated the benefits of these mobile attributes, creating category need. The iPad had to adopt a similar need-generating approach in its launch communications.

Brand awareness

brand awareness
The consumer's ability to identify a manufacturer's or retailer's brand in sufficient detail to distinguish it from other brands

The consumer must be able to identify – recognize or recall – a manufacturer's or retai- ler's brand within the category in sufficient detail to make a purchase. **Brand aware- ness** means that the manufacturer or retailer must make its brand stand out, initially through product attributes supported by distinctive promotional activity. Sony wants consumers to be aware of its products rather than those from LG or Panasonic. In most marketing communications there is the objective of establishing brand awareness among target consumers.

brand attitude
A consumer's particular impression of a brand, formed by emotions and logic or cognitive beliefs

Brand attitude

Emotions and logic or cognitive beliefs combine to give the consumer a particular im- pression of a product. This **brand attitude** directs consumer choice towards a par- ticular brand. Companies need customers to have a positive view of their brands. Much promotional mix activity and the creation of the promotional message relate to developing a favourable brand attitude, but other marketing mix ingredients also impact on these perceptions, notably product design, features and performance.

brand purchase intention
The consumer's decision and efforts to purchase the particular product

Brand purchase intention

Once a category need and brand awareness are established, if the consumer's brand attitude is favourable, he or she will decide to purchase the particular product and take steps to do so, showing **brand purchase intention**.

purchase facilitation
Circumstances that make it possible for the consumer to purchase the product: availability, location, price and familiarity of vendor

Purchase facilitation

Having decided to buy, the consumer requires the product to be readily available at a con- venient location, at a suitable price and from a familiar dealer: **purchase facilitation**.

A manufacturer or supplier must ensure that other marketing mix factors – product, people, place (distribution) and price – do not hinder the purchase. Sony customers expect wide distribution from reputable retailers, with no budget pricing. Sony produces high-quality goods, but it has several well-respected competitors and must ensure product availability and continued product improvement to prevent brand switching.

To provide a better understanding of how promotion can move people closer to the acceptance of goods, services and ideas, the next section focuses on the major promotional methods available to an organization – the promotional mix – and integrated marketing communications.

The promotional mix

Several types of promotional methods can be used to communicate with individuals, groups and organizations. When an organization combines specific ingredients to promote a particular product, that combination constitutes the promotional mix for that product. The four tradi-

promotional mix
The specific combination of ingredients an organization uses to promote a product, traditionally including four ingredients: advertising, personal selling, publicity and public relations and sales promotion

tional ingredients of a **promotional mix** are advertising, personal selling, publicity/public relations and sales promotion. Increasingly, sponsorship and direct mail are elements of the promotional mix in their own right (see Figure 13.6).[17] The Internet and direct marketing are relatively recent additions to the promotional mix. For some products, organizations use all of these ingredients; for other products, two or three will suffice. Each has its pros and cons, but each must be pertinent to the product category's accepted norms, to targeted buyers' expectations and behaviours, and to the product's adopted brand positioning and tone of voice. This section analyzes the major ingredients of a promotional mix and the chief factors that influence an organization to include specific ingredients in the promotional mix for a specific product.

Promotional mix ingredients

advertising
A paid form of non-personal communication about an organization and its products that is transmitted to a target audience through a mass medium

At this point consideration is given to some general characteristics of advertising, personal selling, publicity and public relations, sales promotion, sponsorship, direct mail, the Internet and direct marketing.

Advertising **Advertising** is a paid form of non-personal communication about an organization and its products that is transmitted to a target audience through a mass medium such as television, radio, newspapers, magazines, direct mail, public

FIGURE 13.6
Possible ingredients of an organization's promotional mix

transport, outdoor displays, catalogues or increasingly the Internet and mobile devices. Individuals and organizations use advertising to promote goods, services, ideas, issues and people. Because it is highly flexible, advertising offers the options of reaching an extremely large target audience or focusing on a small, precisely defined segment of the population. For instance, McDonald's advertising focuses on a large audience of potential fast-food consumers, ranging from children to adults, whereas advertising for DeBeers' diamonds focuses on a much smaller and specialized target market. The main uses of advertising include the promotion of products or an organization in order to create awareness among targeted audiences, the stimulation of demand, the off-setting of competitors' advertising, to support personal selling drives, for the education of a target market about a brand and its enhanced marketing mix or product benefits and attributes, to increase consumption and the perceived uses of a product, to remind and reinforce with intended customers, and to even-out seasonal sales fluctuations or manage production cycles.

Advertising offers several benefits. It can be an extremely cost-efficient promotional method because it reaches a vast number of people at a low cost per person. For example, if the cost of an eight-colour, one-page advertisement in the *Sunday Telegraph* is £34 000, and the newspaper reaches 500 000 readers, the cost of reaching 1000 subscribers is only £68 per person. Advertising also enables the user to repeat the message a number of times. Unilever advertises many of its products – cleaning products, foods, cosmetics – on television, in magazines, via the Web and through outdoor advertising. Advertising repetition has been found to be especially effective for brand name extensions beyond the original product category.[18] In addition, advertising a

A Web presence: now routine behaviour

Topical insight

During the 1990s many corporate giants avoided using banners, buttons and other early forms of Internet advertising, believing them to be inefficient and ineffective. Now most large companies embrace Internet advertising and digital communications. McDonald's uses websites, banners and buttons, instant messaging, online games and pop-up windows to engage with consumers through interactivity. *McDonald's on your mobile* and *Wraps on YouTube* are just two examples of McDonald's digital activity. As the company's director for media explains, 'We're not going to sell burgers online, but we can extend the experience of the brand online and bring McDonald's to life online'.

Digital experts believe few consumer or business brands can now avoid harnessing web-based marketing communications, particularly if – as in the case of McDonald's – the target audience is young and made up of consumers who have been brought up as 'digital dream kids' used to twenty-four hour online access anywhere they happen to be, hooked into their online communities.

Nike has many websites, some of which promote specific brands, linking into its sponsorship of entertainers and sports stars. Guerrilla moves, such as mentioning its websites or celebrity tie-ins in chat room messages have been hugely successful for the company in attracting hundreds of thousands of visitors to its websites for specific online promotions and advertising campaigns. Sports-focused video clips, downloadable tracks, musical ePostcards suitable for personalization, and games have proved a big hit with the youth market targeted by so many Nike products.

As with many brands, a digital presence on Twitter, Facebook and YouTube are now routinized expectations for Pepsi consumers and the company's brand managers. Pepsi online provides entertainment, promotions, news, merchandise offers and access to a digital community of consumers sharing interests and lifestyles in which Pepsi plays a part. With 'Every Pepsi Refreshes the World', the Pepsi refresh project has harnessed the Web to good effect ... consumers are invited to dream it, submit it, get the votes, and then Pepsi will help fund the initiative. Playgrounds, support programmes for domestic violence victims, aid to disadvantaged groups and entertainment ideas, are just some of the schemes receiving online votes and thereby Pepsi's dollars, all facilitated by Pepsi's online community and digital presence. Pepsi is harnessing the Web to advertise its wares, but also to build its brand.

Sources: McDonald's, Nike and Pepsi, with thanks to *Advertising Age* and *Campaign*.

product in a certain way can add to its value. For example, BMW cars are advertised as having more sophistication, style and technical innovation than Honda, Toyota and other Japanese companies' vehicles. The visibility that an organization gains from advertising enhances the company's public image. There clearly is a link between a product's brand positioning and the role of marketing communications.

Advertising also has several disadvantages. Even though the cost per person reached may be low, the absolute monetary outlay can be extremely high, especially for advertisements shown during popular television programmes. These high costs can limit, and sometimes prevent, the use of advertising in a promotional mix. Moreover, advertising rarely provides rapid feedback. Measuring its effect on sales is difficult, and it ordinarily has a less persuasive impact on customers than, for example, personal selling.[19] With the growth in satellite channels, the creation of ever greater numbers of consumer and trade magazines, the role of the Web for advertisers and interactive television, the choice of media for advertisers is growing increasingly complex and prone to error unless handled by specialist media buyers.

As illustrated in Figure 13.7, there are eight stages in creating an advertising campaign:

1 The identification and understanding of the advertising target audience, which relates to the company's target market strategy and a deep appreciation of targeted consumers' or business customers' expectations, perceptions, requirements and buying behaviour, as explored in Chapters 4 and 5.

2 The scoping of objectives for the campaign, such as sales levels, increased awareness of the brand, a specific impact on a competitor or a change in the target audience's perceptions and attitudes.

3 The creation of the advertising platform which has relevance to the target audience and seeks to differentiate the brand from rivals, such as Andrex's puppies or BMW's *The Ultimate Driving Machine.*

4 Agreement on the available advertising budget, which is often a specific project amount, the percentage of sales approach or an amount set to match a specific competitor's activity.

5 The highly specialized act of establishing a media plan, which with the proliferation of TV channels, consumer magazines, local radio stations, eChannels and viral possibilities, has become far more flexible but much more complex.

6 The creation of the specific message, such as Direct Line's triumphant red phone proposition or Asda's value-led deals.

7 The execution of the campaign using the agreed platform, message, media and associated IMC activities.

8 The evaluation of the effectiveness of the campaign and assessment of its apparent benefits.

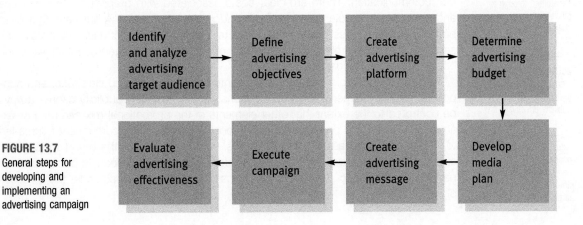

FIGURE 13.7
General steps for developing and implementing an advertising campaign

Personal selling Selling that involves informing customers and persuading them to purchase products through personal communication in an exchange situation is called **personal selling**. The phrase 'to purchase products' should be interpreted broadly to encompass the acceptance of ideas and issues. **Telemarketing**, described as direct selling over the telephone, relies heavily on personal selling.

Personal selling has both advantages and limitations when compared with advertising. Advertising is general communication aimed at a relatively large target audience, whereas personal selling involves more specific communication aimed at one person or several people. Reaching one person through personal selling costs considerably more than doing so through advertising, but personal selling efforts often have a greater impact on customers. Personal selling also provides immediate feedback, which allows marketers to adjust their message to improve communication. It helps them determine and respond to customers' needs for information.

When a sales person and customer meet face to face, they use several types of interpersonal communication. Obviously, the predominant communication form is language – both speech and writing. In addition, a sales person and customer frequently use **kinesic communication**, or body language, by moving their heads, eyes, arms, hands, legs or torsos. Winking, head nodding, hand gestures and arm motions are forms of kinesic communication. A good sales person can often evaluate a prospect's interest in a product or presentation by watching for eye contact and head nodding. **Proxemic communication**, a less obvious form of communication used in personal selling, occurs in face-to-face interactions when either person varies the physical distance that separates the two people. When a customer backs away from a sales person, for example, that individual may be indicating that he or she is not interested in the product or may be expressing dislike for the sales person. Touching, or **tactile communication**, can also be used; shaking hands is a common form of tactile communication in many countries. Management of sales people is very important in making this component of promotion effective. Sales people who are directly involved in planning sales activities develop greater trust in their company and have increased sales performance.[20]

Publicity and public relations Publicity refers to non-personal communication in news-story form about an organization or its products, or both, that is transmitted through a mass medium at no charge. Examples of publicity include magazine, newspaper, radio and television news stories about new retail stores, new products or personnel changes in an organization. Although both advertising and publicity are transmitted through mass communication, the sponsor does not pay the media costs for publicity and is not identified. Nevertheless, publicity should never be viewed as free communication. There are clear costs associated with preparing news releases and encouraging media personnel to broadcast or print them. A business that uses publicity regularly must have employees to perform these activities, or obtain the services of a public relations consultancy or an advertising agency. Either way, the company bears the costs of the activities.

Publicity must be planned and implemented so that it is compatible with, and supportive of, other elements in the promotional mix.[21] However, publicity cannot always be controlled to the extent that other elements of the promotional mix can be. For example, just as Toyota prepared for new model launches, major component failures led to a series of embarrassing product recalls, causing issues for the brand's reputation and credibility which suddenly had to be addressed by the company's public relations partners. The **public relations** mechanism manages and controls the process of using publicity.[22]

Marketing public relations, now so important because of information availability online and growing digital consumer-to-consumer communications via social media, promotes products or brands, while corporate public relations focuses on the company and its impact on society, with all stakeholders and not just intended customers. Marketers make use of PR events, campaigns and programmes. In addition to using a company's web pages to communicate information, PR practitioners use press releases, feature articles, press conferences, interviews, visits and stunts. Harnessing social media chat and digital endorsements from celebrities is increasingly the norm, often now forming the basis for many PR campaigns. Third party endorsement of a product or company by trusted and respected independent authorities and personalities can prove very effective. In addition to creating product or brand awareness and generating interest, public relations is very important in handling crises and combating any negative publicity engineered by competitors or stemming from the media, regulatory bodies or public interest groups.

sales promotion
An activity or material that acts as a direct inducement by offering added value to or incentive for the product to resellers, sales people or consumers

Sales promotion A **sales promotion** is an activity or material that acts as a direct inducement by offering added value to, or incentive for, the product to resellers, sales people or consumers.[23] Examples of sales promotion include coupons, on-pack deals, trade shows, bonuses and contests used to enhance the sales of a product. The term sales promotion should not be confused with promotion; sales promotion is but a part of the more comprehensive area of promotion that encompasses advertising, personal selling, publicity and public relations, sponsorship, direct mail, the Internet and direct marketing. Some sales promotions, however, are closely associated with additional elements of the promotional mix. Currently, marketers spend about half as much on sales promotion as they do on advertising. Sales promotion appears to be growing in use more than advertising.

Marketers frequently rely on sales promotion to improve the effectiveness of other promotional mix ingredients, especially advertising and personal selling. For example, some organizations allocate 25 per cent of their annual promotional budget to trade shows in order to introduce new products, meet key industry personnel and identify likely prospects.[24] For many business-to-business marketers, sales promotions are very important.

Marketers design sales promotion to produce immediate, short-run sales increases. For example, the major brewers, such as Heineken and Coors, use a continuous programme of sales promotion techniques to boost sales in the highly competitive beer and lager market: free drinks and prize competitions, scratch cards and trade incentives.

Generally, if a company employs advertising or personal selling, it either depends on them continuously or turns to them cyclically. However, a marketer's use of sales promotion tends to be irregular. Many products are seasonal. For example, Thomas Cook and the Cooperative Travel promote summer package holidays predominantly in the winter and spring months. Flymo pushes its lawn mowers and other gardening equipment from Easter onwards. On the whole, sales promotions are infrequent, *ad hoc* campaigns.

Consumer sales promotions encourage consumers to patronize a specific retail store or to try a particular product, or they strive to bring forward purchases by existing customers. Techniques include coupons, free samples, demonstrations, competitions, frequent-user incentives and loyalty programmes, point-of-sale materials, money refunds, premiums, product bundling and price-off offers. Trade sales promotions encourage wholesalers, retailers or distributors to stock a product, increase display space and market the product. Popular techniques include buy-back allowances, buying allowances/temporary price reductions, count and re-count promotions, free merchandise, point-of-sales materials, merchandise allowances, cooperative advertising, dealer listings, money to incentivize sales personnel, sales competitions and dealer loaders/gifts.

sponsorship
The financial or material support of an event, activity, person, organization or product by an unrelated organization or donor

Sponsorship The financial or material support of an event, activity, person organization or product by an unrelated organization or donor is called **sponsorship**. Funds are

Facebook can be a marketer's best friend

Topical insight

Founded in 2004, Facebook was initially created just to connect students at Harvard and other Ivy League universities; it soon expanded to include family, friends and colleagues. Since being opened to the general public, it has grown to support more than 500 million users worldwide. Although it still serves its original purpose, Facebook has acquired diverse new roles, even changing how people use the Internet. When conducting research, many people now seek recommendations from social media friends before conducting other kinds of searches. Facebook users share more than 5 billion pieces of Web content each week.

Marketing strategists say businesses now must worry about how to connect to consumers via social media. One of the ways is to create a fan page, of which Facebook has billions. The average user becomes a fan of four pages each month. Fan pages use widgets, which help companies keep track of information on who is becoming a fan of their page. Businesses can use widgets to learn about and track their customers in order to better understand and serve them. These pages are inexpensive and easy to produce, making them accessible to all businesses.

Businesses must tread carefully, however. Generally, Facebook users do not want to feel as if they are being subjected to sales pitches. In order to make fans feel connected to a company without making them feel like they are being pressured to buy something against their will, companies must dedicate time to responding to fan posts and providing relevant information. Problems aside, fan pages and other uses of widgets are a cheap way for companies to advertise their goods and services while also garnering information about consumers. Art Meets Commerce – a marketing firm commissioned to promote Broadway and Off-Broadway shows – has used Facebook with great success, as it is the company's number-one source of ticket sales. Given the popularity of fan pages and the low cost commitment, Facebook may be the future of advertising for some brands.

Source: Bill Pride and O.C. Ferrell, *Marketing*, Cengage South-Western, 2012.

made available to the recipient of the sponsorship in return for prominent public recognition of the benefactor's generosity, and display of the sponsor's name, products and brands. Sponsorship is no longer confined to the arts or the sporting world, although many galleries, theatrical companies, sports events and teams could not survive without sponsorship. Research and development, buildings, degree courses, charitable events – all often benefit from sponsorship. The donor or sponsor gains the benefits of enhanced company, brand or individual reputation and awareness, as well as, possibly improved morale and employee relations. Note the number of prestigious or well-known brands sponsoring the Olympics or football's World Cup. It is important to select sponsorship partners with care, as negative publicity about one may in turn tarnish the reputation of the other.

direct mail
A method of communication used to entice prospective customers or charitable donors to invest in products, services or worthy causes

Direct mail The direct mail industry takes a significant slice of the promotional budgets for many companies and organizations. Few households and companies fail to receive direct mail solicitations. **Direct mail** is used to entice prospective customers or charitable donors to invest in products, services or worthy causes. Throughout Europe, direct mail is used as a pre-sell technique prior to a sales call, to generate orders, qualify prospects for a sales call, follow up a sale, announce special or localized sales, and raise funds for charities and not-for-profit organizations. Good database management is essential, and the material must be targeted carefully to overcome the growing public aversion to 'junk mail'.

Internet
A network of computer networks stretching across the world, linking computers of different types and sharing information

The Internet From humble beginnings as a 'talking shop' for boffins and computer buffs, the **Internet** – a network of computer networks stretching across the world, linking computers of different types – is now firmly established in many office workers' daily routines, accessed in millions of households and by many consumers on the move through smartphones and tablets. Marketers have been quick to identify this additional medium as an opportunity for providing existing and potential customers with company, product and brand information. Most large companies now have their own websites, while the major Internet servers such as Microsoft, Google and Yahoo! are targeting small businesses and providing e-commerce capability at affordable prices.[25] Web-based marketing is particularly important in many business-to-business markets. Use of the Internet is not uniform across all parts of society, although it is no longer the pastime of only the young, affluent and well educated. Scrambling of confidential information such as credit card and bank account details has enabled the recent explosion in the number of purchases made online.

digital marketing
The use of particularly the web and mobile, as well as radio, TV and any other form of digital media, to attract, engage and build relationships with customers and other target audiences

The surge in consumers' 'on-the-move' access to the web and their constant use of sites such as Facebook or Twitter fostered by **digital marketing**, have presented huge new challenges for marketers. Many consumers are readily accessible wherever they are with tailored propositions and messaging, often interactively and instantly. However, such access is easily open to competing brands. Perhaps more challenging, consumers are instantly linked with their friends and peers for positive or negative influences on their purchasing decisions. The growth of consumer-to-consumer (C2C) communications, facilitated by the web/mobile digital communications and enabled via **social media**, has transformed the sources of information used by consumers in making decisions about brands and products. This development has taken a great deal of control away from marketers in terms of how messages about their brands and products are communication and in the pecking order of what information is valued and trusted by consumers. Increasingly, marketers are seeking to influence views on social media and spread their own messages via C2C.

social media
Social media incorporate the online technology and methods through which people can share content, personal opinions, different perspectives and insights, using text, images, audio and video, via social networks, video and photo sharing, micro-blogs, wikis and news aggregators

As a promotional mix ingredient, the Internet provides a tool that can be interactive, updated or modified quickly, and that can produce material aimed at very tightly defined target groups or even individual consumers. **Mobile marketing** has extended these advantages further, placing consumers accessible 24/7. From Interflora to Tesco to JCB, the Internet is increasingly part of the promotional mix and, for direct marketers, the actual point of the sales transaction. Many television and press advertisements for services or consumer goods now direct their target audience to associated websites for additional information. Consumers can then interact with these hosts, in many instances, via e-mail chatrooms and interactive web page information request facilities. Websites still must be tailored to match the target customer buying behaviour and expectations, and must be informative but not mesmerizing, while reflecting the existing branding and product positioning already established by an organization's marketers. They require expert design and updating, as with any ingredient in the promotional mix.

mobile marketing
A set of practices that enables organizations to communicate and engage with their audience in an interactive and relevant manner through any mobile device or network, fostering 'on the move' marketing

Intranets – internal in-company Internet networks – have improved communications within many organizations, becoming an important facet of internal marketing.

direct marketing
A decision by a company's marketers to select a marketing channel which avoids dependence on marketing channel intermediaries and to focus marketing communications activity on promotional mix ingredients which deal directly with targeted customers

Direct marketing First used in the 1960s, until recently direct marketing described the most common direct marketing approaches: direct mail and mail order. Currently experiencing a surge in popularity, direct marketing now encompasses all the communications tools that enable a marketer to deal directly with targeted customers: direct mail, telemarketing, direct response television advertising, door-to-door/personal selling and the Internet. **Direct marketing** is a decision by a company's marketers to both:

- select a marketing channel that avoids dependence on marketing channel intermediaries
- focus marketing communications activity on promotional mix ingredients that deal directly with targeted customers.

Direct marketing is now adopted by a host of organizations ranging from fast-moving consumer goods companies, business-to-business marketers, charities and even government departments.[26] Of all elements of the promotional mix, it is reported to be the fastest growing, but this is partly a reflection of the large number of promotional mix ingredients it includes and the role of the web.[27]

In terms of the promotional mix, there are several key implications. Direct mail is on the increase. Telemarketing has grown and will continue to do so, with more organizations turning to the direct marketing toolkit aided by advances in automated call centres. Door-to-door selling and leaflet dropping, visible forms of direct marketing encountered by most householders, are also on the increase. Direct response advertising – containing a call for action within the advertisement by coupon, telephone or web – now makes up close to a third of all advertising as marketers turn to direct marketing, and as the growth in satellite and cable television channels enables more direct response television advertising. The Internet, too, is used by direct marketers to communicate with current and prospective customers. The deployment of any direct marketing campaign must strive to reflect targeted customer behaviour, needs and perceptions; provide a plausible proposition that is clearly differentiated from competitors' propositions; and match an organization's corporate goals and trading philosophy. Direct marketing is not a substitute for the traditional promotional mix. Direct marketing is an increasingly popular deployment of marketing, resulting from marketers' choices regarding their preferred marketing channel and selection of promotional mix ingredients.

Integrated marketing communications (IMC)

integrated marketing communications (IMC)
The coordination and integration of all marketing communication tools, avenues and sources within a company into a seamless programme that maximizes the impact on consumers and other end users, at minimal cost

Currently popular is the concept of **integrated marketing communications (IMC)**. This is the coordination and integration of all marketing communication tools, avenues and sources within a company into a seamless programme of marketing communications activities. The intention of IMC is to maximize the impact on consumers or business customers and other target audiences, at minimal cost. IMC avoids the waste and duplication inherent in some organizations in which each element of the promotional mix is controlled by separate managers and may even be executed through different external agencies. There is nothing worse than when an advertising campaign on radio created by one agency has little resemblance to a television campaign running at the same time, and created by another advertising agency. This is often compounded by the public relations, sponsorship, packaging and sales promotions being implemented by yet more agencies in a poorly coordinated fashion. On one occasion, five different agencies were developing marketing communications for market-leading Gordon's Gin, each using different shades of green – the brand's famous identity – and adopting various typefaces for the logo.

IMC is the integration of the whole promotional mix, but also all business-to-business, marketing channel, customer-focused and internally directed communications. IMC as a concept is focused on complete coordination and harmonized execution of various campaigns across the elements of the promotional mix. Rather than treating all aspects of the promotional mix and internal marketing separately, often utilizing many different departments and external agencies in an uncoordinated manner, the company instead opts to fully harmonize these activities. This does not have to result in only one supplying agency being commissioned: coordination ensures shared goals and common approaches to execution in a carefully scheduled manner. The benefits of IMC include greater clarity to customers, marketing channel members, employees and suppliers, as well as reduced costs, stronger impact in the marketplace and more effective branding.

Advertising, along with the rest of the promotional mix, exists to help implement a brand's target market strategy by communicating the product appeal and the brand positioning image to intended customers and other key stakeholders (see Chapter 6). Occasionally, a creative execution can be sufficiently memorable and strike a chord so well with the target audience, that an organization rethinks its whole marketing mix for a brand or product. BMW had already decided to focus its whole strategy on the driving experience, but the inception of the memorable *The Ultimate Driving Machine* positioning strapline has for over 35 years steered the strategy. While Mercedes emphasizes the comfort and luxury of its cars to all in the cabin, German rival BMW designs its vehicles around the driver, whose experience is indeed more rewarding than that of cabin passengers. The company prides itself on its engineering and technology innovation, updating new models with dozens of improvements and innovative gadgets, but all orientated primarily around the driver's position and use, along with the drivability of the vehicle. The brand's marketing communications, using all aspects of the promotional mix (just go to www.bmw.co.uk for some examples) in an integrated programme, emphasize both the driving experience and the technical prowess of the range, under *The Ultimate Driving Machine* brand positioning. Sainsbury's upturn in its performance owes much to its agency's use of chef Jamie Oliver in the company's advertising, but in-store demonstrations, point of sale promotions and displays, online activity and publicity also all featured the well known TV chef in a co-ordinated IMC programme. The strategy for marketing communications was linked to many aspects of the marketing mix to provide Sainsbury's shoppers with a co-ordinated proposition. In-store displays, merchandising, product bundling and even some pricing all were aligned around the separate campaigns run under the Jamie Oliver programme.

Now that the basic components of an organization's promotional mix have been discussed, it is important to consider how that mix is created to create a marketing communications programme. The factors and conditions that affect the selection of the promotional methods a specific organization uses in its promotional mix for a particular product need to be examined.

Selecting promotional mix ingredients

Marketers vary the composition of promotional mixes for many reasons. Although all ingredients can be included in a promotional mix, frequently a marketer chooses not to use them all. In addition, many organizations that market multiple product lines use several promotional mixes simultaneously.

An organization's promotional mix (or mixes) is not an unchanging part of the marketing mix. Marketers can and do change the composition of their promotional mixes. The specific promotional mix ingredients employed and the intensity with which they are used depend on a variety of factors, including the organization's promotional resources, objectives and policies; characteristics of the target market; characteristics of the product; and the cost and availability of promotional methods.

Promotional resources, objectives and policies The quality of an organization's promotional resources affects the number and relative intensity of promotional methods that can be included in a promotional mix. If a company's promotional budget is extremely limited, the business is likely to rely on personal selling because it is easier to measure a sales person's contribution to sales than to measure the effect of advertising. A company must have a sizeable promotional budget if it is to use regional or national advertising and sales promotion activities. Organizations with extensive promotional resources can usually include more ingredients in their promotional mixes. However, larger promotional budgets do not necessarily imply that the companies will use a greater number of promotional methods.

An organization's promotional objectives and policies also influence the types of promotion used. If a company's objective is to create mass awareness of a new convenience good, its promotional mix is likely to lean heavily towards advertising, the web, sales promotion and possibly publicity. If a company hopes to educate consumers about the features of durable goods, such as home electrical appliances, its promotional mix may combine a moderate amount of advertising, possibly some sales promotion efforts designed to attract customers to retail stores and a great deal of in-store personal selling, this being an excellent way to inform customers about these types of product. If a company's objective is to produce immediate sales of consumer non-durables, such as paper products and many grocery goods, the promotional mix will probably stress advertising and sales promotion efforts. Business-to-business marketers often use detailed trade advertising, personal selling through sales representatives, sales promotions – often in the guise of bulk discounts and trade show exhibits – and direct mail of brochures and price lists.

Characteristics of the target market The size, geographic distribution and socio-economic characteristics of an organization's target market also help dictate the ingredients to be included in a product's promotional mix. To some degree, market size determines the composition of the mix. If the size is quite limited, the promotional mix will probably emphasize personal selling, which can be quite effective for reaching small numbers of people. Organizations that sell to in-dustrial or business markets, and companies that market their products through only a few wholesalers, frequently make personal selling the major component of their promotional mixes. When markets for a product consist of millions of customers, organizations use advertising and sales promotion because these methods can reach masses of people at a low cost per person.

The geographic distribution of a company's customers can affect the combination of promo-tional methods used. Personal selling is more feasible if a company's customers are concen-trated in a small area than if they are dispersed across a vast region. When the company's customers are numerous and dispersed, advertising an online activity may be more practical.

The distribution of a target market's socio-economic characteristics, such as age, income or edu-cation, may dictate the types of promotional technique that a marketer selects. For example, personal selling may be much more successful than print advertisements for communicating with poorly edu-cated people, because it allows meaning or product attributes to be explained face to face.

Characteristics of the product Generally, promotional mixes for industrial or business products concentrate on personal selling and the Web. In promoting consumer goods, on the other hand, advertising plays a major role. This generalization should be treated with caution, however. Indus-trial goods producers do use some advertising to promote their goods, particularly in the trade press. Advertisements for computers, road-building equipment and aircraft are not altogether un-common, and sales promotion is deployed to promote industrial goods. Personal selling is used extensively for services and consumer durables, such as insurance, leisure and education, home appliances, cars and houses, and consumer convenience items are promoted mainly through advertising and sales promotion. Publicity appears in promotional mixes for industrial goods, con-sumer goods and services. Many organizations use direct mail, and more are now examining the growing use of corporate sponsorship. Most organizations are also developing websites and embracing eMarketing.

Marketers of highly seasonal products are often forced to emphasize advertising, and possibly sales promotion, because off-season sales will not support an extensive year-round salesforce. Although many toy producers have salesforces to sell to resellers (retailers), a number of these companies depend to a large extent on advertising to promote their products.

The price of a product also influences the composition of the promotional mix. High-priced pro-ducts call for more personal selling because consumers associate greater risk with the purchase of such products and usually want the advice of a sales person. Few consumers, for example, would be willing to purchase a refrigerator or personal computer from a self-service establishment. For low-priced convenience items, marketers use advertising rather than personal selling at the retail level. The profit margins on many of these items are too low to justify the use of sales people, and most customers do not need advice from sales personnel when buying such products.

A further consideration in creating an effective promotional mix is the stage of the product life cycle (see Chapter 8). During the introduction stage, a good deal of advertising may be neces-sary for business-to-business and consumer products to make potential users aware of a new product. For many products, personal selling and sales promotion are also helpful at this stage. In the case of consumer non-durables, the growth and maturity stages call for a heavy emphasis on advertising. Business products, on the other hand, often require a concentration of personal selling and some sales promotion efforts during these stages. In the decline stage, marketers usually decrease their promotional activities, especially advertising. Promotional efforts in the decline stage often centre on personal selling and sales promotion efforts.

The intensity of market coverage is yet another factor that affects the composition of the promotional mix. When a product is marketed through intensive distribution, the organization depends strongly on advertising and sales promotion. A number of convenience products – such as lotions, cereals and coffee – are promoted through samples, coupons and cash refunds. Where marketers have opted for selective distribution, marketing mixes vary considerably in terms of amount and type of promotional method. Items handled through exclusive distribution frequently demand more personal selling and less advertising. Expensive watches and high-quality furniture are products that are typically promoted heavily through personal selling. Intensive, selective and exclusive distribution are discussed in Chapter 11.

A product's use also affects the combination of promotional methods. Manufacturers of highly personal products, such as non-prescription contraceptives, feminine hygiene products and haemorrhoid treatments, count on advertising for promotion because many users do not like to talk to sales personnel about such products.

Cost and availability of promotional methods The cost of promotional methods is a major factor to analyze when developing a promotional mix. National advertising and sales promotion efforts require large expenditures. For example, some detergent brands have annual advertising budgets of £20 to £30 million. Tesco and Morrisons each spent £18 million in the run up to Christmas. However, if the efforts are effective in reaching extremely large numbers of people, the cost per individual reached may be quite small, possibly a few pence per person. Moreover, not all forms of advertising are expensive. Many small, local businesses advertise their products through local newspapers, magazines, radio stations, outdoor signs, public transport and the Web.

Another consideration that marketers must explore when formulating a promotional mix is the availability of promotional techniques. Despite the tremendous number of media vehicles, a company may find that no available advertising medium reaches a certain market effectively. For example, a product may be banned from being advertised on television, as are cigarettes in many countries. A stockbroker may find no suitable advertising medium for investors in Manchester United Football Club – should the stockbroker use financial publications, sports magazines or general media?

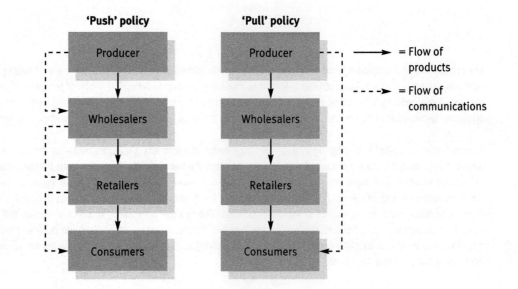

FIGURE 13.8
Comparison of push and pull promotional policies

The problem of media availability becomes even more pronounced when marketers try to advertise in other countries. Some media, such as television, simply may not be available to advertisers. Television advertising in Scandinavia is minimal. In the UK 12 minutes of advertising are permitted per average hour of terrestrial television. The media that are available may not be open to certain types of advertisement. For example, in Germany, advertisers are forbidden to make brand comparisons in television advertisements. Other promotional methods have limitations as well. An organization may wish to increase the size of its salesforce but be unable to find qualified personnel. In the United States, some state laws prohibit the use of certain types of sales promotion activities, such as contests. Such prohibited techniques are thus 'unavailable' in those locations.

Push policy versus pull policy

push policy
A promotional policy in which the producer promotes the product only to the next institution down the marketing channel

Another element that marketers should consider when they plan a promotional mix is whether to use a push policy or a pull policy. With a **push policy**, the producer promotes the product only to the next institution down the marketing channel. For instance, in a marketing channel with wholesalers and retailers, the producer promotes to the wholesaler, in this case the channel member just below the producer (see Figure 13.8). Each channel member in turn promotes to the next channel member. A push policy normally stresses personal selling. Sometimes sales promotion, direct mail and advertising are used in conjunction with personal selling to push the products down through the channel.

pull policy
A promotional policy in which an organization promotes directly to consumers in order to develop a strong consumer demand for its products

As Figure 13.8 shows, a company using a **pull policy** promotes directly to consumers with the intention of developing a strong consumer demand for the products. It does so through advertising, sales promotion, direct mail, the Web, sponsorship and packaging that helps manufacturers build and maintain market share.[28] Social media-led campaigns can create a swell of interest and demand, forcing retailers to seek supplies of a particular line. Because consumers are persuaded to seek the products in retail stores, retailers will in turn go to wholesalers or the producer to buy the products. The policy is thus intended to 'pull' the goods down through the channel by creating demand at the consumer level.

A push policy can be combined with a pull policy. Mars, for example, has a pull policy aimed at the consumer: sponsorship of events and advertising create awareness; packaging, sales promotions – such as competitions or discounts – and direct mail prompt product trial and adoption. Simultaneously, the company's push policy of trade advertising, sales promotions and personal selling persuades channel members to stock and retail its products.

Summary

The primary role of *promotion* is to communicate with individuals, groups or organizations with the aim of directly or indirectly facilitating exchanges. Promotion is commonly known as marketing communications. The nature of promotion in the marketing mix has altered radically in recent years owing to the Web's immediacy and tailored messages, along with far more rapid consumer-to-consumer communication about brands, products and experiences via social media networks and mobile comms.

Communication is a sharing of meaning through the transmission of information. The communication process involves several steps. Using the *coding process*, the *source* first converts the meaning into a series of signs that represent concepts. The source should employ signs that are familiar to the *receiver* or receiving audience, and choose signs that the receiver or *receiving audience* uses for referring to the concepts or ideas being promoted. The coded message is sent through a *medium of transmission* to the receiver or receiving audience. The receiver or receiving audience then uses the *decoding process* to convert the signs into concepts and usually supplies *feedback* to the source. When the decoded message differs from the encoded one, a condition called noise exists. Occasionally, *channel capacity* is reached when the volume of information can no longer be handled effectively.

Marketing communication is the transmission of persuasive information about a product, service or an idea, targeted at key stakeholders and consumers within the target market segment. Marketing communications centre on the promotional mix, which comprises advertising, public relations, personal selling, sales promotion, direct mail, sponsorship and the Internet. Cause-related marketing links product purchases to a 'good' cause. The recent growth of social marketing largely hinges on the effective use of appropriate communications to convey messages to relevant target audiences for wellbeing and sustainability causes.

One long-run purpose of promotion is to influence and encourage customers to accept or adopt goods, services and ideas. The ultimate effectiveness of promotion is determined by the degree to which it affects product adoption or increases the frequency of current buyers' purchases. The *product adoption process* consists of five stages: (1) in the *awareness stage*, individuals become aware of the product; (2) people move into the *interest stage* when they seek information about the product; (3) in the *evaluation stage*, individuals decide whether the product will meet certain criteria that are crucial for satisfying their specific needs; (4) during the *trial stage*, the consumer actually uses or experiences the product for the first time; (5) in the *adoption stage*, the consumer decides to use the product on a regular basis. Product rejection may occur at any stage. People can be divided into five major *adopter categories – innovators, early adopters, early majority, late majority and laggards* – according to how long it takes them to start using a new product.

There are *five communication effects*. A manufacturer or retailer must establish a *category need* for a product. Consumers must have *brand awareness* and a *favourable brand attitude* towards the products. If the consumer decides to make a purchase – *brand purchase intention* – the company's overall marketing policy must guarantee distribution, suitable product quality and attributes and set the relevant price points – *purchase facilitation*.

The *promotional mix* for a product traditionally included the four major promotional methods – advertising, personal selling, publicity/public relations and sales promotion. Now it is usually defined as also including sponsorship, direct mail and the Web. The Internet and direct marketing are currently very popular additions to companies' promotional mixes.

Advertising is a paid form of non-personal communication about an organization and its products that is transmitted to a target audience through a mass medium. *Personal selling* is a process of informing customers and persuading them to purchase products through personal communication in an exchange situation. *Telemarketing* often supports personal selling. *Kinesic, proxemic* and *tactile communication* are important in personal selling. *Publicity* is non-personal communication in news-story form about an organization or its products, or both, that is transmitted through a mass medium at no charge, and controlled by the *public relations* mechanism. *Sales promotion* is an activity or material that acts as a direct inducement by offering added value to, or incentive for, the product to resellers, sales people or consumers. *Sponsorship* involves financial or material support of an event, activity, person organization or product in return for prominent public recognition and display of the sponsor's name, products and brands. *Direct mail* is used to entice prospective customers or charitable donors to invest in products, services or worthy causes. The *Internet*, networked independent computers, sharing information through organizations' websites is a growing part of promotional activity, led in no small way by the growth in *digital marketing, mobile marketing* on the move and *social media* networking.

Many businesses are turning to *direct marketing*, which is a decision to avoid the use of marketing channel intermediaries and to focus marketing communications activity on promotional mix ingredients that deal directly with targeted customers, such as personal selling, direct mail, direct response advertising, telemarketing and the Internet.

Currently popular is the concept of *integrated marketing communications (IMC)*. IMC is the coordination and integration of all marketing communication tools, avenues and sources within a company into a seamless programme that maximizes the impact on consumers and other end users at a minimal cost. It is integration of the whole promotional mix but also all business-to-business, marketing channel, customer-focused and internally directed communications. Rather than treating all aspects of the promotional mix and internal marketing separately, often utilizing many different departments and external agencies in an uncoordinated manner, a company instead opts to fully harmonize these activities. The benefits of IMC include greater clarity, reduced costs, stronger impact in the marketplace and more effective branding.

There are several major determinants of what promotional methods to include in a promotional mix: the organization's promotional resources, objectives and policies; the characteristics of the target market; the characteristics of the product; and the cost and availability of promotional methods. Marketers must also consider whether to use a push policy or a pull policy, or a combination of the two. With a *push policy*, the producer promotes the product only to the next institution down the marketing channel. A company that uses a pull *policy* promotes directly to consumers, with the intention of developing a strong consumer demand for the products. Once consumers are persuaded to seek the products in retail stores, retailers in turn go to wholesalers or the producer to buy the products.

Key links

This chapter overviews the role of promotion – marketing communications – within the marketing mix. It should be read in conjunction with:

- Chapter 8, which features the product adoption process in developing products.
- Chapter 6, which examines brand positioning.
- Chapter 14, which covers branding.

Important terms

Promotion
Cause-related marketing
Communication
Marketing communication
Source
Receiver
Receiving audience
Coding process
Medium of transmission
Decoding process
Noise
Feedback
Channel capacity
Product adoption process
Awareness stage
Interest stage
Evaluation stage
Trial stage
Adoption stage
Adopter categories
Innovators
Early adopters
Early majority
Late majority
Laggards

Five communication effects
Category need
Brand awareness
Brand attitude
Brand purchase intention
Purchase facilitation
Promotional mix
Advertising
Personal selling
Telemarketing
Kinesic communication
Proxemic communication
Tactile communication
Publicity
Public relations
Sales promotion
Sponsorship
Direct mail
Internet
Digital marketing
Mobile marketing
Social media
Direct marketing
Integrated marketing communications (IMC)
Push policy
Pull policy

Discussion and review questions

1 What is the major task of promotion?

2 What significant developments have impacted most on marketers' use of marketing communications?

3 What is communication? Describe the communication process. Is it possible to communicate without using all of the elements in the communication process? If so, which ones can be omitted?

4 Identify several causes of 'noise'. How can a source reduce noise?

5 Describe the product adoption process. In certain circumstances, is it possible for a person to omit one or more of the stages in adopting a new product? Explain your answer.

6 Describe a product that many people are in the process of adopting. Have you begun the adoption process for this product? If so, what stage have you reached?

7 What is category need? Illustrate your answer with examples.

8 Identify and briefly describe the major promotional methods that can be included in an organization's promotional mix.

9 How does publicity differ from advertising?

10 What forms of interpersonal communication in addition to language can be used in personal selling?

11 List the communications tools that direct marketing encompasses and explain the recent surge in popularity of this promotional tool.

12 How do target market characteristics determine which promotional methods to include in a promotional mix?

13 Assume that a company is planning to promote a cereal to both adults and children. Along what major dimensions would these two promotional efforts have to be different?

14 How can a product's characteristics affect the composition of its promotional mix?

15 Explain the difference between a pull policy and a push policy. Under what conditions should each be used?

16 What is integrated marketing communications (IMC) and what are the benefits of this approach?

Recommended readings

Belch, G. and Belch, M., *Advertising and Promotion: an Integrated Marketing Communications Perspective* (McGraw-Hill, 2011).

De Pelsmacker, P., Geuens, M. and van den Bergh, J., *Marketing Communications: A European Perspective* (FT/Prentice-Hall, 2010).

Fill, C., *Marketing Communications: Interactivity, Communities and Content* (FT/Prentice-Hall, 2009).

Pickton, D. and Broderick, A., *Integrated Marketing Communications* (FT Prentice-Hall, 2011).

Shimp, T.A., *Integrated Marketing Communications in Advertising and Promotion* (South Western College, 2009).

Internet exercise

Most leading brands embrace a mix of promotional techniques, including advertising, sales promotions, publicity, the Web and the rest of the promotional mix. Pepsi is no exception.

Pepsi's *Pepsi World* award-winning website is an important part of the company's promotional activity, integrating advertising, sales promotions activity and publicity releases with customer involvement. Brand information, TV advertisements, music links, sports, promotions and street motion – there is much on offer on Pepsi's web pages. Log on to **www.pepsi.com/home**.

1 In what ways and with what messages is Pepsi engaging with customers through the pages of its website?

2 How do these approaches support the brand's positioning?

3 How do the web pages relate to the brand's television advertising?

Applied mini-case

Whether from Nintendo, Sony or Microsoft, gamers are well used to the 'next big thing'. The Wii, PS3 or Xbox all strive to create maximum impact when launching or introducing their next generation. Straightforward broadcast adverts have, over the years, been supplemented with celebrity blogs, publicity stunts, competitions, in-store displays, PR campaigns, and significant social media activity. While gamers tend to look forward with relish to impending developments and launches, these companies require also much broader interest amongst current non-users, in order to leverage their heavy investments in these new products, grow their market shares and volumes, and dent competitors' fortunes.

Question

As marketing manager for Nintendo, Sony or Microsoft, tasked with launching the next generation of your gaming platform, how would you gain the attention of existing customers but also that of consumers not currently hooked on in-home gaming? What would be the core messages and what ways could be used to communicate these messages?

Häagen-Dazs: discover indulgence

Case study

Häagen-Dazs makes the best-selling superpremium ice cream in North America. Its luscious ingredients include chocolate from Belgium, vanilla from Madagascar, coffee from Brazil, strawberries from Oregon and nuts from Hawaii. The packaging serenely asserts that it is the world's best ice cream.

London's Leicester Square shop served close to one million ice cream lovers in its first year. The success of the Victor Hugo Plaza shop in Paris, now the company's second busiest, led to the establishment of its first European factory in France. Häagen-Dazs shops have opened in Italy, Spain, Benelux and Scandinavia, among other countries. The appealing flavours can now be found not only in the company's shops but also at airports, in cafés and in carefully selected delicatessens, with rapidly growing popularity.

The product's high quality has been essential in maintaining a loyal customer following, but it was promotional work that led to the successful take-off of what was previously an unheard-of brand in Europe. Sales promotion in the guise of free tasting was a major part of the promotional mix: over 5 million free cupfuls of ice cream were given away during the company's European launch. Thousands of retailers, cafés and delis were supplied with branded freezers both to display and carefully look after the new premium ice cream. As part of its European launch, Häagen-Dazs spent £30 million on advertising, stressing the deluxe ingredients, unusual flavours and novelty of its product. Europeans currently eat 25 per cent of the 3 billion gallons of ice cream each year consumed worldwide. Häagen-Dazs plans to increase consumption by appealing to more than traditional ice cream-loving children.

The summer afternoon stroll with an ice cream cornet, the family trip to a fun park or beach, a snack during a film or concert, the sticky climax of a birthday party feast had long been the core market for Wall's and Nestlé. Ice Cream Mars changed all that by creating an ice cream bar suitable for any occasion and particularly attractive to adults. Häagen-Dazs went further. Award-winning press adverts, artistically shot, often in black and white, featured lithe, semi-nude couples entwined in exotic poses while feeding each other Häagen-Dazs ice cream. The appeal of vanilla ice cream bars hand-dipped in Belgian chocolate and rolled in roasted almonds now seems hard to resist for adults everywhere. The advertising imagery promotes an adult, upmarket, glamorous positioning for this superpremium ice cream.

The Häagen-Dazs range has grown, expanding to include frozen yoghurts, sorbets and now ice cream novelties, such as the ice cream sandwich made with cookies. Formats, too, have evolved, from sharing tubs to minis, stick-bars to novelty lines. Product development and quality controls are important to Häagen-Dazs' brand positioning as an upmarket, indulgent treat for adults, but so is the company's innovative promotional mix and the messages at the heart of its advertising. Industry observers suggest that despite the exceptional quality and novel flavours, without marketing communications Häagen-Dazs would not have been so successful. Certainly its current campaign, *Win A Date* with well-known heart-throb celebrities, promoted on-line and via blogs, has captured the attention of many adults seeking indulgence.

Sources: Sainsbury's, 2004–11; 'Dairy produce', *Campaign*, 15 March 1996, p. 34; 'Häagen-Dazs cinema first', *Campaign*, 26 March 1995, p. 5; 'Pillsbury's global training plan', *Crossborder Monitor*, 19 April 1995, p. 9; G. Mead, 'Sex, ice and videod beer', *Financial Times*, 26 September 1992, p. 5; 'Saucy way to sell a Knicker-bocker Glory – Häagen-Dazs' new ice cream campaign', *Financial Times*, 8 August 1991, p. 8; 'Häagen-Dazs is using sex to secure an up market niche in Britain's £400m ice cream market', *Observer*, 4 August 1991, p. 25; M. Carter, 'The luxury ice cream market', *Marketing Week*, 22 May 1992, p. 30; **www.haagen-dazs.com**, July 2004, January, 2008 and June, 2011; **www. haagen-dazs.co.uk**, June, 2011.

Questions for discussion

1 Why did the London launch of Häagen-Dazs utilize more than just advertising?

2 Why did Häagen-Dazs target the adult market rather than families or children?

3 Was the 'adult' positioning and promotional execution risky? Why did Häagen-Dazs deploy this positioning strategy?

CHAPTER 14

Branding and packaging

"Marketers must create and manage powerful, differentiated and compelling brands"

Objectives

- To recognize the importance of brands and brand equity

- To understand the types and benefits of brands and how to select, name, protect and license them

- To explore the concepts of brand loyalty, brand advocacy and brand communities

- To appreciate the best practice guidelines for creating strong brands

- To examine the roles of brand attributes, brand values and brand personality in brand development

- To understand the role of branding at the corporate level

- To become aware of the major packaging functions and packaging design considerations

- To consider the ways in which packaging is used in marketing strategies

- To examine the functions of labelling and the legal issues associated with labelling

INTRODUCTION

Effective marketing requires product or service differentiation. Such differentiation entails product design, features and attributes, customer service, branding and the other ingredients of the marketing mix. These need to appeal to targeted consumers or business customers more than competing brands. Branding is seen as a core activity of a company's marketing function. Inside most businesses there is little disagreement: marketers are responsible for brand strategy and brands.

Brands enable customers to readily identify their favoured products and marketers to more easily communicate their advantages. Marketers invest vast sums in persuading targeted customers to prefer their products over and above those supplied by competitors, as they strive to create brand loyalty or brand preference. Effectively creating a well-differentiated and memorable image for the brand is a core requirement for a marketing-oriented organization.

Brand equity is increasingly important in many boardrooms and results from the financial and marketing value that can be placed on a brand owing to its market position and standing. Brand awareness, brand loyalty, perceived brand quality and brand associations create brand equity. An effective brand has what is termed 'brand strength', and generally to achieve a strong brand marketers will have defined brand attributes, values and personality for their brands. These constructs are explored in this chapter.

Packaging and labelling are also part of the marketing process. Packaging includes the immediate container (the primary packaging) and the shipping packaging (the secondary packaging). Both need to exhibit functionality in order to protect and convey the product inside, and facilitate its easy use and storage. Additionally, packaging should support the product's branding and differentiation. Many products, particularly many found in supermarkets, explicitly use their pack designs to support their brand identities.

Polos: are you a sucker? Or, are you a cruncher?

At a factory in York, each day a mountain of thumbnail-sized tyre-shaped white mints is deemed slightly imperfect: chipped, broken or improperly moulded. The sight is awe-inspiring, but gives a clue as to the volume of perfectly formed Polo mints manufactured: 20 million are produced each day in York, and Nestlé makes 5.2 billion each year. 150 mints are eaten every second. Nestlé's take-over of Rowntree assured the world domination of Polo, 'the mint with the hole'.

Polo is the UK's top-selling mint and has established leadership in many other countries too. It was not too long before trial flavours and strengths were tested by product developers at Nestlé. In India there is a cinnamon flavoured Polo to 'spice things up, while being refreshing'.

However, the end of 1998 saw one of the most successful spin-offs from the original Polo concept: the sugar-free Polo Supermint, for 'instant refreshment'. This was not only a masterful brand extension of the Polo name but also proved to be an inspired packaging execution.

The Polo Supermint from Nestlé was even awarded 'Millennium Products' status by the Design Council, an accolade reserved for just a few new designs. The new mini-mints 'with the hole' weigh only a tenth of the original, yet contained four times the amount of peppermint oil in relation to their size. This super-strength mint not only appealed to traditional Polo mint buyers, but also enabled the brand to compete head to head with the plethora of extra-strong mints produced by rival manufacturers such as Trebor.

The new size and extra-strong Polo would inevitably have caught the eye of confectionery buyers on the back of the Polo heritage and the extensive distribution network established by the mighty Nestlé.

Marketers at Nestlé wanted to ensure a successful launch and were determined to make the new item distinctive and appealing in its own right. The innovative packaging design and eye-catching styling made an immediate impact in a rather crowded marketplace. The Supermints were packed in plastic dispensers, developed by RPC Market Rasen, which were shaped as giant versions of the original and very familiar Polo mint. The pack housed a pop-up hatch that enabled it to dispense individual mini-Polos and to be resealed easily. The regular user soon developed the ability to dispense one-handed and in suitable quantities to appease friends also requiring a refreshing treat. The plastic dispenser was packaged in a cool blue, square container with eye-catching graphics, permitting easy stocking and shelf displays.

Nestlé explained that while the mini-Polos were launched to celebrate the Polo brand's 50th birthday, the new item emerged as one of the company's greatest successes ever. Nestlé believed this demonstrated that it is possible to innovate with a brand now over sixty years old. The Supermints line matched the brand values and positioning of the original Polo mint: an effective brand extension must have an affinity with existing brand values. This, and other related Polo product developments, reflected competitor moves and responded to consumer tastes. With the Polo Supermint, the combination of astute branding and clever packaging certainly created a very successful product for Nestlé and a welcome alternative for Polo fans. Few products have been able to achieve such strong branding on the basis of shape and distinctive packaging.

Sources: The Museum of Brands, 2011/12; Nestlé Rowntree, York, 1999; One Stop, 2012; *Marketing*, 4 February 1999, p. 22; **www.nestle.co.uk**, May 2004 and January, 2008; **www.nestle.in**, January, 2008; **www.polomint.co.uk**, June, 2-11.

Source: © Finnbarr Webster / Alamy

B rands and packages are part of a product's tangible features, the verbal and physical cues that help customers identify the products they want and influence their purchase choices. For Nestlé's Polo Supermints, branding and packaging have been central to the product's success. A good brand is distinctive and memorable; without one, companies could not differentiate their products and shoppers' choices may, essentially, be arbitrary. A good package design is cost effective, safe, environmentally responsible and valuable as a promotional tool.

This chapter first defines branding and explains its benefits to customers and sellers; it examines brand loyalty, the role of digital brand communities and brand advocacy; then examines the importance of brand equity, brand attributes, values and personality, strong brands and the various types of brand. The chapter should be read in conjunction with Chapter 6 of *Marketing Essentials*, which explored brand positioning, the creation of a suitable image for a brand. The next section of this chapter examines how companies choose brands, how they protect them, the various branding policies that companies employ and brand licensing. The chapter goes on to discuss how organizations manage brands and how they ensure that they contribute effectively to a company's fortunes. Packaging is then the focus, as part of the product and how it is marketed: the functions of packaging, issues to consider in packaging design, packaging development and how the package can be a major element in marketing strategy. After considering criticisms of packaging, the chapter concludes with a brief discussion of labelling.

Branding

Most marketers believe a key focus for their activity is the differentiation of their product proposition vis-à-vis competing products and services. For many consumers, services or business products, such differentiation entails a mix of product design, features and attributes with the creation of a distinctive image. This generally involves creating a brand and brand identity for products or services. Indeed, without distinctive branding, many service products in particular would struggle to differentiate themselves against rivals (see Chapter 10).

brand
A name, term, design, symbol or any other feature that identifies one seller's good or service as distinct from those of other sellers

In addition to making decisions about actual products, as described in Chapter 8, marketers must make many decisions associated with branding, such as brands, brand names, brand marks, trademarks and trade names. A **brand** is a name, term, design, symbol or any other feature that identifies one seller's good or service as distinct from those of other sellers. A brand may identify one item, a family of items or all items of that seller.[1] A **brand name** is that part of a brand that can be spoken – including letters, words and numbers – such as Coca-Cola or Channel Four. A brand name is often a product's only distinguishing characteristic. Without the brand name, a company could not identify its products. Note how many TV channels display their channel identifier or logo throughout a programme and how much brand building goes on with short brand inserts between programmes or either side of news bulletins. To consumers, brand names are as fundamental as the product itself. Brand names simplify shopping, guarantee a specific level of quality and allow self-expression. Table 14.1 details the world's most valuable brands. For many marketers, establishing a distinctive brand, which is easily remembered and recognized by targeted customers, is one of the primary activities of effective marketing management.

brand name
That part of a brand that can be spoken, including letters, words and numbers

brand mark
The element of a brand that cannot be spoken – often a symbol or design

The element of a brand that is not made up of words but is often a symbol or design is called a **brand mark**. One example is the symbol of a baby on Procter & Gamble's Fairy Liquid detergent. Occasionally, brand marks are modified for local markets. For example, Microsoft topped its brand name with a butterfly in France, a fish in Portugal and a sun in Spain. A **trademark** is a legal designation indicating that the owner has exclusive use of a brand or a part of a brand, and that others are

trademark
Legal designation indicating that the owner has exclusive use of a brand

TABLE 14.1 Top 50 European countries by revenue for 2011

Rank	Company	Country	Sector	Revenue US$m
1	Royal Dutch Shell	Netherlands	Oil and gas	378 152
2	BP	UK	Oil and gas	308 928
3	Total	France	Oil and gas	186 055
4	Volkswagen	Germany	Automobile	168 041
5	AXA Group	France	Insurance	162 236
6	ING Group	Netherlands	Diversified finance	147 052
7	Glencore International	Switzerland	Commodities	144 987
8	ENI	Italy	Oil and gas	131 756
9	Daimler	Germany	Automobile	129 481
10	BNP Paribas	France	Banking	128 726
11	Allianz	Germany	Insurance	127 379
12	E.ON	Germany	Power and gas	125 064
13	Carrefour	France	Food and drug retail	120 297
14	Assicurazionia Generali	Italy	Insurance	120 234
15	GDF Suez	France	Power	111 888
16	Nestlé	Switzerland	Food	105 267
17	Crédit Agricole	France	Banking	105 003
18	HSBC Holdings	UK	Banking	102 680
19	Siemens	Germany	Multi-industry	102 657
20	Banco Santander	Spain	Banking	100 350
21	Enel	Italy	Power and gas	97 185
22	Lloyds Banking Group	UK	Banking	95 682
23	Tesco	UK	Food and drug retail	94 185
24	Aviva	UK	Insurance	90 211
25	Metro	Germany	Food and drug retail	89 081
26	Statoil	Norway	Power and gas	87 646
27	Éectricité de France	France	Power and gas	86 309
28	BASF	Germany	Multi-industry	84 597
29	Société Générale	France	Banking	84 350
30	ArcelorMittal	Luxembourg	Steel products	83 443
31	Deutsche Telekom	Germany	Telecommunications	82 674
32	Telefónica	Spain	Telecommunications	80 444
33	BMW	Germany	Automobile	80 099
34	EXOR Group	Italy	Investment	78 123
35	Munich Re Group	Germany	Insurance	76 220
36	Peugeot	France	Automobile	74 251

TABLE 14.1 Continued

Rank	Company	Country	Sector	Revenue US$m
37	Prudential	UK	Insurance	73 598
38	Vodafone	UK	Telecommunications	71 344
39	Deutsche Post	Germany	Logistics	71 121
40	Repsol YPF	Spain	Energy	70 456
41	Dexia Group	Belgium	Finance	69 491
42	Groupe BPCE	France	Telecommunications	69 297
43	Royal Bank of Scotland	UK	Banking	68 088
44	Zurich Financial Services	Switzerland	Banking and insurance	67 850
45	RWE	Germany	Power and gas	67 179
46	Aegon	Netherlands	Finance	65 136
47	Barclays	UK	Banking	63 661
48	Robert Bosch	Germany	Multi-industry	62 593
49	France Télécom	France	Telecommunications	61 965
50	EADS	Germany	Military and security	60 597

Source: Courtesy of CNN **http://money.cnn.com/magazines/fortune/global500/2011/europe/**

trade name
The full and legal name of an organization

prohibited by law from using it. To protect a brand name or brand mark a company must register it as a trademark with the appropriate patenting office. Finally, a **trade name** is the full and legal name of an organization, such as Ford Motor Company, rather than the name of a specific product.

Benefits of branding

Branding provides benefits for both buyers and sellers.[2] Brands help buyers identify specific products that they do and do not like, a process that in turn facilitates the purchase of items that satisfy their needs and reduces the time required to purchase the product. Without brands, product selection would be quite random, because buyers could have no assurance that they were purchasing what they preferred. Imagine the chaos in a supermarket if every shopper entered not knowing which products and brands to purchase! Research indicates, however, that the bulk of supermarket shoppers are highly brand loyal. So much so, that in-store redesigns and new shelf-space allocations cause significant distress and generate high levels of customer complaints.

A brand also helps buyers evaluate the quality of a product, especially when they are unable to judge its characteristics. In other words, a purchaser for whom a brand symbolizes a certain quality level will transfer that perception of quality to the unknown item. A brand thus helps to reduce a buyer's perceived risk of purchase. In addition, it may offer the psychological reward that comes from owning a brand that symbolizes status. Certain brands of watches (Rolex) and cars (Rolls-Royce) fall into this category.[3]

Sellers benefit from branding because each company's brands identify its products, which makes repeat purchasing easier for consumers. Branding helps a company introduce a new product that carries the name of one or more of its existing products, because buyers are already familiar with the company's existing brands. For example, Heinz regularly introduces new tinned products. Because consumers are used to buying the brand and have a high regard for its quality, they are likely to try the new offerings. The same applies to Tesco's *Finest* range. Branding also facilitates promotional efforts because the promotion of each branded product indirectly promotes all other products that are similarly branded.

Branding helps sellers by fostering brand loyalty. **Brand loyalty** is a strongly motivated and long-standing decision to purchase a particular product or service. To the extent that buyers become loyal to a specific brand, the company's market share for that product achieves a certain level of stability, allowing the company to use its resources more efficiently.[4] Loyal customers are highly desirable and much marketing activity is aimed at reassuring existing customers and canvassing their ongoing support and interest. It should be stated that some experts argue that there is not really true brand loyalty as many consumers are quite prepared to try alternatives when the mood takes or promos inspire them to do so, but there is certainly in most markets evidence of stated brand preference amongst many consumers. When a company succeeds in fostering some degree of customer loyalty to a brand, it can charge a premium price for the product. For example, brand loyal buyers of Anadin aspirin are willing to pay two or three times more for Anadin than for a generic brand of aspirin with the same amount of pain-relieving agent. Tilda rice commands a significant price premium over competing brands of rice, partly due to its brand reputation.

However, brand loyalty is argued to be declining, partly because of marketers' increased reliance on discounted sales, coupons and other short-term promotions, and partly because of the sometimes overwhelming array of similar new products from which consumers can choose. The growth of consumer-to-consumer communication, fostered by social media networking, quickly creates interest in a product or brand, prompting others to experiment or try out the much tweeted about brand. For example, if a well-known celeb tweets about a great experience with a brand, many followers will try it out, too. To stimulate loyalty to their brands, some marketers are stressing image advertising, mailing personalized catalogues and magazines to regular users, and creating membership clubs for brand users, for example, Tesco's ClubCard or Sainsbury's Nectar points. Many brands have created digital or virtual communities in order to foster interest and some degree of loyalty in their proposition. Sometimes consumers make repeat purchases of products for reasons other than brand loyalty. Spurious loyalty is not stable and may result from non-availability of alternative brands or the way in which products are displayed in retail outlets.

An interesting spin-off from increased web access and the growth of social media has been the creation of brand communities. Designed to foster both loyalty to a particular brand and interest in its products/services, a **brand community** is a group of consumers and observers focused on a particular brand, often web-based, centred on a set of social relations and interactions amongst admirers of the brand. The digital Harley Davidson Owners' Club is a typical example, and one well-adopted by fans of this brand. Brand communities generally are controlled and instigated by the brand's owner for commercial gain, but buy-in from followers of the brand creates much of the activity and dialogue. Mobile phone provider Geocell in Georgia created a separate brand targeted at its youth consumers, centred on an online community. Lai-Lai offers its cellular network subscribers live music events, merchandise, special tariffs, game and music downloads and the opportunity to create their own friendship groups. In this way, Geocell has created a strongly bonded set of consumers tied in to its Lai-Lai brand, which is aimed at 15 to 25 year-olds.

Blog communities, such as the Nike Blog – *The Art of Speed* was one of the first – or Google Blog, are an enhancement, where spokespersons for a brand share their views in blogs, permitting one-to-one tailored communication with members and between members of the digital brand community. Technology in the form of digital brand communities and blogs enables so-termed **dynamic branding**, with very rapid communication and sharing of brand information and almost instant take-up by the brand's followers. Companies increasingly view such digital brand community activity as core to

brand loyalty
A strongly motivated and long-standing decision to purchase a particular product or service

brand community
A group of consumers and observers focused on a particular brand, often based on social media, centred on a set of social relations and interactions amongst admirers of the brand

blog communities
Where spokespersons for a brand share their views in blogs, permitting one-to-one tailored communication with members and between members of the digital brand community

dynamic branding
Digital brand communities and blogging enable dynamic branding, with very rapid communication and sharing of brand information and almost instant take-up by the brand's followers

brand advocacy
When consumers are encouraged to share very positive feelings towards a brand with other consumers, whether word-of-mouth, online or in the print and broadcast media

their attempts to build loyalty and to create brand advocacy. **Brand advocacy** is where consumers are encouraged to share very positive feelings towards a brand with other consumers, whether word-of-mouth, online or in the print and broadcast media. Many people believe in the views of others who are 'like them' more than they trust the statements of companies and brands. Creating a set of brand advocates or evangelists is on the increase.

The strategy literature has suggested that the concept of brand advocacy is more important than tracking customer satisfaction or even loyalty, as it is a business strategy built on trust. In a digital world in which rapid communication of positives and negatives is possible, often from consumer-to-consumer outside of the brand manager's control, having a set of brand 'super fans' who truly trust the brand and will both defend it and promote it, may even be a competitive advantage. *Harvard Business Review* explains that a customer brand advocate differs from being a supporter, influencer, loyalist or satisfied customer. A brand advocate supports the brand, actively promotes the brand and is also emotionally attached to the brand. S/he will silence detractors, build a positive customer experience, and share exemplars of the brand 'going that extra mile'. It is likely that more and more brands will develop both brand communities and a sub-set of super fans acting as brand advocates. One leading food brand has created a 'club' of consumers who adore its products, who are given inside information about new launches and invitations to special events, such as live sessions with well-known chefs. These enthusiasts readily share their positive views of this brand with their families, friends and colleagues, so becoming brand advocates or super fans. While communicating one-to-one with such advocates is more costly per capita than television advertising, many brand experts argue such consumer-to-consumer advocacy is very cost-effective in terms of its impact and for persuading others to trial a brand. This theme has been explored further in Chapter 13 of *Marketing Essentials*.

For most marketing managers, two long-established performance metrics are to assess the level of repeat purchasing and customer loyalty to a brand. There are three degrees of brand loyalty: recognition, preference and insistence.

brand recognition
A customer's awareness that a brand exists and is an alternative to purchase

Brand recognition **Brand recognition** exists when a customer is aware that a brand exists and views it as an alternative to purchase if the preferred brand is unavailable or if the other available brands are unfamiliar to the customer. This is the mildest form of brand loyalty. The word loyalty is clearly being used very loosely here. One of the initial objectives of a marketer introducing a new brand is to create widespread awareness of the brand in order to generate brand recognition.

brand preference
The degree of brand loyalty in which a customer prefers one brand over competitive offerings

Brand preference **Brand preference** is a stronger degree of brand loyalty in which a customer definitely prefers one brand over competitive offerings and will purchase this brand if it is available. However, if the brand is not available, the customer will accept a substitute brand rather than expend additional effort finding and purchasing the preferred brand. A marketer is likely to be able to compete effectively in a market when a number of customers have developed brand preference for its specific brand.

brand insistence
The degree of brand loyalty in which a customer strongly prefers a specific brand and will accept no substitute

Brand insistence **Brand insistence** is the degree of brand loyalty in which a customer strongly prefers a specific brand, will accept no substitute and is willing to spend a great deal of time and effort to acquire that brand. If a brand-insistent customer goes to a store and finds the brand unavailable, rather than purchasing a substitute brand, he or she will seek the brand elsewhere. Brand insistence is the strongest degree of brand loyalty. It is a marketer's dream. However, it is the least common type of brand loyalty. Customers vary considerably regarding the product categories for which they may be brand insistent.

Brand equity

A well-managed brand is an asset to an organization. The value of this asset is often referred to as brand equity. **Brand equity** is the marketing and financial value associated with a brand's strength in a market. Besides the actual proprietary brand assets, such as patents and trademarks, four major elements underlie brand equity. These components are brand name awareness, brand loyalty, perceived brand quality and brand associations, as shown in Figure 14.1.[5] Brand equity is a function of the goodwill and positive brand recognition built up over time, which underpin sales volumes and financial returns. Strong brand equity should equate to higher sales and margins vis-à-vis competing brands.

> **brand equity**
> The marketing and financial value associated with a brand's strength in a market, which is a function of the goodwill and positive brand recognition built up over time, underpinning the brand's sales volumes and financial returns

Being aware of a brand leads to brand familiarity, which in turn results in a level of comfort with the brand. A familiar brand is more likely to be selected than an unfamiliar brand because often the familiar brand is viewed as reliable and of acceptable quality compared to the unknown brand. The familiar brand is likely to be in a customer's evoked set (see Chapter 4), whereas the unfamiliar brand is not.

Brand loyalty is a valued component of brand equity because it reduces a brand's vulnerability to competitors' actions. Brand loyalty allows an organization to keep its existing customers and avoid having to spend enormous amounts of resources gaining new ones. Loyal customers provide brand visibility and reassurance to potential new customers. And because customers expect their brand to be available when and where they shop, retailers strive to carry the brands known for their strong customer following.

Customers associate a certain level of perceived overall quality with a brand. A brand name itself stands for a certain level of quality in a customer's mind and is used as a substitute for actual judgement of quality. In many cases, customers cannot actually judge the quality of the product for themselves and instead must rely on the brand as a quality indicator. Perceived high brand quality helps to support a premium price, allowing a marketer to avoid severe price competition. Also, favourable perceived brand quality can ease the introduction of brand extensions, as the high regard for the brand is likely to translate into high regard for the related products.

The set of associations linked to a brand is another key component of brand equity. At times a marketer works to connect a lifestyle, or in some instances a certain personality type, with a particular brand. For example, customers associate Volvo cars with protecting family members; a De Beers diamond with a loving, long-lasting relationship (a diamond is for ever); and Drambuie

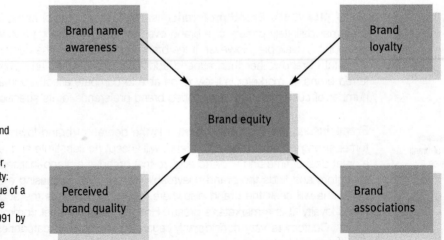

FIGURE 14.1
Major elements of brand equity

Source: David A. Aaker, 'Managing Brand Equity: Capitalizing on the Value of a Brand Name', The Free Press. Copyright © 1991 by David A. Aaker

liqueur with a unique taste. These types of brand association contribute significantly to the brand's equity.

Although difficult to measure, brand equity represents the value of a brand to an organization. An organization may buy a brand from another company at a premium price because outright brand purchase may be less expensive and less risky than creating and developing a brand from scratch – for example, Kraft acquiring Cadbury's strong portfolio of brands. Brand equity helps to give a brand the power to capture and maintain a consistent market share, which provides stability to an organization's sales volume. The top brands with the highest economic value are shown in Table 14.1. Any company that owns a brand listed in Table 14.1, such as Nestlé with Nescafé, would agree that the economic value of that brand is likely to be the greatest single asset in the organization's possession. A brand's overall economic value rises and falls with the brand's profitability, brand awareness, brand loyalty, perceived brand quality and strength of positive brand associations.

Brand personality, values and attributes

brand attributes
The bullet-point specific benefits to the customer from purchasing or using the brand

Most companies have identified specific attributes that should be linked to their brands and emphasized in associated brand communication. **Brand attributes** are the bullet-point selling-type features listed in brochures or in an advertisement: the specific benefits to the customer from purchasing or using the brand. Two decades ago, it became fashionable to also identify brand values to help differentiate a brand and build its

Marketing tools and techniques

Practitioners' use of the brand development theory: the brand personality grid

Leading branding exponents, such as Prophet (David Aaker) and Interbrand, suggest that organizations identify core values that are reflected in their business capabilities and their brands' positionings, and in the perceptions of their target stakeholders. In addition, specific features or attributes that can be construed as brand benefits should be defined. In order to truly make a brand 'come alive' and be distinctive in the marketplace, leading branding experts argue that a *brand personality* should be specified and communicated to stakeholders. Such personality traits are the emotive characteristics of the brand, whereas the brand benefits are more tangible and specific attributes, as outlined opposite.

1 *Personality*
   What sets the company apart/describes its character and personality emotionally

2 *Values*
   The heart of the organization's ethos as conveyed internally

3 *Brand benefits/attributes*
   Detailed/specific features of benefit to the customer

Fujitsu's evolving branding is a good example of this.

Japanese-based Fujitsu is one of the world's biggest businesses, focusing mainly on electronics and IT services. The company had traded under different names across the world and in the UK was familiar to business clients as ICL. Fujitsu decided to maximize its global standing under the Fujitsu name and looked to create a leading brand. Globally, Fujitsu is the world's number three IT services company, is growing and is increasingly successful. In the UK, Fujitsu handles IT outsourcing and management for major banks and retailers, central and local government, the Post Office and many manufacturers.

The old brand in the UK was somewhat staid: hardware-led, overly 'techy', 'grey' and stood for ICL's old values from when the company focused on producing mainframe computers rather than offering innovative IT solutions and management options to leading-edge businesses. The new-look Fujitsu is a dynamic, progressive, forward-thinking business, partnering other leading-edge suppliers to address clients' fast-changing IT requirements and to help clients to transform their business practices.

There are many providers of IT support and many may be able to offer the brand benefits stated on the following page, in the right-hand column. However, fewer B2B companies could claim to have a reputation for being caring, passionate, likeable, dependable and knowledgeable about clients' business issues. Certain rivals would struggle to be described by clients as caring, likeable or dependable. In IT services, interpersonal relationships between the supplier and the client are of paramount importance. Clients also perceive high risks in handing over their IT – on which the success of their operations may depend – to a third party. The brand values and brand personality suggested in this analysis would be highly attractive to many senior executives in current or potential business clients.

Having developed a brand proposition – personality, values and attributes – as hypothesized in the example to the right, the marketing challenges are then to ensure that both:

● all promotional activity reflects this overall message

● any interface with clients and suppliers or partners conveys these sentiments, whether in print format, e-communications, broadcast media or even with any personnel meeting and when working with clients.

In addition to developing suitable marketing communications materials, therefore, there is a core requirement to ensure that a company's workforce understands and utilizes the brand proposition developed, not only a company's marketers. There is a requirement for internal marketing.

The brand personality grid for Fujitsu could easily look like this:*

Fujitsu
The Possibilities are Infinite

Brand Personality	Brand Values	Brand Benefits
Friendly People	**Knowledge** Customer's business Across sectors	**Infrastructure Management**
Customer-focused	**Dependability** Trusted to deliver 30/40 year track record	**Free-up Resources** **Operational Efficiency**
Confident	**Technical Excellence** At forefront of change	**Customers Enabled to Focus on *Their* Business Imperatives**
Dynamic	Tap into Fujitsu's huge R&D	
Future-focused	**Passion** Staff are passionate Deliver for customers	**Latest Technology** **Total Solutions**
Passionate		**Leading-edge Partnerships**
Likeable Staff	**Collaboration** Working together	**Reliable**
Global	Networking with partners	**Cost Effective**

© Dibb/Simkin

* The suggested brand personality grid for Fujitsu is an external observer's view and does not necessarily reflect the company's own analyses or intended brand strategy.

---

brand values
The emotional benefits and less tangible identifiers attached to the brand inside the organization, providing reassurance and credibility for employees and, indirectly, targeted consumers or business customers

appeal to target audiences, particularly those within an organization. **Brand values** are the emotional benefits and less tangible identifiers attached to the brand, creating a sense of identity and purpose within the organization, providing reassurance and credibility for employees and, indirectly, targeted consumers or business customers, and supplementing the specific brand attributes in making the brand attractive to current or potential purchasers. Brand values focus on those inside the organization, to help foster a collegiality around the brand that ultimately will manifest itself to customers and suppliers. For example, IT services company Fujitsu has many brand attributes, including its ability to manage business clients' IT infrastructure, offer the latest technology and thinking, and be cost effective and reliable. Its brand values are defined as knowledge, dependability, technical excellence, reassurance and passion, but to staff the message is that 'we tell it as it is'. These values are far more emotional than the brand attributes. Together, the brand values and brand attributes constitute a more compelling proposition in the marketplace and to staff to understand for what the brand stands.

Many branding experts argue that in addition to brand attributes and brand values, an effective brand strategy should identify brand personality variables in order to facilitate greater differentiation in relation to competitors' products and to form a stronger affinity with customers. **Brand personality** traits are the psychological cues and less tangible desirable facets of a well-presented brand. In Fujitsu's case, the brand personality variables include having friendly, customer-focused personnel who are confident, technically savvy and passionate about assisting clients to improve their organizations. In the market for IT services to large corporations, these are desirable traits. Many

brand personality
The psychological cues and less tangible desirable facets of a well-presented brand

companies readily identify the brand attributes and, after a little deliberation, they are able to scope out a few brand values. However, the identification of an attractive set of brand personality traits is often more difficult, yet once developed, such emotive sentiments often 'bring the brand to life' and help to establish differentiation vis-à-vis rivals. Brand personality traits and brand attributes together combine to present a compelling proposition to targeted consumers or business customers, offering both the emotion of the brand and specific attributes deemed desirable to these targeted customers. The Marketing Tools and Techniques box below illustrates this approach to effective branding.

Implicit in this discussion is the need to determine a strong and relevant brand image that is managed effectively. As explained in Chapter 6's examination of brand positioning, a management team must determine the desired brand proposition and manage its portfolio of brands in order to ensure that the target market recognizes the specified brand attributes, values and personality. Targeted customers should never be left to deduce for themselves a brand's proposition and messages. The role of the brand manager and the management of portfolios of brands are examined in Chapter 9.

Types of brand

There are three categories of brand: manufacturer brands, own label brands (also called private brands, store brands or dealer brands) and generic brands.

manufacturer brands
Brands initiated by producers to ensure that they are identified with their products at the point of purchase

Manufacturer brands **Manufacturer brands** are initiated by producers and ensure that they are identified with their products at the point of purchase – for example, Green Giant, Apple and Wall's ice cream. A manufacturer brand usually requires a producer to become involved in distribution, promotion and, to some extent, pricing

FIGURE 14.2
There are many examples of retailer own-label brands, but Marks & Spencer deliberately created a stand-alone brand for its own, highly popular, range of Per Una clothing emulating the major manufacturer brands

Source: copyright © Marks and Spencer plc.

decisions. Brand loyalty is encouraged by promotion, quality control and guarantees; it is a valuable asset to a manufacturer. The producer tries to stimulate demand for the product, which tends to encourage middlemen to make the product available (stock).

own label brands
Brands initiated and owned by resellers – wholesalers or retailers

Own label brands Own label brands are initiated and owned by resellers (wholesalers or retailers). The major characteristic of own-label brands is that the manufacturers are not identified on the products. Retailers and wholesalers use these brands to develop more efficient promotion, to generate higher gross margins and to improve store images. Own label brands give retailers or wholesalers freedom to purchase products of a specified quality at the lowest cost without disclosing the identity of the manufacturer. Wholesale brands include Roca, Family Choice, Happy Shopper and Lifestyle. Familiar retailer brand names include St Michael and Per Una (Marks & Spencer), Yessica (C&A) and George (ASDA). Many successful own label brands are distributed nationally and are as well-known as most manufacturer brands. Sometimes retailers with successful distributor brands start manufacturing their own products to gain more control over product costs, quality and design in the hope of increasing profits. While one might think that store brands appeal most strongly to lower-income shoppers or to upmarket shoppers who compare labels, studies indicate that buyers of own label brands have characteristics that match those of the overall population.[6] Indeed, many consumers now perceive the own label ranges from the likes of Tesco, M&S or John Lewis to be superior to many 'true' brands stocked by these retailers. One reason for the growth of store brands is that retailers advertise the manufacturer brands, which brings customers to their stores, but sell the store brands, especially to price-sensitive customers.[7] Another reason is that retailers with store labels negotiate better prices from producers of manufacturer brands.[8]

generic brand
A brand that indicates only the product category and does not include the company name or other identifying terms

Generic brands Some marketers of products that have traditionally been branded have embarked on a policy of not branding, often called generic branding. A **generic brand** indicates only the product category – such as aluminium foil – and does not include the company name or other identifying terms. Usually generic brands are sold at prices lower than those of comparable branded items. Although at one time generic brands may have represented as much as 10 per cent of all retail grocery sales, today they account for less than 1 per cent.[9] They are popular for pharmaceuticals and in some discount grocery stores.

The battle of the brands Competition between manufacturer brands and own label brands – sometimes called 'the battle of the brands' – is intensifying in several major product categories, particularly tinned foods, breakfast cereal, sugar and soft drinks. Own label brands now account for around 45 per cent of all supermarket sales.[10] Both men and women are quite favourable towards own label brands of food products, with women – still the major grocery purchasers – even more favourable than men. For manufacturers, developing multiple manufacturer brands and distribution systems has been an effective means of combating increased competition from own label brands. By developing a new brand name, a producer can adjust various elements of a marketing mix to appeal to a different target market. For example, Scott@Brand has developed lower-priced brands of paper towels; it has tailored its new products to a target market that tends to purchase own label brands.

Manufacturers find it hard to ignore the marketing opportunities that come from producing own label brands for resellers. If a manufacturer refuses to produce an own label brand for a reseller, a competing manufacturer will. Moreover, the production of own label brands allows the manufacturer to use excess capacity during periods when its own brands are at non-peak production. The ultimate decision whether to produce an own label or a manufacturer brand depends on a company's resources, production capabilities and goals.

Choosing a brand name

Marketers should consider a number of factors when they choose a brand name. The name should be easy for customers – including foreign buyers, if the company intends to market its products in other countries – to say, spell and recall. Short, one-syllable names such as Mars or Tide satisfy this requirement. The brand name should indicate the product's major benefits and, if possible, should suggest in a positive way the product's uses and special characteristics: negative or offensive references should be avoided. For example, a deodorant should be branded with a name that signals freshness, dryness or long-lasting protection, as do Sure, Right Guard and Arrid Extra Dry. The brand should be distinctive, to set it apart from competing brands. If a marketer intends to use a brand for a product line, it must be compatible with all products in the line. Finally, a brand should be designed so that it can be used and recognized in all of the various types of media.

Finding the right brand name has become a challenging task, because many obvious product names have already been used. The Marketing Tools and Techniques box outlines the role played by brand name consultancies in the naming process.

How are brand names derived? Brand names can be created from single or multiple words – for example, Bic or Apple iPod Nano. Initials, numbers or sometimes combinations of these are used to create brands such as IBM. At times, words, numbers and initials are combined to yield brand names such as Mazda MX5 or Mitsubishi 3000GT. To avoid terms that have negative connotations, marketers sometimes use fabricated words that have absolutely no meaning at the time they are created – for example, Kodak and Esso. Occasionally, a brand is simply brought out of storage and used as it is or modified. Companies often maintain banks of registered brands, some of which may have been used in the past. Cadillac, for example, has a bank of approximately 360 registered trademarks. Possible brand names are sometimes tested in focus groups or in other settings to assess customers' reactions.

Who actually creates brand names? Brand names can be created internally by the organization. Sometimes a name is suggested by individuals who are close to the development of the product. Some organizations have committees that participate in brand name creation and approval. Large companies that introduce numerous new products annually are likely to have a department that develops brand names. Increasingly, outside consultants are used in the process of developing brand names. An organization may also hire a company that specializes in brand name development.

Even though most of the important branding considerations apply to both goods and services, services branding has some additional dimensions. The brand of the service is usually the same as the company name. For example, American Express, Vidal Sassoon, ProntoPrint and Sheraton are names of companies and the services that they provide. Whereas companies that produce tangible goods (such as Procter & Gamble) can use separate brand names for separate products (such as Daz, Head & Shoulders, Flash and Camay), service providers (such as British Airways) are perceived by customers as having one brand name, even though they offer multiple products (first class, business class and economy or holiday packages). Because the service brand name and company name are so closely interrelated, a service brand name must be flexible enough to encompass a variety of current services, as well as new ones that the company may offer in the future. For example, British Airways (BA) has Club World or Euro Traveller (economy) services, each separately branded, but both strongly branded as BA. Geographical references like 'western' and descriptive terms like 'trucking' limit the scope of associations that can be made with the brand name. Northwest Airlines becomes less of a good name as the company begins to fly south and east more regularly.[11] Frequently, a service marketer will employ a symbol along with its brand name to make the brand distinctive and to communicate a certain image.

Protecting a brand

Marketers need to design brands that can be protected easily through registration. Among the most difficult to protect are generic words, such as aluminium foil, surnames and descriptive geographic or functional names.[12] Research shows that, overall, consumers prefer descriptive and suggestive brand names, and find them easier to recall than fanciful and arbitrary names.[13] Because of their designs, some brands can be legally infringed upon more easily than others. Although registration provides trademark protection, a company should develop a system for ensuring that its trademarks will be renewed as needed. To protect its exclusive rights to a brand, the company must make certain that the selected brand is not likely to be considered an infringement on any existing brand already registered with the relevant patent office. This task may be complex because infringement is determined by the courts, which base their decisions on whether a brand causes consumers to be confused, mistaken or deceived about the source of the product. McDonald's is one company that aggressively protects its trademarks against infringement; it has brought charges against a number of companies with 'Mc' names because it

---

Marketing tools and techniques

Who thought of that name?!

Burger King, Coca-Cola, JCB, Nike, Sony or Virgin – no matter what the brand, someone, somewhere, sometime created the names now recognized instantly by millions of loyal customers. David Rivett, former CEO of Design Bridge, responsible for many new product development projects and the creation of brand names, believes that all too often clients focus on the physical properties of their new products – features, size, colours, quality, operation – at the expense of name consideration, which is 'tacked on' to the new product development process just prior to launch. Branding consultancies believe that creating the right atmosphere and having a very clear understanding of both client culture and target market characteristics are fundamental to the creation of a suitable brand name. Very often a creative workshop is used by the consultancy to probe the minds of the client personnel in order to establish buzzwords or emotive trigger descriptions for the new product that may be incorporated into the brand name.

The real difficulty comes not from creating a suitable name, but in registering the preferred choice. Intellectual property lawyers now specialize in trademark registration and searching. Qualitative research, such as focus groups, often throws up many brand names consumers believe might be appropriate. Marketing strategy workshops amongst managers in a company frequently do the same. The result is that some organizations compile extensive lists of names with potential for their types of product, which are then registered, even though at the time there is no expectation of using these names. Companies such as Cadbury and Ford have large lists of already registered brand names which at some time they may use but that are no longer available to any other company. This is not 'sharp practice', merely a logical extension of marketers hearing good suggestions from colleagues, distributors and consumers and marking them down for possible future use.

Another consideration for branding consultancies is how the new product's name will work alongside the client's umbrella brand. For example, Per Una range is given independence from owner Marks & Spencer and Cap Colombie from Nescafé; whereas the Focus, Mondeo and Fiesta names are very much tied to the Ford umbrella brand, just as Apple's products link together. There is no right or wrong in this dilemma. Some companies, such as Nescafé with Cap Colombie, want to create sub-brands that, in the eyes of target consumers, are apparently free-standing. For Ford, the logic of cross-promotion and economies of scale in creating brand awareness, have persuaded senior marketers to always utilize the Ford brand alongside the individual model name.

Most brand names are, at some point in the creation process, tested out on consumers, but such tests have to be carefully constrained so as not to allow consumer suggestions to set the process back to square one. Ultimately, a good name cannot overcome product deficiencies, poor distribution, ineffectual promotion, incorrect pricing or inferior customer service, nor can it combat the superiority of a competitor's marketing strategy. A poor, inappropriate, confusing, unmemorable or misleading name can, though, do much harm to an otherwise good product offering.

FIGURE 14.3
Unilever opts to develop individual brands, in this case for its range of deodrants, including the feminine Impulse and the masculine-focused Lynx

Source: Image courtesy of The Advertising Archives

fears that the use of the 'Mc' will give consumers the impression that these companies are associated with or owned by McDonald's.

If possible, marketers must guard against allowing a brand name to become a generic term used to refer to a general product category.[14] Generic terms cannot be protected as exclusive brand names. For example, names such as aspirin, escalator and shredded wheat – all brand names at one time – were eventually declared generic terms that refer to product classes; thus they could no longer be protected. To keep a brand name from becoming a generic term, the business should spell the name with a capital letter and use it as an adjective to modify the name of the general product class, as in Kellogg's Rice Krispies.[15] Including the word 'brand' just after the brand name is also helpful. An organization can deal with this problem directly by advertising that its brand is a trademark and should not be used generically. The company can also indicate that the brand is a registered trademark by using the symbol ®.

Companies that try to protect a brand in a foreign country frequently encounter problems. In many countries, brand registration is not possible; the first company to use a brand in such a country has the rights to it. In some instances, a company has actually had to buy its own brand rights from a company in a foreign country because the foreign company was the first user in that country.

Marketers trying to protect their brands must also contend with brand counterfeiting. In many countries, for instance, it is possible to buy fake General Motors parts, fake Rolex watches, fake Chanel perfume, fake Microsoft software, fake Walt Disney character dolls and a host of other products illegally marketed by manufacturers that do not own the brands. Many counterfeit products are manufactured overseas – in South Korea, Italy, Taiwan and China, for example – but some are counterfeited in the countries in which they are sold. The International Anti-Counterfeiting Coalition estimates that roughly $600 billion in annual world trade involves counterfeit merchandise. The sale of this merchandise obviously reduces the brand owners' revenues from marketing their own legitimate products.

Brand counterfeiting is particularly harmful because the usually inferior counterfeit product undermines consumers' confidence in the brand and their loyalty to it. After unknowingly purchasing a counterfeit product, the buyer may blame the legitimate manufacturer if the product is of low quality or – even worse – if its use results in damage or injury. Since counterfeiting has become such a serious problem, many companies are taking legal action against counterfeiters. Others have adopted such measures as modifying the product or the packaging to make counterfeit items easier to detect, conducting public awareness campaigns and monitoring distributors to ensure that they stock only legitimate brands.

Branding policies

Before it establishes branding policies, a company must first decide whether to brand its products at all. If a company's product is homogeneous and similar to competitors' products, it may be difficult to brand. Raw materials – such as coal, salt, sand and milk – are hard to brand because of the homogeneity of such products and their physical characteristics. Marketers must also consider the degree to which consumers differentiate among brands of a product. For example, while brand may be an important factor in the purchase of coffee, snacks and frozen foods, it is not usually so important a consideration in buying light bulbs, cheese and cling film.

If a company chooses to brand its products, it may opt for one or more of the following branding policies: individual, overall family, line family and brand extension branding.

individual branding
A policy of naming each product differently

Individual branding Individual branding is a policy of naming each product differently. Procter & Gamble relies on an individual branding policy for its line of fabric washing products, which includes Tide, Bold, Daz and Dreft. There are several Procter & Gamble brands in the UK's top 50 biggest consumer brands, including Pampers, Ariel and Oral B.

A major advantage of individual branding is that if an organization introduces a poor product, the negative images associated with it will not contaminate the company's other products. An individual branding policy may also facilitate market segmentation when a company wishes to enter many segments of the same market. Separate, unrelated names can be used, and each brand can be aimed at a specific segment. Such a policy also encourages internal competition for growth and success between the different brand teams.

overall family branding
A policy of branding all of a company's products with the same name, or at least part of the name

Overall family branding In overall family branding, all of a company's products are branded with the same name, or at least part of the name, such as Kraft, Heinz, Microsoft or Ford. In some cases, a company's name is combined with other words to brand items. Heinz uses its name on its products along with a generic description of the item, such as Heinz Salad Cream, Heinz Baked Beans, Heinz Spaghetti and Heinz Tomato Soup. The quality image of its products increases consumer confidence in what they are buying. This brand consistency is stressed in Heinz advertisements (see Figure 14.4). Unlike individual branding, overall family branding means that the promotion of one item with the family brand promotes the company's other products.

line family branding
A policy of using family branding only for products within a single line

Line family branding Sometimes an organization uses family branding only for products within a single line. This policy is called line family branding. Colgate–Palmolive, for example, produces a line of cleaning products that includes a cleanser, a powdered detergent and a liquid cleaner, all with the name Ajax. Colgate also produces several brands of toothpaste, none of which carries the Ajax brand name.

brand extension branding
A company's use of one of its existing brand names as part of an improved or new product, usually in the same product category as the existing brand

Brand extension branding Brand extension branding occurs when a company uses one of its existing brand names as part of a brand for an improved or new product that is usually in the same product category as the existing brand. Unilever, the makers of Timotei shampoo, extended the name to hair conditioner and skincare products. There is one major difference between line family branding and brand extension branding. With line family branding, all products in the line carry the same name, but with brand extension branding this is not the case. The producer of Arrid deodorant, for example, also makes other brands of deodorant. Waterford, an upmarket Irish

FIGURE 14.4
Heinz uses its name on its products, along with a generic description of the item
Source: © H.J. Heinz Company Limited.

brand of crystal, extended its name to writing instruments when seeking sales growth beyond closely related giftware product categories, such as china, cutlery and table linens.[16]

Choice of branding policy An organization is not limited to a single branding policy. Instead, branding policy is influenced by the:

- number of products and product lines the company produces
- characteristics of its target markets
- number and type of competing products available
- size of its resources.

Anheuser–Busch, for example, uses both individual and brand extension branding. Most of the brands are individual brands; however, the Michelob Light brand is an extension of the Michelob brand. Sometimes companies must update brands so that they remain fresh and interesting.

Brand licensing

A recent trend in branding strategies involves the licensing of trademarks. By means of a licensing agreement, a company may permit approved manufacturers to use its trademark on other products for a licensing fee. Royalties may be as low as 2 per cent of wholesale revenues or higher than 10 per cent. The licensee is responsible for all manufacturing, selling and advertising functions, and bears the costs if the licensed product fails. Not long ago, only a few companies licensed their corporate trademarks but today the licensing business is worth billions of pounds and is growing. Harley-Davidson, for example, has authorized the use of its name on non-motorcycle products such as cologne, wine coolers, gold rings and shirts. Disney also licenses its brand for use on a range of products. JCB and Coca-Cola both now license ranges of clothing sold in high-street stores.

The advantages of licensing range from extra revenues and low cost to free publicity, new images and trademark protection. For example, Coca-Cola has licensed its trademark for use on glassware, radios, trucks and clothing in the hope of protecting its trademark. Similarly, Jaguar has licensed a range of leisure wear. However, brand licensing is not without its drawbacks. The major disadvantages are a lack of manufacturing control, which could hurt the company's name, and the undesirability of bombarding consumers with too many unrelated products bearing the same name. Licensing arrangements can also fail because of poor timing, inappropriate distribution channels or mismatching of product and name.

Managing brands

With the need for brands to create product differentiation, assist in establishing a competitive edge and encourage product awareness, marketers must manage their brands with care.[17] This involves understanding when a brand requires repositioning, modifying, deleting or simply being left alone. Most companies operate with a portfolio of separate brands and products, and must make difficult decisions in terms of which are to receive support and the bulk of an organization's marketing resource, and which are to be killed off or given only minimal support. Chapter 9 of *Marketing Essentials* explores these strategic choices.

As explained in Chapter 4's discussion of consumer buying behaviour, without an understanding of brand loyalty and brand switching, it is difficult to manage an organization's brands effectively. It is essential, therefore, for companies to make an effort to research brand loyalty and brand perceptions to help them make sensible decisions that accurately reflect consumers' views.

successful brands
Brands for which a company must prioritize quality, offer superior service, get there first, differentiate brands, develop a unique positioning concept, have a strong communications programme and be consistent and reliable

Research shows that to create **successful brands**, a company must:

- prioritize quality – the top brands are all high quality in their product fields
- offer superior service – less easily copied by competitors than pure product attributes
- get there first – not necessarily technologically but, in the minds of targeted customers, by:
  - exploiting new technology (Sony, Apple)
  - new positioning concepts (Body Shop, First Direct)
  - new distribution channels (Amazon, Direct Line)
  - new market segments (Orange, Ocado)
  - using gaps resulting from environmental change (Ecover, Toyota Prius)
- differentiate its brands – so that consumers perceive the brands on offer as being different
- develop a unique positioning concept – making the brand and its differentiating characteristics stand out with a clear image and positioning message against rival brands
- support the brand and its positioning with a strong communications programme – so that target consumers are aware of the brand and its positioning proposition
- deliver consistency and reliability over time – keeping the brand's values trustworthy as perceived by target consumers.

Branding expert Peter Doyle[18] stated that, to build effective brands, it is essential for an organization to understand that there is more to a brand than simply a catchy name and visible logo.

brand strength
A function of the product's attributes and functionality, its differentiation, plus any demonstrable added value to the purchaser or user

Doyle argued that **brand strength** is a function of the product's attributes and functionality, its differentiation, plus any demonstrable added value to the purchaser or user. For example, Nike sports shoes are designed for serious running and are fit for this core purpose, but Nike has a reputation for innovation and progression, so the brand is perceived as a 'first mover', providing differentiation versus rival brands. For the purchaser, the reputation of the brand for being state-of-the-art and highly desirable, provides 'street cred', which is the added value to the consumer.

levels of brands
The tangible product, the 'basic' brand, the 'augmented' brand and the 'potential' of the brand

There are, in fact, four **levels of brands**: the tangible product, the 'basic' brand, the 'augmented' brand and the 'potential' of the brand. Level 1, the tangible product, is the degree of quality, performance, features and actual attributes. Level 2, the 'basic' brand, is the identity, differentiation and positioning. Level 3, the 'augmented' brand, is the aggregated impact from including supplementary products and service support. Level 4, the 'potential' of the brand, is reached when customers will not willingly accept substitutes and are unhappy to switch to rival brands; psychological benefits and barriers in the minds of target customers are important determinants of brand potential.

There are three essential acid tests for determining whether a brand is successful. Although most companies consider only the overall profit contribution to the end-of-year financial annual report and accounts, when determining a brand's success they should ask the following three fundamental questions:

1 Has the brand captured the leading share in its market segment or distribution channel?

2 Does the brand command prices sufficiently high enough to produce a large profit margin?

3 Will the brand sustain its strong share of profits when rival and generic versions of the product enter the market?

Using these core criteria, many brands are relatively unsuccessful. For marketers, managing brands must include knowing when a brand is succeeding, when it is faltering but may be saved, and when a brand is a lost cause and should be deleted from the company's range of brands. Chapter 9 examines this difficult issue in more detail.

Corporate branding

corporate branding
The application of product branding at the corporate level, reflected visibly through the company name, logo and visual presentation and in the organization's underlying values

Corporate branding involves applying the principles of product branding at the corporate level. Corporate branding is reflected in visible manifestations such as the company name, logo and visual presentation, and also in the organization's underlying and guiding values. Thus Apple, McDonald's, Wal-Mart and Manchester United Football Club each has a corporate brand that is based around the organization itself. Sometimes the terms **corporate image** and **corporate identity** are also used in relation to corporate branding. The concepts of corporate identity and corporate branding overlap: both referring to what the company transmits about itself.[19] Corporate image reflects the perceptions that external audiences hold about the organization.[20]

corporate image
Reflects the perceptions that external audiences hold about an organization

Corporate branding plays a role in guiding all of a company's marketing activities. The corporate brand is transmitted through tangible and intangible features. The tangible dimensions include visual features of the corporate brand, such as corporate logo and symbols, typography, colour, buildings, staff uniforms, vehicles and stationery. For example, Unilever has recently overhauled its corporate identity to fit with the company's mission: 'creating a better future for every day'. The corporate brand is reflected in a new logo and images showing the everyday contributions its products make to people's lives. Less tangible features include how the corporate brand is portrayed through what people inside and outside the organization believe and say about it.

corporate identity
Overlapping with the corporate branding concept: branding at the corporate level

To be effective, the corporate brand should be embedded in all company actions. This means that all aspects of the company's communication, including internal communication with employees and external marketing activities ranging from the annual report through to its advertising and PR, must convey a consistent message about the corporate brand. Corporate branding is particularly important for services organizations, because customers look for help in understanding and visualizing the services product. A strong corporate brand can therefore help buyers to overcome the intangibility of some of these products. For example, first direct bank has worked hard to build a corporate image based on service quality and easy access, which reflects the company's reliability and flexible approach to meeting customer needs. This has helped to build a corporate image based around the notion of good service. The fact that this image is also reflected in research examining service in the financial services sector adds credibility to the bank's offering.

Packaging and labelling

Packaging and labelling are also part of the marketing process and are linked to brand identity. They impact upon the image of the product, its functionality and, ultimately, upon the customer's perception of satisfaction. At times, they create differentiation vis-à-vis rival products. For example, Coca-Cola introduced limited-edition packaging for its iconic glass bottle to appeal to upmarket consumers. Working with fashion designer Matthew Williamson, the designer bottle was available in three wrap-around prints, each taken from Williamson's summer clothing collection. The bottles were retailed only through selected style bars and restaurants.[21] Major rice companies Tilda and Uncle Ben's developed innovative packaging to allow two-minute steaming of pre-cooked micro-wavable rice, opening up a whole new category and creating significant growth of rice sales to convenience-oriented time-pressured consumers previously unlikely to cook rice at home.

packaging
The development of a product's container and label, complete with graphic design

Packaging involves the development of a container and label, complete with graphic design for a product. A package can be a vital part of a product, making it more versatile, safer or easier to use. Like a brand name, a package can influence customers' attitudes towards a product and thus affect their purchase decisions. For example, several producers of sauces, salad dressings and ketchups have packaged their products in squeezable containers to make use and storage more convenient. Package characteristics help shape buyers' impressions of a product at the time of purchase or during use. This section examines the main functions of packaging and considers several major packaging decisions. The role of the package in marketing strategy is also analyzed.

Packaging functions

Effective packaging means more than simply putting products into containers and covering them with wrappers. First of all, packaging materials serve the basic purpose of protecting the product and maintaining its functional form. Fluids such as milk, orange juice and hairspray need packages that preserve and protect them; the packaging should prevent damage that could affect the product's usefulness and increase costs. Since product tampering has become a problem for marketers of many types of goods, several packaging techniques have been developed to counter this danger. Some packages are also designed to foil shoplifters.

Another function of packaging is to offer convenience for consumers. For example, small, sealed packages – individual sized boxes or plastic bags that contain liquids and do not require refrigeration – appeal strongly to children and young adults with active lifestyles. Putting McVitie's Jaffa Cakes into lunch box-sized plastic tubs greatly boosted sales of this well-known brand by adding a level of functionality and convenience for packed lunches and school snacks. The size or shape of a package may relate to the product's storage, convenience of use or replacement rate. Small, single-serving tins of fruit, such as Del Monte's Fruitini, may prevent waste and make storage easier. Low, regular-shaped packets may be easier to stack and use cupboard space more efficiently. A third function of packaging is to promote a product by communicating its features, uses, benefits and image. At times, a reusable package is developed to make a product more desirable. For example, some ice-cream containers can be used again as food storage containers.

Major packaging considerations

Packaging must support a product's brand image and positioning, helping develop differentiation vis-à-vis rival products. When developing packages, marketers must take many factors into account. Some of these factors relate to consumers' needs; others relate to the requirements of resellers. Retailers, wholesalers and distributors will be required to handle and stock the products, and in many instances to display and deliver them. Packaging solutions must reflect the needs of these channel members in addition to the requirements of end-user customers. Obviously, one major consideration is cost. Although a variety of packaging materials, processes and designs are available, some are rather expensive. In recent years buyers have shown a willingness to pay more for improved packaging, but there are limits. Marketers should try to determine, through research, just how much customers are willing to pay for packages.

Developing tamper-resistant packaging is very important. Although no package is totally tamper-proof, marketers can develop packages that are difficult to tamper with and that also make any tampering evident to resellers and consumers. Because new, safer packaging technologies are being explored, marketers should be aware of changes in packaging technology and legislation, and be prepared to make modifications that will ensure consumer safety. One packaging innovation includes an inner pouch that displays the word 'open' when air has entered the pouch after opening. Marketers now also have an obligation to inform consumers of the possibilities and risks of product tampering by educating them to recognize possible tampering and by placing warnings on packaging.[22] For example, the tops of many sauce and condiment bottles now have plastic seals around them, so that consumers can be confident they have not been opened. Baby food manufacturers, such as Cow & Gate and Heinz, have taken this protection method one step further by using special metal jar tops with pop-up discs showing when a jar has been opened. This move followed cases of tampering in which foreign bodies were introduced into baby foods. Now the special tops expressly warn consumers to watch out for tampering. Although effective tamper-resistant packaging may be expensive to develop, when balanced against the costs of lost sales, loss of consumer confidence and a company's reputation, and potentially expensive product liability lawsuits, the costs of ensuring consumer safety are minimal.[23]

Marketers should consider how much consistency is desirable in a company's package designs. The best policy may be not to attempt consistency, especially if a company's products are unrelated or aimed at vastly different target markets. To promote an overall company image, a company may decide that all packages are to be similar or include one major element of the design. This approach is called **family packaging**. Sometimes it is used only for lines of products, as with Campbell's soups, Weight Watchers foods and Planters nuts.

family packaging
An approach in which all of a company's packages are similar or include one major element of the design

A package's promotional role is an important consideration. Through verbal and non-verbal symbols, the package can inform potential buyers about the product's content, features, uses, advantages and hazards. A company can create desirable images and associations by its choice of colour, design, shape and texture. Many cosmetics manufacturers, for example, design their packages to create impressions of richness, luxury and exclusiveness. Many perfumes are in packs deliberately designed to suggest sensuality and sex appeal. A package performs a promotional function when it is designed to be safer or more convenient to use, if such characteristics help stimulate demand.

To develop a package that has a definite promotional value, a designer must consider size, shape, texture, colour and graphics.[24] Beyond the obvious limitation that the package must be large enough to hold the product, a package can be designed to appear taller or shorter. For instance, thin vertical lines make a package look taller; wide horizontal stripes make it look shorter. A marketer may want a package to appear taller because many people perceive something that is taller as being larger.

Colours on packages and in branding are often chosen to attract attention. People associate specific colours with certain feelings and experiences, as outlined below:

Blue is soothing, it is also associated with wealth, trust and security.
Grey is associated with strength, exclusivity and success.
Orange can stand for low cost.
Red has connotations of excitement, stimulation and danger.
Yellow is associated with cheerfulness and joy.
Purple is linked with dignity and stateliness.
Black is associated with being strong and masterful.[25]

For example, BMW always uses the blue and grey colour palettes in its advertising and brochures, while easyJet's planes famously are adorned in orange. Uncle Ben's rice is familiar in its orange packaging as it emphasizes convenience and value for money, while more up-market competitor Tilda – focusing on premium quality and superior taste – utilizes blue in its branding and smart new packaging.

When selecting packaging colours, marketers must decide whether a particular colour will evoke positive or negative feelings when it is linked to a specific product. Rarely, for example, do processors package meat or bread in green materials, because customers may associate green with mould. However, recent concern about the state of the environment has, in general, led to an increase in the use of green-coloured packaging and neutral shades/textures. Marketers must also decide whether a specific target market will respond favourably or unfavourably to a particular colour. Cosmetics for women are more likely to be sold in pastel-coloured packaging than are personal care products for men. Packages designed to appeal to children often use primary colours and bold designs.

Packaging must also meet the needs of resellers. Wholesalers and retailers consider whether a package facilitates transportation, storage and handling. Packages must allow these resellers to make maximum use of storage space, both in transit and in the shops. Products should be packed so that sales staff can transfer them to the shelves with ease. The shape and weight of packaging are also important. Resellers may refuse to carry certain products if their packages are cumbersome. Figure 14.5 shows how these factors have been taken into consideration in developing the product's packaging.

FIGURE 14.5
Manufacturers, particularly of children's toys, often use bright coloured packaging to attract youngsters to their products.

Source: © Niels Poulsen / Alamy

A final consideration is whether to develop packages that are environmentally responsible. A CNN report on the growing refuse disposal problem in the USA stated that nearly 50 per cent of all rubbish consists of discarded plastic packaging, such as polystyrene containers, plastic soft drink bottles, carrier bags and other packaging items. Plastic packaging material does not bio-degrade, and using paper requires the destruction of valuable forest lands. Consequently, a number of companies are recycling more materials and exploring packaging alternatives, helped by packaging experts such as Tetra Pak. Heinz, for example, is looking for alternatives to its plastic squeezable ketchup bottles.

Companies that decide to develop environmentally responsible packaging have not always received a positive response. For example, customers' responses to US burger chain Wendy's paper plates and coffee cups were mixed; some customers prefer the old non-biodegradable foam packaging. Other companies searching for alternatives to environmentally harmful packaging have experienced similar problems. Thus, marketers must carefully balance society's desires to preserve the environment against consumers' desires for convenience. Green concerns are forcing changes to packaging.

Packaging development

packaging development
A mix of aesthetic considerations and structural necessities to guarantee the functionality of the design

Packaging development requires a mix of aesthetic considerations and structural necessities to guarantee the functionality of the design. There are cartons, bottles, tubes, cans, tubs and jars, multipacks, clamshells and blister packs, CD boxes, gift packs, plus many innovative formats for storing, displaying and dispensing products in a manner that is ahead of the competition. Material selection is an important stage in the design process, as are the specification and application of surface graphics and typography. Decisions must be made concerning information layout and the hierarchy of messages, front-of-pack versus back-of-pack detailing, choice of language and jargon, the photography and images to be selected, illustrations and use of colour, deployment of symbols and icons, final finishes and effects. There are often practical requirements to consider, such as weights, measures, ingredients, nutritional information and barcoding to display. Legal requirements for health and safety have forced changes to packaging, while legal requirements relating to the labelling of ingredients, sourcing and health-related issues have forced producers to include more information on-pack.

Packaging and marketing strategy

Packaging can be a major component of a marketing strategy. A new cap or closure, a better box or wrapping, or a more convenient container may give a product a competitive edge. The right type of package for a new product can help it gain market recognition very quickly. In the case of existing brands, marketers should periodically re-evaluate packages. Particularly in the case of consumer convenience products, marketers should view packaging as a major strategic tool. Tilda re-launched its *Rizazz* microwavable rice pouches as *Tilda Steamed Basmati* rice in smarter, more up-market packaging with improved graphics so as to adequately reflect the superiority of the recipes and ingredients, with significant success in terms of appealing to its target market consumers. This section examines ways in which packaging can be used strategically.

Altering the package At times, a marketer changes a package because the existing design is no longer in style, especially when compared with competitive products. Smith & Nephew redesigned its Simple range of toiletries to show that the products have evolved with the times. A package may also be redesigned because new product features need to be highlighted on the package, or because new packaging materials have become available. A company may decide to change a product's packaging to make the product more convenient or safer to use, or to reposition the product. A major redesign of a simple package costs about £25 000, and the redesign of a line of products may cost up to £300 000. Choosing the right packaging material is an important consideration when redesigning. Different materials vary in popularity at different times. For example, glass is becoming more popular as views on the environment and the need for recyclability come to the fore.

secondary use package
A package that can be reused for purposes other than its initial use

Secondary use packaging A **secondary use package** is one that can be reused for purposes other than its initial one. For example, a margarine container can be reused to store left-overs, a jam jar can be used as a drinking glass and shortbread tins can be reused for storing cakes and biscuits. Secondary use packages can be viewed by customers as adding value to products. If customers value this type of packaging, then its use should stimulate unit sales.

category-consistent packaging
The packaging of a product according to the packaging practices associated with a particular product category

Category-consistent packaging Category-consistent packaging means that the product is packaged in line with the packaging practices associated with a particular product category. Some product categories – for example, mayonnaise, mustard, ketchup and jam – have traditional package shapes. Other product categories are characterized by recognizable colour combinations – red and white for soup; red and yellow for tea; red, white and blue for Ritz-type crackers. When a company introduces a brand in one of these product categories, marketers will often use traditional package shapes and colour combinations to ensure that customers will recognize the new product as being in that specific product category. Few pizza brands are not packaged in square flat boxes coloured red, yellow and black!

Innovative packaging Sometimes, a marketer will employ a unique cap, design, applicator or other feature to make the product competitively distinctive, as illustrated in Figure 14.6. Such packaging can be effective when the innovation makes the product safer or easier to use, or when the unique package provides better protection for the product. In some instances, marketers use innovative or unique packages that are inconsistent with traditional packaging practices, to make the brand stand out relative to its competitors. Procter & Gamble, for example, uses an innovative, crush-proof cylinder to package its Pringles potato crisps. Innovative packaging generally requires considerable resources, not only for the package design itself but also to make customers aware of the unique package and its benefit. Sometimes, innovative packaging can change the way in which consumers use a product. The introduction of cardboard-boxed, single serving soft drinks made it easier for consumers to have a drink while travelling by car, train and plane. Even cyclists can drink with ease while on the move.

multiple packaging
Packaging that includes more than one unit of a product, such as twin packs, tri-packs and six-packs

Multiple packaging Rather than packaging a single unit of a product, marketers sometimes use twin packs, tri-packs, six-packs or other forms of **multiple packaging**. For certain types of product, multiple packaging is used to increase demand because it increases the amount of the product available at the point of consumption – in consumers' houses, for example. However, multiple packaging does not work for all types of product. Consumers would not use additional table salt simply because an extra box was in the cupboard. Multiple packaging can make products easier to handle and store, as in the case of six-packs for soft drinks; it can also facilitate special price offers, such as two-for-one sales. In addition, multiple packaging may increase consumer acceptance of the product by encouraging the buyer to try the product several times.

FIGURE 14.6
Leading packaging supplier Tetra Pak promotes the functionality and applicability of its cartons

Source: Image courtesy of Tetra Pak (UK) Ltd

Handling improved packaging Packaging of a product may be changed to make it easier to handle in the distribution channel – for example, changing the outer carton, special bundling, shrink wrapping or palletizing. In some cases the shape of the package may need to be changed. For example, an ice cream producer may switch from a cylindrical package to a rectangular one to facilitate handling. In addition, at the retail level, the ice cream producer may be able to get more shelf facings with a rectangular package as opposed to a round one. Outer containers for products are sometimes changed so that they will proceed more easily through automated warehousing systems.

As package designs improve, it becomes harder for any one product to dominate because of packaging. However, marketers still attempt to gain a competitive edge through packaging. Skilled artists and package designers who have experience in marketing research, test out packaging to see what sells well, not just what is aesthetically appealing. Since the typical large store stocks 15 000 items or more, products that stand out are more likely to be bought.

Criticisms of packaging

The last few decades have seen a number of improvements in packaging. However, some packaging problems still need to be resolved. Some packages simply do not work well. The packaging for flour and sugar is, at best, often not much better than poor. Both grocers and consumers are very much aware that these packages leak and are easily torn. Can anyone open and close a bag of flour without spilling at least a little bit? Certain packages, such as biscuit tins, milk cartons with fold-out spouts and potato crisp bags, are frequently difficult to open. The traditional shapes of packages for products such as ketchup and salad dressing make the products inconvenient to use. Have you ever questioned, when slapping a ketchup bottle, why the producer did not put the ketchup in a mayonnaise jar?

Certain types of packaging are being questioned with regard to their recyclability and biodegradability. For example, throw-away bottles take considerably more resources to produce than do reusable glass bottles. Social concerns and regulatory pressures are bringing green issues to the fore, with significant implications for marketers and packaging designers.

Although many steps have been taken to make packaging safer, critics still focus on health and safety issues. Containers with sharp edges and easily broken glass bottles are sometimes viewed as a threat to safety. Certain types of plastic packaging and aerosol containers represent possible health hazards.

At times, packaging is viewed as being deceptive. Package shape, graphic design and certain colours may be used to make a product appear larger than it actually is. The inconsistent use of certain size designations – such as 'giant', 'economy', 'family', 'king' and 'super' – can certainly lead to customer confusion. Although customers have traditionally liked attractive, effective, convenient packaging, the cost of such packaging is high. For some products, such as cosmetics, the cost of the package is higher than the cost of the product itself.

Labelling

labelling
Packaging information that can be used for a variety of promotional, informational and legal purposes

Labelling is very closely related to packaging and can be used for a variety of promotional, informational and legal purposes. The label can be used to facilitate the identification of a product by presenting the brand and a unique graphic design. For example, Heinz's ketchup is easy to identify on a supermarket shelf because the brand name is easy to read and is coupled with a distinctive, crown-like graphic design. Labels have a descriptive function. For certain types of product, the label indicates the grade of the product, especially for tinned fruit. Labels can describe the source of the product, its contents and major features, how to use the product, how to care for the product, nutritional information, type and style of the product and size and number of servings. The label can play a promotional function through the use of graphics that attract attention. The food and drug administrations and consumer protection agencies in different countries have varying requirements concerning warnings, instructions, certifications and manufacturers' identifications. Increasingly, however, the EU is demanding similar standards in all member countries. Despite the fact that consumers have responded favourably to the inclusion of this type of information on labels, evidence as to whether they actually use it has been mixed. Several studies indicate that consumers do not use nutritional information, whereas other studies indicate that the information is considered useful. Labels can also promote a manufacturer's other products or encourage proper use of products, resulting in greater customer satisfaction with them.

universal product code (UPC) or barcode
A series of thick and thin lines that identifies the product, and provides inventory and pricing information readable by an electronic scanner

The label for many products includes a **universal product code (UPC) or barcode** – a series of thick and thin lines that identifies the product, and provides inventory and pricing information that can be read by an electronic scanner. The UPC is read electronically at the retail checkout counter. This information is used by retailers and producers for price and inventory control purposes.

Colour and eye-catching graphics on labels overcome the jumble of words – known to designers as 'mouse print' – that have been added to satisfy government regulations. Because so many similar products are available, an attention-getting device or 'silent salesperson' is needed to attract interest. As one of the most visible parts of a product, the label is an important element in a marketing mix.

Labelling is an integral part of packaging that can be used effectively to convey product information and benefits to customers, and to promote a brand's positioning image. There are increasing legal considerations that marketers must address, such as EU regulations in terms of food sourcing, ingredient content, nutritional information, weights and measures, as well as cooking or application instructions. Ethical marketing requires that consumers are not misled or 'over-sold' owing to the information provided on labels. In 2004, Coca-Cola had to withdraw its 'pure still water' Dasani after a batch was contaminated with an excess of the cancer-causing mineral, bromate. Just before Dasani's withdrawal from the market, the Food Standards Agency in the UK had been examining the manufacturer's claim that the product – heavily filtered tap water – was 'pure'. Partly in response, the members of the Natural Mineral Water Association, including Danone Waters, Nestlé Waters, Spadel and Highland Spring, launched an over-arching symbol to appear on the packaging of their respective brands, indicating their products as pure, natural mineral water: 'Natural Mineral Water Certified'. This 'purity' symbol is intended to signify which brands are unadulterated pure mineral water, in a highly competitive and fast-evolving market, with a plethora of flavoured and modified waters now widely available.[26] Concerns about obesity and diabetes are forcing manufacturers of foods to include nutritional and healthy-eating information on their packaging. This provides a window of opportunity for healthier brands to compete with many leading brands whose domination was once viewed as impregnable. *Innocent* smoothies have stolen market share from the colas in most supermarkets, and Innocent's humorous packaging stresses its wholesome and healthy qualities.

Summary

A *brand* is a name, term, design, symbol or any other feature that identifies one seller's good or service as distinct from those of other sellers. A *brand name* is that part of a brand that can be spoken, including letters, words and numbers; the element that cannot be spoken – often a symbol or design – is called a *brand mark*. A *trademark* is a legal designation indicating that the owner has exclusive use of a brand or part of a brand, and that others are prohibited by law from using it. A *trade name* is the legal name of an organization.

Branding helps buyers identify and evaluate products, helps sellers facilitate repeat purchasing and product introduction and fosters *brand loyalty* – a customer's strongly motivated and long-standing decision to purchase a particular product or service.

A recent build on brand loyalty has been marketers' use of online brand communities and blog communities. In a *brand community* a group of consumers and observers who admire a brand are encouraged to share their positive feelings, often online through social media. *Blog communities* permit one-to-one tailored communication with and between members of the digital brand community. Such developments permit *dynamic branding*, with very rapid communication and sharing of brand information. In order to nurture loyalty, brands are turning to *brand advocacy* and investing in creating brand advocates, who will share their positive feelings and experiences of a brand in return for insider knowledge and access to bespoke events.

The three degrees of brand loyalty are recognition, preference and insistence. *Brand recognition* exists when a customer is aware that a brand exists and views it as an alternative to purchase if the preferred brand is unavailable. *Brand preference* is the degree of brand loyalty in which a customer prefers one brand over competing brands and will purchase it if it is available. *Brand insistence* is the degree of brand loyalty in which a customer will accept no substitute. *Brand equity* is the marketing and financial value associated with a brand's strength in a market. It represents the value of a brand to an organization. The four major elements underlying brand equity are brand name awareness, brand loyalty, perceived brand quality and brand associations.

Branding experts believe that well-managed, strong and desirable brands should identify a set of specific tangible benefits to attach to the brand, known as *brand attributes*, a set of reassuring and more emotive *brand values* which help develop a unified sense of purpose among staff as well as support differentiation with external audiences, plus a set of appealing and desirable *brand personality* traits. Implicit in this view is the importance of effectively creating a well-differentiated and memorable image for the brand that is carefully controlled.

A *manufacturer brand*, initiated by the producer, makes it possible to associate the company more easily with its products at the point of purchase. An *own label brand* is initiated and owned by a reseller, such as a retailer. A *generic brand* indicates only the product category and does not include the company name or other identifying terms. Manufacturers combat the growing competition from own label brands by developing multiple brands.

When selecting a brand name, a marketer should choose one that is easy to say, spell and recall, and that alludes to the product's uses, benefits or special characteristics. Brand names are created inside an organization by individuals, committees or branding departments, or by outside consultants. Brand names can be devised from words, initials, numbers, nonsense words or a combination of these. Services as well as products are branded, often with the company name and an accompanying symbol that makes the brand distinctive or conveys a desired image.

Producers protect ownership of their brands through patent and trademark offices. Marketers at a company must make certain that their selected brand name does not infringe on an already-registered brand by confusing or deceiving consumers about the source of the product. In many countries, brand registration is on a first-come, first-served basis, making protection more difficult. Brand counterfeiting, increasingly common, has potential for undermining consumer confidence in, and loyalty to, a brand.

Companies brand their products in several ways. *Individual branding* designates a unique name for each of a company's products; *overall family branding* identifies all of a company's products with the same name; *line family branding* assigns all products within a single line the same name; and *brand extension branding* applies an existing name to a new or improved product. Trademark licensing enables producers to earn extra revenue, receive low cost or free publicity, and protect their trademarks. Through a licensing agreement, and for a licensing fee, a company may permit approved manufacturers to use its trademark on other products.

Successful brands tend to prioritize quality, offer superior service, get to market or the targeted segment first, be clearly differentiated from rival brands, have a unique positioning concept supported by a strong communications programme and be consistent over time. *Brand strength* is a function of the product's attributes and functionality, its differentiation, plus any demonstrable added value to the purchaser or user. Strong brands usually create product differentiation, help establish a competitive edge, encourage product awareness and demand a significant amount of management and control. Four *levels of brands* need to be addressed: the tangible product, the 'basic' brand, the 'augmented' brand and the 'potential' of the brand. To be successful, a brand should capture the leading share in its market segment or distribution channel, command prices sufficiently high to offer high profit margins and be likely to maintain its profit position after more brands and generic versions enter the market. Many companies should be more effective in managing their brands, many of which do not live up to these success criteria.

Corporate branding involves applying the principles of product branding at the corporate level. Corporate branding is reflected in visible manifestations such as the company name, logo and visual presentation and also in the organization's underlying and guiding values. Sometimes the terms *corporate image* and *corporate identity* are also used in relation to corporate branding. Corporate branding plays a role in guiding all of a company's marketing activities. Corporate branding is transmitted through tangible and intangible features and, to be effective, should be embedded in all company actions.

Packaging involves the development of a container and label, complete with graphic design for a product. Effective packaging offers protection, economy, safety and convenience. It can influence the customer's purchase decision by promoting a product's features, uses, benefits and image. When developing a package, marketers must consider costs relative to how much the target market is willing to pay. Other considerations include how to make the package tamper-resistant; whether to use *family packaging, secondary use packaging, category-consistent packaging* or *multiple packaging*; how to design the package as an effective promotional tool; how best to accommodate resellers; and whether to develop environmentally responsible packaging.

Packaging development involves aesthetic and structural choices. Other considerations include: material selection, surface graphics, typography, information layout and hierarchies, front-of-pack versus back-of-pack detailing, language and jargon, photography and illustrations, use of colour, symbols and icons, final finishes and effects, labelling practicalities and barcoding/tracking. There are numerous primary packaging options: cartons, bottles, tubes, cans, tubs and jars, multipacks, clamshells, blister packs, CD boxes, gift packs and a host of innovative solutions for storing, displaying and dispensing products.

Packaging can be a major component of a marketing strategy. Companies choose particular colours, designs, shapes and textures to create desirable images and associations. Producers alter packages to convey new features or to make them safer or more convenient. If a package has a secondary use, the product's value to the consumer may be increased. Category-consistent packaging makes products more easily recognized by consumers, and innovative packaging enhances a product's distinctiveness. Consumers may criticize packaging that doesn't work well, is not biodegradable or recyclable, poses health or safety problems or is deceptive in some way.

Labelling is an important aspect of packaging that can be used for promotional, informational and legal purposes. Because labels are attention-getting devices, they are significant features in the marketing mix. Various regulatory agencies can require that products be labelled or marked with warnings, instructions, certifications, nutritional information and the manufacturer's identification. Increasingly, most products – even cars – have a *universal product code (UPC) or barcode*. There are ethical considerations for marketers as customers should not be misled or mis-sold owing to the information conveyed on a product's packaging.

Key links

- This chapter, about effective branding, should be read in conjunction with the section of Chapter 6 that addresses the linked concept of brand positioning.
- The branding strategy must reflect the characteristics of the product, too, as explored in Chapter 6.
- Many companies operate a portfolio of brands and often must select some for priority investment and marketing spend, as described in Chapter 9.

Important terms

Brand
Brand name
Brand mark
Trademark
Trade name
Brand loyalty
Brand community
Blog communities
Dynamic branding
Brand advocacy
Brand recognition
Brand preference
Brand insistence
Brand equity
Brand attributes
Brand values
Brand personality
Manufacturer brands
Own-label brands
Generic brand
Individual branding
Overall family branding
Line family branding
Brand extension branding
Successful brands
Brand strength
Levels of brands
Corporate branding
Corporate image
Corporate identity
Packaging
Family packaging
Packaging development

Secondary use packaging
Category-consistent packaging
Multiple packaging
Labelling
Universal product code (UPC) or barcode

Discussion and review questions

1　What is the difference between a brand and a brand name? Compare and contrast the terms brand mark and trademark.

2　How does branding benefit customers and organizations?

3　What are the advantages associated with brand loyalty?

4　In what ways have social media and the Web enabled brands to create communities of supporters?

5　Why are companies seeking to identify or create brand advocates amongst their customers?

6　What are the distinguishing characteristics of own label brands?

7　Given the competition between own label brands and manufacturer brands, should manufacturers be concerned about the popularity of own label brands? How should manufacturers fight back in the brand battle?

8　Identify and explain the major considerations consumers take into account when selecting a brand.

9　The brand name Xerox is sometimes used generically to refer to photocopying machines. How can Xerox Corporation protect this brand name?

10　Identify and explain the four major branding policies and give examples of each. Can a company use more than one policy at a time? Explain your answer.

11　What are the major advantages and disadvantages of licensing?

12　Why is there more to a brand than its name? Explain your response.

13　What are the most commonly found foundations for successful brands? Illustrate your response with brand examples.

14　What constitutes brand strength?

15　What are the differences between brand attributes, brand values and brand personality?

16　What is brand equity and why is this notion increasingly important?

17　What are the three core criteria for assessing the success of a brand?

18　Describe the functions that a package can perform. Which function is most important? Why?

19 When developing a package, what are the major issues that a marketer should consider?

20 In what ways can packaging be used as a strategic tool?

21 What are the major criticisms of packaging?

22 What are the major functions of labelling?

Recommended readings

Aaker, D.A., *Building Strong Brands* (Pocket Books, 2010).

Aaker, D.A. and Joachimsthaler, E., *Brand Leadership* (Pocket Books, 2009).

Ambrose, G. and Harris, P., *Packaging The Brand: The Relationship Between Packaging Design and Brand Identity* (AVA Publishing, 2011).

Calver, G., *What is Packaging Design?* (RotoVision SA, 2004).

Davis, M., *Fundamentals of Branding* (AVA Publishing, 2009).

De Chernatony, L., McDonald, M. and Wallace, E., *Creating Powerful Brands* (Butterworth-Heinemann, 2010).

Doyle, P., *Marketing Management and Strategy* (FT/Prentice-Hall, 2002).

Kapferer, J.-N., *The New Strategic Brand Management: Creating and Sustaining Brand Equity Long Term (New Strategic Brand Management: Creating & Sustaining Brand Equity)* (Kogan Page, 2008).

Keller, K.L., *Strategic Brand Management* (FT/Prentice-Hall, 2008).

Kirkpatrick, J., *New Packaging Design* (Laurence King, 2009).

Ries, A. and Ries, L., *The 22 Immutable Laws of Branding: How to Build any Product or Line into a World Class Brand* (Profile Books, 2002).

Internet exercise

Packaging has to reflect manufacturers' requirements and also evolving consumer issues. Log on to: www.tetrapak.com. Consider the information on this leading packaging company's website, notably the information offered about the company, its ethos, core values, vision and mission, innovation and new product development.

1 To what extent and in what ways is Tetra Pak addressing changing and evolving manufacturer and consumer issues?

2 What innovative packaging solutions is Tetra Pak currently developing?

Applied mini-case

In the 1980s, one of Europe's retailing success stories was the creation by George Davies of fashion chain Next. Leading out-of-town grocery retailer ASDA persuaded Davies to leave Next and to rekindle the fortunes of its clothing range. The result was the *George* range of men's, women's and children's clothing, positioned as a low price, high style fashion brand. 'Styles straight off the catwalk' at affordable prices, targeted at ASDA's value-conscious shoppers, proved incredibly successful. In the highly competitive clothing market, in 2004, the George range in ASDA grocery superstores overtook Debenhams to become the UK's third biggest retailer of clothing. A few years ago, George Davies moved on and, to the surprise of many onlookers, was approached by erstwhile arch-rival Marks & Spencer to help improve the former market leader's fortunes. The result for Marks & Spencer was the highly successful range of stylish fashion, branded *Per Una*.

Both ASDA with *George*, and Marks & Spencer with *Per Una* decided to utilize freshly created brands for their new clothing ranges. In the case of Marks & Spencer, this was even more remarkable, as previously all of its merchandise retailed under the *St Michael* retailer's own label brand, familiar to generations of shoppers. It is believed that without brand identities so deliberately far removed from the host retailers' own brands, neither *George* nor *Per Una* would have been so successful. Both brands have themselves enabled their owners to extend their operations: *George* is available by catalogue and online, and both *George* and *Per Una* have now been given fashion-only high-street branches.

Sources: George/ASDA, 2004; Marks & Spencer stores, 2003/2004; Rachel Barnes, 'ASDA to highlight style in George repositioning', *Marketing*, 25 March 2004, p. 4: **www.marksandspencer.com/peruna**, June, 2011; direct.asda.com/george, May, 2011.

Question

Why did ASDA and Marks & Spencer both opt to launch clothing ranges with new brand identities that were different to the host retailers' brands?

Case study

Online traditionally focused on direct response forms of marcomms activity rather than brand building and 'slow-burn' programmes. However, the use of online media to support branding has grown significantly, now accounting for 15 per cent of online marketing spend, up from only 5 per cent in 2009. The maturity of broadband access readily available for most consumers and the rise of social media activity have provided the impetus for this growth. According to Jude Brooks, Coca-Cola's digital activation manager, the exponential growth of online video has created an appetite amongst marketers for creating brand building video content for a wider audience online.

The view is that the online medium has transitioned from being predominately a source of information to an entertainment channel, presenting marketers with an opportunity to attach their brand messages to viewers' online content. It has been a long-held desire by many marketers to make markets a series of conversations, in which their brands are positively endorsed, but the digital arena and social networking phenomenon have established this as today's reality. This of course poses challenges.

As Accenture's Sarah Bentley explains, many marketers fear digital because of the growth of consumer-to-consumer controlled content, which might not be positive about a brand manager's brand. Now there is the growth of consumers influencing what is said about a brand, in quickly shared digital communications. The recent invasions by protesters of Top Shop and Vodafone stores because of alleged tax minimization by these companies would have passed unnoticed by most consumers and indeed users of these brands. Thanks to Facebook, Flickr, YouTube and Twitter, large parts of the population were made aware of these sit-ins and store occupations, along with the brand-damaging reasons for such direct action by these tax activists.

Accenture's Bentley argues that consumers have always voiced opinions about brands and their experiences, but previously in tightly defined circles with little newsworthy material reaching the mainstream. Now it is relatively straightforward for these 'private' discussions to create a strong following and become news for many other consumers. The result is that marketers face a quandary: on the one hand they increasingly wish to include their brand and its messages in online and particularly social media for brand building and greater awareness, but on the other hand, they risk losing control over what is being said about their brand. The digital arena certainly poses threats as well as opportunities for brand building and brand reputation.

Sources: Sarah Bentley, Accenture; Jude Brooks, Coca-Cola; 'Brand-builders look to online space for growth', *Marketing Week*, November, 2010, pp. 42–43.

Questions for discussion

1 Why might marketers wish to use the digital environment for brand building?

2 Highlight how marketers are not in control of their own destiny online.

3 What are the threats and opportunities to a brand from the growth of social media networking?

PART FOUR
Managing Marketing

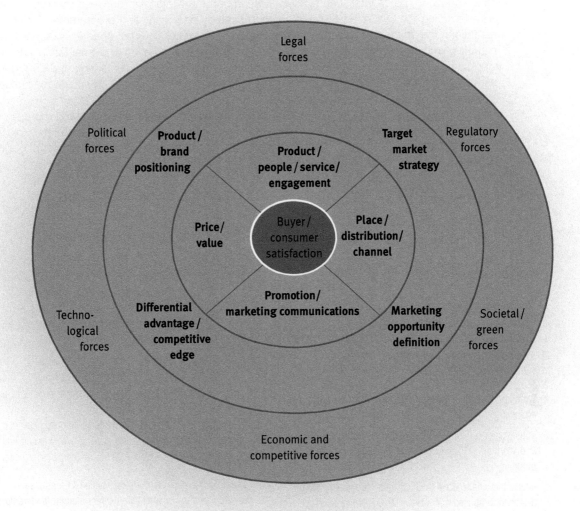

F igure 1.5, the generic tasks of marketing strategy, were identified as marketing opportunity analysis, target market strategy, marketing mix development and marketing management. Parts One to Three of *Marketing Essentials* examined the first three of these generic tasks. Chapter 2 discussed marketing strategy in detail, and target market selection was explored in Chapter 6. The focus of Part Four is on the core aspects of marketing management: implementation and control of marketing strategy and marketing activity, in particular the popular and important technique of marketing planning. Control of performance is very important. Monitoring performance and the effectiveness of marketing strategies and programmes and taking remedial action to rectify shortfalls, are essential activities for marketers and senior managers.

Part Four of *Marketing Essentials* explores the central issues of marketing management: marketing planning, implementing strategies, internal marketing relationships and measuring performance.

Chapter 15, 'Planning and Implementation', examines the marketing planning process and how organizations practise marketing planning. The chapter presents an overview of a 'typical' marketing plan. The chapter then highlights the important relationship between marketing analysis – including the SWOT analysis – marketing strategy and marketing programmes for implementation: the *marketing process* as described in Chapter 1. The chapter examines the marketing implementation process, various approaches to marketing implementation and the importance of internal marketing. The discussion next focuses on implementing and controlling marketing activities. The chapter closes with a look at popular methods and criteria for evaluating marketing strategies and performance.

By the conclusion of Part Four of *Marketing Essentials*, readers should understand more about the complexities of managing marketing strategies and marketing programmes, the role of marketing planning, evaluating marketing performance and ways of implementing marketing strategy.

Fujitsu

1. What excites me most about marketing?

Working in marketing means that you are in a privileged position, working across all parts of a business at all levels, for the good of the whole company. The excitement comes from many areas:

- Working/influencing (challenging) executives on strategic direction.
- Implementing change – identifying new strategies and working with the company to implement the thinking.
- Intellectual challenge – thinking through complex organizational problems and developing strategies to support these.
- Working with smart people – because while the work is important to the company, you get to work with the smartest people (internally and externally).
- Creativity – you are continually having to come up with new and innovative ways of doing things. Working in an innovative environment is fun and exciting.

2. What are the biggest challenges for marketing?

For the IT sector, it's how do we respond to/make money from cloud computing.

For marketing, it's (1) being able to demonstrate the value marketing delivers, and (2) exploiting/using social media to its full potential (to develop relationships).

3. What does marketing contribute?

Marketing is a process that everyone in the company is involved with (satisfying customer needs, at a profit). So everyone is in marketing!!

The marketing function must be configured to use appropriate skills and techniques to support this ambition and be able to demonstrate value. In a B2B environment this includes:

- Increasing the customers predisposition to purchase – brand awareness, relationship events, thought leadership.
- Lead generation – thought leadership, direct marketing, etc.
- Relationship creation – forums, social media, events.
- Evidence – case studies and references.
- Sales force training and development.
- Account development – account-based marketing.
- Market and customer insight.

IAN HUNTER
HEAD OF MARKETING
FUJITSU SERVICES

Reebok races into the urban market

Strategic case

Reebok's UK founder, Joseph Foster, produced some of the first ever running shoes with spikes, as athletes in the late 1890s wanted to run even faster. In 1924, J.W. Foster & Sons was making by hand the running shoes used in the 1924 Summer Games, as depicted in the hit film *Chariots of Fire*. In 1958, two of the founder's grandsons started a sister company called Reebok, named after a type of African gazelle. By 1979, three running shoe styles were introduced to the USA: at US $60 per pair, they were the most expensive on the market. In 1982, Reebok caught the market unawares with the launch of Freestyle, the first ever athletic shoe designed specifically for women. By the 1980s, Reebok was a publicly quoted company active in more than 170 countries. Continual product innovation and customer research gave the company leadership in most of its key target markets. But Nike emerged.

Step Reebok followed in 1989, a totally revolutionary workout programme that led to millions of users across the globe. By 1992 the company was broadening its ranges to include footwear and clothing products linked to many sports. These moves were supported with major sponsorship deals linked with leading sports stars, teams and sporting events. Venus Williams was one of the Reebok stars. In the summer of 2008, Reebok and driving ace Lewis Hamilton announced a multi-year partnership at a spectacular 3-D event in Amsterdam, home of Reebok's European Headquarters. At the event, Reebok unveiled 'The Athlete within the Driver', giving media a rare insight into Hamilton's demanding fitness regime. Hamilton revealed how Reebok's Smoothfit training footwear and apparel range helped him to train better than ever before.

Flying JUKARI

Recently, Reebok has again transformed the way in which people train, with the creation of the JUKARI Fit to Fly workout programmes, based on Cirque du Soleil's artistry and Reebok's knowledge of fitness, as always building on the company's philosophy that it should be fun to stay in shape and that sport and life are entwined for the good of the individual. The workouts have been created on a specially-designed piece of equipment called the FlySet. The result is a workout that gives the sensation of flying while strengthening and lengthening the body through cardio, strength, balance and core training.

Reebok has also made a pledge to tone the butts and legs of women around the world with its innovative EasyTone footwear. Featuring first-of-its-kind balance pod technology, the shoe generates incredible results thanks to proprietary technology invented by a former NASA engineer.

German Adidas-owned Reebok wants to give front-runner Nike a run for its money in the race for market share in athletic footwear, clothing and equipment. Reebok, now based in Massachusetts, USA, gained speed from the 1980s into the early 1990s by marketing special aerobics shoes for women, before Nike pulled ahead with new clothing and equipment endorsed by high-profile athletes such as Michael Jordan and Tiger Woods. Nike has remained the market leader, completely outdistancing all competitors to dominate the industry with a 35 per cent share of the market. In contrast, Reebok's market share is about half that of Nike's. Now Reebok is seeking to close the gap by changing its selection of target markets. In the process, Reebok is aiming to change consumers' perceptions of and attitudes towards its brand and its products, with the objective of boosting both sales and profits.

Breaking tradition with hip-hop

Traditionally, manufacturers of athletic shoes have captured market attention by signing successful or up-and-coming sports stars to promote their shoes. Reebok still likes to link its brand to popular sports and individual champions. The fierce rivalry with Nike continues on the playing field: Reebok has lucrative contracts to make branded hats for the US National Basketball Association (NBA) and to supply the US National Football League (NFL) with uniforms and equipment, while Nike has an exclusive contract to provide performance wear to all 30 Major League Baseball teams. Many other sports around the world are similarly supported by Reebok and Nike, including stadia, teams and individual players.

Looking beyond sports, Reebok's marketers investigated the urban market, where fashion, rather than performance, is the deciding factor in buying decisions. Urban teens tend to be extremely style-conscious, buying as many as ten pairs of athletic shoes a year so they can be seen in the very latest thing. In the States, many are also fans of hip-hop music and buy clothing designed by hip-hop celebrities such as Jay-Z, Sean 'P. Diddy' Combs and Russell Simmons. Reebok's marketing research confirmed this market's considerable buying power and the influence of hip-hop artists. To reach this market effectively, Reebok needed a new brand, new products and new promotional efforts: the

Reebok brand did not have a suitably desirable image with this youth market in any of the company's principle countries of operation. First, the company took the focus off its mainstream Reebok brand by creating Rbk as a new brand specifically for the urban market. Next, it partnered with hip-hop artists such as Jay-Z and 50 Cent to develop special footwear collections, backed by targeted promotional efforts emphasizing style with attitude.

New street credibility

Reebok found it was tapping into a significant marketing opportunity. Soon after it introduced its soft leather, flat-soled S. Carter shoes – after Jay-Z's original name, Shawn Carter – the line sold out. Demand for the US$100 shoes quickly peaked, leading to eager buyers bidding up to US$250 for one pair on the eBay auction website. Within eight months, the company had shipped 500 000 pairs to retailers around the USA and was preparing to launch a second S. Carter shoe.

On the back of this success, Reebok introduced G-Unit footwear, named after a hit song by rapper 50 Cent, who says that 'Reebok's Rbk Collection is the real thing when it comes to connecting with the street and hip-hop culture.' Hip-hop's Eve was also asked to design a shoe. 'She is one of the first artists in the campaign who has male and female appeal, urban and suburban', observed Reebok's director of global advertising; 'she is as much a fashion icon as a music icon'.

The company also found a way to bring sports and hip-hop together by launching the 13 Collection line of shoes by basketball star Allen Iverson. Iverson promoted the line by appearing in a series of fast-paced adverts filmed in rap video style. Although he was shown playing basketball for a second or two, the adverts focused more on his off-court style than his on-court technique.

Despite the added credibility that such celebrities bring to the Rbk brand, the strategy entails some risks. Fads in street fashion and music can come and go at a dizzying pace, which means a shoe that is 'red hot' on one day may be 'ice cold' the next. Reebok could also suffer from negative repercussions if one of its celebrities runs into trouble. Still, the company's chief marketing executive is committed to the strategy. 'With athletes, they wear the shoes for the length of a basketball season,' he comments. 'With hip-hop, the publicity is intense but short, just like movies.' The advantage, in his view, is that, 'you'll know very quickly whether you hit or miss'.

Targeting urban markets in China

In pursuit of growth, Reebok is also targeting promising global markets, with China high on its list of priorities. Interest in sports is skyrocketing in China, thanks in part to Chinese basketball star Yao Ming's move to the NBA. According to the company's research, 93 per cent of Chinese males aged 13–25, a prime market for athletic shoes, watch NBA broadcasts on a regular basis. Reebok's Asia Pacific general manager cites one projection showing 50 per cent annual growth in footwear sales, stating that, 'it's hard to say what the [actual sales] numbers are going to be, but they are going to be huge'. China's successes at the 2004 Olympics in Athens merely fuelled market growth, which simply exploded when China then staged the 2008 Games.

To make the most of this opportunity, Reebok set up 'Yao's House' basketball courts around central Shanghai. Each features the Reebok trademark and a giant *Sports Illustrated* cover showing the basketball star. By giving teens and young adults a place to hone their slam-dunks, Reebok hopes to shape their attitudes towards its products. 'The trends [in China] are made in the urban areas and on street basketball courts, just like in the United States', says one Reebok executive. Reebok is not the only athletic shoe manufacturer entering this market. Nike sponsors a basketball court in Beijing, New Balance is building awareness of its shoes, and Pony is selling sneakers in Beijing, Shanghai and Guandong.

Reebok's 'vector'

Nike has one of the most recognized trademarks in the world and now Reebok has its Vector, a streamlined trademark designed to communicate the brand's attributes in a fast and fun way. The idea is to make the Vector synonymous with Reebok, just as the Swoosh is synonymous with Nike. 'Our research suggests that consumers react better to logos than words, and it's a very effective marketing tool', stresses Reebok's head of marketing.

In addition, the company is giving its brand a touch of glamour with 'showcase stores' in major cities. In New York City, for example, Reebok opened a new men's store right next to its women's store. Both feature footwear, clothing and accessories, and both share the building with the Reebok Sport Club/NY. The displays are as stylish as the products, showing a mix of cashmere sweaters, jackets, wrist-watches and sunglasses along with shoes. 'We want people to say, "I didn't know Reebok made that"', noted Reebok's director of retailing.

Questions for discussion

1 In what ways will marketing planning assist an organization such as Reebok?

2 How best should Reebok assess its performance and execution of its marketing strategies and programmes?

3 In such a diverse business operating across so many markets, what problems of control will Reebok face?

Source: **http://corporate.reebok.com/en/reebok_ history/default.asp**. July 2011.

CHAPTER 15

Planning and Implementation

Planning identifies opportunities and creates engagement programmes, but also aligns the organization to these priorities and establishes control

Objectives

To understand the marketing planning process

To gain an overview of the marketing plan

To examine the relationship between marketing analysis, marketing strategy and marketing programmes in marketing planning

To examine the role of the SWOT analysis in marketing planning

To examine the marketing implementation process

To learn about the impediments to marketing implementation success

To appreciate the role of internal marketing

To understand how to assess the effectiveness of marketing activities and measure performance

INTRODUCTION

Manipulation of the marketing mix to match target market needs and expectations constitutes a daily activity for most marketing personnel. However, as explained in the first two chapters of *Marketing Essentials*, fundamental strategic decisions need to be made *before* the marketing mix(es) are formulated and marketing programmes are executed. To expedite this process and link the strategic decision-making to the development of actionable marketing programmes, many organizations – small and large – turn to marketing planning. This chapter examines the nature of marketing planning.

Marketing planning is a systematic process involving the assessment of marketing opportunities and resources, the determination of marketing objectives, and the development of a plan for implementation and control. Marketing planning is widely deployed by organizations, helping direct and control the activities of marketers.

The chapter's focus switches to issues surrounding the effective execution of marketing plans and programmes, highlighting the most common problems and suggesting approaches for managing implementation. The need to assess the performance of marketing activities is part of the this execution process.

Planning for growth

When US defence, space and electronics giant, Lockheed Martin, embarked on a new round of marketing planning in its European operations, the company wanted to re-think its priority activities and opportunities, re-aligning its operations accordingly. The MD recognized that this would prove a demanding task, diverting many executives from their daily business and requiring careful management. A central team was created to explore emerging commercial opportunities, diversification possibilities, mergers and acquisitions. Separately, the core planning process focused on each business unit, with their leadership teams instructed to produce updated plans and budgets for their markets and product groups.

An external advisor was appointed to help structure this process and guide the various directors involved with undertaking the planning process. The central business development function was strengthened, recruiting more analysts and networking with those knowledgeable of the company's markets. The two senior business development executives were given the remit of controlling and mentoring the whole process.

The planning process was broken into distinctive phases. For each, guidance was provided to those inputting and templates for capturing their outputs were created. These reflected accepted best practice and the tools explained in *Marketing Essentials*. They were constructed so as to steer the subsequent phase of the planning process. In this way, phase I's market analyses and opportunity assessment – which involved financial performance, marketing environment, trend, customer, competitor and capability analyses – informed the company's strategic decisions in phase II. Here, trade-offs were made between existing activities and freshly identified opportunities to pursue, identifying the most attractive realistically attainable set of pursuits and target markets. Phase III explored the required positioning in order to attract the selected customers and how best to establish competitive advantages. Having made certain that the company had compelling propositions to take to growing and highly attractive markets, the next phase considered how best to engage with intended customers and the creation of appropriate sales and marketing programmes. Finally, phase V provided budgetary and operational frameworks to faciliate roll-out of the plan.

The process required four months of intensive activity. While a few managers were dedicated to this task, most executives were juggling inputting to the planning process alongside their existing daily activities and line management responsibilities. The result was a well-considered strategy with a fully specified marketing plan to guide execution of the strategy. Those involved in the process bought-in to the outputs and soon other colleagues shared in the intended direction and detailed implementation programmes. Commercially, significant growth resulted from the re-alignment of resources and re-thought target market priorities. Marketing planning of this sort is essential to provide topical direction informed by market circumstances and developments.

Source: iStock, 06-22-09 © Dmitry Demidovich

This chapter begins with a discussion of the marketing planning process and an overview of the marketing plan. The chapter then discusses the relationship between marketing analysis – including the popular SWOT analysis – marketing strategy and marketing programmes for implementation. The chapter proceeds to examine the management of implementation of marketing strategies, plans and programmes, before concluding with a discussion of the major methods for assessing performance or effectiveness in marketing management.

Marketing planning

marketing planning
A systematic process of assessing marketing opportunities and resources, determining marketing objectives and developing a thorough plan for implementation and control

Marketing planning is a systematic process that involves assessing marketing opportunities and resources, determining marketing objectives and developing a thorough plan for implementation and control. Research shows that good-quality marketing planning can lead to a positive impact on business performance.[1] A core output of marketing planning is the **marketing plan**, a document or blueprint that details requirements for a company's marketing activity. The marketing planning process involves analyzing the marketplace, modifying or updating the recommended marketing strategy accordingly and developing detailed marketing programmes designed to implement the specified marketing strategy.[2]

marketing plan
A document or blueprint detailing requirements for a company's marketing activity

Figure 15.1 illustrates the **marketing planning cycle**. Note that marketing planning is a cyclical process. As the dotted feedback lines in the figure indicate, planning is not one way. Feedback is used to coordinate and synchronize all the stages of the planning cycle, to update market insights, re-think target market strategy and opportunity selection and to re-orientate marketing programmes. Markets are dynamic and endure promiscuous buyers, pesky competitors and poor operation of marketing programmes, so inevitably marketing plans must be modified and re-engineered during their life. Most businesses produce marketing plans annually, typically with a three-year perspective. The immediate 12 months' marketing activity is presented in detail, with overviews provided for years two and three in the three years featured. Once up and running, this process involves revising the previous year's plan by updating the essential marketing analyses, revising the recommended strategy accordingly, before determining detailed marketing mix action plans. Once an organization has gone through the demanding, intensive and resource-hungry process of developing a marketing plan for the first time, subsequent annual revisions are much less taxing. The resulting plan is normally presented to the board or leadership team for approval and budget before becoming a documented set of actions for sales and marketing personnel to follow.

marketing planning cycle
A circular process that runs in two directions, with planning running one way and feedback the other

The duration of marketing plans varies. Plans that cover a period of up to a year are called **short-range plans**. **Medium-range plans** are usually for two to five years. Marketing plans that extend beyond five years are generally viewed as **long-range plans**. These plans can sometimes cover a period of up to 20 years. Marketing managers may have short-, medium- and long-range plans all at the same time. Long-range plans are relatively rare, for good reason, given the volatility evident in many markets. Most marketing plans are revised annually.[3] Organizations choose to update fully and revise their marketing plans, modifying their marketing programmes and changing the detail of their marketing mix(es) as a result. Strategic market plans, as described in Chapter 2, are unlikely to face annual changes of such magnitude, although strategy modifications will always be needed to respond to changes in customer needs, the marketing environment and competitors' activities.

short-range plans
Plans that cover a period of up to a year

medium-range plans
Plans that usually cover two to five years

long-range plans
Plans that extend beyond five years

Most companies have corporate plans, which are big picture views of investment plans, merger and acquisition targets, new product developments, diversifications, innovation programmes, market developments and entry strategies, and associated

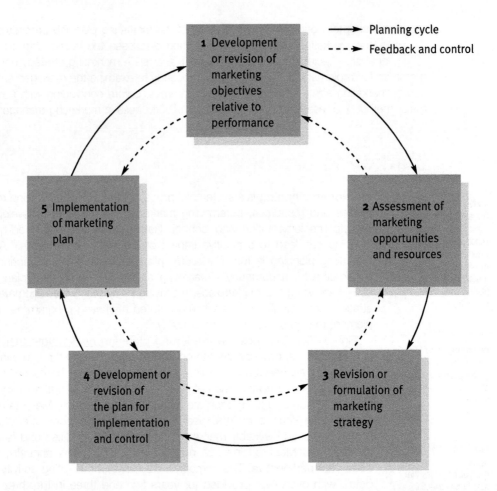

FIGURE 15.1
The marketing
planning cycle

structure, financial and resourcing requirements. Marketing as a function inputs to these strategic plans, particularly with market insights gained from examining the forces of the marketing environment, competitors' moves and changing customer expectations. In addition to the corporate plan or strategy, there is the marketing plan, controlling current operations and the immediate-term opportunities and target markets. While other functions often input to these, such marketing plans tend to be controlled by marketing teams or brand managers.

The extent to which marketing managers develop and use plans varies. Although marketing planning provides numerous benefits, some managers do not use formal marketing plans because they spend almost all their time dealing with daily problems, many of which would be eliminated by adequate planning. However, planning is becoming more important to marketing managers, who realize that planning is necessary to develop, coordinate and control marketing activities effectively and efficiently.[4]

In the authors' *Marketing Planning*, a practitioner text, the benefit of marketing planning is stated as being to provide the basis for an organization:

- serving the 'best' target customers
- beating the competition
- keeping abreast of market developments
- maximizing returns for the organization
- using resources to best advantage

- minimizing threats
- recognizing the organization's strengths and weaknesses.

Malcolm McDonald, a leading authority on marketing planning, argues that marketing planning facilitates:

- coordination of the activities of many individuals whose actions are interrelated over time
- identification of expected developments
- preparedness to meet changes when they occur
- minimization of non-rational responses to the unexpected
- better communication among executives
- minimization of conflicts among individuals that would result in a subordination of the goals of the company to those of the individual.

Well-known American marketing academic Philip Kotler summed up, 'one of the most important outputs of the marketing planning process is the marketing plan'.

When formulating a marketing plan, a new enterprise or a company with a new product does not have current performance to evaluate or an existing plan to revise. Therefore, its marketing planning focuses on assessing opportunities and analyzing capabilities appropriate for these emerging opportunities. Managers can then develop a marketing strategy and specify marketing objectives. Many organizations recognize the need to include information systems in their plans so that they can have continuous feedback and keep their marketing activities oriented towards objectives. Research suggests that companies that increase the level of

FIGURE 15.2
Apple have a very careful marketing planning process

Source: Image courtesy of The Advertising Archives

resources put into planning out-perform those that reduce their allocation to these activities. Marketing plans should do the following:

1 Execute the agreed marketing strategy by detailing appropriate marketing programmes.

2 Specify expected results so that the organization can anticipate what its situation will be at the end of the current planning period.

3 Identify the resources needed to carry out the planned activities so that a budget can be developed.

4 Describe in sufficient detail the activities that are to take place so that responsibilities for implementation can be assigned and schedules determined.

5 Provide for the monitoring of activities and the results so that control can be exerted.[5]

6 Reflect customer needs and market developments.

7 Emphasize any differential advantages or strengths over rivals.

8 Provide clarity of purpose within an organization.

There is a logical and relatively straightforward approach to marketing planning:

1 Analysis of markets, the marketing environment, customer expectations, competitors and trends.

2 Identification and selection of opportunities to pursue and existing business to support.

3 Determination of core target markets relevant to these priorities.

4 Identification of a basis for competing and a differential advantage or competitive edge.

5 Statement of specific goals and desired product or service positioning.

6 Development of marketing mixes to create marketing programmes to implement plans.

7 Determination of required budgets.

8 Specification of schedules and the allocation of marketing tasks to those responsible for their execution and control.

9 Assessment of progress, taking remedial action as is necessary to execute effectively the plan.

10 Monitoring of performance and evolving market conditions, ready to inform next year's planning process.

Table 15.1 illustrates these aspects of the marketing planning process in more detail. A good marketing plan addresses each of these aspects thoroughly and objectively, ensuring it is truly customer-focused. To succeed, a company must have a plan that is followed closely yet is flexible enough to allow for adjustments to reflect changes in the marketing environment.[6] Obviously, the marketing plan document needs to be written carefully in order to satisfy these objectives. The next section of this chapter takes a closer look at the marketing plan itself.

The marketing plan

The marketing plan is the written document, or blueprint, governing all of a business's marketing activities, including the implementation and control of those activities.[7] A marketing plan serves a number of purposes:

● offers a 'road map' for implementing a company's strategies and achieving its objectives

● assists in management control and monitoring of the implementation of a strategy

● informs new participants in the plan of their role and function

● specifies how resources are to be allocated

● stimulates thinking and makes better use of resources

● assigns responsibilities, tasks and timing

● makes participants aware of problems, opportunities and threats

TABLE 15.1 The core steps of the marketing planning process

Analysis
The marketing environment and trends
Company's strengths, weaknesses, opportunities and threats (SWOT)
Customers' needs, buying behaviour and perceptions
Market segmentation and brand positioning
Competition and competitors' strategies
Marketing opportunities
The balance of the product portfolio and ABC sales: contribution analysis
Financial performance
Strategy
Selection of opportunities to pursue and existing business to continue to support
Determination of associated core target markets; basis for competing/differential advantage; desired product/brand positioning
Agreement on marketing objectives and goals
Specification of sales targets and expected results
Programmes for implementation
Specification of plans for marketing mix programmes:
• products
• promotion
• place/distribution
• people (service) levels
• pricing
Allocation of tasks/responsibilities; timing; costs; budgets
Internal marketing of the plan's goals, strategy, key programmes, metrics, timelines and responsibilities
Ongoing work:
• Monitoring progress and benchmarking performance
• Filling gaps in market insight

Source: Sally Dibb and Lyndon Simkin, *Marketing Planning* and *The Marketing Planning Workbook* (Cengage: 2008 and 1996).
Reprinted with permission.

- assists in ensuring that an organization is customer focused, aware of market and competitive movements, realistic in its expectations, and prudent in its use of resources.

A company should have a plan for each marketing opportunity that it pursues and each target market. Because such plans must be modified as company circumstances and forces in the marketing environment change, marketing planning is a continuous process. Many companies have separate marketing managers or teams addressing different product groups, markets or market segments. Each team would typically have its own marketing plan relevant to its market-place. In such cases, the marketing director would produce an over-arching all-inclusive market-ing plan summarizing the key aspects of each team's plan. Organizations use many different formats when devising marketing plans. Plans may be written for strategic business units, prod-uct lines, individual products or brands, or specific markets.

Most plans share some common ground by including an executive summary; a statement of objectives; background to the market; market analysis and examination of realistic marketing op-portunities (a description of environmental forces, customers' needs, market segments and inter-nal capabilities); competitor activity; an outline of marketing strategy, target market priorities, differential advantage, brand and product positioning; a statement of expected sales patterns; the detail of marketing mixes required to implement the marketing plan; controls; financial re-quirements and budgets; and any operational considerations that arise from the marketing plan (see Table 15.2).

A leading defence conglomerate wanted to use its technological expertise in non-defence markets to generate business opportunities. For example, certain sensors developed for missiles

TABLE 15.2 Parts of a typical marketing plan

1	Management or executive summary

2   Marketing objectives

a Company mission statement
b Detailed company objectives
c Product group goals

3   Product/market background

a Product range and explanation
b Market overview and sales summary
c ABC sales: contribution financial performance assessment
d Directional policy matrix evaluation of the product portfolio

4   Marketing analyses

a Marketing environment and trends
b Customers' needs and segments
c Competition and competitors' strategies
d Strengths, weaknesses, opportunities, threats (SWOT) analysis

5   Marketing strategies

a Selected opportunities to pursue and current activities to support
b Core target markets (segments) related to the priority pursuits
c Basis for competing/differential advantage
d Desired product/brand positioning

6   Statement of expected outcomes, sales forecasts and results

7   Marketing programmes for implementation

a Marketing mixes
b Tasks, responsibilities and timelines

8   Controls and evaluation: monitoring of performance

9   Financial implications/required budgets

a Delineation of costs and budgets
b Expected returns on investment for implementing the marketing plan

10 Operational considerations

a Personnel issues/requirements
b Internal marketing relationships, reporting and communications
c Research and development/production needs
d Marketing information needs and ongoing market insight work

11 Appendices

a SWOT analysis details
b Background data and information
c Marketing research findings

Sources: Sally Dibb and Lyndon Simkin, *The Marketing Casebook* (Routledge, 1994). Reprinted with permission. Updated from Sally Dibb and Lyndon Simkin, *Marketing Planning* (Cengage, 2008).

have applications in ocean drilling, fire protection systems and even baby monitors in hospital. Marketing planning enabled this defence company to task its marketers to identify possible opportunities for the company to use its expertise in the oil, alarm, automotive and rail sectors. These opportunities were checked out fully, narrowed down and then addressed with appropriate marketing programmes, through the marketing planning process. The resulting marketing plan was able to articulate the nature of the set of opportunities in non-defence markets and persuade the company's leadership team to sanction the resources required to enter these new markets.

The following sections consider the major parts of a typical marketing plan, as well as the purpose that each part serves.

Management or executive summary The management summary, or executive summary (often only one or two pages), should be a concise overview of the entire report, including key aims, overall strategies, fundamental conclusions and salient points regarding the suggested marketing mix programmes. Not many people – especially CEOs – read an entire report, tending to 'dip in' here and there, so the management summary should be comprehensive and clear.

Marketing objectives Objectives are for the benefit of the reader, such as senior executives or new recruits, to give perspective to the report. Aims and objectives should be stated briefly but should include reference to the organization's mission statement and corporate goals, objectives and any fundamental desires for core product groups or brands. This section describes the objectives underlying the plan. A **marketing objective** is a statement of what is to be accomplished through marketing activities. It specifies the results expected from marketing efforts. A marketing objective should be expressed in clear, simple terms, so that all marketing personnel and other colleagues understand exactly what they are trying to achieve. The marketing objective should be written in such a way that its accomplishment can be measured accurately. If a company has an objective of increasing its market share by 12 per cent, the company should be able to measure changes in its market share accurately. A marketing objective should also indicate the timeframe for accomplishing the objective. For example, a company that sets an objective of introducing three new products should state the time period in which this is to be done, as well as anticipated sales targets.

> **marketing objective**
> A statement of what is to be accomplished through marketing activities – the results expected from marketing efforts

Objectives may be stated in terms of the degree of product introduction or innovation, sales volume, profitability per unit, gains in market share, heightened dealer interest, media endorsement or improvements in customer satisfaction or awareness of the company's products and brands. They must also be consistent with the company's overall organizational goals. Progress against these metrics should be formally monitored as part of the planning process and cycle.

Product/market background Product/market background is a necessary section. Not everyone reading the plan will be fully familiar with the products and their markets. Senior managers may be unfamiliar with specific aspects of the product or market. This section 'scene sets', helping the readers – for example, a chief executive or advertising manager – to understand the context for the marketing plan and its agreed priorities.

Marketing analysis The analysis section is the heart of the marketing planning exercise: if incomplete or highly subjective, the recommendations are likely to be based on an inaccurate view of the market and the company's potential. This section of the plan provides a sound foundation to the recommendations and marketing programmes. It includes analyses of the marketing environment, market trends, customers, competitors, competitive positions and competitors' strategies, the suitability of the business's product portfolio and the financial performance of products, market segments and even certain customers. As this lengthy list of subjects implies, effective marketing planning is about much more than just being customer focused.[8] Marketers therefore need to be careful to include all of these areas in their analyses. However, while the analysis stage is a huge part of the marketing planning process, non-marketer colleagues do not want to read too much detail, so only headlines and highlights should be included in the actual plan, to help explain the strategy choices and underpin the required actions.

The market attractiveness – business strength matrix and the ABC sales: contribution analysis detailed in Chapter 9 are popular tools employed by marketers to assess portfolio performance.

The marketing environment section of the marketing plan describes the current state of the marketing environment, including the legal, political, regulatory, technological, societal/green, economic and competitive forces, as well as ethical considerations. It also makes predictions about future directions of those forces. As discussed in Chapter 3, environmental forces can hamper an organization in achieving its objectives. This section of the marketing plan also describes the possible impact of these forces on the implementation of the marketing plan. Most marketing plans include extensive analyses of competitive, technological, legal and regulatory forces, perhaps even creating separate sections for these influential forces of the marketing environment. It is important to note here that because the forces of the marketing environment are dynamic, marketing plans should be reviewed and modified periodically to adjust to change.

Marketing exists to enable an organization to meet customers' needs properly. This is particularly true in the marketing planning process. The views, needs and expectations of current and potential customers are important as a basis for formal marketing planning. Without such an understanding and analysis of likely changes in customer requirements, it is impossible to safely target those markets of most benefit to the organization's fortunes. It is also impossible to specify a correct marketing mix (or mixes).

The analysis of the marketing environment includes competitive forces and trends. As explained in Chapter 2, a meaningful marketing plan and associated programmes for implementation necessitate a prior comprehensive analysis of an organization's competitive position in its markets and territories, together with an understanding of rival organization's marketing strategies. The failure to understand or anticipate competitors' likely actions is a major weakness in most businesses.[9] Marketers should consider how key competitors will react to their proposed plans, incorporating follow-up programmes prepared to combat hostile reaction from such rivals. In practice, too few companies properly understand their competitors' strategies or capabilities, so fail to realistically appreciate how competitors will react and impact on their plans. This should not be the case: marketers have a responsibility to glean competitor insights and to share these with senior colleagues.

SWOT analysis
Analysis that determines a company's situation by examining four factors: strengths, weaknesses, opportunities and threats

The **SWOT analysis** is an important foundation for any marketing plan, helping to produce realistic and meaningful recommendations. The section in the main body of the report should be kept to a concise overview, with detailed market-by-market or country-by-country SWOTs – and their full explanations – kept to the appendices. Most marketers and senior management teams conduct SWOT analyses (the letters SWOT stand for strengths, weaknesses, opportunities and threats). The first half of this analysis – strengths and weaknesses – examines the company's position and capabilities, or that of its product, vis-à-vis customers, competitor activity, environmental trends and company resources. The second half of the SWOT takes this review further to examine the opportunities and threats identified, and to make recommendations that feed into marketing strategy and the marketing mix actions. The marketing environment analysis often reveals potential opportunities and threats. Understanding and then responding to these opportunities and threats enables a business to make the most of the environmental context in which it operates. Even a potential threat can be transformed into an opportunity if appropriate action is taken.[10] The result of the SWOT analysis should be a thorough understanding of the organization's status and its standing in its markets. A SWOT analysis must be objective, with evidence provided to support the points cited. The focus should be on issues likely to concern customers. As explained in Chapter 2, which offers illustrative SWOT analyses, the checklist-style SWOT analysis is popular with marketers, particularly as part of a marketing plan, few marketing plans do not include one.

Marketing strategies Strategies should be self-evident if the analyses have been objective and thorough: the opportunities to pursue, the target markets most beneficial to the company, the basis for competing and differential advantage or competitive edge in these markets, and the desired product or brand positioning. This strategy statement must be realistic and detailed enough to act upon, providing clear direction throughout the organization and for the leadership team.

This section of the marketing plan provides a broad overview of the plan for achieving the marketing objectives and, ultimately, the organizational goals. Marketing strategy focuses on identifying opportunities to be pursued, defining a target market and developing a marketing mix to gain long-run competitive and customer advantages. There is a degree of overlap between corporate strategy and marketing strategy. Marketing strategy is unique in that it has the responsibility to assess buyer needs and the company's potential for gaining competitive advantage, both of which, ultimately, must guide the corporate mission.[11] In other words, marketing strategy guides the company's direction in relationships between customers and competitors. The bottom line is that a marketing strategy must be consistent with consumer needs, perceptions and beliefs. Thus this section should describe the company's intended target market(s) and how product, people, promotion, place/distribution and price will be used to develop a compelling proposition and product or brand positioning that will satisfy the needs of members of the target market(s).

Expected results Having highlighted the strategic direction and intention, it is important to explain the expected results and sales volumes to show why the strategies should be followed. These forecasts should be quantified – typically as expected units of sales and possible market shares. This stage is important if the required marketing mix budgets are to be approved by senior managers.

Marketing programmes for implementation Marketing programme recommendations are the culmination of the various analyses and statements of strategies: exactly what needs to be done, how and why. This is the detailed presentation of the proposed marketing mixes to achieve the goals and implement the strategies. In poor marketing plans, there is a lack of analysis and strategy, with the focus falling on the tactical marketing mix recommendations. Robust planning requires the recommendation of detailed marketing mixes, but only after time has been taken to thoroughly address the core marketing analyses and determine a detailed marketing strategy.

Each market segment to be targeted may require its own, tailor-made marketing mix. This section of the marketing plan is of paramount importance, as it gives the specific details of the marketing activity required to implement the marketing plan and to achieve the organization's strategic goals. Each element of the marketing mix should be discussed in turn, with specific recommendations explained in sufficient detail to enable managers to put them into action. Product, people (service), pricing, place/distribution and promotion (marketing communications) must all be addressed. Associated tasks should be allocated to personnel and responsibilities for action clearly identified. This is the core output of marketing planning: the detailed plan of action for the business's marketing programmes. Organizations must also be prepared to adapt their implementation plans if unexpected events arise that were not predicted by the plan. Research shows that in smaller businesses, marketing and business success are linked to how good they are at improvising if the unexpected happens.[12]

Controls and evaluation It is essential that controls be established along with measures to assess the ongoing implementation of the marketing plan. This section of the plan details how the results of the plan will be measured. For example, the results of an advertising campaign designed to increase market share may be measured in terms of increases in sales volume or improved brand recognition and acceptance by consumers. Next, a schedule for comparing the results achieved with the objectives set forth in the marketing plan is developed. Finally, guidelines may be offered outlining who is responsible for monitoring the programme and taking remedial action. Financial measures such as sales volumes, profitability and market shares will be included. 'Softer' issues, such as brand awareness and customer satisfaction, should also be monitored.[13]

Financial implications/required budgets The full picture may not be known, but an indication of required resources and the financial implications must be given. The financial projections and budgets section outlines the returns expected through implementation of the plan. The costs incurred will be weighed against expected revenues. A budget must be prepared to allocate resources in order to accomplish marketing objectives. It should contain estimates of the costs of implementing the plan, including the costs of advertising, digital activity, brand building, salesforce training and remuneration, development of distribution channels and marketing research.

Operational considerations These strategies and marketing programmes may have ramifications for other product groups, sectors or territories, for research and development, for engineering or production and so on. The operational implications must be highlighted, but too much detail may be inappropriate and politically sensitive within the organization.

Appendices The main body of the report should be as concise as possible. The document must, though, tell the full story and include evidence and statistics that support the strategies and marketing programmes being recommended. The use of appendices – as long as they are fully cross-referenced in the main body of the report – helps to keep the report concise and well focused.

Conducting marketing planning

Experienced marketers produce their own marketing plans, often with the involvement of colleagues from other functional areas within the organization and particularly the members of the sales team, who have knowledge of market trends and customer issues. Most companies set a point in the year when each business unit is expected to submit a detailed marketing plan, with fully costed marketing programmes set against detailed sales expectations and market share targets. Most marketing teams will spend at least the month before the deadline updating their marketing analyses and strategic thinking, before detailing revised marketing mix programmes.

In organizations embarking on marketing planning for the first time, there is often a significant learning curve to address, with the first round of marketing analyses requiring a long lead time and much resourcing. The managers involved have to learn new skills and accommodate the planning tasks alongside their normal tasks.[14] By year three, the marketing planning process has generally become part of the organization's fabric and the required analyses are being updated routinely throughout the year by marketers well versed in the planning process's requirements.[15] Initially, though, 'naive' organizations – those not experienced in the marketing planning toolkit – often seek the help of external experts and facilitators, as outlined in the Marketing Tools and Techniques box below.

Marketing tools and techniques

JCB's adoption of marketing planning

Some time ago, the then incumbent marketing director of construction equipment leader JCB went to study strategic marketing at INSEAD in France. On his return to the UK headquarters of JCB he introduced a formal marketing planning process to the company. Recognizing the cultural diversity and complexity of a global business, the marketing director opted to focus initially on the UK. At the time the company had four core product groups, including backhoe loaders and telehandlers, plus some quickly emerging new product categories, such as skid steers and mini-excavators. Each product group had its own set of marketers, thus each team produced a marketing plan.

As the marketing planning process was new to the company, external trainers were brought in to establish a stage-by-stage sequence of activities, and to provide the company's sales and marketing staff with the required analytical toolkit. Stage one included the core marketing analyses: financial performance of the company's products and sales analysis; the marketing environment forces active in each product group's target markets; the buying behaviour characteristics and evolving customer needs; competitors' products, strengths, weaknesses and projected plans; the company's brand positioning vis-à-vis leading rivals; plus, JCB's capabilities.

These tasks proved time-consuming for already busy personnel, so some external support was commissioned in order to research customers and competitors. Small teams from within the marketing function were allocated to the different forces of the marketing environment: technological developments, regulatory pressures, economic trends and so forth. These teams reviewed secondary sources for information, networked with JCB and dealer personnel, met with subject experts to solicit their views, and created a dialogue with industry observers. To examine competitors, the JCB marketers visited trade shows, talked with customers and dealers, analyzed rivals' products and marketing programmes, reviewed financial performance and engaged with industry-watchers. Marketing research in the form of one-to-one depth interviews and focus groups gleaned customers' views of JCB, its products and customer service, changing customer needs and the customers' views of competitors. Some of these analyses were undertaken by teams of marketers working across JCB's product groups and target markets, while much research was specific to the separate marketing teams handling each product group in the company.

Within six weeks, a significant amount of marketing intelligence had been derived, updated, collated and analyzed. Stage two, externally moderated by consultants, involved brainstorming workshops with sales and marketing personnel reflecting on current strategies in the light of the various marketing analyses conducted. As a result, the target market priorities were modified, new products commissioned, revised marketing communications created, modified pricing considered, dealer plans revisited and customer service improved. An important aspect of stage two was the sharing of marketing intelligence – particularly about competitors, opportunities and threats – between the separate marketing teams. The final stage of the process involved the formalization of appropriate marketing programmes to operationalize the revised marketing strategy, coordination of the separate teams' proposed marketing programmes, plus the allocation of budgets, personnel, schedules and responsibilities to these emerging tasks.

In year two, when the summer marketing planning period was reached, JCB's subsidiary companies overseas were also included, producing top-line marketing plans. Managers overseas were able to learn from their UK colleagues and emulate the format of their resulting marketing plans. For the UK marketers in their second season, there was the opportunity to address outstanding marketing analysis gaps from the previous year and to focus on utilizing the marketing planning toolkit rather than learning about its scope and tools.

By year three, the rest of JCB's non-UK operation had become involved, while in the UK the growing understanding of the marketplace facilitated by two years' marketing planning and marketing intelligence gathering led to the creation of new target market segments. The marketing plans by year three were segment-specific, ignoring the product groups created by JCB for operational convenience. This led to the formation of the company's Compact Division, recognizing that customers of mini-excavators or mini-skid steers had different purchasing behaviour to customers buying the larger-scale versions of such products.

After three years, one manager described the marketing planning process thus:

In the first year it was really hard – hell: learning new skills; realizing we had inadequate or incomplete knowledge of market trends, competitors and even customers; adjusting to undertaking the planning work alongside our 'day jobs' … just finding the time. The process now is routine: we never miss the opportunity to find out about customer views, examine competitors or discuss market developments with 'those in the know'. We're also much quicker in producing and delivering the marketing plan. The big difference is that now the company's strategic planning and budgeting are guided by the analyses and market understanding provided by the marketing plan. More to the point, we're selling more machines, in a larger number of segments to more satisfied customers. Even better, whether in our French subsidiary, Indian plant or American sales office, we're all addressing the market in a coordinated manner and everyone is aware of the requirements for effective marketing planning. But it has taken three years. Finding the time was hard to start with. It did 'hurt' in the first year!

Marketing implementation

marketing implementation
Processes and activities deployed to action the marketing strategy or roll out the marketing plan

Marketing implementation is the 'how?', 'what?', 'when?', 'by whom?' of marketing strategy; it involves processes and activities directed at actioning marketing strategies or rolling out the marketing plan's recommendations. The implementation process can determine whether a marketing strategy is successful. Increasingly marketers are recognizing the importance of managing implementation and planning for the execution of marketing programmes.[16] For example, the output of marketing planning used to be the specification of the marketing mix. Now, a robust marketing plan is not deemed complete until the 'how', 'by whom', 'when' and 'how much' issues are addressed: allocation of budgets, personnel, schedules and performance measures to the specific marketing mix recommendations. Often managers question what could go wrong … having created a strategy or plan, they seek to identify the likely blockers to progress so that they might pre-empt these problems. In providing these details, marketers identify deficiencies and inadequacies in their capabilities and resources that they must address in order to implement their marketing plans effectively. These impediments often relate to operational and managerial issues. In short, good marketing strategy combined with bad marketing implementation is a recipe for certain failure. Marketing has to be made to happen!

The exponents of marketing planning have for many years realized that internal organizational barriers are likely to impede or restrict the implementation of marketing plans and marketing strategies.[17] They propose that senior managers address the people and cultural concerns detailed in Figure 15.4 before embarking on developing marketing plans, new market segmentation schemes or marketing strategies.[18] These issues reflect the importance of addressing the internal market in effectively pursuing the implementation of marketing strategies and the deployment of recommended marketing mix programmes. Failure to control internal audiences and develop suitable control strategies will reduce the viability of the marketing function's recommended strategies and marketing plan recommendations in the external marketplace.

Already-busy managers developing marketing plans or involved with revising market segmentation schemes need to be managed, cajoled, motivated and rewarded. Any planning process requires access to marketing intelligence; and the involvement of personnel with knowledge of the marketplace, customers, competitors, trends and new developments. Those directly involved must have access to their colleagues and be empowered to conduct the necessary analyses and develop appropriate strategies. 'Buy-in' from managers and colleagues, whose remit may change as a result of the planning, warrants facilitation. The necessary analytical skills and time to strategize must be provided. Senior management should be aware of the invasive nature of marketing planning or creating an updated marketing strategy, and schedule other activities

FIGURE 15.3
The development of a new car model may take six years, but its success in terms of sales volume depends as much on the implementation of the target market strategy as on the design and features of the car

Source: © Duncan Snow / Alamy

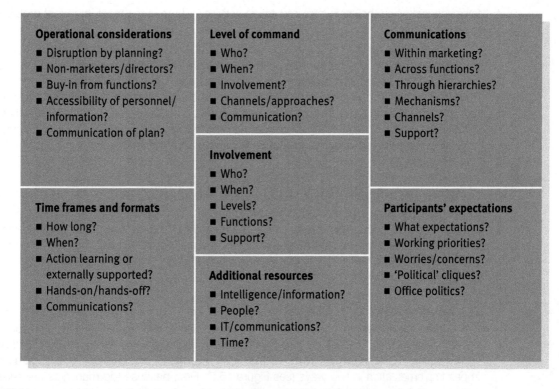

Operational considerations
- Disruption by planning?
- Non-marketers/directors?
- Buy-in from functions?
- Accessibility of personnel/ information?
- Communication of plan?

Level of command
- Who?
- When?
- Involvement?
- Channels/approaches?
- Communication?

Communications
- Within marketing?
- Across functions?
- Through hierarchies?
- Mechanisms?
- Channels?
- Support?

Involvement
- Who?
- When?
- Levels?
- Functions?
- Support?

Time frames and formats
- How long?
- When?
- Action learning or externally supported?
- Hands-on/hands-off?
- Communications?

Participants' expectations
- What expectations?
- Working priorities?
- Worries/concerns?
- 'Political' cliques?
- Office politics?

Additional resources
- Intelligence/information?
- People?
- IT/communications?
- Time?

FIGURE 15.4
People and culture prerequisites to effective marketing and marketing planning programmes
Source: adapted from: Sally Dibb, Lyndon Simkin and John Bradley, *The Marketing Planning Workbook* (London: Thomson, 1998)

requisites for implementation
Process, skill, leadership, empowerment, communication, timing, information, resource and participation decisions

intended strategy
The strategy on which the company decides during the planning phase

realized strategy
The strategy that actually takes place

accordingly. The **requisites for implementation** include process, skill, leadership, empowerment, communication, timing, information, resource and participation decisions. The learning point is straightforward: appreciation of the checklist issues outlined in Figure 15.4 *prior* to embarking on marketing planning or the creation of a new marketing strategy will significantly enhance the likelihood of a successful outcome. Unfortunately, many organizations only realize the importance of planning and facilitating the strategising activity *after* problems have emerged, progress has been baulked and key stakeholders within the organization are failing to cooperate.[19]

An important aspect of the implementation process is understanding that marketing strategies almost always turn out differently from expected. In essence, all organizations have two types of strategy: intended strategy and realized strategy.[20] The **intended strategy** is the strategy that the organization decided on during the planning phase and wants to use. The **realized strategy**, on the other hand, is the strategy that actually takes place; it comes about during the process of implementing the intended strategy. The realized strategy is not necessarily any better than the intended strategy, though it is often worse.

Problems in implementing marketing activities

Why do marketing strategies sometimes turn out differently from that expected? The most common reason is that managers fail to realize that the marketing implementation is just as important as marketing strategy.[21] Both strategy and implementation are important to strategic planning. The relationship between strategic planning and implementation creates a number of problems for managers when they plan implementation activities. Three of the most important problems are described below:[22]

Marketing strategy and implementation are related Companies that experience this problem typically assume that strategic planning always comes first, followed by implementation. In reality, marketing strategies and implementation activities should be developed simultaneously. The content of the marketing strategy determines how it will be implemented. Likewise, implementation activities may require that changes be made in the marketing strategy. Thus it is important for marketing managers to understand that strategy and implementation are highly entwined, iterative processes.

Marketing strategy and implementation are constantly evolving This second problem refers to how strategy and implementation are both affected by the marketing environment. Since the environment and market circumstances are constantly changing, both marketing strategy and implementation must remain flexible enough to adapt. The relationship between strategy and implementation is never fixed; it is always evolving to accommodate changes in customer needs, government regulation or competition.

The responsibilities for marketing strategy and implementation are separated This problem is often the biggest obstacle in implementing marketing strategies. Typically, marketing strategies are developed by the top managers in an organization. However, the responsibility for implementing those strategies rests at the front line of the organization. This separation can impair implementation in two ways (see Figure 15.5). First, because top managers are separated from the front line, where the company interacts daily with customers, they may not grasp the unique problems associated with implementing marketing activities. Second, people, not organizations, implement strategies. Front-line managers and employees are often responsible for implementing strategies, even though they had no voice in developing them. Consequently, these front-line employees may lack motivation and commitment.[23]

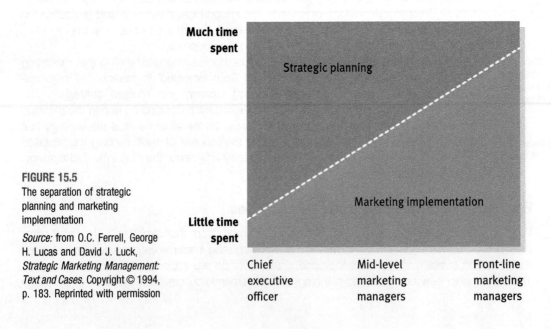

FIGURE 15.5
The separation of strategic planning and marketing implementation

Source: from O.C. Ferrell, George H. Lucas and David J. Luck, *Strategic Marketing Management: Text and Cases.* Copyright © 1994, p. 183. Reprinted with permission

Components of marketing implementation

The marketing implementation process has several components, all of which must be synchronized if the implementation is to succeed. These components are shown in Figure 15.6. The systems component refers to work processes, procedures and the way in which information is structured – elements ensuring that the organization's day-to-day activities are carried out. Typical organizational systems include marketing information systems, strategic planning systems, marketing planning processes, budgeting and accounting systems, manufacturing and quality control systems and performance measurement systems.

The people component in Figure 15.6 refers to the importance of employees in the implementation process. It includes such factors as the quality, diversity and skills of the workforce within the organization, and also covers the human resources function. Issues like employee recruitment, selection and training have great bearing on the implementation of marketing activities.[24] Closely linked to the people component is leadership, or the art of managing people. It involves such issues as employee motivation, communication and reward policies.

At the centre of marketing implementation are shared goals, which draw the entire organization together into a single, functioning unit. These goals may be simple statements of the company's objectives. On the other hand, the goals may be detailed mission statements, outlining corporate philosophy and direction. Shared goals appear in the centre of Figure 15.6 because they hold all the other components together to ensure successful marketing implementation.[25] Without shared goals, different parts of the organization might work towards different goals or objectives, thus limiting the success of the entire organization. These ideas have been embraced within the related concepts of *internal marketing* and *relationship marketing,* as discussed later in this chapter.

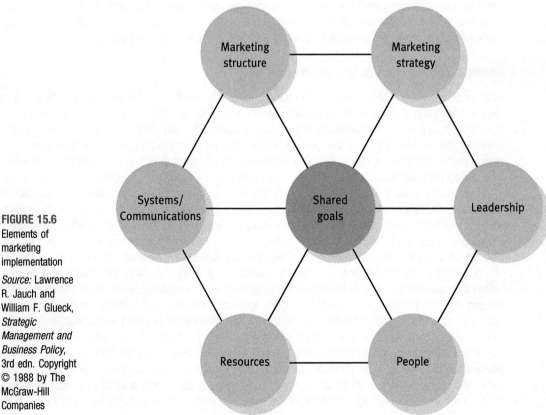

FIGURE 15.6
Elements of marketing implementation

Source: Lawrence R. Jauch and William F. Glueck, *Strategic Management and Business Policy*, 3rd edn. Copyright © 1988 by The McGraw-Hill Companies

Motivating marketing personnel

An important element in implementing a marketing strategy or the marketing plan is motivating marketing personnel to perform effectively. People work to satisfy physical, psychological and social needs. To motivate marketing personnel, managers must discover their employees' needs and then develop motivational methods that help them satisfy those needs. It is crucial that the plan for motivating employees be fair, ethical and well understood by them. Additionally, rewards to employees must be tied to organizational goals. In general, to improve employee motivation, companies need to find out what workers think, how they feel and what they want. Some of this information can be obtained from an employee attitude survey. A business can motivate its workers by directly linking pay with performance, by informing workers how their performance affects department and corporate results, by following through with appropriate compensation, by promoting or implementing a flexible benefits programme and by adopting a participative management approach.[26]

Consider the following example. Suppose a sales person can sell product A or B to a particular customer, but not both products. Product A sells for £200 000 and contributes £20 000 to the company's profit margin. Product B sells for £60 000 and has a contribution margin of £40 000. If the sales person receives a commission of 3 per cent of sales, he or she would obviously prefer to sell product A, even though the sale of product B contributes more to the company's profits. If the sales person's commission was based on contribution margin instead of sales, and the company's goal was to maximize profits, both the company and the sales person would benefit more from the sale of product B.[27] By tying rewards to organizational goals, the company encourages behaviour that meets organizational goals.

Besides tying rewards to organizational goals, managers must motivate individuals by using different motivational tools, based on each individual's value system. For example, some employees value recognition more than a slight pay increase. Managers can reward employees with money, plus additional fringe benefits, prestige or recognition, or even non-financial rewards such as job autonomy, skill variety, task significance and increased feedback. A survey of *Fortune* 1000 companies found that 'the majority of organizations feel that they get more for their money through non-cash awards, if given in addition to a basic compensation plan'.

Communicating within the marketing unit

With good communication, marketing managers can motivate personnel and coordinate their efforts. Marketing managers must be able to communicate with the company's high level management to ensure that marketing activities are consistent with the company's overall goals. Communication with top-level executives keeps marketing managers aware of the company's overall plans and achievements. It also guides what the marketing unit is to do and how its activities are to be integrated with those of other departments – such as finance, production or human resources – with whose management the marketing manager must also communicate in order to coordinate marketing efforts. For example, marketing personnel must work with production staff to help design products that customers want. To direct marketing activities, marketing managers must communicate with marketing personnel at the operations level, such as sales and advertising personnel, researchers, wholesalers, retailers and package designers.

To facilitate communication, marketing managers should establish an information system within the marketing unit. The marketing information system should allow for easy communication among marketing managers, sales managers and sales personnel. Marketers need an information system to support a variety of activities, such as planning, budgeting, sales analyses, performance evaluations and the preparation of reports. An information system should also expedite communications with other departments in the organization and minimize destructive competition between departments for organizational resources. Managers must be encouraged to communicate freely, sharing ideas, insights, marketing intelligence, strategies and tactical recommendations. Such channels of communication should be across business functions and hierarchies.

Stone-walling, gatekeeping, ring-fencing and misinformation – all facets of petty 'office politics' – offer no benefits.

Coordinating marketing activities

Because of job specialization and differences related to marketing activities, marketing managers must synchronize individuals' actions to achieve marketing objectives. In addition, they must work closely with managers in research and development, production, finance and human resources to see that marketing activities mesh with other functions of the company.

Practitioners' implementation management of marketing planning: the Dibb/Simkin checklists

Marketing tools and techniques

When a company commences marketing planning for the first time, already-busy sales and marketing personnel are going to be expected to find time to produce the marketing plan. Hardly any companies employ specialist marketing planners. The organization must recognize the time pressures and resourcing issues associated with asking staff to become involved in marketing planning. Senior managers must be seen to be appreciative, but they must also create channels of communication between functions in the business so that marketing intelligence may be gathered, ideas generated and the resulting plan disseminated across the company. Rather than await problems of information availability, time pressure, poor internal communications, ineffective leadership and so forth, it is better to be aware of these issues from the outset.

The Dibb/Simkin checklist below was developed for a global B2B services company that examined how to improve its annual marketing planning activity. Such a checklist should be considered by those instigating marketing planning – senior managers and the marketing function – before the launch of a marketing planning programme.

- Who to involve, what to tell them, how to control them, how to free up their time.

- Who to put in charge, their level of hands-on involvement, their liaison with other functional areas and senior managers.

- The expected timeframe for completion of the marketing plan and the timing of the planning activity given other commitments in the business.

- Resources required in terms of people, marketing information, IT and administrative support.

- Facilitation of communications within the marketing planning team, across business functions, through the hierarchies of the company.

- Coordination of the inputs from non-marketers, the buy-in to the process by managers, and the roll-out of emerging actions.

- The marketing planning process to utilize, its stages/activities and core requirements.

- The implementation of the resulting marketing plan, its launch, internal communication, external execution, required roll-out resourcing.

- A sequence of ongoing reviews to ensure effective implementation of the marketing plan occurs and any required remedial action is taken.

As explored earlier in this chapter, it is also necessary to adhere to a robust marketing planning process. This should involve:

- marketing analysis – so that the business is properly informed about current market dynamics and the reality of its standing

- a period of strategy development – to ensure that the target market strategy and defined basis for competing reflect the realities of the marketplace

- the creation of marketing mix programmes – designed to execute the devised marketing strategy, and

- a process of controls and reviews – to facilitate the rollout and execution of the marketing plan.

Once the marketing strategy or the plan has been developed, it must be implemented. This partly involves ensuring that specific actions from the plan have been allocated to individual managers, with clearly defined timeframes, budgets and performance measures. The facilitation of implementation also requires reviews and monitoring of progress.

'Review days' are often utilized. These generally take one of two forms:

1 business unit teams present to senior managers and explain their progress in rolling-out their part of the company's marketing plan

2 cross-functional workshops are held in order to more fully review progress, explore emerging issues and determine appropriate remedial actions.

The B2B company cited above introduces its review workshops thus:

Review Workshop – Agenda

- Review the current strategy.
  Focus on the plan's product/service propositions and how effectively they are being taken to the specified target market segments.

- Examine what is working and what is not!
  Lessons to emulate and problems to fix.

- Determine appropriate actions.
  Specify tasks and responsibilities as a result of the discussion.

Generally, such a discussion revolves around:

- the product/service propositions developed to take to market, and their fine-tuning

- the message clarity of the propositions and their communication to target markets

- marketing communications campaign development and execution

- communication across the company of the plan and its imperatives

- orientation of channel partners/members to the revised direction of the plan

- specialist skills required to help roll out the plan

- strategy for establishing/managing channel and customer relationships

- controls and incentives required to change colleagues' behaviours in order to enact the new-look marketing strategy and marketing plan.

Often, a marketing plan changes a company's thinking and direction, so a programme of change management is required in order to realign managers, budgets, the sales force and so forth. Without the detailed planning of how best to align an organization's resources around a marketing plan, successful implementation is unlikely.

While the sentiments above have focused on marketing planning, the same procedures and tips apply to the implementation of a marketing strategy or revised target market strategy.

Sources: © Dibb/Simkin. This process is adapted from and based on material from Sally Dibb, Lyndon Simkin and John Bradley, *The Marketing Planning Workbook* (London: Thomson) and Sally Dibb and Lyndon Simkin, *The Market Segmentation Workbook* (London: Thomson).

Marketing managers must coordinate the activities of marketing staff within the business and integrate those activities with the marketing efforts of external organizations – advertising agencies, resellers (wholesalers, retailers and dealers), researchers and shippers, among others. Marketing managers can improve coordination by using internal marketing activities to make each employee aware of how his or her job relates to others, and how his or her actions contribute to the achievement of marketing plans.

Concepts related to marketing implementation

This section discusses three concepts that exist for their own purposes, but that also relate to marketing implementation: relationship marketing, internal marketing and total quality management. These approaches, which represent mindsets that marketing managers can adopt when organizing and planning marketing activities, are not mutually exclusive. Indeed, many companies adopt a combination of these approaches when designing marketing activities.

Relationship marketing

relationship marketing
Places emphasis on the interaction between buyers and sellers, and is concerned with winning and keeping customers by maintaining links between marketing, quality and customer service

As outlined in Chapter 1, **relationship marketing** has attracted considerable attention in the marketing literature.[28] It focuses on the interaction between buyers and sellers, and is concerned with winning but *also* keeping customers by maintaining links between marketing, quality and customer service.[29] The term *relationship marketing* has been defined as attracting, maintaining and – in multi-service organizations – enhancing customer relationships.[30] The notion hinges on selling organizations taking a longer-term view of customer relationships to ensure that those customers converted are also retained. Rather than focusing on the worth of an individual transaction, the relationship marketing concept is concerned with the lifetime value of the customer relationship and in winning a larger share of a customer's spending over a prolonged period. There has been a shift from transaction-based marketing towards a relationship focus, as explained by a leading exponent: 'Transaction marketing of the 1980s placed the emphasis on the individual sale. Relationship marketing of the 1990s placed the emphasis on individual customers and seeks to establish a long term relationship between customer and company.'[31]

The fundamental message is that ongoing, longer-term relationships are essential for a business's viability and market performance. While marketers are encouraged to devote greater resources to developing such customer relationships, the relationship marketing literature explains that such long-term commitment stems not only from treating customers differently, but also from addressing other audiences. As detailed in the **five markets model of relationship marketing** in Figure 15.7, these audiences include:

five markets model of relationship marketing
In addition to customer markets, the core audiences of influencers, referrals, employee recruitment, suppliers and internal markets

- referral markets, such as insurance brokers and advisers
- suppliers
- employee recruitment markets
- influencer markets, such as government bodies, EU officials and the central bank
- internal markets.

In highlighting this final 'market' or domain of the five markets model, relationship marketers are acknowledging the damage that can be done if employees do not understand their role in ensuring that marketing recommendations are adequately actioned. In order to exploit this internal market effectively, thought must be devoted to: the establishment of communication channels; leadership qualities and people skills; associated resources; information content, access and sharing; IT support systems; management controls; clear internally focused propositions and messages; as well as priorities for which employees are primary targets.

Internal marketing

internal marketing
The application of marketing internally within the company, with programmes of communication and guidance targeted at internal audiences to develop responsiveness and a unified sense of purpose among employees

Much appears to depend on **internal marketing**, which is the application of marketing internally within the company, with programmes of communication and guidance targeted at internal audiences. For example, it has been shown that there is a relationship between satisfied employees, marketing orientation and organizational performance.[32] Internal marketing plays a vital role in developing a customer-focused organization and helps ensure coherent relationship marketing.[33] Internal marketing is based on communication, the development of responsiveness and a unified sense of purpose among employees. It aims to develop internal and external customer awareness, and to remove functional or human barriers to organizational effectiveness. Internal marketing centres on the notion that every member of the organization has a 'supplier' and a 'customer'. Long-term, ongoing relationships require improved customer service. High levels of service depend on individuals ensuring that

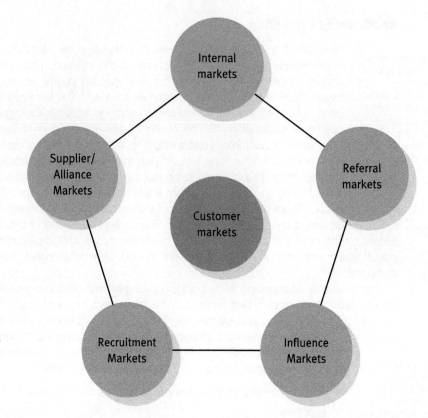

FIGURE 15.7
Six markets stakeholder model

Source: M. Christopher, A. Payne and D. Ballantyne, (2002) *Relationship Marketing: Creating Stakeholder Value, 2nd edition* (Oxford: Butterworth-Heinemann)

their suppliers and customers are happy. The concept also requires that all members of staff work together, in tune with the organization's mission, strategy and goals. The aim is to ensure that all staff represent the business in the best possible way in all transactions they have with suppliers, customers and other staff. A new marketing strategy or modified marketing plan will not be implemented if personnel within the organization do not understand the direction being recommended, fail to appreciate their role in executing the strategy or refuse to comply. Internal marketing is a philosophy for managing human resources with a marketing perspective.[34]

In order to achieve this internal cohesiveness, internal marketers propose six steps:[35]

1 the creation of internal awareness
2 identification of internal 'customers' and 'suppliers'
3 determination of internal customers' expectations
4 communication of these expectations to internal suppliers
5 internal suppliers' modifications to their activities to reflect internal customers' views
6 a measure of internal service quality and feedback to ensure a satisfactory exchange between internal customers and suppliers.

Marketing activities cannot be implemented effectively without the cooperation of employees. Employees are the essential ingredient in increasing productivity, providing customer service and beating the competition. Thus, in addition to marketing activities targeted at external customers, companies use internal marketing to attract, motivate and retain qualified internal customers (employees) by designing internal products (jobs or roles) to satisfy employees' wants and needs. Generally speaking, internal marketing refers to the managerial actions necessary to make all members of the marketing organization understand and accept their respective roles in implementing the marketing strategy. This means that all of them, from the CEO of the company to

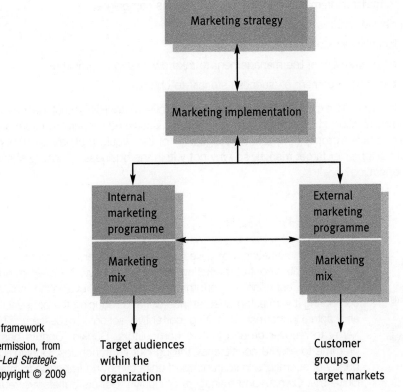

FIGURE 15.8

The internal marketing framework

Source: reprinted by permission, from Nigel F. Piercy, *Market-Led Strategic Change, 4th edition.* Copyright © 2009

the hourly workers on the shop floor, must understand the role they play in carrying out their jobs and implementing the marketing strategy. Everyone must do his or her part to ensure that customers are satisfied. All personnel within the company, both marketers and those who perform other functions, should recognize the tenet of customer orientation and service that underlies the marketing concept.

Like external marketing activities, internal marketing may involve market segmentation, product development, research, distribution and even public relations and sales promotion. The internal marketing framework is shown in Figure 15.8. As in external marketing, the marketing mix is used in the internal marketing approach to satisfy the needs of employees. For example, an organization may sponsor sales competitions to encourage sales personnel to boost their selling efforts. Some companies encourage employees to work for their companies' customers for a period of time, often while continuing to receive their regular salaries. This helps the employees, and ultimately the company, to better understand customers' needs and problems, enables them to learn valuable new skills and heightens their enthusiasm for their regular jobs. In addition, many companies use planning sessions, workshops, letters, formal reports and personal conversations as tools of internal distribution to ensure that employees understand the corporate mission, the organization's goals and the marketing strategy. The end result is more satisfied employees, and improved customer relations.

Internal marketing requires the acceptance of the need for improved internal communication, information sharing and liaison across business functions and managerial hierarchies.[36] The core requirements are:

- information sharing of marketing intelligence/market insight
- orientation sessions to familiarize staff with marketing strategies and marketing plans
- multi-functional team interaction

- formalized internal marketing communications campaigns
- debrief and feedback sessions
- incentivized staff motivation
- empowerment of line management to take ownership of problems
- the encouragement of 'success stories' to champion.

In order to exploit the internal market effectively, thought must be devoted to establishing communication channels, leadership qualities, associated resources, information and clear internally focused propositions and messages. All of this would routinely be undertaken for an external customer or target market, so why not within the business to ensure staff understanding and cooperation?

Controlling marketing activities

marketing control process
One that establishes performance standards, evaluates actual performance and reduces the differences between desired and actual performance

To achieve marketing objectives as well as general organizational goals, marketing managers must control marketing efforts effectively. The **marketing control process** consists of establishing performance standards, evaluating actual performance by comparing it with established standards, and reducing the differences between desired and actual performance, taking corrective action if necessary. This process helped Xerox to recover ground lost to competitors. Dunkin' Donuts has developed a programme to ensure consistency throughout its franchises. Dunkin' Donuts controls the quality of operations in its franchised units by having franchisees attend Dunkin' Donuts University. Owners and managers of Dunkin' Donuts outlets are required to take a six-week training course, covering everything from customer relations and marketing to production, including a test of making 140 dozen doughnuts in eight hours. As part of the test, an instructor selects six of the 1680 doughnuts made at random, to ascertain that they weigh around 350 grams (12 ounces) and measure just under 20 centimetres (eight inches) when stacked. The Dunkin' Donuts University was opened to guarantee uniformity in all aspects of the company's operations throughout the 1700 franchise units.[37]

Although the control function is a fundamental management activity, it has until recently received little attention in marketing. There are both formal and informal control systems in organizations. The formal marketing control process involves performance standards, evaluation of actual performance and corrective action to remedy shortfalls (see Figure 15.9). The informal control process, however, involves self-control, social or group control, and cultural control through acceptance of a company's value system. Which type of control system dominates depends on the environmental context of the business.[38]

Most well-run organizations monitor the roll-out of their marketing strategies and marketing plans. For example, Raytheon's senior managers hold quarterly review meetings with the business unit managers tasked with implementing the annually agreed marketing plans. At each meeting, problems in effectively actioning the plan or barriers impeding progress are highlighted and appropriate steps specified to remedy the problems. This may result in senior managers forcing others in the organization to comply with the plan's recommendations or reallocating resources as required. Often, the review meeting itself is sufficient motivation for the business unit managers to increase momentum. Implicit in this approach is the need to specify deliverables from the marketing strategy, marketing plan or marketing programme that may be assessed in order to determine the extent of successful implementation and the effectiveness of the marketing activity in the marketplace.

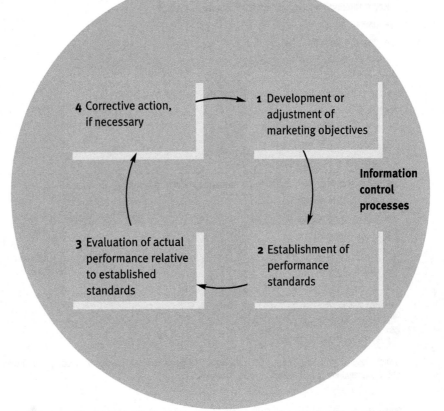

FIGURE 15.9
The marketing
control process

Establishing performance standards

Planning and controlling are closely linked because plans include statements about what is to be accomplished. For purposes of control, these statements function as performance standards. A

performance standard
An expected level of
performance against
which actual performance
can be compared

performance standard is an expected level of performance against which actual performance can be compared. Examples of performance standards might be the reduction of customers' complaints by 20 per cent, a monthly sales quota of £150 000, a 10 per cent increase per month in new customer accounts or an increase in a measure of brand awareness. Performance standards are also given in the form of budget accounts – that is, marketers are expected to achieve a certain objective without spending more than a given amount of resources.

Performance standards can relate to product quality and should be tied to organizational goals. Table 15.3 details the most frequently used performance standards adopted among the professional members of the UK's Chartered Institute of Marketing. A more recent addition to performance standards is that of value-based marketing, utilizing the concept of marketing shareholder value analysis.

Evaluating actual performance

To compare actual performance with performance standards, marketing managers must know what marketers within the company are doing and must have information about the activities of external organizations that provide the business with marketing assistance. Records of actual performance are compared with performance standards to determine whether a discrepancy exists and,

TABLE 15.3 Currently popular performance standards

Key marketing financial performance standards include:

- revenue growth
- return on investment (ROI)
- product profitability
- customer profitability
- earning before interest taxes depreciation and amortization (EBITDA)
- return on sales
- total return to shareholders
- return on capital employed
- sales per square metre (for retailers).

Leading non-financial marketing performance standards include:

- customer satisfaction
- delivery performance
- new customers gained
- market share
- customer loyalty
- customer dissatisfaction brand awareness
- lost customers
- price level achieved
- customer brand attitudes.

Source: adapted from Sally Dibb and Lyndon Simkin, *Marketing Briefs: a Revision and Study Guide* (Oxford: Elsevier, 2004); plus a survey of UK Chartered Institute of Marketing members' views.

if so, how much of one. For example, a sales person's actual sales are compared with his or her sales quota. If there is a significant negative discrepancy, the sales manager takes corrective action. A marketing research company may be contracted to produce quarterly surveys, providing the analyzed results within ten days of each survey's completion. If the report is late and the sampling or analysis inaccurate, the marketer will probably switch to an alternative supplier.

Taking corrective action

Marketing managers have several options for reducing a discrepancy between established performance standards and actual performance. They can take steps to improve actual performance, or they may review the performance standard and possibly redefine it. Changes in actual performance may require the marketing manager to use better methods of motivating marketing personnel or to find more effective techniques for coordinating marketing efforts. In order to prescribe corrective action, it is necessary to diagnose problems and investigate the challenges facing a company's marketers.

Requirements for an effective control process

A marketing manager should consider several requirements in creating and maintaining effective marketing control processes.[39] Effective control hinges on the quantity and quality of information available to the marketing manager and the speed at which it is received. The control process should be designed so that the flow of information is rapid enough to allow the marketing manager to quickly detect differences between actual and planned levels of performance. A single control procedure is not suitable for all types of marketing activity, and internal and environmental changes affect an organization's activities. Therefore, control procedures should be flexible enough to adjust to both varied activities and changes in the organization's situation. For the control process to be usable, its costs must be low relative to the costs that would arise if controls were lacking. Finally, the control process should be designed so that both managers and subordinates can understand it and its requirements.

Problems in controlling marketing activities

When marketing managers attempt to control marketing activities, they frequently run into several problems. Often, the information required to control marketing activities is unavailable or available only at a high cost. Even though marketing controls should be flexible enough to allow for environmental changes, the frequency, intensity and unpredictability of such changes may hamper effective control. In addition, the time lag between marketing activities and their effects limits a marketing manager's ability to measure the effectiveness of marketing activities.

Because marketing and other business activities overlap, marketing managers cannot determine the precise cost of marketing activities. Without an accurate measure of marketing costs, it is difficult to know if the effects of marketing activities are worth their expense. Marketing control may be difficult because it is very hard to develop exact performance standards for certain marketing personnel.

Methods of evaluating performance

There are specific methods for assessing and improving the effectiveness of a marketing strategy. A marketer should state in the marketing plan what a marketing strategy is supposed to accomplish. These statements should set forth performance standards, which are usually stated in terms of profits, sales, market share, brand awareness, customer satisfaction levels or the variables detailed in Table 15.3. Actual performance must be measured in similar terms so that comparisons are possible. This section describes sales analysis and marketing cost analysis, two general ways of evaluating the actual performance of marketing strategies. 'Softer' measures, such as brand awareness and customer satisfaction levels, are also important and feature in the performance standards adopted by marketing-led businesses. An emerging tool for assessing performance is also described in this section: marketing shareholder value analysis.

Sales analysis

sales analysis
The use of sales figures to evaluate a business's current performance

Sales analysis uses sales figures to evaluate a company's current performance. It is probably the most common method of evaluation, because sales data partially reflect the target market's reactions to a marketing mix and are often readily available, at least in aggregate form.

Marketers use current sales data to monitor the impact of current marketing efforts. However, that information alone is not enough. To provide useful analyses, current sales data must be compared with forecast sales, industry sales, specific competitors' sales or the costs incurred to achieve the sales volume. For example, knowing that a store attained a £600 000 sales volume this year does not tell management whether its marketing strategy has been successful. However, if managers know that expected sales were £550 000, they are then in a better position to determine the effectiveness of the company's marketing efforts. In addition, if they know that the marketing costs needed to achieve the £600 000 volume were 12 per cent less than budgeted, they are in an even better position to analyze their marketing strategy precisely.

sales measurements
Data regarding sales transactions that are used to analyze performance, usually in terms of cash volume or market share

Sales measurements Although there are several types of **sales measurement**, the basic unit of measurement is the sales transaction. A sales transaction results in a customer order for a specified quantity of an organization's product sold under specified terms by a particular sales person or sales group on a certain date. Many organizations record these bits of information about their transactions. With such a record, a company can analzse sales in terms of cash or sales volume, or market share.

Companies frequently use cash volume sales analysis because currency is a common denominator of sales, costs and profits. However, price increases and decreases affect total sales figures. A marketing manager who uses cash volume analysis should factor out the effects of price changes.

market share
The company's sales of a product stated as a percentage of industry sales of that product

A company's **market share** is the company's sales of a product stated as a percentage of industry sales of that product. For example, KP, Golden Wonder and Walkers account for around 70 per cent of the UK savoury snacks market. In the carbonated drinks sector, Coca-Cola has a leading share by volume.[40] Market share analysis permits a company to compare its marketing strategy with competitors' strategies. The primary reason for using market share analysis is to estimate whether sales changes have resulted from the company's marketing strategy or from uncontrollable environmental forces. When a company's sales volume declines but its share of the market stays the same, the marketer can assume that industry sales declined – because of some uncontrollable factors – and that this decline was reflected in the company's sales. However, if a company experiences a decline in both sales and market share, it should consider the possibility that its marketing strategy is not effective. The *competitive positions proforma* analysis described in Chapter 2 of *Marketing Essentials* incorporates market share analysis to infer the relative performance of the competitive set within a market segment.

Even though market share analysis can be helpful in evaluating the performance of a marketing strategy, the user must interpret results cautiously. When attributing a sales decline to uncontrollable factors, a marketer must keep in mind that such factors do not affect all companies in the industry equally. Not all companies in an industry have the same objectives, and some change their objectives from one year to the next. Changes in the objectives of one company can affect the market shares of one or all companies in that industry. For example, if a competitor increases promotional efforts significantly or drastically reduces prices to increase market share, a company could lose market share despite a well-designed marketing strategy. Within an industry, the entrance of new companies or the demise of established ones also affects a specific business's market share, and market share analysts should attempt to account for these effects. KFC, for example, probably re-evaluated its marketing strategies when McDonald's introduced its own chicken products. Most fast-food companies revised their strategies and performance expectations in the light of media attention about obesity problems and drives for healthier eating.

Marketing cost analysis

Although sales analysis is critical for evaluating the effectiveness of a marketing strategy, it gives only part of the picture. A marketing strategy that successfully generates sales may also be extremely costly. To obtain a complete picture, a company must know the marketing costs associated with using a given strategy to achieve a certain sales level. **Marketing cost analysis** breaks down and classifies costs to determine which are associated with specific marketing activities. By comparing the costs of previous marketing activities with results generated, a marketer can better allocate the business's marketing resources in the future. Marketing cost analysis lets a company evaluate the effectiveness of an ongoing or recent marketing strategy by comparing sales achieved and costs incurred. By pinpointing exactly where a company is experiencing high costs,

marketing cost analysis
The breakdown and classification of costs to determine which are associated with specific marketing activities

this form of analysis can help isolate profitable or unprofitable customer segments, products or geographic areas.

For example, the market share of Komatsu, a Japanese construction equipment manufacturer, began to decline in the United States when prices increased because of the high yen value. Komatsu responded by developing an equal joint venture with Dresser Industries, making it the second largest company in this industry. The joint venture with Dresser allowed Komatsu to shift a large amount of its final assembly to the United States, to Dresser plants that had been running at 50 per cent capacity. By using Dresser's unused capacity and existing US plants, Komatsu avoided the start-up costs of new construction and gained an immediate manufacturing presence in the United States.[41] This cost control tactic enabled Komatsu to use price more effectively as a marketing variable to compete with industry leader Caterpillar.

In some organizations, personnel in other functional areas – such as production or accounting – perceive marketers as primarily concerned with generating sales, regardless of the costs incurred. Marketers often do commit a large proportion of resources to launching products, achieving distribution or creating promotional campaigns. By conducting cost analyses, marketers can counter this criticism and put themselves in a better position to demonstrate how marketing activities contribute to generating profits. Even though hiring a sports figure such as David Beckham is costly, in many sectors sales goals cannot be reached without large expenditures for promotion. Many advertisers believe that using celebrities helps to increase sales. Research shows that the public are good at identifying which personalities are linked to advertised brands. Ultimately, cost analysis should show if promotion costs are effective in increasing sales.

A robust marketing plan is not complete without a detailed budget which, when balanced with the sales forecast, marketing analyses, strategic thinking and detailed marketing mix programmes, explains the required marketing spend. In effect, a sound marketing plan should offer a cost – benefit analysis in terms of setting the anticipated costs of rolling out the proposed marketing programmes against the expected sales levels and revenue gains. Marketing cost analysis is a necessary facet for managing a well run marketing department.

The task of determining marketing costs is often complex and difficult. Simply ascertaining the costs associated with marketing a product is rarely adequate. Marketers must usually determine the marketing costs of serving specific geographic areas, market segments or even specific customers. The ABC sales: contribution analysis outlined in Chapter 9 is a useful tool in this endeavour.

A first step in determining the costs is to examine accounting records. Most accounting systems classify costs into **natural accounts** – such as rent, salaries, office supplies and utilities – which are based on how the money was actually spent. Unfortunately, many natural accounts do not help explain what marketing functions were performed through the expenditure of those funds. It does little good, for example, to know that £80 000 is spent for rent each year. The analyst has no way of knowing whether the money is spent for the rental of production, storage or sales facilities. Therefore, marketing cost analysis usually requires some of the costs in natural accounts to be reclassified into **marketing function accounts**, which indicate the function performed through the expenditure of funds. Common marketing function accounts are transport, storage, order processing, sales, advertising, sales promotion, marketing research, consultancy and customer credit. Most companies allocate out-goings to cost codes for auditing purposes.

Natural accounts can be reclassified into marketing function accounts, as shown in the simplified example in Table 15.4. Note that a few natural accounts, such as advertising, can be reclassified easily into functional accounts because they do not have to be split across several accounts. For most of the natural accounts, however, marketers must develop criteria for assigning them to the various functional accounts. For example, the number of square metres of floor space used was the criterion for dividing the rental costs in Table 15.4 into functional accounts. In some instances, a specific marketing cost is incurred

natural accounts
The classification of costs based on how money was actually spent

marketing function accounts
A method of indicating the function performed through the expenditure of funds

TABLE 15.4 Reclassification of natural accounts into functional accounts

Profit and loss statement		Functional accounts					
Sales	£250 000						
Cost of goods sold	45 000	**Advertising**	**Personal selling**	**Transport**	**Storage**	**Marketing research**	**Non-marketing**
Gross profit	205 000						
Expenses (natural accounts)							
Rent	£ 14 000		£ 7 000		£6 000		£ 1 000
Salaries	72 000	£ 12 000	32 000	£7 000		£1 000	20 000
Supplies	4 000	1 500	1 000			1 000	500
Advertising	16 000	16 000					
Freight	4 000			2 000			2 000
Taxes	2 000				200		1 800
Insurance	1 000				600		400
Interest	3 000						3 000
Bad debts	6 000						6 000
Total	£ 122 000	£29 500	£40 000	£9 000	£6 800	£2 000	£34 700
Net profit	£ 83 000						

to perform several functions. A packaging cost, for example, could be considered a production function, a distribution function, a promotional function or all three. The marketing cost analyst must reclassify such costs across multiple functions.

Marketing shareholder value analysis

Building on the rationale for marketing cost analysis, the concept of value-based marketing has emerged in recent years. **Value-based marketing** is the inclusion of the value of a marketing strategy and programme in an organization's financial analysis of shareholder value. To achieve this, **marketing shareholder value analysis (MSVA)** divides the estimation of the value to the business created by a marketing strategy into two components:

1 the present value of cash flows during the strategizing and planning phases

2 the continuing value following implementation of the strategy.

MSVA provides a means of demonstrating the contribution of marketing to the organization's financial performance. This also enables marketing assets, such as marketing knowledge, brands, customer loyalty and strategic relationships, to be included in the shareholder value analysis (SVA), as each can be shown to have quantifiable financial value to the business. MSVA enables marketers to communicate the expected results of their marketing strategies in terms comprehended by top management and investors. The analysis supports marketers' requests for budgets, notably those traditionally most at risk of cost cutting in times of reduced demand, such as advertising and marketing research.

In many organizations, the lack of a true marketing orientation has allowed the finance function to take over the notion of shareholder value analysis (SVA).[42] According to leading marketing strategist Peter Doyle, by focusing on short-term profits and ignoring intangible assets – such as brand awareness and customer satisfaction – traditional accounting practices have marginalized marketing activity. However, SVA can in fact bring the core strategic drivers of marketing to the fore in the form of MSVA. Marketing has struggled to quantify results in order to demonstrate its value. By adopting MSVA, marketers can reverse this state of affairs. MSVA can help justify marketing actions in terms of their propensity to bring financial value to the business. MSVA offers marketing a greater theoretical base and encourages profitable marketing investment. MSVA also penalizes arbitrary cuts to the marketing budget, something encountered regularly by marketers when a company's fortunes decline suddenly.

Performance measures

marketing performance
The assessment of the effectiveness of marketing programmes to implement recommended marketing strategies, fulfil corporate financial expectations and achieve the required levels of customer satisfaction

The evaluation of **marketing performance** – the assessment of the effectiveness of marketing programmes to implement recommended marketing strategies, fulfil corporate financial expectations and achieve the required levels of customer satisfaction – is a necessary control mechanism in the marketing process. Table 15.3 presented some popular performance measures adopted by marketers to assess overall markets, specific segments or product lines. Most UK companies are notoriously short term in their thinking, focusing on profitability as their over-riding measure. Other financial measures include return on investment, return on capital employed and, for retailers, **sales per square metre** of selling space. In business generating a lot of cash, **EBITDA** is important: earnings before interest, taxes, depreciation and amortization. Units produced and units sold are included as measures by most manufacturers, leading to an assessment of production capacity utilization. Market share is a vital criterion for judging performance.

sales per square metre
A financial measure retailers might use to assess marketing performance

While it is, unquestionably, important for businesses to be financially viable – making adequate profits to be able to fund future investments in production, people, new products, new target markets and so forth – increasingly marketers have accepted the need to evaluate performance on additional, more customer oriented measures. Marketing aims to satisfy customers, so it is sensible to monitor customer satisfaction. A qualitative measure of marketing performance, assessing **customer satisfaction** involves surveying customers' perceptions and expectations over time in order to determine the effectiveness of the marketing programme in servicing their needs. Over time, such surveys should reveal an improvement in customer satisfaction levels, otherwise it could be argued that the marketing strategy and programme are failing to fully address target customer needs and expectations. Most hotel companies operate room card surveys of guest satisfaction in order to monitor customers' experiences and improve the performance of their staff, services and facilities. A measure of **brand awareness** is also monitored by a growing number of marketers, usually through qualitative marketing research surveys, to ensure that their marketing programmes are effectively bringing their brands and products to their target market's attention. While such tracking involves qualitative marketing research, measures of customer satisfaction and brand awareness should be integral to a business's assessment of performance, alongside the important traditional financial performance measures.

EBITDA
The acronym for earning before interest taxes depreciation and amortization

customer satisfaction
A qualitative measure of marketing performance that involves surveying customers over time

brand awareness
A qualitative measure of marketing performance that determines whether a company's brands capture the attention of their target markets

Marketing communications is a major part of marketers' activity and accounts for a significant proportion of the marketing budget. Performance in the promotional mix, however, has taxed experts for decades and there remain few proven objective solutions to determining the value of promotional spend to the business's overall fortunes. It is possible in public relations to use a **clippings service** to count the frequency of mentions of a specific brand or company in selected media, but this approach fails to assess the positive/negative mix of citations and cannot extrapolate to draw conclusions relating to sales gains resulting specifically from this PR activity. 'Hits' on a company's website are counted, but do these lead to sales or an enhanced corporate reputation? If an order is placed via the Internet a link can be shown, but if not it is difficult to demonstrate a causal relationship between the website and sales. Even if an order is placed via the Internet, it is possible that the customer was in fact responding primarily to a press or TV advertisement or to an earlier in-store demonstration. It is possible to track YouTube hits or Twitter follower numbers, but again, it is still not evident whether such digital activity led to an actual sale or order. Sponsorship agencies monitor the awareness of clients' brands when linked to sporting events or the performing arts, but cannot prove that such awareness leads directly to increased sales of products, better profitability or rising market share.

clippings service
A service that counts the frequency of mentions of a specific brand or company in selected media

Salesforce managers assess individual sales personnel in terms of the ratio of calls to orders. In addition, the salesforce is directly involved in the selling process and instantly judges its own performance. What stands for a good ratio of orders to calls is still a subjective assessment. Sales promotions are perhaps the safest to measure as they generally require customers to redeem coupons and vouchers or submit competition applications, all of which may be counted. However, subjective judgement is still used in determining what constitutes a 'good' redemption rate. Most problematic is the assessment of advertising effectiveness. This is unfortunate as advertising often accounts for the largest individual proportion of the marketing budget. It is possible to monitor target audience awareness of advertising but not to prove that exposure to a specific advertisement has led to a specific sale. At the moment, there are no easy solutions to this dilemma, yet marketers must attempt to assess the performance of their activities, seeking to validate their promotional mix spending. The tools described here are far from perfect but they demonstrate a willingness to assess promotional effectiveness. Many businesses, unfortunately, fail to utilize even these simplistic tools.[43]

Ultimately, a well-managed, customer-oriented company should use a mix of financial and qualitative measures, such as those listed in Table 15.3, to judge its performance and the effectiveness of its marketing. A company should adopt a balanced set of performance measures, mixing the short-term view of profitability with the often longer-term perspective of market share gains. It often requires considerable resources to increase market share at the expense of rivals, which may reduce short-term profitability. However, market share increases are likely to bring longer-term security and rewards. In addition to the financial performance measures, marketers should insist on being assessed on dimensions such as customer retention, customer satisfaction and brand awareness. If marketing programmes are effective, these three customer-oriented criteria should all show signs of improvement. Whatever the selected criteria for assessing marketing performance, it is essential that marketers incorporate performance monitoring within their control and management processes.

Summary

In order to manipulate the marketing mix to create marketing programmes matching target market needs and achieve organizational goals, a company must address fundamental strategic decisions. To expedite this process and to set appropriate goals, many companies use marketing planning.

Marketing planning is a systematic process that involves assessing marketing opportunities and resources, determining marketing objectives and developing a full plan for implementation and control. A core output of marketing planning is the *marketing plan,* a document or blueprint containing the requirements for a company's marketing activity. The marketing planning process involves (1) analyzing the marketplace, (2) modifying the recommended marketing strategy accordingly and (3) developing detailed marketing programmes designed to implement the specified marketing strategy. The *marketing planning cycle* is a cyclical process of planning and feedback that allows for revision. Most companies update their plans annually, typically with a three-year focus. However, *short-, medium-* and *long-range plans* are available.

A key part of the marketing plan is the *marketing objective,* a statement of what is to be accomplished through marketing activities. Objectives should be measurable, indicate a timeframe and be consistent with a company's overall organizational goals.

The heart of the marketing plan is the analysis section. The elements analyzed include the marketing environment and market trends, customers, competitive positions and competitors' strategies, plus the company's capabilities to respond to marketing opportunities, the appropriateness of its product and brand portfolio and an analysis of financial performance. A *SWOT analysis,* which identifies strengths, weaknesses, opportunities and threats, helps to produce realistic and meaningful marketing recommendations.

The strategy recommendations within the marketing plan examine the opportunities to be pursued and existing activities to be supported, associated target market priorities, the basis for competing, differential advantage and desired brand or product positioning. Marketing strategy guides the company's direction in relationships between customers and competitors. Marketing programmes implement the recommended marketing strategy. They discuss each element of the marketing mix in detail and the allocation of schedules and tasks, personnel, budgets, responsibilities and monitoring of ongoing performance. Without such details of the operationalization of the marketing plan, it is unlikely the plan's recommendations would be implemented.

Marketers produce marketing plans for each business unit, product group or target market, and a synthesized overview plan for the board of the company. Usually, cross-functional teams are involved. In companies embarking on marketing planning for the first time, there is a steep learning curve and the required marketing analyses are very invasive. After three years, the planning process becomes routinized. External consultants are often brought in to support a senior management team's initial attempts to develop a marketing plan.

Marketing implementation, a process that involves activities to put marketing strategies into action, is an important part of the marketing management process. The *requisites for implementation* include process, skill, leadership, empowerment, communication, timing, information, resource and participation decisions. Failure to address these issues prior to embarking on marketing strategy formulation or the development of a marketing plan may result in the failure to produce recommendations that are implemented.

To help ensure effective implementation, marketing managers must consider why the intended marketing strategies do not always turn out as expected. The *intended strategies* often differ from the *realized strategies* because of the three problems of implementation: marketing strategy and implementation are related; they are constantly evolving; the responsibility for them is separated. Marketing managers must also consider other vital components of implementation – resources, systems, people, leadership and shared goals – to ensure the proper implementation of marketing strategies.

Implementation is an important part of the marketing management process. Proper implementation of a marketing plan depends on internal marketing to motivate personnel who perform marketing activities, effective communication within the marketing unit and the coordination of marketing activities. Managers can motivate personnel by linking rewards, both financial and non-financial, to organizational goals. A company's communication system must allow the marketing manager to communicate with high-level management, with managers of other functional areas in the company and with personnel involved in marketing activities both inside and outside the organization. Finally, marketing managers must coordinate the activities of marketing personnel, and integrate these activities with those in other areas of the company and with the marketing efforts of personnel in external organizations.

Related approaches that organizations may use to help facilitate marketing implementation include *relationship marketing, and internal marketing*. In relationship marketing, the focus is on winning and keeping customers by maintaining links between marketing, quality and customer service. This requires a company to satisfy not only customers but also those audiences in the *five markets model of relationship marketing:* referral, supplier, employee recruitment markets, influencer and internal markets. *Internal marketing* is the application of marketing internally within the company, with programmes of communication and guidance targeted at internal audiences to develop responsiveness and a unified sense of purpose among employees. It is a philosophy for managing human resources with a marketing perspective so that all members of the marketing organization understand and accept their respective roles in implementing the marketing strategy.

The *marketing control process* consists of establishing performance standards, evaluating actual performance by comparing it with established standards and reducing the difference between desired and actual performance. *Performance standards,* which are established in the planning process, are expected levels of performance against which actual performance can be compared. In evaluating actual performance, marketing managers must know what marketers within the business are doing and must have information about the activities of external organizations that provide the company with marketing assistance. Then actual performance is compared with performance standards. Marketers must determine whether a discrepancy exists and, if so, whether it requires corrective action, such as changing the performance standards or improving actual performance.

Effective marketing control hinges on the quantity and quality of information and the speed at which it is received. The control of marketing activities is not a simple task. Problems encountered include environmental changes, time lags between marketing activities and their effects, and difficulty in determining the costs of marketing activities. In addition to these, it may be hard to develop exact performance standards for marketing personnel.

Control of marketing strategy can be achieved through *sales* and *marketing cost analyses. Sales measurements* are usually analyzed in terms of either cash volume or *market share.* For a sales analysis to be effective, it must compare current sales performance with either forecast company sales, industry sales, specific competitors' sales or the costs incurred to generate the current sales volume. A sales analysis can be performed on the company's total sales, or the total sales can be disaggregated and analyzed by product, geographic area, sales person or customer type.

Marketing cost analysis involves an examination of accounting records and, frequently, a reclassification of *natural accounts* into *marketing function accounts.*

Value-based marketing is the inclusion of the value of a marketing strategy and marketing activity in an organization's financial analysis of shareholder value. *Marketing shareholder value analysis (MSVA)* enables marketing strategies and programmes to be incorporated within this financial appraisal of shareholder value. The value to the business of a marketing strategy is estimated, based on (1) the present value of the business during the strategizing and planning stage, and (2) the continuing value of the business after the plans have been implemented and actioned.

Performance measures popular in evaluating *marketing performance* include assessing overall markets, specific segments or product lines in terms of financial profitability, contribution or return on investment; market share; *customer satisfaction* levels; and qualitative measures of customer *brand awareness.* Retail marketers additionally favour a measure of *sales per square metre* of store selling space. *EBITDA* is important in businesses generating a lot of cash. A *clippings service* can be used to count the frequency of mentions of a particular brand or company in the media: there are many measurements possible like this, covering most aspects of marketing mix activity.

Key links

This chapter, examining marketing planning and sales forecasting, should be read in conjunction with:

- Chapter 1, on scoping out the marketing process
- Chapter 2, which deals with exploring the role of marketing planning within marketing strategy

Important terms

Marketing planning
Marketing plan
Marketing planning cycle
Short-range plans
Medium-range plans
Long-range plans
Marketing objective
SWOT analysis
Marketing implementation
Requisites for implementation
Intended strategy
Realized strategy
Relationship marketing
Five markets model of relationship marketing
Internal marketing
Marketing control process
Performance standard
Sales analysis
Sales measurements
Market share
Marketing cost analysis
Natural accounts
Marketing function accounts
Value-based marketing
Marketing shareholder value analysis (MSVA)
Marketing performance
Sales per square metre
Customer satisfaction
Brand awareness
EBITDA
Clippings service

Discussion and review questions

1 What is marketing planning? How does it help companies address their marketplaces better?

2 What is the difference between a marketing plan and a corporate plan?

3 What is the timespan for a marketing plan?

4 What are the main tasks involved with producing a marketing plan?

5 In what ways do marketing environment forces affect marketing planning? Give some examples.

6 What is a SWOT analysis? How does it lead to an understanding of realistic marketing opportunities?

7 Why is it important to seek a differential advantage?

8 Why does it take three years before the use of marketing planning typically is routinized in a company?

9 In what ways does marketing planning help with establishing controls for a marketing function?

10 What are the implementation requisites for marketing strategies and plans?

11 Why is motivation of marketing personnel important in implementing marketing plans?

12 How does communication help in implementing marketing plans?

13 What attributes distinguish relationship marketing from transaction-based marketing?

14 What is internal marketing? Why is it important in implementing marketing strategies?

15 What are the major steps of the marketing control process?

16 Discuss the major problems in controlling marketing activities.

17 What is a sales analysis? What makes it an effective control tool?

18 What performance measures are favoured by marketers?

19 Why should more than one performance metric be adopted by an organization to assess its marketing outcomes?

Recommended readings

Blythe, J. and Megicks, P., *Marketing Planning: Strategy, Environment and Context* (FT/Prentice-Hall, 2010).

Dibb, S. and Simkin, L., *Marketing Planning* (Cengage, 2008).

Dibb, S., Simkin, L. and Bradley, J., *The Marketing Planning Workbook: Effective Marketing for Marketing Managers* (Thomson Learning, 1998).

Gilligan, C. and Wilson, R.M.S., *Strategic Marketing Planning* (Oxford: Butterworth-Heinemann, 2009).

McDonald, M.H. and Wilson, H., *Marketing Plans: How To Prepare Them, How To Use Them* (John Wiley, 2011).

Wood, M.B., *Essential Guide To Marketing Planning* (FT/Prentice-Hall, 2010).

Doyle, P., *Value-Based Marketing* (Wiley, 2000).

Nikbin, D., *Internal Marketing and Strategy Implementation: The impact of Internal Marketing Practices on Employees Satisfaction and Commitment in Implementing Firms Strategic Orientations* (LAP Lambert, 2010).

Internet exercise

A core task in developing a strong marketing plan is the analysis of competitors. There are many ways of finding information about competitors, as described in Chapters 2 and 7. One useful source of intelligence about rivals is to review their websites. Marketers look for the strengths cited by brands and for products on their websites. Additionally, by examining a range of competitors' websites, it is possible to infer their deficiencies. This is achieved by identifying themes popular on many rivals' websites but ignored on only one or two.

Take the example of food processors, mixers and blenders. Look at the websites for a selection of leading brands, such as Breville, Dualit, Kenwood, KitchenAid, Magimix, Morphy Richards, Moulinex and Philips. What are the respective apparent strengths and weaknesses of these brands and products?

Applied mini-case

Despite various economic blips and global troubles, many consumers still seek adventure and escapism, which is good news for theme park operators such as Disney or Alton Towers. In the UK, Alton Towers aims to maintain its market leadership, and invests continually in new rides and facilities. It opened a £20 million holiday village next to the park – for the leisure market and the growing business conference market – and spent £10 million on the leading white-knuckle Oblivion ride. It now promotes its rides, waterpark, spa and hotels as a resort destination. The strategy is to attract new visitors to the park, from the UK and from continental Europe, while encouraging repeat visits from current users. Key target customers are young adults aged 15 to 24, families with children, school parties and, increasingly, the corporate sector. Business clients use Alton Towers for sales incentive schemes and corporate events, such as AGMs, product launches or salesforce parties. The corporate sector was a leading reason for developing good-quality on-site hotel accommodation. Originally conceived as a day-tripper, family-oriented park, Alton Towers has monitored demographic changes and competitor activity, and has continually modified its rides, amenities and services to reflect the requirements of its evolving target market segments. The growth of corporate clients – for conferences and away-days – reflects this constant updating of the theme park's marketing strategy and associated marketing planning.

Question

In producing a marketing plan for a theme park such as Alton Towers, what would be the most important elements of the marketing planning process? Explain why.

Dell plans for a new future

Case study

Dell originally made its name selling personal computers directly to customers through its catalogues, phone orders and more recently, websites. Over the years, it has expanded into related product lines while battling aggressive rivals such as Hewlett-Packard and Apple. A few years ago, Dell decided to enter the world of consumer electronics, hoping to drive an ever large portion of revenues and profits from a wider mix of products for use beyond the home office. Flat screen television was one consumer electronics market the company targeted aggressively, seeking to take on Philips, Panasonic and Sony.

With a long history of marketing technology-based products, Dell has become a well-known US brand. Management saw the brand as a strength and set out to exploit it by marketing new flat-screen televisions, tiny digital music players, and other non-computer products. 'We've come out of nowhere to be the number three consumer brand in the United States in less than five years, while Coca-Cola has been doing it for 100 years,' said Dell's general manager of consumer business for the United States, adding, 'We're not in this to be number three. Number one is the only target around here'.

However, despite considerable research and marketing investment, Dell's consumer electronics strategy did not succeed. In fact, it was not long before the company reversed course, pulling back from diversifications to refocus on its core computer expertise. Indeed, many computer sector observers perceived that the diversification had deflected Dell from its core market, enabling computer competitors such as Acer to make inroads.

Unfortunately for Dell, it had launched its consumer electronics items just as major technological developments were changing how consumers bought and used such products. Dell's affordable handheld computers initially sparked a flurry of customer interest, but instigated a price war with Hewlett-Packard as the two fought for market share. However, when Apple, Samsung, Nokia and others began marketing new generation smartphones with built-in computer capabilities and multiple entertainment functions, customers found those offerings more appealing than the kind of stand-alone handhelds that Dell offered.

In addition, Dell was caught in the crossfire of intense competition. At the start of its consumer electronics initiative, the company introduced the *Dell Digital Jukebox*, and the *Dell Music Store*, putting it on a competitive collision course with Apple's popular iPods and iTunes store. Apple had so much momentum that Dell discontinued its own brand of music players and instead resells products made by Samsung and other manufacturers. This allows Dell to satisfy customer demand for certain consumer electronics items but without the expense of researching, developing, manufacturing and marketing the products under the Dell name.

Although Dell is not looking to pioneer revolutionary new lines for early adopters, today the company is expanding into proven markets by introducing products that align with consumer demand. For instance, Dell formed a mobile device division to create products such as mobile phones and other portable devices. After two years of research, Dell entered into an agreement with AT&T to carry its Mini 3 Smart Phone that uses Google's Android software, providing an entry into the growing smartphone market. See **www.dell.com/us** for an overview of Dell's full range of activities. Meanwhile, by remaining innovative in its product designs, Dell continues to be a major player in the computer industry. Moving away from its traditional policy of only selling directly to customers, Dell began distributing its brand of computers, monitors, printers and accessories through WalMart, PC World, Staples office supply stores and other retailers around the world.

The company is also polishing its brand by improving customer service, an especially important step as PC sales grow more slowly throughout the industry and competitors dig in to defend market share. Dell's relentless cost cutting had damaged its ability to handle technical questions and complaints, which in turn reduces customer satisfaction scores. Dell is rebuilding relationships by increasing its service budget and encouraging customers to have their say.

Dell has been forced to re-think its strategy, re-do its marketing plans and execute a whole new set of marketing programmes. Forecasting and planning have been pivotal to reshaping its strategy, informed by market insights and smarter awareness of customers' expectations and changing requirements.

Questions for discussion

1 To what extent should planning have helped Dell to avoid the problems encountered when it first diversified into consumer electronics?

2 In what stage of the product life cycle are personal computers? What are the implications for marketing planning in Dell?

3 Explain how marketing planning might underpin Dell's ongoing selection of opportunities and target markets.

Notes

Chapter 1

1 Kohli, A. and Jaworski, B. J. (1990) 'Market orientation: the construct, research propositions and managerial potential', *Journal of Marketing* 54(2):1–18.

2 Lynch, J. (1994) in Norman Hart (ed.) *Effective Industrial Marketing,* London: Kogan Page.

3 Dibb, S., Simkin, L. and Bradley J. (1996) *The Marketing Planning Workbook,* London: International Thomson Business Publishing.

4 Munro, H. J., Brodie, R. J. and Coviello, N. E. (1997) 'Understanding contemporary marketing: development of a classification scheme', *Journal of Marketing Management* 13(6):501(22).

5 Kotler, P. (1988) *Marketing Management: Analysis, Planning, Implementation and Control*, 6th ed., Englewood Cliffs, NJ: Prentice-Hall, p. 6.

6 Ferrell, O. C. and Lucas, G. (1987) 'An evaluation of progress in the development of a definition of marketing', *Journal of the Academy of Marketing Science* 15(3):12–23.

7 Gronoos, G. (1989) 'Defining marketing: a market oriented approach', *European Journal of Marketing* 23(1):52(9); Srivastava, R. K., Shervani, T. and Fahey, L. (1998)'Market-based assets and shareholder value: a framework for analysis', *Journal of Marketing* 62(1):2–18.

8 Wood, L. M. (1996) 'Added value: marketing basics?' *Journal of Marketing Management* 12 (8):735(21); Robertson, T. (1994) 'New developments in marketing: a European perspective', *European Management Journal* 12(4):362(4).

9 Sheth, J. N. and Sisodia, R. (1995)'More than ever before, marketing is under fire to account for what it spends', *Marketing Management* 4(2): 13–14.

10 Gronoos, G. (1994) 'From marketing mix to relationship marketing; towards a paradigm shift in marketing', *Management Decision* 32(2):4–20; Payne, A., Christopher, M., Clark, M. and Peck, H. (1998) *Relationship Marketing for Competitive Advantage,* Oxford: Butterworth-Heinemann.

11 Saren, M., et al., *Critical Marketing: Defining the Field*; Tadajewski, M. and Brownlie, D. *Critical Marketing: Issues in Contemporary Marketing*.

12 Polonsky, M. J., et al. (2003) 'The Harm Chain', *Marketing Theory*, 3(3):345–64; Smith, C., et al. (2010) 'Marketing's consequences', *Business Ethics Quarterly* 20(4):617–41.

13 Laczniak, G. R. and Lusch, R. F. (1986) 'Environment and strategy in 1995: a survey of high-level executives', *Journal of Consumer Marketing* 3(2):28.

14 Dibb, S. and Simkin, L. (1996) *The Marketing Segmentation Workbook*, London: Thomson.

Chapter 2

1 Weitz, B. A. and Wensley, R. (1988) *Readings in Strategic Marketing*, Chicago, IL: Dryden.

2 Varadarajan, P. R. (1999) 'Strategy content and process perspectives revisited', *Journal of the Academy of Marketing Science* 27(1):88–100.

3 Homas, G., Hult, M., Cravens, D. W. and Sheth, J. (2001) 'Competitive advantage in the global marketplace: a focus on marketing strategy', *Journal of Business Research* 51(1):1–3.

4 Dibb, S., Simkin, L. and Bradley, J. (1996) *The Marketing Planning Workbook*, London: Thomson.

5 Abell, D. F. and Hammond, J. S. (1979) *Strategic Market Planning*, Englewood Cliffs, NJ: Prentice-Hall, p. 10.

6 Varadarajan, P. R., Clark, T. and Pride, W. (1990) 'Determining your company's destiny', working paper, Texas A&M University.

7 Peter, J. P. and Donnelly, J. H., Jr (1991) *A Preface to Marketing Management*, 5th ed., Homewood, IL: Irwin, p. 9.

8 Adapted from Peter and Donnelly, *A Preface to Marketing Management*, pp. 8–12.

9 Abell, D. F. (1978) 'Strategic windows', *Journal of Marketing* 42(3):21.

10 Abell and Hammond (see note 5 above), p. 213.

11 Fahey, L., King, W. K. and Naraganan, V. K. (1981) 'Environmental scanning and forecasting in strategic planning – the state of the art', *Long Range Planning* 14(1):38.

12 Georgaff, D. M. and Mundick, R. G. (1986) 'Managers' guide to forecasting', *Harvard Business Review*, January–February, 120.

13 Kotler, P. (1980) 'Strategic planning and the marketing process', *Business*, May–June, 6–7.

14 Piercy, N. (1992) *Market-Led Strategic Change*, Oxford: Butterworth-Heinemann Ltd.

15 Di Benedetto, C. A. (2003) 'The relationship between strategic type and firm capabilities in Chinese firms', *International Marketing Review* 20(5):514–34.

16 Kerin, R. A., Majahan, V. and Varadarajan, P. R. (1990) *Contemporary Perspectives on Strategic*

Marketing Planning, Boston, MA: Allyn & Bacon.

17 Grover, R. (1989) 'When Columbia met Sony ... a love story', *Business Week*, 9 October, 44–45.

18 Hooley, G. and Saunders, J. (1993) *Competitive Positioning: The Key to Market Success*, London: Prentice-Hall.

19 Varadarajan, P. R. (2002) 'Marketing strategy and the Internet: an organizing framework', *Journal of the Academy of Marketing Science* 30(4):296–313.

20 Ries, A. and Trout, J. (1986) *Marketing Warfare*, New York: McGraw-Hill; Saunders, J. (1987) 'Marketing and competitive success', in M. Baker (ed.) *The Marketing Book*, London: Heinemann.

21 Takada, H. (1998) 'Multiple time series analysis of competitive marketing behaviour', *Journal of Business Research* 43(2):97–107.

22 Doyle, P. (1994) *Marketing Management and Strategy*, London: Prentice-Hall.

23 Aaker, D. A. (1988) *Strategic Market Management*, 2nd ed., New York: Wiley, p. 35.

24 Saunders, J. (1987) 'Marketing and competitive success', in M. J. Baker (ed.) *The Marketing Book*, London: Heinemann, pp. 10–28.

Chapter 3

1 Becherer, R. C. and Maurer, J. G. (1997) 'The moderating effect of environmental variables on the entrepreneurial and marketing orientation of entrepreneur-led firms', *Entrepreneurship Theory and Practice* 22(1):47–58; Achrol, R. S. (1997) 'Changes in the theory of interorganizational relations in marketing: toward a network paradigm', *Journal of the Academy of Marketing Science* 25(1):56–71.

2 Kotler, P. (1986) 'Megamarketing', *Harvard Business Review*, March–April, 117–24.

3 *Britain 1990: An Official Handbook* (1990) London: Central Office of Information.

4 Plummer, J. (1974) 'The concept of application of life style segmentation', *Journal of Marketing* 38(1):34.

5 *The IBA Code of Advertising Standards and Practice* (1977) London: Independent Broadcasting Authority, December, p. 3. (The IBA is now the ITC.)

6 Bremner, B. (1989) 'A new sales pitch: the environment', *Business Week*, 24 July, 50.

7 Knight, R. and Dimmler, E. (1989) 'The greening of Europe's industries', *U.S. News & World Report*, 5 June, 45–46.

8 Reprinted by permission from Herbert Simon (1973) 'Technology and environment', *Management Science* 19(10):1110–21. Copyright 1973, The Institute of Management Sciences.

9 Business Link, http://www.businesslink.gov.uk/bdotg/action/detail?itemId=1075422931&type=RESOURCES, 1 March 2011.

10 Accenture Interactive, https://microsite.accenture.com/Accenture_Interactive/Pages/AI_PaidSearch_Digital_Marketing.aspx?c=mul_gdailfelpsgs_0610&n=g_Accenture_Digital_Marketing/a_0_k/digital_marketing&KW=4770b756-7b9c-2868-c21b-0000459ae40b, 1 March 2011.

11 Mobile Marketing Association, www.mmaglobal.com, 1 March 2011.

12 Bradley, A., www.gartnerinsight.com, 1 March 2011.

13 Alderson, W. (1965) *Dynamic Marketing Behavior*, Homewood, IL: Irwin, pp. 195–97.

14 Porter, M. (1980) *Competitive Strategy*, New York: The Free Press.

15 Kotler, P., Armstrong, G., Saunders, J. and Wong, V. (1999) *Principles of Marketing*, Hemel Hempstead: Prentice-Hall.

16 Abell, D. (1980) *Defining the Business: The Starting Point of Strategic Planning*, Englewood Cliffs, NJ: Prentice-Hall.

17 Doyle, P. (1998) *Marketing Management and Strategy*, Hemel Hempstead: Prentice-Hall.

18 Ansoff, H. I. and McDonell, E. (1990) *Implementing Strategic Change*, Englewood Cliffs, NJ: Prentice-Hall.

19 Brownlie, D. (1987) 'Environmental analysis', in M. Baker (ed.), *The Marketing Book*, Oxford: Butterworth-Heinemann.

20 Dibb, S., Simkin, L. and Bradley, J. (1996) *The Marketing Planning Workbook*, London: Thomson.

21 Diffenbach, J. (1983) 'Corporate environmental analysis in large US corporations', *Long Range Planning* 16(3):107–16.

Chapter 4

1 Engel, J. F., Blackwell, R. D. and Miniard, P. W. (1993) *Consumer Behavior*, 7th ed., Hinsdale, IL: Dryden Press, p. 4.

2 Howard, J. A. and Sheth, J. N. (1969) *The Theory of Buyer Behavior*, New York: Wiley, pp. 27–28.

3 Baumeister, R. F. and Mick, D. G. (2002) 'Yielding to temptation: self-control failure, impulsive purchasing, and consumer behavior', *Journal of Consumer Research* 28(4):670–77.

4 Foxall, G. (1995) 'Consumer decision-making', in M. Baker (ed.) *The Marketing Book*, 3rd ed., London: Heinemann/Chartered Institute of Marketing.

5 Keller, K. L. and Staelin, R. (1987) 'Effects of quality and quantity of information on decision effectiveness', *Journal of Consumer Research*, September, 200–213.

6 Biehal, G. and Chakravarti, D. (1986) 'Consumers' use of memory and external information in choice: macro and micro perspectives', *Journal of Consumer Research* 12(4):382–405.

7 Calder, B. J. and Sternthal, B. (1980) 'Television commercial wearout: an information processing

view', *Journal of Marketing Research* 17(2):173–86.

8   Houston, M. J., Childers, T. L. and Heckler, S. E. (1987) 'Picture-word consistency and the elaborative processing of advertisements', *Journal of Marketing Research* 24(4):359–69.

9   Westbrook, R. A. (1987). 'Product/consumption-based affective responses and postpurchase processes', *Journal of Marketing Research* 24(3): 258–70.

10   Bougie, R., Pieters, R. and Zeelenberg, M. (2003) 'Angry customers don't come back: the experience and behavioral implications of anger and dissatisfaction in services', *Journal of the Academy of Marketing Science* 31(4):377–94.

11   Capraro, A. J., Broniarczyk, S. and Srivastava, R. K. (2003) 'Factors influencing the likelihood of customer defection: the role of consumer knowledge', *Journal of the Academy of Marketing Science* 31(2): 164–75.

12   Denny, N. (1998) 'Why complaining is our new hobby', *Marketing*, 26 November, 16.

13   Sellers, P. (1989) 'The ABC's of marketing to kids', *Fortune*, 8 May, 115.

14   Waldrop, J. (1989) 'Inside America's households', *American Demographics*, March, 20–27.

15   Houston, Childers and Heckler (see note 8), pp. 359–69.

16   Robertson, T. S. and Gatignon, H. (1986) 'Competitive effects on technology diffusion', *Journal of Marketing* 50(3):1–12.

17   Ibid., pp. 1–12.

18   Ries, A. and Trout, J. (1986) *Positioning the Battle for Your Mind*, New York: McGraw-Hill Book Co.

19   Bettman, J. R. (1979) *An Information Processing Theory of Consumer Choice*, Reading, MA: Addison-Wesley, pp. 18–24.

20   Aaker, D. and Stayman, D. (1992) 'Implementing the concept of transformational advertising', *Psychology and Marketing*, May and June, 237–53.

21   Myers, J. H. (1997) 'Determinant buying attitudes: meaning and measurement', *Marketing Management* 6, Summer.

22   Alba, J. W. and Hutchinson, J. W. (1987) 'Dimensions of consumer expertise', *Journal of Consumer Research* 13(4):411–54.

23   Rao, A. R. and Monroe, K. B. (1988) 'The moderating effect of prior knowledge on cue utilization in product evaluations', *Journal of Consumer Research* 15(2):253–64.

24   Ibid.

25   Baumgartner, H. (2002) 'Towards a personology of the consumer', *Journal of Consumer Research* 29 (2):286–93.

26   Lastovika, J. L. and Joachimsthaler, E. A. (1988) 'Improving the detection of personality-behavior, relationships in consumer research', *Journal of Consumer Research* 14(4):583–87.

27   Moore, M. T. (1989) 'Spring break: brand names chase sales', *USA Today*, 17 March, B1.

28   Donkin, A., Lee, Y. H. and Toson, B. (2002) 'Implications of changes in the UK social and occupational classifications in 2001 for vital statistics', *National Statistics*, Spring, 23–29.

29   Rogers, E. (2004) 'Adland takes up fat challenge', *Marketing*, 11 March, 19.

30   De Mooij, M. (2003) 'Convergence and divergence in consumer behavior: implications for global advertising', *International Journal of Advertising* 22(2): 183–203.

31   Berry, L. L. (1979) 'The time-sharing consumer', *Journal of Retailing*, Winter, 69.

32   Li, C. and Bernoff, J. (2008) *Groundswell*, Boston, MA: Harvard Business Review, p. 43.

33   Bucklin, R. E. (1998) 'Determining segmentation in sales response across consumer purchase behaviours', *Journal of Marketing Research* 35(2): 189–97.

Chapter 5

1   Jarillo, J. C. and Stevenson, H. H. (1991) 'Cooperative strategies: the payoffs and the pitfalls', *Long Range Planning* 24(1):64–70.

2   Coppett, J. I. (1988) 'Auditing your customer service activities', *Industrial Marketing Management* 17:277–84; Powers, T. L. (1988) 'Identify and fulfill customer service expectations', *Industrial Marketing Management* 17:273–76.

3   Bitner, M. J., Booms, B. H. and Tetreault, M. S. (1990) 'The service encounter: diagnosing favorable and unfavorable incidents', *Journal of Marketing* 54: 71–84.

4   Royal, W. F. (1995) 'Cashing in on complaints', *Sales & Marketing Management*, May, 88–89.

5   Uddin, M. (2001) 'Loyalty programmes: the ultimate gift', *DSN Retailing Today* 40(5):12.

6   Shaw, J., Giglierano, J. and Kallis, J. (1989) 'Marketing complex technical products: the importance of intangible attributes', *Industrial Marketing Management* 18:45–53.

7   Webster, F. E. and Wind, Y. (1996) 'A general model for understanding organizational buyer behaviour', *Marketing Management*, Winter/Spring, 52–57.

8   Gummesson, E. (1987) 'The new marketing: developing long-term interactive relationships', *Long Range Planning* 20(3):10–20.

9   Hakansson, H. (1982) *International Marketing and Purchasing of Industrial Goods*, Chichester: Wiley.

10   Christopher, M., Payne, A. and Ballantyne, D. (1991) *Relationship Marketing*, Oxford: Butterworth-Heinemann.

11   Ford, D. (1982) *Understanding Business Marketing and Purchasing*, London: Thomson Learning.

12 McKenna, R. (1991) *Relationship Marketing*, Reading, MA: Addison-Wesley.

13 Campbell, N. C. G., Graham, J. L., Jolibert, A. and Meissner, H. G. (1988) 'Marketing negotiations in France, Germany, the United Kingdom and the United States', *Journal of Marketing* 52(2):49–62.

14 Jarillo, J. C. and Stevenson, H. H. (1991) 'Cooperative strategies: the payoffs and the pitfalls', *Long Range Planning*, February, 64–70.

15 *Standard Industrial Classification Revision* (1979) London: Central Statistical Office.

16 Doyle, P. and Saunders, J. (1985) 'Market segmentation and positioning in specialized industrial markets', *Journal of Marketing* 49(2):25.

Chapter 6

1 Weinstein, A. (2004) *Handbook of Market Segmentation: Strategic Targeting for Business and Technology Firms*, New York: Haworth Press.

2 Stewart, D. W. (1998) 'Segmentation and positioning for strategic marketing decisions', *Journal of Marketing Research* 35(1):128–29.

3 Frank, R. and Wind, Y. (1972) *Market Segmentation*, Englewood Cliffs, NJ: Prentice-Hall; Wind, Y. (1978) 'Issues and advances in segmentation research', *Journal of Marketing Research* 15(3): 317–27.

4 Schaffer, C. M. and Green, P. E. (1998) 'Cluster-based market segmentation: some further comparisons of alternative approaches', *Journal of the Market Research Society* 40(2):155–63.

5 Wedel, M. and Kamakura, W. (2000) *Market Segmentation: Conceptual and Methodological Foundations*, Boston, MA: Kluwer Academic Publications.

6 Peppers, D. and Rogers, M. (1999) *The One-to-One Manager*, New York: Currency Doubleday.

7 Postma, P. (1998) *The New Marketing Era: Marketing to the Imagination of a Technology-Driven World*, New York: McGraw-Hill.

8 Sheth, J. H., Sisodia, R. S. and Sharma, A. (2000) 'Customer-centric marketing', *Journal of the Academy of Marketing Science* 28(1):55–66.

9 Peppers, D. and Rogers, M. (1999) *The One-to-One Manager*, New York: Currency Doubleday.

10 Chaffey, D., Mayer, R., Johnston, K. and Ellis-Chadwick, F. (2000) *Internet Marketing*, Harlow: Pearson Education.

11 Saunders, J. (1994) 'Cluster analysis', *Journal of Marketing Management* 10:13–28; Saunders, J. (1980) 'Cluster analysis for market segmentation', *European Journal of Marketing* 14:422–35.

12 McNeal, J. U. (1999) *Kids Marketing: Myths and Realities*, Ithaca, NY: Paramount Market Publishing.

13 Albonetti, J. G. and Dominguez, L. V. (1989) 'Major influences on consumer goods marketers' decision to target US Hispanics', *Journal of Advertising Research*, February–March, 9–11.

14 Lastovicka, J. L. and Joachimsthaler, E. A. (1988) 'Improving the detection of personality-behavior relationships in consumer research', *Journal of Consumer Research*, March, 583–87.

15 Plummer, J. T. (1974) 'The concept and application of life style segmentation', *Journal of Marketing*, January, 33.

16 Engel, J. F., Blackwell, R. D. and Miniard, P. W. (1990) *Consumer Behavior*, Orlando, FL: Dryden Press, pp. 348–49.

17 Haley, R. I. (1968) 'Benefit segmentation: a decision-oriented research tool', *Journal of Marketing* 32(3):30–35.

18 Wind, Y. and Cardoza, R. (1974) 'Industrial market segmentation', *Industrial Marketing Management* 3: 153–66.

19 Beane, T. P. and Ennis, D. M. (1987) 'Market segmentation: a review', *European Journal of Marketing* 21(5):20–42.

20 Bonoma, T. and Shapiro, B. P. (1983) *Segmenting the Industrial Market*, Lexington, MA: Lexington Books.

21 Blumberg, D. F. (1987) 'Developing service as a line of business', *Management Review* 76:61.

22 Diamantopoulos, A. and Schlegelmilch, B. (1997) *Taking the Fear out of Data Analysis*, London: Dryden Press; Saunders, J. (1994) 'Cluster analysis', *Journal of Marketing Management* 10:13–28; and Saunders, J. (1980) 'Cluster analysis for market segmentation', *European Journal of Marketing* 14: 422–35.

23 Lilien, G. L. and Kotler, P. (1983) *Marketing Decision-Making: A Model Building Approach*, New York: Harper & Row; Naert, P. and Leeflang, P. (1978) *Building Implementable Marketing Models*, Leiden: Martinus Nijhoff.

24 Maier, J. and Saunders, J. (1990) 'The implementation of segmentation in sales management', *Journal of Personal Selling and Sales Management* 10(1):39–48.

25 Saunders, J. (1994) 'Cluster analysis', *Journal of Marketing Management* 10:13–28; Saunders, J. (1980) 'Cluster analysis for market segmentation', *European Journal of Marketing* 14:422–35.

26 Diamantopoulos, A. and Schlegelmilch, B. *Taking the Fear out of Data Analysis*, London: Dryden Press, 1997; Saunders, J. (1994) 'Cluster analysis', *Journal of Marketing Management* 10:13–28; and Saunders, J. (1980) 'Cluster analysis for market segmentation', *European Journal of Marketing* 14: 422–35.

27 Thomas, J. S. and Sullivan, U. Y. (2005) 'Managing marketing communications with multichannel customers', *Journal of Marketing* 69(4):239–51.

28   Boulding, W., Staelin, R., Ehret, M. and Johnston, W. J. (2005), 'A customer relationship management roadmap: what is known, potential pitfalls, and where to go', *Journal of Marketing* 69(4):155–66.

29   Peppers, D. and Rogers, M. (2004) *Managing Customer Relationships – A Strategic Framework*, New Jersey: John Wiley and Sons.

30   Nguyen, B. and Simkin, L. (2011) 'Effects of firm customization on the severity of unfairness perceptions and (mis)behaviour: the moderating role of trust', paper presented at The Academy of Marketing Conference, Liverpool, UK, July.

31   Ibid.

32   McDonald, M. (1995) *Marketing Plans*, Oxford: Butterworth-Heinemann.

33   Dibb, S. and Simkin, L. (1997) *Marketing and Marketing Planning: Still Barriers to Overcome*, EMAC, Warwick, May.

34   Doyle, P., Saunders, J. and Wong, V. (1986) 'A comparative study of Japanese marketing strategies in the British market', *Journal of International Business Studies* 17(1):27–46.

35   Kotler, P. (1988) *Marketing Management: Analysis, Planning, and Control*, 6th ed., Englewood Cliffs, NJ: Prentice-Hall, p. 257.

36   Wind, Y. (1980) 'Going to market: new twist for some old tricks', *Wharton Magazine*, 4.

37   Harrison, T. (1987) *A Handbook of Advertising Techniques*, London: Kogan Page, p. 7.

38   Ries, A. and Trout, J. (1981) *Positioning: The Battle for Your Mind*, New York: McGraw-Hill; Trout, J. and Rivkin, S. (1996) *The New Positioning: The Latest on the World's #1 Business Strategy*, New York: McGraw-Hill.

Chapter 7

1   Birks, D. (1994) Chapter 10, in M. Baker (ed.) *The Marketing Book*, Oxford: Butterworth-Heinemann.

2   'Pizza Hut studies effects of "pizza deprivation" on college and high school students' (2001) *PRNewswire*, via AmericaOnline, 30 May.

3   Wind, J. (1997) 'Marketing research forum: state of the art in quantitative research', *Marketing Research*, Winter.

4   Dibb, S. and Simkin, L. (2004) *The Marketing Casebook*, London: Routledge.

5   'Research league tables top 65' (2004) *Marketing*, 14 July, 37–46.

6   Johansson, J. K. and Nonaha, I. (1987) 'Market research the Japanese way', *Harvard Business Review*, May–June, 16–22.

7   Tull, D. and Hawkins, D. (1990) *Marketing Research*, New York: Macmillan.

8   Mittal, V. and Kamakura, W. A. (2001) 'Satisfaction, repurchase intent, and repurchase behavior: investigating the moderating effects of customer characteristics', *Journal of Marketing Research* 38 (1):131–42.

9   'Internal secondary market research' (2001) *Small Business Owner's Toolkit*, www.lycos.com/business/cch/guide-book.html?lpv=1&docNumber=P03_3020, 23 June.

10   Vaughn, R. L. (1984) 'Demographic data banks: a new management resource', *Business Horizons*, November–December, 38–42. See also Chapter 5.

11   Conant, J. S., Smart, D. T. and Walker, B. J. (1990) 'Main survey facilitation techniques: an assessment and proposal regarding reporting practices', working paper, Texas A&M University.

12   Riche, p. 8.

13   Billing, S. M. (1982) 'Go slow, be wary when considering switch to computer assisted interviewing system', *Marketing News*, 26 November, sec. 2, p. 2.

14   Tull and Hawkins, 1990 (see note 5).

15   Yorkshire Television's *The Marketing Mix series*.

16   Sokolow, H. (1985) 'In-depth interviews increasing in importance', *Marketing News*, 13 September, 26.

17   Bush, A. J. and Parasuraman, A. (1985) 'Mall intercept versus telephone interviewing environment', *Journal of Advertising Research* 25(2):42.

18   Bush, A. J. and Hair, J. F., Jr (1985) 'An assessment of the mall intercept as a data collecting method', *Journal of Marketing Research* 22(2):162.

19   Singh, J., Howell, R. D. and Rhoads, G. K. (1990) 'Adaptive designs for Likert-type data: an approach for implementing marketing surveys', *Journal of Marketing Research* 27(3):304–21.

20   Hart, N. and Stapleton, J. (1981) *Glossary of Marketing Terms*, Oxford: Butterworth-Heinemann.

21   'Closer encounters' (2004) *Marketing*, 14 July, 48–49.

22   Jackson, P., Adsearch, Richmond.

23   Diamantopoulos, A. and Schlegelmilch, B. (1997) *Taking the Fear out of Data Analysis*, London: Dryden Press.

24   Olivette, M. J. (1987) 'Marketing research in the electric utility industry', *Marketing News*, 2 January, 13.

25   Utter, D. (1998) 'Information-driven marketing decisions: development of strategic information systems', *Journal of the Academy of Marketing Science*, Spring.

26   Goal, L. N. (1992) 'High technology data collection for measurement and testing', *Marketing Research*, March, 29–38.

27   Ferrell, O. C. and Skinner, S. J. (1988) 'Ethical behavior and bureaucratic structure in marketing research organizations', *Journal of Marketing Research* 25(1):103–4.

28   Kavanaugh, M. (1998) 'Masked brawl', *Marketing Week*, 15 October, 65.

29 Colemar, L. (1988) 'It's selling disguised as research', *Marketing News*, 4 January, 1.

30 Allen, B. (1987) 'Make information services pay its way', *Harvard Business Review*, January–February, 57.

Chapter 8

1   Part of this definition is adapted from James D. Scott, Martin R. Warshaw and James R. Taylor (1985) *Introduction to Marketing Management*, 5th ed., Homewood, IL: Irwin, p. 215.

2   Levitt, T. (1981) 'Marketing intangible products and product intangibles', *Harvard Business Review*, May–June, 94–102.

3   Haas, R. W. (1986) *Industrial Marketing Management*, 3rd ed., Boston, MA: Kent Publishing, pp. 15–25.

4   Putsis, W. P., Jr and Bayus, B. L. (2001) 'An empirical analysis of firms' product line decisions', *Journal of Marketing Research* 38(1):110–18.

5   Thomas, M. J. (1987) 'Product development management', in M. Baker (ed.) *The Marketing Book*, London: Heinemann/The Chartered Institute of Marketing.

6   Radas, S. and Shugan, S. M. (1998) 'Seasonal marketing and timing new product introductions', *Journal of Marketing Research* 35(3):296–315; Adams, M. E. (1998) 'Enhancing new product development performance: an organizational learning perspective', *The Journal of Product Innovation Management* 15(5):403–22.

7   Lukas, B. A. and Ferrell, O. C. (2000) 'The effect of market orientation on product innovation', *Journal of the Academy of Marketing Science* 28(2):39–47.

8   Lynn, G. and Reilly, R. (2002) 'How to build a blockbuster', *Harvard Business Review* 80(10):18–20.

9   Benady, D. (2004) 'Chopping brands', *Marketing Week* 10:22–25.

10 Tellis, G. and Golder, P. (1996) 'First to market, first to fail? Real causes of enduring market leadership', *Sloan Management Review*, Winter, 65–75.

11 'Guinness in facelift as volume dips' (2004) *Marketing Week*, 20 May, 8.

12 Parry, C. (2004) 'Cadbury axes Trebor 24–7 after poor sales', *Marketing Week*, 15 April, 5.

13 Levitt, T. (1981) 'Marketing intangible products and product intangibles', *Harvard Business Review*, May–June, 96.

14 Hart, C. W. L. (1988) 'The power of unconditional service guarantees', *Harvard Business Review*, July–August, 54–62.

Chapter 9

1   Sethi, R. (2000) 'New product quality and product development', *Journal of Marketing* 64:1–14.

2   Bennet, R. C. and Cooper, R. G. (1984) 'The product life cycle trap', *Business Horizons* 27(5):7–16.

3   Phillips, D. F. (1990) 'Product development: where planning and marketing meet', *Journal of Business Strategy* 11(5):13–16.

4   Cooper, L. G. (2000) 'Strategic marketing planning for radically new products', *Journal of Marketing* 64(1):1–16.

5   Troy, L. C., Szymanski, D. M. and Varadarajan, P. R. (2001) 'Generating new product ideas: an initial investigation of the role of market information and organizational characteristics', *Journal of the Academy of Marketing Science* 29(1):89–101.

6   Drucker, P. F. (1985) 'The discipline of innovation', *Harvard Business Review*, May–June, 67–68; Couchen, W. (1999) 'A proposed method for the design of consumer products', *Journal of International Marketing and Marketing Research*, February.

7   Levine, J. B. (1989) 'Keeping new ideas kicking around', *Business Week*, 128.

8   Rindfleisch, A. and Moorman, C. (2001) 'The acquisition and utilization of information in new product alliances: a strength-of-ties perspective', *Journal of Marketing* 65(2):1–18.

9   Hyatt, J. (1989) 'Ask and you shall receive', *Inc.*, Sepember, 90–101.

10 Moorman, C. and Miner, A. S. (1998) 'The convergence of planning and execution: improvisation in new product development', *Journal of Marketing* 62(3):1–20; Padmanabhan, V., Rajiv, S. and Srinivasan, K. (1997) 'New products, upgrades, and new releases: a rationale for sequential product introduction', *Journal of Marketing Research* 34(4):456–72.

11 Bayus, B. L., Jain, S. and Rao, A. G. (2001) 'Truth or consequences: an analysis of vaporware and new product announcements', *Journal of Marketing Research*, February, 3–13.

12 Miller, C. (1993) 'Little relief seen for new product failure rate', *Marketing News*, 21 June, 5.

13 Kim, C. K., Lavack, A. M. and Smith, M. (2001) 'Consumer evaluation of vertical brand extensions and core brands', *Journal of Business Research* 52(3):211–22.

14 Grime, I., Diamantopoulos, A. and Smith, G. (2002) 'Consumer evaluations of extensions and their effects on the core brand: key issues and research propositions', *European Journal of Marketing* 36(11, 12):1415–38.

15 Adapted from Everett M. Rogers (1962) *Diffusion of Innovations*, New York: Macmillan, pp. 81–86.

16 Hooley, G. J. and Saunders, J. (1993) *Competitive Positioning: The Key to Market Success*, Englewood Cliffs, NJ: Prentice-Hall.

17 DeBruicker, F. S. and Summe, G. L. (1985) 'Make sure your customers keep coming back', *Harvard Business Review*, January–February, 92–98.

18 Gordon, G. L., Calantone, R. J. and di Benedetto, A. (1991) 'Mature markets and revitalization strategies: an American fable', *Business Horizons* 34(3):42.

19 Clark, K. B. and Fujimoto, T. (1990) 'The power of product integrity', *Harvard Business Review*, November–December, 108–18.

20 Phillips, L. W., Chang, D. R. and Buzzell, R. D. (1983) 'Product quality, cost position and business performance: a test of some key hypotheses', *Journal of Marketing* 47(2):26–43.

21 Lambert, D. M. and Sterling, J. U. (1988) 'Identifying and eliminating weak products', *Business* 38:3–10.

22 Guiltinan, J. P. and Paul, G. W. (1982) *Marketing Management: Strategies and Programmes*, New York: McGraw-Hill, p. 31.

23 Day, G. S. (1977) 'Diagnosing the Product Portfolio', *Journal of Marketing* 41(2):30–31.

24 Dibb, S. and Simkin, L. (1996) *The Market Segmentation Workbook*, London: Thomson.

25 Day, *Analysis for Strategic Market Decisions*, p. 10.

26 Cravens, D. W. (1983) 'Strategic marketing's new challenge', *Business Horizons*, March–April, p. 19.

Chapter 10

1 Berry, L. L. and Parasuraman, A. (1991) *Marketing Services: Competing Through Quality*, New York: Free Press, p. 5.

2 Voss, G. B., Parasuraman, A. and Grewal, D. (1998) 'The roles of price, performance, and expectations in determining satisfaction in service exchanges', *Journal of Marketing* 64(4):46–61; Wirtz, J. and Bateson, J. E. G. (1999) 'Consumer satisfaction with services: integrating the environment perspective in services marketing into the traditional disconfirmation paradigm', *Journal of Business Research* 44(1):55–66.

3 Cowell, D. (1984) *The Marketing of Services*, London: Heinemann.

4 Based on K. Douglas Hoffman and John E. G.Bateson (1997) *Essentials of Services Marketing*, Fort Worth, TX: Dryden Press, pp. 25–28; and Zeithaml, V. A., Parasuraman, A. and Berry, L. L. (1990) *Delivery Quality Service: Balancing Customer Perceptions and Expectations*, New York: Free Press.

5 Bateson, J. E. G. (1979) 'Why we need service marketing', in O. C. Ferrell, S. W. Brown, and C. W. Lamb, Jr (eds) *Conceptual and Theoretical Development in Marketing*, Chicago, IL: American Marketing Association, pp. 131–46.

6 Zeithaml, V. A. (1981) 'How consumer evaluation processes differ between goods and services', in J. H. Donnelly and W. R. George (eds.) *Marketing of Services*, Chicago: American Marketing Association, pp. 186–90.

7 Berry, L. L., Zeithaml, V. A. and Parasuraman, A. (1984) 'Responding to demand fluctuations: key challenge for service businesses', in R. Belk, et al. (eds.) *AMA Educators' Proceedings*, Chicago: American Marketing Association, pp. 231–34.

8 Moores, B. (1986) *Are They Being Served*? Oxford: Philip Allan.

9 Peter, J. P. and Donnelly, J. H. (2000) *A Preface to Marketing Management*, Burr Ridge, IL: McGraw-Hill/Irwin, p. 203.

10 Priluck, R. 'Relationship marketing can mitigate product and service failures', *Journal of Services Marketing* 17(3):37–52.

11 Arnett, D. B., German, S. D. and Hunt, S. D. (2003) 'The identity salience model of relationship marketing success: the case of nonprofit marketing', *Journal of Marketing* 67(2):89–106.

12 Reardon, J., Miller, C., Hasty, R. and Waguespack, B. J. (1996) 'A comparison of alternative theories of services marketing', *Journal of Marketing Theory and Practice* 4(4):61–71.

13 Lovelock, C. H. (1983) 'Classifying services to gain strategic marketing insights', *Journal of Marketing*, Summer, 15.

14 Lovelock, C. H. (1984) *Services Marketing*, Englewood Cliffs, NJ: Prentice-Hall, pp. 46–64.

15 Wind, Y. (1987) 'Financial services: increasing your marketing productivity and profitability', *Journal of Services Marketing* 1(2):8.

16 Goodwin, C. (1997) 'Marketing strategies for services: globalization, client-orientation, deregulation', *International Journal of Research in Marketing*, July.

17 Lovelock, *Services Marketing*, pp. 279–89.

18 Ibid.

19 Berry, Zeithaml and Parasuraman, pp. 231–34.

20 Zeithaml, V. A., Parasuraman, A. and Berry, L. L. (1990) *Delivering Quality Service: Balancing Customer Perceptions and Expectations*, New York: Free Press.

21 Parasuraman, A., Berry, L. L. and Zeithaml, V. A. (1990) 'An empirical examination of relationships in an extended service quality model', *Marketing Science Institute Working Paper Series, Report no. 90–122*, Cambridge, MA: Marketing Science Institute, p. 29.

22 Zeithaml, V. A., Berry, L. L. and Parasuraman, A. (1988) 'Communication and control processes in the delivery of service quality', *Journal of Marketing* 52(2):35–48.

23 Zeithaml, V. A., Berry, L. L. and Parasuraman, A. (1993) 'The nature and determinants of customer expectations of service', *Journal of the Academy of Marketing Science* 21(1):1–12.

24 Hartline and Ferrell, *Service quality implementation*, p. 36.
25 Bitner, M. J. (1990) 'Evaluating service encounters: the effects of physical surroundings and employee responses', *Journal of Marketing* 54(2):70.
26 Hartline and Ferrell, '*Service quality implementation*, pp. 17–19.
27 Glassman, M. and McAfee, B. (1992) 'Integrating the personnel and marketing functions: the challenge of the 1990s', *Business Horizons* 35(3): 52–59.
28 Blois, K. J. (1994) 'Marketing for non-profit organisations', in M. J. Baker (ed.) *The Marketing Book*, London: Heinemann, p. 405.
29 Whyte, J. (1985) 'Organisation, person and idea marketing as exchange', *Quarterly Review of Marketing*, January, 25–30.
30 Garrison, J. (1987) 'Telethons – the positive story', *Fund Raising Management*, November, 48–52.
31 Kotler, P. (1982) *Marketing for Non-profit Organisations*, 2nd ed., Englewood Cliffs, NJ: Prentice-Hall, p. 37.
32 Ibid.
33 Davids, M. (1987) 'Doing well by doing good', *Public Relations Journal*, July, 17–21.
34 Pitt, L. F. and Abratt, R. (1987) 'Pricing in nonprofit organisations – a framework and conceptual overview', *Quarterly Review of Marketing*, Spring–Summer, 13–15.
35 Walker, K. (1984) 'Not-for-profit profits', *Forbes*, 10 September, 165.

Chapter 11
1 Anderson, E., Day, G. S. and Rangan, V. K. (1997) 'Strategic channel design', *Sloan Management Review* 38(4):59.
2 Montoya-Weiss, M. M., Ross, G. B. and Grewal, D. (2003) 'Determinant of online channel use and overall satisfaction with a relational, multichannel service provider', *Journal of the Academy of Marketing Science* 31(4):448–59.
3 Ferrell, O. C. and Pride, W. M., National sample of 2,042 households.
4 Alderson, W. (1957) *Marketing Behavior and Executive Action*, Homewood, IL: Irwin, pp. 201–11.
5 Goodman, L. E and Dion, P. A. (2001) 'The determinants of commitment in the distributor–manufacturer relationship', *Industrial Marketing Management* 30(3):287–300.
6 Hlavacek, J. D. and McCuistion, T. J. (1983) 'Industrial distributors: when, who, and how?' *Harvard Business Review*, March–April, 97.
7 Erdem, S. A. and Harrison-Walker, L. J. (1997) 'Managing channel relationships: toward an identification of effective promotional strategies in vertical marketing systems', *Journal of Marketing Theory and Practice* 5(2):80–87.
8 Lewis, J. D. (1990) 'Using alliances to build market power', *Planning Review* 18(5):4–9, 48.
9 Aspinwall, L. (1961) 'The marketing characteristics of goods', in *Four Marketing Theories*, Boulder: University of Colorado Press, pp. 27–32.
10 Magrath, A. J. (1991) 'Differentiating yourself via distribution', *Sales & Marketing Management*, March, 50–57.
11 Cravens, D. W., Ingram, T. N. and LaForge, R. W. (1991) 'Evaluating multiple sales channel strategies', *Journal of Business and Industrial Marketing* 6(3): 3–4.
12 Rosenbloom, B. (1987) *Marketing Channels: A Management View*, Hinsdale, IL: Dryden, p. 160.
13 Ibid., p. 161.
14 Bowersox, D. J. and Cooper, M. B. (1992) *Strategic Marketing Channel Management*, New York: McGraw-Hill, pp. 177–78.
15 Alderson, W. (1965) *Dynamic Marketing Behavior*, Homewood, IL: Irwin, p. 239.
16 Seideman, T. (1998) 'Get with the program', *Inbound Logistics*, September, 29.
17 Skinner, S. J., Gassenheimer, J. B. and Kelley, S. W. (1992) 'Cooperation in supplier-dealer relations', *Journal of Retailing* 68(2):174–93; Hakansson, H. (1982) *International Marketing and Purchasing of Industrial Goods*, Chichester: Wiley.
18 Cronin, J. J., Jr, Baker, T. L. and Hawes, J. M. (1994) 'An assessment of the role performance measurement of power-dependency in marketing channels', *Journal of Business Research* 30(3): 201–10.
19 Kumar, N., Scheer, L. K. and Steenkamp, J.-B. (1998) 'Interdependence, punitive capability, and the reciprocation of punitive actions in channel relationships', *Journal of Marketing Research* 35 (2):225–35; Lusch, R. F. (1996) 'Interdependency, contracting, and relational behavior in marketing channels', *Journal of Marketing* 60(4):19–38.
20 Hibbard, J. D., Kumar, N. and Stern, L. W. (2001) 'Examining the impact of destructive acts in marketing channel relationships', *Journal of Marketing Research* 38(1):45–61.
21 El-Ansary, A. I. (1979) 'Perspectives on channel system performance', in R. F. Lusch and P. H. Zinszer (eds) *Contemporary Issues in Marketing Channels*, Norman: University of Oklahoma Press, p. 50.
22 Hardy, K. G. and Magrath, A. J. (1988) 'Ten ways for manufacturers to improve distribution management', *Business Horizons* 31(6):68.
23 Michman, R. D. and Sibley, S. D. (1980) *Marketing Channels and Strategies*, Columbus, OH: Grid Publishing, pp. 412–17.

24 Keith, J. E., Jackson, D. W. and Crosby, L. A. (1990) 'Effect of alternative types of influence strategies under different dependence structures', *Journal of Marketing* 54(3):30–41.

25 Gaski, J. F. and Nevin, J. R. (1985) 'The differential effects of exercised and unexercised power sources in a marketing channel', *Journal of Marketing Research* 22(2):139.

Chapter 12

1 Gourville, J. and Soman, D. (2002) 'Pricing and the psychology of consumption', *Harvard Business Review* 80(9):91–96.

2 Lichtenstein, D., Ridgway, N. M. and Netemeyer, R. G. (1993) 'Price perceptions and consumer shopping behavior: a field study', *Journal of Marketing Research* 30(2):234–45.

3 Desiraju, R. (1999) 'Strategic service pricing and yield management', *Journal of Marketing* 63(1):44–56.

4 Samier, S. (1987) 'Pricing in marketing strategies of U.S. and foreign based companies', *Journal of Business Research* 15(1):15–23.

5 Winkler, J. (1987) 'Pricing', in M. Baker (ed.) *The Marketing Book,* London: Heinemann.

6 JCB company literature, 1992.

7 Guiltinan, J. P. (1987) 'The price-bundling of services: a normative framework', *Journal of Marketing* 51(2):74–85.

8 Zeithaml, V. A. (1988) 'Consumer perceptions of price, quality and value: a means-end model and synthesis of evidence', *Journal of Marketing* 52:2–22.

9 Anderson, E. and Simester, D. (2003) 'Mind your pricing cues', *Harvard Business Review*, September, 97–103.

10 Griffith, D. E. (1997) 'The price of competitiveness in competitive pricing', *Journal of the Academy of Marketing Science* 25(2); Sivakumar, K. (1997) 'Quality tier competition: how price change influences brand choice and category choice', *Journal of Marketing* 61(3):71–84.

11 Wilcox, J. B., Howell, R. D., Kuzdrall, P. and Britney, R. (1987) 'Price quantity discounts: some implications for buyers and sellers', *Journal of Marketing* 51(3):60–61.

12 Eccles, R. G. (1983) 'Control with fairness in transfer pricing', *Harvard Business Review*, November–December, 149–61.

13 Morris, M. H. (1987) 'Separate prices as a marketing tool', *Industrial Marketing Management* 16(2):79–86.

14 Trout, J. (1998) 'Prices: simple guidelines to get them right', *The Journal of Business Strategy* 19(6):13–16.

Chapter 13

1 Pollay, R. W. (1987) 'On the value of reflections on the values in "The distorted mirror"', *Journal of Marketing* 51(3):104–9.

2 Holbrook, M. B. (1987) 'Mirror, mirror, on the wall, what's unfair in the reflections on advertising', *Journal of Marketing* 51(3):95–103.

3 Farmer, R. N. (1987) 'Would you want your granddaughter to marry a Taiwanese marketing man?' *Journal of Marketing* 51(4):111–16.

4 Coulson-Thomas, C. (1986) *Marketing Communications*, London: Heinemann; Ailawadi, K. L. and Neslin, S. A. (1998) 'The effect of promotion on consumption: buying more and consuming it faster', *Journal of Marketing Research* 35(3):390–98.

5 Engel, J., Warshaw, M. and Kinnear, T. (1994) *Promotional Strategy: Managing the Marketing Communications Process*, Boston, MA: Irwin.

6 Rossiter, J. and Percy, L. (1987) *Advertising and Promotion Management*, New York: McGraw-Hill.

7 In case you do not read Chinese, this says, 'In the factory we make cosmetics, and in the store we sell hope'. Prepared by Chih Kang Wang.

8 Shimp, T. A. and Delozier, M. W. (1986) *Promotion Management and Marketing Communication*, Hinsdale, IL: Dryden Press, pp. 25–26.

9 Wagner, J. A., Klein, N. M. and Keith, J. E. (2001) 'Selling strategies: the effects of suggesting a decision structure to novice and expert buyers', *Journal of the Academy of Marketing Science* 29(3):289–306.

10 McClenahen, J. S. (1995) 'How can you possibly say that?' *Industry Week* 17:17–19.

11 Szymanski, D. M. (2001) 'Modality and offering effects in sales presentations for a good versus a service', *Journal of the Academy of Marketing Science* 29(2):179–89.

12 Jones, D. (1994) 'Setting promotional goals: a communications' relationship model', *Journal of Consumer Marketing* 11(1):38–49.

13 Adapted from Everett M. Rogers (1962) *Diffusion of Innovations*, New York: Free Press, pp. 81–86, 98–102.

14 Marks, L. J. and Kamins, M. A. (1988) 'Product sampling and advertising sequence, belief strength, confidence and attitudes', *Journal of Marketing Research* 25(3):266–81.

15 Rogers (see note 13 above), pp. 247–50.

16 Rossiter, J. and Percy, L. (1987) *Advertising and Promotion Management*, New York: McGraw-Hill.

17 Shannon, J. R. (1996) 'The new promotions mix: a proposed paradigm, process, and application', *Journal of Marketing Theory and Practice* 4(1):56–69.

18 Lane, V. R. (2000) 'The impact of ad repetition and ad content on consumer perceptions of incongruent extensions', *Journal of Marketing* 64(2):80–91.

19 Flandin, M., Martin, E. and Simkin, L. (1992) 'Advertising effectiveness research: a survey of agencies, clients and conflicts', *International Journal of Advertising* 11(3):203–14.

20 MacKenzie, S. B., Podsakoff, P. M. and Rich, G. A. (2001) 'Transformational and transactional leadership and sales person performance', *Journal of the Academy of Marketing Science* 29(2):115–34.

21 Hunt, T. and Grunig, J. (1994) *Public Relations Techniques*, Fort Worth: Harcourt Brace.

22 Dibb, S., Simkin, L. and Vancini, A. (1996) 'Competition, strategy, technology and people: the challenges facing PR', *International Journal of Advertising* 15(2):116–27.

23 This definition is adapted from John F. Luick and William L. Ziegler (1968) *Sales Promotion and Modern Merchandising*, New York: McGraw-Hill, p. 4.

24 Kerin, R. A. and Cron, W. L. (1987) 'Assessing trade show functions and performance: an exploratory study', *Journal of Marketing* 51(3):87–94.

25 Kavanagh, M. (1999) 'Free ISPs spur Net market growth', *MarketingWeek*, 11 March, pp. 30–31.

26 Evans, M. J., O'Malley, L. and Patterson, M. (1996) 'Direct marketing communications in the UK: a study of growth, past, present and future', *Journal of Marketing Communications* 2(1):51–65.

27 *Marketing Week*, 5 July, 1996, p. 13.

28 Achenbaum, A. A. and Mitchel, F. K. (1987) 'Pulling away from push marketing', *Harvard Business Review*, May–June, 38.

Chapter 14

1 Bennett, P. D. (ed.) (1988) *Dictionary of Marketing Terms*, Chicago, IL: American Marketing Association, p. 18.

2 Doyle, P. (1993) 'Building successful brands: the strategic options', *The Journal of Consumer Marketing* 7(2):5–20.

3 Bell, J. (1998) 'Brand management for the next millennium', *The Journal of Business Strategy* 19 (2):7–10; Rooney, J. A. (1995) 'Branding: a trend for today and tomorrow', *The Journal of Product and Brand Management* 4(4):48–56.

4 Assael, H. (1992) *Consumer Behaviour and Marketing Action*, 4th ed., Boston, MA: PWS-Kent.

5 Aaker, D. A. (1991) *Managing Brand Equity: Capitalizing on the Value of a Brand Name*, New York: Free Press, pp. 16–17.

6 Walker, C. (1991) 'What's in a name?' *American Demographics*, February, 54–57.

7 'British retailing: chemistry upset' (2001) *The Economist*, 24 February, 68.

8 Corstjens, M. and Lal, R. (2000) 'Building store loyalty through store brands', *Journal of Marketing Research* 37(3):281–91.

9 Miller, A. (1991) 'Gains share in dollars and units during 1990 third quarter', *Private Label*, January–February, 85–89.

10 Nelson, T. (1999) 'Sofres superpanel'.

11 Berry, L. L., Lefkowith, E. E. and Clark, T. (1988) 'In services, what's in a name?' *Harvard Business Review*, September–October, 2–4.

12 Cohen, D. (1986) 'Trademark strategy', *Journal of Marketing* 50(1):63.

13 Kohli, C. and Suri, R. (2000) 'Brand names that work: a study of the effectiveness of different brand names', *Marketing Management Journal* 10(2): 112–20.

14 Gurhan-Canli, Z. and Maheswaran, D. (1998) 'The effects of extensions on brand name dilution and enhancement', *Journal of Marketing Research* 35 (4):464–73.

15 'Trademark stylesheet', U.S. Trademark Association, no. 1A.

16 Lane, V. R. (2000) 'The impact of ad repetition and ad content on consumer perceptions of incongruent extensions', *Journal of Marketing* 64(2): 80–91.

17 Hurrell, G. (1997) 'Solpadol – a successful case of brand positioning', *Journal of the Market Research Society* 39(3):463–80.

18 Doyle, P. (1994) *Marketing Management and Strategy*, London: Prentice-Hall; M. Baker (ed.) (1995) *The Marketing Book*, Oxford: Butterworth-Heinemann, Chapter 20.

19 de Chernatony, L. (1999) 'Brand management through narrowing the gap between identity and brand reputation', *Journal of Marketing Management* 15(1–3):157–79.

20 Simoes, C. and Dibb, S. (2001) 'Rethinking the brand concept: new brand orientation', *Corporate Communications: An International Journal* 6(4): 217–24.

21 Rogers, E. (2004) 'Coca-Cola introduces designer glass bottles', *Marketing*, 25 March, 19.

22 Morgan, F. W. (1988) 'Tampered goods: legal developments and marketing guidelines', *Journal of Marketing* 52(2):86–96.

23 Ibid.

24 Wansink, B. (1996) 'Can package size accelerate usage volume?' *Journal of Marketing* 60(3):1–14.

25 Madden, T. J., Hewett, K. and Roth, M. S. (2000) 'Managing images in different cultures: a cross national study of color meanings and preferences', *Journal of International Marketing* 8(4):90.

26 Johnson, B. (2004) 'Mineral water companies to launch "purity" symbol', *Marketing Week*, 29 April, 8.

Chapter 15

1 Pulendran, S., Speed, R. and Widing, R. E., II (2003) 'Marketing planning, orientation and business performance', *European Journal of Marketing* 37(3,4):476–501.

2 Leeflang, P. S. H. and de Mortanges, C. P. (1996) 'An empirical investigation of marketing planning', *Journal of Euro-Marketing* 6(1):77–101.

3 Dibb, S., Simkin, L. and Bradley, J. (1996) *The Marketing Planning Workbook*, London: Thomson.

4 Simkin, L. (1996) 'People and processes in marketing planning: the benefits of controlling implementation in marketing planning', *Journal of Marketing Management* 12(5):375–90; Simkin, L. (2000) 'Delivering effective marketing planning', *Targeting, Measurement and Analysis for Marketing* 8(4):335–50; and Simkin, L. (2002) 'Barriers impeding effective implementation of marketing plans – a new research and training agenda', *Journal of Business and Industrial Marketing* 17(1): 8–22.

5 Luck, D. J., Ferrell, O. C. and Lucas, G (1989) *Marketing Strategy and Plans*, 3rd ed., Englewood Cliffs, NJ: Prentice-Hall, p. 328.

6 Sashittal, H. C. and Jassawalla, A. R. (2001) 'Marketing implementation in smaller organisations: definition, framework, and propositional inventory', *Journal of the Academy of Marketing Science* 29(1): 50–69.

7 McDonald, M. (1989) *Marketing Plans: How to Prepare Them, How to Use Them*, Oxford: Butterworth-Heinemann.

8 Bowman, D. and Gatignon, H. (1995) 'Determinants of competitor response time to a new product introduction', *Journal of Marketing Research* 32(1): 42–53.

9 Simkin, L. and Chang, A. (1997) 'Understanding competitors' strategies', *Marketing Intelligence & Planning* 15(3):124–34.

10 Wind, Y. and Robertson, T. S. (1983) 'Marketing strategy: new directions for theory and research', *Journal of Marketing* 47:12.

11 Sashittal, H. C. and Jassawalla, A. R. (1996) 'Marketing implementation in smaller organisations'.

12 Simkin, L. (1996) 'Addressing organisational prerequisites in marketing planning programmes', *Marketing Intelligence and Planning* 14(5):39–46.

13 Simkin, L. (2002) 'Barriers impeding effective implementation of marketing plans: a new research and training agenda', *Journal of Business and Industrial Marketing* 17(1):8–22.

14 Simkin, L. (2000) 'Delivering effective marketing planning', *Targeting, Measurement and Analysis for Marketing* 8(4):335–50.

15 Dibb, S. and Simkin, L. (1994) *The Marketing Casebook*, London: Routledge.

16 Simkin, L. (2000) 'Delivering effective marketing planning', *Targeting, Measurement and Analysis for Marketing* 8(4):335–50.

17 McDonald, M. (1992) 'Ten barriers to marketing planning', *Journal of Business & Industrial Marketing* 7(1):5–18; McDonald, M. (1992) 'Strategic marketing planning: a state-of-the-art review', *Marketing Intelligence & Planning* 10(4):4–22; Simkin, L. (1996) 'People and processes in marketing planning: the benefits of controlling implementation', *Journal of Marketing Management* 12:375–90; and Simkin, L. (1996) 'Addressing organisational pre-requisites in marketing planning programmes', *Marketing Intelligence & Planning* 14 (5):39–46.

18 Dibb, S. and Simkin, L. (2001) 'Overcoming segmentation barriers: four case studies', *Industrial Marketing Management* 30(8):609–25.

19 Simkin, L. (2002) 'Barriers impeding effective implementation of marketing plans – a new research and training agenda', *Journal of Business and Industrial Marketing* 17(1):8–22.

20 Based on Orville C. Walker, Jr and Robert W. Ruekert (1987) 'Marketing's role in the implementation of business strategies: a critical review and conceptual framework', *Journal of Marketing* 51(3): 15–33.

21 Piercy, N. F. (1998) 'Marketing implementation: the implications of marketing paradigm weakness for the strategy execution process', *Journal of the Academy of Marketing Science* 26(3): 222–36; Strutton, D. (1997) 'Marketing strategies: new approaches, new techniques', *Journal of the Academy of Marketing Science*, Summer.

22 Howard, R. (1990) 'Values make the company: an interview with Robert Haas', *Harvard Business Review*, September–October, 132–44.

23 Ferrell, O. C., Lucas, G. H. and Luck, D. (1994) *Strategic Marketing Management*, pp. 190–200.

24 Glassman, M. and McAfee, B. (1992) 'Integrating the personnel and marketing functions: the challenge of the 1990s', *Business Horizons*, May–June, 52–59.

25 Ferrell, Lucas and Luck, *Strategic Marketing Management*, pp. 190–200.

26 Jones, D. C. (1987) 'Motivation the catalyst in profit formula', *National Underwriter*, 13 July, 10–13.

27 McAdams, J. (1987) 'Rewarding sales and marketing performance', *Management Review*, April, 36.

28 Kotler, P., Armstrong, G., Saunders, J. and Wong, V. (1998) *Principles of Marketing*, Hemel Hempstead: Prentice-Hall.

29 Christopher, M., Payne, A. and Ballantyne, D. (1991) *Relationship Marketing*, Oxford: Butterworth-Heinemann; Gronroos, C. (1994) 'From marketing mix to relationship marketing: towards a paradigm

shift in marketing', *Management Decision* 32(2): 4–20.

30 Berry, L. L. (1983) 'Relationship marketing', in L. L. Berry, G. L. Shostack and G. Upah (eds) *Emerging Perspectives on Services*, Chicago, IL: American Marketing Association, pp. 25–28.

31 Payne, A. (1994) 'Relationship marketing – making the customer count', *Managing Service Quality* 4(6): 29–31.

32 Harris, L. C. and Ogbonna, E. (2001) 'Strategic human resource management, market orientation and organizational performance', *Journal of Business Research* 51(2):157–66.

33 George, W. R. (1990) 'Internal marketing and organizational behaviour: a partnership in developing customer conscious employees at every level', *Journal of Business Research* 20:63–70; Lings, I. and Brooks, F. (1998) 'Implementing and measuring the effectiveness of internal marketing', *Journal of Marketing Management* 14(4):325–51.

34 Gummesson, E. (1987) 'Using internal marketing to develop a new culture', *Journal of Business and Industrial Marketing* 2(3):23–28.

35 Reynoso, J. and Moores, B. (1996) 'Internal relationships', in F. Buttle (ed.) *Relationship Marketing: Theory and Practice*, London: Chapman.

36 Dibb, S. and Simkin, L. (2004) *Marketing Briefs*, Oxford: Elsevier Butterworth-Heinemann.

37 'Higher education in doughnuts' (1988), *Ann Arbor News*, 9 March, B7.

38 Jaworski, B. J. (1988) 'Toward a theory of marketing control: environmental context, control types, and consequences', *Journal of Marketing* 52(3): 23–39.

39 See Haimann, T., Scott, W. G. and Connor, P. E. (1985) *Management*, 5th ed., Boston, MA: Houghton Mifflin, pp. 478–92.

40 'Carbonates and concentrates' (1990), Marketing Intelligence, January, 2.10–2.17.

41 Kelly, K. and Gross, N. (1988) 'A weakened Komatsu tries to come back swinging', *Business Week*, 22 February, 48.

42 Doyle, P. (2000) *Value-Based Marketing*, Chichester: Wiley.

43 Flack, J.-A. (1999) 'Measure of success', *Marketing Week*, 4 March, 45–49.

Glossary

ABC sales: contribution analysis An approach that examines the financial worth to a company of its products, product groups or customers

Accessory equipment Tools and equipment used in production or office activities that do not become part of the final physical product

Accumulation The development of a bank of homogeneous products with similar production or demand requirements

Actual product A composite of the features and capabilities offered in a product, quality and durability, design and product styling, packaging and brand name

Adopter categories Five groups into which customers can be divided according to the length of time it takes them to adopt a product: innovators, early adopters, early majority, late majority and laggards

Adoption stage The final stage of product acceptance, when customers choose a specific product

Advertising A paid form of non-personal communication about an organization and its products that is transmitted to a target audience through a mass medium

Allocation The breaking down of large homogeneous inventories into smaller lots

Allowance A concession in price to achieve a desired goal

Ansoff matrix Ansoff's product–market matrix for determining competitive strategies: market penetration, market development, product development or diversification

Area sampling A sampling method that involves selecting a probability sample of geographic areas and selecting units or individuals within the selected areas for the sample

Assorting The grouping of products that buyers want to have available in one place

Assortment A combination of products put together to provide customer benefits

Attitude An individual's enduring evaluation, feelings and behavioural tendencies towards an object or activity

Attitude scale A series of adjectives, phrases or sentences about an object used by a subject to indicate his or her feelings towards that object

Augmented product Support aspects of a product, including customer service, warranty, delivery and credit, personnel, installation and after-sales support

Awareness stage The beginning of the product adoption process, when individuals become aware that the product exists but have little information about it

Base point pricing A geographic pricing policy that includes the price at the factory, plus freight charges from the base point nearest the buyer

Basis for competing A company's combined strengths as identified in a SWOT analysis and any differential advantage, which should form the leading edge of the company's marketing strategy

Benefit segmentation The division of a market according to the benefits consumers want from the product

Blog communities Where spokespersons for a brand share their views in blogs, permitting one-to-one tailored communication with members and between members of the digital brand community

Brand A name, term, design, symbol or any other feature that identifies one seller's good or service as distinct from those of other sellers

Brand advocacy When consumers are encouraged to share very positive feelings towards a brand with other consumers, whether word-of-mouth, online or in the print and broadcast media

Brand attitude A consumer's particular impression of a brand, formed by emotions and logic or cognitive beliefs

Brand attributes The bullet-point specific benefits to the customer from purchasing or using the brand

Brand awareness A qualitative measure of marketing performance that determines whether a company's brands capture the attention of their target markets

Brand awareness The consumer's ability to identify a manufacturer's or retailer's brand in sufficient detail to distinguish it from other brands

Brand community A group of consumers and observers focused on a particular brand, often based on social media, centred on a set of social relations and interactions amongst admirers of the brand

Brand equity The marketing and financial value associated with a brand's strength in a market, which is a function of the goodwill and positive brand recognition built up over time, underpinning the brand's sales volumes and financial returns

Brand extension branding A company's use of one of its existing brand names as part of an improved or new product, usually in the same product category as the existing brand

Brand insistence The degree of brand loyalty in which a customer strongly prefers a specific brand and will accept no substitute

Brand loyalty A strongly motivated and long-standing decision to purchase a particular product or service

Brand manager The person responsible for a single brand

Brand mark The element of a brand that cannot be spoken – often a symbol or design

Brand name That part of a brand that can be spoken, including letters, words and numbers

Brand personality The psychological cues and less tangible desirable facets of a well-presented brand

Brand positioning The creation of a desirable, distinctive and plausible image for a brand in the minds of targeted customers

Brand preference The degree of brand loyalty in which a customer prefers one brand over competitive offerings

Brand purchase intention The consumer's decision and efforts to purchase the particular product

Brand recognition A customer's awareness that a brand exists and is an alternative to purchase

Brand strength A function of the product's attributes and functionality, its differentiation, plus any demonstrable added value to the purchaser or user

Brand values The emotional benefits and less tangible identifiers attached to the brand inside the organization, providing reassurance and credibility for employees and, indirectly, targeted consumers or business customers

Business (or business-to-business) buying behaviour The purchase behaviour of producers, resellers, the public sector, government units and institutions

Business analysis A company's evaluation of a product idea to determine its potential contribution to the company's sales, costs and profits

Business cycle Fluctuations in the economy that follow the general pattern of prosperity, recession, depression and recovery

Business market Individuals or groups that purchase a specific kind of product to resell, use directly in producing other products or use in general daily operations

Business market The customers are not consumers, private individuals or households: instead the target customers are other businesses and organizations that purchase a specific type of product or service for resale, for use in making other products or for use in their daily operations

Business marketing Activities directed towards facilitating and expediting exchanges between businesses

Business services Services such as repairs and maintenance, consulting and professional advice, installation, equipment leasing, marketing research, advertising, temporary office personnel and caretaking services

Buying behaviour The decision processes and actions of people involved in buying and using products

Buying centre The group of people within an organization who are involved in making business-to-business purchase decisions

Buying power Resources such as goods, services and financial holdings that can be traded in an exchange situation

Capabilities A company's distinctive competencies to do something well and efficiently

Cash cows Products with a dominant share of the market but low prospects for growth

Cash discount A simple price reduction given to a buyer for prompt payment or payment in cash

Category need The consumer's perception of his or her need for a product in a certain category

Category-consistent packaging The packaging of a product according to the packaging practices associated with a particular product category

Causal research Data collection that assumes that a particular variable X causes a variable Y

Cause-related marketing Links the purchase of a product to philanthropic efforts for a particular 'good' cause

Cause-related marketing The linking of an organization's products to a particular social cause on a short-term or ongoing basis

Channel capacity The limit on the volume of information that a particular communication channel can handle effectively

Channel of distribution (or marketing channel) A group of individuals and organizations that direct the flow of products from producers to customers

Channel power The ability to influence another channel member's goal achievement

Client publics In non-profit organizations, direct consumers of a product

Client-based relationships Interactions that result in satisfied customers who use a service repeatedly over time

Clippings service A service that counts the frequency of mentions of a specific brand or company in selected media

Coding process The process of converting meaning into a series of signs that represent ideas or concepts; also called encoding

Cognitive dissonance Doubts that occur as the buyer questions whether s/he made the right decision in purchasing the product or service.

Commercialization The process of refining and settling plans for full-scale manufacturing and marketing

Communication A sharing of meaning through the transmission of information

Competition Those companies marketing products that are similar to, or can be substituted for, a given business's products in the same geographic area or marketing channel

Competition Commission An independent body in the UK that investigates monopolies to determine whether they operate against the public interest

Competition-based pricing A pricing approach whereby an organization considers costs and revenue to be secondary to competitors' prices

Competitive advantage The achievement of superior performance vis-à-vis rivals, through differentiation to create distinctive product appeal or brand identity; through providing customer value and achieving the lowest delivered cost; or by focusing on narrowly scoped product categories or market niches so as to be viewed as a leading specialist

Competitive positions Competitors' roles in the marketplace, which influence their marketing strategies and programmes

Competitive positions proforma A tool for scoping the competitive set, helping a company to understand the competitive positions in its target markets and diagnosing the effectiveness of a marketing strategy

Competitive set All competing organizations and brands, irrespective of size and history, including substitutable solutions to customers' needs, as defined by the target market customers

Competitor monitoring The process by which a company studies the actions of its major competitors in order to determine what specific strategies they are following and how those strategies affect its own; also used by marketers as they try to develop competitive advantages, adjust current marketing strategies and plan new ones

Competitor scanning The monitoring of competitive positions and competitors' strategies

Competitors Organizations viewed as marketing products similar to, or substitutable for, a company's products, when targeted at the same customers

Component parts Parts that become a part of the physical product and are either finished items ready for assembly or products that need little processing before assembly

Comprehensive spending patterns The percentages of family income allotted to annual expenditures for general classes of goods and services

Computer-assisted telephone interviewing A survey method that integrates questionnaire, data collection and tabulations, and provides data to aid decision-makers in the shortest time possible

Concentration strategy A process by which an organization directs its marketing effort towards a single market segment through one marketing mix

Concentric diversification A process that occurs when new products related to current products are introduced into new markets

Concept testing Seeking potential buyers' responses to a product idea

Conglomerate diversification A process that occurs when new products unrelated to current technology, products or markets are introduced into new markets

Consumable supplies Supplies that facilitate production and operations but do not become part of the finished product

Consumer buying behaviour The buying behaviour of ultimate consumers – those who purchase products for personal or household use

Consumer buying decision process A five-stage process that includes problem recognition, information search, evaluation of alternatives, purchase and post-purchase evaluation

Consumer market Purchasers or individuals in their households who personally consume or benefit from the purchased products and do not buy products primarily to make a profit

Consumer movement A diverse collection of independent individuals, groups and organizations seeking to protect the rights of consumers

Consumer products Items purchased to satisfy personal or family needs

Consumer purchase diaries A marketing research tool in which consumers record their purchases

Consumer services Services such as education, healthcare, leisure, catering, tourism, financial, entertainment, home maintenance and other services to help consumers

Consumer spending patterns Information indicating the relative proportions of annual family expenditures or the actual amount of money spent on certain kinds of goods and services

Consumer-to-consumer (C2C) communication Consumer-to-consumer (C2C) communication is now routine, enabled by the digital era and social media in particular. Consumers readily and rapidly share views, experiences and information with each other. A positive or negative customer experience is tweeted instantly, blogged or shared on Facebook with potentially very many fellow consumers.

Consumer-to-consumer communication (C2C) Refers to communication taking place between consumers through online or other electronic media.

Consumers' Association A private organization, funded by members' subscriptions, that works to further consumer interests

Convenience products Inexpensive, frequently purchased and rapidly consumed items that demand only minimal purchasing effort

Core product The level of a product that provides the perceived or real core benefit or service

Corporate branding The application of product branding at the corporate level, reflected visibly through the company name, logo and visual presentation and in the organization's underlying values

Corporate identity Overlapping with the corporate branding concept: branding at the corporate level

Corporate image Reflects the perceptions that external audiences hold about an organization

Corporate strategy A strategy that determines the organization's vision and goals, and how they are to be addressed, in which markets, with what advantages over competitors, and so aligning resources in key functions accordingly across the business

Cost-based pricing A pricing approach whereby a monetary amount or percentage is added to the cost of a product

Credence qualities Attributes that cannot be assessed even after purchase and consumption

Critical marketing Critical marketing involves challenging orthodox views that are central to the core principles of the discipline. Sometimes this involves promoting radical philosophies and theories in relation to the understanding of economies, society, markets and consumers, which may have implications for the practice of marketing. Critical marketing is connected with the growing area of critical management

CRM Data capture about customers and their buying habits, analysis and profiling of such behaviours, so that tailored propositions and communications may be created in order to maintain an ongoing relationship and continue to interest customers in the company's brand, products and activities

Culture All the things around us that are made by human beings: tangible items, such as food, furniture, buildings, clothing and tools; and intangible concepts, such as education, the legal system, healthcare and religion; plus values and behaviours

Cumulative discounts Quantity discounts aggregated over a stated period of time

Customer contact The level of interaction between the provider and customer needed to deliver the service

Customer relationship management (CRM) The identification of the most worthwhile and valuable customers within targeted segments and the development of ongoing relationships to foster loyalty and repeat purchasing

Customer satisfaction A qualitative measure of marketing performance that involves surveying customers over time

Customer satisfaction A state that results when an exchange meets the needs and expectations of the buyer

Customer's zone of tolerance The difference between the customer's desired level of expectations and the customer's acceptable level of expectations

Decline stage The last stage of a product's life cycle, during which sales fall rapidly

Decoding process The process in which signs are converted into concepts and ideas

Defensive warfare A policy of striking a balance between waiting for market developments or competitor activity and proactively parrying competitors' actions

Demand-based pricing A pricing approach based on the level of demand for a product, resulting in a high price when demand is strong and a low price when demand is weak

Demographic factors Individual characteristics such as age, sex, race, ethnic origin, income, family life cycle and occupation

Dependent variable A variable that is contingent on, or restricted to, one value or a set of values assumed by the independent variable

Depression A period during which unemployment is extremely high, wages are very low, total disposable income is at a minimum and consumers lack confidence in the economy

Depth (of product mix) The number of different products offered in each product line

Depth interview A lengthy, one-to-one structured interview, examining in detail a consumer's views about a product

Derived demand Demand for business products that arises from the demand for consumer products

Descriptive research Data collection that focuses on providing an accurate description of the variables in a situation

Descriptors Variables used to profile or build a fuller picture of target segments brand's desired stature

Diary tests Experiments in which households log their weekly purchases and consumption patterns

Differential advantage An attribute of a brand, product, service or marketing mix that is desired by the targeted customer and provided by only one supplier

Differential advantage Something desired by the customer that only one company – not its rivals – can offer

Differentiated strategy A strategy by which an organization directs its marketing efforts towards two or more market segments by developing a marketing mix for each

Digital marketing Digital marketing tools and techniques are used by marketers to improve their proposition to customers and overall competitiveness, with a value adding website and interrelated digital marketing techniques to drive traffic, conversion, positive experience and referrals

Digital marketing The use of particularly the Web and mobile phones, as well as radio, TV and any other form of digital media to attract, engage and build relationships with customers and other target audiences

Direct mail A method of communication used to entice prospective customers or charitable donors to invest in products, services or worthy causes

Direct marketing A decision by a company's marketers to select a marketing channel which avoids dependence on marketing channel intermediaries and to focus marketing communications activity on promotional mix ingredients which deal directly with targeted customers

Directional policy matrix A market attractiveness and business strength/capability assessment tool ideal for trade-off analyses for identifying resourcing priorities

Directional policy matrix (DPM) A more commonly used name for the market attractiveness – business position model

Discretionary income Disposable income that is available for spending and saving after an individual has purchased the basic necessities of food, clothing and shelter

Disposable income After-tax income, which is used for spending or saving

Diversified growth Growth that occurs when new products are developed to be sold in new markets

Dogs Products that have a subordinate share of the market and low prospects for growth

Dual distribution A channel practice whereby a producer distributes the same products through two different channels

Dynamic branding Digital brand communities and blogging enable dynamic branding, with very rapid communication and sharing of brand information and almost instant take-up by the brand's followers

Early adopters People who choose new products carefully and are often consulted by people from the remaining adopter categories

Early majority People who adopt products just prior to the average person

Ebitda The acronym for earning before interest taxes depreciation and amortization

Ecommerce The use of the Internet for marketing communications, selling and purchasing

Economic and competitive forces Factors in the marketing environment – such as the effects of general economic conditions; buying power; willingness to spend; spending patterns; types of competitive structure, competitive tools and competitive behaviour – that influence both marketers' and consumers' decisions and activities

Economic value to the customer (EVC) The underlying principle that a premium price can be charged while still offering the customer better value than the competition

Environmental analysis The process of assessing and interpreting the information gathered through environmental scanning

Environmental factors Uncontrollable forces such as politics, competitive and economic factors, legal and regulatory issues, technological changes and socio-cultural issues

Environmental scanning The process of collecting information about the marketing environment to help marketers identify opportunities and threats, and assist in planning

Evaluation stage The stage of the product adoption process when customers decide whether the product will satisfy certain criteria that are crucial for meeting their specific needs

Evoked set The group of products that a buyer views as possible alternatives after conducting an information search

Exchange The provision or transfer of goods, services and ideas in return for something of value

Exclusive dealing System by which a manufacturer forbids an intermediary to carry the products of competing manufacturers

Exclusive distribution Market coverage in which only one outlet is used in a geographic area

Exclusive distribution The use of only one outlet in a relatively large geographic area to distribute a product

Experience qualities Attributes that can be assessed only after purchase and consumption, including satisfaction and courtesy

Experimentation Data collection that involves maintaining certain variables as constant so that the effects of the experimental variables can be measured

Exploratory research Deliberately flexible data gathering used to discover the general nature of a problem and the factors that relate to it

Extended marketing mix for services In addition to the standard '4Ps' marketing mix – product, promotion, price and place/ distribution – there are 3Ps: process, physical evidence (ambience) and people

Extensive decision making Behaviour that occurs when a purchase involves unfamiliar, expensive, high-risk or infrequently bought products for which the buyer spends much time seeking information and comparing brands before deciding on the purchase

External reference price A comparison price provided by others

External search One that focuses on information not available from the consumer's memory

Family packaging An approach in which all of a company's packages are similar or include one major element of the design

Fast movers Smaller rival companies not yet destined to be major challengers, but growing rapidly on a smaller scale

Feedback The receiver's response to a message

Field settings 'Real world' environments in which experiments take place

Financial price The basis of market exchanges; the quantified value of what is exchanged

Five communication effects Communication aims that include category need, brand awareness, brand attitude, brand purchase intention and purchase facilitation

Five competitive forces Together these determine competition in an industry or market: rivalry amongst existing like-for-like players; the threat of new entrants; the threat of substitute solutions; the bargaining power of buyers; and the bargaining power of suppliers

Five markets model of relationship marketing In addition to customer markets, the core audiences of influencers, referrals, employee recruitment, suppliers and internal markets

Five-category classification A method of analyzing services according to five criteria: type of market, degree of labour intensiveness, degree of customer contact, skill of the service provider and goal of the service provider

Fob destination price A price quotation indicating that the producer absorbs the costs of shipping the merchandise

Fob factory price The price of the merchandise at the factory before it is loaded on to the carrier vehicle, which must be paid by the buyer

Focus group A semi-structured discussion involving six to twelve people, led by a moderator

Focus group interview A survey method that aims to observe group interaction when members are exposed to an idea or concept

Freight absorption pricing A pricing policy in which the seller absorbs all or part of the actual freight costs

Functional middlemen Intermediaries who do not take title to products

Functional modifications Changes that affect a product's versatility, effectiveness, convenience or safety

General publics In non-profit organizations, indirect consumers of a product

Generic brand A brand that indicates only the product category and does not include the company name or other identifying terms

Generic routes to competitive advantage Cost leadership, differentiation and focus; not mutually exclusive

Geodemographic segmentation Clustering people according to postcode areas and census data

Geographic pricing Pricing that involves reductions for transport costs or other costs associated with the physical distance between the buyer and the seller

Good A physical entity that can be touched

Good A tangible physical entity

Government markets Departments that buy goods and services to support their internal operations, and to provide the public with education, water, energy, national defence, road systems and healthcare

Green movement The trend arising from society's concern about pollution, waste disposal, manufacturing processes and the greenhouse effect

Growth stage The stage at which a product's sales rise rapidly and profits reach a peak, before levelling off into maturity

Guarantee An agreement specifying what the producer or supplier will do if the product malfunctions

Heterogeneity Variability in the quality of service because services are provided by people, and people perform inconsistently

Heterogeneous markets Markets in which all customers have different requirements

Home placements Experiments in which a product is used in a home setting

Horizontal channel integration The combination of institutions at the same level of channel operation under one management

Horizontal diversification A process that occurs when new products not technologically related to current products are introduced into current markets

Hypothesis An informed guess or assumption about a certain problem or set of circumstances

Idea A concept, philosophy, image or issue

Idea generation The process by which companies and other organizations seek product ideas that will help them achieve their objectives

Ideas Concepts, philosophies, images or issues that provide the psychological stimulus to solve problems or adjust to the environment

Immediate drop An option that drops an unprofitable product immediately

Impulse buying Behaviour that involves no conscious planning but results from a powerful, persistent urge to buy something immediately

In-depth interview The collection of data from an individual by interview

In-home interview 45- to 90-minute interview in which the researcher visits the respondent in his or her home

Income The amount of money received through wages, rents, investments, pensions and subsidy payments for a given period

Independent variable A variable not influenced by or dependent on other variables in experiments

Individual branding A policy of naming each product differently

Individual factors The personal characteristics of individuals in the buying centre, such as age, education, personality, position in the organization and income level

Industrial distributor An independent business that takes title to industrial products and carries inventories

Industrial or business products Items bought for use in a company's operations or to make other products

Industrial, organizational or business-to-business marketing *See business market*

Industrial/business services The intangible products that many organizations use in their operations, including financial, legal, marketing research, computer programming and operation, caretaking and printing services

Inelastic demand Demand that is not significantly affected by a price increase or decrease

Information inputs The sensations received through sight, taste, hearing, smell and touch

Innovators The first people to adopt a new product

Input–output data Information on what types of industries purchase the products of a particular industry

Inseparability In relation to production and consumption, a characteristic of services that means they are produced at the same time as they are consumed

Institutional markets Organizations with charitable, educational, community or other non-business goals

Intangibility An inherent quality of services that are performed and therefore cannot be tasted, touched, seen, smelled or possessed

Integrated growth Growth that occurs in three possible directions: forwards, backwards or horizontally

Integrated marketing communications (imc) The coordination and integration of all marketing communication tools, avenues and sources within a company into a seamless programme that maximizes the impact on consumers and other end users, at minimal cost

Intended strategy The strategy on which the company decides during the planning phase

Intense growth Growth that occurs when current products and current markets have the potential for increasing sales

Intensive distribution Market coverage in which all available outlets are used for distributing a product

Intensive distribution The use of all available outlets for distributing a product

Interest stage The stage of the product adoption process when customers are motivated to obtain information about the product's features, uses, advantages, disadvantages, price or location

Internal marketing The application of marketing internally within the company, with programmes of communication and guidance targeted at internal audiences to develop responsiveness and a unified sense of purpose among employees

Internal reference price A price developed in the buyer's mind through experience with the product

Internal search One in which the buyer searches his or her memory for information about products

Internet A network of computer networks stretching across the world, linking computers of different types and sharing information

Interpersonal factors The relationships among the people in the buying centre

Introduction stage A product's first appearance in the marketplace, before any sales or profits have been made

Intuition The personal knowledge and past experience on which marketing managers may base decisions

Involvement The level of interest, emotion and activity the consumer is prepared to expend on a particular purchase

Joint demand Demand that occurs when two or more products are used in combination to produce another product

Key account management Dedicated and close support for individual business customers whose volume of business is significant and warrants one-to-one handling

Kinesic communication Body language, including winking, head nodding, hand gestures and arm movements

Knowledge Familiarity with the product and expertise – the ability to apply the product

Labelling Packaging information that can be used for a variety of promotional, informational and legal purposes

Laboratory settings Central locations at which participants or respondents are invited to react or respond to experimental stimuli

Laggards The last people to adopt a new product, suspicious of new products and oriented towards the past

Late majority People who are quite sceptical about new products but eventually adopt them because of economic necessity or social pressure

Learning Changes in a person's behaviour caused by information and experience

Learning relationships understanding better a customer's needs and behaviours

Level of involvement The level of interest, emotional commitment and time spent searching for a product in a particular situation

Levels of brands The tangible product, the 'basic' brand, the 'augmented' brand and the 'potential' of the brand

Limited decisionmaking Behaviour that occurs when buying products purchased only occasionally, for which a moderate amount of information gathering and deliberation is needed

Line extension A product that is closely related to existing products in the line, but meets different customer needs

Line family branding A policy of using family branding only for products within a single line

Long-range plans Plans that extend beyond five years

Macro marketing environment The broader forces affecting all organizations in a market: political, legal, regulatory, societal/green, technological and economic/competitive

Mail panels Groups of consumers selected to represent a market or market segment, who agree to be interviewed regularly by mail

Mail surveys Questionnaires sent by mail to respondents, who are encouraged to complete and return them

Major equipment Large tools and machines used for production purposes

Manufacturer brands Brands initiated by producers to ensure that they are identified with their products at the point of purchase

Market An aggregate of people who, as individuals or within organizations, have a need for certain products and the ability, willingness and authority to purchase such products

Market attractiveness – business position model A two-dimensional matrix that helps determine which SBUs have an opportunity to grow and which should be divested

Market challengers Non-market leaders that aggressively try to capture market share from their rivals

Market density The number of potential customers within a unit of land area

Market development A strategy of increasing sales of current products in new markets

Market followers Low-share competitors without the resources, market position, research and development, or the commitment to challenge for extra sales and market share

Market leader The single player enjoying the largest individual share in the market

Market nichers Companies that specialize by focusing on only a very narrow range of products or on a select band of consumers

Market penetration A strategy of increasing sales of current products in current markets

Market requirements Requirements that relate to customers' needs or desired benefits

Market segment A group of individuals, groups or organizations sharing one or more similar characteristics that cause them to have relatively similar product needs and buying characteristics

Market segmentation The process of grouping customers in markets with some heterogeneity into smaller, more similar or homogeneous segments. The identification of target customer groups in which customers are aggregated into groups with similar requirements and buying characteristics

Market share The company's brand or product share of total sales in a particular target market or market segment, versus competing brands

Market share The company's sales of a product stated as a percentage of industry sales of that product

Marketing Individual and organizational activities that facilitate and expedite satisfying exchange relationships in a dynamic environment through the creation, distribution, promotion and pricing of goods, services and ideas

Marketing assets Customer, distribution and internal capabilities that managers and the marketplace view as beneficially strong

Marketing communication The transmission of persuasive information about a product, service or an idea, targeted at key stakeholders and consumers within the target market segment

Marketing concept The philosophy that an organization should try to provide products that satisfy customers' needs through a coordinated set of activities that also allows the organization to achieve its goals

Marketing control process One that establishes performance standards, evaluates actual performance and reduces the differences between desired and actual performance

Marketing cost analysis The breakdown and classification of costs to determine which are associated with specific marketing activities

Marketing environment External changing forces within the trading environment: laws, regulations, political activities, societal pressures, economic conditions and technological advances

Marketing environment The external forces that directly or indirectly influence an organization's acquisition of inputs and generation of outputs, comprising six categories of forces: political, legal, regulatory, societal, technological and economic/competitive

Marketing era The period in which product and aggressive selling were no longer seen to suffice if customers either did not desire a product or preferred a rival brand, and in which customer needs were identified and satisfied

Marketing function accounts A method of indicating the function performed through the expenditure of funds

Marketing implementation Processes and activities deployed to action the marketing strategy or roll out the marketing plan

Marketing information system (MIS) The framework for the day-to-day management and structuring of information gathered from sources both inside and outside an organization

Marketing intelligence The composite of all data and ideas available within an organization, which assists in decision-making

Marketing intermediary A middleman who links producers to other middlemen or to those who ultimately use the products

Marketing management A process of planning, organizing, implementing and controlling marketing activities to facilitate and expedite exchanges effectively and efficiently

Marketing manager The person responsible for managing the marketing activities that serve a particular group or class of customers

Marketing mix The tactical 'toolkit' of the marketing programme; product, place/distribution, promotion, price and people variables that an organization can control in order to appeal to the target market and facilitate satisfying exchange

Marketing objective A statement of what is to be accomplished through marketing activities – the results expected from marketing efforts

Marketing opportunities circumstances and timing that allow an organization to take action towards reaching a target market

Marketing opportunity One that exists when circumstances allow an organization to take action towards reaching a particular group of consumer or business customers

Marketing orientation A marketing-oriented organization devotes resources to understanding the needs and buying behaviour of customers, competitors' activities and strategies, and of market trends and external forces – now and as they may shape up in the future; inter-functional coordination ensures that the organization's activities and capabilities are aligned to this marketing intelligence

Marketing performance The assessment of the effectiveness of marketing programmes to implement recommended marketing strategies, fulfil corporate financial expectations and achieve the required levels of customer satisfaction

Marketing plan A document or blueprint detailing requirements for a company's marketing activity

Marketing plan The written document or blueprint for specifying, implementing and controlling an organization's marketing activities and marketing mixes

Marketing planning A systematic process of assessing marketing opportunities and resources, determining marketing objectives and developing a thorough plan for implementation and control

Marketing planning cycle A circular process that runs in two directions, with planning running one way and feedback the other

Marketing process Analysis of market conditions, the creation of an appropriate marketing strategy, the development of marketing programmes designed to action the agreed strategy and, finally, the implementation and control of the marketing strategy and its associated marketing programmes

Marketing programme A marketer's marketing mix activities and implementation processes designed to operationalize the marketing strategy

Marketing research The process of gathering, interpreting and reporting information to help marketers solve specific marketing problems or take advantage of marketing opportunities

Marketing shareholder value analysis (MSVA) Divides the estimation of the value to the organization created by a marketing strategy into two components: (1) the present value of cash flows during the strategizing and planning phases (2) the continuing value after implementation of the strategy

Marketing strategy The selection of which marketing opportunities to pursue, identification of associated target market(s), creation of a basis for competing and 'wow' positioning, and the development and maintenance of an appropriate marketing mix to satisfy those in the target market(s)

Marketing-oriented pricing A pricing approach whereby a company takes into account a wide range of factors including marketing strategy, competition, value to the customer, price – quality relationships, explicability, costs, product line pricing, negotiating margins, political factors and effect on distributors/ retailers

Maturity stage The stage during which a product's sales curve peaks and starts to decline, and profits continue to decline

Mechanical observation devices Cameras, recorders, counting machines and other equipment that records physiological changes in individuals

Medium of transmission The tool used to carry the coded message from the source to the receiver or receiving audience

Medium-range plans Plans that usually cover two to five years

Merchants Intermediaries who take title to products and resell them

Micro marketing environment The more company-specific forces reflecting the nature of the business, its suppliers, marketing intermediaries, buyers, all types of competitors – direct, substitute and new entrant – and its publics

Mobile marketing A set of practices that enables organizations to communicate and engage with their audience in an interactive and relevant manner through any mobile device or network, fostering 'on the move' marketing

Mobile marketing A set of practices that enables organizations to communicate and engage with their audience in an interactive and relevant manner through any mobile device or network

Modified re-buy purchase A new task purchase that is changed when it is reordered or when the requirements associated with a straight re-buy purchase are modified

Monopolistic competition A market structure that exists when a business with many potential competitors attempts to develop a differential marketing strategy to establish its own market share

Monopoly A market structure that exists when a company turns out a product that has no close substitutes or rivals

Motive An internal, energy-giving force that directs a person's activities towards satisfying a need or achieving a goal

Mro items Consumable supplies in the subcategories of maintenance, repair and operating (or overhaul) supplies

Multi-channel marketing The decision to reach target consumers or business customers through more than one channel

Multiple packaging Packaging that includes more than one unit of a product, such as twin packs, tri-packs and six-packs

Multiple sourcing A business's decision to use several suppliers

Multivariable segmentation Segmentation using more than one characteristic to divide a total market

Natural accounts The classification of costs based on how money was actually spent

Negotiation Mutual discussion or communication of terms and methods in an exchange situation

New product development The process a product goes through before introduction, involving seven phases: idea generation, screening ideas, concept testing, business analysis, product development, test marketing and commercialization

New task purchase An organization's initial purchase of an item to be used to perform a new job or to solve a new problem

Noise A condition that exists when the decoded message is different from that which was encoded

Non-cumulative discounts One-off quantity discounts

Non-price competition A policy in which a seller elects not to focus on price but to emphasize other factors instead

Non-profit marketing Activities conducted by individuals and organizations to achieve some goal other than the ordinary business goals of profit, market share or return on investment

Observation methods Methods by which researchers record respondents' overt behaviour and take note of physical conditions and events

Offensive warfare A policy whereby challengers aggressively seek market share by identifying any weaknesses in the leader's and other challengers'

marketing mixes and developing a genuine corresponding strength

Office of Fair Trading UK government office set up to oversee the trading practices of organizations and individuals in the UK

Oligopoly A market structure that exists when a few sellers control the supply of a large proportion of a product

On-site computer interviewing A survey method that requires respondents to complete a self-administered questionnaire displayed on a computer monitor

One-to-one marketing Involves developing long-term relationships with individual customers in order to understand and satisfy their needs

Online survey Questionnaires that are sent to an individual's e-mail account or that are available over the Internet or via a website

Opinion leader The member of a reference group who provides information about a specific sphere of interest to reference group participants seeking information

Opportunity cost The value of the benefit that is given up by selecting one alternative instead of another

Organizational factors Include the buyer's objectives, purchasing policies and resources, as well as the size and composition of its buying centre

Overall family branding A policy of branding all of a company's products with the same name, or at least part of the name

Own label brands Brands initiated and owned by resellers – wholesalers or retailers

Packaging The development of a product's container and label, complete with graphic design

Packaging development A mix of aesthetic considerations and structural necessities to guarantee the functionality of the design

Patronage motives Those motives that influence where a person purchases products on a regular basis

Penetration pricing A pricing strategy of setting a price below the prices of competing brands in order to penetrate a market and produce a larger unit sales volume

People variable The aspect of the marketing mix that reflects the level of customer service, advice, sales support and after-sales back-up required, involving recruitment policies, training, retention and motivation of key personnel

Perceived value for money The benefit consumers perceive to be inherent in a product or service, weighed against the price demanded

Perception The process of selecting, organizing and interpreting information inputs to produce meaning

Perceptual mapping A tool used by marketers and marketing researchers to visually depict consumer perceptions and prioritising of brands and their perceived attributes

Perfect competition A market structure that entails a large number of sellers, not one of which could significantly influence price or supply

Performance standard An expected level of performance against which actual performance can be compared

Perishability A characteristic of services whereby unused capacity on one occasion cannot be stockpiled or inventoried for future occasions

Personal influencing factors Demographic, situational and level of involvement factors unique to a particular individual

Personal interview survey Face-to-face situation in which the researcher meets the consumer and questions him or her about a specific topic

Personal selling The use of personal communication in an exchange situation to inform customers and persuade them to purchase products

Personality All the internal traits and behaviours that make a person unique

Persuasion The act of prevailing upon someone by argument to facilitate an exchange

PEST analysis/PESTLE analysis PEST is a popular name for an evaluation of the marketing environment, looking at political – including legal and regulatory issues – economic, social and technological developments, and assessing the implications of such issues. Another term used by marketers is PESTLE – political, economic, societal, technological, legal and environmental forces

Phase out An approach that lets the product decline without a change in marketing strategy

Place/distribution variable The aspect of the marketing mix that deals with making products available in the quantities desired to as many customers as possible and keeping the total inventory, transport and storage costs as low as possible

Population All elements, units or individuals that are of interest to researchers for a specific study

Positioning The process of creating an image for a product in the minds of target customers

Positioning statement A plausible, memorable image-enhancing written summation of a product's or brand's desired stature

Prestige-sensitive consumers Individuals drawn to products that signify prominence and status

Price The value placed on what is exchanged

Price competition A policy whereby a marketer emphasizes price as an issue, and matches or beats the prices of competitors

Price differentiation A pricing strategy involving charging different prices to different buyers for the same quality and quantity of product

Price discrimination A policy in which different prices are charged in order to give a particular group of buyers a competitive edge

Price skimming A pricing strategy whereby a company charges the highest possible price that buyers who most desire the product will pay

Price variable The aspect of the marketing mix that relates to activities associated with establishing pricing policies and determining product prices

Price-conscious consumers Those striving to pay low prices

Pricing objectives Overall goals that describe what a company wants to achieve through its pricing efforts

Pricing strategy An approach to influencing and determining pricing decisions

Primary data Information gathered by observing phenomena or surveying respondents

Probability sampling Every element in the population has a known chance of being selected for study

Problem children Products that have a small share of a growing market, generally requiring a large amount of cash to build share

Problem definition The process of uncovering the nature and boundaries of a situation or question

Process materials Materials used directly in the production of other products, but not readily identifiable

Procompetitive legislation Laws enacted to preserve competition and to end various practices deemed unacceptable by society

Producer markets Buyers of raw materials and semi-finished and finished items used to produce other products or in their own operations

Product A good, service or idea

Product Everything, both favourable and unfavourable, tangible and intangible, received in an exchange of an idea, service or good

Product adoption process A series of five stages in the acceptance of a product: awareness, interest, evaluation, trial and adoption

Product adoption process The stages buyers go through in accepting a product: awareness, interest, evaluation, trial and adoption

Product deletion The process of eliminating a product that no longer satisfies a sufficient number of customers

Product development A strategy of increasing sales by improving present products or developing new products for current markets

Product development The phase in which the organization determines if it is technically and financially feasible to produce a new product

Product item A specific version of a product that can be designated as a distinct offering among a business's products

Product life cycle The four major stages through which products move: introduction, growth, maturity and decline

Product line A group of closely related product items that are considered a unit because of marketing, technical or end-use considerations

Product manager The person responsible for a product, a product line or several distinct products that make up an interrelated group within a multi-product organization

Product mix The composite group of products that a company makes available to customers

Product modification The alteration of one or more characteristics of a company's product

Product portfolio analysis A strategic planning tool that takes a product's market growth rate and its relative market share into consideration in determining a marketing strategy

Product variable The aspect of the marketing mix that deals with researching consumers' product wants and designing a product with the desired characteristics

Product-specific spending patterns The annual monetary amounts families spend for specific products within a general product class

Production era The period of mass production following industrialization

Profiling The task of building up a fuller picture of the target segments

Projective techniques Tests in which subjects are asked to perform specific tasks for particular reasons, while actually being evaluated for other purposes

Promotion Communication with individuals, groups or organizations in order to facilitate exchanges by informing and persuading audiences to accept a company's products

Promotion variable The aspect of the marketing mix that relates to marketing communications used to inform one or more groups of people about an organization and its products

Promotional mix The specific combination of ingredients an organization uses to promote a product, traditionally including four ingredients: advertising, personal selling, publicity and public relations and sales promotion

Promotional pricing Pricing related to the short-term promotion of a particular product

Prosperity A period during which unemployment is low and total income is relatively high

Proxemic communication A subtle form of communication used in face-to-face interactions when either person varies the physical distance that separates the two

Psychological factors Factors that influence consumer behaviour, including perception, motives, learning, attitudes and personality

Psychological pricing A pricing strategy designed to encourage purchases that are based on emotional rather than rational responses

Public relations Managing and controlling the process of using publicity effectively. It is the planned and sustained effort to establish and maintain goodwill and understanding between an organization and its target publics

Public sector markets Government and institutional not-for-profit customers and stakeholder groups

Publicity Non-personal communication in news-story form about an organization and/or its products that is transmitted through a mass medium at no charge

Pull policy A promotional policy in which an organization promotes directly to consumers in order to develop a strong consumer demand for its products

Purchase facilitation Circumstances that make it possible for the consumer to purchase the product: availability, location, price and familiarity of vendor

Push policy A promotional policy in which the producer promotes the product only to the next institution down the marketing channel

Quali-depth interviews 25- to 30-minute intercept interviews that incorporate some of the in-depth advantages of focus group interviews with the speed and flexibility of shopping mall/pavement intercept interviews

Qualitative research Research that deals with information too difficult or expensive to quantify, such as subjective opinions and value judgements, typically unearthed during interviews or discussion groups

Quality The core product's ability to achieve the basic functional requirements expected of it

Quality modifications Changes that affect a product's dependability and durability

Quantitative research Research aimed at producing data that can be statistically analyzed and whose results can be expressed numerically

Quantity discounts Reductions off the list price that reflect the economies of purchasing in large quantities

Questionnaire Base document for research purposes, providing the questions and structure for an interview or self-completion, and providing space for respondents' answers

Quota sampling A sampling method in which the final choice of respondents is left to the interviewers, who base their choices on two or three variables (such as age, sex and education)

Random sampling A sampling method in which all the units in a population have an equal chance of appearing in the sample

Raw materials The basic materials that become part of physical products

Realized strategy The strategy that actually takes place

Receiver An individual, group or organization that decodes a coded message

Receiving audience Two or more receivers who decode a message

Recession A period during which unemployment rises and total buying power declines

Reciprocity An arrangement unique to business-to-business marketing in which two organizations agree to buy from each other

Recovery The stage of the business cycle in which the economy moves from depression or recession to prosperity

Reference group A group with which an individual identifies so much that he or she takes on many of the values, attitudes or behaviour of group members

Refusal to deal Situation in which suppliers will not do business with wholesalers or dealers simply because these wholesalers or dealers have resisted policies that are anticompetitive or in restraint of trade

Relationship management The process of encouraging a match between the seller's competitive advantage and the buyer's requirements over an item's life cycle

Relationship marketing All of the activities an organization uses to build, maintain and develop customer relations

Relationship marketing Places emphasis on the interaction between buyers and sellers, and is concerned with winning and keeping customers by maintaining links between marketing, quality and customer service

Relationship marketing era In which the focus is not only on expediting the single transaction but on developing ongoing relationships with customers to maintain lifetime share of wallet

Reliability The quality of producing almost identical results in successive repeated trials

Requisites for implementation Process, skill, leadership, empowerment, communication, timing, information, resource and participation decisions

Research design An overall plan for obtaining the information needed to address a research problem or issue

Research objective The desired outcome from the marketing research project being undertaken

Reseller markets Intermediaries, such as wholesalers and retailers, who buy finished goods and resell them to make a profit

Restricted sales territories System by which a manufacturer tries to prohibit intermediaries from selling its products outside designated sales territories

Retailers Intermediaries that purchase products and resell them to final consumers

Role A set of actions and activities that a person in a particular position is supposed to perform, based on the expectations of both the individual and surrounding people

Routine response behaviour Behaviour that occurs when buying frequently purchased, low-cost, low-risk items that need little search and decision effort

Run out A policy that exploits any strengths left in the product

Sales analysis The use of sales figures to evaluate a business's current performance

Sales era The period from the mid-1920s to the early 1950s when competitive forces and the desire for high sales volume led a company to emphasize selling and the sales person in its business strategy

Sales measurements Data regarding sales transactions that are used to analyze performance, usually in terms of cash volume or market share

Sales per square metre A financial measure retailers might use to assess marketing performance

Sales potential The amount of sales possible for a particular brand or product in the context of market conditions in a specific period of time

Sales promotion An activity or material that acts as a direct inducement by offering added value to or incentive for the product to resellers, sales people or consumers

Salience The level of importance a buyer assigns to each criterion for comparing products

Sample A limited number of units chosen to represent the characteristics of a total population

Sampling The selection of representative units from a total population

Scientific decision-making An orderly and logical approach to gathering information

Screening ideas The process by which a company assesses whether product ideas match its organizational objectives and resources

Search qualities Tangible attributes of a service that can be viewed prior to purchase

Seasonal discount A price reduction given to buyers who purchase goods or services out of season

Secondary data Information compiled inside or outside the organization for some purpose other than the current investigation

Secondary use package A package that can be reused for purposes other than its initial use

Segmentation Targeting The decision about which market segment(s) an organization decides to prioritize for its sales and marketing efforts

Segmentation variables or bases The dimensions or characteristics of individuals, groups or businesses that are used for dividing a total market into segments

Selective distortion The changing or twisting of currently received information

Selective distribution Market coverage in which only some available outlets in an area are chosen to distribute a product

Selective distribution The use of only some available outlets in an area to distribute a product

Selective exposure The selection of inputs that people expose to their awareness

Selective retention The process of remembering information inputs that support personal feelings and beliefs, and of forgetting those that do not

Self-concept A person's perception of himself or herself; self-image

Service An intangible product involving a deed, a performance or an effort that cannot physically be possessed

Service The application of human and mechanical efforts to people or objects in order to provide intangible benefits to customers

Service The application of human and mechanical efforts to people or objects in order to provide intangible benefits to customers

Service expectations A factor used in judging service quality involving impressions from past experiences, word-of-mouth communication and the company's advertising

Service quality Customers' perception of how well a service meets or exceeds their expectations

Service quality factors Factors that increase the likelihood of providing high-quality service: understanding customer expectations, service quality specifications, employee performance, managing service expectations

Shopping mall/pavement intercept interviews Personal interviewing of a percentage of individuals who pass by certain 'intercept' points in a shopping centre or on a pavement

Shopping products Items chosen more carefully than convenience products; consumers will expend effort in planning and purchasing these items

Short-range plans Plans that cover a period of up to a year

Single variable segmentation Segmentation achieved by using only one variable, the simplest type of segmentation to perform

Single-source data Information provided by a single marketing research company

Situational factors External circumstances or conditions that exist when a consumer is making a purchase decision

Social class An open group of individuals who have similar social rank

Social factors The forces other people exert on buying behaviour

Social marketing Social marketing uses tools and techniques from commercial marketing to encourage positive behavioural changes, such as quitting smoking, reducing alcohol consumption, minimizing anti-social behaviours or reducing carbon footprint. The health and well-being of individuals, society and the planet are at the core of social marketing

Social marketing Social marketing uses tools and techniques from commercial marketing to encourage positive behavioural changes, such as quitting smoking, reducing alcohol consumption, minimizing

anti-social behaviours or reducing carbon footprint. The health and well-being of individuals, society and the planet are at the core of social marketing

Social media Social media incorporate the online technology and methods through which people can share content, personal opinions, different perspectives and insights, using text, images, audio and video, via social networks, video and photo sharing, micro-blogs, wikis and news aggregators

Societal forces Individuals and groups, and the issues engaging them, that pressure marketers to provide high living standards and enjoyable lifestyles through socially responsible decisions and activities

Sole sourcing A buying process that involves the selection of only one supplier

Sorting activities Functions that let channel members divide roles and separate tasks

Sorting out Separating products into uniform, homogeneous groups

Source A person, group or organization that has an intended meaning it attempts to share with an audience

Speciality products Items that possess one or more unique characteristics; consumers of speciality products plan their purchases and will expend considerable effort to obtain them

Sponsorship The financial or material support of an event, activity, person, organization or product by an unrelated organization or donor

Standard Industrial Classification (SIC) system A system that provides information on different industries and products, and classifies economic characteristics of industrial, commercial, financial and service organizations

Stars Products with a dominant share of the market and good prospects for growth

Statistical interpretation An analysis of data that focuses on what is typical or what deviates from the average

Straight re-buy purchase A routine repurchase of the same products under approximately the same terms of sale

Strategic business unit (SBU) A division, product line or other profit centre within a parent company

Strategic channel alliance Arrangement for distributing the products of one organization through the marketing channels of another

Strategic market plan An outline of the methods and resources required to achieve an organization's goals within a specific target market

Strategic objectives Includes intense growth, diversified growth or integrated growth

Strategic window A temporary period of optimum fit between the key requirements of a market and the particular capabilities of a company competing in that market

Strategic windows Major developments or opportunities triggered by changes in the marketing environment

Stratified sampling A sampling method in which the population of interest is divided according to a common characteristic or attribute; a probability sampling is then conducted within each group

Style modifications Changes that alter a product's sensory appeal – taste, texture, sound, smell or visual characteristics

Sub-cultures Sub-divisions of culture according to geographic regions or human characteristics, such as age or ethnic background

Successful brands Brands for which a company must prioritize quality, offer superior service, get there first, differentiate brands, develop a unique positioning concept, have a strong communications programme and be consistent and reliable

Supplier analysis A formal and systematic evaluation of current and potential suppliers

Supply chain management Long-term partnerships among marketing channel members that reduce inefficiencies, costs and redundancies in the marketing channel and develop innovative approaches to satisfying targeted customers

Survey methods Interviews by mail, telephone, web and personal interviews

Swot analysis Analysis that determines a company's situation by examining four factors: strengths, weaknesses, opportunities and threats

SWOT analysis The examination of an organization's strengths and weaknesses, opportunities and threats, usually depicted on a four-cell chart

Syndicated data services Organizations that collect general information and sell it to clients

Tactile communication Interpersonal communication through touching, including shaking hands

Target market A group of people for whom a company creates and maintains a marketing mix that specifically fits the needs and preferences of that group

Target market strategy The choice for which market segment(s) an organization decides to develop marketing programmes

Target public A collective of individuals who have an interest in or concern about an organization, a product or a social cause

Technology The application of knowledge and tools to solve problems and perform tasks more efficiently

Technology assessment A procedure by which managers try to foresee the effects of new products and processes on their company's operation, on other commercial organizations and on society in general

Telemarketing Direct selling over the telephone, relying heavily on personal selling

Telephone surveys Surveys in which respondents' answers to a questionnaire are recorded by interviewers on the phone

Test marketing The limited introduction of a product in geographic areas or a channel chosen to represent the intended market

Third sector Includes charities, the voluntary sector, not-for-profit organizations and NGOs

Trade name The full and legal name of an organization

Trade or functional discount A reduction off the list price given by a producer to an intermediary for performing certain functions

Trademark Legal designation indicating that the owner has exclusive use of a brand

Transfer pricing The type of pricing used when one unit in a company sells a product to another unit within the same company

Trial stage The stage of the product adoption process when individuals use or experience the product for the first time

Tying contract Arrangement whereby a supplier (usually a manufacturer or franchiser) furnishes a product to a channel member with the stipulation that the channel member must purchase other products as well

Undifferentiated (or total market) approach An approach which assumes that all customers have similar needs and wants, and can be served with a single marketing mix

Undifferentiated targeting strategy When a company targets an entire market for a product with a single marketing mix

Uniform geographic pricing Pricing in which the same price is charged to all customers regardless of geographic location

Universal product code (UPC) or barcode A series of thick and thin lines that identifies the product, and provides inventory and pricing information readable by an electronic scanner

Unsought products Items that are purchased when a sudden problem arises or when aggressive selling is used to obtain a sale that would not otherwise take place

Validity A condition that exists when an instrument measures what it is supposed to measure

Value analysis An evaluation of each component of a potential purchase

Value share The proportion of total market monetary sales attracted by an individual brand or product within a particular market

Value-based marketing The inclusion of the value of a marketing strategy and marketing activity in an organization's financial analysis of shareholder value

Value-based marketing Value-based marketing recognizes that marketing must prove its long term financial worth and be accountable to organizations, which involves showing that marketing enables both the creation of short-term customer value and longer-term value for shareholders

Value-conscious consumers Those concerned about price and quality of a product

Venture or project team The group that creates entirely new products, perhaps aimed at new markets, and is responsible for all aspects of the products' development

Vertical channel integration The combination of two or more stages of the channel under one management

Vertical marketing system (VMS) Marketing channel in which a single channel member coordinates or manages channel activities to achieve efficient, low-cost distribution aimed at satisfying target market customers

Wealth The accumulation of past income, natural resources and financial resources

Wholesalers Intermediaries who purchase products for resale to retailers, other wholesalers and producers, governments and institutions

Width (of product mix) The number of product lines a company offers

Willingness to spend A disposition towards using buying power, influenced by the ability to buy, expected satisfaction from a product and numerous psychological and social forces

Zone prices Regional prices that take advantage of a uniform pricing system

Index

Why Marketing?

Marketing as a function should continue to represent the end consumer in any company... Marketing should have its finger on the consumer's pulse.

VIJAY VAIDYANATHAN, TILDA

The power of ideas... Marketing demands that the left brain (analysis and insights) informs the right brain (imaginative product and communication concepts), to create a competitive advantage for your brand and business.

JOHN WRINGE, THE MARKETECTS

Excitement has to be about insight... getting to the bottom of what makes the customer tick. Sometimes excitement comes from dealing with consumers who aren't like you and can't be like you, and the insights they bring.

PETER JACKSON, ADSEARCH

As thousands of businesses emerge crawling from the wreckage of the past few years, what better opportunity for Marketing to be taken more seriously than for them to lead their company-wide charge to re-define themselves in the strange new surroundings we all find ourselves in.

ROBERT BEAN, THE ROBERT BEAN BRANDING CO. LTD.

Anything is possible and everything is in play, and a new generation of challengers is showing us that - was there ever a more inspiring and exciting time to be in Marketing?

ADAM MORGAN, THE EATBIGFISH BRANDING CONSULTANCY

Working in Marketing means that you are in a privileged position, working across all parts of a business at all levels, for the good of the whole company.

IAN HUNTER, FUJITSU

Marketing provides the opportunity to influence the direction of a company and as a consequence to feel part of the success of the company.

SIOBHAN MCKELVEY, NYNAS NV

The real key is that Marketing provides us with the discipline to look at our business in a logical and structured way... enabling us to focus on the important issues and not to be distracted by all the other 'noise' around us and by 'hearsay' evidence.

ANNE HUGHES, WILLIS NETWORKS/WILLIS INSURANCE